Praise for William Korey's
NGOs and the Universal Declaration of Human Rights

"[a] valuable study. . . useful and thorough . . ."

—*New York Review of Books*

"Korey's painstaking research and lucid writing style have produced a book that adds to our understanding of the role that NGOs have played in the struggle for human rights during the past half century . . . authoritative and masterful . . ."

—*American Foreign Policy Interests*

"Korey's book, which provides a detailed and stimulating treatment [of NGOs] will be of interest to all students of human rights . . . a lively and informative study . . ."

—*The International History Review*

D0981467

NGOs and the Universal Declaration of Human Rights

"A Curious Grapevine"

William Korey

palgrave

NGOS AND THE UNIVERSAL DECLARATION OF HUMAN RIGHTS
Copyright © William Korey, 1998.
All rights reserved. No part of this book may be used or
reproduced in any manner whatsoever without written permission except in the case of brief quotations embodied in critical
articles or reviews.

First published in hardcover in 1998 by St. Martin's Press
First PALGRAVE™ edition: February 2001.
175 Fifth Avenue, New York, N.Y. 10010 and
Houndmills, Basingstoke, Hampshire, England RG21 6XS
Companies and representatives throughout the world.

PALGRAVE is the new global publishing imprint of St. Martin's
Press LLC Scholarly and Reference Division and Palgrave Publishers Ltd (formerly Macmillan Press Ltd).

ISBN 0-312-16255-3 hardcover
ISBN 0-312-23886-X paperback

Library on Congress Cataloging-in-Publication Data

Korey, William, 1922-
    NGOs and the Universal Declaration of Human Rights:
"A Curious Grapevine" / William Korey.
    p. cm.
    Includes bibliographical references and index.
    ISBN 0-312-23886-X
    1. Human rights. 2. United Nations. General Assembly.
Universal Declaration of Human Rights. 3. Non-governmental
organizations.
    I. Title.
JC571.K5951998
323'.06'01--dc21   98-37846
                                                      CIP

Design by Acme Art, Inc.

First PALGRAVE edition: February 2001
10 9 8 7 6 5 4 3 2 1

Printed in the United States of America

To Es, My Loving Wife,
Companion and Counselor

CONTENTS

ACKNOWLEDGMENTS

It was my last study of the Helsinki process (*Promises We Keep: Human Rights, the Helsinki Process and American Foreign Policy*, St. Martin's Press, 1993) that initially pointed me in the direction of a volume on nongovernmental organizations (NGOs). The remarkable role that had been played by NGOs in East Europe, in the face of extraordinary obstacles, paved the way for the collapse of the mighty Soviet empire and the disintegration of the seemingly invulnerable Berlin Wall. Perhaps those NGOs were not at all unique. Might they not be symptomatic of a significant trend in modern society that would make the fulfillment of the Universal Declaration of Human Rights a central aspiration of an international human rights NGO movement?

With the encouragement of Ambassador Max Kampelman—"Mr. CSCE"—the very embodiment of the Helsinki process, who had brilliantly tapped the resources of NGOs both in the East and the West, I embarked upon this journey of scholarly inquiry. He brought my proposal to the attention of the U.S. Institute of Peace, which made possible the indispensable travel and research funding of the project. Robert Crane, the President of the Joyce Mertz-Gilmore Foundation, also was keenly interested in the subject and provided additional and essential financial support for the intense three-year study.

The inquiry could not be said to have been launched in a personal, intellectual and historical vacuum. A quarter of a century ago, on the occasion of the twenty-fifth anniversary of the Universal Declaration of Human Rights, I was asked to write the introduction to a picture album about Eleanor Roosevelt. It was then that I found her comment about the "curious grapevine" that would carry the message of the Universal Declaration of Human Rights and its violations through stone walls and across barbed wire erected by totalitarian and authoritarian regimes. Anticipated in that provocative and prescient phrase of the great champion of human rights was the role of nongovernmental organizations. Research on the work of Eleanor Roosevelt, together with an earlier study of the Universal Declaration, commissioned by the Carnegie

Endowment for International Peace, helped shape and focus my personal labors as an NGO lobbyist at the United Nations for some two decades.

Even as Rita Hauser, the U.S. Ambassador to the UN Commission on Human Rights in the late sixties, offered help to my lobbying efforts, so too has she once again extended aid to this work. Additional assistance came from Seymour Reich, former President of B'nai B'rith and Chairman of the Conference of Presidents of Major American Jewish Organizations. Reich stood in the great tradition of B'nai B'rith leaders, like Philip Klutznick and Label Katz, who made the rescue of Soviet Jewry a top priority of the organization.

This labor of love never could have been completed without the detailed assistance of major human rights nongovernmental organizations, which provided through interviews, documentation and studies insights into how they operate, what they seek to accomplish and the extent to which they have succeeded in this effort. I express my heartfelt thanks to the leaders of these organizations and to the many staff members upon whom I have relied. A special thanks goes to Felice Gaer, the Director of the Blaustein Institute for the Advancement of Human Rights, who, with her rich experience drawn from years at the Ford Foundation, the International League for Human Rights, the United Nations Association (UNA) and most recently the Blaustein Institute, was a constant source of advice and documentation.

NGOs were not alone in offering encouragement and help. I was given considerable assistance by human rights professionals at the United Nations and in various government agencies.

This is not intended to be the final word on the subject of human rights NGOs. Their achievement has been enormous in serving as the "curious grapevine" that has made human rights a vital component of international concern and discourse. I hope that I have opened the door to a continuing exploration of an astonishing resource that has helped transform the last half-century and laid the basis for even greater activism in the next century.

When I initially embarked upon this undertaking, I didn't reckon with the magnitude of the research task. Fortunately I had the assistance of several gifted university students who explored a number of subjects which would be incorporated into the study. They were Maria Biancheri Thompson, Kathryn Reardon and Baldwin Robertson, and I herewith extend my deepest appreciation and thanks for their contributions. Especially am I grateful for the valuable research help of Robertson, who was present at the beginning of the project and returned to it after a year of study in Beijing.

Finally, I must acknowledge here an indebtedness of extraordinary proportions to Marie Sassi, who not only typed this massive manuscript, but also meticulously proofread every page. She is a unique talent and there is simply no way I can convey my personal gratitude for her untiring labors and her dedicated devotion to a difficult and burdensome task.

Introduction

Eleanor Roosevelt once said that "within all of us there are two sides. One reaches for the stars, the other descends to the level of beasts."[1] It is the second level that has characterized much of the twentieth century with its history of genocide, mass killings, tortures, disappearances, racial, ethnic and religious discrimination and repression, and the suppression of the basic freedoms. Yet, emerging from the depths of the century's most horrendous bestiality—the Holocaust—was the instrument that would provide the compass for humankind's journey to the stars. The Universal Declaration of Human Rights, which Mrs. Roosevelt helped shape and, more importantly, helped bring into existence fifty years ago, remains the fundamental standard for measuring progress or retrogression in civilized society. It was to serve as the guidepost for setting goals for the future and to which states should aspire.

The Holocaust was not perpetrated by some extrinsic force, alien to the civilized society of Germany. Recent research demonstrates how many ordinary citizens enthusiastically participated in the orgy of its atrocities.[2] At the same time, the very memory of it, even if indirect and at times borrowed by a new generation, provided the motivation for those who would seek to prevent its recurrence by erecting walls to stem the tide of bigotry and hatred. The former top legal advisor for a leading human rights organization consciously dedicated his principal work to his grandparents who perished in the gas chambers. The highest official of another human rights group related that a principal motivation of his career choice was the fact that his parents had sought refuge from Nazism and thereby survived its later juggernaut.

But how could the Universal Declaration achieve the aim of preventing future horrors and of making vital and viable the popular slogan "Never Again!" that would begin to reverberate? Early on, this became a key question Eleanor Roosevelt rhetorically sought to address and with which René Cassin, her major colleague in the drafting of the Declaration, intellectually wrestled. The answer was to be found not in the states, but rather in nonstate actors, in nongovernmental organizations. It was the NGOs who would take on the challenge of transforming the words of the Declaration from a standard into reality; it was they who would assume the function of implementing the demands of international morality. The Universal Declaration itself, in the course of time, would be transformed from a mere moral manifesto or a common standard into "customary international law" that carried a veritable obligatory character. This transformation was pressed by NGOs.

Nor would the Declaration itself ever have been conceived of as an instrument were it not preceded by the UN Charter, whose human rights provisions were products of NGO determination and persistent lobbying in which the American Jewish Committee played the leading role. The Charter was the first general international treaty that would accord human rights a central place and would also provide for a special institution—the UN Commission on Human Rights—to focus exclusive attention on human rights issues. Similarly, various provisions of the Declaration were the handiwork of NGOs, as would be the provisions of the covenants and certainly of the later conventions or treaties on human rights adopted by the UN.

In 1945, when the Charter was adopted, and in 1948, when the Universal Declaration of Human Rights was approved, there were but few NGOs holding consultative status with the UN and a much smaller number that were fully or partly preoccupied with human rights. A recent study offers the following data: only 41 NGOs held consultative status with the UN Economic and Social Council in 1948; 20 years later, in 1968, the total reached nearly 500; 25 years later, by 1992, the figure surpassed 1000.[3] Were account taken of NGOs involved with some aspect of UN work, whether on a regional, subregional, national or local level, the total today would run into the tens of thousands. The developing world (especially in Asia) has seen a veritable explosion in the number of NGOs; one writer in *Foreign Affairs* cited an estimate of 35,000 while acknowledging that "it is impossible to measure a swiftly growing universe that includes neighborhood, professional, service and advocacy groups, both secular and church-based, promoting every conceivable cause. . . ."[4]

Not until the fifties, sixties and seventies would there be created the prominent international human rights NGOs with which the contemporary world is familiar. It was these NGOs, both the early pioneers of the forties and the later more specific rights groups, that put human rights on the journalistic and academic map of the world. In the forties and fifties, the phrase "human rights" hardly was noted in the media and scarcely was mentioned in official circles except for narrowly provincial circles of the UN. And even there, any implementation initiative was treated with a certain condescension, if not contempt.

As for academia, the major standard work on international relations, Hans Morgenthau's *Politics Among Nations,* never mentioned the phrase nor even referred to the Universal Declaration of Human Rights in its first five editions, the last published in 1973.[5] Not until the book's sixth edition, published in 1986, after Morgenthau's death, was a section on of several pages entitled "Human Rights and International Morality" added.[6] But the new material, in keeping with Morgenthau's overall view, insists upon "the impossibility of enforcing the universal application of human rights." At the same time, Morgenthau recognized that "history has shown that the Soviet Union may yield under certain conditions to private pressure."

Today, the issue of human rights is the focus of endless discussion in and beyond the media. It is very much a vital element in international discourse and a subject that statesmen are required to address. Those who have played a decisive role in transforming the phrase from but a Charter provision or a Declaration article into a critical element of foreign policy discussions in and out of governmental or intergovernmental circles are the NGOs. They simply have revolutionized the language of international relations, which statesmen of an earlier era and even some of a recent period would have found strange and unacceptable. Henry Kissinger, in his two volumes of memoirs covering his service as National Security Adviser, made no reference to human rights; in a volume on diplomacy published in 1994, he acknowledged the existence of the subject in some half-dozen pages with scarcely any enthusiasm.

Human rights NGOs have operated on several levels, including, initially, standard-setting and fact-finding. Later, they would serve as a kind of ombudsman intervening on behalf of "prisoners of conscience" or on behalf of the oppressed. Finally, NGOs would become actively involved in the creation of various types of implementing agencies or institutions.[7] At the beginning, standard-setting—that is, the establishment of international norms by which the conduct of states can be measured or judged—was the primary preoccupation of NGOs. Without such norms, it would have been impossible to challenge or confront state activity, howsoever brutal it was. Even before the UN Charter was adopted, at least one NGO, the Anti-Slavery Society, had been preoccupied since the eighteenth century with lobbying for the establishment of standards to outlaw one of the oldest human rights abuses—slavery.

After the norms of the Universal Declaration were adopted and eventually given a legally binding status with two covenants in the sixties, the international community had to wait two decades for the significant advancement of norm-setting with the adoption of the Covenant Against Torture and the Convention of the Rights of the Child. Both dealt with the grave evils unearthed by NGOs in another capacity, i.e., fact-finding. And more significantly, both were, in large part, creations of NGOs, whether in the drafting process or the lobbying process.

Since the Universal Declaration, the total number of major human rights treaties adopted by the UN is six. These treaties address civil and political rights, economic and social rights, racial and ethnic discrimination, discrimination against women, torture and the rights of the child. (The sixth convention against apartheid has become moot.) To this total a seventh should be added—the Convention on the Prevention and Punishment of the Crime of Genocide—whose adoption actually preceded the approval of the Universal Declaration of Human Rights, thus making it the oldest UN human rights instrument. This was scarcely accidental as the UN itself was, to a significant degree, a response to the horror of the Holocaust. The enactment of this Convention was largely the work of a single individual, Raphael Lemkin, who acted as a one-person NGO, while being backed by several mainly Jewish groups, in persuading or cajoling governments to support his unprecedented initiative.

Some of the covenants and conventions carry optional protocols (requiring a separate ratifying process) that permit individuals, not states, to bring their cases of human rights violations to a specific monitoring body created by the treaty itself. While many states have refrained from ratifying the optional protocols, the great majority of them—over 75 percent—have ratified the seven treaties. The United States has ratified four of the treaties—those pertaining to genocide, civil and political rights, racial discrimination and torture. At the same time, the United States, like other major powers, has attached "reservations" to its accession that limit applicability to the contracting party.

The drafting of legally binding norms is only the beginning of the standard-setting work of NGOs. The binding agreements must be ratified by a solid group of governments in order to be brought into force.

Ratification by any particular government often will depend upon pressure exerted by the NGOs in that country. In the case of the United States, the procedure is complicated by the constitutional provision requiring the "advice and consent" of two-thirds of the Senate. None of the seven major treaties were approved by the Senate until 1988, when positive action finally occurred on the historic genocide treaty. But this was possible only because a coalition of NGOs that had initiated the struggle for ratification in 1964 would not relinquish their battle for over a quarter of a century despite continuing frustrations and disappointments. Once ratification of the genocide treaty took place, the tradition of opposition to human rights treaties was subverted and other treaties became subject to ratification. It also enabled the United States to play a major role in pressing the UN Security Council to establish ad hoc International Criminal Tribunals.

As important as the drafting, approval and ratification of treaties was the use of the treaties' implementing machinery, applicable in all cases except genocide, to raise questions with governments about human rights abuses. It is only the NGOs that have made the machinery viable by submitting, usually on an informal basis, documentation to members of the implementing organ. Especially is this the case with the International Covenant on Civil and Political Rights, whose implementing organ, the Human Rights Committee, is almost totally dependent upon NGO briefings, documentation and advice. If the treaties and their enforcement mechanisms are perceived as the foundation of a future international human rights legal community, NGOs stood and still stand at the cutting edge of the early initiatives that would make this future possible.

The public knows NGOs less for their role in standard-setting as for their function in fact-finding and information-gathering with respect to human rights abuses. The information and documentation often would be made available to UN organs such as the Commission on Human Rights and its Sub-Commission on Prevention of Discrimination and Protection of Minorities. Or it would be given to governments and increasingly to the media directly, with the hope and expectation that bringing public shame upon an abuser regime, embarrassing it in the world arena or otherwise damaging its image would bring about a change in the policy of the targeted government. The use of the media became even more important—and, indeed, necessary—after the UN Commission on Human Rights adopted in 1947 a ruling denying that it had any authority whatsoever to deal with human rights complaints.

This declaration of impotence, when coupled with an intensification of ideological and diplomatic tensions between the superpowers during the Cold War epoch that lasted some forty years, obliged NGOs to seek out alternative means for alerting the international community concerning violations of the Universal Declaration of Human Rights. The condition of NGOs was further worsened by the arrival at the UN of a host of new states, mainly from Africa, which were both lacking in human rights traditions and suspicious of NGOs whose headquarters were based in the West. All the more would their antagonism grow when international NGOs would subject the new states to human rights criticism.

Some NGOs were prepared to weather the changed and hostile atmosphere at the UN and submit documentation that carried a criticism of governments, mostly only indirectly. If they assumed what others might have thought to be a courageous posture, it was less because they considered themselves martyrs than that they felt a responsibility to the traumatic memory of the Holocaust. Thus, B'nai B'rith would not be silent about the treatment of Soviet Jews by the Kremlin and about their right to leave the USSR for Israel and the West, if only to survive as a people. Others, too, like the International League for the Rights of Man, would address UN bodies with the withering force of factual data. What followed was a witch hunt conducted by the USSR and its allies in the Third World that threatened those NGOs daring to speak out with deprivation of their consultative status at the UN.

But the fact-finders would not be intimidated, even if some felt it more prudent to avoid using the UN as an outlet for their documentation. Indeed, the seventies constituted a decade when information-gathering on abuses was all the more urgent. Horrendous genocidal episodes were occurring in Asia and, to a lesser extent, in Africa; military seizures of state power were occurring in several major Latin American countries, followed by the ruthless repression of human rights including the use of torture, disappearances and extrajudicial killings. It was the outstanding research work of the London-based NGO Amnesty International that, drawing upon fact-finding missions and fieldwork as well as the painstaking accumulation of data from a variety of sources—the press, letters and interviews—could and did produce reports that spotlighted the gross human rights violations. The exposés, which sensitized world opinion, won for Amnesty the Nobel Peace Prize; it was the only NGO to have been awarded this distinction.

Paralleling the emergence of a growing public awareness of human rights abuses was the emergence of a dramatically changed attitude on the part of the United States toward international human rights. The appropriate term should be "reemergence," rather than "emergence," as the United States in the immediate postwar period had been—partly in response to NGO pressures—the champion of human rights in adopting the UN Charter, in developing the Universal Declaration of Human Rights, in creating the historic Nuremberg Tribunal and in winning adoption of the Genocide Convention by the UN General Assembly. A new isolationism in the early fifties, joined with McCarthyism and xenophobia, had reversed the earlier trend. UN human rights treaties would languish unratified. Later, with Henry Kissinger as National Security Adviser to President Richard Nixon and afterwards, as Secretary of State, human rights was dismissed as a factor serving American international interests.

Realpolitik could not, however, survive the utter disillusionment generated by the U.S. support of repressive regimes and the seemingly endless Vietnamese conflict. Beginning in 1973, with the encouragement and assistance of several key Washington NGOs, Congress enacted legislation of a strong human rights character that linked United States aid and military assistance to whether a government grossly mistreats its own citizens. Congress, too, would require the establishment within the State Department of a special bureau on human rights, and the United States government became the first in the world to launch such a bureau. And, equally impressive, the State Department was to annually prepare a study of the status of human rights in every country. Again, it was only the United States that was required by law to document human rights practices in foreign countries.

Among the various legislative initiatives was the Jackson-Vanik amendment, enacted by Congress in 1974, which linked trade benefits from the United States to whether a Communist country permitted its citizens to emigrate when they sought to do so. It was ultimately to exert an enormous impact upon the Soviet Union and, to a lesser extent, upon Romania, in allowing Jews to leave for Israel and the West. What made this legislation possible, in the face of implacable resistance by Nixon and Kissinger, was a determined American Jewish community that supported the National Conference of Soviet Jewry, an NGO comprising a variety of separate Jewish organizations. The grassroots struggle also involved the Union of Councils, a coalition of separate militant groups in a dozen cities. Backing the Jewish community were a significant number of religious, civil rights and labor groups.

With the election of Jimmy Carter, human rights came to occupy a prominent place in American foreign policy and responsiveness to NGOs was fairly high. The American human rights role was especially significant with respect to the Latin American military dictatorships and with respect to the Helsinki process in Europe. The latter role was critical and was continued in a vigorous way by President Reagan and Secretary of State George Shultz. What was totally reversed was Kissinger's policy of indifference to the Helsinki process; now the human rights provisions of the Helsinki Final Act would be seized upon and promoted on every occasion and, particularly, at Helsinki forums. In this endeavor, the Carter Administration, assisted by the largely congressional U.S. Helsinki Commission, would utilize extraordinarily helpful documentation provided by NGOs in the USSR and in East Europe.

Especially important as sources of information were the Helsinki Watch Group of Moscow and other ethnic Helsinki groups in the capitals of several other Soviet Union republics. Vital, too, were the reports of Charter 77 of Czechoslovakia and Solidarity of Poland. In the United States the National Conference on Soviet Jewry, together with other ethnic NGOs, was extremely active along with an older NGO, Freedom House, and the recently formed U.S. Helsinki Watch. The last was of considerable importance in providing moral support through visits to the various Helsinki groups in East Europe.

The central figure in linking together in the Helsinki process the Carter and Reagan administrations, the United States Helsinki Commission and the various NGO groups in East Europe and the United States was the gifted and articulate Ambassador Max Kampelman. If East Europe was swept by revolutions in 1989, notably the "velvet" one in Czechoslovakia under Vaclav Havel and the others in Poland and Hungary, the dramatic transformation was a testimonial to those elements willing to use the Helsinki process for the promotion of human rights. Besides the U.S. Helsinki Commission and the American NGOs that helped bring it into existence and sustained it were a constant source of encouragement to Andrei Sakharov, Yuri Orlov, Anatoly Shcharansky and the other dissidents of the USSR. To the extent that the collapse of the Soviet empire can be considered one of the two great human rights milestones of the latter part of the twentieth century, NGOs can be said to have played a prominent role in that historic achievement.

The second great human rights milestone was the disintegration of the apartheid system in South Africa, which coincided approximately in time with the collapse of the Soviet system in Europe. Between 1989 and 1991 what had seemed like permanent fixtures of evil on the international scene simply disappeared—though not without leaving a heritage of injustice, the torment of which has yet to be resolved and placated or at least eased. In the overthrow of the apartheid system, Nelson Mandela's African National Congress (ANC), of course, was the central actor. But a key role was played by an American NGO, the American Committee on Africa. From the sixties onward this NGO organized a remarkable public effort, involving the civil rights movement, which ultimately led to a massive popular disinvestment and boycott endeavor to which churches, students, universities and city and state governments subscribed. It was climaxed by the imposition through congressional action of sanctions on a variety of levels.

Accompanying the Helsinki process and the antiapartheid struggle during the eighties were human rights developments at the United Nations that had a revolutionary character. Until then, no effective mechanisms existed for dealing with or responding to human rights complaints. The tens of thousands of complaints flooding the UN system annually were treated—ludicrously enough—with a system of confidentiality. NGOs would now assume their third major function—spurring the creation of special UN mechanisms and providing those instruments with the assembled documentation to make their investigations productive. The new mechanisms, established by the Commission on Human Rights, were Working Groups on Disappearances and on Detention and Special Rapporteurs on Torture or on Arbitrary and Extrajudicial Killings. Later, there came Special Rapporteurs on such other themes as violence against women and race hatred. Special Rapporteurs also were created for particularly egregious human rights violators like Cuba, Sudan, Burma (Myanmar), Burundi and Rwanda.

In most instances, the new special procedures were the product of the creative thinking of various NGOs as well as their determined lobbying. What fed the new special procedures was the flow of information, documentation and data from NGOs. In that sense, they were similar to the recently created or strengthened treaty enforcement mechanisms. The basic truth, which knowledgeable officials at the UN clearly understood, was that without NGOs, the entire human rights implementation system at the UN would come to a halt. Eleanor Roosevelt had anticipated the indispensable value of NGOs when, just before the vote on the Universal Declaration of Human Rights, she projected the image of a "curious grapevine" that would penetrate closed societies. Such a "grapevine" could transmit the messages of human rights abuses to the international community.

Still, the modified UN system is far from adequate. Reports of the Working Groups and the Special Rapporteurs are given only the most cursory of attention by the Commission on Human Rights at its sessions in Geneva. The UN's public relations structure has scarcely been oriented to giving the reports media exposure. Geneva, moreover, is not a major news media center. Thus, only rarely, does a valuable report get any public attention. Besides, Special Rapporteurs on specific countries have been appointed only for the smaller, less influential countries. None of the great powers have ever been subjected to this type of inquiry.

If China's abuses are notorious and widely known, Beijing's power and political lobbying has led to so-called no action resolutions on several occasions in the nineties. While the enormous effort by China to prevent a resolution on condemnation testifies to the significance it attaches to the international community's possible use of moral sanction on its human rights practices, the success of Beijing's political maneuvering and lobbying demonstrates that the Commission on Human Rights in no way provides a level playing field and a reasonably objective manner for judging abusers. In striking contrast, Israel, lacking any political influence at the UN, for years has been treated as a perpetual pariah, subject to continuing investigation, endless resolutions of condemnation and speeches that, at times, resurrect ancient themes of anti-Jewish bigotry.

Politics obviously plays a decisive role at the Commission and, given the typical composition of the 53-member body, it is not always apparent that it will be swayed by human rights considerations. Analysis of Freedom House surveys indicate that a clear majority of its members can be described as but "partly free" or "non-free." The data are hardly conducive to a strong positive perspective on human rights. NGOs have been the main instruments for overriding negative political factors and making progress. In the mobilization of support for the unsuccessful resolution on China, Human Rights Watch repeatedly has striven to mount a major campaign. That NGO, nonetheless, did prove to be effective in a remarkable initiative with the International Olympic Committee to deny Beijing the opportunity to become the site of the Olympic Games in the year 2000. In the absence of a purely political forum, China's fierce determination to prevail could not overcome this crusading human rights effort.

Keenly aware of the unceasing pressure of the NGOs to target abusers and advance human rights objectives, some members of the Commission—especially those, like Cuba, which have been a subject of United States and NGO criticism—during 1997 have launched a dangerous initiative to hinder or prevent further positive steps in advancing the valuable special procedures. It goes without saying that the leading NGO human rights activists have mobilized the NGO community to vigorously oppose these disturbing plans aimed at turning the UN human rights clock back. Uncertainty about the eventual outcome prevails.

Perhaps the most important of the NGO initiatives in creating effective mechanisms for implementing the Universal Declaration of Human Rights came in 1993 with the World Conference on Human Rights held in Vienna. A critical item that would be placed on the world agenda through pressure exerted by NGOs at regional preparatory meetings was the establishment of a UN High Commissioner for Human Rights. The idea had been publicly expressed and promoted in 1964 by Jacob Blaustein of the American Jewish Committee. The Office of the High Commissioner, as initially conceived, would provide a certain minimum implementation of international standards. But Soviet opposition, along with Third World indifference and frequently resistance, killed the first genuine effort of a particular type of compliance mechanism.

Yet the idea once again took shape on the eve of the World Conference on Human Rights in 1993 and an international lobbying effort by established NGOs, supported by a massive push from newly arisen national NGOs, especially in Asia, but also including NGOs in Latin America and Africa as well. What happened at the World Conference was an incredible display of NGO activism for an instrument that was perceived as one that would finally pry open the door to the fulfillment of the dream of Eleanor Roosevelt. It was U.S. diplomacy, once the idea of a High Commissioner was given a blessing by the Clinton Administration, that made possible the victory for the NGO vision both at Vienna and, more importantly, at the UN General Assembly in the fall in New York. It need hardly be said that in the shaping of the Administration's thinking on the proposal, the lobbying in Washington by representatives of major NGOs played a crucial role.

The World Conference deliberations and conclusions served two other purposes of great concern to the NGOs and for which they lobbied intensively and, in the end, triumphantly. One purpose involved addressing a mounting challenge from a coalition of mainly authoritarian regimes in Asia, with the support of China, questioning the "universality" of the Universal Declaration of Human Rights. For these regimes, a set of values—"Asian values"—were presumed to characterize their culture as distinct from Western values and Western culture. In the "Asian values" system, the community was considered to be supreme, rather than the individual—and, thus, order and unity were held to be the proper goals of their society. And, economic and social rights were regarded in the view of the Asian authoritarians to be more important than civil and political rights, which were thought to be the principal concern in the Western perspective. "Universality" would win out in the struggle over language but with a modest compromise by which the "particularities" of culture were accorded a certain recognition. Strikingly, it was the NGOs of Asia that were decisive in advocating universality over the objections of their authoritarian governments.

The second purpose of the NGO community to which the World Conference favorably responded related to women's rights. Until the World Conference, general human rights meetings did not attempt to weave women's rights into the substance of their deliberations. A coordinating women's NGO, the Center for Women's Global Leadership, launched as early as 1991 a "Global Campaign" to link together women's groups throughout the world and focus upon violence against women. The initial target was the Vienna Conference, where it was hoped that women's rights would be declared to be very much part of human rights. This was seen as a critical preparatory step for the World Conference on Women scheduled for Beijing in 1995.

At Vienna, women constituted almost one-half the total number of participants. The Center for Global Leadership made certain through a vast petition campaign prior to the Conference, lobbying at the Conference and a moving, theatrically structured "Tribunal on Violation of Women's Human Rights," to raise the consciousness of the general NGO human rights constituency. Women's rights were equated with human rights. Crimes against women were held to be crimes against humanity. The climax of the women's NGO initiative came at Beijing. There the prevailing theme was declared to be "women's rights are human rights" and an electrifying address by Hillary Rodham Clinton emphasized that "it is no longer acceptable to discuss women's rights as separate from human rights."

Beijing marked a milestone in the struggle for women's rights. With 35,000 in attendance it was both the largest women's conference ever and the largest NGO conference ever. The principal chronicler of the women's rights movement and of the Beijing Conference, Felice Gaer of the Blaustein Institute, has emphasized that there would be no turning back from this historic moment. Partial validity was provided by decisions reached by the first Chief Prosecutor of the International Criminal Tribunals at The Hague, Richard Goldstone: rape against Bosnian Muslim women and Tutsi women in Rwanda, he said, would be treated as a crime against humanity.

The establishment of the International Criminal Tribunal in The Hague in 1993 was itself a landmark decision of the UN Security Council. Not since the postwar Nuremberg trials of Nazi war criminals had the international community accorded recognition of accountability for war crimes, crimes against humanity and genocide. NGOs, particularly Human Rights Watch, played a vital role in urging the establishment of a Tribunal and providing it with an endless flow of documentary evidence on the details of ethnic cleansing. The same NGOs also gave invaluable public support to the Tribunal and pressed for it to be adequately financed and for major NATO governments to apprehend indicted war criminals.

NGOs assumed other functions at The Hague as well. Some volunteered services to deal with delicate emotional problems of witnesses, whether victims or firsthand observers of crimes, including the crime of rape. Others, like the Physicians for Human Rights, made available forensic scientists, who through exhumation of grave sites and examination of corpses provided the most essential type of evidence. To the extent that a watershed was reached in ending impunity and in laying the groundwork for a permanent International Criminal Court, perhaps before the end of the twentieth century, NGOs—sometimes separately, sometimes in coalition with one another—have shown themselves to be invaluable to this remarkable historical process of rendering justice. They have frequently found the United States as an ally; indeed, some members of the Clinton Administration, like Madeleine Albright, actually have encouraged the formation of a coalition-type NGO to promote, publicize and lobby for international justice.

The raging episodes of genocide that punctuated the nineties but had earlier post-Hitlerian manifestations in Burundi, Cambodia and Iraq—and in each of which NGOs were active in accumulating documentation—highlighted the fact that ethnic tensions were a principal source of contemporary conflict and war. In addition to the crumbling of empires and the collapse of multinational states, there was the demand of minorities for rights that could include autonomy or even secession. In any case, it had become clear that ethnicity and minority rights had suddenly surfaced as requiring urgent and immediate attention. Genocide was at times the ultimate expression of unresolved ethnic disputes. Europe, not surprisingly, was quick to give expression to the concern. When the Conference on Security and Cooperation in Europe (CSCE) and its successor, the Organization of Security and Cooperation in Europe (OSCE), moved to have an "early warning system" in the form of a High Commissioner on National Minorities, it set in motion the processes of conflict prevention and crisis management.

The High Commissioner on National Minorities, Max van der Stoel, demonstrated the enormous value of an NGO when he established in The Hague the Foundation for Inter-Ethnic Relations, which provided the information and expertise that helped him facilitate the reduction of tensions in some ten countries in East Europe already plagued by ethnic hostility. Its work has yet to be replicated elsewhere.

While most NGOs focused upon ethnic tensions and the urgent need to deal with them, whether by conflict resolution or by institutions of a special international judicial type, at least one U.S. domestic NGO, Freedom House, shifted to another category of abuse that it thought had been neglected. Religious repression, as conducted by Communist states—notably China—as well as by extremist Muslim states such as Sudan and Iran, was targeted as requiring urgent U.S. governmental attention. While the subject had, in fact, been given considerable focus by other NGOs, it was never handled in quite as dramatic a fashion as that arranged by Freedom House's Puebla Institute, which sought to tap the religious passions of the Christian evangelical movement. The impact of the mass lobbying was considerable.

Among the punitive measures initially advanced in proposed legislation to end religious persecution was the use of U.S. voting power in world financial institutions to transform them into significant levers of change. Since these international lending institutions were of critical importance to the growing economies of the Third World, as well as to some in the former Communist world of East Europe, and since they also served as models for regional lending institutions, they potentially could serve as powerful instruments for combating human rights abuses.

Were the international bodies to link loans to internal governance patterns in which human rights practices are a consideration, a valuable device for halting abuse by Third World regimes would become available. The United States exercised major influence in these institutions, and legislation could oblige it to use its influence to reject loans to abuser states. During the middle and late seventies, the use of this type of legislation had been advanced in connection with gross violations of human rights. One NGO, the Lawyers Committee for Human Rights, was especially interested in the potential leverage of international lending institutions and gave this concept prominent, trailblazing attention.

Sanctions were quite another matter. Use of this weapon was eschewed by most powers, and President Clinton made it clear in 1994 that sanctions would not be applied by the United States to China, a leading abuser of human rights. China's huge market acted as a powerful attraction for Western traders and investors. Commercial considerations, along with security considerations, trumped human rights for the Clinton Administration. If the United States was prepared to use sanctions in the case of abusive small powers where the economic and commercial stakes were not high—for example, with Myanmar (Burma)—it would not apply sanctions to China.

For international NGOs, U.S. reluctance to exert determined pressure upon China (or upon other leading Asian states) posed a serious problem. What alternative strategy should be applied? Some urged adherence by Western businessmen to a code of conduct requiring at least a modest degree of human rights activism, mostly in upholding decent wage standards, avoiding child labor and forced labor and according trade unions a certain authority. Others, like the Lawyers Committee for Human Rights, recommended that the United States and various Western states, together with business groups and NGOs, insist upon the drafting of and adherence to the rule of law. The rule of law was seen as critical to the very nature of business transactions and essential for capitalist enterprises.

But if NGOs were compelled to consider alternative strategies, they would not retreat on the principle of universality of human rights. Strikingly, they were supported in the principle of universality by Asian NGOs, along with NGOs in Latin America and Africa. At the same time, Third World NGOs endorsed the need for the international community—as well as international NGOs—to pay greater attention to economic and social rights, which they felt had been for too long neglected or subordinated to civil and political rights. At a special and unusual retreat for NGO representatives from around the globe, sponsored by Harvard Law School and the Human Rights Internet and held in Crete in June 1989, Third World NGOs expressed considerable criticism of Western-based international NGOs for failing to monitor economic and social rights, even if they pose difficulties in assessing and defining.[8]

Major international NGOs like Human Rights Watch and Amnesty International for several years have been debating the extent to which they should enter the area of economic and social rights, in the absence of specific international standards of measurement, even though they agree that the Covenant on the subject is equal in importance to the Covenant on Civil and Political Rights. Human Rights Watch, in September, 1996, after a year-long "strategic review," agreed to begin reporting on economic and social rights "either when violations of . . . [these] rights are the direct consequence of a serious violation of CP [civil and political] rights, or when respect for . . . [economic and social] rights is an essential part of remedying serious CP violations."[9]

One of the reasons offered for the new posture was that "many local human rights activists around the world" do promote economic and social rights within their countries and "some of them believe we [international NGOs] risk undermining their work" by tacitly questioning the legitimacy of the Covenant on Economic, Social and Cultural Rights. Still the proposed new inquiry into economic and social rights was circumscribed by limitations that accorded recognition to the difficulties in measuring fulfillment of Covenant obligations. At the Crete NGO retreat, references were made to land confiscation, or the removal of inhabitants from land they occupy in order to make room for giant industrial or agricultural projects planned by transnational corporate enterprises, or by state infrastructure-building projects like dams. Another type of economic and social right to which NGO conferees referred was the right of workers to organize unions and the latter's right to bargain collectively.

It is quite likely that increased emphasis on this subject will deepen throughout the human rights field. In several speeches, the UN High Commissioner for Human Rights, Mary Robinson, has given economic and social rights an especially prominent focus.

It should be recognized that the issue of the universality of human rights and the absoluteness of the Universal Declaration was by no means resolved from the perspective of various authoritarian regimes. A number of Third World powers during 1997 intensified their earlier clamor that the "right of development" be added to the International Bill of Human Rights.[10] More disturbing was an accompanying demand, in some quarters, that the Universal Declaration be reviewed and, by implication, revised. Until now, the International Bill of Human Rights has been treated as sacred, not to be weakened or defiled by additions or subtractions. The new attempt by authoritarian and totalitarian states to tamper with documents haloed by time, including the half-century-old Universal Declaration, testifies indirectly to the power of those documents, the increasing magnetism of the standards they set and the binding obligations they demand.

But the recent maneuvering also illuminates the significance of NGOs who, from the beginning, have been critically instrumental in shaping the Universal Declaration; in utilizing its provisions despite threats and intimidation; in creating mechanisms to give it greater vitality and thereby enabling it to be more effectively implemented; and in augmenting its impact with additional Conventions and Declarations so that its application can be made more specific to different types of abuses and human rights violations.

It is hardly surprising that the same forces seeking to weaken the Universal Declaration and its associated instruments also are engaged in efforts to limit the influence of NGOs at the UN Commission on Human Rights and to circumscribe the authority of the Commission and its special mechanisms. That the NGOs are certain to resist the new challenges to the Universal Declaration and to their own role is self-evident. They have come a long way and are not about to capitulate to initiatives that undermine their very purpose.

Besides, there is the matter of unfinished NGO business. Very much the products of the Holocaust, human rights efforts have yet to put into place the crucial institution that is designed to end impunity and institutionalize accountability. It is not only the Universal Declaration of Human Rights which was adopted fifty years ago on December 10, 1948; just a day earlier, the UN General Assembly unanimously adopted the Genocide Convention. If neglected or observed in the breach since the sixties, the Genocide Convention has helped prompt NGOs to press for and provide evidence and other forms of assistance to ad hoc international Tribunals for Yugoslavia and Rwanda. Much remains to be done to enable these Tribunals to succeed in their purpose. What has yet to be realized, however, is not another ad hoc Tribunal, but a permanent International Criminal Court. NGOs have been in the forefront of this effort and the possibility of its coming into being before the end of a century marked by not a few episodes of genocide appears quite promising.

To a considerable extent, progress made at various special UN preparatory conferences during 1996-98 to draft a statute for a permanent International Criminal Court, was the result of an extraordinary, highly coordinated effort by hundreds of NGOs to persuade governments of the proposed Court's urgent necessity. Their effort was crowned with some success when a conference of plenipotentiaries voted to create the statute of the Court. The United States stood in opposition to the final effort which could not fail to mar the achievement.

Accountability means not only the rendering of justice, but also the making of amends for crimes. A study by the UN Sub-Commission on Prevention of Discrimination and Protection of Minorities points the way to reparations. And, at least one NGO—the World Jewish Congress—has shone a bright light on the hidden, somewhat nefarious, conduct of the government of Switzerland and particularly its bankers in depriving Holocaust survivors of the savings deposited by them or by their intimate relatives who had been massacred in gas chambers and Nazi concentration camps. In this case, exposure ultimately led to some compensation.

Beyond justice and reparation, accountability also has meant disclosures of the horrors and evils of grossly repressive systems, including apartheid. Truth Commissions have come into being in the last two decades to reveal the terrifying realities behind these systems. Not surprisingly, NGOs have played a major role in getting such commissions started, providing them with documentation and promoting them with the public.

Precisely how the NGOs operated to achieve the remarkable human rights transformation of the past half-century is the focus of this study. NGOs, in most instances, are treated individually and each is accompanied by a kind of biographical sketch examining when, how, and why it came into existence; how it was funded; the nature of its constituency; the manner in which its policies were formulated and carried out and in what ways it has changed over the years. Each NGO is described in the context of a particular advance in human rights with which it was involved or associated. Thus, in some ways, the chapters unfold in a general chronological fashion and, thereby, provide a broad historical picture of the evolution of international human rights in the last half-century. Within each chapter, however, when the focus is upon a particular NGO, emphasis is placed on the biography and role of the NGO and therefore may not conform precisely with the chronological sequence. At all times, however, the international and political context within which the NGO works is provided as vital background.

The NGOs have been required to assume a multiplicity of tasks. Felix Ermacora, who knew them better than most scholars and statesman, having served for many years in official UN and European human rights bodies, characterized the breadth of their activity in the following way:

> NGOs have built up a system of international pressure on the development of human rights. NGOs are the initiators of projects, they press state delegations to act, they influence intergovernmental staff who prepare documents and studies, they provide material and information about human rights problems and situations, they give legal aid to victims of

violations of human rights and they fulfill—to a certain extent—the role
of an international ombudsman for human rights.[11]

Indeed as ombudsmen, some NGOs, in their various missions abroad,
would intervene in a quiet diplomatic manner on behalf of one or another
"prisoner of conscience" or seek intervention by a Western diplomatic
official.[12] Even the powerful Kremlin during the seventies was not
immune from ombudsman-type activity that might link public exposure
with quiet intervention on behalf of a selected dissident. During the last
decade, NGOs have gone far beyond these broad functions to embrace
major peacekeeping operations and to warfare and facets of weaponry
that violate international humanitarian laws and principles.

Not every human rights NGO has been surveyed in this volume,
although most of the major ones are covered. A particularly prominent
NGO, the International Commission of Jurists, already has been given
extensive coverage in a large-scale work, which explains why the subject
is but briefly treated here, although its important achievements are noted.
Judgment, too, had to be made about whether one or another NGO
would be reviewed in some detail. While coverage of all, in some fashion,
certainly would have been warranted, time and space required limitations
that made for a certain arbitrariness in the selection process. Hopefully,
this has not affected the overall thrust and purpose of the study: to
demonstrate the significance of NGOs in making human rights a vibrant
and major force on the agenda of international diplomacy and discourse.

In achieving this objective, NGOs, especially those that are American-based, inevitably sought to impact upon U.S. government policy. A
subtext that emerges from the study suggests that the official U.S. role
in advancing the interests of human rights coincided with and was
prompted frequently by NGOs. At the beginning of the postwar period
and until the early fifties, the human rights purposes of NGOs won the
support of the American government. That relationship then came to an
end and would not be resumed until the late seventies, although
congressional initiatives pressed by NGOs laid the groundwork for a new
and positive human rights thrust on the part of the Carter Administration
and of subsequent Administrations.

Some of the greatest achievements of NGOs in the recent period
were the result of the diplomatic muscle used by the Clinton Administration—the establishment of the High Commissioner for Human
Rights, the acceptance of the principle of universality at the World
Conference on Human Rights, the creation of ad hoc International

Criminal Tribunals for the Former Yugoslavia and for Rwanda and the equating of women's rights with human rights at the Beijing Conference on Women in 1995. Yet, on a number of major occasions, the Administration has subordinated human rights to security and economic concerns. Pentagon concerns prevailed in the case of a landmines treaty in late 1997 and with respect to the creation of an International Criminal Court in July 1998. At the same time, commercial considerations, all too often, have transcended vital human rights obligations.

One form of the evidence underscoring the growth of the significance of NGOs is in the current responsiveness of the Clinton Administration notwithstanding the above-noted failures. No former U.S. Administration, at its highest levels, has been anywhere near as responsive to NGOs. The Clinton Administration was the first ever to welcome receiving officially a formal document from NGOs: "A Human Rights Agenda for the Clinton Administration," prepared by ten leading U.S.-based NGOs in July 1997. The Administration also arranged for the heads of these organizations to meet first with Samuel Berger, the National Security Adviser, on September 9, and then, toward the end of the year, on November 5, with Secretary of State Madeleine Albright. The last meeting was reported as wide-ranging and unusually lengthy.[13]

The proposed agenda for the Clinton Administration would find hardly any government, even the most democratic, agreeing without qualification with its fundamental propositions. The agenda would require the Administration to affirm human rights to be "an essential element" of American foreign policy and to agree that "human rights concerns are central" to that foreign policy. However, putting aside themes of "centrality" and "essentiality," and focusing upon what the group selected as "priorities" for Clinton's second term, the ten proposals that they offered appeared to be both logical and realistic.

Three proposals stand out. First, the United States was called upon to prevent genocide and other human rights catastrophes. This consideration was to be regarded as "a pillar of American foreign policy" and to be dealt with by force if necessary. Second, the United States must seek to assure that individuals who commit genocide and other atrocities are brought to justice before a national or international court.

The third proposed priority moved into the area of sharp criticism. While calling for firmness and consistency in combating serious human rights violations, the document asked that the abuser state be dealt with in a manner unrelated to whether the state was held to be important to U.S. economic or security interests. China was the focal point of this priority, and a host of linkages to Beijing's policy priorities was set forth involving high-level visits, trade, membership in the World Trade Organization and a critical UN Commission on Human Rights resolution.

When the ten NGO leaders met with Secretary of State Albright, they were crossing a threshold. No previous Secretary of State ever had met with leading international human rights activists, whether individually or as a group. The seriousness of the session was underscored by the fact that Albright included several of her top aides—Under Secretaries Thomas Pickering and Tim Wirth, Assistant Secretary of State for Democracy, Human Rights and Labor, John Shattuck, and Ambassador at Large for War Crimes, David Scheffer. The schedule called for a fairly short 30-minute discussion, which turned into a 70-minute session with the Secretary keenly attentive to everything being said.

From the perspective of the NGO leaders, as reported by a participant, it was a "very successful" meeting, not least because the Secretary of State indicated that she would welcome follow-up sessions. This was precisely the aim of the NGOs. The human rights community, conceivably, could be entering a new era in which it might share its views directly with the U.S. government's highest foreign affairs officials and, at the same time, exchange opinions with them. The first follow-up meetings came in the Spring, 1998. On March 26, the NGOs met with Secretary Albright in a wide ranging discussion mainly on the China issue, but covering other critical subjects. For the human rights activists, the encounter was serious and gratifying. On May 28, they met with Berger. China again dominated the exchange, with the NGOs pressing for some significant act by President Clinton on his scheduled visit. The NGOs also urged positive action by the Administration on the International Criminal Court, on elections in Nigeria and on ratification of a women's rights convention (CEDAW). It may be that these meetings, with respect to China, helped prompt President Clinton to assume a more activist defense of human rights and democracy in his Beijing press conference and his lecture to the Beijing University student body.

Indicative of the NGO community's reaction to the initial exchanges with top Administration foreign policy officials came toward the end of 1997 with the comments of an important NGO leader, Gay McDougall. As director of the Washington-based International Human Rights Law Group, she was asked to introduce President Clinton to one of the largest assemblages of NGOs on the eve of Human Rights Day. McDougall in her remarks acknowledged that "this Administration has opened its doors and provided unprecedented access to human rights advocates, fostering frank policy discussion with officials at the highest levels of the Administration."[14] In the course of her remarks, she praised the Administration for its "leadership on important human rights issues. . . ."

The occasion for the NGO assemblage was the opening of year-long commemorative ceremonies of the fiftieth anniversary of the Universal Declaration of Human Rights. It is of interest to note that the President, in his formal presentation, said: "Advancing human rights must always be a central pillar of America's foreign policy." The language was close to that articulated in the NGO document which had urged that human rights be considered as a "pillar of foreign policy" and that it be considered "central" and "essential."[15] One hardly could escape the similarity in formulation.

Strikingly, the President chose to hold the reception for diplomats, NGOs and prominent personalities to mark the fiftieth anniversary ceremony at the recently opened New York Museum of Jewish Heritage, which was dedicated to the memory of the Holocaust. He must have been acutely aware that the struggle for human rights was sparked by the trauma of the Holocaust and that the phrase "Never Again"—referring to the Hitlerian atrocities—became a major slogan of many in the NGO community.

Even as McDougall lauded the Administration, she made it clear that the NGO community was by no means satisfied, stating: "there is so much more to be done if the United States is to play an effective role in protecting human rights around the world." What she was articulating is precisely the appropriate posture of the human rights advocate. Lobbying must continue until the promise of the Universal Declaration is fully realized. Just a few days before the commemorative ceremonies, perhaps the most prominent of the American-based NGOs, Human Rights Watch, released its annual *World Report* which scathingly criticized the United States for its "Great Power Arrogance on Human Rights."[16] On a host of human rights issues, the NGO community is and will continue to be critical of the United States.

The very next day—December 10—more than 80 U.S. organizations announced the creation of a national coalition sponsored by the Franklin and Eleanor Roosevelt Institute that would conduct a year-long campaign aimed at ending human rights abuses worldwide. Publicly unveiled by the Chairperson of the coalition's steering committee, Felice Gaer, was a community action guide to maximize public efforts directed at winning U.S. ratification of the UN convention barring discrimination against women, establishing an international criminal court, obtaining the arrest of indicted war criminals for genocide in Bosnia and Rwanda and providing greater protection for the rights of children.

In considering the escalation of NGO influence, other factors demand attention. Jessica Mathews, of the Carnegie Endowment for International Peace, observed in a provocative essay that the growth of the influence of human rights NGOs was a reflection of the changed distribution of power in state—nonstate relations since the end of the Cold War.[17] The traditional modern state, with its almost absolute sovereignty features over the territory it rules, has been obliged to contend with other non-sovereignty factors such as transnational business, international organizations and NGOs. Both the marketplace, affected by the globalizing economy, and international public opinion, exercised through international NGOs, have intruded in a variety of ways into the heretofore absolute authority of state power.

Technological factors of a revolutionary character have facilitated the change in the distribution of powers, with nonstate actors gaining at the expense of state power. Computers and the extraordinary transformation of the telecommunications industry have broken forever an earlier government monopoly on the collection, management and transmission of vast amounts of information. Instantaneous access to information and the ability to put it to use immediately give NGOs, among others, the megaphone power to be heard quickly and loudly. Take the example of Human Rights in China, an NGO founded by Chinese scientists and scholars in March 1989. Based in New York and initially sharing office space at Human Rights Watch headquarters, Human Rights in China has acquired its own Web site and gopher menu, which enables it to provide information about human rights conditions in China. In addition, it posts action alerts, press releases and other material on the Internet through which it is in touch with 100,000 Chinese students and scholars worldwide. In a recent paper, the organization commented: "With mainland China's access to the Internet exploding, the potential for conducting human rights advocacy and education electronically is enormous."[18]

The Internet, along with e-mail, enhances enormously NGO clout. The nonprofit Association for Progressive Communications provides 50,000 NGOs in 133 countries access to tens of millions of Internet users for the price of a local call.[19] NGOs in one country can interact immediately with like-minded NGOs in distant places so as to generate a groundswell of activity and public statements affecting one or more governments. Weaker NGOs in the developing countries can win a quick show of support from more experienced, better-funded and more powerful colleagues in the United States or the United Kingdom. American-based or British-based NGOs can impact on the international media and mobilize support from their own governments on behalf of the human rights interests of NGOs in developing countries.

Technology is assisted by the ability of NGOs to tap various sources of funding from both private and public sources. Except for several totalitarian regimes, like those of China or North Korea, and authoritarian regimes, mostly in the Arab world (except Egypt), where civil society is severely restricted, the number of NGOs and their influence have greatly expanded in the last five years. The financial resources, together with expertise and know-how, of some NGOs are so large that they sometimes exceed those of smaller governments and even segments of international organizations. The head of the UN Centre for Human Rights in Geneva jealously complained in 1993 that "we have less money and fewer resources than Amnesty International and we are the arm of the UN for human rights. This is clearly ridiculous."[20]

Even with the big impact that human rights NGOs exert today upon the world scene, voices in and out of the NGO community are critical as to how successful they actually are. In a two-year study (1992-94), sponsored by the Ford Foundation, that examined mainly Amnesty International and, to a lesser extent, Human Rights Watch and the Lawyers Committee for Human Rights, Professor Stanley Cohen of Hebrew University concluded that there was "widespread awareness and frustration that so much effort is invested [by NGOs] in compiling yet more information—which then sinks into a public and media black hole."[21] Cohen concluded that "the amount of work that goes into producing a standard human rights report . . . is not balanced by much thinking about the impact of this information."[22]

What most troubled Cohen was the failure of the major NGOs to evaluate "whether and how information is actually received" by the various audiences to which it is addressed. While the problem of measuring the effectiveness of communication may be recognized, he found, the NGOs did not seek to examine what impact the reports they release actually have. Either missing or rare were the standard techniques for "reflective discourse" in evaluating particular strategies—conferences, workshops, specialized research or commissioned articles. Cohen's perspective for the future was less than enthusiastic. Despite the "growing visibility and credibility" of human rights NGOs over the last 25 years, public support, from the pessimistic perspective which he cited, "has now leveled out."[23] Solid evidence was not offered for this outlook. Even more questionable was Cohen's conclusion that the human rights movement has not "emerged as a major force in mobilizing public opinion," whether within countries or on the international scene.

That the Cohen paper would spark discussion in various branches of the human rights community, academic as well as practitioner, not least in the Foundation that had sponsored it, could not but be expected. In fact, the discussion had begun earlier with the Vienna World Conference on Human Rights, where it became evident that the human rights movement lacked "a long term capacity to chart sound directions on . . . agenda-setting, [and] policy analysis. . . ."[24] This "capacity" was especially seen as missing for the numerous NGOs that but recently had made their appearance in the Third World. In July 1994, a consultation was held at Cambridge University devoted to the questions of applied policy research and evaluation. A basic paper prepared by Helena Cook, formerly head of Amnesty International's Legal Office, set the frame of reference. In her view, applied policy research on international human rights issues, or rather its absence, constituted a crucial problem. What was needed, Cook emphasized, was a research structure that would serve "as a genuinely international body" and make "research accessible to the wider human rights community. . . ."[25]

A Founding Board, comprised of a half-dozen leading academics from several countries, established the International Council on Human Rights Policy in the summer of 1996. By September, 1997 it acquired a Director to oversee a small Secretariat based in Geneva. The Secretariat is to hold "conferences, seminars and workshops" in which practitioners and scholars will meet to discuss complex issues as well as strategy-related aspects of planned or ongoing research projects.

How, when and in what way the Council will relate to the needs and strategies of NGOs is yet to be defined. In the meantime, it would be premature to question the strength and vitality of NGOs, especially after the Ottawa Landmines Treaty ceremony on December 3-4, 1997 and the subsequent Nobel Peace Award ceremony in Oslo on December 10. NGOs first were accorded widespread international attention and praise almost thirty years after the adoption of the Universal Declaration of Human Rights. In 1977, the Nobel Peace Prize was awarded to Amnesty International for stirring the world's conscience in its numerous campaigns to implement the Universal Declaration. At the time, the group was only at the beginning of a career that would rocket it to human rights fame, and several other important international human rights

NGOs were not yet even born, a circumstance applicable as well to the thousands of NGOs in the Third World that only later would make their historical appearance.

Only two decades later, in the fall of 1997, an announcement was made in Oslo that an NGO, "The International Campaign to Ban Landmines," together with its coordinator, Jody Williams, would again be awarded the 1997 Nobel Peace Prize. It was to be given in recognition of their effort to obtain an international treaty banning landmines. The coordinating or coalition NGO, The International Campaign to Ban Landmines, was composed of some 1,000 separate NGOs in over 60 countries. Playing very prominent leadership roles in the Campaign were Human Rights Watch, especially one of its key negotiators, Steve Goose, and the Physicians Committee for Human Rights.

The Treaty for which the NGOs had lobbied was signed in Ottawa on December 3-4, 1997 by the representatives of nearly 125 states of the world. It banned the production, use, stockpiling and transport of antipersonnel landmines, the deadliest of this type of weapon, which kills and maims thousands of soldiers and civilians each year. The signers also pledged resources and funds for the removal of the 100 million landmines still dispersed around the world. Among the major Western democratic powers only the United States failed to sign, on the reported grounds that the weapon was indispensable for preventing a North Korean invasion of South Korea through the demilitarized zone. It is clear that the United States was embarrassed to be a non-signer since President Clinton had been an advocate of the treaty ban since 1993. His aides have sought to correct the tarnished image by announcing a major effort to remove landmines elsewhere in the world.

What was especially striking and, perhaps unique, was the speed by which the landmark treaty was adopted and the even greater tempo expected on the ratification process. It was only in 1992 that the campaign was launched by a handful of peace groups and human rights organizations. In the course of but five years, they won the support of the vast majority of the globe's governments, led by Canada. Only Russia, China, India and Pakistan, of the major countries—besides the United States—remained holdouts. More significant was the expectation of Canada's Foreign Minister, Lloyd Axworthy, that the treaty would come into force within a year. The treaty technically becomes operational six months after at least 40 countries have ratified it. Axworthy obviously expects the tempo of the signing to be maintained in the ratification process.

To judge from the energy, determination and commitment of the NGOs in attendance at Ottawa, the Canadian Foreign Minister hardly could have been much in error. When the International Landmines coordinator, Jody Williams, spoke at the signing ceremony, she offered a bit of evidence that "the tide of history has changed": NGOs, she emphasized, have come into their own as a significant factor in international relations. "Together," said Williams, "we are a super-power."[26] Well, maybe not quite a "superpower"; but surely their impact could not be dismissed.

CHAPTER ONE

Genesis:
NGOs and the UN Charter

That the United Nations Charter, in its specific references to human rights, marked a milestone in mankind's long history was quite apparent to those familiar with international treaties. Earlier treaties may have had references to religious tolerance, minority rights or the banning of slavery, but none had used the language of human rights, and more importantly, none had directly linked peace and security or "stability" to observance of human rights and fundamental freedoms. In addition, the Charter would explicitly, and unprecedentedly, provide for an institution whose function it was to promote human rights. A gifted lyrical poet and later Librarian of Congress who, at the time, was an Assistant Secretary of State, Archibald MacLeish, caught the significance of the moment: "Here, for the first time in the history of the world is an effort to extend to mankind everywhere the fundamental rights so painfully won"[1] by the United Nations during World War II.

But what is especially striking, and generally not known, is that the historic breakthrough never would have taken place without the commitment, determination and pressure of a group of American nongovernmental organizations. It was their initiative, exerted at the founding conference of the United Nations in San Francisco in April, 1945, which made the difference. A keen observer and authority on human rights in the Charter later would comment that, "inconceivable as it may now seem," without the American nongovernmental representatives, the Charter would have carried at most "only a passing reference" to human rights.[2] The writer was John P. Humphrey, later Director of the UN's Division on Human Rights.

After calling attention to the Charter's concern for "human rights and fundamental freedoms" as that which "distinguishes it most sharply from the Covenant of the League of Nations," he stressed the role of NGOs in making the distinction possible.[3]

An obscure plaque hanging on the wall of the Garden Room in San Francisco's famed Fairmont Hotel offers a glimpse of the role of NGOs. Like an unearthed archeological artifact, it suggests the reality of a half-century ago, in which governments—even victorious ones—were hardly enthusiastic about taking revolutionary steps in a human rights direction. "In this room," the plaque reads, "met the Consultants of forty-two national organizations assigned to the United States Delegation at the Conference on International Organizations in which the United Nations Charter was drafted." Then comes the disclosure: "Their contribution is particularly reflected in the Charter provisions for human rights. . . ." The wording is preceded by the date—"25 April–26 June 1945."[4]

The consultants were representatives of very prominent public and civic organizations who had been invited by the U.S. State Department. Presumably, they were to advise the official eight-member U.S. delegation to the Charter talks. It was an "unprecedented move," according to an informed observer, Dorothy Robins, but the innovation turned out to have a most "fortunate circumstance." When and how the idea of "consultants" appeared is by no means clear. Their role, Robins observed, was "as yet unwritten" and, indeed, was "somewhat uncertain and undefined."[5] Of course, voluntary nongovernmental organizations stood at the very core of American public life and, no doubt, Washington policymakers were keenly aware that President Woodrow Wilson's push for American involvement in the League of Nations was frustrated by opposition in the Senate. Popular support for the UN, including strong pressure from public organizations, could neutralize a resumption of isolationist sentiment in the Senate.

In fact, the Administration had encouraged the public discussion of the Dumbarton Oaks Proposals that had laid the groundwork for the United Nations. And, according to Secretary of State Edward Stettinius, in his formal report to President Harry Truman, the idea for creating consultants was "the direct result" of the interest that the discussion had aroused.[6] Stettinius quite appropriately called the idea an "innovation in the conduct of international affairs" that ultimately made "an important contribution to the Conference itself."[7]

Consultants to the American delegation were selected from such principal national organizations as the National Association of Manufacturers, the Chamber of Commerce, the American Federation of Labor, the Congress of Industrial Organizations, the American Farm Bureau Federation, the Federal Council of Churches and the American Association of the United Nations. The consultants were usually the heads of the respective invited organizations.

It was the consultants who constituted what the San Francisco conference analyst called "an experiment in democracy in action on the diplomatic level."[8] No one was quite sure how the unique experiment would work. What was clear was that the American government wanted to involve major segments of its citizenry in the process and, ineluctably, this meant seeking their assistance. Stettinius, in his first meeting with the consultants on April 26, 1945 expressly requested "your assistance," which included, in his view, "your guidance, counsel and advice."[9] The Secretary of State acknowledged that it was an "experiment," utterly "new in international conferences."

The consultants' status, nonetheless, remained undefined. Their names were not listed in conference documents as part of the American delegation although they were included in Stettinius's official report to the President. The official U.S. delegation held regular meetings with the consultants, usually in the morning and approximately every second day. All meetings were off-the-record, and "precise" note-taking was discouraged.

While the Department frowned upon "bloc" lobbying, it strongly invited an "exchange of opinions" between the consultants and the American delegation. From the perspective of the consultants, the parameters suggested that they might function most effectively were they to meet, as the occasion warranted, in small groups with official delegation members. The separate groups would reflect specific interests. Four interests were quickly delineated by the consultants when they met on May 1: (1) dependent areas; (2) economic matters; (3) a bill of rights and (4) educational and cultural questions.

It was from the small group dealing with the third subject that a revolution in international diplomacy would emerge. But, equally important, was the very initiation of a process that underscored the value of nongovernmental organizations. Even if the "consultants" were restricted only to the American delegation at San Francisco—no other delegation included anything similar—an experiment had been launched with historic ramifications.

The catalytic force at San Francisco for making NGOs a significant element in the Charter was Professor James T. Shotwell, a distinguished historian at Columbia University who also served at the time in two other key capacities: as President of the Carnegie Endowment for International Peace and as Chairman of the Commission to Study the Organization of Peace. He had taken part, after World War I, in creating the Statute for the International Labor Organization (ILO), which provided for tripartite representation on national delegations of labor, industry and government. NGOs from labor and industry officially were accorded equal status with governmental representatives as part of official delegations. The experience of the ILO had so impressed Shotwell that he believed that its organizational pattern, appropriately modified, should become a standard for other non-labor international structures. He became convinced that the UN Charter should include a provision legitimizing consultation between the international organization and NGOs.

Under Shotwell's leadership, the consultants from several groups drew up a proposal that recommended that a new and key UN institution—the Economic and Social Council (ECOSOC)—should establish a pattern of formal consultations with national and international NGOs. The proposal was submitted to the U.S. delegation on May 17.[10] A perceptive consultant summed up the view of many of the group:

> . . . we are now embarking on a hope that possibly we may be able to bring into a world organization the common people of the world. I think this thing, if it could be sold to the other nations, will have opened a great door.[11]

The U.S. delegation accepted the proposal of the consultants and won the support of the other delegations at the San Francisco conference. Article 71 specified that ECOSOC "may make suitable arrangements for consultation with nongovernmental organizations which are concerned with matters within its competence." Secretary of State Stettinius accorded full credit to the consultants for the incorporation of Article 71 in the Charter. In his report to President Truman, he said that the article was the result of "the close and fruitful cooperation between the United States Delegation and its consultants."

U.S. responsiveness to the American NGOs, of course, was not altogether surprising. Voluntarism stood at the very center of American culture. At subsequent UN meetings, it was characteristic of Washington policymakers to invite leaders of various communal organizations and groups to serve as "public" members of official U.S. delegations. In contrast, no other foreign delegation to the San Francisco conference had appointed consultants from the public sector. Voluntarism was hardly a basic element of foreign cultures. Never would any of them select representatives of major voluntary groups to serve as "public" members of official UN delegations.

If the new status accorded NGOs was to mark a significant *procedural* development in international affairs, the far more crucial breakthrough came in the *substantive* area of human rights and fundamental freedoms, the concern of the bill of rights group. Of the 42 American consultants, five played critically important leadership roles with respect to human rights. Most prominent was again Professor Shotwell. As early as April, 1943, his Commission to Study the Organization of Peace had urged that the new legal order that would be established by the UN must include a "Bill of Human Rights."[12]

A second important public figure of the bill of rights group was Dr. O. Frederick Nolde, representing the Federal Council of Churches, which was the coordinating body of the Protestant churches. Later, the name "Federal Council" would be changed to "National Council." Dr. Nolde was the Director of the Commission of the Churches on International Affairs, a body that would continue to play an activist role in promoting human rights. At the same time, he served as Dean of the Graduate School of the Lutheran Theological Academy in Philadelphia. A third leader was Clark Eichelberger, who would head up the principal citizen's lobbying group for the United Nations, the American Association for the United Nations, out of which would emerge the United Nations Association (UNA).

But the sparkplugs of the group and of the lobbying effort were Judge Joseph Proskauer, president of the American Jewish Committee (AJC) and Jacob Blaustein, Chairman of its Executive Committee. Proskauer, the senior partner of a prestigious New York law firm, was especially articulate and, along with Nolde, often acted as spokesman of the group. Blaustein was a prominent Baltimore industrialist. That the American Jewish Committee's leaders were the driving force of the lobbying effort was attested to by Professor Shotwell, who later recalled that they did "the major and strenuous part of the thinking" that enabled the consultants to impact decisively upon the San Francisco deliberations.[13]

What especially disturbed the five leaders was the failure of the Dumbarton Oaks conference, an assemblage of world leaders in 1944, to offer anything substantive about human rights, only making an incidental reference to it. The proposals of the conference, designed as a guidepost for the San Francisco meeting, were issued in October, 1944. The disappointment was all the more dismaying when it was learned that both the United Kingdom and the Soviet Union strongly resisted the inclusion of any human rights commitments in the proposed UN Charter.

From the perspective of the American Jewish Committee, it was absolutely essential to make human rights a core element of the UN Charter. As an agency formed in 1905 to defend Jewish interests and the rights of minorities, the Committee was keenly aware of the failure of interwar treaties aimed at protecting minorities in a few countries in East Europe. It was also profoundly sensitive to how the Nazis had stoked the embers of bigotry and hate in Germany, ultimately causing aggressive war, massive abuses of human rights and the Holocaust. Committee leaders were convinced that only if the rights of all peoples were protected could the rights of any particular ethnic, racial and religious minority be assured. And, moreover, only through the protection of human rights could future conflicts and war be avoided.[14]

Recognizing that Professor Shotwell's Commission to Study the Organization of Peace was the major axis upon which the plans for the future UN Charter might turn, Committee leaders made contact with him well before the San Francisco conference. Shotwell later related that his Commission "came in contact" with the AJC and "formed a sub-committee that linked up" with the Committee leaders. In Shotwell's opinion, it was the Committee leaders that provided "the brilliant leadership" for the human rights struggle.[15] Central to the "joint work" of the Commission subcommittees and the AJC, Shotwell observed, was the key "suggestion that there should be, within the new international organization, a commission on fundamental freedoms and human rights. . . ."

As early as 1944, the AJC supported the publication by Columbia University Press of the seminal work, *The International Bill of the Rights of Man* by the distinguished British legal scholar Hersch Lauterpacht. The purpose was to make the proposed bill of rights the heart of UN activities. By the end of 1944, the Committee formally issued a call for an "International Bill of Rights." The appeal was signed by 1,300 distinguished Americans of all faiths and races and released on December 15, 1944. More importantly, the Committee published in February, 1945 a booklet, *To the Counselors of Peace*, which stipulated that human rights must be made a principal purpose of the world organization. The booklet also indicated that the UN should establish a Commission whose aim would be the practical one of implementing the hoped-for human rights provisions of the UN Charter. Both ideas already had been spelled out in a letter by Proskauer to U.S. Secretary of State Edward Stettinius dated November 28, 1944.

The most important political step taken by the AJC was a meeting with President Franklin D. Roosevelt on March 21, 1945, one month before the San Francisco conference. At their meeting in the White House, Proskauer and Blaustein, while stressing at the very beginning that Jews had been the principal victims of Hitler's persecution, nonetheless wanted it understood that their primary objective was "to establish a world order that is just to every human being, irrespective of race, creed or nationality."

The meeting with President Roosevelt was a climactic one. The President's response was more than encouraging. As recalled by Blaustein, Roosevelt urged them to go to San Francisco and "work to get those human rights provisions into the Charter so that unspeakable crimes like those by the Nazis will never again be countenanced by world society."[16] And, he authorized them to say that he was "profoundly interested" in an International Bill of Rights.[17]

The President went on to explain that human rights provisions in the Charter "would be of the greatest significance because they go to the very root of what is fundamental to the well-being and the very lives of all people. . . ." But only two weeks after the meeting with the Committee leaders, President Roosevelt died. His comments to the Committee were quite consistent with his major pronouncements during World War II. In his address to Congress on January 6, 1941, the President spoke of how mankind must "look forward to a world founded upon four essential freedoms"—freedom of speech, freedom of expression, freedom of religion and freedom from fear.[18] Eight months later, on August 14, the President joined Prime Minister Winston Churchill in signing the Atlantic Charter, which provided "assurance that all men in all the lands may live out their lives in freedom from fear and want."

There can be little doubt that Roosevelt's reiteration of human rights themes served as a powerful inspiration to the Jewish leaders and their associates in the Council of Churches and the Carnegie Endowment for Peace. The themes, by implication, suggested, too, a crucial and basic assumption upon which to establish a linkage between peace and human rights. Internal repression, the argument would go, is an indispensable agent for external aggression. Freedoms are important values not only in themselves, but also because they dissipate and weaken the drive to war and conflict. President Truman, in his speech to the closing session of the San Francisco Conference on June 26, 1945, stressed that without human rights and fundamental freedoms, "we cannot have permanent peace."

Frederick Nolde found the argument more than persuasive. In a work published in 1949, he wrote that "as a result of recent events, men have become increasingly convinced that the observance of human rights everywhere is an imperative requirement for world peace and order."[19] But the struggle of the consultants for human rights in the Charter was only at its very beginning. Roosevelt's assistance could no longer be relied upon. British and Soviet opposition for the inclusion of human rights remained intense. Differences within the U.S. delegation and within the State Department were sharp. Blaustein later recalled that the consultants "were shocked to get the news that our recommendations bearing upon human rights . . . were not to be incorporated into the Charter."[20]

At about the same time, a leading figure of the official U.S. delegation, Dean Virginia Gildersleeve, who had served as chief officer at Barnard College, told Clark Eichelberger that the idea of a Commission on Human Rights was unlikely. Instead, the official U.S. delegates appeared to support the view that only the UN Economic and Social Council could "be empowered to appoint whatever commissions would be necessary."

Desperately, the five activists decided to draft quickly a sharply defined written position paper to be sent to Secretary Stettinius. They were joined by Jane Evans, the head of the National Peace Conference and later Director of the National Federation of Temple Sisterhoods. Drawing upon past position papers of their respective organizations, they assigned Judge Proskauer the task of preparing a fresh text, which he promptly dictated to Eichelberger's assistant, Margaret Olsen.

In the new and urgent memorandum to Stettinius prepared on May 2, the NGO activist group pressed the Secretary of State and the American delegation to take "a position of leadership" on the issue of human rights. The role of leadership must be exercised, they said, in three specific areas: (1) human rights must be identified as a "purpose" of the UN; (2) all member states of the UN must assume the obligation of guaranteeing human rights; and (3) establishment of a "human rights commission" must be stipulated by name in the Charter. It was the determined contention of the activists that the "conscience of the world demands an end to persecution" and that it is a "matter of international concern to stamp out infractions of basic human rights." They went on to warn that it would be "a grievous shock" were the Charter not to make "adequate provision" for human rights fulfillment. They reminded Stettinius that expectations had been raised by the Atlantic Charter and the Four Freedoms and, therefore, they were certain that American leadership on behalf of human rights "would win the enthusiastic support of the American people and . . . command their hearty approval."[21]

High level lobbying was urgently and immediately conducted on May 2 by the NGO leadership team, especially by Blaustein. Besides talking to the various official delegation members, he met with a fellow Baltimorean, Dr. Isaiah Bowman, President of John Hopkins University, who also served as an adviser to Secretary Stettinius. Bowman was asked to brief the Secretary about the concerns of the consultants and about their desire to meet with him. Blaustein's immediate task was to win the approval of the 42 organizations that the consultants represented.

By the time of the meeting in the late afternoon of May 2, the leadership group had won formal approval from 21 organizations. The others, Proskauer acknowledged, could not be reached "in the short time allotted to us." It was significant that all those who had been reached agreed to sign, without a single refusal. It was very likely that the bulk, if not all, would have accepted the ideas of the memorandum had they been reached.

Dr. Nolde of the Council of Churches made the initial "forceful" presentation to Stettinius. He was followed by Judge Proskauer, who delivered an "eloquent appeal." Proskauer's autobiography records its essence, which carried a powerful emotional wallop:

> I said that the voice of America was speaking in this room as it had never spoken before in any international gathering; that voice was saying to the American delegation: "If you make a fight for these human rights proposals and win, there will be glory for all. If you make a fight for it and lose, we will back you up to the limit. If you fail to make a fight for it, you will have lost the support of American opinion—and justly lost it. In the event, you will never get the Charter ratified."[22]

It was tough talk, which could not fail to remind the Secretary of State of President Wilson's failure to convince the American public of the need for a League of Nations. The moment that followed was tense, dramatic and historic. Proskauer wasn't certain that he spoke for any of the other representatives and he proceeded to ask whether any of the "consultants" disagreed with his presentation. Only one person arose— Philip Murray, the President of the Congress of International Organizations (CIO)—but he represented considerable domestic political power. Proskauer wasn't certain where Murray stood on the issue, but his comments brought the events to an exhilarating climax.

Murray thrust a finger at Stettinius. "Mr. Secretary," he said, "I didn't sign the paper." For a moment, he paused, and everyone turned excruciatingly attentive. "The only reason I didn't sign it," Murray went on, "was that they didn't get it to me." His point was then driven home not without the relish of power and authority: "I am here to tell you that I believe I am speaking not only for the CIO but for all labor when I say that we are 100 percent behind the argument which has just been made."[23]

Proskauer was to savor that moment. He would recall that Stettinius rose to his feet, "impulsively" declaring that "he had no idea of the intensity of the feeling on this subject. . . ." The Secretary of State must have assumed that the consultants would simply be polite and supportive with respect to the official Washington policy issue and not independent, as well as demanding. He promised to bring the matter to the attention of the delegation that evening. That he was clearly persuasive was soon apparent. The U.S. delegation agreed to sponsor the consultants' proposed human rights amendments to the Dumbarton Oaks proposals—and to fight for them.

In turn, the lobbying of the U.S. delegation was quite obviously effective. The three other great powers—Britain, France and even the USSR—agreed to join the United States in sponsoring the human rights proposals. It was on May 5, only three days after the consultants effectively had persuaded Stettinius to make human rights a major item of the UN Charter that he publicly announced that the initiative of the NGO consultants had prevailed. The United States, on behalf of the major European powers, would formally submit the NGO proposals to the San Francisco conference. Stettinius acknowledged that "the assistance and advice of the consultants to the United States Delegation have been invaluable."[24]

In a personal word addressed to the consultants, the Secretary raised a rare kind of toast: "I am sure that you recognize your own proposal" as the one "we advanced, agreed, and accepted," following "the meeting I held with you the other night." One of his principal aides, Walter M. Kotschnig, who would later hold important positions in the State Department, offered a final extraordinary and telling comment. He told the consultants: "It seems to me that I have never seen democracy in action demonstrated so forcefully as it was forcefully demonstrated at this conference."[25]

Several small powers at the time had been lobbying hard in San Francisco for a stronger commitment to human rights than the

Dumbarton Oaks proposals offered. They included Chile, Cuba and Panama, each of whom ultimately would assume a military-authoritarian character. At the time, however, they constituted democratic societies and vigorously advanced strong human rights initiatives. Indeed, they articulated ideas that would have obligated the world organizations to guarantee the protection of specified human rights, and not merely their promotion.[26]

Far more consequential than the efforts of the tiny group of small Latin American powers was the lobbying of important American nongovernmental groups. They planted several firm human rights seeds in the UN that, in time, would bear considerable fruit. The secret of their strategy was to persuade the U.S. government of the value of human rights in the Charter, relying upon its leadership to affect decisively the perspective of others. It was a strategy that would be pursued at various intervals later on in UN history. And it was, to a large extent, the key to human rights advancement. Only rarely would a major breakthrough in human rights occur at the UN without the determination and power exercised by Washington.

So it happened that the single most important treaty of the twentieth century, the United Nations Charter, which led to the creation of mankind's most elaborate international institution ever, was obliged to incorporate not a passing and extremely limited note about human rights but rather seven major references to human rights, several of enormous consequences. The preamble carries the famed ringing and unprecedented call: "We the peoples of the United Nations [are] determined . . . to reaffirm faith in fundamental human rights. . . ." It is in Article 1 of the Charter that the consultants left a most substantial mark. The promotion and encouragement of human rights was placed on the same footing as the maintenance of international peace and security. A third Charter reference was to be found in Article 13, which authorized the General Assembly to initiate studies and make recommendations for the purpose of assisting in the realization of human rights and fundamental freedoms.

Articles 55 and 56, each with a distinctive reference to human rights, stood linked together as the very core of the Charter. The former spelled out how the UN must promote the "universal respect for, and observance of, human rights and fundamental freedoms for all without distinction as to race, sex, language or religion." But this almost all-encompassing list had even greater significance in that it specified that the very promotion of the specified rights had as its object the creation of conditions of stability that were necessary for peaceful and friendly relations among nations.

If Article 55 virtually set forth the ideological or intellectual purpose of the UN in promoting human rights, the following Article 56 created the only clear legal obligation in the Charter for all member states to fulfil the provisions of Article 55. Through Article 56, "all members pledge themselves to take joint and separate action in cooperation with the Organization for the achievement of the [human rights] purpose" set forth in Article 55. Certainly, Article 56 inevitably would inhibit future efforts to prevent UN human rights initiatives on alleged grounds that they constituted intervention into the internal affairs of member states. From the beginning, Article 56 had the potential not just for economic sanctions, but even for military action, provided that a solid majority, including the major powers, supported it.

Another Charter reference to human rights was to be found in Article 62, which stipulated that a major UN organ, the Economic and Social Council, "may make recommendations for the purpose of promoting respect for, and observance of, human rights and fundamental freedoms for all." More pertinently, Article 62 notes that the Council may undertake or initiate studies as well as prepare draft conventions and hold international conferences on matters falling within its competence.

Article 68 created precisely the body whose primary function was oriented to realizing these critical aims by preparing studies along with Declarations and Conventions (most notably the Universal Declaration of Human Rights and the International Covenants on Human Rights). In the language of the Article, the Economic and Social Council "shall set up Commissions in economic and social fields and for the promotion of human rights. . . ." Created here was a unique official international institution, never previously established in human history. Subordinate to this institution there later would be created the Sub-Commission on Prevention of Discrimination and Protection of Minorities, a body of presumed experts that would assume the burden of launching studies that exerted a certain and at times considerable impact.

The seventh and final reference to human rights in the Charter was in Article 76, which dealt with the UN's Trusteeship system. One of its purposes was "to encourage respect for human rights and for fundamental freedoms for all without distinction as to race, sex, language, or religion and to encourage recognition of the interdependence of the people of the world." As the UN Trusteeship system during the next decade would be sharply reduced, the human rights reference inevitably would diminish in significance.

When comparison is made between the actual proposals of the consultants, as dictated by Judge Proskauer, with the human rights references in the Charter itself, one is struck by the remarkable impact that the ideas and language of NGOs exerted on the very genesis of human rights in the UN system.[27] The Proskauer touch went far beyond the dictation. It was the power of his articulate persuasiveness that carried the moment. Professor Shotwell later would comment that Proskauer had "made the most eloquent and convincing argument that I have ever listened to in my life." The Columbia University scholar went on to add that the event "is destined to become one of the chapters in American history."[28]

Accompanying the proposals of Proskauer were a set of "principles" aimed at guiding the Secretary of State and the American delegation. One of them was especially natural for a specifically Jewish organization to articulate. It spoke of "Hitlerism" as demonstrating how "persecution by a barbarous nation" placed an enormous "burden" upon "peace-loving nations." That "burden" involved the achieving of "redress" for the victims of Nazism. It obviously was meant to include what is today termed accountability. Jews, with the experience of the Holocaust still tormenting and traumatizing them, not surprisingly, would give emphasis to this theme. No doubt, this traumatization provided a potent motivation for a Jewish organization to be in the forefront of the struggle for stirring "the conscience of the world" to finally put an "end to persecution."[29] The principles as set forth by the Committee transformed the Holocaust concern into a universal axiom. Yet, if the U.S. delegation, and then shortly afterward, the other major powers, and, finally, the entire United Nations had come to accept the need for incorporating important human rights references into the UN Charter, a central element of the consultants' "principles"—an "International Bill of Rights"—was not acted upon. A fundamental obstacle stood in its path. Were the Charter, which constituted a treaty and was, therefore, politically binding, to encompass a bill of rights, the rights, too, would become binding. But there had been no preliminary discussion of human rights at Dumbarton Oaks. And there were certain to be sharp differences of opinion about what constituted human rights.

A binding agreement on human rights was out of the question for the time being, but everyone understood that the initial primary function of the proposed human rights commission would be the preparation of an International Bill of Rights.[30] President Harry Truman, who had succeeded President Roosevelt, gave solid expression to this prevailing belief in his speech at the San Francisco closing session. Referring to the Charter, he said that "under this document we have good reason to expect the framing of an international bill of rights acceptable to all the nations involved."[31]

In fact, a beginning of the discussion on the subject came but a year after the San Francisco conference. On April 29, 1946, a so-called nuclear Commission on Human Rights of nine members, appointed by the Economic and Social Council, met at New York's Hunter College campus. It was given the task of preparing an "international bill of human rights." Eleanor Roosevelt, for over a decade a crusader for human rights both in the United States and abroad, was promptly chosen by acclamation as the body's first chairman. The "nuclear" Commission's session was short—but three weeks. After elaborating the structure and membership of the permanent Commission (comprising 18 governments), the "nuclear" group assigned the Commission the "real work" of determining "when the actual writing of an international bill of rights will have to be undertaken."[32]

Deliberations were begun by the newly established Commission on Human Rights on January 27, 1947, under Mrs. Roosevelt's chairmanship. Politically acute and sensitive, she was keenly aware that a binding agreement on human rights was, for the time being, out of the question. An atmosphere of growing East-West tensions was making agreement on fundamental issues concerning rights and other matters extremely difficult. Besides, Moscow's perception of the relationship of the individual to the state was totally antithetical to that of the West.

The Soviet delegate on the Commission, V. Tepliakov, for example, found the rights enumerated in various drafts prepared by the Secretariat in the UN Division of Human Rights to be totally inapplicable. He wanted deletion of the following: rights to life and personal liberty; the prohibition of slavery and compulsory labor; the right to petition national governments and the UN; the right of property; freedom of movement and freedom to resist oppression. Tepliakov declared that these rights were either superfluous, went beyond the power of the UN or impinged upon local customs and the laws of national states.[33]

An internal American factor also had to be recognized. Mrs. Roosevelt was profoundly aware of the uniqueness of the American treaty-making process. The Senate would have to approve a legally binding treaty by a two-thirds vote. Whether such a sizable majority could be obtained on sensitive human rights issues was questionable. Moreover, in the absence of a determined and absolute majority, there was always the danger of an interminable filibuster in the Senate by willful opponents.

A drafting committee of the Commission, under Mrs. Roosevelt's guidance, decided that the International Bill of Rights would be comprised of two documents: a Declaration that would constitute a broad set of human rights principles establishing therewith "a common standard of achievement" for all states, and a binding Covenant or Convention together with measures of implementation. The first, a Declaration, warranted immediate consideration. Roosevelt sensed that any delay by the Commission would dissipate the great public support for human rights that the UN tentatively enjoyed. She observed that people everywhere were expecting "the Commission on Human Rights to do something."

When the Soviet delegate to the Commission proposed at the second session of the body that priority be given to a Declaration, Mrs. Roosevelt immediately voted for the proposal. The decision later would be approved by the UN's major organs. Roosevelt's initial decision turned out to be remarkably prescient. While the Declaration would be completed and adopted in less than two years, it was almost twenty years before the UN in 1966 approved the International Covenant on Human Rights.

A tough taskmaster, Mrs. Roosevelt kept the Commission totally engaged for nearly an entire year in drafting a Universal Declaration that would rank in historic significance with the Magna Carta, the French Declaration of the Rights of Man and the American Declaration of Independence. At her side throughout was the brilliant and creative international legal specialist of France René Cassin, later chosen as Nobel Laureate, as well as Charles Malik of Lebanon, a gifted lawyer and Christian humanist who served first as Rapporteur of the Commission's deliberations and, strategically, more importantly, as Chairman of the General Assembly's Third Committee, which later would work on and endorse the document.

The Commission's draft had to pass muster with the UN General Assembly. Its Third Committee, dealing with Social, Cultural and Humanitarian Affairs and serving as a kind of Committee of the whole was seized with the draft for two and a half months. Eighty-one sessions and countless subcommittee meetings were given over to examining each article and 168 amendments.

It was three o'clock in the morning of December 10, 1948 at the Palais de Chaillot in Paris when the exhausted delegates to the third session of the UN General Assembly by a unanimous vote—with 8 abstaining and 2 absent—adopted the Universal Declaration of Human Rights. U Thant would later call it the "Magna Carta of Mankind," and Alexander Solzhenitsyn, in his brilliant undelivered Nobel Laureate lecture in 1970, declared it to be the "best document" ever produced by the UN. The weary delegates, exhausted with fatigue in those early hours a half-century ago, recognized their indebtedness to Mrs. Roosevelt's guiding hand. In a tribute rare in UN annals, they rose as one to give her a standing ovation.

The 30 articles of the Declaration embrace the totality of rights with which democratic societies and the international community had been concerned in modern times. Two broad categories of rights can be clearly distinguished: civil and political rights, and economic, social and cultural rights. The first category embraced the right to life, liberty and security of person and prohibited slavery, torture, cruel and inhuman treatment, arbitrary arrest and detention. It specified the right to a fair trial, the presumption of innocence and the prohibition of ex post facto laws. The rights to privacy and to private property were spelled out.

The basic freedoms—speech, religion, assembly and movement (including travel and emigration)—were emphasized, along with the right to asylum and to a nationality. Key political and electoral rights were stressed. Nondiscrimination with respect to race, sex and opinion was considered fundamental.

The second category of rights was noted as being "indispensable" for a person's "dignity" and the "free development" of his or her "personality." Spelled out were rights to social security, to work, to equal pay for equal work, and to a "just and favorable remuneration." Included in the category were rights to leisure and rest, and an adequate standard of living along with security in the event of unemployment, sickness or unforeseen tragic circumstances. Emphasized too, was the right to an education (which was to be free at least in the "elementary and fundamental stages").

The Universal Declaration of Human Rights was to be the point of departure for the concern and activism of nongovernmental organizations when they focused on human rights, whether in whole or in part. In the absence of a legally binding covenant, the Universal Declaration could serve as the lodestar for criticizing nonadherence by governments of international obligations.

If NGOs played a central part in insisting that the UN Charter incorporate human rights obligations and in creating the mechanism for drafting the Universal Declaration, it would be expected that NGOs would have a hand in the drafting of the provisions of the Declaration. Regrettably, no researcher has undertaken a study along these lines. But, three disclosures by authoritative sources indicate that various NGOs continued to be involved either with the staff of the UN Division on Human Rights, who prepared drafts of articles in the Universal Declaration, or with delegation heads who participated in the deliberations of the Commission on Human Rights or of the General Assembly's Third Committee.

One crucial source was none other than the Commission's Rapporteur and the Chairman of the General Assembly's Third Committee, Charles Malik. In a speech on December 10, 1973, on the occasion of the Declaration's twenty-fifth anniversary, he revealed:

> They [the NGOs] were profoundly concerned, especially the religious among them, whether Jewish, Catholic or Protestant, in the fate and dignity of man in the modern world; they kept in close touch with us, and we received them and adopted many a sound counsel from them, and you can trace in the text of the Declaration a word here, a clause there, or a whole article, back to their inspiration.[34]

Equally revealing was a disclosure by a principal architect of the Universal Declaration, René Cassin. In a speech in Paris commemorating the twentieth anniversary of the Declaration, he recalled "the encouragement and assistance received by national delegations" from NGOs, whether at the level of the Commission or at the General Assembly. Those who were involved in the drafting process, Cassin said, owed a "debt of gratitude" to the NGOs who, "thanks to their cooperation and judicious comments," made constant improvements in the successive drafts of the Declaration. Particularly grateful was he, personally, to the various women's organizations, "whose contribution was especially valuable when the definitive provisions of the Declaration regarding marriage, the family and children were being worked out."[35]

The third source was UN Secretary-General U Thant. Addressing the same NGO Paris conference. U Thant said that "during 1947 and 1948, non-governmental organizations participated at every stage in the strenuous process of preparing the Universal Declaration of Human Rights. . . ."[36] He particularly emphasized a political role they played: "on the numerous occasions when deadlocks threatened," NGOs sought determinedly "to find successful solutions." According to a well-known human rights legal scholar, "NGOs were instrumental in the drafting of the Universal

Declaration of Human Rights." He especially stressed that "their personal expertise and prestige" was influential in the drafting process.[37] Regrettably, details of the instrumental role of NGOs were not spelled out.

That the interested NGOs "kept in close touch" with the drafters of the Declaration would not be surprising, but pertinent data about when, how, in which respect and in what precise way NGOs made their recommendations known have thus far not been established. One prominent NGO, Roger Baldwin of the International League for the Rights of Man related in an oral history interview that he and his associates attended every session of the Commission that deliberated on the Declaration. His relationship with Mrs. Roosevelt, a League Board member, was friendly. Another NGO who, according to Mrs. Roosevelt, "attended almost every session of the Commission on Human Rights" was Dr. Nolde of the Federal Council of Churches. So perceptive was he, noted Mrs. Roosevelt, that he "sometimes gauges the mood of the members [of the Commission] more accurately than we ourselves do."[38]

The vacuum in public knowledge about the precise role of NGOs in the drafting of the Universal Declaration was partly filled quite recently by Theo van Boven, a former Director of the UN Division of Division Rights and currently a professor in the Netherlands. In a scholarly analysis for a legal journal, he made use of the so-called Travaux Préparatoires of the International Bill of Human Rights, which were unpublished preparatory background papers prepared by the staff of the Division of Human Rights in the late forties. Those preparatory papers reveal, van Boven noted, that "NGOs did participate in the debates on the drafting of texts." However, because they were prohibited from moving "proposals in their own names," their specific ideas and lobbying activities could not be delineated for the record or for historical purposes.[39]

NGOs were totally dependent, at the time, upon the willingness of governmental delegations to sponsor one or another of their ideas. Van Boven cited Charles Malik as characterizing NGOs as "batteries of unofficial advisers to the various delegations supplying them with streams of ideas and suggestions." At best, the drafting of the Universal Declaration, van Boven concluded from the background working papers, was a "dynamic process" involving various minds, legal systems and ideological orientations. For example, the language of such a key article as Article 18 covering freedom of religion and belief, he noted, can "largely be attributed to Dr. Nolde. . . ."

Mrs. Roosevelt, as a principal architect, was keenly aware that between the enunciation of rights and their fulfillment stood a wide gap. Indeed, she was profoundly cognizant that the Communist perception of the relationship between the individual and the state was totally antithetical to the purpose of the Universal Declaration. The top Soviet spokesman at the General Assembly when the Universal Declaration was adopted was Deputy Foreign Minister Andrei Y. Vyshinsky. He had acquired notoriety as the "Grand Inquisitor," the ruthless prosecutor at the infamous "Great Purge" trials in Moscow in the late thirties. Now, in Paris, he would articulate the Soviet views that "the rights of human beings cannot be considered outside the prerogatives of governments, and the very understanding of human rights is a governmental concept."[40]

Implicit in the Vyshinsky thesis was the rejection of the fundamental democratic view that the individual has inherent and inalienable rights. Vyshinsky made repeated efforts to circumscribe the absoluteness of the various basic rights of speech, organization and movement, but in each case he was voted down. Mrs. Roosevelt dealt with him and the Soviet bloc with great tactfulness, meticulously avoiding any response to repeated provocatory remarks, and always seeking ways to placate their concerns.

What impressed the very pragmatic American human rights champion, she told the Russians, was "the significant fact" that some fifty states that ordinarily "find it difficult to reach a common basis of agreement" on many issues, nonetheless, "found such a large measure of agreement in the complex field of human rights." That which prompted the consensus, she said, was "man's desire for peace," which reflected "our common aspiration."

The delicacy of Mrs. Roosevelt's tactfulness was reinforced by a "real enthusiasm" that had seized the UN delegates, as noted by the President of the General Assembly. They were "gripped" by a sense that a great historical development was in the making. It seemed to a prominent UN diplomat, Carlos Romulo of the Philippines, that the approval of the Universal Declaration had assumed a status of almost transcendental importance. A mood had seized the delegates, he said before the final vote, that the very "continued existence" of the United Nations was at stake, and that, indeed, it was "on trial for its life." Under the circumstances, for the Soviet Union to play the role of spoiler with a negative vote would have jeopardized its image as a major partner in the UN future. Moscow finally chose to abstain, along with the Ukraine, Byelorussia, Poland, Czechoslovakia and Yugoslavia. They were joined by South Africa and Saudi Arabia. (Yemen and Honduras were absent.)

But if the Soviet Union had permitted a unanimous favorable vote for the Universal Declaration, it was most unlikely that it would permit any challenge or inquiry into whether and how it complied with the provisions of the Declaration. Mrs. Roosevelt was deeply conscious of the totalitarian character of Soviet society and chose to raise, in an indirect manner, a portentous question just after the successful vote in the Third Committee on December 7, 1948 in favor of the Universal Declaration. How would the repressed and oppressed ever know what their rights were under the Universal Declaration of Human Rights? The question was not specifically articulated. Instead, cunningly, she provided an answer to an unasked query. A "curious grapevine" would carry the words and significance of the Universal Declaration to all peoples, even to those shielded from it by the censors of totalitarian regimes. "Information" from the "curious grapevine," she commented, "may seep in even when governments are not so anxious for it."[41]

The impact of the "curious grapevine" could have revolutionary implications. Mrs. Roosevelt noted that "all the governments, even the totalitarian regimes which completely control the means of information are affected by what their people want." She may have never defined her striking phrase of a "curious grapevine," but it is not at all unlikely that she was thinking of nongovernmental organizations. It was they, after all, which had insisted upon inclusion in the UN Charter of references to human rights, which had demanded an institution that would elaborate an International Bill of Rights, and which had already left their imprint upon the first stage of that bill—the Universal Declaration of Human Rights.

If the "curious grapevine" could carry information about the provisions of the Universal Declaration beyond the censors of totalitarian and authoritarian regimes, it also could perform the alternative task of bringing out information concerning the nature of repression and discrimination or about violations of human rights. The "curious grapevine" was pregnant with possibilities. The impact of the nongovernmental organizations ultimately would be felt in international affairs in a major way.

What gave their task a certain foundation, though one not completely solid, was that the Universal Declaration, over time, took on the character of something more than a "statement of basic principles," as Eleanor Roosevelt cautiously had described it.[42] Cassin, at the same time, claimed that the Declaration "could be considered as an authoritative interpretation of the [UN] Charter." But Mrs. Roosevelt was extremely reluctant to take that perspective, insisting that the Declaration "was not a treaty or international agreement and did not impose legal obligations."

In contrast to the narrow and restrained Roosevelt definition, a leading scholar on the subject who had served as deputy director of the UN Division on Human Rights, Egon Schwelb, later pointed out that a number of legally binding international conventions on human rights, as well as general peace treaties, incorporated direct references to the Declaration.[43] In the legislative work of the UN, the Declaration quickly became a final arbiter and standard of reference to which every new text on human rights had to conform. Strikingly, references to the Declaration and its provisions were incorporated in the constitutions of almost 20 of Africa's new states. Similarly, the constitutions of such new states as Cyprus, Jamaica, and Trinidad and Tobago clearly were inspired by the Declaration. Even national courts have made reference to the Declaration and, in several instances, have juridically applied it.

The legislative history of the General Assembly in the early sixties further helped erode the concept of the Declaration being merely a "statement of principles." In December 1960, the Assembly adopted, by a vote of 89 to 0, the Declaration on the Granting of Independence to Colonial Countries and Peoples, which specifically required that "all States shall observe faithfully and strictly the provisions of the . . . Universal Declaration of Human Rights." It was hardly a statement about a "standard of achievement," but rather one of immediate and current necessity and law.

Based upon this legislative history and related legal developments, the UN Office of Legal Affairs, in 1962, offered a new interpretation of the term "Declaration" that carried clear implications for the Universal Declaration. The official definition of the "Declaration" read:

> It may be considered to impart, on behalf of the organ adopting it, a strong expectation that Members of the international community will abide by it. Consequently, in so far as the expectation is gradually justified by State practice, a declaration may by custom become recognized as laying down rules binding upon States.[44]

The ruling would win strong support from a major conference of leading international authorities on human rights that met in Montreal, Canada from March 22 to March 27, 1968. A formal statement adopted by the conference declared that the Universal Declaration of Human Rights "constitutes an authoritative interpretation of the Charter of the highest order, and has over the years become a part of customary international law."[45]

The NGO community saw its initial task to be that of sensitizing international opinion concerning the provisions of the Universal Declaration. The "curious grapevine" could become more effectively operable were there to exist a modicum of awareness about the Declaration. René Cassin later would say that "education for [world] citizenship" was considered by the Declaration's authors to be of "prime importance, even more important than any measures they might take in the national or international fields."[46] He found that NGOs had performed this role admirably with a flow of informational brochures, periodicals and articles in scientific publications, and with the convening of innumerable conferences in various countries and regions. In Cassin's view, the NGOs were "the first to make the principles of the Declaration widely known" and it was they who kept "public opinion informed" of both "positive achievements" and "obstacles encountered."[47]

The leading "obstacle" would turn out to be inherent in a crucial section of the Charter itself. Article 2, paragraph 7 of the Charter read: "Nothing contained in the present Charter shall authorize the United Nations to intervene in matters which are essentially within the domestic jurisdiction of any state. . . ." Not surprisingly, many, if not most, governments in 1945-48 and later gave the term "intervene" the broadest possible interpretation. They would argue that the "domestic jurisdiction" clause precluded consideration in any UN forum of their respective government practices. It would constitute the guidepost of the worst human rights violators. NGOs, seeking to function as a "curious grapevine," ineluctably would have to confront this enormous obstacle.

CHAPTER TWO

The "Curious Grapevine": NGO Rights and Limitations

That American nongovernmental organizations had been the moving force for the genesis of the UN Charter's human rights provisions was not accidental. The significant role of voluntary organizations in American public life had impressed a host of prominent observers and commentators of the American scene. Thus, Alexis de Tocqueville, as early as 1835, noted: "In no country of the world has the principle of association been more successfully used or applied to a greater multitude of objects than in America." He went on to clarify and illustrate: "wherever at the head of some new undertaking you see the government in France, or a man of rank in England, in the United States you will be sure to find an association."

U.S. power and involvement with the creation of the United Nations, of course, made it possible for the American NGO to play a distinctive role. In the same way, American influence helped to create provisions to the UN Charter that legitimized the role of NGOs in the UN system itself. Article 71 of the Charter authorized an almost unprecedented development in international affairs.

The Covenant of the League of Nations had not provided for a formal relationship between League bodies and NGOs. If informal contacts between NGOs and the League had existed and, indeed, had increased in scope and variety over the years, a statutory basis for the relationship was absent, thereby hindering the effectiveness and influence of NGOs. In only one international institution had NGOs of a certain type acquired, before the UN Charter was adopted, formal legitimacy and power. The International Labor Organization, headquartered in Geneva, in its constitution enacted in 1919 authorized one representative each from an employer's and a worker's organization within a country. Authorization for NGO consultative status was extended by ECOSOC in 1946, only a year after the Charter was adopted. The purpose of the status was clear. Consultation would enable ECOSOC and its subordinate organs, including the Commission on Human Rights, to tap expert information and advice from qualified and competent organizations. Appropriate UN organs and bodies also would be able to hear the views of those representing important and broad segments of public opinion. In this way, the international institution could be kept alert to community attitudes and concerns.

Tentative principles governing the consultative relationship were approved. These included criteria for selection of NGOs, distinctive categories into which they would fall for specific types of functions, and a listing of forms of activity. To acquire consultative status, an NGO had to be concerned, to an undefined extent, with issues within ECOSOC's competence. The aims of the NGO applicant had to conform with the purposes of the UN Charter. Except in rare instances, the NGO seeking status had to be international in structure and had to represent a large, though unspecified, percentage of the organized group within its field of operations.

In February 1950, these tentative principles were incorporated in ECOSOC Resolution 288B, which became the standard for almost two decades. Resolution 288B delineated three types of categories: A, B and C. The "A" category was designed to include NGOs whose concerns embraced a broad spectrum of ECOSOC's activities; the "B" category involved NGOs that focused on a more limited number of ECOSOC activities; and the "C" category included groups whose focus was mainly on the dissemination of UN information. When the resolution was altered 18 years later, the alphabetic symbols of A, B and C were changed to I, II and "Roster."

Rights given NGOs in Categories A and B under Resolution 288B were of a kind that could affect the deliberations of ECOSOC and its subordinate organs. These NGOs were allowed to submit written statements that would then be officially circulated or they could address these bodies in oral statements or undertake both kinds of actions. It was apparent that NGOs were extended an unusual authority to affect decision-making. In the case of Category A, the NGO could even propose items for the agenda of the ECOSOC and its organs.

Some NGOs in consultative status that focused upon human rights to a significant extent represented special interest groups such as labor, veterans, the press or women. Others were linked to a religious community—Catholic, Protestant or Jewish. (Later, other religious communities, like Muslims and Bahai, were added.) Very few were exclusively concerned with human rights. The most prominent at the time were the New York–based International League for the Rights of Man and the Paris-based International Federation for the Rights of Man. The Anti-Slavery Society, headquartered in London, concentrated upon the particular issue of forced servitude. Later, in 1952, the International Commission of Jurists, located in Geneva, and in 1961, Amnesty International, based in London, would join the few preeminently devoted to general human rights questions.

Access to UN human rights mechanisms was of course extremely valuable for those NGOs concentrating either entirely upon human rights or tangentially, as part of their special interest concern. What became crucial to these NGOs, with all the potential extended to them to influence policy, was whether ECOSOC would allow them to refer critically in their written or oral statements to human rights situations in specific countries. How much value did their access to decision-making machinery have if they could not refer to specific instances of human rights abridgements? The answer, over time, turned out to be discouraging. Until 1952, ECOSOC had interpreted liberally the implied NGO right to comment critically upon given country situations when they officially submitted written or oral statements.

Under new rules introduced in 1952 that were formally incorporated into ECOSOC Resolution 728F, communications from NGOs or other private sources alleging violations of human rights in particular countries no longer could be officially circulated or, indeed, discussed in open session of ECOSOC and its subsidiary bodies. Fear by states of embarrassment in a world arena on a kind of public stage was the driving force for this limitation.

But even more significant in restricting the human rights NGOs was a decision taken by the Commission on Human Rights at a very early stage in its history. This authoritative organ, which was created to oversee human rights issues, arbitrarily ruled in August, 1947 that "it has no power to take any action in regard to any complaints concerning human rights."[1] A stunning abdication of responsibility, the resolution was labeled as a "self-denying" rule by Dr. Egon Schwelb. It had no basis either in the UN Charter or in its own original terms of reference.[2] The rule was restricted to what the Commission could do or say, not yet what NGOs might do or say.

Repeated suggestions were made in subsequent years to amend the self-denying rule.[3] In 1949, for example, the UN Secretary-General proposed that the Commission recommend to ECOSOC that in cases affecting a great number of people or in situations having international repercussions, the Commission might examine communications from NGOs and private persons as well as the governments' replies to them. During the same year, the Sub-Commission on Prevention of Discrimination and Protection of Minorities submitted to the Commission a draft resolution recommending that communications alleging the existence of urgent problems in the field of discrimination should be examined by the Sub-Commission.

Neither of the two useful suggestions was acted upon. Equally unsuccessful was a significant effort launched by the Commission in 1958-59. It appointed a committee to reexamine the self-denying rule "with a view to establishing a procedure for handling communications which is better calculated to promote respect for, and observance of, fundamental human rights."[4] The Committee, however, favored reaffirmation of the 1947 rule and ECOSOC formally endorsed the decision in 1959 in its classic Resolution 728F.

Self-denial was accompanied by a complex bureaucratic procedure that created a special Alice-in-Wonderland world of nonexistence. This is the way it worked: a confidential list of "communications"—the technical word for complaints—was drawn up and distributed at a closed meeting of the Commission early in its annual session; the identity of the authors of the complaints was not divulged, except in cases where they expressly indicated that they had no objections to their names being revealed; also distributed were any comments by governments against which the complaints were lodged; and no discussion was permitted to take place at the closed meeting, except on procedural grounds.

The final step in this bureaucratic nightmare required the UN Secretary General to inform the writer of the "communication" that the complaint would be handled in accordance with Resolution 728F and that the Commission had no power to take any action with regard to human rights complaints. One is reminded of Humpty-Dumpty's comment to Alice that when he uses a word, it means what he chooses it to mean. Human rights "communications" were to be understood as not having any meaning at all. The contrast with the operations of the UN Trusteeship systems was overpowering. Article 87 of the Charter authorized the Trusteeship Council to "accept petitions and examine them in consultation with the administering authority." Between 1947 and 1959, the Trusteeship Council received 16,232 petitions that it considered and acted upon.[5]

Notwithstanding the clearly enunciated abdication of responsibility by the Commission of Human Rights, NGOs and ordinary citizens continued to address complaints to it. The overall figures on communications during the fifties were striking in suggesting how euphoria about the United Nations would not quickly be dissipated. The average annual number of complaints during 1950-58 ranged from 2,000 to 6,000. Some years brought forth a huge volume; in 1951-52, the complaints reached the level of 25,000, and in 1957, ran to 63,700.[6]

From the very beginning, the question of creating implementation machinery was a central one. At the preliminary or "nuclear" session of the Commission on Human Rights, the UN organ agreed that there was an urgent need for "an international agency of implementation entrusted with the task of watching over the general observance of human rights."[7] The watchdog agency would have two separate functions: (1) implementation of the observance of human rights—the implied reference was to the Charter's Articles 55 and 56; and (2) implementation of an international bill of rights. ECOSOC supported the Commission's views with the assertion that the human rights purposes of the United Nations "can only be fulfilled if provisions are made for the implementation of human rights and of an international bill of human rights."[8]

In the early deliberations of the Commission, two key proposals for an international agency were advanced. Australia, in 1947, proposed the creation of an international court of human rights to which states, national or international organizations, individuals or groups of individuals could be parties. The idea found initial support in various quarters and, with some modification, received endorsement in late 1947 by the so-called Working Group on Implementation, which had been appointed by the Commission. Soon, thereafter, interest in the idea dissipated and it passed into the limbo of UN history.

But the idea would not be interred. It reappeared in several variations. Colombia in 1962 proposed in the General Assembly that the question of creating an international tribunal for the protection of human rights should be placed on the provisional agenda of the 1963 session. Interestingly, the Colombia plan was vigorously defended by such U.S. Supreme Court Justices as William J. Brennan and Arthur J. Goldberg, but it eventually was withdrawn.[9]

New impetus for an international court came from a prominent African jurist, T. O. Elias, Attorney-General of Nigeria and Commissioner of Justice, in a study for a UN-sponsored International Conference on Human Rights in February 1968. He emphasized that "what is urgently needed now is the establishment [of] international machinery and techniques for the implementation of human rights."[10] Elias advocated that a special UN committee be appointed "to work out detailed proposals for the early establishment of an *International Court of Human Rights.*"

Running parallel to the Australian and Colombian proposals was the idea for an international penal or criminal tribunal. This was based upon the experience of the Nuremberg Tribunal established after World War II as an organ of the international community to try those charged with war crimes and "crimes against humanity." The Tribunal had rested on principles that marked a critical inroad into traditional concepts about exclusive domestic jurisdiction. A basic theme of the Nuremberg tribunal was that certain crimes against humanity were international crimes "whether or not [they were] in violation of the domestic law of the country where perpetrated."

Remembrance of the Nuremberg Tribunal experience inevitably was triggered by the UN General Assembly's adoption of the Convention on the Prevention and Punishment of the Crime of Genocide on December 9, 1948. Its Article 6 projected the idea of an international penal tribunal that would try those charged with acts committed "with intent to destroy, in whole or in part, a national, ethnical, racial or religious group, as such." At the request of the General Assembly in 1949, the International Law Commission of the UN considered the idea of an International Penal Tribunal and judged it to be both possible and desirable.

On this basis, the General Assembly proceeded to appoint two committees that would draft the statute of an international criminal court. After the committees met in 1951 and 1953 and prepared the statute, the Assembly in December, 1957 chose to defer the discussion of a penal court until it had the opportunity of dealing with two related questions: a definition of aggression and an elaboration of a code against the peace and security of mankind. Until those matters were completed, approval of the Tribunal statute would have to be shelved.

As provocative as the Australian court plan (or its later variation) had been, so too was a proposal advanced by Uruguay in 1950 calling for the establishment of a United Nations Attorney General, with the second title of High Commissioner for Human Rights. An earlier formulation of the idea came in a presentation offered by René Cassin in December 1947. He called for the creation of an international bureau of human rights, composed of independent persons of eminent repute, which would receive petitions about human rights violations from nongovernmental organizations or individuals. The bureau would have an Attorney General who would act as a "cover" for the NGO or individual before the International Court of Justice should a bureau recommendation be appealed to The Hague. Only states have standing before the International Court of Justice and thus a "cover" was essential if the advocacy role of nongovernmental groups or persons was to be exercised and protected.

In 1950 and 1951, Uruguay fleshed out its initial concept of a UN Attorney General. He or she would be authorized to receive and examine formal human rights violations submitted by international and national NGOs. Examination was but a prelude to executive authority to engage in negotiations with the concerned state party. He or she also would be able to conduct on-the-spot inquiries and to summon and hear witnesses. The Attorney General was seen as a vital link to the yet-to-be drafted International Covenant on Civil and Political Rights.

Almost from the inception of the idea when it was proposed by René Cassin, the Soviet Union took aim at it. In 1948, the Soviet delegate to the Commission of Human Rights lumped it with the international court proposal as "a system of international methods or pressure" rather than "a system of measures for ensuring that human rights are implemented."[11] Presumably, the "pressure" was perceived as being exerted by the West upon the Communist bloc. Still, the Uruguayan plan was given repeated attention in the debates of the Commission during 1951-54, when it focused upon draft implementation clauses of a proposed Covenant on Civil and Political Rights.

Still, the core of the proposal, including its other title for the office—High Commissioner for Human Rights—would not evaporate. A decade after it disappeared from Commission discussions, it reappeared when Jacob Blaustein of the American Jewish Committee gave its key elements a public airing in a lecture at Columbia University. That lecture, given as part of the Dag Hammarskjold Lecture series in the fall of 1963 actually was drafted by John Humphrey, the Director of the UN's Human Rights Division.[12] How the idea came about is somewhat complex but bears relating if only to demonstrate the interrelationship between NGOs and government as well as friendly UN officials.

Apparently, the initial impulse for the idea as formulated in 1963 came from Marietta Tree, the U.S. representative to the UN Commission on Human Rights. In April of that year, she had sent Richard Gardner, Deputy Assistant Secretary of State for International Organizations, an article from the *Manchester Guardian,* describing the work of New Zealand's new Ombudsman together with a note asking: "Can this *ever* be suggested for the UN?"[13] During the following month, Gardner's interest was further sparked when he was asked by the American Jewish Committee to participate in a seminar in New York about the international protection of human rights. In the agenda for the seminar, prepared by the Committee's UN representative, Sidney Liskofsky, was the item, "High Commissioner (Attorney General, or 'Ombudsman') for Human Rights." Gardner's interest was now very much piqued.

In July, he held a number of meetings in the State Department with the thought of having the proposed institution incorporated in a speech by President John F. Kennedy to the General Assembly in September. It was opposed by almost every regional and functional bureau of the Department, recalled Gardner, on grounds that a High Commissioner might embarrass some of the totalitarian regimes with which the United States was allied and could even embarrass the American government. Such concern was, indeed, warranted, unless, of course, one was interested in institutionally advancing human rights purposes. What killed the proposal within the Administration was not opposition from the State Department, but rather rejection of the proposal's timing by U.S. Attorney-General Robert Kennedy. He and his associates in the Department of Justice were preoccupied with the enactment of the Civil Rights Act, which was then stalled in Congress.

On September 26, Gardner and Marietta Tree were authorized to discuss the proposal with the UN's John Humphrey. In the latter's memoirs, he stressed that he was "convinced that the idea had merit," and he was "determined not to let it die." When Blaustein asked him to write the Columbia University speech, Humphrey agreed because, he later noted, "Blaustein had influence at the State Department. . . ."

Humphrey did not neglect other NGOs as potential channels for promoting the idea of a High Commissioner. Early in 1964, while on a visit to London, he met with a small group of NGOs at the offices of Amnesty International and it was agreed that all would take steps to give UN legislative shape to the proposal. In the summer of 1964, the NGOs met in the offices of the ranking official of the International Commission of Jurists, Sean MacBride. A draft resolution on the High Commissioner was readied for presentation to the friendly Ambassador from Costa Rica, Fernando Volio Jimenez.

At the UN Commission of Human Rights, the proposal for a High Commissioner was first advanced by Costa Rica in 1965. Its establishment was seen as "an effective means of implementing the rights proclaimed in the Universal Declaration of Human Rights."[14] Later that year, the Costa Rican delegation submitted to the General Assembly a memorandum and draft resolution that defined the functions of the High Commissioner. He "would act as spokesman for the conscience of the world" and he would seek "to secure the observance of the Universal Declaration."

At the session of the Commission on Human Rights in 1966, the Communist member-states sharply opposed the High Commissioner proposal, arguing that the office would "unquestionably impair the sovereignty of States" and violate the Charter's insistence upon "non-intervention in . . . internal affairs."[15] However, the majority, by a vote of 16 to 5, authorized the appointment of a 9-member working group to study the proposal. The working group found the expressed fear of the Communist members to be unwarranted.[16]

Based upon the favorable reaction of the working group, the Western sponsors of the Office of High Commissioner drafted a resolution that was designed to alleviate fears of the Communist states and other UN members anxious about the prerogatives of state sovereignty. The result was a much watered down version of the original Uruguay plan. The High Commissioner, the sponsors observed, "would in no way impose his will upon governments" and "his assistance would be extended to States only at the request of the Government concerned."[17] The vote for approval of the Office was 20 to 7 with 2 abstentions.

The resolution provided that the Office was "to be so organized within the framework of the United Nations that the High Commissioner will possess the degree of independence and prestige required for the performance of his functions under the authority of the General Assembly."[18] The proposed mandate of the Office would strike a balance between the prohibitions flowing from the Charter's Article 2(7) and the felt need for an implementation institution in the human rights field. Emphasis was placed on reporting and conciliation. There would be no adjudicatory function. Even the technique of public exposure was sharply limited. The High Commissioner would be required to "maintain close relations" with other major UN organs. If they asked him to perform a quiet form of diplomatic mediation between states over a human rights dispute, the consent of both parties would be essential. Any report of assistance and services rendered by the High Commissioner would require "the consent of the State concerned."[19]

The most important function proposed for the High Commissioner was related to the thousands of communications on human rights violations received by the UN under ECOSOC Resolution 728F and promptly pigeonholed in an elaborate bureaucratic procedure. The Office's mandate would permit the High Commissioner to have "access to communications concerning human rights addressed to the United Nations," and "whenever he deems it appropriate, bring them to the attention of the Government . . . to which any such communications explicitly refers." Here was the promise of a slight breakthrough in implementation. The possibility of at least a modest redress or minimal satisfaction for those making complaints would exist.

Restrictions upon the power of the High Commissioner were evident. He was to be assisted by a panel of seven expert consultants appointed by the Secretary-General who was to take account of "equitable representation of the principal legal systems and of geographical regions." As resistance to the entire concept was rooted in the Communist world and much of the Third World, the panel was certain to act as a powerful restraint. Moreover, the resolution made clear that any conciliation function the High Commissioner enjoyed must be assigned to him by other UN organs with the consent of individual states. Still, opposition from totalitarian and authoritarian regimes was too strong. ECOSOC may have approved the Commission's recommendation in June 1967, but the following fall, the General Assembly postponed action on it. The postponement took on a near permanent character.

Not until a quarter of a century later, in 1993, would the concept be revived and, indeed, be strengthened and favorably acted upon. Not surprisingly, it would be the international NGO community, whose forces were by then significantly reinforced with new national NGOs in Third World countries, that would resurrect the dormant idea that had been initially proposed and sponsored by various NGOs.

A final implementation proposal, this time focused not upon special external institutions but rather upon the cooperation of member states of the UN themselves, was suggested a few years after the self-denying decision had been accepted. The proposal was designed to demonstrate at least some UN interest in bringing about a modicum of compliance with the Universal Declaration. In 1950, René Cassin proposed that member states "forward annually to the Secretary-General of the United Nations, for consideration by the Commission, a report on the steps they have taken to ensure respect for, and the promotion of human rights in the course of the preceding year."[20] The key phrase "consideration by the

Commission" implied at least a modest form of scrutiny and evaluation and therefore a certain implementation. It was the initial projection of a periodic reporting system.

A formal periodic reporting system finally was approved in 1956. It was, however, strongly emphasized that "the role of the Commission was not to criticize individual governments on the basis of reports," but rather simply to "ascertain the results obtained and difficulties encountered" in attaining compliance with the Universal Declaration.[21] After examining the reports, the Commission was to be restricted to making comments and recommendations, of "an objective and general character." The word "general" was designed to exclude references to specific countries or situations.

Instead of annual reports, ECOSOC decided upon triennial reports by member states with summaries prepared by the Secretary-General for consideration by the Commission. The system proved utterly unproductive. Many governments failed to respond at all and, when they did, they focused upon the technically legal human rights situation rather than the actual situation. Evaluation and self-criticism by governments were nonexistent. In the hope of correcting a flagrant distortion of the periodic reporting process, the Commission, on the basis of a report by its six-member Committee on Periodic Reports, NGOs were called upon "to submit comments and observations of an objective character on the situation in the field of human rights." But, at the same time, the Commission warned them that "allegations of violations of human rights in individual countries would be inadmissible."[22] The warning, in effect, neutralized the appeal to NGOs.

When a further set of reports turned out to be inadequate, whether in terms of the number of states submitting replies or in terms of the substance in the reports, which generally took the form of a whitewash, the Commission chose to transfer the procedure to the Sub-Commission on Prevention of Discrimination and Protection of Minorities. It was called upon to study the government reports and the "objective information" submitted by NGOs, along with comments made by states that NGOs may have criticized. Since some Sub-Commission "experts" tended to be more responsive to NGOs than Commission members, member states generally suspicious of NGOs lodged a sharply worded critique of most NGOs as Western-based and as issuing reports that were often "tendentious."[23]

But the Commission chose for the moment to disregard the angry reaction to NGOs. Instead, it seemed partially to institutionalize the procedure with but one modification: the triennial cycle would be divided into annual reportage geared to separate categories of rights. During the first year, the focus would be on civil and political rights; during the second, on economic, social and cultural rights; and, during the third, on freedom of information. Whatever the structural arrangement, the key issue would come to center on NGOs.

If machinery for airing and coping with human rights violations repeatedly was blocked, there were yet the forums of the Sub-Commission on the Prevention of Discrimination and Protection of Minorities and the Commission on Human Rights, to which NGOs had a certain access, whether in submission of documentation or in oral statements. Particularly was the access open when these organs explicitly invited NGOs to submit information on a specific subject. An unusual opportunity present itself in late 1959, when a swastika daubing that desecrated a synagogue in Cologne, the Federal Republic of Germany, triggered a worldwide epidemic. Hundreds of swastika daubings and other forms of desecration of Jewish institutions and temples throughout Europe and the Americas stunned a world that had not yet forgotten the horrors of Nazism.

The Commission, meeting in March, 1960, requested NGOs to submit documentation on "Manifestations of Anti-Semitism and Other Forms of Religious Intolerance." Extensive information was provided by two Jewish NGOs, the Coordinating Board of Jewish Organizations (CBJO—comprised of B'nai B'rith, the British Board of Jewish Deputies and the South African Board of Jewish Deputies) and the World Jewish Congress. Particularly rich was the report of B'nai B'rith on behalf of CBJO since its research arm on anti-Semitism, the Anti-Defamation League, already had tracked and assembled a vast array of data on the daubings. But since the Commission request was not limited specifically to swastika desecrations, but rather included all forms of anti-Semitism, B'nai B'rith could and did include a detailed picture of official Soviet discrimination against Jews and Jewish culture as well as other manifestations of anti-Semitism in the USSR.

The reaction of B'nai B'rith, the oldest Jewish service organization—its birth was in 1843—was in keeping with a new trend among world Jewry. An informed source, in a volume published in 1967, described the emergence of a fundamental change in strategy:

A few years ago when Jewish leaders began asking themselves what to do about the problem of Soviet Jewry, many said: "Sha." ["Keep quiet"] They claimed that even loud protest and outcry would serve to anger the Soviets and harm the Jews in the Soviet Union. Only when all attempts at discussions with the Soviet authorities failed and when the burden of eye-witness accounts continued to grow—only then did Jewish organizations, some slowly, others more rapidly, begin to raise their voices on behalf of the Jews of the Soviet Union.[24]

When B'nai B'rith and the spokespersons of other Jewish organizations added oral testimony on the subject at the Sub-Commission on Prevention of Discrimination and Protection of Minorities, they were met with a vehement harangue by the Soviet "expert," Valentin Sapozhnikov, who repeatedly interrupted testimony each time USSR policy toward Jews was mentioned. Such references, he shrilly insisted, were "slanderous."[25] Especially criticized was the President of the 500,000-member B'nai B'rith (who also served as Chairman of CBJO), whose oral comments were pointedly sharp and precise. In Sapozhnikov's repeated rebuttals, the Soviet Constitution had assured freedom "for all peoples regardless of race" and, therefore, neither anti-Jewish discrimination nor anti-Semitism prevailed.

The significance of the Commission's inquiry about anti-Semitism would be diminished by a large-scale influx in the early sixties of newly independent African states into the UN that radically changed the character of the General Assembly, ECOSOC and the Commission of Human Rights. Manifestation of anti-Semitism would cease to be the primary issue on the Commission's agenda; it was replaced by the issue of racial discrimination. It was decided in the early sixties that the UN organ initially would prepare a Declaration and then a binding treaty—i.e., a "Convention"—on "the Elimination of All Forms of Racial Discrimination." Only later would the Commission prepare a Declaration and Convention on the Elimination of All Forms of Religious Intolerance. These latter instruments were seen as related to Jewish concerns. "Religious intolerance" would not be seen as a priority objective, and it would be a long time before the Commission would draft the appropriate instruments.

Ad hoc UN studies by certain of its organs, prompted by sudden events, may not have been useful for NGOs except, of course, for stirring the public conscience. However, when UN bodies undertook long-term studies of various provisions of the Universal Declaration of Human Rights, NGOs could play significant roles. No better example of the potentiality of creative NGO research might be demonstrated than by how B'nai B'rith (of CBJO) dealt with the decision in 1960 by the Sub-Commission on Prevention of Discrimination and Protection of Minorities to have a Special Rapporteur conduct a study of discrimination with respect to Article 13(2) of the Universal Declaration of Human Rights. That article concerned "the right of everyone to leave any country, including his own, and to return to his country."

For B'nai B'rith, the study offered a rare opportunity to focus on a major concern of world Jewry. A central anxiety of the group was the right to emigrate from any state that threatens Jews or deprives them of basic freedoms. If Jews have no possibility of emigrating, when all avenues of life and opportunity are closed off to them, it conceivably could mean a return of the Holocaust. Especially relevant was the problem facing Jewry in the Soviet Union. On the one hand, Soviet Jews were confronted with religious and cultural discrimination by the Kremlin, as well as virulent Judeophobic propaganda.[26] On the other, they together with all Soviet citizens found it extremely difficult to emigrate.

In October, 1960, B'nai B'rith submitted a documented study to the Sub-Commission focusing generally upon emigration and specifically upon the question of Jewish emigration from the Soviet Union.[27] It was to have strong immediate and, more importantly, long-term ramifications. The study showed that, while Moscow's policy on the right to leave was generally negative, the Kremlin made exceptions in the case of several ethnic groups—Spaniards, Greeks, Germans and Poles—who sought to be reunited with kin in home countries.

The B'nai B'rith document pointedly asked why these numerous exceptions did not include Soviet Jewry, many of whose families had been ripped asunder and separated by the Nazi Holocaust and who, not surprisingly, yearned to reunite with family and kin already living in Israel. As historic cultural and religious opportunities for Jews in the Soviet Union were limited, reunion of families had become a pressing aspiration.

For the Special Rapporteur, José D. Inglés, a talented Filipino jurist and diplomat, the B'nai B'rith perspective carried considerable weight. His 115-page study,[28] a landmark, constituted a powerful reminder of the significance of Article 13(b) of the Universal Declaration. It is still considered in various quarters as one of the most important human rights analyses ever published by the UN.

Inglés's principal theme ran as follows: next to the right to life, the right to leave one's country is probably the most important of human rights. For, however fettered in one country a person's liberty might be and however restricted his longing for self-identity, for spiritual and cultural fulfillment and for economic and social enhancement, the opportunity to leave that country and seek a haven elsewhere can provide the basis for life and human integrity. If Inglés avoided making specific reference to the plight of Soviet Jews, there were sufficient indirect references and open hints to make the Moscow target fairly clear. Besides, he went out of his way to laud B'nai B'rith (or rather CBJO) documentation as "substantive."

Inglés noted that the right to leave is one of the oldest of human rights. Socrates is cited for the thesis that the right to leave is an "attribute of personal liberty." And the Magna Carta, Inglés observed, incorporated the right for the first time into "natural law." The French Constitution of 1791 gave it a special sanction, as did an Act of the American Congress in 1868 that called it "a natural and inherent right of all people, indispensable to the enjoyment of the rights of life, liberty and the pursuit of happiness."

In the opinion of the Rapporteur, the right to leave was a precedent for the exercise of other rights. Thus he noted that if a person is restrained from leaving a country, he thereby may be "prevented" from observing or practicing the tenets of his religion; he may be frustrated in efforts to marry and found a family; he may be "unable to associate with kith and kin"; and he may be prevented from obtaining the kind of education that he desires. Thus, Inglés concluded that a government's disregard of the right to leave "frequently gives rise to discrimination in respect of other human rights and fundamental freedoms, resulting at times in the complete denial of these rights and freedoms." To this point, he added the overwhelmingly persuasive thesis that, for a man who is being persecuted, denial of the right to leave "may be tantamount to the total deprivation of liberty, if not life itself." Appended to this was a psychiatric feature. Denial of the right, he said, produced a "spiralling psychological effect" leading to "a sort of collective claustrophobia." Inglés saw this as the outcome for those who "belong to a racial, religious or other group which is being singled out for unfair treatment." For them, the result of being unable to exercise the right leads to a "morbid fear of being hemmed in."

Inglés completed his study in January, 1963, and it immediately became a subject of heated discussions at the session that month of the Sub-Commission on Prevention of Discrimination and Protection of Minorities. It was the Soviet intention to frighten Inglés into withdrawing references to NGO documentation. Moscow assigned one of its top agents to serve as its "expert" on the Sub-Commission and perform this required task. He was Boris S. Ivanov, a tough, ruthless and articulate spokesman. Later, it was revealed by a high level Soviet defector at the UN, Arkady Shevchenko, that Ivanov was no ordinary diplomat; rather, he was the chief KGB official "rezident" in New York, operating under diplomatic cover.[29] By the early seventies, Ivanov had risen to Major-General in the KGB and was the operating head of its extremely important First Directorate.

Ivanov, in his effort at intimidation, focused upon B'nai B'rith. He called the documentation, previously lauded by Inglés, "slanderous," "tendentious" and "colored by cold war considerations."[30] A warning that carried an implied threat to Soviet Jews followed: "By its provocative acts, 'B'nai B'rith' could only do a disservice to that [Soviet Jewish] population."[31] Ivanov's efforts were in vain. Inglés would not reject the B'nai B'rith documentation. The U.S. expert on the Sub-Commission explained to a researcher: "The Soviet Union tried to get Mr. Inglés to retreat from including the NGO information. When the Soviet representative discovered that he would not retreat, he was simply shocked."[32]

The "NGO information" in the Inglés study would not be forgotten by the USSR. On the occasion of a review of the status of NGOs some six years later, the Kremlin would lead a ferocious drive to deprive B'nai B'rith (i.e., the Coordinating Board of Jewish Organizations) of its consultative status at the UN, an effort in which it very nearly succeeded. But consultative status meant precisely the responsibility of examining government conduct to ascertain how it corresponded with obligations it assumed under the UN Charter. The American expert, Morris Abram, explained to an academic interviewer that it was the function of NGOs to "undertake . . . scrutiny" of governmental conduct for "most governments endeavored to justify their actions. . . ."[33]

If the USSR perceived the Inglés study to be a serious challenge to its policy on emigration, it was not altogether in error. By the late sixties and early seventies, Soviet Jewish activists seized upon Inglés's work and the specified Article 13(b) of the Universal Declaration of Human Rights to justify in scores of appeals and letters they wrote to Soviet and world leaders their strong desire to leave so that they might be reunited with kin and family.[34]

While the potential human rights value of UN studies, drawing upon the NGOs, was patently evident, much less clear was the value of the UN forum, whether the Commission on Human Rights or its Sub-Commission on Prevention of Discrimination and Protection of Minorities. The "self-denying" rule may have erected an almost insuperable obstacle but limited evidence suggests that, if the intervention was at a sufficiently high level, a precise human rights issue involving a specific country could be raised. One example was the session of the Sub-Commission in March, 1964. At that time, various quarters in the West had learned of an unusually vicious anti-Semitic book, *Judaism Without Embellishment,* published in the Soviet Union, by the Ukrainian Academy of Sciences. Written by Trofim Kichko, a virulent Soviet propagandist against Judaism, the work was replete with traditional anti-Semitic canards of a particularly obscene character. Most disturbing were several pages that carried crude cartoons of Jewish stereotypes in a style remarkably similar to that found in Nazi propaganda.[35]

An NGO, Jewish Minority Research, had sent copies of pertinent translated sections of the book along with the vulgar cartoons to every member of the Sub-Commission. The American expert who was also President of the American Jewish Committee, Morris Abram, raised the subject in an especially vigorous manner.[36] The Abram intervention, reported in the media, set in motion a worldwide outcry, including many protests emanating from Western left-wing and Communist sources. So embarrassing had the situation become for the Soviet Union that the Communist Party Ideological Commission took the very rare initiative of condemning the book as a "serious mistake," while Soviet Premier Nikita Khrushchev ordered the book removed from bookstalls.[37]

The Kichko example offered a minor example of how the "self-denying" rule could be overlooked. In fact, it simply was bypassed on all interventions, whether governmental or nongovernmental, that related to the evils of apartheid in South Africa. How this exception was sanctioned and eventually resulted in one of the greatest human rights triumphs of the NGO community will be discussed separately. Here, it might be observed that the treatment of apartheid in the UN forum almost led in the mid-sixties to a fundamental modification of the "self-denying" rule. Almost, but not quite.

On March 4, 1966, ECOSOC, determined to move rapidly ahead in ending apartheid as well as racial discrimination, invited the Commission to consider the question of violations of human rights and fundamental freedoms "including policies of racial discrimination and segregation and of apartheid in all countries. . . ."[38] The Commission meeting that same month, reacted swiftly to the invitation. It declared that:

> . . . in order completely to deal with the question of violations of human rights and fundamental freedoms in all countries, it will be necessary for the Commission to consider fully the means by which it may be more fully informed of violations of human rights with a view to devising recommendations for measure to halt them.[39]

Were the Commission to fully inform itself of human rights violations, the self-denying rule would have to be junked. The next year witnessed radical developments at the Commission level.

In March, 1967, the UN human rights organ appeared to embark upon a totally new procedure that opened the door to NGO interventions. The Commission asked ECOSOC to authorize it and its Sub-Commission to examine the previously unexamined communications from individuals and nongovernmental organizations for purposes of ascertaining information about "gross" human rights violations. It went further. The Commission now would be permitted to study situations that might reveal a "consistent pattern" of human rights violations. "Gross" and "consistant" were the key words. They seemed to suggest to Commission members the kind of practices inherent in and applicable to apartheid. But supposing enterprising NGOs found "gross" and "consistent patterns" of human rights violations in countries and situations unrelated to apartheid?

That is precisely what was found by the very important NGO Amnesty International in its research concerning Greece and Haiti, which it submitted to the Sub-Commission on Prevention of Discrimination and Protection of Minorities. The report was carefully drafted to meet all the necessary UN legal requirements by Professor Frank Newman of the University of California Law School at Berkeley. Newman was a towering figure in the international human rights field who constantly would seek to devise ways in order to hurdle the obstacle of the "self-denying" rule. Later, he would serve as a member of the California State Supreme Court. His creativity would serve as a model for the other NGOs striving to cope with the bureaucratic absurdities of the UN system.

In Greece, a brutal military junta had seized power, ending democratic rule and suspending all constitutional liberties. Arbitrary detention and torture became common practices. Haiti, under the rule of "Papa"

Duvalier, for some time already had acquired a special notoriety for cruelty and barbarity. The Sub-Commission, at its October, 1967 session, critically examined the Amnesty International material and other NGO reports. Certainly the terms "gross" and "consistent patterns" of human rights violations seemed appropriate guidelines for application to Greece and Haiti. The Sub-Commission recommended the establishment of a special committee of experts to investigate the situation in the two countries and in other countries with similar situations. At about the same time, the Commission had established an Ad Hoc Working Group of Experts on South African Prisoners and Detainees.[40] Why not also establish a special committee of experts on similar situations involving "gross" and "consistent patterns" of human rights violations?

The reaction of the Commission at its February-March, 1968 session was quite different than the one expected by NGOs and the Sub-Commission.[41] Haiti chose to send to the Commission session its Permanent Representative at the UN, who denied all charges and proceeded to launch a counterattack. As a black state, Haiti charged that the Sub-Commission was attacking it in order to divert attention from the evils of apartheid. The Greek representative defended at some length the conduct of his government and castigated the Sub-Commission for singling it out.

Far more politically threatening were the angry warnings hurled by both Haiti and Greece. If the Commission permitted itself to condemn governments on the basis of unofficial communications received by the United Nations from individuals and nongovernmental organizations, then no government would be safe from condemnation. Haiti called attention to the fact that an unnamed certain power had been accused of genocide in Vietnam and that a certain unnamed European power had been accused of denying religious freedom to Jews. Clearly, the references were to the United States and the USSR respectively. The threat hardly differed from crude blackmail.

The intimidation was extended beyond the major superpowers. For example, the Greek representatives, fully aware that Nigeria was a member of the Commission, observed that the Athens delegate had been approached by Biafran spokesmen concerning alleged mistreatment of Ibos by Nigeria. If Haiti and Greece could be denounced, why not Nigeria? Or any state with a human rights problem?

The warnings proved decisive. Strikingly, not a single Western state, aside from Sweden, proposed that the evidence provided by NGOs, which the Sub-Commission had supported, warranted action by the

Commission. The action of the delegate of Tanzania proved decisive. Initially, he submitted a draft resolution that would have censured the Sub-Commission, and at the same time, required it to limit its reports on gross violations exclusively to southern Africa. Then, he threatened that if the Sub-Commission were to continue focusing attention on areas other than southern Africa, he would request it to consider violation of human rights in Vietnam and in the United States itself. The blatant and intimidating threat worked; the United States withdrew a very mild draft and the Commission agreed not to take any action on the Sub-Commission's recommendation.

And to make certain that the Sub-Commission would restrict itself to studying exclusively "consistent patterns" of human rights violations in southern Africa, Tanzania pushed through a resolution asking ECOSOC to increase the membership of the Sub-Commission from 18 to 26, adding "experts" principally from Africa and Asia. "Equitable geographical representation" was the key phrase used in the resolution to express the changed character of UN membership. A specific figure was appended to the phrase: 12 experts were to come from Africa and Asia. With 3 experts to be selected from Communist East Europe, it was certain that the Sub-Commission no longer would dare to venture forth beyond the human rights situation in southern Africa, except when expressly permitted by the dominant new bloc in its midst.

The year 1968 marked the twentieth anniversary of the Universal Declaration of Human Rights but most disturbing human rights issues of the sixties found no airing in the Commission of Human Rights or in other UN chambers. Even mass killings of Chinese and native leftists in Indonesia by an xenophobic military that had seized power went unnoticed. A similar indifference in the United Nations could be noticed in the case of large-scale massacres of Ibos in Nigeria or the mass ouster of Pakistanis and Indians from commercial and political positions in Kenya.

When dozens of NGOs met in Montreal in March to commemorate the anniversary of the Declaration, one of its principal leaders told the participants that there was a "conspiracy of governments" to evade and avoid their responsibility under the Charter and the Universal Declaration. The speaker was the gifted Sean MacBride, Secretary General of the International Commission of Jurists, who had served as a Foreign Minister of Ireland.[42] Few, if any, of the NGOs would have disagreed with the MacBride thesis.

The evidence of indifference could be found in the official UN-sponsored International Conference on Human Rights held in Teheran in May, 1968.[43] Many governments did not even bother to attend; of 134 states invited, only 84 came. And, of those who participated, few were represented by top-level officials in their respective countries. The principal result of three weeks of debate was the so-called Proclamation of Teheran, which, in most respects, was a rehash of various UN resolutions without any considerations given at all to the vital question of implementation machinery. It was scarcely accidental that public attention to the proceedings flagged and then disappeared.

Summing up the experience of two decades, a perceptive academic authority in the human rights field, Professor Richard Bilder, concluded that most governments have little real interest in how other states treat their citizens. The responsibility of government officials, after all, is first and foremost the protection and promotion of their own state's national interest. Moreover, many officials consider human rights to be a dangerous Pandora's box. If it were to be opened, no government would be safe from attack. Thus, it is the better part of valor to keep the lid closed lest one's own shortcomings be exposed, marring the image a government is attempting to project.[44] How the Commission dealt in 1968 with crucial human rights issues appeared to validate the Bilder perspective.

Still, if the Commission's record on implementation was unimpressive, it did undertake significant initiatives in standard-setting. In the early sixties, it began working on a draft Convention on the Elimination of All Forms of Racial Discrimination, which primarily interested the new UN members from Africa and Asia. Perceived at the time as especially noteworthy was the Convention's implementing organ—the Committee on the Elimination of Racial Discrimination (CERD). Its 18 members were to be elected for a 4-year period by and from the contracting parties to the treaty. CERD was to receive biennial reports from the contracting parties describing the measures taken by them to fulfil the specific obligations set forth in the treaty.

Significant, too, was the establishment by the Convention of an optional petition system for individuals; whereas under international laws, only states have standing before courts or judicial bodies, this treaty would permit, under certain circumstances, an individual or group of individuals who believed their rights under the treaty to be violated to submit complaints to CERD. The circumstances were quite limiting. The contracting state party against which the complaint was lodged must have beforehand formally declared that it recognized the authority of CERD to accept complaints from individuals.

It is a measure of how reluctant states have been and are to accept any challenge by individuals to their absolute sovereignty that as of the mid-1990s, less than 20 states have accepted the optional clause of CERD. In contrast, 140 states have ratified the racial convention. Individuals, too, have been keenly aware of the system's limitation and, at the same time, very much fearful of how, if their names were known, they might be subject to state pressures and punishment. Only a handful of individual petitions have been brought to the attention of CERD over the years.[45] What might have made the system more useful would have been if NGOs had been granted the right to submit complaints. But such authority was not given them; only an individual or individuals were authorized to do so.

Of far greater significance as a standard than the race convention was the International Covenant on Human Rights. It was projected as early as 1948 as the second stage of an International Bill of Rights, the first stage of which was the Universal Declaration of Human Rights. The Covenant, in contrast to the Declaration, would be a legally binding document compelling contracting parties to assume obligations for fulfilling the provisions of the Covenant.

After over a decade of deliberations marked at times by heated debates that reflected clashing Cold War ideological perspectives, the Commission finally adopted by unanimous vote on December 16, 1966 two separate Covenants—the Covenant on Economic, Social and Cultural Rights and the Covenant on Civil and Political Rights. Of very special importance was the approval at the same time of an Optional Protocol to the Covenant on Civil and Political Rights, which, borrowing from the race convention, provided for individual petitions and, therefore, for a certain standing in international law for individuals. Unlike the race convention, the Protocol here was deliberately created as a separate instrument. While in both instances, the system of individual petitions was optional, in the race convention, the petition device was incorporated into the treaty itself.

Nobel Laureate René Cassin stressed that NGOs played an important role in pushing governments to support and approve the Covenants that "provided for the application of the principles stated in the [Universal] Declaration. . . ."[46] It was NGO "perseverance," he said, that brought about this "partial victory." Cassin did not name the specific groups, but the major international NGOs, including the International League for the Rights of Man and the International

Commission of Jurists, were known to have been involved in promoting the Covenants.

The Covenant on Civil and Political Rights was drafted with greater juridical specificity than was the Universal Declaration, even if the catalog of rights covered was largely the same as those in the Declaration. But there were important exceptions. The Covenant enumerated more rights, especially one that obligated states not to deny members of ethnic, religious or linguistic minorities the right "in community with other members of their group to enjoy their own culture, to profess and practice their own religion or to use their own language." Of great potential, for purposes of implementation, was the Covenant's creation of a distinctive organ—the Human Rights Committee—aimed at achieving a certain, if extremely limited, degree of compliance. It was to be composed of 18 members chosen by and from the contracting powers to the Covenant. Implementation largely was restricted to a compulsory reporting function by those states ratifying the instrument. They were obligated to submit reports on the measures they had taken to comply with the provisions of the Covenant one year after it came into force and whenever afterward the Human Rights Committee requested them. After studying the reports, the Committee was required to forward them to the various contracting parties along with "such general comments as it may consider appropriate."

Initially, the implementation machinery was not intended to be a device for challenging in any meaningful way state authority with respect to compliance. But, eventually the Committee assumed a number of prerogatives—to be discussed later—that have enhanced its competence and effectiveness. Such prerogatives emerged from the guidelines and procedures the Committee adopted over time for dealing with the reports. In the course of this development, NGOs would come to play an invaluable role.

The optional Protocol merits special attention. It provides that an individual who claims a violation of the Covenant by his government *and* who has exhausted all available domestic remedies may submit a written communication to the Human Rights Committee. The Committee will consider the petition in closed meetings and then transmit it to the government against whom the allegation has been made. The contracting party to the Protocol is required to forward to the Human Rights Committee "written explanations or statements clarifying the matter and the remedy, if any, that may have been taken." The Committee's authority is then limited to merely considering the explanation and forwarding its views to both the individual petitioner and the states against which a complaint has been made.

That neither René Cassin nor human rights NGOs were enthusiastic about such a weak implementing instrument is obvious. Besides, resistance to even this instrument was so widespread that not until a decade later, in 1976, would it receive sufficient ratifications to come into force. Still, the Optional Protocol established the principle of individual petitions, a principle that was missing in the original draft prepared by the Commission and for which NGOs had lobbied. More importantly, in recent years, there has taken place a dramatic increase in the number of contracting parties to the Optional Protocol as well as a significant jump in individual communications. The way the Committee dealt with this growth in the use of the instrument led to the development of "a valuable body of case law interpreting and applying the Covenant and Protocol."[47]

Especially important was the NGO role, Cassin observed, in obtaining a favorable vote on the Optional Protocol, even if its provisions fell "far short of what they sought." Without NGO lobbying, there simply would have been no Optional Protocol at all. He emphasized that "but for the counsel given by the competent non-governmental organizations to the governmental delegations to the [General] Assembly, the protocol, inadequate though it is, would never have been adopted."[48]

Completing the International Bill of Rights was the Covenant on Economic, Social and Cultural Rights, which, while containing a longer and more comprehensive listing of rights than was to be found in the Universal Declaration, did not call upon contracting parties to comply immediately with them. Instead, the ratifying state obligated itself to take steps "to the maximum of its available resources" in order to achieve "progressively the full realization" of these rights. In essence, the rights were goals to be realized over time and commensurate with availability of state resources.

The Covenant provided for no implementing organ, like the Human Rights Committee of the Covenant on Civil and Political Rights. The only compliance requirement was a reporting system whereby the contracting parties were obliged to report to ECOSOC what measures they had taken in implementing their obligation, and the progress they had made to achieve fulfillment of the listed rights. They may also submit comments on any general recommendations made by ECOSOC. By the late eighties, in consequence of decisions taken by ECOSOC, a UN Committee on Economic, Social and Cultural Rights was created. Its establishment would transform the Covenant into an instrument for requiring contracting parties to fulfil the provisions of the treaty as early as possible.

Clearly, standard-setting, while constructive over the long run, could not and did not offer remedies for a UN human rights system unsympathetic to implementation and to NGOs that would lobby for implementation. While the Covenants and the racial convention were signal achievements, it would be decades before they would become operational, or at least partly operational, in terms of effectiveness.

CHAPTER THREE

Silencing
the NGOs at the UN

"**R**ubbish Which Should Be Thrown Out" read the headline of a lead article in *Izvestiia,* the Soviet government newspaper, on April 9, 1969. The *Izvestiia* article went on to describe unnamed NGOs as "weeds in the field" that desecrated the UN landscape and that required uprooting. For those observing the review proceedings of a relatively unknown United Nations body—the Committee on Non-Governmental Organizations—the headline carried ominous overtones. The Committee was a subordinate organ of the important UN Economic and Social Council (ECOSOC). Heretofore, the small body had attracted practically no public attention. Its formal function, exercised for a several-week period every year, was the routine approval of selected international NGOs for official consultative status with ECOSOC.

Now its utterly unexciting commonplace and routine function would be radically altered. The Committee would become the center-piece of a major assault upon NGOs and the NGO system of the UN. A veritable witch hunt would be unleashed within the Committee on almost all human rights NGOs, threatening their status and casting a permanent chill upon their ability to raise human rights concerns in UN organs. Especially targeted were Jewish NGOs, most notably the Coordinating Board of Jewish Organizations (CBJO) of which B'nai B'rith was the primary constituent. The assault would last some three years and, while the immediate practical impact was hardly significant, the consequences for NGO initiatives proved to be great. For the NGO system itself, the results in the broad area of UN human rights were devastating and almost disastrous.

What transformed the UN Committee on NGOs into a potent force was the entrance into the UN structure in the late fifties and early sixties of a large number of African (and to a lesser degree Asian) countries that had been formerly colonial dependencies of West European empires. UN membership had nearly doubled in size, thereby shifting the balance of power within the international organization sharply away from the West. The political interests of the new states were radically different from those of the European and North American democracies. And, since their experience with voluntary nongovernmental organizations was virtually nonexistent, it was hardly surprising that the new UN members would cast a suspicious eye upon international NGOs whose headquarters were almost exclusively located in the West. Only those Western NGOs that were preeminently concerned with anticolonialism or with the struggle against apartheid might win their support.

The anti-Western orientation of the new UN member states ineluctably enhanced the status of the Soviet Union. It was Moscow, after all, that had championed the anticolonial struggle within the UN, most notably by sponsoring in 1960 the historic Declaration on the Granting of Independence to Colonial Countries and Peoples. In 1961, the General Assembly demanded by a vote of 97 to 0 with 4 abstentions that the provisions of the Declaration be implemented without delay. During the following year, the Assembly reaffirmed the Declaration's obligations by a vote of 101 to 0 with 4 abstentions.

A kind of tacit alliance focusing upon anticolonialism had come into being. For the Soviet Union, the altered balance of power offered the potential for ending the continuing human rights criticism from international NGOs and permanently silencing them, especially those that had engaged in a continuous exposé of the Kremlin's suppression of human rights. The new African and Asian states were scarcely sympathetic with the bulk of these NGOs and, indeed, might welcome clamping down on NGO criticisms of the human rights practices of member-states. Besides, the very political nature of most new states, preeminently authoritarian in character, was hardly conducive to welcoming human rights advocacy.

Illuminating the character of the tacit alliance whose purpose was the imposition of silence upon NGO allegations about most human rights violations was an extraordinary and, in fact, unprecedented UN episode that occurred in January, 1967 at a meeting of the Sub-

Commission on Prevention of Discrimination and Protection of Minorities. The Sub-Commission had appointed one of its members, Judge Zeev Zeltner, as Special Rapporteur, to prepare a study covering "salient development and trends" in the human rights field as drawn from periodic reports submitted by both governments and nongovernmental organizations. He found the government reports to be inadequate and, therefore, he said, it was impossible to "point out trends and developments."[1]

The Special Rapporteur also prepared a separate document of eleven pages summarizing allegations made by a half-dozen prominent NGOs about civil and political rights violations in almost every major geographical area. Among the NGOs were the International League for the Rights of Man, Amnesty International, the International Federation of Christian Trade Unions and the World Young Women's Christian Association. The range of NGO charges was quite broad, stretching from enforced servitude to deprivation of freedom of thought, conscience or religion; from violations of freedom of opinion and expression to restrictions upon the formation of trade unions.[2]

Moscow's "expert" on the Sub-Commission, Yevgenii Nasinovsky, reacted with almost apoplectic vehemence to the Special Rapporteur's document of NGO allegations. In a stormy tirade, he denounced NGOs for violating the UN Charter's "domestic jurisdiction" clause and demanded that the official Sub-Commission document be suppressed. Parenthetically, it should be observed that Nasinovsky was hardly an independent "expert" on human rights as required by UN procedures. Indeed, he served as a member of the permanent Soviet delegation to the UN.

But in the fundamentally changed UN political structure, Nasinovsky's views carried weight. "Expert" Sub-Commission members from Africa and Asia, similarly lacking in human rights specialization even while serving on their governments' permanent delegations to the UN, were angered by allegations that might have targeted their countries.

The open appeal for suppression of the UN document may have been unique in UN annals. But the stunning demand, clearly symptomatic of a new Orwellian strain in the UN bodies, carried the day. By a vote of 8 to 6 with 4 abstentions, the majority took the unprecedented step of suppressing an official Sub-Commission document. Two months after the Sub-Commission decision, the Commission on Human Rights followed a somewhat similar route. What was at issue was the traditional report of the Commission's proceedings by its own Rapporteur, who was always chosen by his colleagues at the opening session. A particularly noteworthy event of the Commission's meeting was the unexpected appearance of U.S. Ambassador Arthur J. Goldberg, the head of the U.S. delegation to the UN.

Heads of delegations ordinarily did not participate in Commission sessions. They restricted their formal UN participation to either Security Council or General Assembly meetings. But in March, 1967, Goldberg felt it important to focus world attention upon a particularly dangerous human rights trend in the USSR, that of the brutal silencing of dissenters. Word had leaked out of Moscow about the secret and infamous Sinyavsky-Daniel trial. (Andrei Sinyavsky and Yuli Daniel were two prominent literary dissidents who were placed on trial for their writings.) The American Ambassador, strongly motivated on human rights matters, decided to address the Commission about "current and serious transgressions" against freedom of expression in the USSR. Inevitably, the essentials of the Goldberg address found their way into the official Rapporteur's report. Specifically, it contained three paragraphs which summarized the Goldberg speech. The Soviet delegate was outraged and insisted that the three paragraphs be expunged from the record. By a vote of 10 to 8 with 4 abstentions, the startling act of expurgation was completed.[3]

At the heart of the earlier successful censorship initiative within the Sub-Commission was the question of whether NGOs had the right to criticize specific countries for human rights violations. Until 1952, ECOSOC offered a fairly liberal interpretation of the authority of NGOs to comment on the human rights practices of specific governments. Whether in oral or written statements, NGOs in consultative status could submit documentation to ECOSOC and its subsidiary organs detailing violations of human rights in individual countries. However, in that year—1952—new rules were introduced that rejected written communications from NGO sources that dealt with human rights violations in individual countries. As finally and formally adopted by ECOSOC in 1959, the new guideline, Resolution 728F (XXVIII), prohibited reported violations in specific countries from being officially circulated or discussed in open session of ECOSOC or in its subsidiary bodies.[4]

If the hopes and aspirations of human rights NGOs were to be blocked, the initial instrument by which this would be accomplished would be the ECOSOC Committee on NGOs. It was the UN body that was charged with the responsibility of establishing standards for NGOs, including approval of applications for consultative status. If heretofore it had been hardly a consequential organ, it now assumed a significant role. For the Committee would launch a landmark attempt to intimidate, if not silence, the community of some 200 NGOs.

Who comprised the Committee membership, along with its parent body, ECOSOC, would clearly be a critical factor. As a result of the entrance into the UN of numerous African and Asian states, the composition of almost all UN organs (except for the Security Council) would be radically altered. The Committee on NGOs was enlarged from 7 to 13 members (and ECOSOC membership jumped from 18 to 27). Western democracies earlier had virtually monopolized the Committee membership. In 1955, for example, the only non-Western member was the USSR. By 1968, the Western majority had sharply diminished, even though it still could count on a very slim majority of at least seven votes.[5]

But the beginning of 1969 brought a fundamental shift in power within the Committee, with the West losing its majority. The Swedish chairman was replaced by an Indian, who tended to be supportive of anti-Western interests. And the 2 Latin American seats, which generally supported the West, were reduced to 1 seat—Uruguay. In the now 12-member Committee, the West could be certain of only 5 votes. Moscow, of course, was poised to exploit the new balance of forces. Committee deliberations could be turned into a device for reversing the rules that permitted NGOs to criticize governments, whether directly or indirectly. Perhaps, some of the more activist human rights NGOs might be totally silenced or even excluded from the UN.

What triggered the Soviet initiative was an effort by the United States and the West at the Committee meeting in March, 1967 to block applications for consultative status of well-known Soviet "front" organizations—the International Association of Democratic Lawyers and the Women's International Democratic Federation. The West in the past had succeeded in preventing the entrance of additional Communist front organizations, and its close majority in 1967 carried the day. Moscow and its allies appealed to ECOSOC not only to reverse the West's victory but, far more significantly, to lay the groundwork for a detailed review of the criteria and functioning of the NGO system.

Reinforcing the drive for reversal and reevaluation was the disclosure in an obscure California-based radical journal, *Ramparts,* that the Central Intelligence Agency (CIA) had channeled funds into various domestic nongovernmental organizations. When the *New York Times* published the California journal's disclosure in the very same month—March 1967—that the UN Committee on NGOs was meeting, the brouhaha reached an especially high level, even if no U.S.–based NGOs holding consultative status at the UN were named. ECOSOC, meeting shortly after the scandal broke, adopted a Resolution proposed by the United Republic of Tanzania that referred to "recent disclosures" about "certain" NGOs having "received funds from the intelligence agencies of certain states" and, then, asked for a review of the status of each NGO.[6]

In June, 1967, ECOSOC not only admitted the Soviet lawyers' front group; it also opened the door to a wholesale challenge to the UN system on NGOs that had existed since Eleanor Roosevelt's time and had played such a significant role in creating human rights standards as well as calling for their implementation by highlighting egregious violations and violators of the standards. It was the newly adopted ECOSOC Resolution 1225 that now ushered in a new review that would carry the earmarks of a major witch hunt. The centerpiece of Resolution 1225, requiring a review of the NGO system, was an opening perambular statement dogmatically asserting that the existing criteria for NGO consultative status "do not tend to conform to the realities of contemporary experience in the international community." Clearly implied here was that the change in the balance of power at the UN, with the new Afro-Asian group now linked to the Soviet bloc, had made anachronistic a system in which Western-based NGOs were dominant and which enabled them to criticize human rights violations.

The Resolution went on to ask the NGO committee to undertake a multifaceted investigation. It was to review the admissions criteria that had been established in 1950 in the historic Resolution 288B and was to formulate rules for suspending or revoking the status of NGOs. As Resolution 288B had no such provision, the proposed inquiry carried obviously threatening ramifications. The Committee, further, was to require NGOs to submit information on their activities and on their financing. Finally, the Committee was to determine whether any NGO was subject to undue influence by particular states, whether through financial assistance or otherwise, and to recommend appropriate action.

It is scarcely surprising that when the Committee met in January, 1968, the atmosphere was especially heated. An emerging majority would now approve a questionnaire for NGOs that was drafted by India and Tanzania and required them to state whether, in the last ten years, they had ever criticized a state in which they had no constituency. Since most West-based international NGOs had a constituency largely limited to the West, the requirement inevitably carried a McCarthyite flavor. The questionnaire also obliged NGOs to disclose whether they ever had criticized the UN itself. Hardly any activist NGO could have avoided such criticism. The potentiality for intimidation was exceedingly great.

The Soviet representative on the NGO Committee welcomed the questionnaire and vigorously offered a justification for it. He insisted that criticism by NGOs of states in which they had no constituency "could only be irresponsible or malicious" as all such information "could only be second-hand, and came generally from a corrupt press which was only too ready to hawk its lies."[7] The Soviet representative, Yevgenii Nasinovsky, was the same person who, as an "expert," had demanded in the Sub-Commission on Prevention of Discrimination and Protection of Minorities the suppression of an official UN document carrying a summary of NGO charges about human rights violations. For Nasinovsky, only the totalitarian state could be an authority on the human rights of its own citizens; all other reports were lies.

On May 23, 1968, ECOSOC was prepared to alter significantly the rules that had governed NGOs almost since the beginning of the UN. Resolution 1296 was adopted on that day to supersede Resolution 288B. Some of its language would be used to challenge various NGOs once the witch hunt in the NGO Committee was launched. Thus, one paragraph of the Resolution called for a "grouping" of NGOs "where there exists a number of organizations with similar objectives, interests and basic views." This had special implication for Jewish and Catholic NGOs. The individuality and integrity of each such NGO was being called into question.

Another paragraph seemed to focus especially on Jewish groups. Consultative status was to be extended to an NGO if it had "a general international [human rights] concern, not restricted to the interests of a particular group of persons, a single nationality or the situation in a single state. . . ." The powerful bloc of Arab states, together with the Soviet bloc, would contend that Jewish NGOs were only concerned with the interests of their fellow Jews. In the very same paragraph, however, sanction was extended to groups that focused exclusively upon the condition of blacks in South Africa.

The most pointed threat to NGOs came in a special paragraph dealing with the temporary suspension or permanent withdrawal of consultative status. Two different circumstances would warrant such punitive action. Punishment could be invoked if there existed "substantiated evidence of secret government financial influence to induce an organization to undertake acts" contrary to the principles of the UN Charter. The second circumstance was far less precise and, therefore, far more potentially threatening: an NGO could be punished if it "clearly abuses the consultative status by systematically engaging in unsubstantiated or politically-motivated acts against states-members." "Abuses" were but vaguely spelled out while "politically-motivated acts" were left undefined. Almost any activist NGO in the human rights field conceivably might be denounced and punished for charging a specified government with human rights violations.

A major departure from previous requirements was taken by the ECOSOC Resolution. In order to cope with the fact that international NGOs were Western-based, the Resolution provided that "national organizations" might be extended consultative status—with the consent of the government concerned—"in order to help achieve a balanced and effective representation of nongovernmental organizations reflecting major interests of all regions and areas of the world." Heretofore, only international NGOs could be granted consultative status. The new procedure would allow, totally unexpectedly, certain national NGOs in major Western countries to play a major role in the struggle against apartheid. This scarcely reflected the thinking of the Resolution's sponsors, who must have hoped that new national NGOs would appear in Asia and Africa and would reflect a non-European perspective. Later on, such national NGOs indeed would appear on those continents but, strikingly, their perspective was more in keeping with that of the NGOs of Western democracies than with that of their own governments.

One further feature of Resolution 1296 aroused concern among NGOs. It specified that the Committee on NGOs would examine those in consultative status every four years and, therefore, NGOs were expected to prepare and submit detailed reports on their activities at regular intervals. Clearly, a Sword of Damocles now was to be suspended above their heads. The language of the Resolution warned NGOs that their conduct and statements could lead to suspension or exclusion if they did not toe the line.

The NGO Committee began to review specific organizations in September, 1968 with additional sessions in November, and again in February, March and April, 1969. The 1968 sessions were relatively mild as a Swede still occupied the chairmanship of the Committee and the Western majority continued to prevail. The questions, however, were intimidating, with the focus on whether an NGO had criticized during the past decade any government of a country where it had no members, and, if so, which ones and in what way. Similarly NGOs were asked about any criticism of a UN political decision. Finally, questions were asked about budgets and whether any funding came, directly or indirectly, from governments.

The interrogation became more hostile in 1969 when an Indian delegate replaced the Swedish Chairman. Especially coarse was the verbal abuse by the Soviet delegate. His attack upon the highly respected International League for the Rights of Man was characteristic:

> This so-called League is one of the most odious organizations. It wages a systematic campaign of slander and subversion in many member states. Whom does it protect? It protects plotters, kidnappers, criminals, murderers, detainees, fugitives and refugees. It throws mud at member states.[8]

But the vulgarity of the assault upon the League paled before the verbal attack upon the half-dozen Jewish organizations and especially upon B'nai B'rith and the umbrella body it represented at the UN CBJO. All Jewish NGOs were labeled as agents of "Zionist expansionism." B'nai B'rith was accused of engaging in "malicious and slanderous attacks against the USSR" and of seeking to serve "invidiously as counsel" for Soviet Jews and, thereby, of poisoning the atmosphere of the UN. No doubt, the Soviet Union was determined to retaliate against B'nai B'rith's documentation at the UN in the early sixties that sharply had examined Soviet conduct toward its own Jewish community.

Moscow was joined in hurling harsh invective against B'nai B'rith by Arab members of the committee. The Libyan delegate said that B'nai B'rith was "truly an invisible government" in the United States, controlling the telephones of UN delegations and seeking to forbid delegations from entering the UN. The imagery echoed the language of traditional anti-Semitic works, such as the "Protocols of the Elders of Zion," which endow Jews with demonic powers.

Two key non-Jewish NGO representatives, attending the session on behalf of the "Bureau" of NGOS, which served as a kind of NGO Executive Committee, were so dismayed by the proceedings that they wrote a joint letter to the Chairman of the Committee protesting the verbal abuse to which B'nai B'rith had been subjected. The writers were Mrs. John Shepard, who was President of the Bureau and representative of the League of Red Cross Societies, and Miss Margaret Forsythe, representative of the World Young Women's Christian Association (YWCA) and Chairperson of the Bureau's Ad Hoc Committee on Consultative Status. Their letter read:

> In relation to the discussion of the status of the Coordinating Board of
> Jewish Organizations, we want to make clear the serious shock produced

by the proceedings upon the representatives of non-governmental organizations present. The [B'nai B'rith] representative was pilloried for over an hour and was forced to listen to a stream of invalidated charges not only directed against his organization but also touching the people to whom he has the honor to belong.[9]

The ethnic bias also was noted by Western delegations. Mrs. Beryl Chitty of the United Kingdom told the Committee that her delegation "was shocked that the representatives of the Union of Soviet Socialist Republics openly revealed its hostility to organizations whose members hold certain creeds. . . ." She added that this was a "total denial of what we are working for in the United Nations. . . ." The U.S. member of the Committee also decried "the interjection into the debate by certain representatives of political, religious and racial motivations in seeking to exclude or to lower the classifications . . . of certain organizations. . . ." The press was more precise; virtually all the Western correspondents at the UN found the proceedings disturbing. Darius Jhabvala, formerly of the *New York Herald Tribune* writing as the UN correspondent of the *Boston Globe,* noted that "an element of prejudice and discrimination" had been introduced into the NGO Committee's deliberations. The result, he observed, was that "a Jewish organization had been singled out by the Committee to deprive it of its standing. . . ."[10] Jhabvala concluded that the discussions "could decisively affect the role of non-governmental organizations in UN activities. . . ." His prediction was very much on target.

The most striking feature of the Committee's investigation of NGOs was that it found no evidence of CIA infiltration of any of them. It was precisely this allegation that had sparked the formal inquiry, as was made clear by the Tanzanian delegate at the end of the ECOSOC debate on the subject in June, 1969. He initially had prepared, jointly with the Indian delegate, the Resolution calling for a Committee investigation. Their questionnaire had unleashed the tactic of the witch hunt. He now would acknowledge to ECOSOC that, while some national organizations in the U.S. may have been infiltrated by the CIA, this did not apply to international organizations. He went on to express regret that political considerations that he said had not been intended in his proposal had been injected into the review.

The status of all of the NGOs, except B'nai B'rith (or CBJO), would be formally approved by the Committee even if some had a bad scare or close call. The vote on B'nai B'rith's status was a tie—4 to 4 with 3 abstentions. Its parent body was to make a final decision.

Deliberations in the Committee constituted a dress rehearsal for the ECOSOC debate that began in May. Once again, human rights NGOs were singled out for attack by the Soviet Union, supported to a limited extent by several delegations from Africa and Asia (while non–human rights delegations were quickly approved). Thus, the International Commission of Jurists was charged with "slander" of member states, including states where it had no members. The International League for the Rights of Man was accused of having as its officers "renegades" from Socialist countries who had found refuge in the United States and engaged in "campaigns of slander" against their former homelands and other countries. A long list of countries that the League supposedly had maligned was read out by Moscow's representative. He also accused the League of failing to speak out against human rights violations in South Africa. The accusation was completely erroneous, since the League had focused to a considerable extent upon that country as well as upon southern Rhodesia, and, indeed, upon various countries that persecuted Communists, such as Greece and Indonesia. This point was driven home by the Uruguayan and American delegates, citing official League statements.

America was in the forefront of the defense of human rights NGOs and appealed that ECOSOC, "by its vote, would show the nongovernmental organizations that they not fear that silence was the price of consultative status...." Significantly, none of the other major Western powers played as active a role. Only Uruguay followed in vigorous advocacy of the NGOs. Soviet efforts to expel the International Commission of Jurists and the League failed in lopsided votes as did a Soviet effort to demote the Paris-based International Federation of Leagues of Human Rights to a lesser status.

The outcome was somewhat different in the case of Jewish organizations. The principal targets of the Soviet Union and its Arab allies—notably Sudan, Kuwait and the United Arab Republic (Egypt), the last playing a strategic leadership role while serving as an official "observer," not as Commission member—were the World Jewish Congress and particularly, B'nai B'rith. Both were charged by the USSR with conducting a "campaign of slander" that, Moscow indicated, was prompted by the presumed arrogance of the "chosen people" concept. The reference to "the chosen people," articulated with biting sarcasm, was, in fact, a reflection of traditional anti-Semitism. The seminal work of Judeophobia, the "Protocols of the Elders of Zion," made the "chosen people" idea the centerpiece of the thesis that Jews were striving to dominate the world.

For veteran *New York Post* UN correspondent Michael Berlin, the Soviet tactic was clearly a "witchhunt" that was designed to appeal to those holding biased stereotypes about Jews. It was quite apparent, he emphasized, that all Jewish NGOs were subjected by Moscow "to particular harassment."[11] The Uruguayan, who was unusually eloquent in his defense of Jewish NGOs, made the crucial point that the Soviet drive to exclude Jewish groups on ground that they had criticized various governments would "impose censorship all over the world."

The Arab delegates joined in the oral slugfest, repeatedly charging that the Jewish organizations were merely Israeli puppets. Since the session was taking place only two years after the Six-Day War, Jewish organizations became proxies for the endless verbal vitriol of revanche against Israel pursued by the Arab states at the UN. Much was made, particularly by Egypt, of B'nai B'rith's Anti-Defamation League and its campaign against anti-Semitism everywhere. That campaign was condemned as constituting interference in the domestic affairs of states and, therefore, in violation of the UN Charter.

What made the CBJO especially vulnerable was that it had a major constituent in South Africa—the South African Board of Jewish Deputies. The Sudanese delegate, for example, sought to demonstrate that the Board of Jewish Deputies had, among its members, Zionist officials as well as persons holding high positions in South African society. The fact that both B'nai B'rith's Anti-Defamation League and the South African Board of Deputies had vigorously and publicly condemned apartheid was disregarded.

While the U.S. delegate, Ambassador Walter Kotsching, energetically and forcefully supported the Jewish organizations, sharply castigated the bigotry of the "chosen people" reference and proceeded to laud the human rights work of B'nai B'rith, he could not halt the general drumbeat of character assassination. He did succeed, with the support of the West, in winning the necessary votes to enable all the Jewish organizations except B'nai B'rith to continue their consultative status. The decision on B'nai B'rith's permanent status was postponed for one year. In the meantime, on the basis of a U.S. motion that ultimately carried, B'nai B'rith's status, with appropriate rights, was to be continued.

Intense procedural debates preceded the final votes on the American motion, which totaled 11 to 8 with 7 abstentions. The vigor of U.S. lobbying no doubt made the difference. But if B'nai B'rith survived and, in the balloting the following year (1970) had its status formally renewed until the next review, the impact of the debate would not be lost on all

NGOs. The point was powerfully made by Kathleen Teltsch, who had been the *New York Times* correspondent at the UN since its founding and had completed a survey of NGO attitudes to the ECOSOC review. She said that as a result of the strong effort to expel B'nai B'rith after its participation for 22 years in UN deliberations, other NGOs might "become afraid to call attention to governments' violations of human rights lest they too be threatened with expulsion."[12] Her assessment proved correct. For a long period thereafter, NGOs would be reluctant to openly criticize the USSR in a UN setting.

This did not mean that the nongovernmental community would acquiesce to the tactics of intimidation that characterized the review process. Assembling in Geneva at the eleventh General Conference of NGOs in Consultative Status, early in July, 1969, they expressed in a formal Resolution "concern over the manner of the review." They went on to note "with distress that this review was marked by attacks on Non-governmental Organizations with substantial records of contributions to the Human Rights Programme of the United Nations and to human rights in general." The Resolution sharply observed that the attacks upon NGOs were "motivated by considerations extraneous" to the ECOSOC criteria. It then concluded that "such intrusions of extraneous consider-ations" are "an erosion of the principles of the UN Charter and of the Universal Declaration of Human Rights. . . ."[13]

If the NGO General Conference formally called upon its governing body—the Bureau—"to protect the status and integrity" of NGOs in consultative status, it was nonetheless clear that a watershed had been reached. The Soviet Union and its allies, for the time being, would not be halted in their effort to intimidate and silence the NGOs at the UN. Only the United States was prepared to mobilize strong and determined diplomatic forces to prevent expulsions, but it could not alter an atmosphere that had become charged with fear and tension. And that atmosphere would be seen as itself intimidating. NGOs were reluctant to run the gauntlet of scathing rebuke.

One major consequence of the vehement verbal assault upon NGOs was their turning away in the early seventies from using the UN machinery or responding at the UN to human rights violations. Increasingly, NGOs exploited such other techniques as direct publicity in the world media to call attention to the plight of the repressed. Thus, the President of the International League for the Rights of Man, Jerome Shestack, wrote in *The Law Review* of New York University's Law School:

It is striking that almost all . . . examples of efforts by human rights NGOs to restrain government abuses occurred outside of the U.N. structure. This is not an accidental trend. More and more the international NGOs have concentrated their "protest" activities outside of the U.N. and quite likely will continue to do so.[14]

What reinforced this view was the inadequacy of the UN machinery to respond to NGO complaints. Means of implementation remained inadequate and circumscribed, and therefore, noted Shestack, "unfortunately, the U.N. has largely proved to be a futile forum for redress of human rights." Indeed, it was this structured inadequacy that he considered "the principal reason" for bringing about a "futile forum."

The offensive of the totalitarian rulers in East Europe, supported by authoritarian regimes in the Third World, did not end with intimidation alone. The early seventies was marked by an initiative of these powers to move the UN Division of Human Rights out of the UN Headquarters in New York City to Geneva, Switzerland. New York was, of course, the headquarters of a number of major human rights NGOs, including the bulk of Jewish NGOs to which Moscow, its satellites and supporters in the Arab world had registered strong opposition. More significantly, the overwhelming majority of the world media—press, radio and television—was to be found at UN Headquarters or in the city of New York itself. Geneva was hardly a center of the international media; major Western organs had no permanent bureau there but, instead, were serviced by local stringers.

If the offending NGOs were to be isolated and silenced by being cut off from media communications, what better way was there than to move the entire UN human rights system—both the staff professionals and meetings of the Commission on Human Rights—to Geneva. The rationale for the radical and transforming move was given as economic. The staffing of UN offices and the holding of meetings would prove less costly, it was argued, in Geneva than in New York. Critics found the argument tendentious and hypocritical, especially in view of the high cost of living in Geneva, but to no avail. Politically, the idea had too much support. In addition to the Soviet and Third World blocs, France was a vigorous advocate of the move. From the perspective of the cultural ideologues of Paris, French-speaking Geneva was far more suitable for international meetings than New York. Human rights issues were less consequential to France than cultural ego. By the mid-1970s, the move to Geneva was consummated.

But even meetings in Geneva would not give NGOs immunity from governmental onslaught. In February, 1975, at a Commission session in Geneva, the representative of the World Council on Religion and Peace, Homer Jack, berated the Commission members for the extremely slow progress in completing a Convention against religious intolerance. After all, the proposed treaty had been on the Commission's agenda for 11 years. Surely, this should have been enough time to complete the project.[15] Religious bigotry, Jack implied, was an obvious obstacle. He went on to document how the absence of a treaty made possible denials of religious freedom. Examples of such denial in Syria, Egypt, Pakistan, the Philippines and the USSR were offered. For the states concerned, even the mild accusations by an NGO were perceived as intolerable. Egypt charged that the NGO had engaged in an "abuse of freedom of speech." Precisely what was meant by the word, "abuse," was not clarified. Instead, the Egyptian delegate suggested that the NGO's status might be reconsidered. Meeting in closed session, the Commission asked ECOSOC to impose rules that would keep NGOs silent about the status of complaints to the Commission until the latter made a specific recommendation to ECOSOC. And it requested that should an NGO fail to display appropriate discretion in an oral or written statement regarding the state's conduct, it may be subjected to suspension of its consultative status.[16]

Two years later, the intimidation process was intensified; this time the Soviet Union was joined by authoritarian military regimes in Argentina and Chile. In its traditional mode, the USSR found NGO criticism of these military-authoritarian regimes to be slanderous as well as "poisonous to the international atmosphere."[17]

Intimidation was accompanied by the attempted imposition of a value system that was totally antithetical to human rights. Moscow, joined by the Arab bloc, in November, 1975 pushed through a Resolution in the General Assembly that carried distinctive anti-Semitic overtones. Zionism was declared to be "a form of racism and racial discrimination." That is, of course, not how Zionism is defined in major dictionaries. But the Orwellian inversion of language was made possible by a UN vote of 72 to 35 with 32 abstentions. Ironically the date of the vote—November 10—marked the thirty-seventh anniversary of the infamous Nazi "Kristallnacht."

"Zionism," in the lexicon of Moscow, was a code-word for Judaism and Jewishness, just as "cosmopolitanism" had been in the late forties. When the initial vote on the new definition was taken in the Third Committee of the General Assembly on October 17, a British literary critic, Goronwy Rees, while sitting in the Assembly balcony, sought to capture the scene:

> There were ghosts haunting the Third Committee that day; the ghosts of Hitler and Goebbels and Julius Streicher, grinning with delight, to hear not only Israel, but Jews as such denounced in language which would have provoked hysterical applause at any Nuremberg rally.[18]

The dangerous bigotry was immediately recognized by the great Soviet human rights champion Andrei D. Sakharov. He publicly warned that "if this resolution is adopted, it can only contribute to anti-Semitic tendencies in many countries by giving them the appearance of international legality."[19] A leading international affairs analyst, Paul Johnson, expressed fears that the anti-Jewish bigotry would become "the conventional wisdom of international society."[20]

Moscow's leadership in the campaign to win UN adoption of the infamous Resolution was to be found on several levels. First, it directly contributed 7 or 8 votes from East Europe to the final count. Second, several Soviet dependents in the Third World played key sponsoring and lobbying roles. Somalia, the principal sponsor of the Resolution, was at the time totally dependent upon Soviet military assistance. Cuba was a vital link to the Third World and its representatives were everywhere exerting pressure for votes. Dahomey (Benin) was pursuing a similar tactic with respect to Africa.

What motivated the Soviet Union to have the international community adopt the Resolution equating Zionism with racism? Moscow had been pursuing internally a vicious and massive anti-Semitic propaganda drive masquerading as anti-Zionism, since 1971. The campaign could be legitimized were it to receive an international sanction from the foremost global institution. And, indeed, no sooner was the Resolution adopted, than Moscow unleashed a major drive in the media to report the UN debate and vote and to clarify its meaning in ways designed to justify its own internal propaganda campaign.[21]

America's UN Ambassador, Daniel Patrick Moynihan, immediately recognized the implications and ramifications of the UN General Assembly decision. Speaking from the podium, he declared:

> The abomination of anti-Semitism has been given the appearance of international sanction. The General Assembly today grants symbolic amnesty—and more—to the murderers of the six million European Jews.[22]

It wasn't only anti-Semites in the USSR who would justify their bigotry by citing the UN Resolution. The same psychological device could be applied elsewhere as well. Traditional anti-Jewish formulations had come to be regarded as vulgar and lacking in civility. If, however, cloaked in anti-Zionist UN language, hate formulations could find a certain legitimacy in various countries.

Clearly, the seventies had marked the apogee of Soviet power at the UN and the lowest level of U.S. and Western influence. The tide began to turn in the late seventies and eighties and a new balance of forces augured well for NGO initiatives. But Moscow would not be kept from using the "Zionism equals racism" Resolution as part of its drive against NGOs and Jewish NGOs in particular. On February 20, 1987, the Soviet delegation in the NGO Committee challenged the continuation of the UN consultative status of the International Council of Jewish Women on the grounds that the Council had been critical in its literature of the Zionism Resolution. The Soviet delegation even went on to challenge every Jewish NGO, each on different grounds.

In August, 1987, the Soviet "expert" on the UN Sub-Commission on the Prevention of Discrimination and Protection of Minorities, meeting in Geneva, bitterly condemned a Jewish NGO on the grounds that it was allegedly "intrinsically chauvinistic" and "racist." Western delegates publicly expressed dismay at what appeared to be a display of overt anti-Semitism. It was the final anti-Semitic convulsion by Moscow at the UN. A fundamentally altered relationship between Moscow and Washington, as well as a shift in the internal Soviet power structure under Mikhail Gorbachev toward perestroika, glasnost and reform brought relief to the NGO community. A new atmosphere had been created that offered NGOs a far greater opportunity to champion provisions of the Universal Declaration of Human Rights. The virulent 1975 "Zionism equals racism" Resolution finally was revoked by the UN General Assembly in 1991. In this revocation drive, the United States would play a central role. At the same time, B'nai B'rith lobbying both within the United States and with numerous UN missions would prove of critical importance. Its UN representative, Harris Schoenberg, was the principal strategist in this initiative.

In the mid-seventies, however, the powerful Moscow assault upon NGOs, often with the cooperation of significant segments of the Third World, posed a major challenge to organizations committed to advancing human rights. How could they pursue the purposes to which they were dedicated and that their constitutions or bylaws as well as constituencies required them to fulfill? Intimidation, both subtle and crude, involving the overt threat of expulsion and worse, joined to efforts designed to isolate them from formal UN channels of communication raised serious questions about how effective they could be. Besides, a quarter century of experience had demonstrated that efforts to create meaningful implementation machinery at the UN had led nowhere. What instruments existed or were expected to come into existence in the near future were severely restricted. The enthusiasm in the NGO community of the 1945-48 era simply had dissipated. How NGOs would react to the profoundly burdensome challenges and obstacles confronting them would vary.

CHAPTER FOUR

"Honored Guests": NGOs in the Struggle Against Apartheid

Not as "petitioners," but rather as "honored guests"—that was how the former principal United Nations official dealing with apartheid in South Africa characterized NGOs during an interview in May, 1996.[1] E. S. Reddy, a tough-minded Indian in the UN bureaucracy, ran the world organization's Special Committee Against Apartheid from the time it was created in 1963 until his retirement in 1986, and in those two decades, he formed a virtual alliance with certain NGOs that constituted, in his own words, "one of the most significant movements in the 20th century" and one that eventually would lead to the collapse of the notorious apartheid system.[2]

The contrast with human rights NGOs striving to have the UN give effect to the Universal Declaration of Human Rights couldn't be sharper. During the fifties and sixties (and continuing thereafter), activist NGOs were kept at a cool distance from policymaking even as the UN Commission on Human Rights refused to deal with human rights violations. Worse than the effort to isolate and neutralize the NGOs was the virulent initiative in the late sixties and early seventies to frighten them into silence or exclude them altogether. Sisyphean struggle was hardly the fate of the antiapartheid NGOs. On the contrary, Reddy recalled, the UN machinery almost always was responsive to the ideas advanced by NGOs.

Indeed, these NGOs were veritable partners of the special UN machinery. In a work published in 1994, Reddy stressed that leaders of antiapartheid NGOs

> were invited to all conferences and seminars organized by the Special Committee [Against Apartheid], with full rights of participation, and were elected as officers. No United Nations committee had ever developed such intimate relations with non-governmental organizations.[3]

The extent of cooperation, barely known at the time, was extraordinary. In a 1986 paper that Reddy prepared and read at a symposium in Geneva, he disclosed that NGOs "often" provided "useful advice" and often suggested "new initiatives for international action" by his Special Committee. The UN body actually "sent delegations to various capital to consult with international and national NGOs."[4]

Especially striking was Reddy's revelation that his Special Committee, over time, "avoided distinctions between government representatives and NGOs in the conduct of discussions."[5] After several years, the Committee "even began to elect NGO representatives as officers of its conferences and seminars." Later, the Special Committee would organize important international events but formally announce that this was done "in cooperation with" one or more NGOs. The converse type of arrangement, with an NGO as prime sponsor, but "in cooperation with" the Special Committee, also would be followed. The Committee went so far as to provide expenses "within its budgetary possibilities" for NGOs to participate in Committee-sponsored "conferences, seminars and special sessions."[6]

The 1996 interview with Reddy was more than a touch intriguing for the student of UN language and bureaucracy. He disclosed that he held the phrase "human rights" in a certain contempt and sought to avoid it in the struggle against apartheid. Not that the phrase was harmful. The problem was that the words "human rights" were linked to the UN Commission on Human Rights, which was universally regarded as ineffectual. Besides, decisions taken at the Commission level had to be approved at the ECOSOC level before they went to the General Assembly for final action. Far more effective and efficient, Reddy explained, was the system he had worked out with and through the Special Committee. Its decisions and recommendations went directly to the General Assembly or Security Council. In Reddy's view, human rights in the sixties had a "low priority" at the UN, while the struggle against apartheid carried far greater weight and urgency.[7]

As an example of the Special Committee's influence, Reddy related an episode involving Sean MacBride, then the powerful head of the International Commission of Jurists. He had complained on one occasion to Reddy that he received no response from an urgent written inquiry he had made to the Commission on Human Rights. Reddy advised that MacBride repeat the written request, but this time with a show copy sent to him as the Special Committee Secretary. A full response quickly resulted.[8]

Even the power and prerogative of the Commission on Human Rights were reinforced by taking on specific South African issues. Thus, in 1967, the Commission created an Ad Hoc Working Group of Experts to examine and report on South African prisoners and detainees. The inspiration came from the Special Committee on Apartheid and particularly from Reddy himself, who later noted that, while the South African regime pointedly refused to recognize the Committee, it continued to accord formal recognition to other UN organs.[9]

In fact, the Ad Hoc Working Group of Experts was established with a distinctive set of guidelines that the Commission previously had sought to avoid and, indeed, had rejected. For the first time, the UN body provided for an *independent* group of experts to examine a specifically defined human rights violation. In addition, the Ad Hoc Group was authorized to gather information specifically from nongovernmental sources as well as other standard sources. Openly breached was the Commission's Resolution 728F, which stipulated that it had "no power to take any action" with respect to human rights complaints. The significance of the Commission decision was immediately recognized by the Director of the UN's Division on Human Rights. He called the operation of the Ad Hoc Working Group "one of the first occasions that an inquiry of this type had been organized under United Nations auspices."[10]

What emerged from the work of the Ad Hoc Working Group was a trailblazing triumph for both NGOs and human rights. Twenty-five witnesses were heard and 23 written statements were obtained. Maximum public exposure thereby was given to how South African authorities had inflicted torture and other gross human rights violations upon prisoners and detainees. One witness sharply illuminated the rationale of the inquiry when he stated that "the focusing of attention on what is going on and the exposures of what has been happening are likely to exercise something of a brake on the authorities."[11] Only apartheid in South Africa was the target, nothing else.

This focus was by no means accidental. At the very first session of the UN General Assembly in 1946, India formally raised the question of South African racial discrimination. Resolution 44, adopted by the Assembly, called upon South Africa to adhere to the UN Charter's human rights provisions.[12] The Assembly decision was taken, even after South Africa insisted that the proposed Resolution would violate Article 2(7) of the Charter upholding the inviolability of "domestic jurisdiction." With this Resolution, a small breach had been made in the traditional rejection by international diplomacy of action in the human rights field.

It was at the seventh session of the UN General Assembly in September, 1952, that the major breakthrough was made in international diplomacy.[13] Thirteen member states asked that South Africa's apartheid policies be placed on the agenda on the grounds that they violated the Universal Declaration as well as the UN Charter provisions on human rights and, significantly, that they constituted a "threat to international peace." Decisions taken by the Assembly in 1952 and 1953 had removed South African apartheid from the traditional Charter's "essentially domestic" jurisdiction and placed it in the context of "a grave threat to the peaceful relations among ethnic groups in the world."[14] Thus, UN intervention was justified on the basis of the Charter's peacekeeping responsibilities.

Significantly, these landmark steps were taken at a time before the large-scale decolonization of Africa had occurred and, therefore, prior to the massive influx of new African countries into the UN structure. Pretoria found itself a virtual pariah at the UN, which meant that it hardly could fend off strong criticism and, more importantly, action by the Security Council. The newly liberated countries entered the UN in large numbers in the early sixties and, prompted by the flagrant Sharpeville massacre of March, 1960, the Council warned that South Africa's practices endangered peace and security and called upon it to abandon apartheid.[15] Unprecedented punitive action was taken 3 years later in 1963 with Security Council Resolution 181, which called upon all countries "to cease forthwith the sale and shipment of arms, ammunition of all types and military vehicles to South Africa." During the following decade, the military ostracism of South Africa was tightened by various Security Council Resolutions.

The punitive military measures of the Security Council were augmented by an all-purpose Resolution of the General Assembly on November 5, 1976 under the title "Programme of Action Against Apartheid."[16] Member states were called upon to terminate diplomatic, economic, cultural and sport relations with South Africa and to refuse landing and service facilities for South African aircraft. The Assembly Resolution did not carry, by any means, the weight and impact of the Security Council Resolutions, but it indicated the moral and political perspective of the international community.

How the decisions of the UN were brought about and, more importantly, how they were implemented by the leading industrial and commercial powers is the story of certain nongovernmental organizations. It was several of them, located mainly in the United States and the United Kingdom, which helped shape a climate of public opinion that forced the hands of major and vital institutions whose impact upon the South African economy and government proved decisive. What would be wrought ultimately was nothing less than the revolutionary destruction of the apartheid system and its replacement by a democratic system. It was one of most profound political and social transformations of the twentieth century comparable only to the collapse of the Soviet Communist empire in East Europe. Both occurred at about the time the century was entering its last decade and constituted a testimonial to the significance of the Universal Declaration of Human Rights and, notably the "curious grapevine" of NGOs.

Perhaps the first NGO to be involved with South Africa was the New York–based International League for the Rights of Man. (This involvement, barely known today, related not to the apartheid regime directly, but rather to South Africa's effort to incorporate South West Africa, now known as Namibia, and thereby extend its system of racial discrimination and separation to a huge area on its border. The League would take determined steps on a variety of levels to block the South African aspirations. The impact would be felt early upon both the UN system and South Africa itself.

The International League, in the very early years of the United Nations, was but one of very few international NGOs whose exclusive concern was human rights. Most other international NGOs dealt with human rights only tangentially, as part of a myriad of other social concerns. Neither Amnesty International nor the International Commission of Jurists had as yet been established. The only other international human rights NGO was the London-based Anti-Slavery Society. National NGOs concerned with South Africa were still to appear upon the social horizon. The League was already three years old when the UN was launched. It was the creation of Roger N. Baldwin, an enormously energetic human rights activist who had helped found the National Civil Liberties Bureau in 1917, becoming two years later its first Chairman when the group's name was changed to the American Civil Liberties Union (ACLU).

Baldwin consciously modeled his new group upon the prestigious French human rights organization, called the Ligue Francais pour la Défense de Droits de L'Homme et du Citoyen, which had been founded in 1902 on the heels of the infamous Dreyfus affair (whose repetition it was determined to prevent). The French group, whose membership had been sizable—some 200,000—had reached its peak during World War I. Decline set in shortly afterward and, with the Nazi victory during the early part of World War II, its leadership was dispersed and its activities halted.

After several of the Ligue's prominent members had emigrated or escaped to America during the World War II, Baldwin came to the conclusion that they could provide the nucleus of a new international human rights organization. Among the French refugees, several of whom taught at the New School for Social Research in New York, were Henri Laugier, a former Minister in De Gaulle's wartime government who had been pivotal in organizing the escape of French scientists from Occupied France. Another was Charles Malik, the former Foreign Minister of Lebanon, who was to play a very prominent role in the early UN Commission on Human Rights. Also sitting on the Board were Eleanor Roosevelt and other distinguished Americans. Baldwin served as Executive Director and later as Honorary Chairman.

The League, according to a leading academic researcher, "was deliberately created and maintained as a small, private informally organized staff organization" that "accorded well with Roger Baldwin's social philosophy and operational ideology, drawn from 19th century concepts of *noblesse oblige* and private charitable services. . . ."[17] An "old boy" network played a key role in recruiting the board, in forming policy, and in affecting government policy. A mass structure was consciously avoided; at the most, membership stood at 2,000. Political action was accomplished mainly through discreet and indirect pressure or through the U.S. federal judicial process in whose efficacy Baldwin and his associates had a "single-minded faith."[18]

Elaborate funding devices, even with the small membership, were eschewed. "As a matter of principle," the League made clear repeatedly, it would not accept funding from governments.[19] Reliance initially was placed upon membership dues, which initially were $10 per annum and later became a mere $35 per annum.[20] Without a professional staff, other than part-time secretaries, additional funding was not considered essential. Office space was made available rent-free by several board members, and most professional service was extended by volunteers. Not until the League received a sizable bequest of $100,000 in 1968 did it increase a tiny budget of $15,000 to $40,000, and go on to hire its first full-time Executive Director.

Special attention, from the very beginning was given by the League to the United Nations in what Baldwin called "our unspoken faith in building up [the rule of] law for the brighter future. . . ."[21] He recalled the point when interviewed in 1954:

> Our attention was directed mainly to what at first appeared the most hopeful of human rights enterprises, an international Bill of Rights. I attended every meeting, urging in the endless debate what we considered effective enforcement. Mrs. Roosevelt, chairman for the first few years . . . shared our hopeful views.[22]

Disillusionment quickly set in. Nations, he later observed, "were not prepared to make law out of principles. . . ." After the League had criticized Argentina and several Latin American dictatorships, these countries were able to have a Resolution accepted at the UN "sharply curtailing our liberties of criticism."[23]

What gave the League "wider opportunities," Baldwin noted, were the trusteeship areas and the non-self-governing territories, since national sovereignty over them was restricted by the UN Charter. In consequence, self-determination or self-government became a priority human rights objective for the League "and with my personal efforts [occupied] a far greater place." In the early postwar years, the League became closely involved with many anticolonial efforts in both Africa and Asia.

The central issue of the status of South West Africa quickly came to the fore when the Union of South Africa, which had acquired this former German-controlled territory as a trusteeship, and now sought to annex it. (The territory was controlled by the German Empire prior to World War I.) The effort was rebuffed by the General Assembly, which referred the issue to the UN's Trusteeship Council, a body that South Africa refused to recognize. For the League, an opportunity presented itself to challenge publicly both colonialism and apartheid in the form of South Africa. The key question was: would the League be allowed to testify? If so, how could it technically represent the people of South West Africa?

The principal player in the complex political skirmishing that followed was the Reverend Michael Scott, an articulate Anglican clergyman from Johannesburg, who was described in League literature at the time as its "foreign representative."[24] Were he permitted to appear before the Trusteeship Council or the General Assembly's Fourth Committee, which dealt with Trust and non-self-governing territories, a significant precedent would be established for NGOs. On his own initiative in 1947-48, Scott did not succeed in testifying. Roger Baldwin's ACLU had to use considerable energy and persuasive arguments with the American authorities to bring him to the United States in 1949 since he was alleged earlier to have had Communist associations. In order to cope with this obstacle, the League in 1949 formally appointed Scott its consultant and observer to the UN.

Scott arrived in June, 1949 and immediately was joined by Walter White, head of the National Association for the Advancement of Colored People (NAACP) and Max Beer, the League's regular UN representative (a former French journalist, he was a major figure in the League's leadership corps) in an intensive lobbying effort of UN delegates to permit him to appear before the Fourth Committee of the Assembly.

Scott's formal request to be heard by the UN Committee required a certain ingenuity in order to satisfy two separate aims that did not run precisely on the same track. He wrote: "I am here as consultant for the International League on the Rights of Man but come at the request and expense of the South West Africa Herero people" [in order to testify] "on their behalf."[25] On the one hand, he was representing an international NGO that held consultative status; on the other hand, he could testify for an indigenous national group with which he had a certain familiarity. His testimony established clearly that South Africa had breached the trusteeship mandate by denying the native population fundamental civil and political rights.

The League had struck a very early blow on behalf of human rights, especially targeted against South Africa's regime of apartheid. At the very same time, it helped legitimize the right of NGOs to challenge the power of the Pretoria regime. As reported by Max Beer at the League's Board Meeting in December 1949, the League "had gotten very large mouth to mouth publicity through Reverend Scott and is now in very good standing at the UN."[26]

Even more startling than the League's initiative in appearing before a UN body to testify on the South West Africa issue was its effort to appear before the International Court of Justice at the Hague in a friend-of-the-court brief in relation to the same issue. How the matter of South Africa's determination to annex South West Africa came before the

International Court is clear enough. The General Assembly, on the recommendation of the Fourth Committee, formally sought the Court's advisory opinion on the annexation question. South Africa strongly objected to the Fourth Committee's recommendation, but the Assembly brushed aside its objection.

If the Assembly's action was hardly novel, the League's request to appear before the Court was totally unexpected by the authorities at the Court as only states, not nongovernmental organizations, have standing before it. Perhaps because the entire UN system was still in an early stage, a certain confusion resulted from the League's initial inquiry to be heard. On the one hand, the Court's Registrar informed the League by telegram that it could submit a written statement "of the information likely to assist the Court in its examination of legal questions put to it in Assembly request concerning South West Africa."[27] On the other hand, the Registrar, on behalf of the Court, rejected the League's request to appear before the Court. The Registrar set the date of April 10, 1950 for submission of the written statement.

The League's statement, prepared by its counsel, Asher Bob Lans, a Wall Street attorney, contended that NGOs with consultative status "should be permitted to participate in advisory proceedings as fully as a member state of the United Nations." The rather revolutionary thesis was based upon the argument that NGOs "had been closely involved in the drafting of the Charter," and, through the Charter's Article 71, NGOs in consultative status have been involved "in the subsequent activities of the United Nations."[28] As an example, the League statement pointed to its own appearance before the Fourth Committee, which, Lans claimed, actually "precipitated" the current advisory proceedings before the Court.

The purpose of the League's statement was aimed at obtaining permission for the Reverend Michael Scott to appear before the Court and present testimony as well as oral arguments. But, regrettably, the League statement was submitted on May 9, a full month after the required April 10 deadline. Three days later, on May 12, the Court informed Lans that his statement had been received too late to be included in the proceedings and, moreover, the Court had not changed its earlier opinion of not wishing to hear orally from the League.

In the opinion of Professor Roger Clark, who had researched this aggressive legal maneuver of the League, it was "unfortunate that the League's efforts came apart so disastrously." He emphasized that the initiative was the very first time in the history of the International Court of Justice that it had "authorized NGO participation in its proceedings" and, thus, "a valuable opportunity to impress upon the Court the advantage of such [NGO] participation was lost."

In any case, the Court did rule against South Africa's aspiration for annexation and demanded that South Africa adhere to its "international obligations" under the Trusteeship Mandate granted it in 1920. The Reverend Scott would appear frequently before this body, but its impact was limited. In 1966, the General Assembly decided that South Africa had breached its mandate and proceeded to terminate, at least formally, its mandated authority to administer the territory. A new administering authority was established by the Assembly over the newly designated territory of Namibia, formerly South West Africa. It was a decision that was vigorously pushed by the Reverend Scott and the League.

Finally, in 1981, their persistence was rewarded: Namibia gained its independence. Reverend Scott, at the time, was still a member of the League's Board of Directors and could derive personal gratification from the result. In Clark's judgment, it was Scott's "perseverance," supported by the League, which kept the South West Africa issue "in the public spotlight and on the U.N. agenda." Their role turned out to be "an important catalyst in the international legal process."[29]

Preventing the extension of the apartheid system was one thing. Far more difficult was to challenge the system itself by compelling the outside world and, particularly, the major industrial and commercial powers of the West to cripple the apartheid economic structure and, thereby, force a radical change in the political system itself. This would be achieved by a variety of nongovernmental forces, at the center of which stood a fairly obscure NGO, the American Committee on Africa (ACOA). It wasn't even an international NGO and had, initially, no consultative status to ECOSOC, although it would later get consultative status with the Special Committee Against Apartheid. Nor did it have much of a membership. But, in its dedication and commitment, and through its alliances and contacts with major public forces, it helped shape, at least indirectly, an American policy that delivered the decisive blow to the very foundation of apartheid.

A particularly knowledgeable, if surprising, witness to the role of the American Committee on Africa was Les De Villiers, who served during the sixties and seventies as a senior South African diplomat in the United States and Canada. Later, he held the key government post of Deputy Secretary of Information in Pretoria. After the collapse of the apartheid regime, he came to the United States to complete the research for a doctoral dissertation in history at the University of Stellenbosch. His topic was the sanctions campaign in the United States against South Africa, and his study later was turned into an impressive scholarly book.[30]

In focusing upon the ACOA as the "pressure group that pioneered sanctions against South Africa," de Villiers offered a special testimonial to the group's founder, George Houser, who created ACOA in 1952 and whose "life vocation" became the ending of apartheid "at any cost" once he had traveled to South Africa and met with the young leaders of the African National Congress (ANC) who had been driven underground by the apartheid regime.[31] What enormously impressed de Villiers was "the way Houser commanded his troops into battle, so to speak," and "the way he exploited the media and fired up many Americans. . . ." It was a rare form of testimonial from a former tough advocate of the apartheid regime.

Houser, when interviewed in 1996, already had reached the ripe age of 82 but, with his constant smile, warm hazel eyes, distinctive short grayish-white goatee, limber walk and firm build, he appeared at least fifteen years younger.[32] While he had retired in 1981, he continued to serve as consultant to the ACOA and was frequently on the road delivering lectures.

The autobiography of Houser scarcely suggests the image of a revolutionary, even if, as he admitted, he was "a product of the 1930s."[33] It was the "social gospel," the putting into practice of the Christian ethic, that was his credo. A product of the Union Theological Seminary in New York, he chose not to take up the Methodist ministry but rather to link together three callings that intellectually and emotionally had seized him—pacifism, support of trade unionism, and opposition to racial discrimination and segregation. He was attracted to Norman Thomas's brand of socialism. But that which exerted the strongest ideological influence upon him was Mohandas Gandhi and his call for nonviolent struggle. He told de Villiers that Gandhi was his "role model."[34]

Houser's first jobs gave initial expression to his mission. He served in the mid-forties as Executive Secretary of the Congress of Racial Equality (CORE) and, at the same time, was on the staff of the pacifist Fellowship of Reconciliation.[35] Impressed by what he believed to be the nonviolence of the ANC and after its convention of 1948 chose a youthful leadership including Nelson Mandela and Oliver Tambo, with Walter Sisulu as Secretary-General, the CORE leader wrote to Sisulu offering support. Houser recalled that Sisulu responded enthusiastically, saying "maybe you can do some publicity work for us. . . ."

It was in May, 1953 that the American Committee on Africa was created, with its prospectus stating that "one of the world's continents is missing from America's conscience" and that the ACOA "is being organized to help bridge the gap between Africans and Americans."[36] Its policymaking was done by an Executive Committee of some fifteen members meeting monthly. Initially, the Committee had no budget, with office space provided rent-free by the Reverend Donald Harrington's Community Church. Bolstering the activist Executive Committee was a National Committee of some sixty to seventy persons, prominent in various areas. Monies were raised through a direct mail campaign. And since the Committee's mailing list would grow into thousands—ultimately totaling 20,000—fund-raising brought in sufficient dollars to support an office of four persons. Space now could be rented in larger quarters located near civil rights and human rights organizations.

The ACOA even set up a South African Defense Fund that contributed $75,000 toward the legal defense of those South Africans arrested in their Defiance Campaign. Concerned British individuals also had become active. Canon John Collins of St. Paul's Cathedral in London created a Race Relations Fund that contributed $350,000.[37] By the sixties, decolonization increasingly had become a thing of the past. In 1960 alone, 17 African states became independent. Prime Minister Harold Macmillan, in a major speech to the South African Parliament in Capetown on February 3, 1960, defined the new watershed: "the winds of change" were sweeping over Africa.

It was clear that the ACOA could and would alter its focus away from Africa generally to apartheid in South Africa specifically. The traumatic events in Sharpeville on March 21, 1960 helped consummate the total shift. A massacre of blacks exercising their right to demonstrate inevitably concentrated the minds of those concerned about South Africa. That morning in Sharpeville township, a crowd estimated between 5,000 and 7,000 had marched peacefully to the municipal offices of the township in order to protest the hated "pass" system that had kept blacks out of urban areas in South Africa. The police fired into the midst of the crowd, killing 69 persons, including 8 women and 10 children.

Sharpeville triggered an explosive response. Trade unions in various countries, particularly those affiliated with the International Confederation of Free Trade Unions (ICFTU), took steps toward a consumer boycott.

In Britain, a particularly significant development took shape with the organization of a formal Anti-Apartheid Movement (AAM). The initial purpose of the British AAM was a permanent consumer's boycott that would be continued indefinitely. South African produce was the target. An early leaflet of the AAM noted that "we buy nearly one-third of South Africa's total exports"; it was the openly public posture of the movement "to isolate and ostracize apartheid." Housewives and cooperatives were called upon to not buy South African exports. At the same time, sportsmen were asked not to play in South Africa and artists were asked not to perform there.[38] The AAM extended its branches everywhere in Britain, developing a potent grassroots constituency.

For the first time, the UN Security Council, just ten days after Sharpeville, took up the South African issue and eventually, on August 7, 1963, called on all states to cease the sale and shipment of arms, ammunition and military vehicles to South Africa. The United States, under the leadership of President John Kennedy, joined in this initiative. The impact of Sharpeville upon American public opinion was enormous. If, heretofore, interest in South Africa was limited, the brutal arbitrariness of the shootings aroused widespread sympathy, as well as anger, notably among churchgoers. Houser would later tell de Villiers: "Without Sharpeville we would never have had much success. Violence in South Africa was the only way we could have Americans sit up and take notice."[39]

Just three days after Sharpeville, the ACOA held a demonstration in front of the South African Consulate in New York that attracted considerable attention. On April 13, the NGO sponsored a large protest meeting on the steps of New York's Town Hall that urged a boycott of South African goods and announced the creation of a fund for the "victims of apartheid."[40] Among the speakers at the rally was Thurgood Marshall, then general counsel of the NAACP. His presence was symptomatic of a new orientation among blacks in the United States toward the apartheid regime. Heretofore, their concentration was almost exclusively upon the civil rights struggle within the United States. In 1962, the major civil rights groups—NAACP, CORE, the Urban League, the Southern Christian Leadership Conference and the National Council of Negro Women—organized the American Negro Leadership Conference on Africa. It was successful in pressing Washington to halt U.S. naval vessels from visiting all South African ports.

Among the black civil rights leaders, none was more committed to the ACOA and the Negro Leadership Conference than Martin Luther King, Jr. According to a recent biographer, King "made significant moral and financial contributions" to the ACOA. He served as the principal speaker at major public events sponsored by the ACOA and vigorously promoted its appeals. He gave similar priority to the Leadership Conference and its major functions. Especially did he welcome and support economic sanctions and a "massive international boycott" of South Africa because he saw in those tactics "a potent nonviolent path" for the overthrow of the apartheid regime.

The culmination of the post-Sharpeville struggle came in 1966, with a particularly potent blow delivered against the South African economy. It was undertaken by the American Committee on Africa through a specifically created national Committee of Conscience Against Apartheid. The specific aim of the ACOA strategy was the cutting off of traditional bank loans to South Africa by ten leading U.S. banks. The imposition of such potentially powerful sanctions had not been undertaken before. What made it especially significant was the highly visible public relations character of the action involving, as it did, the very heart of America's financial system.

The development grew out of financial difficulties faced by South Africa after Sharpeville, including a drop in investments and loans. To relieve the plight of South Africa, the two leading New York banks—Chase Manhattan and First National City Bank (now Citibank)—organized a consortium of ten prominent banks that established a revolving fund of 40 million dollars for loan purposes. Suddenly, at the prompting of the ACOA's Committee of Conscience, chaired by the great civil rights leader A. Philip Randolph and numbering 120 of America's most distinguished citizens, the banks were confronted by deputations from churches, demanding that bank executives end the revolving fund. Otherwise, the portfolios of these religious bodies would be withdrawn.

In an interview 30 years later, George Houser recalled how his group initially focused upon the area around Columbia University, which embraced Union Theological Seminary and the headquarters of various denominations of the National Council of Churches (at 475 Riverside Drive). A branch of National City Bank was nearby and the Committee of Conscience "set a date for withdrawing accounts at that branch. There was quite a line-up of people who went in there to withdraw their accounts." Houser further recalled how the ACOA sought to duplicate the New York tactic in other major cities, such as Chicago, where the University of Chicago and Northwestern University were focal points, together with nearby churches, of the withdrawal campaign.

Paralleling the direct action with banks was a certain innovative protest action involving corporations that held deposits at the ten banks or engaged in major business activity in South Africa. Houser recalled:

Then we'd go to stockholders' meetings. We would buy a share of stock, various of us. And we would go to the stockholders' meetings and raise the issue. Now, of course, we weren't going to get the vote to carry any motion, but it got . . . public attention.[41]

By 1969, the South African Foreign Minister announced that the consortium loan would be ended "because of the Republic's strong gold and foreign exchange positions."[42] The rationale obviously was designed to soften the public relations impact of a regime capitulating to the pressures being exerted by an American NGO on powerful banks.

A major organizer of the British Anti-Apartheid Movement, in an interview in 1995, recalled that the action of American banks was "the greatest victory of all."[43] It spurred the British activists to put pressure upon the very influential Barclays Bank in London. Trade unions and students were urged to threaten the cancellation of their accounts at Barclays unless it ceased cooperating with the South African government. As in the United States the activists, mainly students, would buy shares in Barclays, as well as with Shell Oil and various goldmining companies. They then would "go to the annual meetings and make a hell of a row there."[44] By the late seventies, the AAM organizer recalled, Barclays did withdraw its South African loan accounts.

A sports boycott was a parallel activity of the AAM. It helped organize in 1969 a massive direct action campaign involving students and militants against a visiting South African cricket team. "Stop the Seventies Tour" was the name of the campaign, which culminated in an official cancellation of the tour by the British Cricket Council.[45]

A central focus of the sports boycott was the effort to keep South Africa from the Olympic Games. As early as 1963, the AAM joined with others in appealing to the International Olympic Committee to exclude South Africa. The appeal was acted upon positively, and at the Olympics in Tokyo in 1964, South Africa was not present. When South Africa offered limited concessions without changing the apartheid system in sports, and the International Olympic Committee appeared responsive, a massive worldwide boycott of the Olympics was threatened by a prominent group of black athletes, headed by the American baseball star Jackie Robinson. The Olympic Committee then decided to exclude South Africa from the Olympic Games in Mexico City in 1968.[46]

With the remarkable precedent having been set with respect to the banking structure, the ACOA now would undertake a major initiative against the giant pillars of American industry whose role in the South

African economy was much greater than that of U.S. banks. U.S. corporations provided 20 percent of the long-term direct investment in the South African economy (with Britain extending almost 50 percent).

"Disengagement" was the name given by Houser for the overall new strategic aim of the ACOA. He used that term in testimony before Congress when he asked for U.S. "disengagement from the South African economy, including official persuasion of U.S. companies to withdraw." What Houser was demanding, well before anyone else, was the imposition of total sanctions upon South Africa's economy. In his testimony, he also called for placing all U.S. exports to South Africa under provisions of the Export Control Act; taxing all companies doing business with South Africa and giving over the proceeds to aiding the "victims of apartheid"; eliminating the U.S. quota for South African sugar; removing U.S. space tracking stations in South Africa and ceasing nuclear cooperation. Ultimately, U.S. legislators would enact most of the ACOA's proposals into law but, at the time, Pretoria's officials, according to the later revelations of a government insider, "dismissed Houser's efforts as the delirious dreams of a radical." After all, they argued that "it would hardly be in America's strategic and economic interests to take such drastic action against a valued ally."[47]

What sparked the new sanctions initiative as well as the intensification of older more traditional educational activity was, as earlier, developments involving violence within South Africa. In June, 1976, thousands of black South African students, spurred by a Black Consciousness Movement, took to the streets of Soweto, the black suburb of Johannesburg, protesting against the imposition of the Boer Afrikaans language as a medium of education in the schools. Of course, the apartheid system itself was also a target of the student demonstrations. Once again, South African police responded, as they had earlier, with egregious violence. In the course of a few days, six hundred to a thousand youngsters were killed. As the demonstrations spread to other cities, the violence followed.

The violence would stir a powerful response from U.S. students on college campuses, where, during the past decade, their activism in the civil rights struggle and in the anti-Vietnam demonstrations had produced extraordinarily significant political consequences. Now the campus quiet of only a couple of years would be shattered. Demonstrations, mass meetings and leaflet distribution, as well as the more radical tactic of confrontation directed at university administrators and trustees, were now again being pursued. The objective was to pressure universities to divest themselves of stocks in all corporations doing business in South Africa.

Student activism was both anticipated and vigorously encouraged by the ACOA. This NGO had employed a staffer whose sole function was to be in continuous contact with student groups on college campuses.[48] By 1979, at least 18 outstanding academic institutions either partly or wholly divested themselves of the stock in corporations doing business in South Africa.[49]

As important as student activism was, the newfound militancy of the churches was even greater. One of George Houser's deputies, Dr. Timothy Smith, directed an ACOA-created group, the Interfaith Center of Corporate Responsibility (ICCR), which embraced more than 100 Protestant and Roman Catholic groups holding well over $25 million in U.S. corporate stock.[50] Divestiture was important in itself, but equally valuable, if not more so, was the access these church groups had to the annual general meetings of most corporations. Even when the proposed divestiture Resolutions of the activists were rejected, their intervention had "a debilitating and disruptive effect at these meetings."[51]

According to Houser in a study for the United Nations Special Committee Against Apartheid, "church bodies have been the most influential sector of American institutional life in pressing corporations involved in South Africa to examine their operations." It is essential to note that the individual Protestant church groups were provided a strong moral and political legitimacy by the powerful parent body, the National Council of Churches of Christ to engage in militant divestiture activism.

A third group, besides students and churches, to which the ACOA oriented itself was the trade union movement. In the early seventies, the International Confederation of Free Trade Unions compiled a list of 1,600 companies with investments in South Africa.[52] At the same time, it called upon unions affiliated with it to refuse to handle goods from South Africa. A number of American unions withdrew general or welfare or pension fund accounts with banks investing in South Africa. Houser, in an interview, recalled the significance of trade unions in terms of their huge mass memberships and financial resources that enabled them to provide valuable assistance to the ACOA.

In the hope of coping with the union pressure as well as the broad moral dimension of the divestiture campaign, those who sought to maintain economic and financial links to South Africa seized upon economic program ideas that offered the possibility of changing or modifying the apartheid regime. An initial example was proposed in early 1971 by Polaroid, the manufacturer of photographic equipment. Following a multiracial "fact-finding mission" sent to South Africa, the company placed certain restrictions on all sales to the South Africa government but, at the same time, adopted the so-called Polaroid experiment which involved a dramatic improvement in the wages and benefits of the company's black workers in South Africa as well as their training for upgraded jobs.

Of far greater breadth and significance was a plan advanced by the Reverend Leon Sullivan, a prominent civil rights leader of Philadelphia who also served on the board of the giant manufacturer, General Motors. He advocated a striking voluntary six-point program that set conditions for American businesses to stay in South Africa:

1. nonsegregation of all races in all eating, comfort and work facilities;
2. equal and fair employment practices for all employees;
3. equal pay for employees doing comparable work;
4. initiation of training programs to prepare blacks in supervisory, administrative and technical jobs in substantial numbers;
5. an increase in the number of blacks in management positions; and
6. improvement the quality of employees lives in such areas as housing, transportation, schooling, recreation and health facilities.

The virtually revolutionary "Sullivan Principles," announced on March 1, 1977, were a testimonial to the impact of the sanctions campaign. Initially 12 huge multinational companies signed up and by the middle of 1985, 170 of 350 American corporations in South Africa had joined. Yet, the moral fervor of the sanctions campaign, constantly reinforced by egregious examples of gross human rights violations in South Africa, particularly during 1985-86, would not be stilled.

A sizable majority of American corporations, in the early eighties, were reported to be spending one-third of their time fighting sanctions pressures.[53] And those pressures continued to escalate. Entire cities and states would adopt legislation that gave corporations without South African links special preferences with respect to governmental purchases and the awarding of contracts. The first such initiatives were taken by Madison, Wisconsin and East Lansing, Michigan, the sites of two leading state universities with activist student bodies and faculties.

Reinforcing the "hassle factor" was the decision by the ACOA to file legal suits against American companies doing business in South Africa, alleging before the courts that they discriminate against blacks in their hiring and promotion policies. The ACOA even succeeded in requiring the *New York Times* to cease carrying advertisements for jobs in South Africa on the basis that such jobs were not available for black Americans and, therefore, violated New York's antidiscrimination law.

When the sanctions movement shifted from the economic arena to the political and legislative arenas, a climactic stage would be reached. Even as U.S. television screens focused upon bloody crackdowns of South African blacks by government police, Senators and Congressmen from both political parties began clamoring for legislation that would curtail investment and impose economic and diplomatic sanctions. The intensifying political drive in Washington, in which Senator Edward Kennedy played a major role, was greatly augmented by a veritable "siege" of the South African Embassy by protesters. Launched on Thanksgiving Day in 1974 by TransAfrica, an NGO headed by Randall Robinson, whose public relations and organizational skills were to become legendary, the "siege" attracted national television attention and, ineluctably, the keen interest of legislators. All the more was this the case when Bishop Desmond Tutu, the prominent black Anglican cleric of South Africa, arrived in Washington and joined the protesters in December, 1984.

By the fall of 1986, Congress was prepared to enact the Comprehensive Anti-Apartheid Act, despite President Ronald Reagan's vigorous opposition. The legislation was "the toughest and most far-reaching sanctions legislation" introduced by any of South Africa's trading partners.[54] It would ban the following: all significant exports to South Africa; most imports from South Africa including the Krugerrand gold coins; landing rights for South African Airways; and all U.S. government purchases of South African goods and services.

If the legislation in itself directed a cataclysmic assault against South Africa's economy, it also included clauses that could compel South Africa's other trading partners to undertake similar enactments or run the risk of jeopardizing their valuable marketing opportunities in the United States. Congress provided U.S. citizens the "legal right" to seek damages against any person who took "commercial advantage of a sanction or prohibition." President Reagan vetoed the legislation adopted in August and September 1986, calling it a policy of "cut and run." The House of Representatives overrode the veto by an overwhelming 313 to 83 vote, and the Senate followed shortly afterward with a 78 to 21 vote. It was the first time since 1973 that the White House "had suffered such a heavy loss on an important foreign policy issue."[55]

Nelson Mandela ultimately recognized that "there is no doubt" that "sanctions played a decisive role in the collapse of apartheid."[56] Once sanctions were applied by the United States, it was only a matter of a few years before the entire structure of apartheid would come crashing down. No UN sanctions Resolution could have been effective without Washington undertaking the central driving role. That is what Les de Villiers discovered in his study of sanctions. But he also discovered that the sanctions policy did not suddenly dawn upon American legislators. It was an NGO—the American Committee on Africa—that had formulated and developed the policy a quarter of a century earlier, shaped it, involved major public forces and spearheaded the extraordinary historic effort that eventually led the U.S. government to act decisively.[57] George Houser was rather modest about his group's achievement:

> First of all, I wouldn't make grandiose claims that the American Committee did all of this. What we did was to get the ball rolling and helped to have it become a national issue. What we did as an organization was . . . to be in contact with all of the sympathetic national bodies, so that it became an agenda item for them.[58]

For a leading scholar of the apartheid system, "NGOs have been indispensable in developing alternative ideas, facts and policies at the national and international level."[59] Precisely because they were the bearers of "alternative ideas"—such as sanctions—they were particularly welcomed by the UN and its Special Committee Against Apartheid administered by E. S. Reddy. He called them "pioneers" who had "originated" many of the proposals submitted by his Committee to the General Assembly and the Security Council.[60]

Besides the "pioneers"—the American Committee on Africa and the British Anti-Apartheid Movement—there were dozens of others, international and national NGOs, who were involved in the struggle. A small booklet published by the International University Exchange Fund with the cooperation of the UN Center Against Apartheid in 1978 listed over fifty of these NGOs.[61] All were advocacy groups.

But there were some national NGOs that focused not on advocacy, but rather on providing legal assistance to the antiapartheid movement both in and out of South Africa. One such NGO merits particular attention because its project ultimately would lead to a special role in the first and historic elections in South Africa in the early nineties.

The organization was the Lawyer's Committee for Civil Rights under Law, established in Washington, D.C., in June, 1963. While the group dealt with a number of domestic programs, it also established the Southern Africa Project, which was funded largely by the Ford Foundation. Central to its purpose was assistance in the legal defense of various South African activists. Particularly useful was its support in the show trials of young leaders of the black consciousness movement who were accused of violating the Terrorism Act. In addition to financial help for the defense, the Project arranged for distinguished legal specialists in the West to visit, observe and report upon such trials.[62]

The Southern Africa Project had a domestic dimension as well. The Lawyers' Committee staff members often were called upon to testify before congressional committees and to assist in drafting legislation on South Africa. The Committee's expertise was specifically shared with those seeking advice on the corporate stock divestiture campaign.[63] The key figure in the Southern Africa Project was Gay McDougall, a veteran civil rights activist who participated in voter registration drives in America's Deep South. For 14 years, she served as the director of the Project.[64] Her principal function, she recalled, was "to work with lawyers inside South Africa who were willing to defend political prisoners." Engaging their services and paying for the legal cost of the defense was one facet of the job. Another crucial facet was helping shape the defense strategy and tracking the litigators.

At the same time, McDougall proved to be an invaluable source of information to the U.S. Congress, obtaining through her South African contacts information about activists who had been secretly seized by the police. She would persuade legislators to read the names of the detainees on the floor of the Congress. The result, she recalled, was "a lot of publicity," and, as a consequence, she and her colleagues "were able to exert significant pressure on the South African government."[65]

What constituted a climactic moment for the Project and McDougall's career until then were the four days of April 26-29, 1994 when South Africa held its first free elections. It was the historic moment that would mark "apartheid's funeral."[66] Ten months earlier, on July 2, 1993, Nelson Mandela and Frederik W. de Klerk had appeared before the cameras of the world to announce that a new interim constitution had been agreed upon and South Africa would hold its first nonracial election the following April. In January 1994, McDougall was appointed to South Africa's new 16-member Independent Electoral Commission; she was the only American accorded this honor and responsibility.

Voter education programs had to be started from scratch. The Lawyers Committee for Civil Rights was active with a variety of civic groups urging the holding of workshops and the building of an administrative structure essential for the election process. That the election process would have a positive outcome was by no means certain. One of the Lawyers Committee representatives commented: "People were afraid that there wouldn't be an election—that it would be violently disrupted, that the turnout would be insignificant, that there would be assassinations or civil war." Instead, and despite widespread anxieties and fears, the election turned out to be remarkably peaceful.

For McDougall, the election was more than an historic watershed. "Through all the work I've done over the past twenty-three years, I never imagined that this would happen at this time," she said. But the unique moment that she especially would remember was the one during which she accompanied Nelson Mandela to the polls: "To be with him when he voted for the first time in his life, after spending a lifetime fighting for this simple right was very special."[67]

McDougall would go on to other responsibilities as the Director of the important International Human Rights Law Group, an NGO that engages in training and empowering human rights advocates in developing countries. In these transitional states the Group seeks to build national institutions of accountability and justice. Strengthening legal systems and reinforcing women's rights are part of its mandate. As a leading figure in the U.S. NGO human rights movement, Gay McDougall was designated by her colleagues to introduce President Clinton when he formally inaugurated the fiftieth anniversary commemorative ceremonies on the Universal Declaration of Human Rights.

Nongovernmental organizations were at the center of the world struggle against apartheid. Not surprisingly, various UN bodies, mainly the General Assembly, adopted 16 Resolutions or reports since 1966 that appealed for assistance from NGOs, in addition to governments, as part of the international antiapartheid campaign.[68] The response of the NGOs did not go unnoticed. Nelson Mandela, in his acceptance speech at the Nobel Peace Prize ceremony in Oslo, Norway on December 10, 1993 publicly credited the "millions of people across the globe" who comprised "the anti-apartheid movement" for helping realize the historic human rights victory in South Africa.[69]

CHAPTER FIVE

The NGO "Prototype": The Anti-Slavery Society

The status of "honored guest" did not, of course, apply to those NGOs whose purpose was the implementation of the broad human rights provisions of the Universal Declaration. The contrary was the case. Should they dare to speak out they faced the threat of expulsion from the United Nations. How intimidating the UN bureaucratic machinery had become was painfully evident in the case of the oldest human rights NGO, the Anti-Slavery Society. The Society was one of the first NGOs to be granted consultative status and had had a distinguished career in combating one of the worst forms of human rights violations. However in 1977 it was sharply attacked for "slander" and early the following year was called to face a serious challenge to its status by the UN's Committee on NGOs. Only a kind of divine intervention halted the immediate threat. A 10-foot snowfall in the early morning hours before the hearing was to begin forced a cancellation of the meeting, ending for the moment the dangerous challenge.[1]

The Anti-Slavery Society enjoyed a unique reputation for helping bring about the adoption of treaties barring slavery and the slave trade even before there was a Universal Declaration of Human Rights. The Declaration, in Article 4, specified that "slavery and the slave trade shall be prohibited in all their forms." And once the Declaration was adopted, the Society urged the adoption of additional international legislation to cope with distinctive modern and nontraditional forms of slavery along with special machinery to give effect to both old and new legislation. Its age made it especially illustrious. No other postwar NGO could trace a lineage back to the late eighteenth century. A prominent British human rights leader and member of Parliament, Peter Archer, called the Society the "prototype" for all later NGOs.[2]

The first antislavery society was formed in 1783 in England by a group of Quakers. They were responsive to a growing body of literature attacking the institution of slavery and, in particular, the terrible conditions faced by the enslaved in the British slave trade. The initial group was augmented by others who had been influenced by a young antislavery scholar at Cambridge, Thomas Clarkson, and, together, they established the Society for the Abolition of the Slave Trade.[3]

The Society found a powerful voice for articulating its views in the Parliament—William Wilberforce. Sketches and busts of this great champion adorn the walls and hallways of today's Anti-Slavery International in London. At his insistence and continuous prodding, the British government under Prime Minister Charles James Fox abolished the slave trade in 1807. And at the historic Congress of Vienna in 1815, British Foreign Minister Viscount Castlereagh prevailed upon his colleagues to extend the ban to all of Europe. This was one of his proudest "trophies" even though he did not go to Vienna "to collect trophies."[4] The antislavery group in England, nonetheless, demanded further action: this time the end of slavery itself in the British Empire. The group's efforts were vigorously assisted by Wilberforce's successor as principal antislavery advocate in Parliament, Thomas Buxton. As of July 31, 1834, slavery was declared abolished in the British Empire.

The formal founding of the Anti-Slavery Society, as distinct from an informal group, came in 1839. Seven years later, it merged with The Aborigines Protection Society, which originally had been created in 1837. The lobbying by the Society during the nineteenth century was impressive. It persuaded the governments of Austria, France, Britain, Prussia and Russia to adopt a treaty in 1841 recognizing the right of each to halt ships on the high seas of any one of the group engaging in the slave trade. In the 1880s, the Society succeeded in getting a number of international treaties adopted suppressing slavery in Africa.[5] The culmination of this effort came in 1890 at the Brussels Conference, which created a permanent International Slavery Bureau to police the Red Sea and Indian Ocean.[6]

While the Bureau was not revived after World War I, the Society pressed the League of Nations to adopt a convention banning slavery. In 1926, through the efforts of the British government, the Assembly of the League adopted the treaty. Six years later, the League created a modest implementation instrument, an Advisory Committee of Experts on Slavery, which, too, was a purposeful aim of the Society.[7] Its activities were not restricted to standard-setting. The Society exposed de facto slavery in Liberia and pressed for and secured the abolition of the slave status in a number of countries.

By the time World War II ended, the Society remained very much in the tradition of both liberal colonialism and paternalism. On the masthead of early issues of its journal, the *Reporter,* the Society invited "all those to whom the maintenance of justice for weaker races of the world appeals as a duty" to join its membership. That organ, with about 25 pages, had a circulation in 1947 of about 2000. In that year, the Society formally changed its name from the previous Anti-Slavery and Aborigines' Protection Society to the Anti-Slavery Society.

The membership was prestigious, embracing elite elements of British society. A top-heavy organizational structure prevailed with 3 Joint Presidents and 18 to 20 Vice Presidents. But the key figure was C. W. W. Greenidge, who served as Secretary. He held that position for 14 years and was replaced only in 1956 by T. S. L. Fox-Pitt, his deputy and editor of the *Reporter.* Internally, the centerpiece of the group was the Annual General Meeting, attended by some 100 members.

The Society in the late forties was preoccupied with slavery mainly, but not exclusively, in African areas controlled by the British colonial administration. One of its Joint Presidents, Lord Winster, in a speech to the House of Lords on March 27, 1956 warned that "during and since" World War II, "vigilance" in combating slavery and the slave trade had "relaxed," with the result that "the traffic in human beings has again become active. . . ."

A sensitivity to the spreading slavery—one estimate at the time offered the figure of 2 million enslaved—was accompanied by an awareness that there were circumstances that bordered on the slave condition even if they were not formally defined as slavery. A promotion flyer of the Society, as early as 1948, referred, for example, to "native labour systems analogous to slavery."[8] This might apply to serfdom, debt bondage, bride purchase and child labor exploitation; each carried distinctive features that made it similar to slavery. From the perspective of the Anti-Slavery Society, two urgent objectives had to be pursued: first, the adoption of a treaty that would reaffirm and strengthen the earlier League of Nations Slavery Convention and would, at the same time, extend it to servile conditions akin to slavery; and, second, the creation of an implementing organ.

As early as 1948, Greenidge traveled to the Commission on Human Rights while it was in the process of drafting the Universal Declaration of Human Rights. His hope was that the Commission might seek to establish the proposed working group of experts on slavery. He met with five of the eleven Commission members, including Eleanor Roosevelt and René Cassin. Cassin was later reported to have been especially sympathetic. When Cassin died in 1976, the Society's house organ reported that "it was largely thanks to his support" that the Economic and Social Council "was requested to study the problem of slavery."[9]

Apparently Greenidge used the occasion of his visit to the Commission to distribute literature on slavery. The Soviet representative referred to the literature of a "voluntary organization" that he said he had found useful. It was an extremely rare testimonial. While Greenidge had doubts about the possibility of the establishment of a working group, he was upbeat about the UN in general but insistent on the need for the Society to do lobbying in order to keep the UN focused on the slavery issue.

Greenidge's lobbying proved effective. In October, 1948, ECOSOC adopted a Resolution that called for a study of slavery. On May 13, 1949, the General Assembly ratified the ECOSOC proposal and requested that the UN Secretary-General appoint a five-member ad hoc Committee of Experts. Perhaps not surprisingly, Greenidge was appointed to the Committee; it was probably the first time that a top official of an NGO was selected for an important, if temporary, UN post. Not until two decades later would the expertise of NGOs be accorded such recognition.

With his new status, Greenidge was in a position virtually to guide decision-making of the UN with respect to slavery. It was apparent, for example, that his Committee was pressing for the Society's aims of creating a permanent UN Working Group of Experts and of extending the 1926 Slavery Convention. In February, 1950, the Committee distributed a questionnaire to both UN member states and non–member states asking whether slavery existed in the recipient's country and also whether practices similar to slavery existed.

What the Committee learned through its questionnaire was described by the UN Department of Public Information in a special release.[10] The Committee, according to the release, found that "only a vestige of crude slavery remains in a few backward areas and is rapidly dying out." The judgment would prove to be premature. The release further noted that the slave trade did not "exist on any considerable scale." But the major evidence that the Committee uncovered, according to the release, was "that forms of servitude not called slavery but leading to a similar result affected a much larger number of people than slavery of the classical kind. . . ."

The outcome was manifestly evident. In the Committee's judgment a Supplementary Convention to the 1926 treaty was needed "to cover these practises." Several years were required to transform the Committee recommendation into a treaty. In 1954, ECOSOC created a 10-member drafting committee to prepare a Supplementary Convention. It met early the following year and, working from a British draft, approved the initial formulation of a supplementary slavery treaty. Significantly, the Anti-Slavery Society was in close contact with the members of the drafting committee and most of its recommendations were adopted.

To facilitate early enactment of the proposed Supplementary Convention on the Abolition of Slavery, the Slave Trade, and Institutions and Practices Similar to Slavery, ECOSOC recommended the holding of a Conference of Plenipotentiaries. Were the usual route of having the General Assembly debate and approve the draft convention followed, two years would elapse because the Assembly's calendar was already heavily crowded. The Conference met for a three-week period in 1956— August 13 to September 4—and after accepting several amendments, approved the text of the drafting committee. The vote was unanimous, 40 to 0. But there were three striking abstentions—Argentina, Chile and the United States. The United States' negative position on ratification of human rights treaties already had been made patently evident in April, 1953 by Secretary of State John Foster Dulles.

The significance of the treaty lay in its recognition of, and, more particularly, its banning of, a host of contemporary practices that were deemed akin to slavery itself: debt bondage, serfdom, bride price, treatment of wives as property and child labor peonage.[11] The definition of "slavery" in the earlier 1926 Convention, which was appropriately reaffirmed in 1956, was precise and pointed: "The status or condition of a person over whom any or all of the powers attaching to the right of ownership are exercised." Clearly, that definition was fully applicable to the status of the various categories that the new Convention delineated.

The Anti-Slavery Society could take great pride in the adoption of the Supplementary Convention. It was the second major human rights treaty approved by the UN and came seven and a half years after the vote upon the Genocide Convention. That the supplementary slavery convention would enjoy broad support was never in doubt. By 1990, 103 countries had ratified it, including the United States. Another 17 did so by 1996. Throughout all the steps in the process of UN approval, the Society played the key role. Greenidge's personal hand in the entire development was quite distinctive. It is significant that, prior to the Conference of Plenipotentiaries, Greenidge visited the United States and appeared before ECOSOC, where he testified about slavery in Saudi Arabia and forced labor in the African colonies of Portugal.

A feature of the Supplementary Convention prompted the Society as well as the UN itself to focus upon certain human rights issues involving women. The entire issue of bride price or purchase, for example, could not fail to raise the question of freely expressed marriage. It was hardly surprising that the Conference of Plenipotentiaries took only one additional action beside completing the Supplementary Convention itself. ECOSOC was called upon, in a special Resolution, "to consider the appropriateness" of undertaking "a study of the questions of marriage with the objective of drawing attention to the desirability of free consent of both parties to a marriage and of the establishment of a minimum age for marriage, preferably of not less than 14 years."[12]

In keeping with this new thrust, the Society in 1957 again changed its name, adding the words "for the Protection of Human Rights" to the title. The name change marked a milestone in the evolution of the Anti-Slavery Society. It rarely had used the phrase "human rights" earlier. If it welcomed the condemnation of slavery in Article 4 of the Universal Declaration of Human Rights, the Society was not averse to criticizing an approach to slavery in the terms of human rights as too absolute and naive. A more appropriate course would be one that was based upon prudence and incrementalism. Thus its leaders contended that the fight against slavery must take account of circumstances and must in no way demand self-determination and the end of colonial rule.[13]

Still, the Society opposed apartheid and sent a delegation to the British government asking it to oppose South Africa's attempt to annex South West Africa and to reject a UN trusteeship over the area. Greenidge and the Reverend Michael Scott led the delegation, which involved several organizations, including the Society, in the meeting with Philip Noel-Baker, Secretary of State for Commonwealth Relations. Reverend Scott's involvement is indicative of the antiapartheid orientation of the Society. By 1963, this activist from Johannesburg, who earlier had served as an instrument of the International League for the Rights of Man and later worked with the American Committee on Africa, entered the leadership of the Society.

More relevant than apartheid to the Society's newly found human rights interests was the issue of women's rights. It is intriguing that the first expression of this interest came in 1949 and concerned what would become the highly controversial issue of female genital mutilation as practiced in Africa. An article in the Society's journal was written by a former official of a midwives' training school in the Sudan. Using the inaccurate phrase "female circumcision," the author described the various forms of this practice in Sudan. While sharply critical of the procedure, the author contended that "if the practice is to be stamped out it can only be with the active aid of the Government." The reason offered was that the Sudanese were so tradition-bound that they "cannot be expected to help themselves in this matter. . . ."[14]

To get the government in Sudan to respond positively to the problem would entail, in the author's opinion, "the assistance of public opinion in Great Britain. . . ." But public opinion in Britain was far less pertinent to the situation than public opinion in the Sudan. Inevitably, the Society was confronted with a reality of a cultural conflict in Africa of such potency that progress in this particular gender area was questionable. One authority captured the limitations of Society pressures. After "many disappointments," he wrote, "African women alone must be seen to wage this war. . . ."[15]

If female genital mutilation was perceived as not warranting further attention in the immediate future by the Society, the question of "bride-price" or "bride-purchase" was regarded as of direct concern to the Society. Traditional cultural habits could not be allowed to do violence to the new legally binding treaty. Greenidge wrote to the UN Commission on the Status of Women that "the Society stands for freedom of choice of one's spouse by persons capable, by reason of their age, of making that choice. . . ." Clearly, the Society had moved cautiously into a human rights field that had been neglected by NGOs. By the late seventies, it would seek to widen its concern about women's rights in order to address not only traffic in prostitutes, but also child labor exploitation. The enlargement of the Society's human rights horizon would have to wait however, until it tackled more vigorously the problem of implementation machinery. That priority concern had been shunted aside as its preoccupation with the Supplementary Convention became a high priority demand.

As early as 1957, Greenidge stressed that it was absolutely essential for the UN to "set up machinery to supervise application of the Slavery Convention. . . ." Addressing a group of NGOs in consultative status on

July 16 of that year, he argued that "the experience of the last century . . . has shown that the making of conventions to abolish slavery and slave trading is not enough to achieve that aim." If the Brussels Conference of 1890 succeeded in halting the slave trade, Greenidge contended, it was "because it contained machinery" of implementation, and if the League of Nations slavery treaty failed, it was because such machinery was not created.[16]

ECOSOC may have debated the slavery issue every year as part of its regular agenda, but it was reluctant to recommend implementation machinery. UN tradition hardly ever had been enthusiastic concerning a compliance apparatus except with reference to apartheid. In the early sixties, NGO pressure, stimulated by the Anti-Slavery Society but now embracing other groups as well, began to be felt by government delegates. A Society lobbyist, Mary Nuttall, noted the increasing lobbying by NGOs for a Working Group during 1962 and commented: "That so many NGOs should ask for the same thing at one time is, I believe, unprecedented and without doubt this had an influence on government delegations."[17]

In 1963, Col. Patrick Montgomery became Secretary of the Society and he assumed the leadership in the campaign to establish a Working Group of Experts. Montgomery retained the post until 1980. An extremely modest step forward in reaching the implementation goal was taken in 1964 when ECOSOC named a Special Rapporteur on Slavery to ascertain the extent of slavery throughout the world and what was required to combat it.[18] Appointed to the post was a prominent Egyptian expert on the Sub-Commission on Prevention of Discrimination and Protection of Minorities, Mohammed Awad. The Anti-Slavery Society provided him with extensive information. Equally important was its recommendation for implementation machinery. In his interim report of 1971, Awad proposed the creation of a UN working group of experts to gather information on slavery and to offer suggestions on combating it.

Awad died soon after the report appeared, but ECOSOC proceeded to act upon his proposal. The Sub-Commission was asked to examine the question of implementation, and, in 1973, it formally urged the establishment of a Working Group of Experts on Slavery, which finally was approved in 1975. The Working Group was to be made up of five members, drawn from the Sub-Commission, which was held to be a body of experts. Each of the five was to be chosen from a major geographical area. Of particular importance was the selection of Ben Whitaker of Britain to represent the West European geographical area. He was a member of the Anti-Slavery Society and also served as Director of an important London-based NGO, the Minority Rights Group.

The Working Group was to meet in Geneva in August for one week every year just prior to the annual session of the Sub-Commission. That it offered a valuable precedent is clear. As yet no other implementing mechanism for a human rights treaty had come into existence. The genocide treaty provided for no special implementing organ. Still, the working group's role was limited. It could not but rely heavily upon information and documentation assembled by NGOs, especially that prepared by the Anti-Slavery Society, for it had no staff to accumulate data and develop studies or programs. But the Working Group could and did forward the information it received from NGOs to the government against whom an allegation had been made.

In any case, violators of slavery treaty obligations were not immune from open criticism and being called to account. Especially was this true if the NGO was persistent and carried a certain clout. That the Anti-Slavery Society would be a persistent agent of exposure and documentation was hardly questionable. From the beginning, the Working Group was heavily dependent on assistance rendered by the Society. Candid acknowledgment of this reality was made by the Ghanaian expert representing Africa, who, in introducing a Resolution to adopt the Working Group report, commented that "the Group could not have fulfilled its task without the help of the Anti-Slavery Society."[19]

Almost no competition existed for the Society. At the first meeting of the Working Group, only Interpol (the International Police Organization)—aside from the Society—provided documentation that, in this instance, involved the trafficking of persons. The following year, during the 1976 session, "almost all" the information came from the Society.[20] In that year, however, for the first time, two other NGOs submitted documentation—the International Commission of Jurists and the Women's International Democratic Federation.

Without clear guidelines, the Working Group did undertake the innovative path of sending a mission to check on an allegation involving Mauritania. Of course, that mission could not have been sent were Mauritania not actively involved in extending the invitation to the Group. Nonetheless, what emerged was a precedent for later UN Commission Working Groups. That which had prompted the development was a report sent to the Society by a Frenchman who related that he personally had witnessed, in February, 1980, in a small Mauritanian town, the open sale of a female. While the Anti-Slavery Society had estimated in a report to the UN that the slave population of Mauritania totaled 100,000, open sale of slaves was rare.

The highlight of the episode came when a representative of Mauritania at the UN appeared before the Working Group and, while admitting the existence of slavery in his country, stated that his government already had assumed the responsibility for enacting "various legislative, administrative and socio-economic measures . . . to put an end to slavery."[21] On various levels, clearly, the Anti-Slavery Society had been successful in fulfilling its two major aspirations.

Without either a national or international constituency, how did it achieve its aims? The secret of its success rested with the power of Britain. It was British diplomacy and pressure that obtained the votes needed by the Society. London, from the later eighteenth century onward, perceived its national interest to require the abolition of slavery and the slave trade. While no doubt image and a Calvinist or Puritan moral rectitude helped shape the national interest, certainly also traditional economic concerns of a free market and a free trade society legitimated the struggle against slavery. Strikingly, membership in the Anti-Slavery Society was almost exclusively British in the beginning, and only later did it incorporate some foreign elements. And the Society's leadership came from the same political class of Britain that was dominant in the state and the governmental apparatus. British diplomats might be members of the Society or have a close relationship with its leaders. With the decline of British power in the world during the last several decades of the twentieth century, the continuing leadership of the Anti-Slavery Society inevitably would decline.

Certainly, however, the Society's interest in child labor would be maintained and, indeed, would grow since such labor was a crucial expression of a widespread and growing form of servitude. An International Labor Organization (ILO) estimate in 1972 placed the number of working children under the age of 15 at 45 million, which constituted 5 percent of all children.[22] At the 1979 meeting of the Working Group of Experts on Slavery, the Society submitted "substantive material" for the discussion on child labor, which was the only source of material used by the Working Group.[23]

The target date for the Society was 1979, which was declared to be the International Year of the Child. It had launched studies as early as 1975 and 1977 on child labor in the Moroccan carpet industry. In 1978, it submitted to the Working Group a preliminary survey of child labor "throughout the world."[24] The areas actually covered in 1978 were

Colombia, India, Portugal and Hong Kong. In the following year, Italy, Malaysia, South Africa, Spain and Thailand were added. Funding for these fairly extensive studies and reports was provided by the Ford Foundation. The culmination of the Society's efforts came at the 1979 meeting of the Sub-Commission on Prevention of Discrimination and Protection of Minorities. The group decided, for the first time, to appoint a Special Rapporteur on the Exploitation of Child Labor. Of course, he would be provided with a considerable amount of research material by the Society's "project officer" on child labor.[25] Ultimately, what would emerge from the various decade-long international efforts— at the center of which was the Anti-Slavery Society—was a Convention on the Rights of the Child adopted by the UN General Assembly on November 20, 1989.

Even with the reportage on child labor exploitation or on the servitude of women, it was apparent that only the surface had been touched. Much of the material was anecdotal. Systematic studies were rare, and probably too burdensome for the Society or the Working Committee of Experts to assume. Was there an alternative route to pursue? That a massive number of complaints existed about servitude akin to slavery scarcely could be doubted. Information that came to the Society suggested as much. The trouble was that the complaints that came to the UN were treated as totally confidential and thus could not be acted upon, let alone examined. The procedure had been scornfully ridiculed by John Humphrey, Director of the UN Division of Human Rights until the mid-sixties, as a "waste-basket" for disposing of victims' pleas.[26] Developments in 1965-66 appeared to offer an alternative route at least for contracting parties to two treaties adopted by the UN.

Resolution 1503, adopted on May 27, 1970, was considered historic at the time for offering a real breakthrough for documentation. The Sub-Commission was given the primary responsibility for review of complaints. It was to appoint a Working Group that would meet several days prior to each Sub-Commission session and examine all communications as well as government replies. The Group then would determine which of those communications "reveal a consistent pattern of gross and reliably attested" human rights violations and then formally bring them to the attention of the Sub-Commission.

The Sub-Commission and later the Commission would determine whether the situation warranted a "thorough study" by the Commission, which then would provide a report and recommendation to ECOSOC. The Commission might choose to avoid that procedure by appointing, with the consent of the state against which charges have been leveled, an ad hoc investigatory committee. In the meantime, all steps in this elaborate procedure would be treated as confidential.

Even this procedure was held in various quarters to be too brazen. How would the Sub-Commission or Commission ascertain which communications to accept and which to reject? A tentative decision was reached in August, 1971. Communications from the following sources were considered acceptable: (1) the alleged victims, whether individuals or groups, and persons or groups with a "direct and reliable knowledge" of violations; or (2) NGOs "acting in good faith in accordance with recognized principles of human rights, not resorting to politically motivated stands . . . and having direct and reliable knowledge of such violation." The aim was clearly to circumscribe the role NGOs might play which was the manifest intention of Resolution 1503. The qualifying language made this clear. In addition all anonymous and abusive communications were to be declared inadmissible as well as those in which domestic remedies had not yet been exhausted. The five-person Working Group would be comprised of representatives of countries chosen from each broad geographical region.

The debate over NGOs reflected a general suspiciousness and hostility. Some openly questioned the objectivity of NGOs in consultative status. Others warned that NGOs might take advantage of consultative status to "slander" states and "deluge" the Working Group. Ultimately, the Sub-Commission avoided the more hostile anti-NGO posture and it did not limit the NGO category. However, the Sub-Commission did not require that NGOs, in contrast to individuals or groups, have "direct and reliable" knowledge nor did it require that the knowledge be "first-hand." What was demanded was that the information NGOs submitted to the Sub-Commission be accompanied by clear evidence.

With the new 1503 procedure now in place, NGOs saw the opportunity of testing its provisions, to see how they would work, and to ascertain whether at least a modest breakthrough had occurred in achieving an implementation instrument. At the August, 1971 session of the Sub-Commission no less than 22 international NGOs called upon the Sub-Commission to appoint the Working Group so that it might take up communications on human rights violations forwarded to the UN, including communications on atrocities then being perpetrated against Bengalis in East Pakistan.[27] The NGOs were to have their hopes dashed, none more so than the Anti-Slavery Society.

It wasn't until three years later, in the spring of 1974, that the Commission was apprised of the results of the inquiry by the Sub-Commission and its Working Group. According to the organ of the Anti-Slavery Society, a total of 23,000 communications or complaints had been received by the UN, and "a friend in court" who "leaked the news" revealed that a mere 8 cases had been accepted.[28] The rest had been rejected. Only a infinitesimal number "appeared to reveal a consistent pattern of gross and reliably attested violations of human rights."

As noted by one authority, the eight cases involved Northern Ireland, Brazil, Burundi, Guyana, Indonesia, Iran, Portugal and Tanzania.[29] The same researcher found that NGOs were responsible for the complaints dealing with three countries—Brazil, Burundi and Tanzania. Presumably, the other complaints came from either victims or knowledgeable witnesses. Perhaps not too strangely, one case that was expected to be approved for submission to the Commission remained stalled in the Sub-Commission files. It dealt with Greece and covered detention and torture by its military regime. The case had been meticulously prepared by Professor Frank Newman of the University of California Law School at Berkeley. Aides of his and observers who were witnesses to the submission viewed it as a "model for briefs on other cases."[30] If it was intended as a standard for future NGO statements related to Resolution 1503, for the time being at least, it was suspended in midair. The brief simply was accorded no recognition by the UN organs.

From the perspective of the Anti-Slavery Society, the 1503 procedure constituted a great disappointment. One of its communications was, in fact, accepted for Commission consideration. The Society, focusing upon early and forced marriage aspects of the Supplementary Convention, complained that a certain Nasreen Hussein, a 15-year-old girl from Tanzania, was forced to marry a member of the Revolutionary Council of Zanzibar. Numerous appeals for her freedom had been made earlier by the Society to the Zanzibar authorities and the President of Tanzania, Julius Nyerere. Those appeals and the new 1503 communication produced nothing. Not until years later did Nasreen, with the assistance of her aunt, succeed in escaping.[31] So discouraged was the Society with the 1503 procedure generally that its Secretary, Colonel Montgomery, wrote in 1990, "The Society has not used the 1503 Procedure again. It is still in use but in the opinion of this writer it amounts to a blank cheque in the hands of the tyrant and the torturer."[32]

The failure of the 1503 procedure would not thwart the determination of the Anti-Slavery Society to fulfill its mission. As early as 1973, it had become seized with an issue involving the trafficking of female Indian slaves in Paraguay and it was determined to raise that issue publicly at the Commission. The matter first was brought to the attention of the Society in 1970 when an anthropologist, Mark Munzel, studying a nomadic Indian group, the Aché, in the southeast corner of Paraguay, disclosed to the Society details of both slave trafficking and genocide carried out by Paraguayan officials.

At a meeting of the Commission on Human Rights in March, 1973, the Society's information was made available. Especially focused upon was a so-called reservation run by state officials where the Aché were hunted, captured, enslaved, tortured and killed. One official was identified as particularly obscene and brutal in hunting and molesting 10- and 11-year-old girls.[33] In keeping with the highly restricted standards at the time for NGOs, the Society representative, while describing the atrocities, meticulously avoided referring to any country. Instead, he spoke of a "small, land-locked state in South America."

According to a report by the Society's Secretary, Colonel Montgomery, written much later, the Commission Chairman asked the Society representative to "have the courage to name the state." At the moment, the Society was reluctant to run the expected gauntlet of official criticism from governments. It initially demurred. But later on, in September, 1973, the Society chose to be specific in a prepared statement to the Sub-Commission on Prevention of Discrimination and Protection of Minorities. After providing details about slavery and genocide in a "South American state," the Society concluded with the following: "These reports are well documented. The government of the country was approached last December and asked to investigate and comment. It has not replied. The country is Paraguay."[34] It was probably the first time that an NGO at a UN organ consciously chose to name a country—other than South Africa—in which gross human rights violations had taken place.

Clearly, the Society could not easily be intimidated. Nor would the threat of the Soviet Union silence the group. It continued to pour out an extraordinary amount of reports to the UN. For the first three meetings of the Working Group on Slavery in the mid-seventies the Society submitted to it 12 reports totaling 250,000 words.[35] And when the UN, facing a budget crunch in 1986, proposed the postponement of scheduled meetings of the Sub-Commission and three subordinate working groups in 1987, the Society led the opposition to the proposal.

Most NGOs as well as many UN agencies and governmental representatives supported the Society's resistance.

The resistance was certain to fail but the Society mounted an alternate effort, holding a three-day NGO Seminar on Human Rights and the United Nations in 1987. With the support of other major NGOs, the Seminar was successfully held. In attendance were representatives from the UN Centre for Human Rights, UNICEF, UNESCO, UNDP and ILO and two-thirds of the members of the Sub-Commission, as well as representatives from almost all Permanent Missions in Geneva. The Seminar proved to be, in the words of the Society's house organ, a "model of how debates in the United Nations ought to be conducted but, alas, so seldom are."[36]

The Society's intervention on behalf of the Aché Indians was intimately related to its very heavy and rather unique involvement with indigenous peoples on several continents. Until 1957, the protection of aborigines was a part of the name of the Society. Even when the name changed that year, concern about the plight of indigenous groups remained. Once the UN embraced decolonization in 1960, the Society began dramatic efforts to assert the right of self-determination and to demand fairer treatment for the indigenous. Its project officer on the subject, Julian Berger, would write in 1994 that they were "victims of the disastrous quartet of Columbus, Cook, Christianity and colonialism...."[37] He emphasized that "contemporary colonialism," from the perspective of the indigenous, takes the form of "development."[38]

In the seventies, the Society intervened on behalf of the natives of East Timor after the Indonesia invasion; the Kurds of Iraq; the Chittagong Hill Tracts in Bangladesh; and, of course, the Aché. But, perhaps, the most significant intervention was on behalf of the Yanoama, an Indian group in Brazil that was facing extinction by the government's support of development. At the Sub-Commission on Prevention of Discrimination and Protection of Minorities, Colonel Montgomery delivered a blistering oral attack upon the Brazilian government's plan, saying that it "seems designed to provide for the extinction of Yanoama in the shortest possible time."[39]

In 1981, the Sub-Commission, with the strong encouragement of the Society, created the UN Working Group on Indigenous Populations. That instrument became a potent official channel for the Society to raise pressing issues relating to tribes, aborigines and other indigenous groups. Thus, the Society could focus some UN attention upon the plight of indigenous groups in Thailand, Burma and West Papua. So that representatives of these groups might attend UN Sub-Commission sessions, the Society and several other European-based groups established in 1984 a Human Rights Fund for Indigenous People. That the indigenous have looked upon the Society with appreciation hardly would be surprising especially since "it always takes indigenous questions up from the perspective of the victims themselves and is prepared to be out-spoken on matters of principle."[40]

A high point in the history of the Society was reached in November, 1990, when the membership adopted a Resolution changing its name to the Anti-Slavery International for the Protection of Human Rights. It was to "reflect a development in the supportive role envisaged for the Society with the emergence of vigorous indigenous agencies in the countries most affected by slavery and slavery-like practices."[41] Besides, antislavery societies had appeared in a number of countries, including France and Norway. But the name change was also symptomatic of a major shift in the character of the organization. "Society" would have served to suggest the older nature of the organization that had prevailed since the beginning.

The Society, in fact, had operated without trained professionals skilled in organizational management and without a fundraising appa-ratus. Until 1978, the staff consisted of only a Secretary and Assistant. In that year, the title of Secretary became Director. Whether Secretary or Director, the top official of the group signed no contract nor was he provided a definite salary. Instead, the staff were paid a sort of honorar-ium. The arrangement was convenient and perhaps appropriate since the holders of staff positions were either retired civil servants or former diplomats or former army officers. But such staff, as well as lay officers had aged palpably and organizational life required a fundamentally changed perspective.

In January, 1990, Lesley Roberts, a former official with Oxfam, a development NGO, was named Director and she set in motion a significant modernization of the Society. At her insistence, the vestiges of a colonial or Victorian society would have to be relinquished. In "personal comments," she recalled that prior to her appointment, the Society never aspired to being an "employer" and "was almost cavalier in its treatment of staff; there were no staff contracts, pension provision, staff meetings."[42] Other standard features of modern organizational life were absent. Until 1991, it had no annual program nor even a budget. Any expenditure above £50 had to be approved by the bimonthly General Committee meetings. Minutes of the General Committee meetings were designated as "secret" and were "not normally accessible to staff."[43] Roberts, in an interview, recalled being asked by the leadership: "What do you want money for?" And her response, as expected, was for the "program." About this essential need she was insistent and persuasive.[44]

Under Roberts the staff was enlarged to number some ten persons with a highly trained and experienced Research Manager, Mike Dottridge—formerly with Amnesty International—and two project officers covering respectively child labor and servile marriage.[45] Funds to the Society were contributed by the individual Scandinavian governments. For a period of time in the eighties, the Ford Foundation provided funding for projects. The membership was also a source of contributions. As many as one-third of the 1,600 members, according to Roberts, provided funding. Private trusts were an increasing source of the organization's income.[46]

Modernization of operations was rather timely. Slavery, together with the various forms it had assumed, had become a matter of considerable public interest in the last decade of the twentieth century. *Newsweek*'s International Edition, in 1992 carried an extensive spread about the extent of the slavery phenomenon, citing the Anti-Slavery International as a source for the figure of 100 million slaves worldwide. The editors stated that their own year-long four-continent investigation showed that "cases of involuntary servitude reach well into the millions." Among the areas covered were the Dominican Republic, Mauritania, Pakistan, the Persian Gulf states, India, Saudi Arabia, Brazil, Thailand and Sudan.[47]

Sudan was a particular focus of international interest. The Khartoum Arab regime, dominated by Muslim fundamentalists, was seeking to crush a liberation movement in the south by blacks who were primarily Christian or animist. A study of the civil war by a Special Rapporteur of the UN Commission on Human Rights, released in 1996, showed "an alarming increase in the number of reports and information emanating from a wide variety of sources on cases of slavery, servitude, the slave trade and forced labour." Especially noted was the evidence of children and women being forced into slavery.

A distinguishing feature of the enslavement was its racist and antiminority character. The "victims," according to the UN report, "are exclusively persons belonging to racial, ethnic and religious minorities from Southern Sudan." The report found "particularly aggravating" the "overwhelmingly racial connotation" of the enslavement. Equally disturbing was the fact that "the slave trade, including traffic in and sale of children and women, slavery, servitude, forced labour and similar practises are taking place with the knowledge of the Government of the Sudan."

Sources for the damning UN report were broad-based. They included representatives of UN agencies working on relief operations in southern Sudan and representatives of international humanitarian and human rights organizations active in the field. Various Sudanese groups and individuals knowledgeable about human rights also provided documentation. As the Special Rapporteur was refused entry into Sudan proper, he had to tap the above sources while on research missions to the neighboring states of Kenya, Uganda and Eritrea.

After the UN study appeared, both Human Rights Watch and Amnesty International weighed in with further supporting material. On the same day—May 29, 1996—they each released a study on Sudan that included the evidence on slavery. The Watch release spoke of the seizure of "women and children for use as slave or forced domestic labor," and attributed the information to "scores of accounts from escaped slaves. . . ." The Amnesty International report referred to "child abduction" and to how "kidnapped children appear to be held in domestic slavery."[48]

The documentation became a broad public political issue in the United States when Louis Farrakhan, the leader of the Nation of Islam, a black nationalist group, expressed doubt about the slavery charges. Indeed, he vigorously had endorsed the Sudanese government while visiting the country on February 8, 1996. He was quoted by the Sudanese government press service as saying that "more than 40 million American Muslims stand with Sudan." The comments prompted Randall Robinson of TransAfrica to say that people familiar with the "de facto practice of slavery in Sudan" would be "shocked and disappointed" with Farrakhan's comments.[49]

Perhaps the most detailed journalistic essay on slavery in Sudan as it related to Farrakhan was written by Nat Hentoff and appeared in *The Village Voice*. He cited videotapes documenting slavery in the Sudan as well as the detailed observations of Professor Ushan Ahmad Mahmoud, a Sudanese expert on slavery, about how government-armed militias, after capturing southern villages, carried women and children back to the Arab north: "The women and children are put to work in the fields— all without pay—and are also available as slave concubines."[50]

What made Hentoff's article in *The Village Voice* especially instructive was its opening paragraph: "During the 19th century, the Anti-

Slavery Society of London was a ceaseless illuminator of the relentless evils of slavery. Until recently, I thought the society was no longer in existence." The author then went on to say: "But Anti-Slavery International, the continuation of the Anti-Slavery Society, states unequivocally: 'Slavery was not abolished in the nineteenth-century. Today it is flourishing unchecked in Sudan.'"

One implication was apparent. The Anti-Slavery International, aside from the new name, had not sufficiently made modernization strides in public relations to enable it to impact significantly upon contemporary consciousness. Regrettably, the remarkable labors of the Society in winning adoption by the UN of the Supplementary Slavery Convention in 1956 (some thirty years after it succeeded in getting the League of Nations to accept the original treaty banning slavery and the slave trade) is scarcely known or has been forgotten. Nor has much attention been paid to its valuable contribution to the UN implementing organ, the Working Committee on Contemporary Forms of Slavery.

Clearly, today, the Anti-Slavery International is no longer the prototype of a nongovernmental organization. Big NGOs, well-funded and with enterprising public relations staffs, frequently monopolize public attention, especially as they focus upon what are the principal new areas of concern of the Anti-Slavery International: child labor, bride purchase and forced marriage, coerced concubinage and female genital mutilation.

In the case of the last item, however, given the increasing focus on women's rights, the work of this key antislavery NGO has commanded widespread attention. If earlier, in the late forties, the Society had postponed public action on the subject until African women themselves became involved, by 1977, it became instrumental in creating a broad NGO Working Group on the subject with one of its members, Kati David, as Chairperson. Workshops, lectures and visits organized by the NGO Working Group in various African countries bore fruit.[51]

In February, 1984, an Inter-African Committee was established, with separate national committees in individual countries. A major step forward in ending the initial silence on the subject came in November, 1990 when an African regional conference held in Addis Ababa formally approved the use of the phrase "female genital mutilation" to characterize the traditional form of excision of genital tissues. Representatives came from 25 countries in Africa. With training courses and the production of educational material considerably extended, the Anti-Slavery International could take pride in initially targeting the subject, in facilitating the breakthrough and in looking forward to the "ultimate elimination of the mutilation."[52]

With respect to the Anti-Slavery International's other new current priorities, it should be recalled that these matters had attracted the scrutiny of its predecessor—the Society—at a key early stage. Even as the Society launched public initiatives on child labor and purchased marriages before anyone else, at the very same time, it stood firm and resisted the onslaught of those governments at the UN that sought to intimidate the NGO community. Two hundred years of experience in fighting one of the great human rights battles would not quickly disappear. Indeed, the International was certain to continue, and from time to time, to make that experience impact upon the public consciousness.

When the United States, in mid-1997, suddenly became cognizant of the veritable enslavement of deaf Mexicans smuggled to major American cities to sell trinkets, the Anti-Slavery International was once again in the news. Its new director since 1996, Mike Dottridge, was interviewed by the *New York Times*'s UN correspondent, and he explained that the word "slavery" has been so "abused" by being applied too loosely people think that "real slavery does not exist." "Unfortunately," he added, "it does."[53] Elaborating, he noted that "debt bondage is practiced on a huge scale in certain parts of the world, particularly in South Asia." A well-organized begging industry subjects Indian children to mutilation and then transports them to Saudi Arabia, where they are stationed near mosques to plead for money. He further reported that in the West Africa countries of Togo and Benin, children are seized from villages and sold into domestic servitude in Nigeria and Gabon.

The recent increase in migration around the world has significantly contributed to slavery, Dottridge observed. The reason, he thought, was self-apparent: after the migrant leaves home, he or she is unlikely to look to the authorities to protect him or her. What the migrant presents to a ruthless exploiter is a high degree of vulnerability. As spelled out by the Anti-Slavery official:

> It is fair to say that in the 1990s, the more oppressive forms of slavery are affecting migrant laborers who are traveling and already vulnerable because they moved from their own societies into quite different societies where they perhaps don't understand the language and are much more easy to exploit.

Bonded child labor, particularly in Pakistan and India, continues to be a central concern of the NGO community. In this area, the Anti-

Slavery International is a prime source of documentation. When Human Rights Watch/Asia produced its excellent study entitled *Contemporary Forms of Slavery in Pakistan,* it relied upon the pioneering research work of the Anti-Slavery International, particularly its reports on the carpet industries that employ bonded child labor and on certain agricultural sectors that depend on bonded agricultural laborers.[54]

In Dottridge's new strategy of combating "the worst forms of child labor," it is more effective to utilize not the UN mechanisms, but rather those of the International Labor Organization (ILO) and particularly its Convention on forced labor and the latter's mechanism.[55] When the ILO adopted a Convention in the early seventies on the minimum age of employment, it was a matter of some interest to the Anti-Slavery Society. The ILO, Dottridge reported, now was moving toward banning the "most intolerable" forms of child labor through a new special Convention. It came as no surprise that he would report further that the Anti-Slavery International was "one of the main NGOs" in shaping "the terms of" the planned treaty. The NGO remains remarkably active.

CHAPTER SIX

An NGO Shifts Its Focus: The "Pioneer" International League for Human Rights

A keen human rights strategist in the NGO community, writing privately in 1974, concluded from the prevailing evidence that for NGOs, "in coping with specific cases" of a human rights nature, "the prospects of a forceful UN 'protective' role" were nonexistent. Of course, apartheid was an exception. But, as for the broad area of human rights, because of the absence of effective implementation machinery at the UN or the reluctance to use machinery that was available, international NGOs had to learn a quick lesson in strategic thinking. "Their principal efforts," he strongly recommended, "would need to be focused for a long time *outside* the UN. . . ."[1] No doubt the intimidation of the NGOs in the late sixties and early seventies reinforced this perspective.

The writer of the proposed strategy change served on the board of the International League for the Rights of Man (the name was changed in 1976 to the International League for Human Rights) and was considered as one of its ablest, if rather cautious, strategists.[2] Roberta Cohen, who was Executive Director of the International League at the time, confirmed to an interviewer that the organization did significantly begin to shift course away from the UN to other arenas.[3] Exerting an impact upon individual governments and upon American government policy became a major focus of the League, although the UN was not to be entirely neglected.

Shifting the focus of concentration and of lobbying did not, by any means, affect all of the international NGOs. The Anti-Slavery Society, if anything, stepped up its UN activism even if this meant weathering a storm of abuse. For the League itself, the trauma of a partial separation from the UN focus was hardly that great. Certainly, it had been intimately involved at a very early stage in combating apartheid and opposing the annexation of South West Africa by South Africa. And, as Roger Baldwin recalled in an Oral History project in 1954, League leaders "were sustained . . . by an unspoken faith in building up laws for the brighter future. . . ." But deep-seated skepticism had already set in with Baldwin concerning the fulfillment of the "sweeping commitments" made in the Universal Declaration whether "in principle, let alone enforcement." As early as 1954, he was prepared to conclude that the nations of the world "were not prepared to make law out of the principles" of the Universal Declaration. What particularly angered him was that the United States was the nation "least of all" determined to press for the rule of law. He was, of course, profoundly and bitterly conscious of the commitment given by Secretary of State John Foster Dulles to the Senate a year earlier that the Administration simply would not seek ratification of any human rights treaty.

After the experience that the League itself had undergone in the course of the UN's investigations of NGOs during 1969-70 as well as the virtual paralysis of the Resolution 1503 procedures, the earlier doubts of Baldwin were greatly strengthened. Its chairman, Jerome J. Shestack, summed up the League's veritable contempt for the UN's record of human rights activity in his 1973 annual report. The occasion was appropriate. A quarter of a century had passed since the Universal Declaration of Human Rights was adopted by the General Assembly: "At the U.N., the Commission on Human Rights has shown an inability to deal effectively, indeed, deal at all with human rights violations. Egregious complaints from individuals and groups have been ignored for political reasons."[4] Shestack then listed the "vital matters" in the human rights field in which "no effective action has been taken." He drove home his outrage by stressing how NGOs were "even harassed" when they sought to bring these violations before the UN.

Total disillusionment took hold in 1975 when NGOs were openly and arbitrarily threatened with expulsion when they attempted to merely follow new procedures that had been accepted and allowed the year earlier. If the unwritten rule at the UN until 1974 had been not to "name names" under any circumstance, NGOs could not fail to notice that, in February 1974, a fundamental change in the application of that rule was allowed. The Commission had invited the wife of the slain President of Chile, Mrs. Salvadore Allende, to address the body. She did not speak in her own capacity as a private citizen; indeed, such authorization was not possible. Mrs. Allende was authorized to address the Commission on grounds that she was serving as a representative of the Women's International Democratic Federation, a leftist NGO headquartered in East Berlin.

If the invitation was unprecedented, so was the presentation. Mrs. Allende, in a highly emotional address, denounced the military dictatorship of General Augusto Pinochet that had assumed power following the 1973 military coup. After cataloguing the ruthless assault upon human rights by the Pinochet regime, she called upon the Commission to condemn the regime for "genocidal repression."[5] Strikingly, neither the Commission Chairman nor any of its members chose to interrupt the speaker. No one raised the question of a violation of the rules of procedure. Chile suddenly had been placed in the same category as South Africa and Israel. It could be directly targeted for abuse on the basis of human rights violations. All others were immune to such verbal denunciation.

A representative of one of the more activist NGOs, Dr. Homer Jack of the World Conference on Religion and Peace, perceived the experience to be a door-opener. If the Commission appeared to give indirect encouragement to an NGO to identify specific violations of human rights, why could not other NGOs delineate a host of human rights violations? Dr. Jack would seek the floor to present a "state of the world" human rights report with considerable detail about both victims and violators.[6] He was not the only one who saw the development as a possible breakthrough. Soon after Homer Jack's statement, Professor Frank Newman, speaking for Amnesty International, would spell out detailed allegations about torture in Chile.

Noting the example of these two NGOs taking heart and moving the human rights debate to the very center of the UN, specifically, the chambers of the Commission of Human Rights—Niall MacDermot, Secretary-General of the prominent International Commission of Jurists, decided to follow a similar course, though not at the UN. He wrote an article for a special issue of the *Times* (of London) in May, 1974 that violated established NGO tradition. He listed, from totally confidential sources, the eight cases from the 1503 procedure that showed "consistent patterns of gross violations."[7] It would have been extremely risky on

MacDermot's part to have divulged the information at the UN proper; his status on behalf of an NGO would have been at stake. But even a disclosure on the outside was certain to raise eyebrows, especially among the eight countries mentioned.

The reaction of governments to Jack's intervention, as noted earlier, was extraordinary. No less than five governmental representatives on the Commission and two governmental observers attending the session asked to speak. The five Commission members were Egypt, Pakistan, the Soviet Union, Turkey and Zaire; the observers were from Syria and the Philippines. None of these states could be described as models of human rights behavior; indeed, the record of each of them with respect to human rights at the time bordered on the notorious. Those who sat on the Commission were chosen for that role because of politics, not because of human rights considerations. If they sought to be elected to the body it was no doubt due to a desire to squelch any exposure of their malpractices.

NGOs were told that they had no right to attack governments. The Egyptian member spelled out the generalized anger of the chastised governments in a subsequent amplifying statement for the record:

> We are extremely concerned about the abuse of freedom of speech practiced by some representatives of nongovernmental organizations. This particular statement . . . by the World Conference on Religion and Peace should not appear in the summary records of this Commission. Indeed, its status should be restudied by the Economic and Social Council.[8]

If the assault upon Jack testified to the extreme sensitivity of governments to exposure of their human rights conduct, it also revealed the lengths to which UN bodies—especially the Commission on Human Rights—would go to forever silence any criticism whatsoever. The airing of NGO human rights complaints would not be tolerated. Meeting in private session, the Commission called upon ECOSOC to impose sharp restrictions on NGO communications about human rights violations.[9] And these restrictions were to apply to all NGO communications whether made in a UN forum or in public statements anywhere. The MacDermot article in the *Times* of London clearly had not gone unnoticed.

What was being advanced here was a form of censorship totally unprecedented. Not only must an NGO in consultative status avoid criticizing governments in a UN setting, but also he or she cannot disclose in a public medium information obtained as a participant in UN deliberations. ECOSOC specifically was asked to notify NGOs that, when they make complaints or allegations about human rights violations, their statements are going to be dealt with "not under the rules of consultative status but under the decisions concerning the inclusion of such material in confidential lists of communications. . . ."[10]

The logical consequence easily could be anticipated. An ECOSOC ruling would abide by the Commission request. Noting that "some non-governmental organizations have occasionally failed to observe the requirements of confidentiality . . . and . . . that the oral interventions of some non-governmental organizations on matters affecting Member-States have often shown disregard for proper discretion," ECOSOC harshly warned that "any non-governmental organization failing to show discretion in an oral or written statement may render itself subject to suspension of its consultative status."[11]

The overt threat to NGOs constituted a stunning challenge to the very nature of the NGO system at the UN. Oddly, the NGO community, whether human rights oriented or not, refused to unite in a joint effort to protest the shocking assault upon their integrity and independence. Were they so indifferent to their freedom of maneuver that they would not protect themselves?[12] Roberta Cohen, the League's executive, disclosed to an interviewer that, indeed, many NGOs refused to press their joint defense on the grounds that it might undermine the "credibility" of their nongovernmental consultative status. For the International League, the premier U.S.-based NGO at the UN, these developments were sufficiently dismaying as to alter fundamentally its institutional focus upon the UN organs. Ms. Cohen now considered the previous policy an "error" and personally lobbied her Board members to concentrate attention in the future upon leverage provided by Western governments.[13]

The League, of course, was keenly aware of the positive UN involvement in the struggle against apartheid in South Africa and how NGOs were intimately linked to that struggle. Apartheid had been and remained a priority issue with the League. It was the failure of the major nations of the UN, along with the smaller ones, to see that human rights violations were to be found everywhere—and not merely in South Africa, the Israeli-occupied areas and most recently Chile—that profoundly undermined the significance of what was called the Universal Declaration of Human Rights. From the League's perspective a "double standard" and a "selective morality" had so penetrated the UN program that, in essence, its human rights activities had become "politicized."

Far greater emphasis now would be given to affecting Washington policy and the policy of other states through the League's affiliates in various countries. If the United States once again were to resume the role it had played in the immediate postwar period to advance human rights through the UN Charter, might not the UN itself be significantly changed and the rule of law promoted? Besides, U.S. power, when effectively exercised, might directly impact upon governments either permitting violations of human rights or actually engaging in such violations. An informed observer who, at the time, worked for the Ford Foundation, noted "that in 1975-76, the way the UN had turned with the anti-Zionism movement, the disappointment with the 1503 process and the legitimization of human rights in foreign policy . . . she [Roberta Cohen] and others felt that the way to go was to focus on the U.S. government and on U.S. groups."[14]

The Ford Foundation was acutely aware that the broad gamut of the Universal Declaration was getting little public attention, whether at the UN or otherwise. A letter of the Foundation, dated October 1, 1976, stated:

> In more countries than is generally realized, torture and repression have become routine facts of life. Actors are arrested for performing controversial plays; universities are closed and scholars are expelled; scientists with unorthodox views are declared mentally ill; dissident journalists and student leaders are killed during police interrogation. . . . As grim acts multiply, the issues of human rights and intellectual freedom assume an urgent importance.[15]

Given this perception, and the inevitable concern that followed, it hardly was unexpected that the Foundation would allocate $500,000 that year to strengthen various NGOs working in the human rights field. The League itself later would benefit from a Ford Foundation grant. Additional fundraising would enable it to increase modestly its budget and staff and to deal more effectively with the radical shift in direction that it would undertake.[16] Funding had been a problem for the League almost since the beginning. Not until now has the source of the problem been publicly revealed. A note in the files of Roberta Cohen discloses that "for about twenty years" before 1977, the League had sought "to obtain tax exempt status in order that it might receive tax deductive contributions from individuals and foundations. . . ."[17]

The requests were met by repeated rebuffs. The "avowed reason" given the League by the government for the denial of tax exempt status was that the organization was a "political" organization that "lobbied" at the UN. To the League, this reasoning was open to serious challenge. Other organizations, after all, undertook similar "political" activities by "lobbying" at the UN and had been extended tax exempt status. It was Ms. Cohen's assumption that "behind the IRS' repeated denials must have been the FBI file." That file had confused Roberta Cohen with someone with the same name who had engaged in radical leftist political activities. Her protests and insistence upon clarification finally brought forth the necessary correction. The correction would have a positive consequence: "In 1977, after the FBI determination of communist domination had been removed from the books, the League re-applied for tax exempt status and received it immediately."[18]

The most striking example of the new orientation of the League was its involvement with Andrei D. Sakharov, who would become the very symbol of twentieth century dissidence and human rights advocacy. In November, 1970, Sakharov, joined by two other Soviet scientists—Valery N. Chalidze and Andrei N. Tverdokhlebov—formed the Moscow Human Rights Committee. Other dissidents, like Pavel Litvinov, became members later. The Committee's purposes were made explicit. Human rights in a socialist society were to be promoted and advanced. All activity was to be conducted "in conformity with the laws of the state." The Committee would undertake "constructive criticism of the present state of the Soviet system of legal safeguards for individual freedom."[19]

Formation of the Moscow Committee constituted a remarkable act of courage. The Soviet regime, since 1966, had entered into a period of deepening repression. Dissidents often were jailed and thrown into the gulag or incarcerated in mental institutions. A ruthless and deadening conformity was insisted upon by the authorities. Virulent anti-Semitism was becoming rampant in the Soviet press even as crude discrimination against Jews had taken hold in higher education and employment.[20]

The Committee took a further step in its confrontation with the arbitrary regime. It formally sought affiliation with the International League for Human Rights. This was at a time when the totalitarian state had embraced a harsh anti-Western stance and its ideology assumed vehement anti-American forms. Actually, the Committee had no detailed, firsthand knowledge about the work of the League. Chalidze only contacted the League after finding its name in a guidebook. What was in his mind, according to a knowledgeable League source, was the need for some legitimacy and some contact "out there."[21] Still, for the League, the decision was a difficult one. Some Board members were fearful that affiliation might lead to reprisals against Moscow Committee members. Only insistence by various Soviet dissidents that "publicity could only strengthen their position [and] that silence helped no one"[22] finally prevailed upon the League Board. Besides, the League, in its new innovative strategy, had embarked upon a course of supporting national affiliates, of which there were 38.

In June 1971, the League took the unprecedented step of adopting the Moscow Human Rights Committee. It was the first time a Western NGO formally had linked itself with one in the Soviet Union. Later, in 1974, Amnesty International would admit into its fold a branch in Moscow.[23] Admission of Sakharov's Committee immediately entailed a burst of activity by the League, in keeping with its responsibility of protecting the Committee by the strategy of openness or transparency. Thus, the League instituted weekly phone calls to its affiliate members in Moscow, to ascertain their well-being and to keep apprised of human rights developments.

Equally important were the League's broad lobbying activities on behalf of the Committee. On the one hand, the League transmitted information received from the Committee to the press and to various groups interested in Sakharov, such as Western scientific organizations. And, of course, U.S. government officials would be asked to intervene. The extraordinary commitment of the League would never be forgotten by Sakharov and his family. His stepdaughter, Tanya Yankelovich, living in Boston, later would acknowledge that the League "was the first Western organization that recognized the Soviet human rights movement and the first organization to collaborate with my father . . . and his friends."[24]

Human Rights Bulletin, the house organ of the League from 1972 onward, became a veritable chronicler of the Moscow Committee. The harassment and detention that any of its members suffered—as well as the members of the Amnesty International branch—were reported upon in detail. When Aleksandr Solzhenitsyn, a member of the Committee, was arrested, the League dispatched cables to Soviet and American officials calling for his release and decrying "the official and concerted campaign to restrict the freedom of opinion and expression." The protest demanded that the Soviet government "not use its power to suppress the Moscow Human Rights Committee and its distinguished members who stand in the forefront of the struggle for individual freedom."[25]

But the primary concern of the League was Sakharov. If the Kremlin was determined to harass the towering moral giant, hoping to intimidate him into silence, the League was equally committed to shredding the isolation screens that shielded the Kremlin's initiatives from public view. The League published Sakharov's speeches and articles, nominated him for the UN Human Rights Prize and exposed the efforts to silence him. Almost every article in the *Bulletin* dealing with the USSR devoted space to a description of Sakharov's efforts on behalf of other dissidents.

After Sakharov was awarded the Nobel Peace Prize in 1975 and the Soviet Union refused to let him go to Oslo to receive the award, the League was provided with an additional weapon to combat Soviet efforts of forced seclusion from public view. It prevailed upon 33 Nobel Laureates to join in a letter urging that Sakharov be given a visa for the Oslo ceremony. World attention came to be focused upon his plight. Sakharov recognized that the League's strategy was geared to halting Moscow's "blockade . . . of my international telephone and mail." In a message to the League, he wrote that wherever human rights advocates are persecuted, "our duty . . . the duty of the League is to defend the liberty and lives of our friends and comrades who fight for human rights in the whole world."[26] In 1976, he was named Honorary Vice-President of the League.

Even though the International League no longer concentrated its attention upon the UN, the Soviet Union decided to use that forum to punish the League, along with Amnesty International. In May, 1977, the Soviet representative to the UN Economic and Social Council, Sergei Smirnov, publicly attacked the two NGOs as having engaged in activities that "poisoned detente and slandered the Socialist countries." He went on to threaten that their "abuses of privileges would lead to cancellation of this consultative status."[27]

The League would not be intimidated. Its Honorary President, Roger Baldwin, called the Soviet attack "highly inappropriate" since his group and other NGOs were only fulfilling their "obligatory role to support UN principles as set forth in the Universal Declaration of Human Rights." Roberta Cohen commented to the press that Moscow's anger was "a measure of our effectiveness" and that by threatening NGOs, the USSR and its allies "are thereby indicting themselves."[28] It was, of course, true that the shift in the League's strategy made it less vulnerable to threats to its UN consultative status.

If the League could not be intimidated, the Kremlin was faced with a difficult problem of seeking to stanch the hemorrhaging of information, disclosures and criticism emanating from the "conscience of mankind," as the Nobel Peace Prize Committee referred to Sakharov. Especially was this the case after the brutal Soviet invasion of Afghanistan in December, 1979.

Sakharov had become the pivotal figure in the conflict between the democratic activists in East Europe and Soviet power. So long as he was around in Moscow and could talk on the phone or meet journalists, totalitarianism could be eroded. The Kremlin decided upon the radical step of arresting him and his wife, Yelena Bonner, on a street in Moscow on January 22, 1980 and forcefully moving them to Gorki, a closed city, off-limits to travelers, journalists and Western colleagues.

The total isolation of Sakharov constituted perhaps the greatest challenge the League ever faced or would ever face. Much was at stake. Without any contact with him and his wife, no one could be certain that the Kremlin's agents might not subject them to bodily harm or even death. Certainly, Moscow was aware of Sakharov's unique status and reputation in the world of science and far beyond. At the same time, a certain desperation had entered into its decision-making. The apprehension and exile of Sakharov and his wife stood in utter violation of basic international *and* Soviet legal procedures.

The circumstances were to test the ingenuity, imagination and various skills the League had developed over the years. Its Executive Director in the eighties, Felice Gaer, recalled: "The League figured out at some point that Sakharov had never been brought before a court of law. We were told he was in exile . . . ."[29] But no formal statement had been made as to precisely where he was located and, in fact, at one point, he was known to have been taken to a psychiatric hospital. League strategists struck upon the idea of using the UN Working Group on Forced and Involuntary Disappearances as the key lever. The creation of the UN Working Group marked a significant new development at the world organization.

Sakharov's situation, the League thought, somehow might be considered as fitting a category that had been applied to the military dictatorships of Argentina, Uruguay and Chile in their horrendous repression of opponents in the late seventies and early eighties. Including Sakharov into the category of involuntary disappearances seemed quite reasonable: "we found out," remembered Gaer, "that the characteristics of the disappeared and what happened to Sakharov could be matched up." So the League "prepared a lengthy and really very impressive document on this. . . ." This was in 1984.

The strategy meant that, once again, the League had returned to its original methodology of focusing upon UN machinery. Felice Gaer acknowledged the change: "I took the League back to the UN." But the return was made possible by recent positive developments in the UN human rights field, including the establishment of working groups on various thematic violations. A lever was provided that served a particularly useful purpose, and the League made the most of it through documentation and public testimony by its Chairman, Jerome Shestack.[30]

While the UN never would be the exclusive focus of the League, still where it offered what Gaer called "a hook," it would be utilized. The "hook" was provided by new mechanisms. If the League were to prepare a report on one or another mission in which it was engaged, it would seek to link the report to "a UN process, a meeting, a review session or into some *hook*. . . ."[31]

The results of the League's creative improvisations turned out to be strikingly successful. Press coverage was extensive. The Soviet Union was forced to respond with "lengthy statements . . . explaining how he [Sakharov] was not disappeared, why he was well and where he was." This information was precisely "what we wanted."[32]

The drumbeat of the League continued. Even if the UN Working Group never acted upon the League's information, the NGO continued to use the UN body as a forum to raise questions about Sakharov's health and especially Bonner's medical condition which required treatment abroad. Most of all, the League sought confirmation of the survival of the two Soviet activists. It even prevailed upon the chairman of the Working Group "timidly to suggest to the Soviets that they have Sakharov send some postcards from time to time so the family [living in Boston] would at least know." During 1985, the *Bulletins* of the League were filled with anxious reports of the Sakharov situation, especially his hospitalization following a hunger strike to compel the authorities to allow Yelena to have eye surgery abroad. League representatives, accompanied by Sakharov's children living in the United States, went to a Helsinki review meeting in Ottawa, Canada in the summer to pointedly focus world attention upon the Sakharov-Bonner plight. Soviet representatives at the conference openly were challenged by delegates from various Western countries precisely on this question. Two weeks later, the USSR released two videotapes, made apparently with hidden cameras, one showing Sakharov as a patient in a hospital in Gorki.

That same film was entitled "To Where Has Sakharov Disappeared?" The reference clearly was to the League campaign brought before the UN Working Group on Disappearances. Indeed, the narrator on the tape specifically described the film's intent as a response to charges made by the League and Sakharov's children. It was a perspective shared by the Sakharov family. According to the family, "the League's actions at the UN Working Group and the Ottawa Experts meeting prodded the Soviets to release the films." What was significant about the films from both the League's and the family's point of view was that "they broke the official barrier of silence and give hope that the Sakharov couple are still alive."[33]

In the end, the League's demands were granted. Approval for Yelena Bonner to travel to the West for medical treatment was given in October, 1985, and, in the following month, Sakharov was permitted to place a telephone call to his family in the United States, the first direct contact he had had with them since 1980. Yelena left the USSR in November and remained abroad, mainly in the United States, recuperating from surgery until June, 1986. At the suggestion of the League, she was met at the Moscow airport by Western diplomats to assure a safe arrival and she then was escorted to her Moscow apartment by two important Congressmen, one of whom, Barney Frank, represented the district of a Boston, Massachusetts suburb where Sakharov's family resided. Just a half-year would elapse before the nightmare dissolved. With glasnost becoming very much the cornerstone of Kremlin policy, Prime Minister Mikhail Gorbachev put through a call to Sakharov lifting his internal exile and authorizing his return to normal life.

Sakharov may have been the League's top priority, but a half-dozen other major human rights issues stood high on its agenda and merit special commentary, if only to indicate the breadth of the League's concern and activism during those years when it was shifting its focus away from the UN. In 1972, the League, joined by the International Commission of Jurists and the International Law Section of the American Bar Association, sent an observer to a patently political trial in Greece involving 15 accused students. An 172-page document was published by the three NGOs describing gross violations of human rights—torture, denial of fair trial and suppression of speech and press.[34]

In 1973, the League, again joined by its NGO colleagues, sent a top-level legal group to Greece to seek the release of the seven lawyers who had defended the students. The Greek junta refused to meet with the mission which had received wide public attention especially in Europe. Shortly afterward, the seven lawyers were released as part of a general amnesty, but Greek observers credited the release to the intervention of the NGOs.[35]

If the League did not hesitate to be critical of Greece, a NATO ally of the United States, it was equally assertive in dealing with America's closest ally, the United Kingdom. In 1972, it took a major part in examining the conduct of British military authorities in the "Bloody

Sunday" massacre of that year in Londonderry where 13 persons were killed. The League sent Samuel Dash, of Georgetown University Law School (later to become famous in the Watergate hearings), and Louis Pollak of Yale Law School to investigate the affair. An official British report by Lord Widgery already had exculpated the British military forces. However, Sam Dash sharply questioned the official finding in a report entitled: "Justice Denied: A Challenge to Lord Widgery's Report on Bloody Sunday."[36]

Major concern was expressed by the League in the seventies about three military dictatorships other than the Soviet Union. Two—Chile and Paraguay—were in Latin America; the third, South Korea, was in Asia. With reference to Chile, League strategists found it advisable to use the United Nations as a focal point, since it was committed to dealing with human rights violations in that country. As early as March, 1974, the League appeared at the UN Commission on Human Rights critically commenting on severe human rights abridgements in Chile. It joined with several other NGOs in a jointly prepared statement calling on the Commission to undertake a study of the outrages perpetrated by the military junta in that country.[37]

For the League, direct personal involvement in fact-finding in Chile was essential if its credibility was to be maintained. In 1976, it sent a high-level New York judge and two prominent New York attorneys on a fact-finding mission. They reported that arrests in Chile were continuing at a higher rate than earlier.[38] More importantly, the League helped establish on December 10, 1978—the date was highly symbolic—the Chilean Commission on Human Rights. That body formally affiliated with the League the following year. Shortly afterward, in 1982, the League launched what it called the Human Rights Defenders Project, which would be copied later by other human rights groups. The project involved campaigning for the release of jailed or exiled human rights monitors through public appeals to offending governments. A report detailing the repression of monitors in a dozen countries was given broad coverage in the West. Among those the League campaigned for and honored was Dr. Jaime Castillo Velasco, a former Chilean Minister of Justice and later President of the country's Commission on Human Rights who had been sent into forced exile. In August, 1983, he was allowed to return.

During the same year, Samuel Dash and League Board member Clyde Ferguson of Harvard Law School traveled to Chile to observe trials of members of the Chilean Commission on Human Rights who were charged with "illicit political association." The result of the League's efforts to focus international attention on these legal proceedings, especially through visits of League observers, "led to the extraordinary suspension of sentences against the defendants," according to its *Annual Report.*

The efforts on behalf of Sakharov and the Chilean Commission on Human Rights ran parallel with League activism concerning South Korea. There, too, the League had a local affiliate—the International Human Rights League of Korea. Once President Park Chung Hee's had assumed unlimited dictatorial power in 1972, repression of dissent became characteristic. The regime, in 1974, placed severe restrictions on the leading Seoul opposition newspaper *Dong-ah-Ilbo.* Strong League protests may have had a positive effect; the restrictions on the newspaper eased. A letter to the League's headquarters in New York from the Chairman of the Korean affiliate, Hwal Lee, stated that, if the repression on the newspaper eased considerably, and recovered a certain "normality," "it was . . . mainly due to the outside opinions, such as yours."

When the most prominent dissenter, Kim Dae Jung, was sentenced to death in a sham trial in September, 1980, the League strongly embraced his cause, with his picture placed on the cover of its house organ.[39] The League's members and contacts were urged to protest to President Chun, who had succeeded Park after the latter's assassination in 1979. Because the South Korean military regime was especially sensitive to American public opinion, it chose first to reduce Kim's sentence to life imprisonment in 1981 and, at the end of 1982, to release him from prison and to send him to the United States "for medical reasons." In 1984, Kim announced that he planned to return to South Korea despite an official warning that he would be imprisoned and forced to serve the rest of a 20-year jail sentence.

The League, fearful that Kim might be assassinated upon arrival (as had been the case in 1983 of the Filipino dissenter Benigno Aquino), arranged, together with the International Human Rights Law Group, an NGO based in Washington, D.C., to hold a "farewell gala" on Capitol Hill. In attendance were prominent Senators and Congressmen, including the Chairman of the Senate Foreign Relations Committee and the Chairman of the House Foreign Affairs Subcommittee on Asia. Father Robert Drinan, a League Board member who had served in Congress for a number of years, wrote that the affair and the press coverage provided "preventive medicine . . . a signal to the South Koreans."[40] Kim ultimately was elected President of South Korea. His survival owes something to the League's precautionary watchfulness.

Paraguay was another priority concern of the League. While the Anti-Slavery Society had targeted the military regime because of its enslavement of the Aché Indians, the League went beyond this charge to accuse the government of Paraguay of a host of gross human rights abuses, including genocide. And, in its criticism of the military dictatorship of Alfredo Stroessner, it focused upon a variety of other human rights violations practiced by the government. The date of the League's initial involvement was late 1973, when it still saw the UN as an instrument offering genuine leverage. It was appropriate to deliver a formal protest to the UN Secretary-General accusing the Paraguay government of "the wholesale disappearance of a group of human beings."

A study documenting the horrors in Paraguay was prepared for the League by Professor Richard Arens of Temple University Law School.[41] He and Roberta Cohen presented the report to the Organization of American States (OAS) and personally appeared before the Inter-American Commission on Human Rights.[42] Protests also were lodged with the U.S. Senate and with the UN Sub-Commission on Prevention of Discrimination which in turn proceeded to chastise Paraguay.[43]

The League's intervention was by no means at an end. It sent a mission to Paraguay whose findings were published in a 58-page report. The Stroessner regime was excoriated for its "massive onslaught on civil liberties." Another mission was sent in 1977. Its lengthy report surveyed the history of abuses since Stroessner had declared a "state of siege" in 1954. But the outcry in the West must have exerted some, if limited, impact even before the second mission. The government released 169 political prisoners, although over 200 others still were listed in the second League report as "disappeared" or in prolonged detention.

More significantly, the military regime offered to provide assistance to the League researchers in the second mission and to receive its advice. The change in the Stroessner perspective was welcomed in an editorial in the *Washington Post.* It commented: "the League mission focused helpfully on the further steps needed to regulate the political process by law. Its report is a how-to guide for a dictator wanting to decompress."[44] Fundamental change in Paraguay's human rights record, however, would have to wait until the authoritarian rule of Stroessner came to an end in 1989.

Totalitarian and authoritarian regimes were not alone in being subjected to League criticism. India, during the administration of Indira Gandhi, was chastised for institutionalized and pervasive abuse of human rights. No other international NGO ever had lodged such a formal protest about India. In June, 1976, the League in an elaborate research document carefully detailed the arbitrary arrest, detention and torture of political prisoners and the suspension of freedom of speech, the press and assembly, along with the suspension of habeas corpus and judicial review. This followed India's emergency proclamation of June, 1975. The research document was submitted to the UN Commission on Human Rights.[45]

Press attention was extensive. The *New York Times* and the *Washington Post* on June 2, 1976 gave the criticism broad coverage. But so did the press of India. New Delhi responded with vehement anger. Its Mission to the UN, in a special press release, stated that "the protection of fundamental human rights is the concern of each sovereign State." The argument was the traditional one used by practitioners of human rights violations.

In the League's shift in strategy away from the UN to individual countries and to the use of the media to bring public shame upon human rights violators, it would have welcomed leverage provided by the United States government. But its appeals during the early seventies for the United States to cut off assistance to particularly virulent practitioners of human rights violence went unanswered. The Administration of President Richard M. Nixon and the foreign policy of his National Security Adviser and later Secretary of State, Henry A. Kissinger, were indifferent to concerns expressed by the League. However, with the election of Jimmy Carter as President, a significant change in U.S. policy took place. In his inaugural address, Carter gave human rights a prominent place.

The Carter rhetoric was important, but even more so was the President's willingness, just a few weeks after his inaugural, to respond openly and warmly to a letter from Andrei Sakharov, the bête noir of the Kremlin. For the League, which had embraced the harassed Soviet physicist and human rights dissenter and had been his major supporter, a turning point had been reached. "Human rights is suddenly chic," Roberta Cohen told a reporter of the *New York Times*. In the interview, she added: "For years we were preachers, cockeyed idealists or busybodies and now we are respectable."[46]

The League quickly became a magnet attracting volunteers, whereas earlier it had had to make a determined effort to find persons like lawyers or physicians who could be of assistance to the organization's aims. Now, reported Ms. Cohen, such professionals as well as students "are calling" since "everybody wants to get into human rights."[47] The sudden interest was pretty heady brew for an organization with only two staffers and several interns just beginning to be funded by the Ford Foundation. Not unnatural was the sense that the new expectations could not be quickly fulfilled.

The League was not the only NGO basking in the human rights glow. The American branch of the London-based Amnesty International, a membership organization, was reported to be swamped with requests for information and membership applications. The Director of Amnesty USA, David Hawk, told a *Times* reporter that the public had become interested in torture and other gross violations and "want to find out what they can do about it."[48]

With a sympathetic Administration in power, the League concentrated its efforts upon offering advice upon what Washington's priorities ought to be. Significantly, the League thought the United States should seek to become deeply involved with the UN and undertake crucial initiatives in order to reverse the prevailing negative human rights trends in the world body.[49] The highest priority for the United States, advised the League, was government ratification of UN human rights treaties, "in particular" the genocide treaty, the racial discrimination convention and the international covenants. Why ratification urgently was warranted was made explicitly clear: "without ratification, the U.S. cannot assume a leadership role in the human rights field."

What now stood at the core of the League's thinking was its earliest vision for the UN a quarter-century ago, namely, the creation as well as the implementation of the rule of human rights law. But, if that vision was to be realized, the United States must stand at the center of the effort, as it had in the initial postwar period. The appeal for American leadership never was sounded so loudly by the League as it was now. Ratification of human rights treaties was vital, the League paper noted, because the United States "cannot credibly take to task those states which violate the provisions of the human rights conventions. . . ." The implication was evident. No one could more effectively blow the whistle on human rights violators than the United States, but it was prevented from doing so by its failure to ratify human rights treaties.

The League further urged the United States to press for adoption of a Convention banning torture and for improved complaint procedures in handling the thousands of petitions to the Commission on Human Rights from individuals and NGOs alleging gross abuses. Requiring special attention, the League believed, was the 1503 procedure, which could become modestly effective only if "vigorously pressed by the U.S." through "a coalition of states" that the United States must help build. At the same time, the League recommended that the United States "undertake initiatives to overcome the double standard" in dealing with UN human rights activists.

All the proposals relative to NGOs were conditional upon a far-reaching involvement by the United States in UN human rights matters. It was the League's thesis that the United States "should assume more of a protective role toward human rights NGOs and expand their access to U.N. forums." At the heart of the League's perception of power realities was the basic belief that significant progress in the UN human rights area could not be made without the political muscle of the United States. Only through U.S. leadership could a breakthrough be made at the UN.

Testifying to the League's positive perception of the importance of the U.S. role in advancing human rights was a letter written by Roberta Cohen to a Washington NGO umbrella group just a few days after she had delivered the League's recommendation to a conference of the United Nations Association (UNA). The Washington group, called "Coalition for a New Foreign and Military Policy," embraced a large number of NGOs or their representatives, some of whom were strongly pacifist or left-leaning. Several focused largely on Latin America and were hostile to Washington's military policy in that area. Cohen's letter was dated April 3, 1977 and was a response to a circular letter sent out by the Coalition a month earlier, on March 7.[50]

The League's letter cited the following from the Coalition's circular of March 7: "By spotlighting the mistreatment of Soviet dissidents, President Carter is trying to coopt public concern over human rights and turn it into a weapon in the continuing U.S.-Soviet propaganda war." For Cohen and her colleagues, that statement was nothing short of "harmful . . . to the human rights movement in the Soviet Union" and, far more disturbingly, it constituted "a dangerous formulation to the cause of human rights generally." Cohen's letter and an earlier telephone call by her to the Coalition's Chairman in which she took "strong exception" to the contents of the Coalition circular may have been sharply worded, but this was scarcely surprising. After all, Sakharov and his Moscow Human Rights Committee were affiliated with the League and, beyond that, were deeply symbolic of the struggle for human rights in the USSR.

Cohen angrily wondered in her letter whether the Coalition was aware of the nature of the human rights movement in the USSR. She was prepared to offer it "documentation" at the disposal of the League. As for the critical importance of the United States "spotlighting" the issue, she offered testimony recently given by the exiled Soviet dissidents Vladimir Bukovsky and Andrei Amalrik, with whom she had recently met. They, along with Valery Chalidze and Pavel Litvinov—both members of the League Board—had "emphasized the importance of US spotlighting . . . the mistreatment of Soviet dissidents. . . ." "Conversely," she added, "they considered harmful efforts which would discourage or seek to alter the President's policy."

Anger turned to explosive fury in responding to the charge that official U.S. concern for human rights was a "cold-war weapon":

> On what grounds can your group possibly ask for selective application of human rights standards?. . . . Human rights must be universally applied and spotlighted all over the world. There can not be one standard on human rights for US allies or aid recipients and another standard for Communist countries. Any effort by the Coalition to perpetuate this point of view is quite dangerous to the solidarity of the human rights movement and destructive to human rights itself.

The toughness of the League's approach on human rights issues complemented what one study of the NGO called its receptivity to "experimentation."[51] The organization was constantly in "search for techniques of effective implementation of human rights legislation," according to the study.

One of its experiments was to have a permanent impact upon the NGO world. The League created in 1975 a special group of young lawyers to consider "class action" legal intervention. It was an outgrowth of the difficulty of coping with the receipt by the League of about 1,000 complaints annually from individuals and groups all over the world alleging human rights violations. If the League was able to undertake standard, traditional approaches to human rights issues through sending observers to political trials or dispatching special missions to conduct on-site investigations in particularly egregious situations, it lacked the research manpower to deal with the vast and growing number of requests for assistance.[52]

In a joint effort with the Council of New York Law Associates, a group of some 1,600 young "public interest" lawyers in the New York City area, the League established the Lawyer's Committee on International Human Rights. Shortly afterward, in 1978, the Committee broke away from the League and became one of the most important NGOs in the human rights field. Today, ironically, it has a far larger budget and much bigger staff than its creator.

A particularly distinctive feature associated with the new organization, namely the targeting of pressure upon multilateral funding agencies such as the World Bank or the International Monetary Fund was actually an experimental idea initially projected by the League. It asked the World Bank to deny a pending loan request from Paraguay on grounds of genocide against the Aché Indians and general political repression by the military regime.[53]

The former Director of the League during the eighties, Felice Gaer, believes that it will be remembered most of all as a "pioneer" of "new techniques."[54] "Time and again," she observed, the League would "take skills that were out there . . . and use them." Another example of the League's creative pioneering was the lobbying it did with the UN Sub-Commission on Prevention of Discrimination and Protection of Minorities in August, 1989 after the horrendous massacre in Tiananmen Square by the Beijing regime. The League was determined to win a breakthrough at the Sub-Commission: to have this UN organ adopt a Resolution criticizing a member of the Security Council. It would be an unprecedented action in any UN body. As reported in a letter by Felice Gaer to her Board in September, the League undertook the following steps: (1) it prepared a detailed 101-page report of the facts about Tiananmen Square demonstrations prior to the violent military crackdown on June 4, 1989; (2) it assisted Chinese students and other eyewitnesses presenting testimony before the Sub-Commission; and (3) it engaged in nonstop lobbying of Sub-Commission members.

"From the first days of the Sub-Commission session," Gaer wrote, "we had a bevy of representatives on hand to meet quietly with delegates, share the documentation with them, and help frame our version of what a resolution should look like." Shestack was particularly active, using his extensive diplomatic contacts and skills acquired during his service as U.S. Ambassador to the Commission on Human Rights in 1979-80. He met with one Sub-Commission after another, advising on a text to be adopted. The League was "at the center of the efforts" to convince the Sub-Commission and the result in the adopted Resolution was positive.

For the "granddaddy" of NGOs, it was a signal achievement for a career that had lasted over a half-century.[55] No American-based international NGO even came close to the League in age and service. Only the Anti-Slavery International was older, but its service was restricted to a specific and narrow mandate, while the League embraced the entire gamut of rights as articulated in the Universal Declaration of Human Rights.

As the century entered its last decade, the "granddaddy's" influence, as a U.S.-based NGO, already was passing to younger, more dynamic organizations with far larger budgets and staff. But its pioneer work would have a permanent impact.

CHAPTER SEVEN

"To Light a Candle": Amnesty International and the "Prisoners of Conscience"

Pomp and circumstance may have distinguished the ceremony in Oslo on December 11, 1977 when the Nobel Peace Committee awarded Amnesty International its distinctive prize. But for the nongovernmental human rights community, it was a substantive, as well as unprecedented, landmark achievement. Never before had a human rights NGO been awarded the Nobel Peace Prize. The inevitable consequence was the enormous enhancement of the image and status of an organization that only had been created 16 years earlier. But equally valuable was the great enhancement of the significance of human rights. No longer would human rights be regarded as an obscure or irrelevant aspect of the international community, including the United Nations. Its legitimacy had been given a firm foundation.

The announcement of the award had been made on October 10, 1977, when the Nobel Committee cited Amnesty as a "bulwark" against increased worldwide brutality and the internationalization of violence and terrorism. Particularly noted were the efforts of Amnesty "on behalf of defending human dignity against violence and subjugation. . . ."[1] To deliver its response to the unique honor bestowed on the organization, Amnesty chose a virtual unknown in the Western world, Professor Mümtaz Soysal of Ankara, Turkey. His Nobel lecture, like himself, carried no heroic quality; rather it was as mundane as his reputation was pedestrian.[2]

"We are gratified," said the Ankara professor, "that the Nobel Committee should see fit to award the 1977 Peace Prize to the 168,000 individuals in 107 countries who comprise the active members and supporters of Amnesty International. I am here in their name." The speech had no soaring or poetic qualities. Its prose read like one of the organization's promotional, if humane, brochures. Still, the Oslo ceremonial event focused world attention upon Amnesty International and its program as never before. The organization's beginnings in London in 1961 were exceedingly modest, the brainchild of a single individual, Peter Benenson. The First Annual Report of Amnesty International, a document of a mere 15 pages, in contrast to the NGO's recent Annual Reports numbering each over 350 pages, related what had prompted him to begin a profound human rights adventure that in the course of a decade and a half would astonish the world.

While traveling to his barrister's office by subway one morning in November, 1960, Benenson was stunned by an article he read in a London newspaper.[3] Two Portuguese students, it appears, were dining in a restaurant in Lisbon. Their conversation involved a certain amount of criticism of the ruthless Salazar dictatorship, which concluded with them raising their glasses in a toast to freedom. Unfortunately, the comments were overhead—a not unusual occurrence in a totalitarian regime—and the students were sentenced to seven years imprisonment for treason. The newspaper article infuriated the 40-year-old lawyer who had served as defense counsel in a number of political trials and was active in a group that had sought to bring about compliance with the Universal Declaration of Human Rights.

Benenson wondered how the Lisbon authorities could be prevailed upon to release the victims, whose only crime was an expression of their opinion. What initially struck him—and, indeed, what would become the very basis of Amnesty International—was the notion that the Salazar regime should be bombarded with letters of protest. Martin Ennals, a later Secretary-General of Amnesty, would comment that the Benenson vision constituted "an amazing contention that prisoners of conscience could be released by writing letters to government."[4]

The initial subway impulse soon would take on a broader dimension: why not a year-long campaign to focus public attention on all political and religious prisoners throughout the world? And, why not begin in 1961, the centenary of the liberation of slaves in the United States and of the serfs in Tsarist Russia? Benenson sought the assistance of two colleagues: Eric Baker, a prominent Quaker, and Louis Blom-Cooper, a highly respected international legal specialist. The three agreed to launch a campaign, "Appeal for Amnesty, 1961," which would urge the release of all those imprisoned simply for expressing their opinion.

"Prisoners of conscience" was the phrase that Benenson soon would use to characterize the focus of the "Amnesty" campaign. His law office was to be the repository for the files of information that the three founders would collect. Soon they were joined by some two dozen of their friends—lawyers, journalists, political leaders and intellectuals.[5] The assistance of David Astor, the longtime editor of the influential Sunday newspaper, the *Observer,* gave the campaign a remarkable headlong start. Astor, a friend of Benenson, offered one entire page for a major story—"The Foreign Prisoner"—that appeared on May 28, 1961. The article described the plight of eight quite different "prisoners of conscience."

The "prisoners" were neatly balanced between the democratic nations, the Communist bloc and the Third World. That division was crucial for Benenson and his associates and followers: each group of perhaps ten Amnesty supporters would adopt three prisoners from the separate categories and work for their release. The device became the centerpiece of Amnesty strategy. Once the *Observer* article was picked up on the very same day by *Le Monde* and then the next day by *Die Welt,* the *New York Herald Tribune,* the *Journal de Geneve,* and the leading publications in Denmark, Sweden, the Netherlands, Belgium, Italy, South Africa, Ireland and India, the movement quickly assumed an international character. Thousands of letters poured into Benenson's office offering support. Sympathizers now could be put in touch with one another within a particular geographic area. Churches, schools and community groups were encouraged to set up their own group of "threes." Prisoners would be adopted, then letters would be written to them and contact made with their families. Relentless pressure was to be exerted on the various authorities to release the prisoners.

Amnesty's newly designed emblem powerfully captured the vision of Benenson. A candle encircled by barbed wire has since 1961 remained the logo and emblem of the organization. The image had come to Amnesty's founder when he recalled the ancient proverb: "Better to light a candle than curse the darkness. . . ." The actual design was crafted, at Benenson's request, by the British artist Diana Redhouse. In Benenson's imagination, the emblem brilliantly summed up the spirit of the movement.

In a prescient symbolic public relations gesture, Benenson arranged for the first candle of the organization to be lit on December 10, 1961— Human Rights Day. The ceremony was held in the historic Wren church at St. Martin's-in-the-Fields, near Trafalgar Square. The obvious link with the Universal Declaration of Human Rights, specifically Articles 18 and 19 dealing with freedom of conscience and freedom of expression, could not be avoided.

Both the design and its purpose vividly recalled Eleanor Roosevelt's reference to the "curious grapevine" that would carry the provisions of the Universal Declaration to the repressed behind barbed wire and stone walls. Strikingly, too, at the memorial service to Mrs. Roosevelt, her distinguished friend Adlai Stevenson characterized her as one who "would rather light candles than curse the darkness. . . ."[6] He would add that the glow of the candles that she had lit "has warmed the world."[7] Amnesty's annual report, in commenting upon its first year of activity, seemed to echo Mrs. Roosevelt's "curious grapevine":

> Perhaps the greatest achievement of AMNESTY in its short life is that Prisoners of Conscience are no longer forgotten. Governments know that it is not possible any more to throw their citizens into jail without there being inquiries and publicity about their actions. Prisoners know that there are friends in the outside world working on their behalf and this gives them hope.[8]

Local chapters quickly mushroomed in the democratic world, first in the United Kingdom and the Federal Republic of Germany, then throughout West Europe and North America. In February, 1962, the budding organization held its first formal meeting, and, in keeping with its emerging international character, the session was held in Luxembourg—at a cafe. The delegates decided upon two key steps. First, the temporary nature of the original Benenson plan for only a one-year program was discarded in favor of a permanent organization. And, second, that organization was formally given the title of Amnesty International.

The almost exclusive priority of the organization was "to work for the immediate and unconditional release of persons imprisoned, detained or restricted for their political, religious or other conscientiously held beliefs, their ethnic origin, sex, color or language who have not used or advocated violence."[9] A second aim was "to work for a fair trial" for political prisoners. And the third objective was the ending of torture, which, later in Amnesty's history, would assume a priority function.

To realize these aims, the organization set to work to create a research library carrying information about approximately 1,200 prisoners. This documentation would be provided to the groups of "threes" who constituted the heart of Amnesty. Also created was a Prisoner of Conscience Fund to assist the prisoners and their families.

From Amnesty's very beginnings, a second distinguishing feature of the organization's strategy, along with the indispensable letter-writing emerged; it involved the dispatching of missions to countries reported to hold prisoners. The purpose of the missions was twofold: (1) to ascertain more detailed information about the state of the prisoners; and (2) to plead at the highest level for their release. During the first year in 1962, four missions were sent—to Czechoslovakia, to Ghana, to Portugal and to East Germany.

The mission to Czechoslovakia was headed by Sean MacBride whose foreign affairs experience and credentials could not easily be equaled. His key role in the organization as a member of its Board of Trustees enabled the group to draw upon his invaluable advice and assistance. The Prague visit concentrated upon Archbishop Josef Beran, who had been held incommunicado by the Czech Communist regime. MacBride was able to meet with Prague's Foreign Minister, Jiri Hajek, and offered the argument that the harsh treatment accorded the Archbishop violated the Czech Constitution of 1960. His powers of persuasion were apparently quite good. The high prelate was released with four other bishops 18 months later, although they were kept under house arrest. Amnesty was warmly thanked by the Archbishop.

The mission to Ghana, headed by Blom-Cooper, focused upon President Kwame Nkrumah's arbitrary incarceration of his political opponents. The intervention proved impressively successful. After only five months, 152 detainees were released. Amnesty linked the mission's success with the concomitant letter-writing campaign. Comprised of the simple technique of letter-writing, followed by a personal visit to the country, Amnesty's method seemed to produce results.[10]

Far less successful was the mission to East Berlin by Prem Khera, an Indian lawyer, which sought a fair trial for Heinz Brandt, a labor activist. Promises to allow Amnesty's observers at his trial were not kept and he was given a long prison sentence in a secret trial. However, a determined public campaign on several levels later was conducted that eventuated in Brandt's release after two years.

At the outset, Amnesty set guidelines for its missions that would become a permanent feature of the operation. No mission was to be sent clandestinely to a country; it must be open and officially approved by the local authorities. While the mission was in the host country, it was to issue no statement to that country's press. Upon the mission's return to London, it was to submit a report to the policymaking body of Amnesty—the International Executive Committee (IEC). Only at this point, and with the approval of the IEC, would a memorandum be prepared spelling out the mission's findings and recommendations.

The letter-writing campaign, even early in Amnesty's history, would have positive consequences. In 1964, Ireland freed 37 prisoners on Human Rights Day and Romania released thousands of political prisoners during the summer. Greece, Egypt and Burma also responded favorably. During June, 1967–June, 1968, 293 of Amnesty's adopted prisoners were released. That figure constituted more than 10 percent of some 2,000 prisoners of conscience in the Amnesty files.[11]

A doctoral study in 1977 that examined the reactions of the adopted prisoners found that Amnesty served as "a reservoir of external resources," an invaluable lifeline for the prisoners of conscience.[12] The nature of the "reservoir" was illuminated by a sampling of letters from prisoners that the researcher found. One noted that the letters from Amnesty "provide me with greater strength and courage to endure the present moments. . . ." It went on to say that "just knowing that there is a concern in other countries for my fate gives me great and invaluable aid."[13] A mother of a young female prisoner reported:

> When, in our anguish, two Amnesty members came to inform us that they had adopted our daughter as a "Prisoner of Conscience," it was like two angels had descended from the Heaven to lift our souls. . . . In our sorrow, it was comfort to know that there were people so far away who cared for the fate of our loved one.

Besides the morale-sustaining quality of the letters, the researcher also found that the prisoners firmly believed that the letters helped achieve their release or ease their condition. A former Soviet prisoner told Amnesty:

> You may think that hundreds of letters to the USSR without a reply can't be doing any good. But they are: they present a tremendous embarrassment, a threat to authorities. Only when you stop sending them do the thousands of political prisoners know the bad side of detente. . . .

Especially dramatic was the testimony of a Dominican trade union leader, Julio de Pena Valdez, who was arrested in 1975 and held naked in an underground cell. Following Amnesty's worldwide appeal on his behalf, mail overwhelmed the small Caribbean country and he was released by President Joaquin Balaguer early the following year. In the prisoner's recollection, the flow of letters determined the course of his rehabilitation and release:

> When the first two hundred letters came, the guards gave me back my clothes. Then the next two hundred letters came and the prison director came to see me. . . . The letters kept coming and coming three thousand of them. . . . The letters still kept arriving and the President called the prison and told them to let me go. After I was released, the President called me to his office. . . . He said: "How is it that a trade union leader like you has so many friends all over the world?"[14]

Amnesty, of course, was keenly aware that the letters had a certain positive effect upon repressive officials. Sean MacBride, who was deeply familiar, as an insider, with governmental attitudes, observed: "The avalanche of mail bags is still the biggest annoyance to most governments."[15] Amnesty data appeared to bolster MacBride's contention. In the seven-year period running from 1970 to 1977, Amnesty adopted more than 15,000 political prisoners. It helped gain the release of more than half of them.[16] In one London news account, more than 9,000 prisoners were released.[17] The same report showed a correlation of a fairly constant character. In 1975, for example, Amnesty adopted 2,015 new cases, and during the approximately same time frame, 1,688 political prisoners were released. Ennals, Amnesty's Secretary-General, was quoted in the account as saying: "The coincidence rate between the cases which were taken up and people released is simply high."

Concerning one quite prominent prisoner, Amnesty found itself in a peculiar and somewhat embarrassing situation. Its mandated requirement obliged the adoption of a person as a "prisoner of conscience" only when he or she had "not used or advocated violence." Perhaps the world's most famous political prisoner, Nelson Mandela of South Africa, was disqualified from this status and, therefore, from adoption after a South African court in 1964 found him guilty of sabotage. Mandela's speech to the court following the judicial verdict justified violence in the struggle against apartheid. A furious debate took place within Amnesty over the issue but the nonviolence requirement was ultimately, if somewhat rigidly, upheld.[18]

The central assumption upon which Amnesty operated and the key to the question of freeing prisoners of conscience was government's fear of negative publicity. As Ennals put it in a carefully crafted analytical essay about his organization: "Amnesty International is founded on the very simple precept that governments respond to public opinion."[19] In essence, governments can be made to respond by being shamed or embarrassed.

To the extent that the Amnesty mandate focused almost exclusively upon prisoners of conscience and—inevitably—the related phenomenon of torture of prisoners, the information it accumulated was sharply and narrowly concentrated, and this was seen as its source of strength. Ennals argued that "the single factor" that has most contributed to Amnesty's growth was precisely "the blinkers with which it approached the controversial human rights track."[20] It meticulously insisted upon upholding this key priority of "prisoners of conscience." Not until 1973 was a second priority added—ending the death penalty. Other human rights issues, including the highly charged issues of ethnic and racial discrimination, were rejected as not within the organization's purview. A leading and longtime Amnesty activist from Canada, David Matas, in a recent historical survey of Amnesty's role, commented that "the prisoner emphasis is a safeguard against Amnesty's becoming a general human rights organization . . . [and therewith losing] its identity and its power to influence."[21]

Critical to the organization—indeed, the basic source of its strength—was the collection, organization, preparation and presentation of information. As Ennals unhesitatingly emphasized, "the entire structure of the movement is designed to collect, distribute and use information."[22] Almost from the beginning, the research department was, and remained until recently, the largest and key unit in the London international secretariat. It collected, assembled and meticulously checked as well as rechecked every piece of information gathered from a great variety of sources and contacts. Amnesty's top researcher on Latin America at the time, Mike McClintock, explained to a *Washington Post* correspondent how meticulously the checking must be done "before you can be sure your information is correct."[23] Subdivided into the obvious geographical regions, the research department had as its objective the identification and interpretation of information about individual prisoners of conscience and the reasons for their detention. The research sections also would suggest ways in which the information was to be used.[24]

What was regarded as absolutely crucial to the organization was the accuracy of its information. Amnesty's very credibility was always "on the line," as it were, and indeed credibility was its principal value. The organization simply "cannot afford to make mistakes," observed Ennals, and if, by accident and despite all careful checking and re-checking, a mistake should occur, then Amnesty was obligated to acknowledge it quickly.[25] A scholar who studied the organization observed: "The long-term credibility of AI [Amnesty] would be badly damaged if its reports and statements could be shown to be false."[26] Clearly, the organization's honesty, independence and integrity were at the core of its self-regard and reputation. Only once in the early years were these qualities called into question, triggering a serious internal crisis. In 1967, Benenson suggested that the British intelligence service had infiltrated Amnesty's International Executive Committee and somehow affected the NGO's decision-making in an obscure matter involving the British outpost in Aden.

Benenson, in turn, was accused of accepting British government funds to help finance Amnesty's relief operations in Rhodesia, which unilaterally had declared its independence in 1965. The founder was forced out and replaced by the cautious, sober and undramatic Ennals, who was instructed to work more closely with the national sections but, at the same time, to create a more efficient and more effective central structure. Centralization became his top priority. In the meantime, the various charges were investigated and found to be unsubstantiated. The internal crisis had ended with scarcely any damage and the organization could almost effortlessly return to its primary purpose of fighting for the release of prisoners of conscience.

It was the power of exposure through publicity of damaging information, or its threatened use, that was and is the source of Amnesty's influence and potency. Amnesty may not have had troop divisions, but, like the papacy, it could exert or potentially exert considerable political weight, at least on certain less powerful countries or in international institutions. A case in point was the way Greece was forced to resign in 1968 from the Council of Europe, which was, at the time, the most important Western institution—other than NATO—in Europe. The military regime, dominated by colonels, had seized power in 1967 and ruthlessly suppressed freedom, imprisoned many and subjected scores to torture. Amnesty's detailed documentation of the repression submitted to the European Commission on Human Rights was expected to lead to an overwhelming vote of expulsion by the Council. To forestall the certain removal of Greece, the Athens military chose to withdraw from the Council.[27]

Amnesty, through submissions of Professor Frank Newman to the UN Commission on Human Rights, sought to do the same thing at the international level in 1968 as had been accomplished on the European level in Strasbourg, but was frustrated by the political balance at the UN.

The organization, which acquired consultative status with ECOSOC in 1964, three years after its own founding, refused to shift gears in the seventies. Its targets were a mix of the general international media and institutions. At the UN, its responsibility was clear: to prepare submissions about prisoners and other victims of human rights abuses. On this purpose, it would not compromise.

The Council of Europe and the UN Commission of Human Rights were not the only crucial target areas for Amnesty information. With the emergence of the U.S. Congress as a focal center of human rights leverage in the early seventies, Amnesty found it essential to initiate lobbying there. The office it opened in Washington, D.C. in mid-1976 had become so effective by the end of the year that an investigative journalist found its impact "extraordinary."[28] Its information and testimony to congressional bodies, he reported, provided "vital input" into the legislative process. The offices of some 40 to 50 Congressmen were responsive to Amnesty's concern and the organization had "close links particularly" with a key subcommittee on international organizations of the House Foreign Affairs Committee.

According to the various NGO activists on the Washington scene, the journalist reported, Amnesty information constituted the bulk of documentation that they used in their lobbying. Amnesty even played an advisory role in drafting a statement signed by over 100 incumbent Senators and Congressmen on the eve of the 1976 election urging that human rights become a priority for American foreign policy. Amnesty's reputation extended beyond Congress to the State Department. One official of the Department's special new human rights bureau was quoted as saying "Amnesty has a very good reputation for credibility."[29]

Amnesty's presence and activism in Washington was certain to impact upon U.S. membership growth. From but a few thousand in 1975, the membership rolls had increased tenfold, and from 7 prisoner adoption groups in 1972, the number had jumped to 80 at the end of 1976, comparing quite favorably with 130 such groups in Britain. Plans were being laid in the United States for doubling the membership, which would make the American section the largest by far of Amnesty's various national sections.

A curious feature of the reportage, as some observers noted, was the uneven nature of the targeting process.[30] As compared with the published material on Latin America, for example, the Soviet Union and its Warsaw Pact allies were given little attention except for Amnesty's publication in 1972 of the samizdat publication, *The*

Chronicle of Current Events. Not until 1975 did Amnesty issue a long report on prisoners of conscience in the USSR. One reason was suggested to a *Washington Post* correspondent by an Amnesty official: it is usually much more difficult to get information about prisoners of conscience in the East bloc states than in Western rightist countries. The correspondent also cited a comment made to him by London's Amnesty researcher, Mike McClintock: "Some governments threaten sanctions against the prisoners we're trying to help if we go public." Whether it was because of the paucity of available information or because of the threats made, Amnesty's noninvolvement in the Helsinki process during the seventies and eighties was striking.

When public use was made of its frequently potent information, Amnesty was careful to avoid claiming credit for the release of one or another prisoner of conscience that might follow. A variety of factors often played a role in achieving such an objective, so that, at best, as Ennals noted, to claim credit for Amnesty would be "only partially true." Besides, he went on, since no government would admit to acting under pressure or yielding to outside circumstances, for Amnesty or any NGO to boast of freeing a prisoner could prove counterproductive, since the repressive government might then delay the release of other prisoners.[31]

Statistics about releases of prisoners, nonetheless, suggested that Amnesty could derive satisfaction from its efforts. Self-evaluation was very much a feature of its activity. Indeed, according to two researchers who studied its operation, Amnesty was unlike most NGOs in that it "systematically" reviewed its goals, structure and operations, at least since 1965.[32] How deeply the evaluation was conducted is questionable.

But in the terms of one set of statistics that might measure accomplishment, there could be little doubt about the organization's effectiveness. Amnesty had grown enormously since its tiny operation in 1961. By the end of 1977, it had well over 150,000 members in over 100 countries. No other specifically human rights organization came close to those membership figures. Indeed, most of the others simply eschewed the aim of being a membership organization, let alone a mass membership organization. A major source of Amnesty's strength was precisely its sizable membership. Only twenty years after Amnesty received the Nobel Peace Prize in 1977, its membership would increase tenfold.

Yet, at the same time, as two scholars emphasized, the organization was "elitist" in certain key respects. Its officers and members who financially contributed to the organization were "primarily upper-middle-class professionals."[33] And, despite its claim to worldwide constituency, the bulk of its membership was located in the West—in Britain, West Europe and, by the end of the seventies, in the United States. Ennals, in an Annual Report in 1980, emphasized Amnesty's "North/South dilemma" of being "very much rooted in the wealthy countries of the North with only tentacles slowly reaching to the South."[34]

Keeping pace with the explosion of membership was the increase in Amnesty's budget. In 1961, the budget was but a few thousand pounds; by 1970, it ran to fifty thousand pounds; and by 1980, it quadrupled to nearly two million pounds.[35] A distinguishing feature of Amnesty's fundraising was its deliberate refusal to accept funds from any government lest its independence and integrity be compromised. No other European human rights NGO followed this course.

The need for a pristine image even affected the issue of whether to accept the Nobel Peace Prize, which included a financial award of over eighty thousand pounds. To avoid the problem, Amnesty, in accepting the prize, announced that the money would be placed in a special account to assist new and growing national sections so that they might become more firmly established.

Membership and fundraising were closely related to the program of campaigning for prisoners of conscience. What frequently attracted members was precisely the opportunity to be personally involved, through letter-writing, with the rescue of prisoners. At times the focus on prisoners would be intensified by special days or weeks selected to concentrate on a particular issue.

Far more dramatic and significant, however, than the struggle on behalf of prisoners of conscience was the initiative Amnesty had undertaken to combat torture, one of the most horrendous evils of the twentieth century. It was on December 10, 1972 that the organization formally launched a worldwide, one-year Campaign for the Abolition of Torture.[36] Its Chairman, Sean MacBride, made the formal announcement of the initiative, with a profoundly insightful commentary about what had already become a commonplace phenomenon in dozens of totalitarian and authoritarian regimes. He called torture an "epidemic" perpetrated by these regimes "to control dissent and maintain power."

It was, of course, appropriate for Amnesty to select December 10, the anniversary of the Universal Declaration of Human Rights, to start the campaign. The organization frequently would use the ceremonial occasion as a launching pad for public initiatives. Besides, the Universal Declaration specifically had prohibited torture. Its Article 5 stipulated that no one should be "subjected to torture or to other cruel, inhuman or degrading treatment or punishment." A careful analyst of the Declaration stressed that a major purpose of the UN was "to eliminate medieval methods of torture and cruel punishment which was practiced in the recent past by the Nazis and fascists."[37] The 1966 Covenant of Civil and Political Rights, in Article 7, similarly banned torture.

Despite the legal prohibition of torture and the moral obloquy to which it was subject, at least in the Western democratic world, the brutal phenomenon nonetheless remained pervasive. Even if precise data was lacking, the evidence was all too obvious for Amnesty, whose accumulation of information from its "prisoner of conscience" campaigns highlighted painful examples that, from time to time, would become public knowledge.

The Campaign for the Abolition of Torture was one of the most successful initiatives ever undertaken by an NGO. In the course of a fairly short time frame, masses of people were involved along with numerous NGOs in pressuring governments and, ultimately, the United Nations General Assembly to brand torture among the vilest of crimes and to erect a set of institutions to combat it. The campaign was impressively orchestrated, with a variety of individual and separate initiatives integrated into the overall effort, each reinforcing the other.

At the heart of the campaign strategy was, not surprisingly—given Amnesty's special research expertise—a detailed survey of the phenomenon. Published in the very midst of the opening phase of the campaign was a comprehensive world survey running to 224 pages and identifying over 60 countries in which torture was being practiced.[38] Even as the research study was being readied for publication, Amnesty sections were engaged in a massive petition effort. The petition was prepared in 30 languages and called upon the UN "to outlaw immediately the torture of prisoners throughout the world."[39] Over a million persons signed the petition by the end of 1973. The enormous figure hardly would have been possible without the assistance of the mass base of Amnesty.

The climax of the first-year effort was to be a high-level international conference on torture scheduled for the twenty-fifth anniversary of the Universal Declaration of Human Rights on December 10, 1973. It was to be held at UNESCO headquarters in Paris. But the very nature of Amnesty's global report on torture created a problem for officials of UNESCO.[40] In the initial arrangements for the conference, Amnesty officers had given assurances that no member states of the UN would be publicly attacked at the conference. From the perspective of UNESCO's Director-General René Maheu, the publication of the torture report was itself a breach of the agreement. But UNESCO's refusal of its facilities for the conference served only to embarrass itself. Front-page stories in *Le Monde* and *Le Figaro* stirred public sympathy for Amnesty even as they challenged the integrity of UNESCO.

The publicity of the conflict spurred greater interest in the International Conference for the Abolition of Torture, held conveniently on a solemn commemorative day. This "major event," as one former high-level Amnesty official described it, brought together over 300 participants from governments, the UN and NGOs as well as from the Amnesty membership. Moreover, the conference was widely covered in the media.[41]

Even before the climactic event of 1973, the impact of the Amnesty campaign was being felt in a profound way in the chambers of the UN. At the 1973 session of the General Assembly in the Fall, several Foreign Ministers, no doubt prompted by Amnesty constituencies as well as by other NGOs, focused their remarks on the prevalence of torture and the need to combat it. The Danish Foreign Minister said he was "alarmed by the many reports of torture." The Netherlands Foreign Minister noted "reports" from various parts of the world that "provide evidence that this appalling practice has become rife. . . ."

When concrete proposals for General Assembly action were advanced in the Third Committee, the role of Amnesty was highlighted. The Swedish delegate called attention to comments made by Amnesty's Chairman, Sean MacBride, to the effect that the eradication of every form of torture was "a common humanitarian duty." The UN Resolution that emerged condemned torture and "other cruel, inhuman or degrading treatment or punishment." More importantly, the Assembly resolved to keep the issue on the UN agenda "as an item of a future session. . . ."[42]

The die had been cast. Amnesty had succeeded in making torture and its practitioners an acceptable and appropriate subject for the UN agenda. Under circumstances in which the UN Commission on Human Rights in the past had rejected any action on human rights violations, except in the rarest of instances, and in which NGOs who had dared to merely raise such issues in UN chambers had been openly threatened with expulsion, the Amnesty achievement could not but appear as a seminal breakthrough. In launching its campaign in December, 1972, Amnesty set for itself the task of making torture "as unthinkable as slavery."[43] And it succeeded.

What enormously facilitated Amnesty's purpose were developments in Chile. The military coup on September 11, 1973, against Salvadore Allende ushered in an era of shocking brutalities, including torture. The regime of Augusto Pinochet could not escape the attention of the UN General Assembly, which began its session only days after the coup. Harrowing events in Chile had become a staple of the press and the media generally. The torture appeal of Amnesty took on a sense of immediacy and urgency.

There was a crucial political dimension to the Chilean factor that heavily affected the nature and, especially, the outcome of the UN discussions. Chile, under Allende, formally belonged to the nonaligned group that comprised the countries of the Third World. Its overthrow was perceived in Third World quarters as a plot of the United States and, therefore, specific attacks at the UN on the new military rulers were considered permissible. Generally, Third World countries were keenly suspicious of any critique of their respective human rights behavior, whether coming from NGOs or other countries. The very opposite situation now obtained.

For Amnesty International, the uniqueness of the political elements provided a distinctive opportunity to accelerate the remarkable momentum in combating torture. The climax of December, 1973 was now extended into 1974 and beyond. To meet the new and continuing political opportunities, Amnesty arranged for its so-called urgent action network, heretofore limited in character, to be the centerpiece of its strategy. The campaign against torture, largely focused upon the UN, now was integrated into the organizational structure of Amnesty itself. Within a very short time frame, hundreds of letters and telegrams could be sent to a variety of governments and sources on behalf of the victims of torture. National sections of Amnesty were mobilized to pump endless energy into the campaign and coordinators were appointed to oversee the stepped-up drive.

The frequency of "urgent action" appeals greatly increased, averaging more than one a week through May, 1975. A significant section of the membership was tapped for active involvement in the campaign, along with other NGOs.[44] The campaign also was extended geographically. Incidents of torture in Iran, Spain, South Korea and the USSR were given special attention. A second revised edition of the classic 1973 *Report on Torture*, published in 1975, included such countries as Chile, North Vietnam, Portugal, Greece, South Korea, Cyprus and Saudi Arabia. The last two were mentioned for the first time.[45]

The "urgent action" network, together with the metastasizing nature of reported torture cases in Chile, inevitably meant that the General Assembly would be seized with the torture issue. The list of states that addressed the subject in the general debate had significantly grown. The

Foreign Ministers of Norway, Belgium, the Netherlands, Luxembourg, Denmark, Eire, Austria, the Federal Republic of Germany and the United States were among those who spoke out. Some, like Norway, paid their respect specifically to Amnesty International for "the campaign against torture which that organization has launched."[46]

Communist East Europe joined in the Assembly's criticism of Chile, even going to the extent of citing data from organizations it had regarded as hostile. Thus Bulgaria referred favorably to a report on Chile by Amnesty. And the USSR referred to testimony submitted to the UN Sub-Commission by several NGOs including Amnesty, the International Commission of Jurists and the Women's International League for Peace and Freedom.

The UN was prepared to take a step beyond mere condemnation of torture as it had done in 1973. By a vote of 125 to 0, with only Zaire abstaining, the Assembly on November 6, 1974 adopted Resolution 3218 (XXIX), which, for the first time, called for specific action by the UN and its agencies.[47] The already scheduled Fifth UN Congress on the Prevention of Crime and the Treatment of Offenders (to be held in Geneva in September, 1975) was requested to prepare "rules for the protection of all persons subjected to any form of detention. . . ."

The UN General Assembly had not as yet adopted a specific form of implementation to cope with the rise of torture, but it came fairly close with its demands for precise ethical and legal norms. The Fifth Congress was obviously of potential historic significance and that was precisely the way Amnesty perceived it. A former top legal official of the organization, Helena Cook, later recalled that Amnesty "spent a year preparing for the Congress—lobbying governments, submitting a 16-page document with a series of recommendations and sponsoring two seminars on torture at the Congress itself."[48] No stone was left unturned. Nigel Rodley, Amnesty's chief legal officer, attended the Congress as an official observer and made certain that the delegates fully grasped the sensitive ramifications of what was at stake.[49]

A prominent American international law professor, Virginia Leary, was greatly impressed with the way in which Amnesty went about its task.[50] Especially noted by her was the "long and intensive preparations for the Congress" that drew upon the "well-organized and professional international secretariat" headed by a "Legal Adviser" of "outstanding competence."[51] At the same time, Amnesty's national sections were called upon to provide appropriate political muscle by asking their respective governments to support Amnesty's recommendations. This, too, impressed Professor Leary.

Of particular tactical importance was the holding by Amnesty, just prior to the Congress, of a seminar in The Hague for senior police officers and representatives of police associations from eight West European countries. Norms for police conduct therewith acquired a powerful built-in support group. A cosponsor of the seminar was the particularly strong Dutch section of Amnesty. It was almost natural and perhaps inevitable that the Dutch delegation to the Congress, and, later, at the UN, would assume the leadership in drafting and guiding to victory a formal act against torture.

Emerging from the Congress was a moving Declaration against torture. The General Rapporteur of the Congress recorded that a "passionate concern over the use of torture . . . had been the most significant and pressing aspect of its work."[52] Amnesty could take particular pride in the manner by which it had accomplished its mission. But there was yet the need to finalize the achievement by having the General Assembly adopt a formal Declaration on the Protection of All Persons from Being Subjected to Torture and Other Cruel, Inhuman or Degrading Treatment or Punishment. From London headquarters, personal messages from the organization's Secretary-General were sent to government leaders and to UN ambassadors urging support for the draft Declaration. Martin Ennals, the Secretary-General, came to New York in October, 1975 to personally lobby the delegations. On December 9, 1975, the Declaration unanimously was adopted.[53]

That it constituted a landmark achievement quickly was recognized. A vital feature of the Declaration was its definition of torture, the first time that the international community had engaged in and completed such a task. Torture was defined as:

> any act by which severe pain or suffering, whether physical of mental, is intentionally afflicted by or at the instigation of a public official on a person for such purposes as obtaining from him or a third person information or confession, punishing him for an act he has committed or is suspected of having committed or intimidating him or other persons.[54]

Only political naivete would have assumed that a UN Declaration would end the continuation and spread of torture. And Amnesty hardly fit that category. After the General Assembly session, Amnesty sought to aid the next Congress on Crime Prevention by preparing draft Professional Codes of Ethics to deal with the reality that "torture is often furthered and supported through the complicity of doctors, lawyers, judges and professional groups."[55]

But the legal field of standard-setting was not the primary or exclusive arena for counteraction. During 1975-76, Amnesty's special new apparatus—the Campaign Against Torture—put out 116 "urgent action" appeals on behalf of 500 victims or potential victims of torture. The practitioners of torture could be found on almost every continent, as its Annual Report indicated.[56] Still, the focal point was Latin America, where the Chilean experience soon would be duplicated elsewhere on that continent.

The immediate target of Amnesty in early 1976 was Uruguay, a country whose traditions of democracy and peace gave it the reputation of the "Switzerland of Latin America." But under its new military dictatorship, torture had become commonplace. Amnesty, beginning on February 19, 1976, held a series of press conferences in major European and North American cities, stressing the widespread use of torture and the deaths of 22 tortured victims of the Uruguayan military apparatus.

Once again a massive petition campaign was launched utilizing the mass base of Amnesty; 350,000 persons from 70 countries signed the petition, which asked for an independent international investigation of torture in Uruguay. Signers included Nobel Peace Prize winners, high government officials, distinguished scholars and cardinals of the Catholic Church, along with former prisoners of conscience in the USSR.[57] The European Economic Community (EEC), with whom Uruguay sought to enlarge trading arrangements, was directly approached by the Amnesty Secretariat. The response was positive, with the EEC rejecting better terms of trade for Uruguay on grounds of "the indefensible methods of the Uruguayan police against political prisoners in that country."

The impact of the highly concentrated and focused campaign upon the government in Montevideo was "considerable," according to Amnesty's Annual Report. Acknowledging that the massive effort was on "an unprecedented scale," Amnesty concluded that the campaign had "succeeded in drawing international attention" to human rights violations in Uruguay. The EEC response reflected that success. An Amnesty study for the year 1976 reinforced the thesis that the Campaign Against Torture had demonstrated a certain degree of effectiveness. Of 149 Urgent Action cases, in at least half of them, the prisoner's situation appeared to have improved, either through the halting of torture, the official acknowledgment of arrests, the release of kidnapped victims or the commutation of death sentences. Professor Leary, in examining the effectiveness of Amnesty's campaign, stressed the "broad based support" provided by its worldwide membership. "Well-developed national sections," she went on, "may be counted on to exercise influence with their national governments." In Leary's views, other NGOs could "not easily" duplicate such "advantages."[58]

But Leary chose to go beyond this theme to a broader area. Citing "recent debates within the General Assembly on torture . . . [which] have helped to create within the U.N. itself an increasing and critical audience for Amnesty International material," she concluded that this NGO "has been able to exercise a significant influence in international organizations."[59] The argument explicitly was intended to reject the view of numerous other NGOs that their "peripheral status" had "prevented them from exercising effective influence" within the UN.[60] In fact, were it not for the singular uniqueness of the Chile problem at the UN, the extent of the victory won by Amnesty hardly would have been as great. And, then too, the Amnesty writ at the UN extended to only one type of human rights violation, albeit the most horrific—torture.

Implementation of the new standard, however, remained a major problem. When the Fifth Congress on Prevention of Crime had submitted its draft Declaration on Torture to the UN, it emphasized that the draft "represented but an initial step. . . ." What was needed was implementation machinery to help bring about compliance with the Declaration.

What prompted the obviously feverish attempt to go beyond the historic, if limited, 1975 initiative was the bombardment of Western governments with documentation about torture. As the Assembly declared in one of its Resolutions, it was "gravely concerned over continued reports from which it appears that in some countries state authorities are systematically resorting to torture and other cruel, inhuman or degrading treatment or punishment."[61] The "reports" were, of course, coming from nongovernmental sources. The "careful work" of these NGOs, a U.S. delegate noted, had "indicated that the current list of practitioners of torture was a long one."[62]

Yet, it was not until 1984 that the UN would approve a legally binding treaty against torture—a total of nine years after the Declaration had been adopted and a full decade after the UN Congress on Prevention of Crime had called for urgent action to deal with the subject. And a full year would elapse after the Treaty before an effective UN instrument would be created.

Moreover, even with the Declaration, 1976 saw the emergence of what became one of the most virulent modern repressive regimes in the Western world, a regime that tolerated, encouraged and practiced torture. On March

12, 1976, a military coup took place in Argentina and launched the notorious "dirty war" against a variety of individuals and groups, some of whom were left-wing, but most of whom were trade unionists, democrats, dissenters, students and journalists. At the core of the "dirty war" was a vicious form of torture. Torture may have been practiced in Argentina since 1930, in spite of its being outlawed by the state's constitution and its penal and military justice codes. But, after the coup, "nothing . . . remotely resembled the scale on which torture was practiced. . . ."[63]

How the electrical shock torture operated at one of the major naval barracks just outside of Buenos Aires was characterized in the following: "It was unhurried and methodical. If the victim was a woman, they went for the breasts, vagina, anus. If a man, they favored genitals, tongue, neck. The aim was to cause disorientation as much as pain."[64] That was but the beginning. Crude, obscene and vile devices were used to extract "confessions." Especially vivid and powerful was the description of the personal experience of a prominent journalist, Jacobo Timerman.[65]

Intimately related to torture, indeed almost totally interwoven with it, was the process of what came to be called "disappearances"— desaparecido, in Spanish. The term originally was coined in Guatemala in the 1960s. Hundreds had been recorded as "disappeared" in Guatemala and Brazil in that decade. Some 700 people disappeared following the military coup in Chile and as many as 300 disappeared in Argentina before the March, 1976 coup. But now, after the coup, this phenomenon would assume a dimension of unprecedented proportions. An Argentine NGO human rights group, the Permanent Assembly of Human Rights, published a list of almost 6,000 who had disappeared; a commission established by the democratic government after the collapse of the military dictatorship compiled a total of nearly 9,000 disappeared. Even this figure was regarded as an underestimate.[66]

A senior diplomat at the U.S. Embassy in Buenos Aires defined disappearances as a euphemism for "unacknowledged detention" by the security forces. The detainees usually were tortured as part of interrogation and eventually executed. According to the authoritative work on the subject, the Argentine disappearances program was different in scale and method from what had preceded it: "Never before had the resources of a state been geared to systematic torture and murder."[67] The military junta had transformed disappearances into "a government policy"— "deliberate, methodical and calculated."

The Permanent Assembly on Human Rights had come into existence in December, 1975 in response to pre-coup killings by a naval terrorist apparatus. This organization was made up of prominent Argentine democratic figures who saw their function to be the methodical collecting of files on individual cases of the disappeared. But the organization eschewed any form of activism, conducted no investigations and organized no protests. State terrorism was too overpowering a phenomenon to challenge.

The only protest came from the Mothers of the Plaza de Mayo. On April 30, 1977, 14 middle-aged women who had been looking for their disappeared children for months decided to go to the central square in Buenos Aires in the hope of meeting with the head of the military regime. From this assemblage emerged the only confrontation with the ruthless military regime. Every Thursday, the group, which eventually reached several hundred, would come to the Plaza de Mayo with white head scarves, silently picket the government offices, particularly the Interior Ministry, and seek information about their disappeared family members. The Mothers were steadfast and could not be intimidated even by police pressure. But they were powerless.

In the early stage of the Argentine military rule, with disappearances still low in numbers and the full force of the state repression not yet exerted, Amnesty asked the regime for permission to send a mission to the country. The junta approved with the intention of demonstrating to the well-known NGO its "firmness and conviction" and, secondly, learning about "their contacts." The two-week visit in November, 1976 was by no means a friendly one.[68] Amnesty's delegation was fairly high-level—Father Robert Drinan, a leading Jesuit scholar and liberal Congressman from Massachusetts; Lord Avebury, coordinator of a British parliamentary human rights group; and Patricia Feeney, the Amnesty professional who ran the organization's Argentine desk.

Four months later, on March 23, 1977, the Amnesty report was published. It was a sober, factual account of the year's killings as well as disappearances. Names, dates and places were set forth in considerable detail. According to an authoritative work, the Amnesty mission to Argentina turned out to be "one of the most significant human rights missions ever undertaken by a non-governmental organization."[69] The international community had been provided with a rich and not easily challenged source of data on the new and horrendous crimes of disappearances. Although the Argentina junta furiously attacked the report as "political," the judgment of the international community was provided elsewhere. On October 10, 1977, the Norwegian Nobel Committee awarded its Peace Prize to Amnesty International for the organization's work in protecting "prisoners" from the kind of treatment that is in "violation of human rights."

The reaction in the military dictatorship of Latin America was a cold fury. A leading Argentine journal declared that the Norwegian decision meant that "the cause of peace for all lost a battle." Chilean radio contended that Amnesty had "played along with international Marxism." A leading newspaper in Uruguay quoted the Minister of Education as characterizing the Nobel Committee's decision as "a joke in bad taste."[70]

Martin Ennals, Amnesty's Secretary-General, greeted the news with the self-effacing comment that "what we would like to be is nonexistent—unemployed." "But," he went on, "torture is now widely practiced and is becoming more systematic. . . ."[71] Symptomatic of the organization's perspective was the publication on October 18, only one week after the Nobel Committee's announcement, of a new Amnesty study of political prisoners halfway around the world, in Asia. In a 146-page report, Indonesia was accused of holding in detention 100,000 political prisoners whose constitutional and legal rights were being violated by "arbitrary" means, including torture.[72]

In a word, it was "business as usual." Ennals himself did not go to Oslo to receive the Nobel Peace Prize on December 10. Instead, he was in Stockholm on that day, participating in a conference that concentrated upon combating the death penalty. Nor would Amnesty's chief legal officer, Nigel Rodley, who had so much to do with creating and advancing the institutional means for opposing torture, be present in Oslo. Rodley was in Geneva for another conference, although he related in an interview how, when he walked into the conference room, a burst of applause greeted him. It was symbolic to him of what Amnesty International had achieved.[73]

The glory of the day and of the prize nonetheless would carry important ramifications, even if the appropriate public posture for Amnesty staffers was one of modesty. Its image was enormously enhanced, as was the cause for which it had fought—human rights. A watershed in the recognition of human rights and its advocates had been reached. Attitudes toward the subject never would be the same again. Still, torture had not diminished; nor had disappearances. Effective action required the cooperation of intergovernmental institutions, most notably, the United Nations. And at the UN there existed an institutional bias against implementation. For a real breakthrough, the influence of a powerful state was necessary.

"A Call for U.S. Leadership": Congress, the Struggle for Human Rights, and the NGO Factor

In March, 1974, an extraordinary document was published by a congressional subcommittee which soon would have a very significant and, to an extent, revolutionary impact upon U.S. policy in the area of international human rights. Entitled "Human Rights in the World Community: A Call for U.S. Leadership," the report was prepared by a panel of the influential House of Representatives Foreign Affairs Committee. The Subcommittee on International Organizations and Movements, headed by Congressman Donald M. Fraser, a Democrat from Minneapolis, Minnesota, had held virtually unprecedented hearings on U.S. human rights policy, a total of 15 hearings with over 40 witnesses between August 1 and December 7, 1973. As some of the most important congressmen sat on the subcommittee and its parent body, the report was certain to attract attention. Notably unusual was its "Call for U.S. Leadership." It reflected an angry rejection of the Nixon Administration policy, of which Secretary of State Henry A. Kissinger was a principal architect, and a demand for a radically new orientation in American policy.[1]

Early on, the Congressional report took aim at its Administration target: "the human rights factor is not accorded the high priority it deserves in our country's policy." The rebuke then became sharper: "Too often, it [human rights] becomes invisible on the vast foreign policy horizon of political, economic and military affairs." Referring indirectly, but clearly, to the Secretary of State, the report noted that the "proponents of pure power politics too often dismiss it [human rights] as a factor in diplomacy." The disregard for human rights was bitterly denounced as harmful to America's interest and image in the world: "The prevailing attitude has led the United States into embracing governments which practice torture and unabashedly violate almost every human rights guarantee pronounced by the world community."[2]

Several case studies were given special attention by the Subcommittee: the large-scale massacre of Bengalis in Pakistan in 1971 and of Hutus in Burundi in 1972; widespread torture in Brazil and Chile; and racial discrimination in South Africa. At best, the Department would contend, said the report, that "serious violations" of human rights should be handled by a "quiet diplomacy" of private inquiries and "low-keyed appeals."

The critique of "quiet diplomacy" was equally applicable to America's détente policy to the Soviet Union. While détente was welcomed, the report warned that "cooperation must not extend to the point of collaboration in maintaining a police state." The Subcommittee detailed the evidence of how the Soviet Union was "intensifying efforts to perpetuate the closed society" and demanded that the United States "be forthright in denouncing Soviet violations of human rights."

A striking feature of the Subcommittee's report was the attention it gave to the role of nongovernmental organizations. Especially stunning was the appreciation rendered by Chairman Fraser, in the report's Preface to a staffer, John Salzberg, who was said to be "indispensable" by bringing to the hearings and the report "the special expertise" of "practical experience in the field" along with careful study. Salzberg earlier had served as the UN representative of the Geneva-based International Commission of Jurists, a point emphasized by Congressman Fraser. International NGOs were praised in the report as "a vital contributor to the international protection of human rights."[3] An entire section was devoted to lauding their independence and objectivity and to a description of how, Amnesty International, in particular, functioned.

The special attention given to the need for underscoring "American leadership" in the human rights field was by no means unique. From the very beginning of the American republic, a distinctive human rights tone often had characterized the formulation of U.S. diplomacy, even if it was not necessarily incorporated within the application of specific foreign policy objectives. The Declaration of Independence invoked a *universal* appeal for "unalienable rights" of the individual. It constituted a revolutionary notion that the rights of the individual were superior to those of the state. Until then, the supremacy of state power was held to be fundamental. The Declaration ineluctably had thrown down the gauntlet to the prevailing international order.

Human rights would be perceived as a special *American* mission to the world.[4] Benjamin Franklin wrote that "establishing the liberties of America . . . will have some effect in diminishing the misery of those who, in other parts of the world, groan under despotism. . . ." President Andrew Jackson, in his Inaugural Address, observed that "Providence . . . has chosen you as the guardians of freedom, to preserve it for the benefit of the human race." On the eve of World War I, President Woodrow Wilson commented that, in time, the world will come to recognize that America puts human rights above all other rights, and that "her flag is the flag . . . of humanity." And President John F. Kennedy pledged, in his inaugural address, to "bear any burden, pay any price" for the sake of freedom.

World War II, together with the Holocaust, brought among policymakers a greater awareness and sensitivity to the significance of human rights. The experience with Nazi totalitarianism demonstrated that an intimate linkage existed between internal repression of human rights and external aggression. Secretary of State George Marshall stressed the relationship in his address to the UN General Assembly in September, 1948: "Governments which systematically disregard the rights of their own people are not likely to respect the rights of other nations and other people and are likely to seek their objectives by coercion and force. . . ."[5] It is almost a truism to assert that modern totalitarian and authoritarian regimes, by suppressing internal dissent and crushing human rights, are less hampered in engaging in declared or undeclared war.

At the closing session of the UN Conference in San Francisco, President Harry Truman clearly sensed the relationship between human rights and conflict resolution. Referring to the UN Charter provisions for human rights and fundamental freedoms, he emphasized that "unless we can attain those objectives for all men and women everywhere . . . we cannot have permanent peace and security."

A further consideration flows from the revolutionary transformation of international communications since World War II. Massive violations of human rights become almost instantaneously known and reach quickly into the living rooms of America through nightly telecasts. Public opinion polls demonstrate that, at a minimum, Americans are opposed to any U.S. support to governments that "perpetuate egregious and gross violations of human rights."[6]

Despite these factors, American foreign policy since the beginning of the Eisenhower Administration had moved away from any human rights focus to a predominant concern with security and stability. The utter disdain Kissinger held for human rights was illustrated in the severe berating he gave to the U.S. Ambassador in Chile who dared to raise human rights issues with the military regime there.[7] As previously mentioned, in the two hefty volumes of Kissinger's memoirs embracing his stewardship of American foreign policy while serving as National Security Adviser, the phrase "human rights" does not even appear in the index of each.[8]

Congressional irritation with Kissinger's indifference to human rights issues and, at times, his actual or seeming support of military dictatorships—whether in Latin America, South Korea or the Philippines—fed a growing revolt. It initially had been spurred by American policy toward Vietnam, which was perceived as cynical and immoral, supportive of only a corrupt military regime in Saigon. The Watergate scandal aggravated the executive-congressional confrontation; increasingly, Congress was prepared to challenge the "imperial presidency," including the foreign affairs area, traditionally regarded as the prerogative of the executive.

The Foreign Assistance Act of 1973, especially its Section 32, pressed by Congressman Fraser, broke new ground. For the very first time, U.S. legislation declared that "it is the sense of Congress that the President should deny any economic or military assistance to the government of any foreign country which practices the internment or imprisonment of that country's citizens for political purposes." Fraser's Subcommittee, in its "Call for U.S. Leadership," specified in its formal Recommendation that the State Department should withdraw "military assistance and sales" along with certain "economic assistance programs" from "governments which are committing serious violations of human rights. . . ."[9] The new Act was designed to formalize the "Call for U.S. Leadership" and provide it with a statutory legitimization.

In September, 1974, Fraser sent Kissinger a letter signed by 105 members of Congress warning that their support for legislation extending foreign aid would be affected by the degree to which State Department policy displayed concern for human rights in recipient countries. The warning was formalized in legislation enacted as Section 502B of the

Foreign Assistance Act. It required the President, except in "extraordinary circumstances," to "substantially reduce or terminate security assistance to any government which engaged in a consistent pattern of gross violations of internationally recognized human rights." The language, as is evident, was drawn from key resolutions adopted by the UN Commission on Human Rights and about which staffer Salzberg was an expert.

Angered by the dilatory tactics of Kissinger regarding the security assistance legislation and concerned about growing atrocities in Chile, Congress moved to new levels of human rights legislation. The conditioning simply of economic assistance would in 1975 supplement the earlier conditioning of security assistance. Freshman Congressman Tom Harkin, a Democrat from Iowa, won support for legislation denying economic assistance to any country that consistently violated internationally recognized human rights. The amendment was identified as Section 116 of the International Development and Food Assistance Act.

The assault upon traditional executive prerogatives was continued into 1976 with the adoption of Section 301 of the International Security Assistance and Arms Export Control Act. In keeping with the recommendation of the "Call for U.S. Leadership" but now extending it, the legislation established within the State Department the position of Coordinator for Human Rights and Humanitarian Affairs, to be appointed by the President. The new statute also required the Secretary of State to submit reports every year on the human rights practices of each country that the Department wished to be a recipient of security assistance. At the same time, the Department was warned that, were the reports not satisfactory nor submitted within 30 days, Congress might reduce or end security assistance to a particular human rights violator by adoption of a joint Resolution.

Congressional toughness in the human rights field also was shown in 1976 with respect to international regional lending institutions in which the United States was represented. New specific legislation obliged the U.S. Executive Directors at the Inter-American Development Bank and the African Development Fund to vote against loans to governments that engaged in gross violations of human rights. Such action could kill the request for a loan. Later, it would be extended to other international lending institutions.

To what extent were NGOs responsible for this extraordinary outpouring of unprecedented international human rights legislation during the last two years of Kissinger's leadership of the State Department? Professor David Weissbrodt, a specialist on human rights law, in the course of documenting a study on "the influence of interest groups" on U.S. human rights legislation, strongly criticized a *Washington Post* story crediting NGOs for the passage of the human rights legislation.[10] Weissbrodt contended that "in fact, nongovernmental organizations generally concerned with human rights devoted no significant attention to Congress during the critical formative period of 1973 through 1975."

But a key State Department official who had spent a long period of time on a grant from the Council of Foreign Relations examining American human rights policy, Sandy Vogelgesang, came to a totally different conclusion. The "human rights lobby" in Washington, she found, comprising representatives of a number of religious groups, labor unions and international NGOs, was "often . . . a decisive factor propelling" human rights developments in Washington.[11] From a mere handful in the early seventies the "lobby" grew to about 50 organizations in the late seventies exercising "considerable clout." One legislator called them a "dogged bank of human righters" who packed considerable importance. Several represented religious groups. Vogelgesang called attention to Edward Snyder of the Friends Service Committee on National Legislation and his counterparts from the National Council of Churches, B'nai B'rith International and the U.S. Catholic Conference as being part of what "irreverent congressional staff members" called the "God squad."[12] That "squad" collected data on human rights violations abroad and engaged in campaigns to educate the public about them.

Particularly singled out was the Washington Office on Latin America (WOLA), headed at the time by Joseph Eldridge. An offshoot of the National Council of Churches, WOLA, with a small staff, nonetheless was able to provide the principal witnesses and documents for congressional hearings and assisted Congressman Tom Harkin in drafting much of his legislation.[13]

Eldridge, interviewed very recently in Washington, confirmed the findings of Vogelgesang twenty years ago and offered fresh details. He had returned in September, 1974 from Chile where he served as a Methodist minister on church missions to the poor. Joining WOLA, which he said was at the time the only NGO with specific connections with the Solidarity movements involving Chile and Argentina, Eldridge "conspired" with Salzberg to "recommend witnesses" to the Fraser Subcommittee. Together with the Friends' Edward Snyder, he observed, they "put together" the congressional hearings.[14]

The choice of panelists was, of course, crucial to the impact the hearings might have and what legislation would emerge. Assistance in drafting legislation was also provided to the congressional staffers of the freshman group of young Democratic legislators headed by Harkin. Called the "Watergate babies," since they first were elected in 1974, the group—very much human rights oriented—was prepared to challenge the assumptions of Kissinger's realpolitik.[15] According to one careful academic researcher, the historically significant Harkin amendment of 1975 was "first drafted" by "staffers of the Quakers and WOLA."[16] No doubt, he was referring here to Ed Snyder of the Friends Committee and Joe Eldridge.

The same researcher found, in a survey of congressional opinion on the impact of NGOs, that these NGOs were particularly effective in raising the "saliency of human rights issues." Their influence may not be decisive with any particular congressman, he added, but, it cannot be excluded. As described by a number of interviewees, the NGO influence was of a "secondary" character, not necessarily decisive. Especially with liberal congressmen did the NGOs carry weight, although, as an aide to Harkin put it: "We are never taken where we don't want to go."[17] But even some conservative congressmen found that the detailed and informed testimony of NGOs on gross human rights violations—for example, in Argentina—could not fail to sway many in Congress.

The "Call for U.S. Leadership" reached its climax not with enactments of unprecedented human rights legislation by Congress but with the election of Jimmy Carter as President. In his Inaugural Address on January 20, 1977, President Carter stressed that "our moral sense dictates a . . . preference for those societies which share with us an abiding respect for individual human rights." Symptomatic of the decisive turn in policy was President Carter's decision several weeks after his inauguration to respond publicly to a letter from Andrei D. Sakharov, the very symbol of dissent and human rights in the USSR, an act that, not unexpectedly, ignited a burning fury at the Kremlin.

Human rights NGOs now would occupy a totally different place in the Washington power structure. Not only Congress, but also the executive branch would be openly responsive to their views. As early as October 2, 1976, prior to the election, Carter staffers met with officials of the Friends Committee who, on behalf of themselves and six other NGOs, outlined orally and in written form various recommendations. And, soon after the inauguration, the International League for Human Rights outlined various policy proposals to the new Administration.[18] Of particular significance was the appointment of Patricia Derian as the Coordinator of Human Rights and Humanitarian Affairs under the tough human rights legislation enacted by Congress in 1976. The title was soon changed to Assistant Secretary of State. Derian had come out of the civil rights movement and was active in a number of domestic rights groups.

When interviewed 20 years later, Patt Derian recalled how she quickly had established a close working relationship with Washington's human rights NGOs who, she firmly believed, were invaluable to the fulfillment of the new Administration's purposes.[19] Especially significant was her appointment in early 1978 of Roberta Cohen as Deputy Assistant Secretary of State. The new Deputy had been the Executive Director of the International League for Human Rights and, therefore, was familiar with many of the substantive issues of concern to NGOs as well as their principal leaders and activists. Moreover, Cohen was assigned, among her various responsibilities, the specific task of dealing with NGOs. The choice hardly could have been more appropriate.

An "Evaluation of Performance" prepared by the State Department at the end of 1978 described some of her achievements, which were altogether striking as well as distinctively new:

> She brought together NGOs with Department officials and Ambassadors [who are] home on consultations in order to create a dialogue on the policy and exchange of information. She helped stimulate and organize NGO human rights study missions to different countries. She has been instrumental in having NGOs make statements on human rights violations in countries when U.S. Government statements would have been fruitless.[20]

Liaison work with the NGO community was of basic importance in providing the State Department with the pressing concerns of NGOs. An example was a memo Cohen drafted for Patt Derian, which the latter sent to the Acting Secretary of State on June 13, 1979.[21] The memo noted that meetings held by Cohen with some 20 international and national NGOs revealed that these groups were "deeply disturbed" by the "declining visibility" of the Carter Administration's human rights advocacy. A detailed list of NGO complaints followed. Particularly emphasized was the "failure" of the executive branch to "strongly work for the ratification of the Genocide Convention" as well as the international human rights covenants and other international agreements.

NGOs also were reported as disappointed with the uneven application of human rights policy. When, for example, security or economic interests were involved, "human rights are ignored." NGOs were troubled too by "diminishing U.S. pressure" on major human rights violators such as South Korea, Argentina, Indonesia, Nicaragua, the Philippines, El Salvador, Guatemala and South Africa. Finally NGOs were irritated by the "continued insensitivity to and lack of knowledge about human rights by many foreign service officers here and abroad."

The memo sought to deal with these concerns by giving concrete suggestions; for example, it suggested toughening America's stance toward major human rights violators and establishing a massive foreign service education program to institutionalize the teaching of human rights. Cohen also recommended the appointment of a top-level individual with expertise to represent the United States at the UN Commission on Human Rights. In 1980, the Chairman of the International League for Human Rights, Jerome Shestack, would be selected for that post and, with Cohen as his Senior Adviser, would bring about a "landmark achievement" with respect to the traumatic and enormously egregious problem of "the disappeared" in Latin America. This achievement was referred to in the Department's "Evaluation" of Cohen in 1980.[22]

Yet access, especially through the human rights bureau, did not mean that NGOs played a decisive or even primary role with respect to policy. The Carter Administration never did attempt to win ratification of the genocide treaty (or other covenants) lest it jeopardize the priority objective of winning ratification of the Panama Canal treaty. When legislation was advanced in Congress in 1979 requiring the Administration to instruct U.S. officials in the World Bank and other international institutions to consider human rights in their financial decisions, the Carter Administration initially opposed it. A review of the evidence on conduct as opposed to rhetoric by one scholar demonstrated "that American policy on human rights remained linked to security and economics."[23]

Nonetheless, a fundamental change in the perception of the role and significance of human rights NGOs had taken place. Even if their greatest influence was with Congress, their legitimacy as an invaluable source of information now would be accorded respect in keeping with the new legitimacy of the rhetoric concerning human rights. The State Department no longer could discount or exclude their views and presence. According to a skeptical analyst, human rights NGOs, by the late seventies, "significantly affected both legislation and State Department operating consideration."[24] The impact of the change in the United States would shortly be felt in regional and international institutions.

Running parallel to the congressional hearings on general human rights that produced the "Call to Leadership" and the subsequent human rights legislation was the congressional challenge to the Administration on a specific but critical human rights issue—the right of Soviet Jews to emigrate. It would be embodied in the so-called Jackson-Vanik amendment. A principal factor in its enactment was an NGO, the National Conference on Soviet Jewry (NCSJ), which acted as a coordinator for several long-established national Jewish NGOs whose various local constituencies embraced the bulk of the organized Jewish community. Unlike most other NGOs, the NCSJ could tap deeply into the grass roots and impact upon Congress in a direct and potent manner. In that respect, it echoed, to a certain extent, the way the American Committee on Africa functioned.

A major study of worldwide emigration policies sponsored by the Twentieth Century Fund and published in 1987 by Yale University Press lauded the Jackson-Vanik amendment as the "single most effective step" taken by the United States to cope with "the new serfdom" of restrictions upon emigration.[25] The comment of the study accorded with the perspective of Jews from the former Soviet Union for whom the amendment constituted a potent—if potential—liberating lever. A similar attitude was held by American Jews, for whom the amendment served as a powerful weapon in the struggle on behalf of their brethren held in virtual bondage. Perhaps even more significant as the view of Jews was the perception of the modern world's great humanist, Nobel Laureate Andrei Sakharov. In an "open letter" to the American Congress on September 14, 1973, he extended the amendment a unique and unprecedented endorsement as a "policy of principle" that could further the purpose of détente, not detract from it.[26]

Yet, the enactment of the Jackson-Vanik amendment was by no means a quick and easy achievement. It required a two-year legislative struggle involving intensive battles with a determined Nixon Administration, bolstered by powerful corporate interests. The Administration's principal opponent was a senior U.S. Senator, Henry M. Jackson, who had a record of vigorously espousing civil liberties at home and strongly criticizing the USSR and Soviet expansionism abroad.

What intellectually appears to have motivated Jackson merits special attention. When he formally introduced his amendment on the Senate floor on March 15, 1973, he specifically referred to Article 13/2 of the Universal Declaration of Human Rights, which held that "everyone has the right to leave any country, including his own, and to return to his country," as the principal source of inspiration for the proposed legislation.[27] His amendment thus became the very first piece of American legislation that expressly drew its inspiration from the Universal Declaration of Human Rights. Relevance of the Declaration to the Jackson-

Vanik amendment was critical. Sakharov was to underscore it in his "open letter."

Senator Jackson went beyond this general point to emphasize a specific attribute of the American tradition, the country's basic character as a "nation of immigrants," which, in his view, justified the introduction of the amendment. For it was precisely because of this character, he insisted, that freedom of emigration was "an American issue." Jackson reminded his colleagues that "I would not be in this chamber today if Norway, the country of my parents' birth, had practiced the sort of emigration policy that the Soviet Union has today."

The issue of emigration for Soviet Jews had become especially pressing after 1967, when the Kremlin had imposed a sharply discriminatory policy in the admission of Jews to higher education, resulting in a consequent reduction of their numbers in the fields of science and technology. The discriminatory policy was accompanied by a vast and virulent anti-Semitic propaganda campaign masquerading as anti-Zionism. For many, who earlier had seen the loss of ethnic and cultural rights, the only hope was emigration to Israel. But that alternative was severely restricted by Moscow. Even a modest emigration was unacceptable to the state, although the barrier was lifted somewhat in March, 1971 to allow some Jewish immigration.

Jackson's initiative was sparked by a secret and extraordinary, if brutal, decision of the Soviet government: the enactment, on August 3, 1972, of a decree requiring would-be emigrants who had acquired a higher education to pay a "diploma tax." On August 14, the decree was reaffirmed by an order of the USSR Council of Ministers, directing appropriate Soviet agencies to establish a scale of fees. These were so exorbitantly high that payment by persons holding advanced degrees was virtually impossible. Soviet Jewish activists, at an August 15 press conference, warned that the effect of the decree would be the creation of a new category of human beings—"the slaves of the twentieth century." The diploma tax was but the latest of a massive series of devices created by the Kremlin to stop the drain of talent. Even as the barrier to emigration had been lifted in March, 1971, the highly educated and technically trained now were compelled to run an obstacle course of prolonged torment.

The Kremlin had not reckoned with the revulsion the tax would generate in the United States. Especially shocked were the scientific and academic communities. Mobilized by the Academic Committee on Soviet Jewry (established by B'nai B'rith and chaired by Professor Hans Morgenthau), 21 Nobel Laureates issued a public statement in the fall of 1972 expressing "dismay" at the "massive violation of human rights" by the imposition of "exorbitant head taxes." Thousands of university professors signed petitions and newspaper advertisements of the Academic Committee demanding that the Kremlin remove "the ransom tax." An even stronger and more bitter, if anxious, reaction took place in the organized Jewish community. At an emergency meeting of the leadership of national Jewish organizations, called on September 26, 1972 in Washington by the National Conference on Soviet Jewry (NCSJ), it was decided that they would move from a largely public relations campaign to a predominantly political one focusing on a particular piece of legislation. Senator Jackson, who had asked to be invited to the gathering, outlined to the 120 participants a legislative proposal that he intended to introduce—the tying of trade benefits to the removal of curbs on emigration. The Jewish leadership audience was enthusiastic.[28]

In part, the Jackson proposal was a response to nearly completed negotiations for a comprehensive trade agreement that had been carried on between American and Soviet officials since the beginning of August. The provisions of the agreement, as finally signed by the two powers in October, had two key features: The United States was to receive from the USSR $722 million as a token of the enormous lend-lease debt owed it since World War II; in return, the Administration pledged to seek congressional authorization for extending to the Soviet Union Most-Favored Nation (MFN) tariff treatment. The American-Soviet agreement was the core element of the Nixon-Kissinger policy toward the Soviet Union, a high priority objective of establishing links that presumably would reduce tensions and erect a "structure of peace."

The amendment would refuse a "nonmarket economy country" MFN status, as well as credits, credit guarantees and investment guarantees, if that country denied its citizens the right to emigrate or imposed more than a nominal tax on emigration. Early in January, 1973, Congressman Charles A. Vanik, a Democrat from Cleveland, Ohio, had assembled a larger list of representatives who agreed to sponsor in the House legislation similar to Jackson's amendment. A massive letter-writing campaign initiated by the NCSJ and organized Jewry was to evoke a powerful response. Local Jewish communal structures and most synagogues were very much part of the NCSJ organizational apparatus as were the separate major Jewish groups, like B'nai B'rith, Hadassah, the American Jewish Committee and the American Jewish Congress. Thus the campaign was profoundly grassroots in character. Attempts were made to reach every legislator on a continuing basis. In addition, a number of groups of a more militant character were established in several communities like Long Island, San Francisco and Cleveland. Support for the amendment also came from various other sources, including the especially important trade union movement and several Christian religious groups. The lobbying was massive, coordinated and constant.

By early February, 238 representatives—more than a majority of the House—had decided to become cosponsors of the proposed legislation. That legislation would be designed to amend an expected administration Trade Reform Act that was scheduled for early introduction.

The Soviet authorities initially sought to meet congressional action head-on. The major target was to be big business in the United States, which was thought to be most susceptible to Soviet blandishments. It was characteristic of the Kremlin to view America through the Marxist class perspective. Lobbying by ethnic groups hardly was envisioned as being as potent as that of the presumed dominant capitalist class. A high-level 15-member Soviet delegation headed by Vladimir Alkhimov, Deputy Minister of Trade, arrived to participate in an American-Soviet trade conference sponsored by the National Association of Manufacturers (NAM). At the opening session in Washington on February 27, which was attended by 800 businessmen, no less than 3 powerful Soviet officials served as panel members. The Soviet panelists quickly learned where Congress stood. Senator Edmund S. Muskie, a powerful Democratic legislator from Maine, told them that Soviet emigration policy constituted a "major roadblock" to expanded East-West trade.

The Russians focused on the softer line of economic inducements, with the NAM providing the required link to Congress. On March 12, Deputy Minister Alkhimov and two Soviet embassy economic officials met with 15 congressmen, among them key Republicans, at a luncheon requested by the Soviet embassy and arranged by NAM officials, to explain the advantages of increased United States–Soviet trade. They were advised that members of Congress are "much concerned with Soviet emigration policies and that we tend to link them with the granting of the most favored nation status."

On March 19-20 the USSR allowed 44 Soviet Jews who had obtained a higher education to leave without paying the diploma tax. On March 21, the Tel Aviv newspaper *Yediot Achranot* published an article by Victor Louis, a Soviet journalist with close KGB connections, which said that the diploma tax "will no longer be enforced." Acknowledging that the Soviet decision was the result of congressional pressure, Louis observed: "It seems that the Soviet citizens who have decided to emigrate from the Soviet Union have won a victory in the six-month war against the education tax." He might have added that the Jackson-Vanik amendment and the National Conference on Soviet Jewry had achieved a remarkable and, probably, unique result—the nullification by the Kremlin of one of its own statutes.

Jackson, speaking at the National Press Club in Washington on March 22, welcomed the Moscow developments as "encouraging signs," but also made it clear that he would continue to press for his amendment to insure that Moscow did not "relapse into the old patterns" of harassment and taxation to limit emigration. The issue, it was clear, remained the right to leave a country. So long as harassment and intimidation of would-be emigrants continued in the USSR, the fundamental problem was by no means resolved.

The Administration followed up with a direct approach to the Jewish community. At Nixon's invitation, 15 prominent Jewish leaders were invited to the White House. They had long sought a meeting with the President to discuss the totality of the Soviet Jewish problem, but had not been particularly successful. Now it was the President who sought the meeting. It lasted 70 minutes and ranged over central aspects of the Soviet Jewish problem. The President explained to the leaders the profound moral dilemma in which he found himself. On the one hand, he had made a commitment to the Kremlin on MFN status, which was perceived as integral to his search for détente. On the other hand, there was the Jackson-Vanik amendment, which would negate that commitment.

Delivered in a delicate manner, the message was clear. The White House hoped the Jewish community would reconsider its adamant support of the Jackson-Vanik amendment. The strategy appears to have temporarily succeeded. After the meeting, Jacob Stein, Chairman of the Conference of Presidents of Major Jewish Organizations; Charlotte Jacobson, Vice-chairman of the National Conference on Soviet Jewry; and Max Fisher, former President of the Council of Jewish Federations and Welfare Funds and an important Republican fundraiser, issued a statement on behalf of all participants, which was as revealing for what it did not say as for what it said. It noted the contents of the Soviet embassy "communications" that had been provided by Kissinger and "asked the help of the President for the 100,000 Soviet Jews who had been refused exit visas." Finally, it reaffirmed "the commitment to Soviet Jews and our determination to continue maximum efforts in their behalf." Nothing was said about the Jackson-Vanik amendment.

The failure of the Jewish leaders' statement to include any reference to the Jackson-Vanik amendment raised doubts on Capitol Hill about the firmness of the Jewish community's position. More importantly, the very ambiguity of the statement also stirred a major grassroots backlash among Jewish communities throughout the United States. Demands for clarification rapidly mounted among the organizations comprising the NCSJ. Parallel and interlocked with this pressure were demands by the amendment's leading congressional sponsors for a strong statement of support, without which their ability to hold their supporters in line was open to question.

The top Jewish leaders were faced with a dilemma that they had sought to avoid. Until their meeting at the White House, they had made every effort to present publicly their support of the Jackson-Vanik amendment as in no way directed against the President. Moreover, they were keenly aware that President Nixon had been a friend of Israel.

A decisive consideration in resolving the dilemma was the attitude of Jewish activists in the Soviet Union itself. When reports about an apparent ambiguity concerning American Jewish support for the Jackson-Vanik amendment reached Moscow, Soviet Jewish activists decided to intervene directly. On April 23, they sent an appeal bearing more than 100 signatures to American Jewish leaders, urging them to continue backing the amendment. Their language was strong and was designed to remind American Jewry of the Holocaust. The closing paragraph was particularly poignant: "Remember the history of our people has known many terrible mistakes. Do not give in to soothing deceit."

Since guilt feelings, associated with the inability of the American Jewish community to prevent the Holocaust, were at the heart of its militant and concentrated involvement with Soviet Jewish survival, the desperate appeal of Soviet Jewish leaders could not fail to evoke a profound anxiety and concern. Clarification of the Jewish community's position was pressed at an enlarged Executive Committee meeting of the NCSJ on April 26. It reached the decision that a prompt public statement of support for the amendment was essential.

While the Administration was unable to sway Congress (or the Jewish community), Leonid Brezhnev thought he might try to do so during a scheduled trip to the United States in mid-June. Two days after his arrival he met with 17 members of the Senate Foreign Relations Committee and 8 members of the House and outlined the prospects for vast Soviet-American trade. He emphasized rather vigorously that the condition for such trade was MFN status for the Soviet Union. Brezhnev received a far more enthusiastic reception from 40 of America's top industrial and banking executives who had been invited by Secretary of Labor George Shultz to a meeting at Blair House on the morning of June 22. They were enormously impressed by the broad picture Brezhnev painted of the potential of trade relations between the two countries.

Yet, for all his lobbying, Brezhnev failed to achieve his primary objective of winning over Congress for the Administration's trade bill. The large majority in both the Senate and House had not retreated from its support of the Jackson-Vanik amendment. The amendment now had 77 sponsors in the Senate and 285 in the House.

Before the bill came up for final vote in the House (scheduled for October 17 or 18), fighting broke out in the Middle East. The Yom Kippur War significantly affected the character of the debate and the strategic maneuvering behind the scenes. For one, the Jewish community, the principal public backer of the amendment, now chiefly was concerned with Israel's survival. At the same time, a major objective of American foreign policy was to bring about a ceasefire in the Middle East, which in turn required the cooperation of the Soviet Union. The circumstances played into the lands of an Administration fiercely opposed to the amendment.

At this point, a curious if somewhat Machiavellian episode took place. On October 23, Kissinger, who had just returned from his whirlwind trip to Moscow, Tel-Aviv and London, met at the White House with Jacob Stein, NCSJ Chairman Richard Maass, and Max Fisher. Toward the end of the meeting, which mainly focused on Middle East matters, Kissinger raised the issue of the Jackson-Vanik amendment. He reiterated that the President favored the elimination of the Title IV (Jackson-Vanik) from the Trade Reform Act and then surprised his listeners by asking whether, in the event that Jackson and Vanik agreed to the elimination of Title IV, the Jewish leadership then would proceed to condemn the legislators. Since the Jewish leaders did not know whether Jackson or Vanik even had been approached by the White House, their answer was evasive. If, indeed, Jackson or Vanik agreed with Kissinger, they said, they would have to ask their constituency for instructions on how to proceed. The White House reinforced the clever Kissinger tactic. Peter Flanigan, its chief adviser on international economic policy, told Jewish leaders that the interests of Israel required the elimination of Title IV.

Jewish leaders had been scheduled to see Jackson on November 5. During the preceding weekend, word of the Administration's proposal leaked out and quickly generated a chorus of anger and concern in the grass roots of the Jewish community. The executive committee of the NCSJ rejected the Kissinger and Flanigan proposals. Instead, Richard Maass of the NCSJ was instructed to talk to Jackson about the White House position and to seek his counsel. The November 5 session with Jackson was the turning point in the year-long campaign. The Senator chose to invite, in addition to Maass and Stein, his principal legislative partner, Senator Abraham Ribicoff. After Maass reported on the conversations with Administration officials, Jackson and Ribicoff addressed the source of the Jewish community's anxiety: that continued support of the amendment might undermine or weaken United States assistance to Israel.

After the meeting, Stein and Maass immediately went to the White House to advise Flanigan that the organized Jewish community would continue to back the amendment. The following week, Maass issued a public statement to this effect. It made clear that backing the amendment did not mean the Jewish leadership had cut its ties with the Nixon Administration or did not appreciate its massive aid to Israel. What the leadership rejected, Maass emphasized, was the attempt to use the issue to weaken or remove the Jackson amendment.

The collapse of Nixon's strategy compelled the Administration to shift in 1974 to a new approach. Kissinger had to recognize the political reality that more than three-quarters of the Senate supported the House-approved legislation. He therefore, for the first time, entered into negotiations with the principal sponsors of the amendment, Senators Jackson, Ribicoff, and Javits. The purpose of the negotiations, which continued throughout the spring, was to find a formula to make the amendment acceptable to the Administration and to the Kremlin.

Ineluctably, the Administration was compelled to conduct parallel and interlocking discussions with Soviet officials to determine what concessions the Kremlin was prepared to make to satisfy the Senate. Kissinger frequently met with Soviet Ambassador Anatoly Dobrynin and saw Soviet Foreign Minister Andrei Gromyko in Geneva in April and at Cyprus in May, to discuss the matter. Two critical aims were central to these discussions: (1) ending the harassment of Soviet Jews who applied for exit visas; and (2) raising the level of Jewish emigration.

The accession of Gerald Ford to the presidency following the resignation of a disgraced Richard Nixon on August 9 was a decisive development. Not only was Ford, in the calculations of the Kremlin, an uncertain factor as far as détente was concerned; he also had committed himself, in his first public act, to a "marriage" with Congress. The Kremlin moved rapidly. Three days after Ford's inauguration, Dobrynin interrupted his vacation to fly to Washington, and the two met on August 14 to discuss the trade measure. The discussion was clearly encouraging. The President called the three Senators to the White House the following morning and offered them his personal guarantee that the Kremlin was prepared to end the harassment of Jewish applicants and to raise significantly the level of emigration.

The Administration-Senate negotiations now entered their final stage, with the NCSJ playing a valuable role. It spurred the opposing sides to reach an agreement, a task that was complicated by personality clashes. Initially, the negotiators agreed that Kissinger would write a letter spelling out the Soviet commitment on eased emigration procedures. Upon the insistence of Stanley Lowell, the new Chairman of the NCSJ, it was agreed that the letter would refer to "assurances" rather than a more vague term. Jackson then would respond by giving his interpretation of the agreement, indicating a precise figure of 60,000 as the expected minimum emigration rate, a compromise between earlier figures.

Announcement of the understanding was made by Senator Jackson on October 18. The prearranged Kissinger letter stated that "punitive action" against would-be emigrants and "unreasonable impediments" no longer would obtain. Only in the case of persons holding "security clearances" would "limitations of emigration" be imposed, and then only for a designated time period. Senator Jackson's prearranged response translated the assurances into specific terms. With respect to "security clearance" cases, he set a date of three years from the time they had been exposed to sensitive information.

On the basis of these understandings, Jackson agreed to propose an additional amendment to the Trade Reform Act that would authorize the President to waive, for a period of 18 months, Title IV restrictions with respect to MFN status and credits. Thereafter, the presidential waiver authority could be extended on a year-by-year basis, through concurrent Resolution of both houses of Congress.

A week after the Kissinger-Jackson exchange, Gromyko handed Kissinger, who was then in Moscow, a letter dated October 26, which complained that the letters presented a "distorted picture of our position." It stated that "we resolutely decline" the interpretation of "elucidations that were furnished by us" on emigration practices as involving "some assurances and nearly obligation on our part." The Gromyko letter was kept from the Senate—and the public. Kissinger made no reference to it during his crucial testimony in support of the Trade Reform Act before the Senate Finance Committee on December 3. He instead insisted to the

Senate committee that "assurances" had been given by Brezhnev, Gromyko, and Dobrynin to the President and himself.

On December 13, the Senate, by a vote of 88 to 0, approved the waiver provision, with the proviso that the President certify to Congress that "he has received assurances that the emigration practices" of the USSR will "lead substantially to the achievement of the objectives" of the Jackson-Vanik amendment. But on the morning of December 18, Moscow suddenly decided to react publicly to the trade measure. Its comments were unusually negative.

The Tass release revealed a totally new Kremlin attitude. Prior to December 18, the Kremlin failed to indicate publicly that it had second thoughts about the understandings reached between the White House and Senator Jackson to which it was a silent partner. What brought the changed perspective? Analysis suggests that it was triggered by another congressional action completely unrelated to the Jackson-Vanik amendment.

By December 14, it had become clear to the Kremlin that the Senate was about to approve an amendment to a bill that extended the life of the U.S. Export-Import Bank (Eximbank) for four years. The amendment, sponsored by Senator Adlai E. Stevenson III, would place a ceiling of only $300 million on credits to the USSR over the entire four-year period. It initially had been voted on favorably by the Senate on September 19. As the House version of the Eximbank bill contained no similar amendment, the issue went before a Senate-House conference committee, which adopted the ceiling on December 12. The Senate then began considering the conference report and after several sessions—the last on December 16—appeared almost certain to adopt it.

As Kissinger later indicated, the amount of credits permitted the USSR under the ceiling was "peanuts in Soviet terms." As compared to more than $1 billion in credits it sought for the next three years, the proposed $75 million per annum was a severe disappointment. From the Kremlin's perspective, the bargain that had been struck involving an agreed-upon exchange of money credits for emigrants had been unfavorably altered.

The puzzling question is why the Administration failed to alert the public and Congress as to what the Stevenson amendment involved in relation to the understandings reached on the Jackson-Vanik amendment. Strikingly, Jewish organizations that had a great stake in the emigration issue were totally unaware of the Stevenson amendment and its potential consequences. Kissinger was reported to have admitted to his aides that he failed to focus on the Eximbank bill and the Stevenson amendment when he should have done so.

An attack now would be mounted by the Kremlin against the entire Trade Reform Act. On December 20, both the Senate and the House approved the Act by large majorities. The very next day, December 21, the official Soviet news agency, Tass, unleashed the new propaganda offensive, denouncing both the Trade Reform Act and the Eximbank legislation as "attempts at interference in the internal affairs of the USSR." Several weeks later, the Kremlin formally scrapped the October, 1972 trade agreement.

The Trade Reform Act, with its historic Jackson-Vanik amendment, became law on January 3, 1975 when President Ford signed the legislation. As the very first piece of legislation that drew its inspiration consciously from the Universal Declaration of Human Rights, the amendment was ultimately to serve as a powerful lever on Soviet emigration practices. Even before Jackson-Vanik became law, it had compelled the Kremlin, in an unprecedented act, to nullify an education tax on exit visas. During a seven-month period while the tax was applied, 1450 Soviet Jews had to pay approximately 7 million dollars to emigrate. How many were kept from applying because of the tax is not known. But never again would Soviet Jews be required to pay an exorbitant ransom tax. The same leverage would be used by the United States with Communist Romania. Granted MFN status in 1975, the Ceausescu regime suddenly sought to impose a huge education tax on would-be Jewish emigrants in November, 1982. After Washington warned that MFN status and Eximbank credits would be withdrawn by June, 1983, Bucharest relented. The exit visa tax was canceled.

Nor would Moscow choose to disregard the message of Jackson-Vanik even after its vehement media outbursts of December, 1974. After 1975, the annual emigration rate of Soviet Jews rose, jumping to 28,000 in 1978 and an unprecedented 51,000 in 1979. During 1978-79, a draft Strategic Arms Limitation Agreement (SALT II) occupied a key place on the American-Soviet agenda, and Moscow sought to win support for Senate ratification of the treaty. Preliminary discussion concerning trade and credits also were taking place at the time. There was little doubt that the Carter Administration, with the backing of the National Conference on Soviet Jewry, was prepared to show flexibility in applying the waiver provision of Jackson-Vanik should an agreement be reached.

The Soviet invasion of Afghanistan in December, 1979 brought an end to the warming trend with the West. The resumption of an even more frigid Cold War ineluctably followed with a concomitant plunging downward of Jewish emigration rates. By 1986, the figure had reached the lowest level since the sixties.

With the emergence of glasnost and perestroika following Mikhail Gorbachev's coming to power, a new era in East-West relations appeared on the horizon. It found expression in the Helsinki process talks held in Vienna, especially during 1987-88. Moscow would commit itself to free emigration and the removal of virtually all obstacles to it. Even on the core issue of the national security device designed to inhibit emigration, Moscow was prepared to impose "stringent time limits" on the "state secrets" obstacle. Gorbachev himself made this commitment in an address to the United Nations General Assembly on December 7, 1988.

Central to Jackson-Vanik was less the commitments than the actual flow of emigrants. Implementation constituted the heart of the amendment and explains why Senator Jackson had insisted that a "benchmark" of 60,000 emigrants per annum was essential for determining whether a waiver of his statute was to be granted. From 1989 onward, that "benchmark" annually was reached and, indeed, exceeded. In 1989 the Soviet Jewish emigration total was 72,000; it jumped to 213,000 in 1990 and 180,000 in 1991. Since 1992, the annual emigration rate from the former Soviet Union has been over 60,000.

Appropriately, the waiver was granted and the Soviet Union and its successor states, most notably Russia, were extended MFN status and Eximbank credits on an annual basis. The very existence of the Jackson-Vanik amendment, together with the annual review, provided the leverage for assuring continuing compliance. President Boris Yeltsin, in view of Russia's positive record and eager to remove any obstacles to American investment and trade, sought to have Jackson-Vanik entirely revoked. When he met with President Bill Clinton at their first summit in Vancouver, Canada, in April, 1993, he vigorously pressed the issue.

At the press conference that climaxed the meeting, Yeltsin observed that the two leaders had "decided to do away with the Jackson-Vanik Amendment." The comment was hardly accurate. Clinton, in his press comments, merely had indicated that only after the White House was certain that restrictions on emigration were no longer being implemented, would he then be prepared to recommend to Congress that the legislation be reconsidered. As it happened, the Administration learned from the NCSJ that the number of refuseniks was disconcertingly sizable.

Given these facts, Clinton was hardly in a position to ask for a change in the status of Russia under Jackson-Vanik. Moscow had to do better and knew it. The next year, Russian Prime Minister Viktor Chernomyrdin came to Washington armed with positive details. It was on June 21, 1994 that he met with several Jewish leaders brought together by the

NCSJ. Besides noting the continuing high level of exodus, Chernomyrdin could call attention to the sharp decline in the number of refuseniks.

But that change would not and could not mean that Jackson-Vanik no longer applied to Russia, which was precisely what Chernomyrdin sought (as had Yeltsin in Vancouver). Enlightenment was provided by the late Senator Jackson's collaborator, former Congressman Charles Vanik. As an invited member of the NCSJ delegation, he told the Russian Prime Minister that the Jackson-Vanik amendment was "firm as concrete" in both American law and the American mind. Besides, only Congress, not the President, could remove Russia from the Jackson-Vanik rubric, and this was most unlikely. In view of Russia's (and the Soviet Union's) past record on Jewish emigration, as well as the continuing instability of authority in Moscow, Congress along with the NCSJ hardly could be certain about future Kremlin conduct.

Still, a significant step under Jackson-Vanik would be taken in recognizing Russia's compliance. President Clinton, with the support of NCSJ, formally affirmed on September 21, 1994 Moscow's "full compliance" with Jackson-Vanik. This affirmation permitted Russia to obtain MFN status and Eximbank credits *without* an *annual* review (by both the Administration and Congress). The removal of the burdensome annual review was strongly welcomed by President Yeltsin when he arrived in Washington shortly after Clinton's announcement.

Sakharov's "policy of principle" had come full circle. Approximately one and a quarter million Jews have emigrated from Russia and the former Soviet Union since Jackson-Vanik first was introduced, a testament to its power, as Yeltsin himself indirectly recognized.[29] But, it was also a testament to the determination of American Jewish NGOs, led by the NCSJ and backed by the Jewish community as a whole, to stand firmly behind the legislation in the great struggle on behalf of their beleaguered Soviet Jewish brethren.

Overcoming "Lingering Brickeritis": The Struggle for Genocide Treaty Ratification

While the call for American human rights leadership, intensely promoted by NGOs, produced a host of positive legislative initiatives that ultimately led to serious changes in a generation-old U.S. policy, and soon would be reflected in the Helsinki process, there was yet a vital human rights area in which time stood still for the United States. Ratification of the historic genocide treaty along with other international human rights treaties had lain in abeyance since the adoption of the Universal Declaration of Human Rights. Nonratification had reached such scandalous proportions that the International League for Human Rights, in offering advice to President Carter at the very beginning of his Administration, gave the subject the highest priority among human rights issues.

Central themes on the current worldwide human rights agenda are accountability and the absolute rejection of impunity for government leaders who perpetrate genocide and crimes against humanity. For that reason, much attention has focused upon the special International Criminal Tribunal for Yugoslavia, established in 1993, and a similar Tribunal for Rwanda, created in 1994. Strikingly, the United States initially occupied center stage. It was no accident for the first Chief Prosecutor of the Yugoslav Tribunal, Richard Goldstone, in a private letter to the American Embassy in The Hague, to call the United States "the strongest supporter and most reliable friend of the Tribunal."[1]

Yet, only a few years ago, the United States would have had no international standing to assert leadership in the struggle against genocide, for it was not among the nearly 100 states that had ratified the Convention on the Prevention and Punishment of the Crime of Genocide. Not until 1988 did Washington formally become a contracting party to that treaty, which had been adopted by the UN General Assembly a stunning 40 years earlier. Numerous examples of genocide had occurred in the four-decade interval—in Biafra, in Indonesia, in Iraq, in Burundi, in West Pakistan, in Cambodia, in Uganda and in East Timor—and, in each of these instances, the United States was silent.

The 40 years of self-imposed exile from the principle of accountability for genocide inevitably were marked by a continuing diplomatic embarrassment. The chagrin proved all the more disconcerting for those who remembered that the United States had initially, during the early postwar years, been the great champion of both the Nuremberg Tribunal and a treaty banning genocide.

What ended the long night of embarrassment and enabled the United States to resume a leadership role in the struggle for accountability is a story about both an individual and an NGO. That story especially as it relates to the NGO is told here for the first time.

An incident in January, 1964, at a meeting of the UN Sub-Commission on Prevention of Discrimination and Protection of Minorities, blatantly illuminated America's embarrassment in international forums in consequence of its failure to ratify human rights treaties.[2] The failure, itself, was a reflection of America's general retreat from the leadership role it had assumed in getting human rights provisions into the United Nations Charter and, later, under Eleanor Roosevelt's guidance, in having the world organization adopt the Universal Declaration of Human Rights.

The subject on the Sub-Commission's agenda was racial and ethnic discrimination; the discussion was preparatory to drafting a binding treaty on the subject. The American expert, Morris Abram, was more than merely knowledgeable on the racial issue. A bright young lawyer from Atlanta, Georgia, with Rhodes Scholar credentials, he had been active in a major civil rights struggle in his state to unmask the Ku Klux Klan. It was quite logical for this human rights activist to espouse the need for "forceful measures of implementation" in coping with racial discrimination.

No sooner was the phrase "forceful measures" out of the American's mouth than the Soviet expert on the Sub-Commission quickly challenged the integrity and good faith of the Atlanta activist. Had not the United States failed to ratify the most basic of human rights treaties, the genocide treaty? he asked. The less-than-subtle hint of hypocrisy filled the UN conference room, with the other Sub-Commission experts as well as NGO observers now focused upon how the American might reply. His response, despite the fact that he was, under ordinary circumstances, an extraordinarily articulate debater, was disconcerting. Obviously embarrassed, the American only could find the words to express "regret, of course that my country has not ratified the convention on genocide."

The harsh reality was that the very first UN human rights treaty, the Convention on Prevention and Punishment of the Crime of Genocide, which had been adopted unanimously by the UN General Assembly on December 9, 1948, one day before it approved the Universal Declaration of Human Rights, was, disconcertingly, not ratified by the United States by the mid-sixties. Nor had Washington acceded to any of the major human rights treaties adopted by the UN and its Specialized Agencies. It would take another quarter-century—exactly 40 years after the genocide treaty had been adopted—before the United States would accede to it.

That which made possible the ending of an American embarrassment and the final act of ratification was the stubborn determination of a group of American NGOs operating under the awkward and almost unknown umbrella rubric, Ad Hoc Committee on the Human Rights and Genocide Treaties. This group's struggle requires relating if only to underscore how NGOs have made extraordinary breakthroughs possible in the human rights field. In the face of serious political and constitutional obstacles, and frustrated by repeated rebuffs and inertia, both high and low, the Ad Hoc Committee held unwaveringly to convictions about the importance of America's role in advancing human rights and the rule of law through the ratification of human rights treaties. In the end, the Committee and its key constituent groups prevailed.

There was, however, a certain prologue to the story of the Committee that involved an NGO in the form of a single person whose lobbying made possible the genocide convention in the first place and, moreover, whose vision served as an inspiration for the Committee. Why he failed in persuading the United States to ratify his treaty, even if that seemed quite certain on December 9, 1948, has very much to do with an era of American history during which international human rights were perceived in a constricted and distorted manner that was provincial and isolationist at its core.

Winston Churchill had called the wartime deliberate mass slaughter of European Jewry "the crime without a name."[3] It was given a name—genocide—by a brilliant Polish-Jewish legal scholar, Raphael Lemkin, in a book he wrote in 1944, *Axis Rule Over Occupied Europe,* published by the Carnegie Endowment for International Peace. Lemkin simply joined the Greek word for racial group to the Latin term for killing. The new construct shortly would enter into common usage and international discourse in an extraordinary way. It became the veritable coin of the twentieth-century realm, as so many episodes of wholesale massacre have required its almost continual linguistic application. But, beyond the term itself was a new concept of international law to which Lemkin committed himself: genocide must be branded as an international crime that the world community must permanently outlaw.

Lemkin's concept ultimately would be crowned with universal acceptance, whether in terms of treaty enactment by the United Nations or through the enactment of implementing legislation on the national level in most of the civilized world. Yet, this remarkable trailblazer is all but forgotten today. The Lemkin name is inscribed nowhere at the United Nations, neither on a wall, nor in the cases that adorn the corridors, nor in special UN documents, nor even in popular UN works.

Lemkin's legal creativity led to his early appointment to the staff of Associate Supreme Justice Robert K. Jackson, who had been named as Chief American Prosecutor at Nuremberg. Lemkin spent four months in London assisting in drawing up the indictment of the war criminals, but he failed in convincing the prosecution to use his newly minted term, "genocide," in the indictment. A driven man, Lemkin flew to two separate peace conferences in the hope of persuading them to adopt a resolution on genocide. Once again, he failed. Dangerously high blood pressure landed him in a Paris hospital. There, listening to the radio, he learned that the UN General Assembly was deliberating about its fall agenda. Physical recovery would have to wait. In great haste, Lemkin checked himself out of the hospital and flew to New York's Lake Success.

The crusader's arrival in New York on October 31, 1946 provided little time for achieving a breakthrough. Only six days remained for having an item on genocide inscribed upon the Assembly's agenda.[4] The deadline was 5:30 P.M., November 5. Lemkin transformed himself into a whirling dervish, lobbying with a burning intensity all the key actors. Crucial to his success was the support of Ambassador Warren Austin of the United States. He was sympathetic and indicated that Lemkin's efforts would have his full support. Similar support was extended by the Ambassadors of France and Britain. Austin and his colleagues, however, advised Lemkin that for his objective to be effectively launched, he should obtain the agreement of several small powers to be sponsors of his proposed resolution.

Lemkin initially concentrated upon Panama's ambassador, Ricardo Alfaro, a distinguished international lawyer in his own right. He agreed to be a sponsor and Lemkin then quickly won over the ambassadors of Cuba and India. On the fifth and final day, the UN's "unofficial man" filed his draft resolution, signed by the essential three sponsors. But his lobbying had only just begun. Writing endless letters appealing for support from delegates and nongovernmental groups, buttonholing everyone who might be helpful and preparing supporting speeches for 30 different delegations, as per their request and, at times, in their own respective languages, he was a veritable perpetual motion machine.

In his lobbying, Lemkin hardly had a moment to himself. A friend observed that any empty office at the UN Lake Success headquarters "became his home." Days on end went by when he ate no more than a sandwich—or no food at all.[5] There were times when he fainted from hunger.

Victory finally came on December 11, 1946, when the General Assembly adopted Resolution 96 (I), which formally declared "that genocide is a crime under international law which the civilized world condemns and for the commission of which principals and accomplices are punishable." The UN vote constituted a virtual revolution in international law. For the first time, genocide was made an international crime. What still was required was the drafting and adoption of an international treaty that spelled out the details for preventing and punishing the crime of genocide. That would take another two years.

Lemkin as a zealous researcher, advocate and lobbyist comprised within himself all the major ingredients of an effective NGO. His was an achievement verging on the miraculous. Only heavily funded NGOs with large staffs can boast nowadays of achievements similar to Lemkin's lone accomplishment as the "unofficial man."

Yet, without the leadership by the United States in the General Assembly, Lemkin hardly could have succeeded. The U.S. role was similar to the one it performed at the precedent-setting Nuremberg Tribunal. As its major architect, the United States was able to provide a firm foundation for recognizing the rule of law as applied to criminal violations of human rights. President Harry Truman would comment in November 1946, a month before the Assembly resolution on genocide, that the "undisputed gain" of Nuremberg is "the formal recognition that there are crimes against humanity."[6] Nuremberg constituted a "revolution in international criminal law," an erosion of the earlier principle that the area of human rights was exclusively the domain of domestic legal jurisdiction. Included in "crimes against humanity" were persecutions on political, racial or religious grounds, whether or not sanctioned by domestic law.

U.S. leadership was particularly impressive in the drafting of the text of the Convention on Prevention of the Crime of Genocide and, equally important, the lobbying that brought about a unanimous vote for the treaty at the General Assembly meeting in Paris at the Palais de Chaillot on December 9, 1948.[7] The United States was the principal actor in the drafting process, while Anglo-American legal theory was the principal source for the text.[8] Indeed, the formulations conscientiously were couched in traditional American common-law concepts, including the very precise wording of common-law crimes long accepted in American jurisprudence. Of critical importance, in this connection, was U.S. insistence that proof of *intent* to commit genocide must be clearly demonstrated before an offender can be convicted. Intent is a central element of U.S. criminal law as distinct from legal notions in other systems of jurisprudence. It stands as the cornerstone of the genocide treaty. Thus, its key Article 2 outlaws "acts committed with an *intent* to destroy, in whole or in part, a national, ethnic, racial or religious group, as such." (Emphasis added.)

Comprising 19 articles, the last ten of which were procedural, the treaty confirmed that genocide is a crime under international law and defined "acts" of genocide as including killing, the causing of serious "mental harm," the inflicting of "conditions of life calculated" to lead to physical destruction and the imposition of measures designed to prevent reproduction of a group. Punishment would be imposed upon those committing, attempting to commit or engaging in a conspiracy to commit genocide. Also to be punished were the direct and public incitement of genocide and complicity in the act of genocide.

Particularly important was the provision stipulating that no one is immune from punishment, whether they are rulers, public officials or private individuals. Persons charged with the crime of genocide were to be tried by a competent tribunal of the state in the territory in which the act was committed. This would require extradition, and the treaty stressed that genocide was not, under any circumstances, to be considered a political crime precluding extradition. While the trial and punishment of genocide was left to national courts, the treaty, in Article 8, permitted a competent organ of the United Nations, like the Security Council, to take action under the Charter to prevent and suppress genocide. In 1993, the Security Council acted in part under this provision to create an ad hoc Tribunal in The Hague to deal with genocide in Bosnia.

A provision—Article 6—conceived of a possible alternative international juridical means of rendering judgment. Should an international penal tribunal be established and should its jurisdiction be accepted by the contracting parties (through a separate treaty) in a given case, then the genocidist could be tried before it. While the International Court of Justice could not try crimes of genocide (its function being restricted to the acts of states, not individuals), it was assigned the task of handling disputes brought before it about the interpretation, application and fulfillment of the treaty.

Adoption of the treaty by the UN General Assembly was a high priority of the United States, as important as the establishment of Nuremberg Tribunal. The thesis of accountability for horrendous crimes against humanity, including genocide, was central to America's concern. The U.S. delegation was headed by a top State Department official, Ernest A. Gross, an Assistant Secretary of State. He made it absolutely clear to all UN delegations that it was crucial that "positive action be taken now."

U.S. efforts were impressively successful. The vote on December 9, 1948 in the Assembly for the very first UN human rights treaty was unanimous. And two days later, on December 11, the U.S. delegation rushed to be among the first to sign the treaty. Signature to a treaty, in the context of international law, is a solemn and formal act. It signifies both a commitment to fulfil the purposes of the treaty and an intent to ratify it. The act of ratification (or accession) makes the treaty legally binding. The process of ratification varies from one country to another. In the case of the United States, the Constitution requires a two-thirds vote of the Senate, thereby providing "advise and consent."

Even with this constitutional obstacle, hardly anyone expected serious difficulties, and, indeed, the required deliberative process appeared to be moving rather swiftly. On June 16, 1949, President Truman transmitted the treaty to the Senate asking for its consent. A Subcommittee of the Senate Foreign Relations Committee held public hearings in January and February, 1950.[9] Testimony from most nongovernmental organizations was strongly favorable. Of a particularly strong nature was the testimony of the Truman Administration. Deputy Under-Secretary of State Dean Rusk emphasized two major points. First, in addition to the value of the treaty itself, ratification was essential to "demonstrate to the rest of the world that the United States is determined to maintain its moral leadership in international affairs." Second, Rusk noted, ratification would indicate that the United States intends "to participate in the development of international law on the basis of human justice."

The two themes—moral leadership and international law—stood at the core of America's foreign policy role during and immediately after World War II. They reflected a major and distinctive stand in policy-making since the era of Woodrow Wilson's administration. But loud negative notes emanating from the important American Bar Association (ABA) challenged the view of the government and the bulk of the NGO community.[10] They carried the sounds of isolation and insularity. More significantly, they carried weight with the Senate, itself largely comprised of lawyers and, therefore, respectful toward a body that considered itself the guardian and guarantor of America's legal tradition.

The testimony of the ABA focused upon two arguments. One argument took its inspiration from former Chief Justice Charles Evans Hughes, who had contended that the treaty-making power of the executive must be used only "with regard to matters of international concern." From the perspective of the ABA, genocide and other human rights issues were essentially a domestic matter and, therefore, did not meet the relevant test of the Supreme Court as to whether the genocide treaty was "properly the subject of negotiations with a foreign country."

In fact, human rights have been dealt with and protected by international treaties since the sixteenth century. The Treaty of West-phalia, for example, provided for equality of religious rights in the various German states. The Congress of Vienna in 1815 outlawed the slave trade and required the free exercise of religion. The peace settlement following World War I embraced several treaties involving the states of Central and East Europe that carried elaborate provisions for the protection of minorities. During the nineteenth century, the United States itself was a party to dozens of treaties regulating the slave trade. How these basic international facts escaped the ABA's attention is puzzling.

Moreover, the ABA argument failed to take account of the fact that the United States had ratified a host of treaties relating to the activities of its own citizens when those activities carried a transnational character. For example, cases might involve narcotics, public health or nature conservation. Certainly, a major lesson of World War II, as the Nuremberg Tribunal would demonstrate, was that genocide is quintessentially an international concern, far more so even than slavery had been in the nineteenth century.

The second major argument of the ABA related to the federal character of the United States and to the balance of federal-state relations. ABA critics of treaty ratifications pointed to the fact that murder was a state crime and, therefore, by making genocide a federal crime through treaty ratification, the balance of power in federal-state relations would tilt toward the federal government. However, this argument failed to take account of the specific constitutional provision that Congress has the power "to define and punish offenses against the law of Nations," and genocide firmly had been declared to be an offense against international law.

Strikingly, when Congress later enacted legislation in the civil rights field in the fifties and sixties, broadening the scope of federal authority in dealing with violence, the ABA continued to hold its earlier narrow perspective. Even when murder in certain circumstances was made a federal offense by Congress following the assassination of President John F. Kennedy, the ABA refused to budge.

In May, 1950, several months after hearings, the Senate Subcommittee reported favorably on the genocide treaty.[11] But, to meet objections made by the ABA, it recommended that a "declaration" be included in a Senate resolution consenting to ratification. That "declaration" would stipulate that Article I of the Constitution explicitly provided for Congress to punish "offenses against the law of Nations." This was intended to address the concern about the federal-state balance being maintained. The Subcommittee also recommended the inclusion of four "understandings" relating to the U.S. interpretation of certain language in the treaty. Particular attention was focused upon the phrase "in part." It was to be "understood" to mean "a substantial portion of the group concerned."

The full Senate Foreign Relations Committee never got a chance to act upon its favorable Subcommittee recommendation for ratification. One month after the Subcommittee vote, North Korea launched the invasion of South Korea that ushered in a new era profoundly affecting the fabric of American society. Powerful xenophobic forces were unleashed, significantly bolstering McCarthyism and the widespread anti-Communist witchhunt in numerous political and cultural quarters. The resurgent nativism buttressed traditional isolationism, which considered the genocide treaty and other international human rights treaties to be undermining American sovereignty.

Paralysis set in among supporters of the treaty. They were overwhelmed by a combination of McCarthyite and nativist forces. The treaty came into force on January 12, 1951 with the twentieth ratification, but the leader in winning its adoption simply had dropped out of the struggle. Indeed, with the ascendancy of a new kind of isolationism that concentrated only upon the Communist "enemy" in international affairs, some nativists were prepared to enact legislation that forever would limit the treaty-making power of the executive and, thereby, ban all human rights treaties.

Senator John Bricker of Ohio lent his name to the movement that would accomplish the task of reducing, across the board, the historic authority of the executive to make treaties with foreign powers.[12] In Bricker's opposition to the forces of internationalism and presumed subversion threatening American sovereignty, the major danger was seen to emanate from the United Nations. It was in the UN Commission on Human Rights that discussions had begun for creating legally binding covenants on human rights that, linked to the Universal Declaration of Human Rights, finally would constitute the International Bill of Rights. Senator Bricker now proposed an amendment to the constitution that would give effect to his narrow vision of America's role in the world and restrict the authority of the executive to approve all treaties, including human rights treaties. The nativist forces that had joined were gathering momentum at an extraordinary speed. Even the newly elected Eisenhower Administration, inaugurated in January, 1953, was fearful that the Bricker amendment would succeed in weakening the authority and power of the President in the international relations field.

To undercut the strong legislative challenge, Secretary of State John Foster Dulles chose a maneuver aimed at depriving the Bricker amendment forces of their primary raison d'être. If firm commitments were made to the Senate, as early as possible, that the Administration never would contemplate signing a human rights treaty, let alone transmitting it to the Senate for its consent, the Bricker phenomenon might disintegrate for want of a meaningful rationale.

Testifying before the Senate Judiciary Committee on April 6, 1953—only two months after the presidential inauguration—Secretary Dulles publicly promised that the Eisenhower Administration never would "become a party to any covenant [on human rights] for consideration by the Senate."[13] No longer would the United States accept "formal undertakings," such as treaties, in the human rights area. If human rights were to be promoted by the United States, it would be accomplished by "methods of persuasion, education and example." Dulles then added to his testimony the rather hoary argument that treaty-making could not be used "as a way of effectuating reforms, particularly in relation to social matters." Dulles concluded with a statement that may have undermined the Bricker amendment, but also deprived American policy since World War II of its moral greatness and legitimacy. It would be a reversal of the "traditional limits" in the exercise of treaty-making, the Secretary of State said, were treaties to be used for the purpose of effecting "internal social changes." But the very objective of inserting human rights into the UN Charter was precisely the attaining of "international social changes." And this was the purpose, too, of the planned International Bill of Rights.

With the Dulles doctrine striking at the very heart of U.S. foreign policy and at goals elaborated during and after World War II, a stunning anomaly in the field of human rights inevitably would present itself. The fifties and sixties saw the adoption by the UN and its Specialized Agencies, most notably the International Labor Organization and UNESCO, of various human rights treaties:

- on the status of refugees;
- on the political rights of women;
- on the status of stateless persons;
- on the abolition of forced labor;
- on the abolition of forms of servitude akin to slavery;
- on the nationality of married women;
- on discrimination in employment and occupation;
- on discrimination in education;
- on the reduction of statelessness; and
- on the free consent to a minimum age of marriage.

What was to be done about them?

These standard-setting instruments were climaxed by the UN's adoption in 1965 of the Convention on the Elimination of All Forms of Racial Discrimination and, in 1966, of both the Covenant on Civil and Political Rights and the Covenant on Economic, Social and Cultural Rights.

But if an elaborate legal structure of binding international human rights standards had been erected—together, in some instances, with rather modest mechanisms for implementation—the world's principal democratic power, which had been the leading advocate of human rights and the rule of law, now formally indicated that it would not embrace the structure. The historic breakthrough in standard-setting by the UN and its Specialized Agencies may have been of some importance to others but the United States would not become contractually involved. This would mean, too, that it could not serve on implementing mechanisms of the racial convention and the covenants, as only contracting states could be elected to them.

No one was more shaken by the Dulles doctrine than Raphael Lemkin. The creator of the genocide treaty considered U.S. ratification of the treaty as pivotal for the fulfillment of his hopes. He may have received world attention for his achievement but significant progress in winning world endorsement depended on the U.S. Senate approval of the treaty, which he said would "be an inspiration to the world."[14] He feared that people quickly would forget the lessons of the Holocaust. As it was, some people, he said, "still believe that Dachau, Auschwitz, and Buchenwald are manufactured war propaganda."

Lemkin, until the end, remained hopeful about the future. Shortly before his death, he commented that "I have made but a small beginning. So much remains to be done to make life secure for those who are oppressed."[15] Some five years later, in early 1964, a small group of professionals from major American Jewish organizations, prompted by a modest, though important, human rights development in Washington, met several times in New York to seek to pick up the torch and fulfil Lemkin's dream. The organizations were the American Jewish Committee, the American Jewish Congress, B'nai B'rith, the Jewish Labor Committee and the National Community Relations Advisory Council. All had been associated with Lemkin's efforts. Of critical importance to his very survival was the Jewish Labor Committee, which had provided him with a monthly check for personal needs.[16]

What had stirred a new initiative were actions taken in 1963 by President Kennedy. For the first time in over a decade, an American President spoke vigorously about the value and significance of human rights. In the course of an American University speech on June 10, 1963, addressed largely to the subject of bringing nuclear weaponry under control by the superpowers, he raised the rhetorical question: "Is not peace, in the last analysis, basically a matter of human rights?" One month later, the President provided the rhetoric with a certain resonance of action that, in essence, repudiated the Dulles doctrine. He sent to the Senate for its "advise and consent" three human rights treaties covering servitude akin to slavery, forced labor and the political rights of women. In his message to the Senate, Kennedy said: "The United States cannot afford to renounce responsibility for support of the very fundamentals which distinguish our concept of government from all forms of tyranny." The White House chose not to transmit again the genocide convention but a spokesman for the President did publicly state that "we share the views that prompted President Truman to urge consent of the Senate."[17]

It was quite natural that Jewish community organizations would use the opening provided by President Kennedy's action to formulate a broad lobbying strategy for human rights treaties that would reverse Washington's Eisenhower era policy and counteract "lingering Brickeritis." But, in formulating the outline of that strategy, top priority was extended to the genocide treaty, in which the generation of the Holocaust had a special stake. Preventing another Holocaust inevitably became a fundamental aim of that traumatized generation.

By the end of 1964, the group chose to create an Ad Hoc Committee on Human Rights and Genocide Treaties and to invite a host of organizations that had expressed interest to join it.[18] Rather quickly, some 40 NGOs, ranging from church, labor, civic, ethnic and women's groups to civil liberties and civil rights organizations, became part of the Ad Hoc Committee. The breadth of the coalition that was created could not fail to impress legislators. By the end of the sixties, it ran to 52 NGOs, a veritable "who's who" of organized groups embracing tens of millions of people. The first Chairman was Dr. Martin Dworkin, President of Manhattan Community College, who soon was succeeded by the energetic head of the Episcopal Church's Division of Christian leadership, the Reverend Herschel Halbert. Elected as Vice-Chairman was an experienced Washington lobbyist, Dr. Vernon Ferwerda, who was the Washington Director of the National Council of Churches.

The key administrative role was played by the Ad Hoc Committee's Executive Secretary, Betty Kaye Taylor, who served also as Assistant National Director of the Jewish Labor Committee. Both dynamic and diplomatic, the pert Ms. Taylor acted as coordinator of a far-flung NGO enterprise seeking to decisively affect national human rights policy in the area of treaty ratification. Assisting her and the NGOs were a number of individuals, mainly lawyers, who were serving the Committee on an *ad personam* basis. Three who stood out were Bruno Bitker of Milwaukee, Wisconsin, Rita Hauser, a liberal Republican of Manhattan and Professor Richard Gardner of Columbia University Law School, who had served as Deputy Assistant Secretary of State dealing with international organizations during the Kennedy era. All were active in the American Bar Association, whose significance, as already noted, was great.

Professor Gardner was asked by the Ad Hoc Committee to testify on behalf of itself and its constituent organizations on March 8, 1967 before a Senate Foreign Relations Committee panel (chaired by Thomas Dodd, Democrat of Connecticut). This was the very first time since 1950 that the Senate was holding hearings on human rights treaty ratification. It was a measure of the Ad Hoc Committee's impact that so soon after coming into existence—a mere three years—hearings were scheduled. Among the Senators who were especially responsive was William Proxmire, Democrat of Wisconsin, with whom Bitker was close. Beginning in January, 1967, Senator Proxmire launched an extraordinary effort of speaking every business day of the Senate on the genocide treaty. He would not falter from his determination to stir the moral consciousness of the country's legislators.

Gardner's testimony was forceful and oriented to demonstrating that human rights treaty ratification was not starry-eyed, but rather concretely served the national interests of the United States. First, he stressed, ratification would encourage other nations, particularly newly independent countries, to adhere to and implement human rights treaties. Second, it would place the United States in "a better legal and moral position to protest infringement of those human rights. . . ." Third, it would increase U.S. influence in the continuing UN process of drafting legal norms in the human rights field. "So long as the U.S. fails to ratify human rights treaties," he emphasized, "its views will carry less weight than they deserve." Finally, Gardner contended that ratification would end "the embarrassing contradiction between our failure to ratify these conventions and our traditional support of the basic human rights with which they are concerned."[19]

The theme of "embarrassment" initially had been projected in the public arena in an article in the *Saturday Review,* a major literary journal, in October, 1964 that described an American-Soviet confrontation relating to the genocide treaty.[20] The principal policy journal in the international affairs field, *Foreign Affairs,* carried an essay in April, 1967 which developed the theme much further.[21] What made the *Foreign Affairs* essay particularly important was that it was the very first time that this quarterly journal of the foreign policy establishment in the United States ever had carried an article on a human rights subject.[22]

The U.S. Ambassador to the United Nations at the time, Arthur J. Goldberg, who earlier had been a prominent Supreme Court Justice, indirectly underscored the "embarrassment" theme when he testified before the Dodd Subcommittee. He told the Senators that, during his tenure as UN Ambassador, he often was asked to explain the American failure to ratify the genocide and other human rights conventions. "Frankly," he continued, "I never found a convincing answer. I doubt that anyone can."[23]

The nearly total isolation of the United States in the area of human rights treaty ratification was suggested in the following data as of 1968: 71 countries had ratified the genocide treaty; 68 the supplementary convention on slavery; 78 the forced labor agreement; and 55 the convention on the political rights of women.[24] Only South Africa, Saudi Arabia, Spain (then under Fascist rule) and several small countries also had accumulated this record of nonaccession to all human rights treaties. Among the major powers and among the leading democratic countries, the United States stood, embarrassingly, alone.

The Ad Hoc Committee, besides pressing for Senate hearings to which it provided strong testimony, also concentrated upon lobbying within the American Bar Association, which had succeeded from the beginning in preventing ratification of human rights treaties. Its influence upon the Senate Foreign Relations Committee was decisive and, indeed, the President of the ABA had asked the Senate Committee to postpone any action on the three conventions concerning which it had held hearings in late February and early March until a key ABA group, the International Law Section, would assemble to discuss them in late April.[25] That section had on its agenda on April 28 a resolution moved by Eberhard P. Deutsch of New Orleans, the powerful chairman of the ABA Standing Committee on Peace and Law through United Nations. The Deutsch Committee asked the ABA to reject the proposed treaties as interference in U.S. domestic matters through the treaty-making power.

Leading the fight against Deutsch was Professor Gardner of the Ad Hoc Committee. Significantly, the International Law Section rejected the Deutsch resolution and, in a "straw vote," supported ratification of the supplementary slavery and forced labor conventions, but not the treaty on the political rights of women.[26] Gardner immediately wired the Senate Foreign Relations Committee to act soon on the human rights treaties "since it is now clear that there will be no common ABA position on the matter." His judgment was somewhat premature, although he was proved correct regarding the supplementary slavery treaty. At the ABA convention in Honolulu on August 9, 1967, the latter treaty was approved for ratification, but the one on forced labor was not.[27]

The Senate Foreign Relations Committee promptly responded with the half-measure of approving the supplementary slavery convention for ratification. The others were, not unexpectedly, rejected. Reverend Halbert, in a letter to the Chairman of the Senate Foreign Relations Committee, Senator J. William Fulbright, expressed deep disappointment with the Fulbright Committee decision. It was a "costly anachronism," he wrote, and he urged that the decision to table the treaties on forced labor and the political rights of women be reconsidered. Halbert also appealed for a vote on the genocide convention that had been "tabled 18 years ago for tactical considerations that no longer prevail."[28]

Fulbright was utterly indifferent even as he treated the Ad Hoc Committee to a certain condescension. Referring to the rather hoary constitutional concerns that the national federal-state balance of relations might be upset by treaty ratification, he added that: "much of the current pressure for action comes from individuals and organizations which have made little or no effort to examine the constitutional issues which . . . [they] raise for the United States."[29]

At the same time, Senator Fulbright was reluctant to close the door to further Foreign Relations Committee action. There was after all favorable testimony from distinguished figures in the legal profession, including Ambassador Goldberg, Professor Gardner and the ABA President, Orison Marden. Their powerful arguments could not be entirely dismissed. Fulbright acknowledged that "the area of human rights is new for treaty making" and "there appears to be no reason why these treaties should not receive further study" and be acted upon "at a later date."[30]

It was small comfort for the Ad Hoc Committee Secretary. In a year-end letter to the constituent organizations, Taylor expressed "grave disappointment" in winning approval for only one ratification. But the battle was not over. "Our efforts must be intensified," she said, urging that until the November, 1968 election, the Committee concentrate in "an all-out effort to see that candidates for election and re-election are asked to state publicly their position on treaty ratification."[31] At the same time, Taylor indicated that the "formidable obstacle" of the ABA must be given special attention.

The lobbying efforts of the Ad Hoc Committee, now largely focused upon the genocide treaty and directed at candidates from both major political parties, were not without positive results. Interest in and support for the treaty had deepened with even the Chief Justice of the Supreme Court, Earl Warren, choosing the twentieth anniversary of the Universal Declaration of Human Rights to publicly criticize the failure to ratify the treaty.

Of particular dramatic significance was the perspective of newly elected President Richard Nixon. On February 19, 1970, he sent a special message to the Senate "urging reconsideration of the Genocide Convention and the granting of its advice and consent to ratification."[32] It was the first time that a President of the United States had called for action on the issue of genocide since 1949, 21 years earlier. He deliberately chose not to refer to any of the other human rights treaties, including those rejected by the Senate Foreign Relations Committee.

One week after the Senate transmittal, the President wrote to the Chairman of the Ad Hoc Committee. It was more than a formal letter. Having learned that constituent groups of the Ad Hoc Committee were assembling in Washington, President Nixon wrote that he "welcome[d] your deliberations" and sought the "active support of your Committee" in pressing for "ratification of Genocide Convention at this time" because it is in the "national interests" of all Americans.[33]

Of special relevance was the role within the Administration played by his newly appointed Ambassador to the UN Commission on Human Rights, Rita Hauser. She vigorously pressed within the Administration for ratification and, indeed, drafted President Nixon's letter to Chairman Halbert.

Ambassador Hauser, who was an individual member of the Ad Hoc Committee, was performing double duty with respect to the genocide treaty. She had been Chairperson of the drafting committee of a special section of the ABA dealing with "Individual Rights and Responsibilities." The section report called upon the ABA House of Delegates, meeting on February 23-25, 1970 to ratify the Genocide Convention on grounds that "opposition" to it "stemmed largely from a fear of expanded use of treaties generally" and that this "fear is no longer relevant as treaties by the thousands have been entered into by the U.S. and others in the past 20 years."

The section voted favorably on the report in August, 1969 and the section council approved it on October 17. It was sent to each member of the ABA House of Delegates in early December and released publicly. The section Chairman, Jerome J. Shestack (recently President of the ABA), issued a statement that noted:

> Two decades have passed since the House of Delegates decided U.S. participation in this [genocide] convention involved risks the nation should not take. The world has changed and the presumed risks have

proved groundless. But the need for the convention is as great or greater than it was 20 years ago. It is past time for action.[34]

Shestack, along with President Nixon, would be greatly disappointed. Powerful legal specialists did raise their voice at the ABA meeting. The Solicitor General of the United States and former Dean of Harvard Law School, Erwin N. Griswold, pleaded for the ABA to help "restore this nation to the great role of leadership in international law." Former Attorney General Nicholas B. de Katzenbach warned the delegates: "The world is regarding you." The President of the ABA told them that, on the genocide treaty, "we stand alone."[35] The lobbying and pleas proved unavailing, although deep inroads had been made into the strength of the dominant leadership elements of the ABA. By a vote of 130 to 126, the ABA's House of Delegates voted against recommending the genocide treaty's ratification by the United States.

In a perceptive scholarly article written later, Shestack would characterize contemporary human rights activists to the mythological Sisyphus fated forever to push a giant boulder up a hill only to see it plunge downward shortly afterward.[36] Shestack's own struggle, together with that of his colleagues in the internal ABA battle, surely provided his imaginative insight with a certain buttressing. Failure in the ABA did not necessarily mean that the effort initiated by Nixon in the Senate was doomed. The ever-optimistic Senator Proxmire, on June 10, 1970, pleaded with his colleagues not to overemphasize the lack of support from an organization—the ABA—that was almost evenly divided "on the question of the Convention." He contrasted this sharp split within just one organization with the "unusually broad and active support" that the treaty enjoyed among the over 50 organizations comprising the Ad Hoc Committee.[37] He proceeded to insert into the *Congressional Record* the name of every constituent group of the Committee, the total of which represented "the majority opinion in this country. . . ."

By the following year, Ambassador Arthur Goldberg was chosen as Chairman of the Ad Hoc Committee replacing Reverend Halbert. Given his national distinction and the strong commitment of the Nixon Administration, hope for ratification inevitably burst forth. Goldberg, joined by Gardner, testified before the Senate Foreign Relations panel on behalf of the Ad Hoc Committee on March 10, 1971. The testimony was forceful and compelling. On March 30, 1971 the Senate Committee, for the first time since the Genocide Convention was turned over to it in May 1950, voted in favor of ratification by a sizable margin—10 to

4. How could "advise and consent" not be forthcoming? Optimists failed to take account of how a small, determined and astute group of parliamentarians can prevent Senate action just by the mere threat of a filibuster, let alone the use of the filibuster.

Opposition was led by a powerful and effective parliamentary tactician from North Carolina, Senator Sam J. Ervin. He and his colleagues exploited the well-known Lt. William Calley conviction in the United States for mass murder of Vietnamese to arouse fear that some foreign government might seek to try Americans on charges of genocide in Vietnam. Several Senators spoke darkly about the possibility that North Vietnam itself would attempt to put captured American soldiers on trial. That such an eventuality had nothing at all to do with America either ratifying or not ratifying the genocide treaty should have been clear. Still the concern somehow carried weight, so much so that the Senate Majority Leader, Mike Mansfield, Democrat of Montana, a key legislative figure, commented in April that the treaty "is in deep trouble. I don't know whether it has the votes."[38]

By the end of the year, Mansfield revealed to colleagues that he was prepared to bring the treaty to a vote by the Senate as soon as he had a clear indication that the body was prepared to take up the issue. This was noted by the prominent Senator Hubert Humphrey, Democrat of Minnesota and former candidate for U.S. President, in a speech in early 1972.[39] Humphrey inserted into the record a new special article on the treaty written by Goldberg and Gardner for the *Journal* of the ABA. A shortened version of the article appeared in the *New York Times* as an Op-Ed piece.[40]

All signs seemed to point to early Senate action. The Goldberg-Gardner essay concluded with the following: "It is inconceivable that we should hesitate any longer in making an international commitment against murder." Four leading Senators—Frank Church, Democrat of Idaho; Jacob Javits, Republican of New York; Hugh Scott, Republican of Pennsylvania and Proxmire sent out a rarely used "Dear Colleague" letter urging the Senators to join them in a bipartisan appeal to Mansfield to bring the treaty to the Senate floor for action.[41] The leadership of the Ad Hoc Committee, expecting finally decisive action, assembled in Washington for last-minute lobbying of uncommitted Senators.

What the Ad Hoc Committee learned was that Senate offices were being flooded by hate mail against the treaty, emanating largely from the extremist Liberty Lobby.[42] Nonetheless, the moment of truth seemed to have arrived, with every sign showing a favorable Senate vote. At this point, on October 5, 1972, Majority Leader Mansfield asked for "unanimous consent . . . that the Senate go into Executive Session and I be permitted to call up the International Convention on the Prevention and Punishment of the Crime of Genocide, and that there be a 4-hour limitation attached to such a request."[43] Senator Ervin, with his lone objection, killed a two-year effort.[44]

Two Senate champions of the genocide treaty—Jacob Javits, Republican of New York, and Proxmire—expressed regret, with the former stating that "every effort will be made to bring it up as expeditiously as possible early next year." Proxmire joined in the hope for action "early next year" because "it is a sad blot on the proud escutcheon of this Nation that we have failed to take action. . . ."[45] The Ad Hoc Committee activist from B'nai B'rith followed up the suggestion of the Senators with an Op-Ed essay calling for action.[46] But there was no indication by the legislators of how the obstacle of Ervin would be overcome. In February, 1974, Javits and Proxmire again moved for treaty approval but a sporadic filibuster by Ervin and like-minded colleagues prevented action, and an unsuccessful vote to end the filibuster killed the effort. The required two-thirds favorable vote to halt a filibuster failed by 6 votes, 55 to 36.[47]

Sisyphus was destined not to end his travail. The NGO community remained steadfast in its determination to prevail. A major breakthrough in the ABA in February, 1976 even encouraged a return to an earlier state of euphoria. The ABA, so long the champion of nonratification of the genocide treaty, completely reversed itself by an overwhelming vote on the issue. Indeed, it became a strong advocate of the treaty, and the Director of its Washington office, Craig Babb, now would play a vigorous and activist role in Ad Hoc Committee meetings as well as in joint lobbying of the Senate.

With Jimmy Carter in the White House in 1977, the Ad Hoc Committee resumed its pressure for early action. The Committee had been greatly impressed that President Carter, in a maiden speech to the UN General Assembly, placed a high priority on the ratification of human rights treaties. A letter from Betty Taylor to the White House on May 6, 1977 commended the President for the human rights perspective in his UN address. She went on to spell out the nature of the opposition from the Liberty Lobby and the John Birch Society and, at the same time, provided a tentative count for a consent-to-ratify vote and asked for the political assistance of the White House. "Without [its] solid help," Taylor's letter said, it would be "impossible" to obtain the 67 votes needed for consent.[48] The response from the White House came in a strong letter of transmittal to the Senate on May 23, 1977. The letter noted that already 83 countries had ratified the Genocide Convention.

Two days of hearings by the Senate Foreign Relations Committee followed, with Bruno Bitker now testifying on behalf of a major ABA section and observing: "Today it [the genocide treaty] is eligible in the Guinness Book of World Records as being the oldest treaty pending before the Senate."[49] It was a wry, if not sardonic, commentary on the mischievous record of the U.S. Senate. Arthur Goldberg testified once again on behalf of the Ad Hoc Committee, whose constituent groups, he said, carry a "total membership . . . in the millions." But neither his prestige nor the powerful legal arguments advanced by him and, now, the ABA could stir the Senate into action. "Lingering Brickeritis" had turned into an almost immovable inertia.

Only a genuinely determined U.S. President, prepared to invest some heavy political capital, could shake up the indifference that had gripped the Senate. But Carter's commitment to human rights was by no means a total one. Priority, he judged, had to be given over to favorable Senate action on a new treaty with Panama concerning the Panama Canal. This was accomplished in 1978. And then there was SALT II (the Strategic Arms Limitation Talks) with the Soviet Union, which consumed his attention in the Senate during 1979. The issue of genocide had to take a back seat. And 1980 was an election year, hardly an occasion for investing political capital concerning a human rights treaty. A letter from Betty Taylor to the Ad Hoc Committee leadership, dated October 29, 1979, summed up and reflected a highly skeptical attitude that the new Senate of 1981 would result in "62-65 firm votes for cloture. . . ."[50]

A new dimension to the genocide struggle was added when President Carter chose to sign on October 6, 1977 and transmit to the Senate three additional human rights treaties that had been adopted by the General Assembly in 1965-66: the Convention on Racial Discrimination and the Covenants on Civil and Political Rights and on Economic, Social and Cultural Rights. It became quite clear during the hearings that favorable Senate reaction on these vitally important treaties was even more unlikely than on the genocide treaty. The genocide treaty was far simpler in character than the others and offered far fewer constitutional problems.

A fundamental assumption and thesis of the Ad Hoc Committee leadership was that if positive action on these treaties ever was to occur, it would have to be preceded by favorable action on the genocide treaty. The latter was the key to the others. Without a favorable vote on the genocide treaty, nothing could be expected with respect to any other human rights treaty. It was the cork in the human rights bottle.

The problem was that inertia also had set in with numerous groups comprising the Ad Hoc Committee. Repeated Sisyphean labors had produced little. Various constituent groups moved on to other priorities. The victory of Ronald Reagan to the presidency hardly was perceived as an augury for a significant positive development in the human rights arena. Moreover, the talented coordinator of the Ad Hoc Committee, Betty Taylor, accepted a high-level position in the New York State Labor Department. (Her place was taken by the skilled Hyman Bookbinder of the American Jewish Committee, who knew the Washington political scene particularly well.)

Yet, the problem of U.S. "embarrassment" had, if anything, worsened. This was keenly felt by U.S. diplomatic representatives at the major Helsinki forums of the Conference on Security and Cooperation in Europe (CSCE). Arthur Goldberg, who headed the American delegation to the CSCE talks in Belgrade in 1977-78, testified before the Senate Foreign Relations Committee on November 14, 1979 that the United States was "hampered in seeking a full and adequate review [on implementation of the Helsinki Final Act] by its failure to ratify the international covenants relating to human rights."[51] He went on to explain that "we were challenged by the Soviet Union and its satellites. . . ." And he cautioned that Moscow probably would do the same at the forthcoming Madrid forum of the CSCE scheduled for November, 1980.

It was precisely the Helsinki process that, at its core, illuminated the ideological conflict between East and West and helped shape the perspective of the Reagan Administration toward the genocide treaty. Initially suspicious of the Madrid CSCE meeting, President Ronald Reagan came to recognize its value in exposing the human rights violations of the Soviet bloc. Elliott Abrams, his Assistant Secretary for Human Rights, urged the State Department to take a strong position on behalf of ratification.

B'nai B'rith, in the face of a declining NGO activism on behalf of the genocide treaty, sought to stir once again a national public interest in Raphael Lemkin and the issue of genocide. With the cooperation Vartan Gregorian, who was President of the New York Public Library and a leading academic, the mass Jewish service organization arranged for a major exhibit of Lemkin's letters, articles, unpublished books and memorabilia. It was to be held in the Library during December 1983–February 1984. The *New York Times* gave the story national attention with a headline reading, "Crusader Against Genocide Recalled."[52] Public interest also was stimulated by a host of Op-Ed pieces for the press, written by a B'nai B'rith professional.[53]

What especially sparked a renewed interest was a decision by President Reagan to use the occasion of B'nai B'rith's biennial international convention in Washington, D.C. to focus his address upon the need to ratify the genocide treaty. His convention speech would take place just two months before the presidential election. The Democratic nominee, Senator Walter Mondale, Democrat of Minnesota, also was to address the B'nai B'rith convention. Inexplicably, he chose to say nothing about the genocide subject.[54] On the very eve of President Reagan's appearance before the convention, he held a press conference and called for early Senate action on genocide in order to assist "our efforts to expand human freedom and fight human rights abuses around the world." It became a front page story nationally.[55]

The leadership provided by the Reagan Administration was crucial. In view of its conservative ideology, opposition from traditional right-wing sources was certain to be less intense and less shrill than it might have been for a liberal or moderate Democratic Administration. Still, the right wing refused to relent. Early in October, 1984, the Senate Foreign Relations Committee unanimously approved ratification, 17 to 0. The resistance only now would begin.

Old conservative fears surfaced about the weakening of American sovereignty, particularly in terms of imagined powers that might be exercised by the World Court. Anxieties among the Senate leadership that a filibuster might ensue, holding up all legislation at a moment when the political election campaigns were heating up, promoted an unprecedented vote not on ratification but on the principles of the genocide treaty. By a huge lopsided vote on October 11 of 87 to 2, the Senate adopted a resolution approving the "principles" of the treaty and pledging to act "expeditiously" on the ratification question at the next legislative session beginning in late January, 1985.

But "early action" in 1985 was not forthcoming. Conservative Senators, under the leadership of Senator Jesse Helms, Republican of North Carolina, who had inherited the mantle of Senator Ervin, insisted upon the acceptance of eight amendments before they might accede. What created conflict was right-wing insistence that the World Court not be given any authority under the treaty provisions except with formal United States approval. Since the United States already had given notice that it would not participate in a case brought to the World Court by Nicaragua, the perspective of the conservatives on the genocide treaty appeared to have little rationale. While the State Department initially opposed the proposed amendment, it finally agreed to accept what had been considered an unnecessary weakening of the treaty text. Strikingly, the amendment on the World Court was similar to the "reservation" made by the Soviet Union and its Communist allies when they had ratified the treaty.

Senate Majority Leader Bob Dole, Republican of Kansas, at a groundbreaking ceremony in October, 1985 for the erection of the Holocaust Museum by the United States Holocaust Council, gave public assurances that he would bring the genocide treaty issue to a vote.[56] It was patently evident to him that the official national focus upon the trauma of the Holocaust was scarcely consonant with the failure to ratify the only international treaty expressly designed to prevent another Holocaust. Senator Dole reiterated his commitment in November to a large assembly of Jewish communal leaders.

However, on December 5, when the Majority Leader sought unanimous consent to bring up the genocide treaty, two Senators objected: Senator Helms and Senator Chic Hecht, Republican of Nevada. This killed the issue for 1985, despite the firm commitment made by the entire Senate on October 11, 1984. A new argument was advanced by the two objecting Senators: that Israel would be the first to be targeted were the treaty to be activated. What this supposition had to do with United States ratification was not made clear. Besides, the supposition itself was open to question, since Israel had been one of the very first countries to ratify the treaty. This it had done on March 9, 1950.

With the onset of the new Senate session in 1986, the determination finally to act on the genocide treaty issue had grown. The Administration was pressing for action. The ABA, now in the forefront of a national effort of the Ad Hoc Committee, intensely was lobbying for a vote. Careful nose-counting indicated that close to 80 percent of the Senate would support ratification and that should a filibuster be launched, sufficient votes for cloture were at hand. (Cloture now required a three-fifths vote, no longer two-thirds.)

"We have waited long enough," said Majority Leader Dole on February 11. Firmly calling for a vote on the treaty (along with the eight amendments), he added: "As a nation which enshrines human dignity and freedom . . . we must correct our anomalous position on this basic rights issue."[57] The vote was indeed overwhelming, 83 to 11. It was a solid endorsement of the treaty, with opposition coming mainly from conservatives of several western and southern states.

The Senate vote almost had ended the four-decade-long American embarrassment at international meetings and regional conferences. However, one additional step—a critical one—was necessary to complete the ratification process. The treaty was not, as are other international treaties, self-executing. Article 5 of the treaty required the adoption of implementing legislation. It would take two more years before the House of Representatives, on April 25, 1988, adopted a draft statute making genocide punishable by life imprisonment and fines up to $1 million. The Senate Judiciary Committee already had approved the proposed legislation the week before, on April 14, 1988—Holocaust Remembrance Day. The Genocide Convention, once again, was in the hands of the Senate.

By early October, 1988 the draft implementing legislation had 59 cosponsors. Fear, however, of a proposed amendment that would add the death penalty as punishment for genocide had slowed progress in the Senate. Such an amendment, if adopted, would kill the bill, since many supporters of the treaty were, in principle, opposed to the use of the death penalty amendment. Senator Strom Thurmond, Republican of South Carolina, had been a strong opponent of the genocide treaty and was among the 11 Senators who voted "nay" on "advise and consent." Now, he was insisting upon a death penalty amendment. Until the very end, staffers of B'nai B'rith and other NGOs from the Ad Hoc Committee kept pressing for a compromise so that a final decision could be approved.

At the last moment, just days before the end of the 100th Congress, a compromise was reached. For several months, confirmation of the nomination of Republican judges had been held up by influential Democratic members of the Senate Judiciary Committee. In response to the threats by the Senator from South Carolina to introduce the death penalty amendment to the Genocide Convention, the nominations, which Senator Thurmond favored, would be accepted only if the Senator gave in on the death penalty. He did. Later Friday afternoon, October 14, 1988—six months after the implementing legislation had been reported out of the Judiciary Committee—with all the pieces in place, it was sent to the floor. Officially called the Proxmire Act, the legislation finally passed at 6:55 P.M.[58]

Senator Proxmire could take special pride in the completion of the ratification process. Since 1967, he had delivered over 3000 speeches on the Senate floor concerning the genocide treaty. It was he who had acted as the conscience of Congress in continuing to press his colleagues for action. On October 20, B'nai B'rith honored him at a reception in the

Dirksen Senate Office Building to which all his Senate colleagues and many NGO lobbyists were invited.[59]

The final step was taken by President Reagan on November 4, when he signed the implementing legislation at a National Air Guard Hangar near O'Hare Airport in Chicago. The President's comments were appropriate: "We finally close the circle today. I am delighted to fulfill the promise made by Harry Truman to all the people of the world—and especially the Jewish people."[60] He also made a point of referring to Raphael Lemkin. The founder of the historic treaty finally had his dream fulfilled.

Ratification had been very late in coming. It was 40 years since the Genocide Convention had been adopted by the United Nations. Ninety-seven nations by 1988 already had ratified or acceded to the treaty. The long dark night of embarrassment had come to an end. The United States once again could assert leadership in the struggle against genocide and in advancing the rule of law. And the task of ratifying other international human rights treaties had been made enormously easier. The seemingly insuperable obstacle to ratification of human rights treaties suddenly had collapsed. During the next few years, the United States would become a contracting party to several crucial treaties, each of which had an implementing organ in which the United States could play an active role. Especially important was the Human Rights Committee of the Covenant on Civil and Political Rights. In 1995, a prominent U.S. expert, Professor Thomas Buergenthal, was chosen for the Committee.

What ultimately brought about the remarkable achievement of ratification was an NGO committee, embracing a variety of groups, that simply would not capitulate. Unlike Sisyphus, its final effort was crowned with success.

CHAPTER TEN

"Heroic Reformers": NGOs and the Helsinki Process

Even while Amnesty International was being uniquely honored for its human rights work by the Nobel Peace Committee in Oslo, the UN General Assembly was engaged in a remarkable inversion of the language of the Universal Declaration of Human Rights. Strikingly, the Soviet delegate to the UN would welcome the "new United Nations approach to human rights" while the West would strongly decry it. But the General Assembly development simply had given legitimacy to trends within the UN that, with some important exceptions, restricted or prevented implementation of the Universal Declaration and sought to silence the NGO community that clamored for compliance.

Yet in striking contrast was the emergence, at about the same time, of a new regional structure in Europe to which the United States and Canada were joined and in which the struggle for human rights would become a central feature, challenging and ultimately undermining a great Soviet totalitarian empire. The new structure, the Conference on Security and Cooperation in Europe (CSCE), created in July, 1973, was given a statutory basis with the Helsinki Final Act adopted on August 1, 1975.[1] That Act linked human rights with security considerations while at the same time endorsing "the right to know and act upon one's rights." Specifically referred to and sanctioned was the International Covenant of Human Rights, as well as the Universal Declaration.

At the heart of the "Helsinki process," embracing all the countries of Europe and North America, except Albania, were forums to which

CSCE members could publicly bring issues, whether of a security or human rights nature (along with economic matters). The process would climax in 1989-90 with the success of democratic revolutions in East Europe, the collapse of the Berlin Wall and the adoption of a second Magna Carta—the Charter for a New Europe. A perceptive analyst called CSCE the "premier post–Cold War political forum"[2] while a leading congressional official, deeply involved in the Helsinki process, citing a roguish commentator, referred to CSCE as "the sexiest new acronym in international diplomacy."[3]

The first CSCE forum—technically, "follow-up meeting"—held in Belgrade, Yugoslavia coincided with the above-mentioned UN General Assembly meeting. If the Belgrade forum, to a certain extent, focused upon individual human rights spelled out in the Universal Declaration, the Assembly adopted resolutions that virtually scrapped the idea of individual rights, replacing it with collective rights. Priority was to be given to the "human rights of peoples" with the focus upon resisting "aggression and threats against national sovereignty" and supporting "national unity and territorial integrity." Of particular importance were the self-determination of peoples and the right of "every nation to exercise full sovereignty over its wealth and national resources."[4]

The Irish delegate expressed West European concern and irritation that "collective rights" now would be considered as taking "priority over the rights of the human person." U.S. Ambassador Andrew Young, despite his sympathy for the Third World, which was a moving force in the new UN thrust, bitterly complained that "the promotion of vital rights of the individual" had been subordinated to the proposed "higher priority." Western efforts to redress the new imbalance failed. An amendment to add the words "of individuals" in specifying rights and freedoms was voted down 54 to 63 with 20 abstentions. Another amendment that would add to the phrase "protection of rights" the words "for all, without distinction as to race, sex, color, language or religion" also was defeated. The resolution, significantly, said nothing about such gross violations of human rights as torture, extrajudicial killings, arbitrary arrest and detention and deprivation of speech, press and assembly.

No wonder the Soviet delegate to the UN embraced the resolution, calling it "significant." After all, it echoed the remarks of Andrei Vyshinsky in the famous exchange with Eleanor Roosevelt in 1948. The Russians at the time had insisted that human rights did not concern individuals but rather was "a governmental concept" that could not be considered outside the "prerogatives of governments." That view had been rejected by the Assembly 30 years earlier, but now was given a stamp of approval. Eleanor Roosevelt's contention that the Universal Declaration was an expression of individual rights and served as the "international Magna Carta of all men everywhere" now appeared to be in abeyance. The Assembly's automatic majorities of the seventies placed in jeopardy traditional concepts of human rights.

The contrast with the regional group, the CSCE, couldn't have been sharper. Here the Western democracies constituted a majority, neutralized however by the absence of any voting mechanism; instead, decisions were to be reached by consensus. To achieve consensus, trade-offs were required, which meant that, if the Soviet bloc wished to freeze postwar borders (and particularly the East German border), as expressed in Principle 3 of the Helsinki Final Act, to advance détente or to reduce military arms, it had to accept positive—even if limited—developments in human rights, as expressed in Principle 7. The adoption of Principle 7 in August, 1975 marked a signal achievement: for the very first time in history, an international agreement specifically recognized human rights among a decalogue of principles regulating relations between states.[5]

Initially perceived as but a modest instrument of détente, the Helsinki process took on an increasingly potent human rights dimension that produced the transformations of 1989 and led to the glowing hosannahs of the following year. What greatly contributed to the historic and revolutionary changes was the role of nongovernmental organizations, most notably those formed in East Europe, which indirectly helped shape the thinking and human rights policy of the West in dealing with the Soviet-dominated world of East Europe. Closely linked to their efforts was the work of certain American NGOs, whether in creating a special, largely congressional body, the U.S. Helsinki Commission, or in providing a rich reservoir of research findings and publicity to change Western attitudes toward totalitarianism and to assist the courageous pioneering human rights groups in the East. Of considerable pertinence was the recent technological revolution in the spheres of communication and information, which enormously facilitated the work of these NGOs.

It was in Moscow that the idea of forming a nongovernmental organization specifically oriented to the Helsinki process first was developed.[6] The originator was Yuri Orlov, a prominent physicist and member of the Armenian Academy of Sciences who, in 1975, had helped form the USSR chapter of Amnesty International. If other dissenters and opponents of Soviet rule—like Aleksandr Solzhenitsyn and Andrei Sinyavsky—saw in the Helsinki Final Act a capitulation to Soviet strategic interests and a betrayal of human rights aspirations, Orlov was struck by its useful, if modest, human rights features: Principal 7, which specified "respect for human rights and fundamental freedoms," and Basket 3, which spelled out the obligations of the signatories to attain a "freer movement of people and ideas."

When the Kremlin chose to publish the entire text of the Helsinki accords in *Izvestiia* in September, 1975, various readers, according to a chronicler of the dissident movement, "were stunned by its humanitarian provision."[7] For Orlov, an invaluable lever had been handed the democrats.[8] "It was the Soviet government itself that gave us something to work with," he observed. An extraordinarily perceptive analyst, he alone quickly recognized that, "if the Soviet government said [Helsinki] was important, it was, in fact, important."

Initially, Orlov proposed—on the basis of the recommendation of his colleague, Anatoly Shcharansky—that dissident and democratic members of the Soviet intelligentsia invite their friends and colleagues in the various Western countries to form NGO groups that would monitor compliance with Helsinki's human rights provisions. Once this was achieved, he thought, he and his associates in Moscow "can create the same sort of [NGO] committee at home with less risk of persecution." But he soon rejected this approach and dumped the already prepared appeal to Western intellectuals. Orlov had concluded that liberals in the West were so preoccupied with disarmament issues that "nobody in Europe will care" about human rights.[9]

The alternative had become clear. "If we wanted compliance with the Helsinki Final Act," Orlov understood, "it was up to us to monitor it." He formed the Moscow Helsinki Watch Group with about a dozen courageous activists who would accumulate a mass of carefully assembled data on all facets of Helsinki human rights abridgements by the Kremlin.

Moscow's Helsinki Watch Group took special note of a Final Act provision calling upon the citizenry of member states to assist in fulfilling their humanitarian obligations and, in its very first statement, urged that NGOs be formed in all signatory states to check on compliance. From these separate national NGOs there would emerge, the Group's statement hoped, "an International Committee for Support." It took several years before this remarkable vision would take root, first by the creation in the United States of a Helsinki Watch NGO and, a decade later, an International Helsinki Federation. In the meantime, the Moscow group prepared and distributed an extraordinary amount of detailed and valuable documentation on human rights compliance—or rather, noncompliance—by the Soviet Union. A modest 26 documents were provided for use by the West at the Belgrade review conference in 1977-78.[10] For the later Madrid review conference, during 1980-83, it prepared the striking figure of 138 documents.

Even as the significance of the Helsinki Final Act and its human rights provisions quickly were grasped by Orlov and his colleagues in the USSR, so, too, did elements of the democratic intelligentsia in Poland recognize that they now had a concrete focus for their opposition to the Polish Communist regime. The first expression of the new core of dissidents was an "open letter" sent on December 5, 1975 by 59 intellectuals, artists, writers and scientists to the Speaker of the Parliament and the Council of State.[11] The *Manifesto,* taking note of the Helsinki Final Act and its reference to the International Covenant of Human Rights, demanded fulfillment of the freedom of expression and of conscience. In concluding the *Manifesto,* the signers observed that the various freedoms, "confirmed at the Helsinki Conference," have "today assumed international importance." A crucial linkage, implied in the Helsinki document, then was emphasized: "Where there is no freedom, there can be neither peace nor security."

The formal nongovernmental organization that would give expression to the views of the *Manifesto* was the Committee of Workers Defense (KOR).[12] It came into existence in September, 1976, although, as a coalition of intellectuals, the yet-unnamed Committee already was functioning as early as June, providing assistance to workers in Radom who had been fired from their jobs after they went on strike. The bond between intellectuals and workers was to be the distinctive feature of Polish dissent as it developed into the mass organization Solidarity. But the key standard to which KOR would cling was the Helsinki accord.

Lech Walesa was to clarify and highlight the Helsinki linkage in his autobiography. After noting that "freedom of expression" was a "central freedom," Walesa commented that it was "a direct corollary of the Helsinki agreement."[13] He saw himself "as part of a vast pattern," and he "began to recognize an international dimension to our [Polish] problems. . . ." In that recognition, he said, he "learned of the existence of human rights groups abroad to whom we could appeal."

The activism of KOR was accompanied by the formation of the Polish Helsinki Committee (later called the Helsinki Committee in Poland).[14] It became the principal channel to the West of documented information on human rights violations accumulated by Solidarity offices throughout the country. Solidarity, as the successor to KOR, but with a greatly enlarged membership drawn from the working class, functioned until December 13, 1980, when the military coup of Marshal Wojciech Jaruzelski banned it. But its underground leadership continued to assemble and transmit documentation to the West.

Czechoslovakia's principal human rights nongovernmental organization, Charter 77, was formed but a few months after Poland's KOR. On January 6, 1977 the new group distributed a petition of 240 signatories listing in detail the violations of human rights in Czechoslovakia and demanding adherence to the Helsinki accord and the UN human rights covenant, which the Prague government had ratified the previous March and, ironically, published in the press in October, 1976.[15] Intimate linkage of Charter 77 with the Helsinki accord was made explicit in a letter signed by the group's leaders, Vaclav Havel, Jiri Dienstbier and Vaclav Benda, and smuggled out of the prison in which they were incarcerated.[16] Sent to the CSCE Madrid review meeting in December 1980, the letter said that "the creation of this [Charter 77] movement concerning human rights was actually motivated by the [Helsinki] Final Act." The aim of Charter 77 was held to be "entirely in harmony" with the Helsinki accords, as the text of the Charter had made "evident."

By 1988, Charter 77 was exerting such a strong public impact that it could hold large public demonstrations against the regime and garner petitions signed by thousands.[17] In November, 1988, the group formed a Czechoslovak Helsinki Committee. During strikes and demonstrations 12 months later, Charter 77 veterans created the Civic Forum, which, after organizing mass rallies and negotiating with the authorities, proceeded to take power in a coalition government on December 10— Human Rights Day. The "Velvet Revolution" had brought the NGO outsider to the very seat of authority.

What gave the Helsinki-created NGOs in East Europe, especially in the USSR, Poland and Czechoslovakia, far greater influence than their numbers would warrant was the recent technological revolution in the electronic field. In the USSR, as of 1980, there were more than 168 million radios and 100 million television sets in a population of 267 million.[18] Radio listening was particularly popular and foreign broadcasts hardly could fail to exert an impact. The major foreign broadcasting services were the Voice of America, Radio Liberty/Radio Free Europe, the British Broadcasting Company (BBC) and Deutsche Welle.

Surveys, while hardly precise but, nonetheless, carefully structured to ascertain the extent of the listening response, estimated that about one-third of the Soviet population listened to foreign broadcasts on a fairly regular basis.[19] Heavy jamming of Radio Liberty (RL) inevitably reduced the size of its audience. Despite the jamming, however, RL surveys indicated that almost seven million persons listened daily to its broadcasting service.[20] Jamming of Radio Free Europe (RFE) broadcasts to Poland and Czechoslovakia was far less effective, which helps explain the fairly high level of their respective listening audiences.[21] According to audience surveys of Poles in 1979, 50 percent of the adult population listened to RFE. The statistic went up to 54 percent in 1980, to 66 percent in 1981-82 and to 68 percent in 1982-83. In Czechoslovakia, too, the figures were quite high: in 1979, the listening audience included 35 percent of all adults and rose to 37 percent in 1982-83.

Programming on Radio Liberty and its sister network, Radio Free Europe, designed for the populations of the satellite Communist regimes, was oriented to the interests and "special concerns" of their listeners.[22] A primary function of NGOs in the USSR or in East Europe was to slip their reports, documents and statements to Western diplomats or travelers who then would make them available to the radios for broadcasting into the forbidden areas. Lech Walesa, Vaclav Havel and Yuri Orlov later would acknowledge how much the impact of their respective movements had been dependent upon the "voices" of the West.[23] Walesa, for example, when asked on November 15, 1989 whether he could estimate the degree to which Radio Free Europe was helpful to Solidarity in its domestic activity, responded: "Ladies and gentlemen, the degree cannot even be described. Would there be earth without the sun?"[24] The power of "the modern electronic media" was of critical importance in the spread of Helsinki ideas. A top Swiss specialist on communism noted that the media had compelled "the East European societies, long isolated behind the Iron-Curtain . . . to open up."[25]

It was in the United States that the studies and appeals of the East European NGOs found their strongest echo. U.S. human rights NGOs were to be vital participants in fundamentally reshaping the policy of the Nixon-Kissinger Administration toward the Helsinki process. That policy was one largely of indifference at best warranting nothing more than "damage control." Human rights, from this perspective, was totally inconsequential. The relationship between NGOs and U.S. policy in the Helsinki process cannot be understood apart from the largely congressional body the Commission on Security and Cooperation in Europe (the so-called U.S. Helsinki Commission), created by an overwhelming favorable legislative vote in May, 1976. It was this Commission that had served and continued to serve as the principal organ by which NGOs interested in the Helsinki process communicated with the U.S. government, although direct contacts by NGOs with the State Department and the White House also were maintained.

The idea for the Commission sprung from the head of Millicent Fenwick, a Republican congresswoman from New Jersey. An intelligent and sensitive first-term legislator, she was powerfully moved, while on a visit to Moscow in the summer of 1975, by traumatic stories of Jewish refuseniks who, desperate to emigrate, had been refused visas and, at the same time, suffered the loss of their jobs.[26] That something ought to be done for the courageous refuseniks was overwhelmingly clear to Mrs. Fenwick. She thought that the provisions of the Helsinki Final Act might prove useful. This perception was strongly reinforced by Yuri Orlov, who told her that, while the Helsinki Final Act was a "weak" document as compared with the Universal Declaration of Human Rights, it was "more important."[27] Upon returning to Washington, the freshman legislator introduced a bill creating a Commission to "monitor" implementation of the Helsinki accord's human rights sections.

The draft legislation, strongly opposed by the Administration, would have gone nowhere without the active intervention of the National Conference on Soviet Jewry (NCSJ) and several ethnic groups, including the Joint Baltic American Committee as well as Polish, Czechoslovak, and Hungarian emigré organizations. They saw the legislation as providing major leverage for assisting their ethnic brethren behind the Iron Curtain and they mobilized powerful, though separate, lobbying efforts to achieve this objective.[28] Strong backing for the proposed legislation also came from Freedom House, the anti-Communist human rights group headquartered in New York.

Once in existence, the Commission proved to be especially responsive to the constituent NGOs that had performed such vital parts in creating it. "Reunion of families"—a priority aim of the NCSJ to allow Soviet Jews to emigrate—became a priority concern of the Commission even as it began using the broader language of "the right to leave a country" or "the right of emigration." A key staff member of the NCSJ, Meg Donovan, went to work for the Commission soon after it was established. Frequent meetings and phone calls between NGO leaders and top Commission staffers remained a basic feature of the Washington scene.

Ultimately, at the end of the Vienna follow-up meeting in January, 1989, the CSCE would accept the new language on the right to leave or to emigrate.[29] The result was a flood of Soviet Jewish emigrants to Israel and the West, which fulfilled a major objective of the Jackson-Vanik legislation. The ramifications of the new language extended beyond ethnic minorities. It provided legitimacy and legal justification for Communist Hungary's refusal in the fall of 1989 to return East German vacationers, allowing them to fulfil their desire to emigrate to West Germany. The resulting torrent of East German emigrants helped spark massive dissent in the puppet East Berlin government, with the consequent collapse of both the Honecker regime in East Germany and the infamous Berlin Wall. The Helsinki process, which initially had been perceived by Moscow as freezing the status quo in East Europe, had achieved the very opposite: the torpedoing of the status quo and of its most important symbol, the Berlin Wall.

Perhaps the most important NGO to become involved in the Helsinki process was not in existence at the time of the Helsinki Commission's creation in 1976. U.S. Helsinki Watch, chaired by Robert Bernstein and directed by Jeri Laber, first emerged in February, 1979. With a top-level board of sponsors—many of whom were human rights activists—and a well-trained research staff, it soon became the recognized NGO spokesman on all Helsinki human rights issues. Because of its strong, generally liberal, civil rights credentials, it added a major dimension of credibility to the Helsinki process. All too often, liberals and left-wing NGOs dismissed or played down allegations about Soviet human rights violations as but an expression of Cold War conflicts and tensions.

The idea for creating U.S. Helsinki Watch came from former Supreme Court Justice Arthur Goldberg, who was chosen by President Jimmy Carter to represent the United States at the first Helsinki review conference. Goldberg was dismayed to find that American press coverage of the Belgrade proceedings was infrequent, limited and displayed little understanding of how the Kremlin and its allies were engaged in massive repression. Equally troubling was the extraordinary opposition he received from NATO allies and from neutral states when he urged that individual cases and names, like those of Orlov, Shcharansky, Sakharov and Havel, be cited at the Helsinki forum to highlight the extent of gross rights violations in East Europe.

In Goldberg's thinking, the grievous plight of the Soviet and East European dissenters was either neglected or discounted. Orlov's principal aide, Ludmilla Alexeyeva, later told international legal specialists that the attitude of European diplomats at Belgrade was summed up in the comment of one of them: "this is a diplomatic conference, not a boxing ring."[30] She recalled that Goldberg's initiative on human rights issues "was blocked almost completely." Orlov himself believed that the

European governments had a "Munich"-like approach to the Soviet Union and, in the interest of détente, were "prepared to sacrifice human rights in the USSR."[31]

Goldberg saw the need for a responsible and highly regarded American NGO that could provide detailed information about Communist repression that might sensitize Western public opinion. After the Belgrade sessions and upon his return to the United States he met with the President of the Ford Foundation, McGeorge Bundy, and prevailed upon him to help create and fund an appropriate NGO.[32] Further negotiations involving the Chairman of the Fund for Free Expression, Robert Bernstein, led to establishment of U.S. Helsinki Watch. A sum of $400,000 from the Ford Foundation for a two-year period initially was given to the newly created NGO.

Letters and documents in the archives of the Ford Foundation disclose the process by which the U.S. Helsinki Watch Group was created.[33] A letter from Bernstein to Bundy, dated May 23, 1978, referred to an "initial meeting with you and Ambassador Goldberg on April 5" in which the Fund for Free Expression would follow up with a request for an appropriation to set up the Watch Committee. The formal request from the Fund indicated that the Watch Committee would be composed of a representative group of prominent U.S. opinion leaders concerned about the need for "international compliance with the human rights provisions of the 1975 Helsinki accords. . . ."[34]

It was the projected "functions" of the Committee that were seen as especially crucial. The new group was to "establish liaison" with Helsinki Watch groups in other countries or in exile. It also was to "encourage the formation of such Committees in any of the signatory countries where no such group presently exists." The vision of the former Supreme Court Justice and the hope of the Ford Foundation were not misplaced. With its careful research findings always meticulously checked before publication, U.S. Helsinki Watch became a major source of information and documentation to the media in the United States and abroad.[35] It also became a leading protector of the East European monitoring groups by issuing a flurry of press releases when they appeared to be in jeopardy. From the perspective of the monitors—whether Charter 77 or the Helsinki Watch group in Moscow—the Bernstein group in New York would become an invaluable source of moral support that helped sustain them during their most trying periods.

In changing strongly held anti-Helsinki perceptions in America and in impacting upon NGOs in East Europe that led to the revolutions in

1989-90, U.S. Helsinki Watch, which began operating only in 1979, could claim considerable credit. Its Executive Director, Jeri Laber, undertook an unusually large number of personal missions to East Europe, visiting with NGO activists in Moscow, Prague, Budapest and Warsaw, and even in Bucharest and East Berlin, where the secret police regimes were strong. Her diary shows that between September, 1979 and June, 1990, she made four trips to Moscow, nine to Prague, four to Budapest, six to Warsaw and one each to Bucharest and East Berlin.[36] On the one hand, she gave the activists a sense that important NGO groups in the West were deeply concerned about their condition and welfare. On the other hand, Laber's talents as a writer enabled her to communicate through articles and Op-Ed essays to the American public the character and extent of repression that they faced.

A sampling of these essays in major newspapers and in *The New York Review of Books* illustrates how she sensitized the West about the problems of freedom that confronted the East European NGOs. In a July, 1980 article entitled, "Moscow vs. Rights," Laber described a meeting she had had the previous autumn in Andrei Sakharov's apartment with the twelve members of the Helsinki Watch Group who, while still "plucky," were "dispirited" by the "severe harassment" to which they were being subjected. In the article, she chastised a high State Department official who had urged that the U.S. diplomatic stance at the forthcoming Madrid meeting in November, 1980 be cooperation rather than confrontation. "To what end?" she asked. Instead, she recommended that the United States "demand that the Soviet Union and Czechoslovakia release their imprisoned Helsinki monitors as well as countless others being punished for their religious or political beliefs."[37]

The following year, writing in the *Washington Post,* Laber described an earlier private meeting in a restaurant at the Moscow Book Fair where Soviet dissident writers had gathered to advise her of the continuing ruthless suppression of free expression.[38] Soon afterward, Laber chronicled, with acute perceptivity and photos, visits with key NGOs in Warsaw, Prague and Budapest. The human rights climate in Warsaw, at the time, was as "unbelievably bleak" as the weather, for it was characterized by beatings of Solidarity activists, arrests and punitive harassments. In Prague, she learned how the regime was "apparently trying to wipe out its disaffected intelligentsia once and for all." In Budapest, where a "goulash communism" prevailed, arbitrariness was far less apparent and the activists could express dissent provided it did not target the Party or the Soviet Union. What especially struck Laber's keen political eye in 1981 was that "the Soviet Union's East European empire is crumbling" even if "the disintegration will not happen overnight. . . ."[39]

A kind of commentary on the role of U.S. Helsinki Watch and Jeri Laber, personally, would later be provided by President Vaclav Havel of the Czech Republic with whom Laber had been in communication, directly or indirectly. On his first visit to the United States after the Velvet Revolution had brought him to power, Havel made it his business to visit the offices of U.S. Helsinki Watch. He told the gathered staffers: "I know very well what you did for us, and perhaps without you our revolution could not be."[40]

Madrid, in November, 1980, was a milestone for the impact of nongovernmental organizations upon international discourse and diplomacy. It was, of course, not the first time since the end of World War II that NGOs had played crucial roles in helping shape the structure and policy of states and international institutions. But it was at the beginning of the Madrid review meeting of CSCE that the power of NGOs, both national and international, would help bring about a fundamental change in the character of the Helsinki process. And that change ultimately would trigger the revolutions that closed the decade.

How Madrid appeared on the opening day of the Helsinki conference was powerfully captured in *Le Monde* with the marvelously descriptive phrase "city of dissidence."[41] The Spanish capital had become a magnet for dissidents and democratic activists from every part of East Europe, along with their human rights champions and advocates in the West. Wives and relatives of Soviet "prisoners of conscience" and refuseniks mingled with representatives of Western nongovernmental human rights organizations in rallies, demonstrations, press conferences and mini–review sessions. Displays and leaflets, films and posters, and books and recordings were everywhere. The corridors of the Helsinki sessions and of nearby hotels were sites for hurried press conferences given by, for example, Nina Lagergren (the half-sister of Raoul Wallenberg) and Anatoly Shcharansky's wife, Avital.[42]

Especially active in arranging for public exposure of Soviet and East European activists who were present was U.S. Helsinki Watch, which leased office space and staffed it with a highly skilled professional. Though only a year old, U.S. Helsinki Watch already was functioning with considerable effectiveness in lobbying CSCE delegations, providing well-researched documentation on human rights violations to the hundreds of media correspondents who had descended upon Madrid and hosting NGO representatives from the Communist world.

To a far greater degree than the meeting in Belgrade, where the first Helsinki conference was held, Madrid had become the stage for grand human rights theater. One reason was its accessibility; the city was close to most Western countries and to NGOs headquarters. A second was the strong democratic character of Spanish society and the Spanish government, in contrast to Yugoslavia, where a certain arbitrariness befitting an authoritarian regime made for caution and restraint in any public display of support for human rights. A third reason was the Western public reaction to Moscow's repression of the several Helsinki Watch groups.[43] Of the 71 individuals who comprised the half-dozen Helsinki monitoring groups in the USSR, 24 had been tried and found guilty, with 19 of them serving a total of 156 years in forced labor or internal exile.

A fourth and final reason was critical. New NGOs had come into existence since Belgrade, fiercely determined to champion human rights without holding to a particular political point of view. Other, older NGOs had become even more active and more effectively organized than that had been earlier. The National Conference on Soviet Jewry, together with newly formed similar Jewish groups from West Europe, Latin America and Israel—which ultimately formed the World Conference on Soviet Jewry—set up a full-time reception center, arranged for continuous lobbying of delegations by a group of professionals who provided meticulously prepared research studies and hosted a variety of functions.

Responsiveness to NGO pressures and activism on the part of Western governments was extraordinary. At Belgrade, not a single West European delegation had chosen to enter into a direct confrontation with the USSR or with its Warsaw Pact allies. Madrid was a historic breakthrough and set a totally new standard. Never in a formal international setting had so many countries raised human rights issues.[44] Twenty-six delegations condemned Soviet human rights actions in Afghanistan. Nine Western delegations raised questions about various aspects of the Soviet treatment of Jews. This was totally unprecedented. One NATO country—Belgium—took the risk of openly accusing Moscow of anti-Semitism. As for the United States, it raised some 65 East European cases during the first six-week period and nearly 250 more during the balance of the Madrid meeting (ending in September, 1983).

Of course, American diplomacy had a great deal to do with the new posture of its NATO allies and the neutrals. Ambassador Max Kampelman, the head of the U.S. delegation, was far more tactful and flexible than the often arrogant Goldberg in negotiations with his colleagues. He also was tough-minded and determined to expose the Soviet Achilles' heel on human rights to public view. Without such exposure, Western public opinion would be unprepared to accept major military steps by the West to offset Soviet military might. As "Mr. CSCE," as he became known, Kampelman strongly championed human rights themes. But, there can be little doubt that what enormously aided him in his objective was the crucial new factor in international affairs or rather regional affairs—NGOs—that played a vital role in motivating states to be responsive in the Helsinki process.

During and after Madrid, major national NGOs became the core of larger, international NGOs. Thus, the National Conference on Soviet Jewry helped create the World Conference on Soviet Jewry. The world body, staffed with professionals from each of the constituents, served as coordinator for the separate geographical groups, a sponsor of joint studies and a regulator of lobbying activities during the various Helsinki meetings. Its most significant achievement came at the Copenhagen CSCE meeting on the human dimension in June, 1990.

The document that emerged in Copenhagen, important in a number of ways, carried a condemnation of xenophobia, racism and anti-Semitism—unprecedented in international agreements—that called upon all CSCE governments to take effective measures to combat various forms of bigotry.[45] Among these measures were public denunciations by high government officials, antidiscrimination laws and educational programs. The specific reference to anti-Semitism was unexpected. At the beginning of the Copenhagen meeting, no delegation had advanced any proposal incorporating that term.

What made the activism of the World Conference and its U.S. constituent—the NCSJ—of vital importance was the fact that the major ingredients of the Copenhagen document would be incorporated in the Charter for a New Europe adopted in Paris in November, 1990 by the heads of the CSCE states. The Charter appropriately would be called the second "Magna Carta" by no less an authority than the British Prime Minister, Margaret Thatcher.

Of particular importance was the decision in 1982 by the U.S. Helsinki Watch to create, with the assistance of the Ford Foundation, similar Helsinki NGOs in a number of European countries, both West and East. Jeri Laber spent most of the year traveling in Europe for that purpose—a "turning point," in the history of the Helsinki NGO movement, she later said.[46] What would emerge by late 1987 was an International Helsinki Federation (IHF), headquartered in Vienna and comprising groups in the Netherlands, the Nordic countries, Austria, Switzerland, Poland, Czechoslovakia, Slovenia and the United States.

By 1988, the IHF was functioning as an effective coordinating instrument for consciousness-raising about human rights. Its former Director, Lotte Leicht, a Danish lawyer, observed that the international NGO's purpose was to make sure "that there will never be an excuse that we didn't know."[47] The lesson of the Holocaust clearly had been driven home. Sharing information on human rights violations, together with lobbying, was the organization's purpose. For documentation and studies, the IHF would rely on the U.S. Helsinki Watch.

At the beginning of the Helsinki process, governments were perceived as the sole actors in what was essentially a forum of interstate diplomacy. If the Helsinki Final Act made several references to NGOs, particularly to their role in science and technology, environmental protection, human contacts, culture and education, they still were viewed as but tangential and incidental to the process. But, by the end of 1991, the Foreign Minister of Norway, Thorwald Stoltenberg, would say that the CSCE was a process involving the interaction of governments with NGOs. The latter, he stressed, "are an important repository of insights, expertise and experience."[48] If building demo-cratic institutions, Stoltenberg went on, was to be "a priority task of the CSCE," then this purpose could be greatly facilitated by construc-tive use of NGO resources.

It was at the Vienna follow-up meeting during 1986-89 that a more integral, if still quite modest, formal relationship of NGOs to the process was set forth. The concluding document at Vienna underscored what already had been apparent at Madrid—that NGOs had the right of access to Helsinki meetings, the right to attend open CSCE sessions, the right to contact delegates, the right to meet with host state citizens and the right to hold assemblages on the periphery of CSCE meetings.[49] A significant step forward was taken at Copenhagen in June, 1990, following the revolutionary changes in East Europe. The document adopted by the human dimension meeting frequently mentioned the NGOs' role in prompting tolerance, cultural diversity and the resolution of questions relating to ethnic minorities. Once again, access to CSCE meetings, delegates and documents was emphasized.

Recognition of the important part performed by NGOs in the Helsinki process finally was adopted at the Paris summit meeting in November, 1990. The heads of the CSCE states expressed appreciation for "the major role that NGOs, religious and other groups and individuals have played in the achievement of the objectives of the CSCE."[50] The Charter promised that the CSCE would "further facilitate their [NGOs'] activities for the implementation of the CSCE commitments by the participating states." Taking note of the new CSCE institutions created at the Paris summit, the Charter assured NGOs that they would "be involved in an appropriate way in the activities and new structures of the CSCE in order to fulfil their important tasks."

NGOs did develop a close relationship with a separate new CSCE institution located in Warsaw: the Office for Democratic Institutions and Human Rights (ODIHR), initially called the Office for Free Elections. But with the deepening of ethnic tensions and open conflict in the Former Yugoslavia and the Former USSR after 1991, the focus of the CSCE came to center upon crisis management and conflict prevention at the expense of the human dimension. ODIHR found itself at the margin of CSCE priorities. From the NGO perspective, this was unacceptable. Especially sensitive to the evidence of genocide in Bosnia, human rights NGOs recognized that conflict prevention and crisis management in ethnic matters could not be dealt with effectively except as a facet of the minority rights issue—and, therefore, as a facet of the human dimension, or human rights.

In January, 1992, the Council of (Foreign) Ministers appeared to take a major step toward blending these two viewpoints.[51] It requested that the forthcoming review meeting scheduled for Helsinki attempt to "strengthen the relations between the CSCE and NGOs in order to increase the role of NGOs in implementing CSCE goals and commitments." More specifically, the review meeting was asked to "develop opportunities and procedures for meaningful NGO involvement in the CSCE and possibilities for NGOs to communicate with structures and institutions." If, clearly, the Council wanted to broaden the role and influence of NGOs, it still shied away from specifics.

NGOs themselves, prior to and during the meeting in Helsinki (March-July, 1992), vigorously argued that they should be included in all aspects of the CSCE process, not merely the human dimension aspect.[52] Guidelines established in Moscow for the human dimension should be extended to all areas, they contended. At the Helsinki meeting, they advanced proposals for unlimited NGO involvement in the entire CSCE process on an equal basis with government delegations.

The Helsinki meeting refused to go that far, although the opening to greater involvement was widened.[53] Guidelines heretofore agreed upon only for "certain CSCE meetings" now were to "apply to all meetings." Briefings and a general broader flow of information to NGOs were extended. Full access was assured to all plenaries, ODIHR seminars and workshops, implementation review sessions and experts' meetings. "NGO liaison persons" were to be designated by all CSCE institutions, foreign ministries and delegations with whom NGOs would have continuing contact and exchanges of views. NGOs also would be able to submit written presentations to CSCE seminars.

However, meetings of the Council of (Foreign) Ministers, the Committee of Senior Officials and working groups of review conferences remained off-limits for NGOs. NGO proposals for involvement on an equal basis with government delegations clearly were rebuffed. One of the more powerful NGOs, Amnesty International, which had become active in CSCE affairs after the democratic revolutions and the collapse of communism in East Europe, reacted with irritation: "Despite a few specific improvements, Helsinki II still leaves NGOs on the outside of the CSCE trying to look in through opaque glass. If the CSCE really wants to develop its 'early warning' capacities, it needs to integrate NGOs into the human rights process."[54]

For the NGOs, especially for such prime movers as IHF and, more recently, Amnesty International, the crucial issues centered on the following: Would the decisive Helsinki power sources include the human dimension facet in their regular deliberations on European security? Would the various CSCE missions, mainly rooted in security concerns, be assigned a human rights component? How could ODIHR be strengthened? And, how could NGOs be empowered so they might be centrally involved at least in the human dimension aspect?

Positive answers were provided by CSCE in the last quarter of 1993, partly in consequence of heavy lobbying by IHF and Amnesty International and a host of other NGOs. At the CSCE Human Dimension Implementation Meeting held in Warsaw, September 28–October 14, 1993, the rules governing NGO access were interpreted very flexibly and liberally.[55] NGOs were allowed to participate actively in plenary sessions and to deliver oral statements in the two subsidiary working groups. The latter development was an altogether new departure. The IHF, for example, delivered four oral statements that included such topics as torture in Turkey and the increasingly difficult situation of the Gypsies. In addition, it raised each of the core issues, noted above, for enhancing the role of NGOs.

Especially important was a crucial step involving NGOs as a means of strengthening ODIHR. NGOs were called upon to "channel information to ODIHR concerning reports of nonimplementation" by CSCE states.[56] Heretofore, CSCE procedures permitted only states to provide its institutions information on noncompliance (although, of course, states often derived such information from their own or other NGOs). Authorization of this new, official NGO function constituted a significant breakthrough.

A limited test case of NGO status was provided at the major CSCE review meeting in Budapest, October 10–December 2, 1994, where the body was renamed the Organization on Security and Cooperation in Europe (OSCE).[57] On the one hand, NGOs were provided with virtually unlimited rights to address the working group dealing with the human dimension and to impact upon its decisions. Those hostile to the enhanced NGO role, like France and Turkey, sought to place obstacles in the path of NGO activism, but they were unsuccessful. On the other hand, NGOs failed to achieve parity with governments in the drafting process of resolutions. And their role in the working groups concerning security issues or conflict prevention remained quite limited. The mixed outcome is unlikely to change to any great extent in the immediate future, although the concluding document of the meeting gave special emphasis to the importance of NGOs and the need for their "increased involvement."

Involvement of NGOs in OSCE, a regional operation, formally linked to the United Nations, became increasingly intense in the last few years. At the Budapest review meeting, a total of 305 NGOs participated, with 57 submitting written presentations. Human Dimension seminars run by ODIHR especially attracted them. A seminar in 1993 entitled "Tolerance" brought 17 of the NGOs to Warsaw for a valuable exchange. More impressive was their participation in 1994 in a seminar on Roma (Gypsies), where a total of 71 NGOs added considerable light in dealing with a difficult problem of prejudice and stereotyping.[58]

That NGOs have begun to move even into the crucial political arena of preventive diplomacy is suggested by a seminar on the subject held in Warsaw in January, 1994. A number of NGOs volunteered how they might play a significant role in early warning problems and conflict prevention. Later that year, in September, the dialogue on the subject was furthered by a special seminar held in Austria that was attended by OSCE officials and heads of OSCE delegations and in which 20 NGOs, active in the field of conflict prevention, played a leading role.

Exploration at a high OSCE level continues into how NGOs can provide even greater assistance. The Budapest Summit of 1994, for example, requested the Secretary-General of the OSCE, its newest and highest administrative official, to prepare a study to ascertain in what way NGO participation can be enhanced further. Inquiry was to be made of each participating OSCE state as well as the 600 NGOs registered with the organization. In September, 1995, the Secretary-General was prepared to move beyond the exploratory phase, offering a number of specific proposals that enhanced NGO status in a variety of technical and procedural ways.

Nowhere at the UN or in its other affiliated regional structures had NGOs succeeded in coming close to the status occupied by NGOs in OSCE. Still, their current role remains a far cry from the politically vital and dynamic activism that had characterized human rights struggles during the Helsinki process of the seventies and eighties. Those struggles, which inevitably carried a certain romantic quality at the time for which the advocates of realpolitik registered disinterest, if not total contempt, nowadays evoke recognition and praise.

Exemplifying this belated change of heart is the archexponent of realpolitik, Henry A. Kissinger. His work, *Diplomacy,* published in 1994, offered an unexpected and uncharacteristic afterthought. Kissinger now acknowledged that Basket 3 (which he earlier had never even noticed) turned out to be "most significant" and "was destined to play a major role in the disintegration of the Soviet satellite orbit. . . ." He went on to add the startlingly unbecoming comment that Basket 3 "became a testimonial to all human rights activists in NATO countries." It was these human rights activists, he suddenly recognized, "who deserve tribute," for it was "the pressures which they exerted" that hastened the end of totalitarian rule. Especially accorded praise were the "heroic reformers in Eastern Europe" who used Basket 3 as "a rallying point" in their struggle against "Soviet domination."

"The Fuel and the Lubricant": NGOs and the Revolution in UN Human Rights Implementation Machinery

In 1979, the Council on Foreign Relations in New York, while seeking to anticipate international human rights developments for the next decade, invited the leading legal specialist of London's prizewinning Amnesty International to speculate about how human rights would fare at the United Nations. Nigel Rodley, despite Amnesty's achievements regarding prisoners of conscience and, especially, torture, was distinctly skeptical and, indeed, quite pessimistic about the future. In a perceptive review and analysis of the existing UN human rights machinery, he concluded that the international organization neither would, nor could, engage "in a systematic and unpartial program of monitoring even the most serious incidents of human rights violations in the world, at least within the next generation."[1]

The best that could be hoped for, said the Amnesty specialist, was the prevention of the "erosion of such gains as have already been achieved." Reviewing the historic Resolution 1503, which many had thought would offer a meaningful mechanism for the protection of human rights, Rodley found that it "has not even yielded . . . one thorough study or investigation." As for the mechanisms created for the implementation of various human rights treaties, like the Covenant on Civil and Political Rights, they "hold out little better prospect." And little, he thought, could be expected from the "fruitlessly debated" issue of a High Commissioner for Human Rights. If authorization was given to the 1975 Chilean investigation—which he recognized as "a significant precedent and as a valuable contribution"—it was only because of "a rare conjunction of widely shared feelings of repugnance for the [Chilean] junta. . . ." Rodley did not expect the "rare conjunction" to reoccur.

In reality and in striking contrast to Rodley's expectations, the eighties were marked by significant human rights breakthroughs at the UN involving the creation of a host of implementation mechanisms, which, while modestly effective, augured encouragingly for the future. The initial revolutionary act that concerned disappearances came in 1980 at the Commission of Human Rights, only one year after Rodley's dark prediction. What was striking about the radical and unprecedented step was that it was pushed through largely by the state power of the United States. Without the leverage, diplomatic and political, offered by a major international player—and in the human rights field only the United States could perform that function—the transforming initiative simply could not have been realized.

That, of course, was the case in the Helsinki process, in which key U.S. officials, bolstered by the U.S. Helsinki Commission, gave voice to the demands of NGOs in the Soviet Union, Czechoslovakia and Poland, as well as those in the United States itself. The very nature of the Helsinki process, with its open and almost continuing forums, its quite specific Final Act provisions in Basket 3 and Principle 7 and its predominantly Western balance, helped sustain a momentum in the direction of broader human rights. At the UN, the obstacles were far greater with the West, and its democratic values were increasingly isolated, outvoted, and even marginalized. But, if the United States were to hope to achieve at the UN what it successfully was realizing in the Helsinki process, it first would be required to reclaim the leadership role in human rights that had characterized it in the early postwar years.

Jimmy Carter came to power in the same year that Amnesty International won the Nobel Peace prize and, from the beginning of his Administration, he took a strong human rights stand—at times only verbally, at other times in reality. One obvious target were the human rights abuses and Helsinki agreement violations in the Soviet empire. Another target inevitably centered on the military dictatorships of Latin America, where the abuses involving disappearances and torture were so egregious as to require some kind of response. Amnesty had set the pace with disclosures involving meticulously documented reports to the UN on disappearances in Chile and later Uruguay and Argentina. Of special significance was the landmark achievement of a Declaration Against Torture.

The documentation and the Declaration, however, did not include machinery oriented to bringing about implementation or compliance, at least in some measure. The Commission on Human Rights was scarcely the kind of institutional structure that easily could create that kind of machinery. From the sixties on, its numerical majority was made up of Third World countries. The Commission membership would be ultimately and arbitrarily fixed at 53 and in a manner to be distinctly anti-Western. Flowing from the huge influx of new members from the Third World in the sixties, the precise figures by the eighties would be 15 for Africa, 12 for Asia, 11 for Latin America and the Caribbean, 5 for East Europe and 10 for the West. But the very political orientation of that majority scarcely harmonized with the purpose of the Commission—the promotion and protection of human rights. Besides, its impact on world public opinion was limited. The last American representative to the Commission before the Carter presidency, Leonard Garment, remembered Geneva as "a nice forgotten place with a sleepy press corps and no spectator interest."[2]

Patricia Derian was President Carter's choice to run the new human rights operation of the State Department.[3] An activist from the civil rights movement in the United States she was determined to press for a vigorous U.S. response to the crass and brutal violations of human rights in Argentina. This inevitably would produce clashes with the traditional foreign service career officials manning the Latin American geographical bureaus whose interest in human rights was not great. But Derian was a tough-minded infighter within the State Department bureaucracy, and she did have the ear of a President. Especially valuable to her was the cooperation of the human rights nongovernmental community. She found the NGOs, particularly Amnesty and Joe Eldridge's WOLA (Washington Office on Latin America), "absolutely essential."[4]

The "disappearances" trauma was very much on Derian's mind from the very beginning of the Carter Administration. Three days before the inauguration, on January 17, 1977, the President-elect received a letter from 12 NGOs urging him to take strong action to halt the disappearances.[5] And two months later, Derian chose to visit Argentina; she took two subsequent trips there in that same year. Her meeting with the military rulers, especially President Jorge Videla, could not be described as warm or friendly. It stood in sharp contrast with her embrace of the

Argentine Mothers of the Plaza de Mayo, with whom she developed the strongest attachment.[6]

Developments at the UN reinforced the Derian perspective. At the 1978 General Assembly, the U.S. representative commented on a report of the Commission of Human Rights with respect to Chile by demanding an "explanation of the problem of missing persons in Chile, since the matter had occasioned too much anguish and torment . . . to be ignored." Significantly, the American added that the problem extended to Argentina and other countries. In view of "its magnitude," he proposed "that a mechanism should be set up to examine the problem."[7]

ECOSOC, shortly afterward, asked the Commission on Human Rights "to consider as a matter of priority the question of disappeared persons, with a view to making appropriate recommendations."[8] The opportunity that the 1980 session of the Commission posed for the United States and for Derian's tough-minded approach was clear. Newly appointed as the U.S. representative on the Commission was Jerome Shestack, who continued to serve as President of the International League for Human Rights. His State Department Deputy for the sessions was Roberta Cohen, his former collaborator from the League, now functioning as Derian's agent. The eventual objective of the U.S. team, though not immediately perceived as such, was nothing short of revolutionary—to create an official Working Group on Enforced or Involuntary Disappearances that would be empowered to review individual cases, take evidence from individuals and consult with NGOs, whether holding or not holding formal consultative status with the UN. Finally, the utterly useless and dormant complaint procedures of the UN could take on a certain vitality. To accomplish this difficult and seemingly impossible task, given the nature of the membership of the Commission on Human Rights, required a variety of skills. The Western representatives had to be solidly unified in support of this aim. Members of the nonaligned bloc from the Third World had to be persuaded to support the proposal, or at least not to oppose it.

Needless to say, the NGO community was determined to give any effective proposal on disappearances its fullest backing. One week after the Commission session had begun, the NGOs in Geneva held a meeting on disappearances and publicized a new Amnesty report that revealed shocking information about 16 secret detention centers in Argentina.[9] The NGO meeting also clearly was designed to stir up enthusiastic support for halting an especially gross human rights violation.

When the proposal to create a Working Group first came to the Commission floor, no government was prepared to speak. The Chair promptly turned to those NGOs in attendance who sought to address the Commission. Amnesty launched the discussion, referring to its documentation on thousands of disappearance cases worldwide. Specific mention was made about Argentina, Afghanistan, Cambodia, Ethiopia, Nicaragua and Uganda.[10] In his comments about Argentina, the Amnesty representative described specific experiences of those who had been tortured and had disappeared while in a secret military detention center. The infuriated government delegate interrupted and challenged the right of an NGO to criticize any government by name. Uruguay and Ethiopia supported Argentina. On the other hand, the United States supported the right of NGOs to mention countries.

The Chair, a Jordanian, gave the NGOs breathing space. He ruled that NGOs could not "attack" governments; however, they could "provide information" about specific countries. The ruling permitted the International Commission of Jurists and the International League for Human Rights to address the subject of disappearances. Still, the crucial responsibility remained with governments—and, specifically the United States. Shestack's determination and diplomatic skill were essential. Far more relevant was the backup role of State Department diplomacy. A half-dozen nonaligned Commission members receiving American aid were approached. NGOs had no direct leverage. At the same time, Shestack prevailed on his Western colleagues to replicate the American effort with various other nonaligned countries on the Commission with which they had a special relationship.[11]

That the lobbying was unusually intense easily could be sensed by anyone present. The Argentine delegation, with the support of Uruguay, desperately was seeking to halt the creation of a new implementation organ. They did succeed in preventing any reference to Argentina in the draft resolution, but this had the tactical effect of permitting the Working Group to examine disappearances everywhere. Two American legal specialists observing the proceedings later would describe the chaotic atmosphere that enveloped the session: "Delegates stepped up the pace, searching each other out, yelling, cajoling and pleading."[12] Congressman Don Bonker (Democrat of Washington state), who was a champion of human rights in the House of Representatives, was especially impressed by Shestack's efforts. Having visited the Geneva session, he wrote to Secretary of State Cyrus Vance, commenting that "our delegation was rated by some the best in recent memory."

On February 29, 1980, a watershed Working Group at the UN was approved by the Commission in a formal Resolution.[13] It did not target

a specific country, but rather was to focus on a specific theme—
"questions relevant to enforced or involuntary disappearances of persons." Carrying a thematic cachet rather than being focused upon an
individual country gave the mechanism a *universal* character. Thus, the
failure to refer to Argentina turned out to provide a "strategically brilliant
breakthrough."[14] The Resolution established the precedent and basis for
the creation during the succeeding decade of a host of thematic
mechanisms. The Working Group on disappearances was to consist of
five Commission members, serving as experts in their individual capacities, not as representatives of governments. They were to be appointed
for one year by the Commission Chairman.

Considerable latitude was given the Working Group to obtain
information on the critical subject. Specifically mentioned as information sources were governments, intergovernmental institutions,
"humanitarian organizations and other reliable sources." For NGOs, the
Resolution offered, indirectly although nonetheless clearly, an avenue for
the distribution of their documentation. Thematic mechanisms of the
UN would become invaluable channels for NGO human rights material.

The procedure won solid endorsement from the UN General
Assembly. It welcomed at the end of 1980 the Working Group on
Disappearances and appealed to all governments to cooperate with it.[15]
The Commission was asked to continue "to study this question as a
matter of priority" and "to take any step" in pursuit of such efforts.
Significantly, the approval by the General Assembly of a landmark
implementation mechanism coincided with its decision to terminate the
utterly irrelevant periodic reporting system that had prevailed since 1956.

During the first several years, the Working Group received reports
on disappearances in some three dozen countries.[16] The reports came
overwhelmingly from national and international NGOs, a hardly surprising result. One of the reports in the mid-eighties listed 44 organizations "with which the [Working] Group has been dealing over the years."
Found in that category, of course, were the major NGOs in consultative
status with the UN—including some strictly human rights NGOs like
Amnesty International or the International League for Human Rights,
as well as NGOs with broader mandates, like the World Council of
Churches or Pax Romana.

The principal technique used by the Working Group became
standard operating procedure for later thematic mechanisms. It initially
would write to a government indicating that it had received "expressions
of concern" about "disappearances" in that country. The communication

was designed to initiate formal contact with a specific government and create a channel to obtain or confirm information. Soon afterward, the technique would be supplemented by requests for direct visits to the specified country by members of the Working Group. If it received a positive response, the mission would undertake to meet with all relevant groups, including, particularly, human rights NGOs.

If the setting up of the Working Group itself constituted a revolutionary step in UN human rights history, a particular procedure adopted by the Group at its first session carried profoundly radical ramifications. The new procedure was designed to deal with "urgent reports" that required "immediate action." It was the very first time that any principal UN organ, other than the Secretary-General, was empowered to take action routinely if there was an immediate threat to life or limb.[17] In the course of a half-dozen years, the Working Group used the "urgent action procedure" in over 1,000 cases. The Group concluded from its experience that "prompt international expression of concern can be effective. . . ."

According to a leading authority on disappearances, Nigel Rodley, the establishment of the Working Group has had a distinctly positive effect.[18] While older cases, in numerous instances, had not been clarified, publicity surrounding them had helped reduce and even halt the incidence of disappearances. In his view, the activities of the Working Group constituted a kind of "international habeas corpus." What was no doubt evident from statistical data was the fact that the incidence of disappearances had diminished since the seventies, although by no means has this gross human rights violation ceased.

By 1997, the number of disappearances in Latin America had greatly declined, according to a report of the Working Group.[19] New cases were reported in Colombia, Honduras, Mexico and Peru, but on a far smaller scale than in the seventies and eighties. Asia had become the continent with the largest number of disappearances. Ranking especially high were Indonesia, Iraq and Sri Lanka. The "disappearances" in the first two countries involve minorities—Timorese and Kurds respectively. Clearly, with reference to the initial source of disappearances, the establishment of the Working Group served a valuable if limited function.

Disappearances were not the only form of a gross violation of human rights that distinguished the seventies and shocked civilized society. Perhaps the centerpiece of the Universal Declaration of Human Rights was the right to life. The international community considered the taking of life by summary or arbitrary execution, whether or not justified to combat insurgency or terror, an assault upon a fundamental right. But such executions perpetrated by authoritarian and totalitarian regimes were grossly augmented in the seventies by extralegal or extrajudicial executions where not even the figleaf of ideological justification was used.

As the Commission on Human Rights already had embarked upon a radically new course in dealing with gross human rights violations in 1980, was it not feasible to take an additional step? After all, the sky had not fallen, governments hadn't collapsed, peace hadn't been breached and sovereignty hadn't been compromised. The Director of the Division on Human Rights, Theo van Boven, appointed in 1978, was prepared to move the Commission in new directions. A Dutch lawyer and academic, he quickly demonstrated his activism at the very first Commission he addressed after his appointment. "It is impossible," he said, "to remain indifferent when confronted with the many appeals which are directed to the United Nations."[20] The widespread character of the problem was highlighted by Amnesty in a study in 1983.[21]

At the opening session of the Commission in 1982, van Boven's introductory statement concentrated upon "deliberate killings perpetrated by organized power" without any legitimacy at all.[22] The response of Commission members was positive. They asked ECOSOC for permission to authorize the appointment of a Special Rapporteur who would examine the problem of arbitrary and extrajudicial executions and submit a comprehensive report on it. Once again, the target was thematic, not directed at a specific government. When ECOSOC agreed three weeks later, the Commission Chairman appointed S. Amos Wako, a highly experienced legal expert of Kenya, as the Special Rapporteur of a second Commission thematic issue. He was authorized to seek information from the traditional sources—governments, intergovernmental institutions and, most importantly, nongovernmental organizations. Basing his finding on such information, the Special Rapporteur, in his first report, listed 39 countries about which he had received allegations of arbitrary executions. In the same report, he observed that during the preceding 15 years, executions not based upon international legal standards had taken place "in many countries." Drawing upon conservative estimates, he calculated data that two million persons had been victims of arbitrary or summary executions.[23]

In 1984, the Special Rapporteur welcomed the technique of urgent action that had been introduced earlier by the Working Group on Disappearances. The Commission already had authorized him "to pay special attention to cases" in which execution was "imminent," and "to respond effectively." For Wako, "this urgent action procedure is an invaluable part of the response of the international community. . . ."[24] In his report of 1985, he did not hesitate to acknowledge that he had received communications from a half-dozen leading international NGOs in consultative status with ECOSOC. Each was listed.

No absolute proof may exist for demonstrating that the Special Rapporteur, particularly through the urgent message procedure, deterred or prevented arbitrary or extrajudicial executions. Still, the very existence of the international mechanism meant that governments had to take account of how they responded to formal queries from the mechanism.

Disappearances and extrajudicial executions were but two of what the new top UN human rights official, Kurt Herndl (who replaced van Boven), called the "three fundamental phenomena . . . affecting the right to life." The third, of course, was torture. It had been the first gross human rights violation with which the UN had been seized. Now, in 1984, nearly a decade later, Herndl, who was given the new title of Assistant Secretary General for Human Rights, pointed out that torture was the only one of the "three fundamental phenomena" lacking "a fact-finding mechanism of its own."[25] Herndl promptly put the issue before the UN. The proposal for a Special Rapporteur on Torture was no longer a revolutionary step. Torture was integral to both disappearances and extrajudicial executions. Prisoners, before being "disappeared" or executed, were in many instances subjected to torture. It was the overwhelming evidence of this practice in Latin America that had shocked the Western world and forced governments to overcome fears that a vigorous international response to the evil somehow would undermine national sovereignty.

Besides, a new survey by Amnesty International, undertaken in April, 1984 and designed to update its historic findings of a decade earlier, demonstrated that torture was still a burning problem.[26] If, in 1974, torture was found to be practiced in 61 countries, ten years later it was reported to have occurred in 66 countries. Clearly, the Declaration of 1975 was not adequate for coping with the spread of the horror. And, to bolster its documentation, Amnesty had its national sections lobby their respective governments (if they served on the Commission) to support the idea of a Special Rapporteur.

Thus, when the Commission met in February, 1985, the statement of its outgoing 1984 Chairman, Peter Kooijmans of the Netherlands, specifically called for "monitoring machinery" on torture.[27] Herndl later gave particular emphasis to "the need for a fact-finding mechanism or special procedure" in order to respond to the problem. What powerfully reinforced these appeals was the position taken by the representative of Argentina, whose new, democratically elected government of Raul Alfonsin, following the collapse of the repressive military regime, introduced the draft resolution for appointing a Special Rapporteur on Torture. It was unanimously adopted on March 31, 1985. In May, Kooijmans was named as Special Rapporteur. He would, in 1993, be replaced by the extraordinarily gifted NGO professional Nigel Rodley.

From the very beginning, the Special Rapporteur on Torture operated in a manner that paralleled his thematic predecessors on disappearances and on arbitrary and extrajudicial executions. He consulted with and received reports from a host of international and national NGOs.[28] He wrote to governments generally asking about what measures had been taken or contemplated to prevent or combat torture. A significant number responded. Where allegations of torture had been brought to his attention—already 33 "country situations" were reported to the thematic mechanism—he wrote to the respective governments asking for "clarification" about the charges.

Since 1980, nearly a dozen thematic mechanisms have been created, radically transforming the character of UN implementation machinery prior to that date and profoundly undermining the skeptical extrapolations and predictions of one of the most knowledgeable and experienced commentators on implementation machinery. Among the more important ones created, besides the major mechanisms, were: Special Rapporteur on Religious Intolerance (1986); Special Rapporteur on the Use of Mercenaries as a Means of Impeding the Exercise of the Right of People to Self Determination (1987); Special Rapporteur on the Sale of Children, Child Prostitution and Child Pornography (1990); Working Group on Arbitrary Detention (1991); Special Rapporteur on Freedom of Opinion and Expression (1993); Special Rapporteur on Racism, Racial Discrimination and Xenophobia (1993) and Special Rapporteur on Violence Against Women (1994).

What is striking about the thematic mechanisms was the fact, noted by analysts, that they have "fundamentally altered what the UN can and to some significant degree does accomplish" in assisting those whose rights are violated.[29] The endless and previously unproductive flow of petitions to the UN from all corners of the globe now has a group or an individual authorized by important UN bodies to examine them. The group or individual legitimately can and does inquire about the condition of the petitioners or of the victim and may move more quickly if circumstances are especially threatening. The persons selected to participate in the mechanisms, whether Working Groups or Special Rapporteurs, were and are independent experts, frequently academics, who have been and generally are insulated from politics. Equally striking is the fact that the pressure for the establishment of the theme mechanisms came from NGOs. It wasn't only that NGOs played central roles in bringing the thematic mechanisms into existence, thereby radically transforming the entire UN process for handling complaints about human rights violations; even more significantly, the NGOs performed the critical function of the mechanism—acquiring and verifying information on human rights abridgements. Indeed, the entire system rested upon the involvement of NGOs. The mandates for the thematic mechanisms created by the Commission on Human Rights and approved by ECOSOC specifically authorize Working Groups and Special Rapporteurs to "seek and receive credible and reliable information" from governments, the specialized agencies of the UN, intergovernmental organizations and NGOs. In reality, the overwhelming bulk of the "credible and reliable" information has been and is provided by NGOs.

A variety of authoritative assertions testify to this monumental function. According to a study prepared especially for the UN-sponsored World Conference on Human Rights of 1993, "NGOs are the main source of information for the thematic machinery, whose reports are themselves influential in the determination of situations appropriate for special scrutiny."[30] In the following year, a meeting of Special Rapporteurs and Working Group experts concluded with an extraordinary plea to NGOs: "We appeal to non-governmental organizations (NGOs) whose work and information is crucial to human rights protection and to the effective discharge of our own mandates to continue providing us with relevant information and ideas."[31]

The appeal almost carried a note of desperation, as if the mandates of thematic mechanisms were utterly dependent upon NGO collaboration. The 1994 experience of a major thematic mechanism—the Working Group on Arbitrary Detentions—illuminated the dependency. No less than 97 percent of the cases the Working Group took up that year were brought by NGOs; 74 percent came from international NGOs and another 23 percent were submitted by national NGOs. A mere 3 percent were provided by the families of the detainees.[32] The Special Rapporteur on Freedom of Expression characterized the contribution of NGOs as nothing short of "primordial."[33]

The thematic mechanisms are part of a key section of the Centre for Human Rights in Geneva. That section is called Special Procedures and encompasses, in addition to thematic mechanisms, Special Rapporteurs dealing with individual countries.[34] In a recent interview, the Director of Special Procedures, Georg Maurtner-Markhof, revealed that 80 to 90 percent of the total reports to his section came from NGOs, whether national or international.[35] The section often would check the evidence submitted by national NGOs, he indicated, with international NGOs. Indeed, many national NGOs channeled their information through the international organizations.

Amnesty International, Maurtner-Markhof asserted, was far and away the principal supplier of documentation to all of the new mechanisms. No other international NGO approached Amnesty in the number of submissions.[36] A former high legal officer of Amnesty, Helena Cook, added documentation supporting this contention in an essay. She reported that Amnesty sent Special Procedures more than 500 communications each year that embraced thousands of cases.[37] A key member of the very first thematic mechanism, the Working Group on Enforced or Involuntary Disappearances, Diego Garcia-Sayan, characterized the input of NGOs as "the fuel and the lubricant which allow the machine to function. . . ."[38] Without NGOs, the entire thematic system would cease to exist.

Paralleling in time the creation of thematic mechanisms in the new Special Procedures branch of the Centre for Human Rights was the establishment of country-specific mechanisms. Once the Commission on Human Rights voted in 1975 to establish an ad hoc Working Group to investigate allegations about Chile's gross human rights violations, a precedent had been set for inquiry into charges made about individual countries. The traditional ECOSOC Resolution 1235, not Resolution 1503, offered the governing principle.[39] The latter Resolution, complex and shielded from any external scrutiny by elaborate steps of confidentiality, precluded virtually any effective investigation. Even if NGOs could trigger the application of the 1503 process with appropriate information, all the subsequent stages were enclosed in a cocoon of silence, so much so that an NGO (or an individual who initially submitted an allegation) could not learn the fate of this submission nor could it submit any additional documentation on the same subject.

Thus, the case by NGOs against the military rulers in Greece involving torture and detention during 1967-74 simply disappeared from public view at the UN. Equally notorious was the case involving mass murder in Uganda under Idi Amin, which initially was brought to the UN under Resolution 1503 in 1974. It later was revealed that in

1977, the confidentiality principle was insisted upon by a majority of the Commission.[40] Only when Amin was fleeing from Uganda following defeat of his forces by the Tanzanian army, supported by anti-Amin insurgents, did the Commission finally decide to take any action. It requested the UN Secretary-General to appoint a Special Representative to examine the situation in Uganda. The action had a farcical quality made doubly amusing by the fact that the request was to be acted upon under the confidential procedure of 1503.

It was not that hope under 1503 entirely would collapse. From 1978 to 1984, at least 28 cases were reported to have been considered by the Commission, mostly from Africa, Asia and Latin America.[41] Two international legal specialists estimated that the referral rate from the Working Group of the Sub-Commission on Prevention of Discrimination and Protection of Minorities—the first of four stages—was 8 to 10 cases a year.[42] According to Felice Gaer, who later served as a public member of the U.S. delegation to the Commission, some 46 countries had been the subject of Commission decisions, none of which involved positive public action. Since the adoption of 1503, in no instance has the Commission undertaken a thorough study of the human rights violation allegations.

The utterly unproductive history of 1503 has raised the question of whether this ECOSOC Resolution has become obsolete. In the judgment of a specialist who prepared a study for the UN-sponsored World Conference on Human Rights, which was concerned with a more effective UN system, it would be "extremely premature" to discard 1503.[43] The procedure, he said, "offers some hope that a minimum of international attention will be focussed on grave situations." Noting that experienced NGOs continue to submit complaints under the procedure, he pointed out that should a targeted state fail to cooperate effectively with the Commission, the latter could call for action under the Special Procedures of the Centre for Human Rights.[44]

But with the new willingness, ever since 1975, of the Commission to use Resolution 1235, nearly a dozen countries, accused by one or another Commission member or by its Sub-Commission of having committed gross violations of human rights, have been subjected to and still remain under the new country-specific mechanism of a Special Rapporteur (also called a Special Representative or, in some instances, simply "Independent Expert"). Among the countries specified in the eighties to be examined were Afghanistan, Guatemala, Equatorial Guinea and Iran. They were joined in the nineties by Iraq, Cuba, Haiti,

El Salvador, Myanmar (formerly Burma), Yugoslavia, Somalia, Cambodia, Sudan, Rwanda, Burundi and Zaire.

The country-specific Special Rapporteurs, as independent specialists, undertake detailed studies of the accused countries that include on-site investigations, but only when the targeted government agrees. The studies are climaxed by reports and recommendations submitted to the Commission on Human Rights and sometimes to the General Assembly. Of considerable significance is the ability of these UN rapporteurs to transmit appeals, sometimes on an urgent basis, regarding individual cases. The authority to intercede carries the potentiality of humanitarian rescue.

While the country-specific Special Rapporteurs operate out of the same branch of the Centre—Special Procedures—as those of thematic mechanisms, report to the same body—the Commission on Human Rights—and were created at approximately the same time, their functions are somewhat different.[45] The country-specific Rapporteurs, with their focus on fact-finding and reporting, ineluctably have a judgmental role. On the other hand, the thematic mechanisms regard themselves as engaged in problem-solving, oriented to a humanitarian objective and not geared to making judgments. At the same time, the thematic Special Rapporteurs tend to relate to individual cases, frequently on the basis of an urgent situation. In contrast, the country-specific Rapporteurs tend to concentrate on the overall situation in the targeted country and rarely engage in urgent action. Thematic mechanisms, because their geographic scope is broad, inevitably will seek to draw conclusions on a comparative basis. In moving in this direction, the Special Rapporteur or Working Group hardly can avoid engaging in judgmental comments. Furthermore, when they produce reports on various country visits, a judgmental reaction is quite likely. Country-specific Special Rapporteurs, all too often, are refused visits by the targeted governments.

One of the Special Rapporteurs, in an interview, spelled out how his report was prepared and how NGOs played a part. Carl-Johan Groth, a prominent former career diplomat from Sweden who once served as its representative to the Commission on Human Rights, has been for several years the Special Rapporteur on Cuba. After submitting an "interim report" to the 1996 General Assembly on the "situation of human rights" in Cuba, he explained to a listener that "I am indebted for almost the whole content of the report to NGOs."[46] In addition to Amnesty International, Human Rights Watch and Freedom House, he relied heavily—as, in fact, he said, do the international NGOs—upon a dozen or so national NGOs in Cuba.[47] Since he repeatedly had been refused a visa by the Castro government, Groth met in New York and Washington, D.C. on August 26-29, 1996, with various NGO representatives, along with experts on Cuba from academia. From these meetings as well as from written material directly from individuals and NGOs in Cuba, he arranged for the staff of the Centre for Human Rights to draft the UN report.

What greatly impressed Groth were the NGOs in Cuba (several of whom he chose not to list). They produced, he said, an "astonishing amount of information," for which they had to "run risks" of a serious nature. In the report, he called the information of "vital importance."[48] From the information, Groth prepared a detailed 19-page study of discriminatory practices in Cuba concerning deprivations of freedom of expression, restrictions of freedom of association and the right to emigrate and limitations on the enjoyment of economic, social and cultural rights.

Virtually every report by a Special Rapporteur, whether on a theme or on a country, has carried references to the contributions of NGOs. A few recent examples will serve to illustrate how the Special Rapporteur has relied upon NGOs. In January, 1997, the Special Rapporteur on Torture spelled out, in a very lengthy report and analysis, the significance of NGOs in his assemblage of information.[49] In an annex, he noted that he "seeks and receives credible and reliable information from . . . non-governmental organizations," and that when he visits a country, he frequently consults with local NGOs.[50] Consultation also takes place with a number of international NGOs in Geneva.[51] The information provided by these NGOs is clearly extensive, detailing who were the victims of torture; who carried out the torture; where the torture occurred; what was the method of torture; whether the local legal system permitted prosecution of torturers and in what way and whether the system offered the possibility of legal assistance.[52] The Special Rapporteur went out of his way in validating reports on torture by Indonesian authorities in East Timor by visiting NGOs in Portugal along with East Timorese victims.[53]

On a totally unrelated theme dealing with the sale of children, child prostitution and child pornography, the Special Rapporteur underscored how NGOs proved invaluable in providing documentation and in extending detailed assistance to child victims.[54] Whether the subject matter concerned the trafficking of children, the luring of girls to dubious jobs in Germany that turn out to involve prostitution or the growing prominence of child pornography, the NGOs constituted for Ofelia Calcetas-Santos the primary source of documentation.[55] In addition, NGOs were very valuable in arranging for medical, psychiatric and social work assistance in coping with the abuse of children.[56]

A characteristic recent country-specific report is one dealing with Myanmar (Burma).[57] This quite detailed 29-page examination of the discrepancy between the regulations of the military dictatorship and the international human rights norms and standards focused heavily upon what the Special Rapporteur, Rajsmoor Lallah said was "much assistance and information from . . . non-governmental sources."[58] Since the military regime refused all requests that he had made to visit the country, the Special Rapporteur related how he traveled to London, Geneva and New York to obtain documentation on human rights violations as well as on the ruthless and arbitrary displacement of perhaps one million minority persons from border regions.[59] Also noted was information about humanitarian assistance rendered by NGOs.

Strikingly dissimilar was the country-specific report on Iraq prepared by the very gifted and knowledgeable Max van der Stoel, the Netherlands' former Foreign Minister who, since 1991, served as the Special Rapporteur on that country.[60] Neither in his report nor in his statement to the Commission on Human Rights on April 11, 1997 introducing his findings did van der Stoel make any reference to NGOs. His report catalogued every conceivable form of human rights abuse by the Saddam Hussein dictatorship, especially emphasizing the huge number of unresolved cases of disappearances that stigmatized Iraq as having "the worst record in the world."[61] Nonetheless, when interviewed in his office at The Hague a month later, van der Stoel admitted that international human rights NGOs were the source of much of his report to the Commission, as since 1991 he repeatedly had been refused permission to visit Iraq.[62] He was particularly grateful to Human Rights Watch/Middle East for its studies and, to some extent, to Amnesty International.

Eleanor Roosevelt would have welcomed the revolution in implementation procedures at the UN. Finally, the "curious grapevine" of NGOs officially could bring serious violations of human rights to the attention of the world community—at times, quite quickly. Hopelessly ineffective machinery was replaced by fairly extensive, although still incomplete, thematic mechanisms and country-specific Special Rapporteurs. The personnel operating the new machinery, according to close analysts, "have used their mandates for all they were worth, including the making of recommendations that push beyond thinking and practice at the UN."[63] Moreover, the timetable for identifying and dramatically illustrating violations of provisions of the Universal Declaration of Human Rights has been enormously accelerated. At the meeting of all those engaged in Special Procedures in June, 1994 where a special, if not desperate, plea was made to NGOs for their assistance, the new UN High Commissioner for Human Rights excited the audience by announcing that he had established a "human rights hotline" to enable emergency information to be dealt with immediately and urgently. The hotline—a special fax number—was to be used "exclusively . . . by victims of human rights violations or relatives or informed NGOs."[64]

While NGOs have provided and continue to provide the basic information and data, they are not in command of the forum of the Commission of Human Rights and its apparatus. What should be a crucial Commission role in examination and follow-up has been almost nonexistent. Given the short, six-week agenda for the annual Commission session, little time is available to focus on the reports. The products of the thematic mechanisms "rarely" have been discussed "in any systematic way," informed observers noted.[65] Only in the context of the general debate on an agenda item or in discussion of gross violations might the thematic reports be considered. The vital on-site observations made by the Working Group or by Special Rapporteurs were and are not discussed. Even the annual resolution welcoming the reports of these mechanisms often refrains from specifically mentioning the places that were visited.

The general public, in most instances, has not received and does not receive information about what has happened after a government, for example, has responded to an inquiry made by the mechanism. The public has no way of learning what, if anything, can be done about inquiries that were unanswered or answered inadequately. In most instances relating to often potentially valuable reports emerging from the mechanisms, silence encompasses the release and presentation of the reports. Part of the problem lies in the relative isolation of Geneva as compared with any major Western city, where a sizable press corps is available.

Almost by historical accident, the emergence in the eighties of new and radical implementing human rights machinery to deal with human rights complaints coincided with the coming into force of older international human rights treaties, the drafting of new ones covering several key subjects and the coming into force of these new treaties. Each had its own implementing organ and, stunningly, these organs, in time, developed a special close relationship with NGOs. The relationship enabled NGOs to play as important a role in the treaty-making process as they did in connection with Special Procedures.

In 1976, the Covenant on Civil and Political Rights came into force and its implementing organ, the 18-member group of experts entitled the Human Rights Committee, began functioning the following year. In addition to receiving and evaluating reports from contracting states, it receives under the Optional Protocol, which also came into force at the same time, an increasing number of complaints from individuals. The Covenant on Economic, Social and Cultural Rights, initially perceived as not requiring immediate obligations from contracting states, took on a rather concrete responsibility in 1990 when its implementing organ—the Committee on Economic, Social and Cultural Rights—decided that the Covenant, indeed, "imposes various obligations which are of immediate effect."[66] The third older treaty, the Convention on the Elimination of All Forms of Racial Discrimination, came into force earlier, in 1969. Its implementing organ, the Committee on the Elimination of Racial Discrimination (CERD), is considered to have lagged behind the Human Rights Committee of the Covenant in strengthening the Convention's reporting system and in prodding contracting states to comply with treaty obligations. Strikingly, the Convention's individual petition system (which came into effect in 1982) has produced only a handful of petitions.[67]

The three older treaties were augmented by three new ones. The Convention on the Elimination of All Forms of Discrimination Against Women (CEDAW) was adopted in 1979 and entered into force two years later. Its implementing organ, a Committee comprised of 23 experts, reviews the periodic reports of state parties but, since it only meets for two weeks a year, it cannot effectively evaluate the reports. Besides, the treaty carries no individual complaint mechanism. The Convention Against Torture and Other Cruel, Inhuman or Degrading Treatment already has been noted. Adopted in 1984, it came into force in 1987. Its implementing organ, the Committee on Torture (CAT), comprising 10 experts, examines reports from contracting parties and undertakes investigations when it receives "reliable information" that torture is being "systematically practiced" in the territory of a contracting state.[68]

The most recently enacted functioning treaty, the Convention on the Rights of the Child, was adopted in 1989 and entered into force in 1990. With its focus on the protection of children, the Convention concentrates upon a variety of threatening dangers, including economic exploitation, the traffic in children, sexual exploitation and abuse and the use of drugs. That the Convention acquired in five short years 190 ratifiers testified to its popularity. Its implementing Committee on the Rights of the Child of 10 experts review the reports of contracting states.

According to a special study prepared in 1993 for the World Conference on Human Rights by Professor Philip Alston of Australia, the adoption of the half-dozen human rights treaties is one of the great achievements of the United Nations.[69] In his view, the treaty system, along with the Universal Declaration of Human Rights, "constitutes the cornerstone of human rights endeavors." Twenty-five years earlier, at the time of the Teheran conference in 1968, not a single human rights treaty body existed. By the time of the second World Conference on Human Rights, 60 percent of the countries of the globe were contracting parties to the Covenants and a significant percentage—40 percent or more— were contracting parties to the other treaties.[70]

The separate implementing organs of the six human rights treaties can be expected to play and—in some cases, already play—important roles in demanding compliance with the provisions of the treaties. Comprised of skilled experts who can challenge and raise questions about the accuracy of a country's report, they are in a position to embarrass governments to some degree. Just as governments do not like to be shamed in the public arena, they also seek to avoid embarrassment about the truth or validity of the reports they submit to world bodies. In the case of the oldest and most experienced Committee, the Human Rights Committee of the Covenant on Civil and Political Rights, which covers the broadest range of rights, it is indisputable that the organ's power has grown significantly over the years. The expert-members today can ask the representatives of states (who are required to be present when their government's reports is up for review) to explain the contents of the reports, clarify materials in the reports, and resolve challenging questions. The experts may further request additional information. The consequence of this authority can be the suggestion of serious compliance problems by a country, made all the more embarrassing by the Committee's ability to focus the attention of all UN member states on these matters by describing the proceeding in the Committee's annual report to the General Assembly.

Two other recent developments point to the growing influence of the Committee. If a state has ratified the Optional Protocol on individual complaints, the Committee now can require that state to report what action it has taken to give effect to the Committee's recommendation.

Finally, with respect to both individual complaints and state reports, increasingly the Committee has adopted the practice of making "General Comments," a phrase that has taken on the character of an advisory opinion on various provisions of the Covenant. A kind of quasi-judicial authority has become apparent. In 1980, none of the existing treaty bodies had adopted any "General Comments." By 1993, the Human Rights Committee had adopted 21 such Comments and the parallel Economic Social and Cultural Committee had adopted 4 Comments.[71]

The General Comments, strikingly interrelate with other aspects of the new mechanisms. Thus, the Special Rapporteur on extrajudicial and arbitrary executions noted that he cited them frequently "as a guide to the interpretation of international standards."[72] The Special Rapporteur on Torture considered that the Human Rights Committee was "a highly authoritative body" and its "views" were to be "taken with the greatest possible seriousness."[73]

It is in the context of the broader significance as well as the wider acceptance through ratification of the UN treaty mechanisms that one can note the enhanced influence of NGOs. They have become, over time, an "essential component" of the human rights treaties' implementing process, according to Helga Klein, who is the top staffer on treaty mechanisms at the Centre for Human Rights.[74] Initially, she noted, NGOs were not even mentioned in the treaties (although in the children's rights treaty, they were hinted at as a source). In the early eighties, she explained, a kind of unofficial and rather mild breakthrough did take place when Amnesty International and the International League for Human Rights began providing the Human Rights Committee with background information on individual countries prior to or during the time their human rights reports came up for review. The intervention of the NGOs took the form of personal verbal contact or a mailing sent to individual experts. The circumstances and communications were totally informal and the experts, even when they used the NGO information, meticulously avoided any reference to an NGO. Should one or another expert challenge a country's presentation, reference might be made to "reliably attested information" as the source of the challenge. Insiders frequently understood that phrase to mean information from an NGO with consultative status.

By the late eighties and early nineties, according to Klein, the contributions from NGOs became "extremely welcome" and, indeed, were "solicited." A knowledgeable analyst of the treaty mechanism has pointed out that "Committee members look for NGO material prior to consideration of each country review."[75] The information enables Committee members to pose questions in a "more precise, factual and less abstract" manner. In essence, the analyst concluded, NGOs "essentially serve as unofficial researchers" to Committee members who hardly can rely on Centre staff for support.

An American expert who serves on the Human Rights Committee, Professor Thomas Buergenthal, confirmed in an interview that NGOs were "absolutely indispensable" to the Committee.[76] Without them, he said, there would be "virtually no sources of information" to question governments on their reports. Those official government reports, he acknowledged, are "usually whitewashes" of the particular regime.

Recently, the Committee experts have become increasingly inclined to refer specifically to their reliance upon NGOs. A startling culmination of the trend came in 1994 at a meeting of the Chairpersons of all human rights treaties' Committees. They recommended that "each treaty body examine the possibility of changing its working methods or amending its rules of procedure to allow nongovernmental organizations to participate more fully in its activities."[77] Specifically, they suggested that NGOs be allowed "to make oral interventions" and "to transmit information" about human rights violations through established "procedures." And, to facilitate greater NGO involvement, the Committees' Chairpersons proposed that information about the reporting by state parties as well as the proposed general comments of the various committees "be made available" to NGOs. The group explicitly sought "to encourage non-governmental organizations to provide input to the [final] drafts. . . ."

Special attention was given by the Chairpersons to national NGOs, from whom "a stronger, more effective and coordinated participation" was requested on the occasion when consideration of their respective governments' reports is planned by the various Committees. Helga Klein, in her interview, took note of the fact that representatives of several major international NGOs always attended the review sessions.[78] Especially mentioned by her was the work and reportage of Human Rights Watch and its UN representative in New York, Joanne Weschner. Also noted by her was the frequent presence of Amnesty International. Like the Chairpersons, Klein, too, wanted more participation by national NGOs. She noted that Latin American national NGOs were significantly involved, as were some Asian NGOs, notably from Japan and Korea. In Africa, however, there was very little national NGO involvement.

The new attention to national NGOs was not intended to diminish the continuing importance of international NGOs. Buergenthal welcomed, for example, the special briefing arranged for the Human Rights Committee in New York, prior to its 1995 session, by the Lawyers Committee for Human Rights. At the same time, Buergenthal was not uncritical of NGOs. He noted that one of them deliberately chose not to antagonize a regional judicial institution lest it affect the future of the NGO to operate in the region. More serious was his criticism of the failure on the part of various international NGOs to distinguish between totalitarian or authoritarian regimes and democratic regimes in their evaluation of human rights. Approaching both in precisely the same way can prove profoundly misleading, he said.

The briefings by the Lawyers Committee marked a novel development and appeared to be responsive to an expressed desire by the UN Human Rights Committee to be thoroughly informed about situations in the various countries under review. No longer was the UN group a passive recipient of information; here, it was actively seeking out information and, was desirous of engaging in dialogue with the NGO—in this case the Lawyers Committee—either to challenge points or to obtain further documentation. Clearly, the Lawyers Committee, as it had in other instances, was blazing a new trail for strengthening the rule of law, especially through the fulfillment of covenant obligations.

An example was a briefing of the Human Rights Committee on March 27, 1997 held on neutral grounds in New York at the Church Center, across the street from the United Nations. The subject was the official report by the government of Colombia that was to be examined by the UN group four days later on March 31–April 1.[79] The principal sponsor of the lunch and of the two-hour briefing session, attended by the bulk of the UN group, was the Lawyers Committee, which was joined by Amnesty International and, more importantly, by a top-level group of legal representatives from human rights groups in Bogota who flew to New York especially for the occasion. The briefing was accompanied by documented studies that were distributed to the guests.

Documentation prepared by the Lawyers Committee was remarkably detailed, spelling out how violence with impunity was persistent and pervasive in Colombia, how governmental declarations of "states of exception" nullifying a variety of fundamental rights had become commonplace, with due process for criminal defendants almost disappearing, and how government forces aided and abetted paramilitary units that were responsible for the most virulent human rights violations.[80] The factual evidence constituted a sharp, pinpointed challenge to the government's official report.

The challenge was underscored with details about the establishment of notorious "faceless" courts. A separate essay by the Lawyers Committee's Coordinator of the Latin American Program, Robert Weiner, revealed that these courts, in which everyone but the defendant is anonymous, account for 40 percent of the nation's criminal-justice docket. Approximately 50 percent of Colombia's prison inmates come from "faceless" court cases.[81] Especially disturbing to the Lawyers Committee and their legal colleagues from Bogota was the threat posed to Colombia's 1991 Constitution by new legal proposals advanced by the Bogota government.

The oral presentations by the Latin American NGO representatives elaborated upon the documentation. Many of the UN Human Rights Committee members took notes and some asked searching questions. By a curious and remarkable coincidence, the *New York Times* on the day before the briefing—March 26—published a long dispatch from its correspondent in Colombia describing the brutal repression by the paramilitary forces.[82]

Colombia, no doubt expecting a strong challenge to its periodic report, sent to the Human Rights Committee hearings a top-level four-member team of governmental officials, headed by the Presidential Advisor on Human Rights. Despite vigorous efforts to defend Bogota's official report, the delegation found that its government's report was subject to continuous criticism as perhaps accurate with respect to the listing of Colombia's laws and official mechanisms for human rights protection but woefully lacking in terms of political reality. Many Committee members sharply questioned the delegation on the militarization of society, on impunity, on paramilitary activity and on "faceless" military tribunals.[83]

Almost every item that had been brought up at the briefings came up during the question period as well as in the concluding comments of the Committee. Some went out of their way to take note of how NGO reportage had shaped their thinking. The Committee expert from Germany, for example, observed that NGO reports documented that Colombia maintained the worst human rights record in the Western Hemisphere. The expert from Ecuador cited a particular NGO, the Andean Commission of Jurists, as a source for information about the acquiescence of state security forces in torture, disappearances and summary executions, all of which undermined the guarantee of the right to life.[84]

Clearly, briefings and documentation by NGOs are extremely effective in guiding the implementing organ of the crucial Covenant on Civil and Political Rights. Whether that organ, however, can sufficiently impact upon the society and government of a given country as to bring about positive change, and not in some distant future, is as yet unpredictable. Much will depend upon the local follow-up through media coverage by national NGOs, as well as by international NGOs.

Significantly, the most recent human rights treaty that has come into force—the Convention on the Rights of the Child—was itself, in large part, a product of the efforts of NGOs. Some 35 of them established in Geneva an NGO Ad Hoc Group in order to develop a coordinated strategy that would impact upon the Special Working Group of the Commission on Human Rights.[85] While some worked separately, the NGO Ad Hoc Group had, as its leader, the Defense for Children International. Many articles of the draft convention, as finally approved, "were proposed or influenced by NGOs," according to van Boven. When the draft convention was submitted to the Commission on Human Rights in March, 1989, the Polish Chairman and Rapporteur of the Working Group, Adam Lopatka, officially acknowledged the prominence of that role. On November 30, 1989, the Convention on the Rights of the Child was adopted by the General Assembly.

In any case, just as a revolution had taken place in the UN machinery of implementation with the emergence of thematic and country-specific mechanisms, so too had it occurred, in somewhat parallel fashion, with respect to both the elaboration of more human rights treaties and the considerable enlargement of their specially created organs of compliance. At the core of this extraordinary change by the beginning of the last decade of the twentieth century were the NGOs. "We would not be what we are today," said a veteran senior staffer of the UN Centre for Human Rights, Tom McCarthy, "without the NGOs."[86]

McCarthy went on to ask rhetorically: "'Do we need NGOs?'" His answer took a similar rhetorical turn, this time, however, carrying a metaphorical variation: "'Does it snow in Minneapolis in the winter?'" The listener in the interview needed no further clarification.

CHAPTER TWELVE

A "Rare, Defining Moment": Vienna, 1993

UN Secretary-General Boutros Boutros-Ghali, in addressing the opening session of the World Conference on Human Rights held in Vienna, June 14-25, 1993, called the affair "one of those rare, defining moments" in modern history. It was a remarkably prescient observation for the then Secretary-General to make. He was not given to analytic predictions and his oratory, always bureaucratically prosaic, hardly ever carried a lilting quality. Indeed, the burst of clairvoyance here actually understated the distinctive extraordinary features of Vienna that would make the moment "rare" and "defining."[1]

The most stunning, if almost totally unexpected, development at the World Conference was a call to the United Nations to establish a High Commissioner for Human Rights, a vision projected at the beginning of the UN, then dropped and later revived in the sixties, only to be interred for what was expected to be forever. And this striking appeal from 171 governmental representatives was a consequence of an unprecedented and unparalleled outburst of lobbying by nongovernmental organizations. It was quite simply an act of massive insurrectionary proportions. "We, the peoples" of the UN Charter finally had risen to demand the fulfillment of an early, almost utopian, vision.

Significantly, the address of Boutros-Ghali carried no reference to a High Commissioner for Human Rights, let alone a recommendation that such an institution be created. Indeed, the opposite was true. He went out of his way to say "that at this moment in time it is less urgent to define new rights than to persuade States to adopt existing instruments and apply them effectively." Just prior to the Conference, the Secretary-

General wrote an essay in the *Washington Post* arguing that "solutions cannot be imposed from the top down."[2] In his view, "proposals for new bureaucracies [and] high level positions" just would "arouse discontent and resistance." And he would continue to oppose the establishment of a High Commissioner until the very last minute, no doubt perceiving it as a challenge to his own authority and preeminence.

Equally pertinent was the absence in the speech of the Secretary-General of any reference to NGOs. Not even the slightest hint was projected that the nongovernmental community had a special stake in the deliberations of the Conference. In essence, he refused to be the spokesman for "we, the peoples" and, instead, chose the safer course of adhering to "existing instruments" of the international community, thereby not frightening the sovereign states comprising the UN body.

The idea for a World Conference on Human Rights was advanced almost accidentally in the fall of 1989, in the wake of euphoria flowing from the historic victory of democracy over totalitarianism in East Europe. What would be updated were the rather modest undertakings of the first World Conference held in Teheran in 1968, precisely 20 years after the Universal Declaration of Human Rights had been adopted. Now, another quarter of a century later, on the eve of the twenty-first century, could not mankind bask in the glory of a burgeoning democratic phenomenon? The questions that were projected for the Conference, while banal, nonetheless had an upbeat character: What progress has been made in the field of human rights since the adoption of the Universal Declaration of Human Rights in 1948? What obstacles remain and how are they to be overcome? How can UN implementation mechanisms be improved so as to advance human rights? These were projected as the agenda items for the 1993 Conference.[3]

Certainly, the decade prior to the World Conference had given birth to a variety of new human rights instruments and mechanisms. But the new international instruments or mechanisms could not, of themselves, bring to a halt egregious violations of human rights. Eradication of abhorrent practices, even with the best of instruments, required a political will on the part of states to utilize the mechanisms or to confer upon them the appropriate authority and capacity to act. The Commission on Human Rights, as late as 1996 comprised of a majority of states that were either "not free" or "partly free," was scarcely the kind of institution that would maximize the use of the valuable data and information assembled by the mechanisms. A researcher of UN Watch, an NGO in Geneva, found that only 36 percent of the Commission could be identified as "free," 43 percent as "partly free" and 21 percent as "not free."[4] Nor would the Commission be inclined, except in the rarest of instances, to press for public exposure of serious and grave human rights violations or pursue the aim of reducing tensions or conflict situations.

As the twentieth century entered its last decade, the three most terrifying of human rights violations, other than genocide itself, actually saw a significant increase in reported cases. The cases, of course, concerned disappearances, arbitrary killings and torture. According to the Working Group on Enforced or Involuntary Disappearances, the year 1991 brought to its attention the highest number of cases it ever had received in a single year. The total was 17,000 disappearances, of which 4,800 were new.[5] An entire decade had elapsed since the Working Group was launched and it appeared startled to note "an unexpected resurgence of the problem in some countries." So numerous were the reported cases that the Working Group acknowledged that it did not have the capacity to process them all in one year. No doubt the significant numerical increase in reported cases was due to the very existence of a reporting mechanism.

The Special Rapporteur on Extrajudicial and Arbitrary Executions similarly found the 1991 record disturbing. He ascertained that not only was there an alarming increase of deaths of persons while in custody of the authorities, but also there was a big upsurge in arbitrary executions in internal conflicts. At the same time, the number of reported death threats had grown significantly. Testifying to the vast and deepening concern was the fact that the Special Rapporteur actually doubled the number of appeals he made to governments as compared to the previous years. A total of 174 communications were sent by the Special Rapporteur to no less than 65 countries. Nine years of experience with the new mechanism had not seen even a token diminution of the problem.[6]

Torture can be described in a similar way. As noted by the Special Rapporteur on the subject, despite the very significant progress taken on an international level since 1975 regarding torture, at the national level, "only failures can be recorded." During 1991, the Special Rapporteur said that he had received "an alarming number of communications." Judging by the fact that the number of countries in which torture was reported to have occurred was twice as large as had been recorded in the first year of the mechanism's operations, the conclusion was self-evident: "the practice of torture is still widespread." Even if many states had gone on record denouncing torture, their actual internal behavior "threatens to discredit the verbally-endorsed campaign against torture."[7]

Amnesty International concluded at the end of 1992 that "violations of the most fundamental human right . . . still occur daily and often on a massive scale in all regions of the world."[8] The view found an echo in the UN Secretary-General's 1992 report on the work of the world organization. He readily acknowledged that the UN "has not been able to act effectively to bring to an end massive human rights violations." In his speech to the World Conference, Boutros-Ghali painted a devastating picture of human rights violations:

> Not a day goes by without scenes of warfare or famine, arbitrary arrest, torture, rape, murder, expulsion, transfer of population and ethnic cleansing. Not a day goes by without reports of attacks on the most fundamental of human freedoms. Not a day goes by without reminders of racism and the crimes it spawns. . . .[9]

Lack of political will by the states comprising both the Commission and the UN itself found reflection in the scandalous budgetary and personnel policy of the world body toward human rights. In a remarkably frank interview in 1993, the Special Rapporteur on Extrajudicial and Arbitrary Executions, Bacre Ndiaye, called UN human rights "absolutely under-funded and under-resourced."[10] Only .75 percent of UN personnel was allocated to the Centre for Human Rights, and its budget constituted but 1 percent of the total UN resources. The Rapporteurs in a joint report in 1993 embarrassingly admitted that "despite our best efforts, we sometimes appear ineffective in critical situations simply because the most basic support structure is not available. . . ."[11] A startling example was offered: "How can we allow piles of individual cases to be unprocessed and unanswered because of inadequate human and material resources?"

Beyond the lack of political will was a UN bureaucracy indifferent to claims or requests made by the Special Rapporteurs. In addition, the sudden emergence of so many mechanisms cried out for some form of coordination to minimize confusion and to maximize their effectiveness. Instead of a coordinating operation aimed at rationalizing the various Special Procedures operations, a vacuum prevailed, making for fragmentation and, at times, chaos. Even the indispensable documentation center and database were lacking.

Equally distressing to Bacre Ndiaye was the "lack of publicity" for the Special Procedures system. He candidly stressed that "many people do not know that procedures exist and that they can do something through the UN system." The tragic reality was that the frequently excellent reports of the Working Groups and Special Rapporteurs went unnoticed: "you cannot find them outside UN offices."[12]

The Special Rapporteur on Extrajudicial and Arbitrary Executions especially highlighted the failure of his colleagues to obtain at times favorable responses from governments that would enable them to undertake official visits to targeted countries. Noting that "visiting is one of the most important parts of the [Special Rapporteur's] job," he bitterly complained that some governments, "despite UN resolutions . . . get away with ignoring requests from the rapporteurs." China, Turkey and Bangladesh specifically were mentioned as perpetrators of this neglect. Precisely because of the various gaps that diminished the great potentiality of the Special Procedures system, a commissioned UN study, in 1993, called for "a top level coordinating official" to "ensure coherence and cooperation" and to make certain that UN human rights machinery be "deployed" to achieve "maximum effort."[13]

The treaty system, with its half-dozen organs of implementation, also augured considerable promise. Especially disturbing was the tendency of many governments to delay sending in the required reports of how they were fulfilling their human rights obligation. An expert's analysis in 1993 of the process found that "the current level of overdue reports . . . is chronic and entirely unacceptable."[14] According to a chart documenting the analysis, as many as half of the contracting parties have been "overdue" in the submission of their reports.[15] Were such delays to continue to be tolerated, he advised, the "credibility of the entire regime" would be placed in question and the "reporting system" would become ineffectual. Moreover, since, at best, only a handful of reports could be reviewed and evaluated at any one time, and the review organs met but a couple of times a year, the ability to cope with serious human rights violations under the treaty system inevitably became problematic.

Bureaucratic inefficiency made solutions even more difficult and, indeed, further complicated the problem. For both the tough-minded NGOs and governments concerned with balanced budgets in the face of excessive expenditures, the splintered and utterly disjointed character of the United Nations human rights operation was distressing. The need for coordination had become urgent especially since the Centre for Human Rights was located in Geneva, while the new dozen and a half UN peacekeeping operations, some with human rights mandates, were headquartered in New York.[16]

While the widespread persistence of gross human rights violations dictated the need for an authoritative office to cope with the problem, and while this need was reinforced by the logic of coordination, there was little certainty that need and logic would prevail. Determined opposition could be expected from leading violators, especially those from the coalition of powerful and fast-growing industrial states of Asia, possibly supported by many of the nonaligned countries from Asia, Africa and even Latin America, who might fear an intrusion of supranational influence emanating from a foreign High Commissioner.

It was NGO determination that would overcome resistance and doubt. What would prove to be a new and decisive factor on the world scene was the very presence of the nongovernmental organization almost everywhere.[17] Prior to the 1968 World Conference in Teheran, the NGOs were too few in number to exert influence and power. By the 1980s, an extensive network of numerous local and regional NGOs had emerged, at times linked with established international NGOs. Many were to be found in the emergent Asian economic powers. Others had appeared in Latin America, especially following the collapse of military dictatorships. And the Helsinki process in Europe stirred the rise of potent popular groups in the former Communist empire west of the Urals.

Governments no longer were being challenged or called to account only at the United Nations or in Helsinki forums. Charges of human rights abuse were now being hurled on local streets or in local media. The power of local NGOs could be maximized by contact with international NGOs, which might channel their concern to the broader arena. The conjunction of need and logic with a burgeoning self-awareness of power on the part of local NGOs would make the difference—even if, initially, local NGOs were not yet fully conscious of what was even on the scheduled Vienna agenda.

The testing ground of NGO concern and strength came at the meetings of the so-called UN Preparatory Committee, which was composed of government representatives. The first meeting of the UN Committee whose objective was the preparation of the agenda of the World Conference was held on September 9-13, 1991. Even before the session began, it was known that the Committee planned to impose severe restrictions on NGO participation in the World Conference.[18] The key proposal that was circulating would limit the NGO presence to public sessions where they might serve as "observers." Oral intervention by an NGO would be allowed *only* at the invitation of the Conference Chairman. Otherwise, no NGO oral intervention would be permitted.

The response from the NGO community was vigorous and uncompromising. Thirty international NGOs signed a joint letter sent to the

Committee Chairman on September 11 arguing that "it is in the interest of both the success and integrity of the World Conference" to permit NGOs to "participate fully in its deliberations." Emphasizing their strong perspective that NGOs "are essential partners in all aspects of human rights work," they warned that without full NGO participation, "the Conference risks becoming cut-off from reality and an empty exercise."[19]

It was a shot across the UN bow, but the Preparatory Committee's acquiescence to the NGO demand was not immediately forthcoming. At the second meeting of the UN Preparatory Committee, held March 30–April 10, 1992, a number of governments were prepared to amend the proposed restrictive rules to allow participation by NGOs that had consultative status with ECOSOC or actively had involved themselves in regional meetings or in Preparatory Committee sessions. However, intense opposition by Asian states prevented acceptance of this liberalized perspective. A final decision about NGO participation was postponed.

By the third Preparatory Committee meeting held on September 14-18, 1992, the firm NGO stand produced a significant concession from Committee members. Participation by NGOs would be considerably broadened. Not only would NGOs holding UN consultative status be officially invited, but also other NGOs active in either the human rights or development fields that had their headquarters in specific regions would be invited to participate. The only qualifying limitation that applied to the latter non-UN consultative group was that they would be invited "in prior consultation with countries of the region." NGOs objected to what appeared to be an authorization for governments to apply a veto. Pressures by NGOs obliged the UN Secretariat eventually to issue an interpretation clarifying the threatening formulation. The Secretariat statement specified that "consultation" did not mean that states of the region could exercise a veto authority.

The fourth and final Preparatory Committee meeting would not be held until April 19–May 7, 1993, the very eve of the World Conference. By then tensions between governments and NGOs (as well as within NGOs) had escalated to a boiling point. What contributed to a deepening suspicion and hostility were several regional preparatory meetings that took place between the third and fourth Preparatory Committee meetings and at which NGOs, increasingly conscious of their own aspirations and, more significantly, of their power, were prepared to display newly discovered muscle. This they did by organizing separate NGO forums that ran parallel to regional meetings and could not but impact upon them.

Contributing heavily to the empowerment of NGOs was an unusual project designed to maximize coordination among a mass of separate and distinctive NGOs, many of whom had little knowledge of what was planned on a world level for June, 1993. The so-called Joint Liaison Project was launched by the International Service for Human Rights in Geneva and the Ludwig Boltzman Institute of Vienna. The specified intention was to achieve "the fullest possible contribution and participation of NGOs particularly from the South."[20] "South" meant the Third—or nonaligned—World. The initiative clearly was designed to involve a group until now almost marginal to international activity in the human rights field.

Central to the project was an NGO *Newsletter,* launched in October, 1992, and distributed to approximately 6,000 NGOs throughout the world. From the *Newsletter,* NGOs from the South could learn about the significance of the World Conference and how they might relate to it. They also would learn about a planned NGO Forum prior to the World Conference. At the same time, they were advised about the possibility of NGO activities being arranged that would run parallel to the World Conference.

The project would soon lead to the formation of a Joint Planning Committee of 15 members drawn from the key coordinating body of international NGOs holding consultative status at the UN, Conference of Non-Governmental Organizations (CONGO), from the Boltzmann Institute and from three regional NGO Committees—Africa, Asia/Pacific and Latin America/Caribbean. The Planning Committee assumed the task of disseminating detailed information about the scheduled World Conference. An important part of its goal was the coordination of the work of NGOs. The Committee further took on the semipermanent job of establishing a continuing liaison with the World Conference Secretariat. In time, it also assumed responsibility for organizing the NGO Forum as well as the parallel NGO activities during the World Conference.

A host of crucial items for the World Conference were emerging, and a coordinated leadership effort was essential for the empowerment of local NGOs. Among these items was the core theme of various authoritarian powers, especially in Asia, that sharply questioned the validity of an automatic universal character to human rights. Cultural "particularities," it was argued, circumscribed the *universality* of human rights obligations. Other core themes, advanced by different parties, concerned the right of development as well as economic and social rights, and women's rights. But equally important was a specific target toward which all NGOs might strive as a means of fulfilling their human rights aspirations. What would emerge at the NGO regional forums as the central theme that linked almost all of them was the notion of a UN High Commissioner for Human Rights. It would become the banner to which they would cling, and the slogan around which they would unify their forces. How the High Commissioner concept, virtually unknown to local NGOs, could take on the character of a revolutionary slogan in the course of several regional meetings over a six-month period in 1992-93 may be mystifying, though not inexplicable.

After all, prompted by urgent human rights needs and deficiencies in the UN machinery for coping with rights violations, activists were spurred to develop and seek out new ideas. The search for new ideas ineluctably was expedited by the awareness that a conference focusing upon the problem soon was to take place. Credit must go to Amnesty International for dusting off a discarded thesis, giving it pertinence and immediacy and setting it afloat. It would become the dominant cry of NGOs at the various regional NGO forums.

The idea first emerged in Amsterdam at a large conference hosted by the Dutch section of Amnesty International. Present were a number of human rights experts and activists who reached a consensus on the need for a new office headed by a high level UN official. The office would be called upon to respond quickly and effectively to gross rights violations, including disappearances and political killings. It would be the hub of a rationalized UN human rights system.

Two months after the Amsterdam meeting, Amnesty International shaped the idea into concrete formulation. Its document, *Facing Up to the Failures,* now would set forth the functions of what it called a "Special Commissioner for Human Rights." The odd language was designed to remove the traditional formulation—"High Commissioner"—because it seemed to recall structures of the British colonial system.[21] Elimination of a hated symbol, it must have been thought, would attract more support from NGOs in the Third World "South." In fact, there was little need for Orwellian verbiage. Once the office of the High Commissioner was clearly defined, the artificial phrase, "Special Commissioner," could be sloughed off.

The very first formal appearances of the High Commissioner concept came at the initial UN regional preparatory meeting that was designed to embrace the African continent. Tunis was the host for the week-long sessions held November 2-6, 1992. It turned out to be the largest human rights conference ever held on the African continent. A total of 163 NGOs were in attendance, including 131 that were strictly local.[22] The latter figure was quite high. In the early eighties, the prominent researcher Professor Harry Scoble found a "relative weakness" of the human rights movement in black Africa due to poverty, the low level of adult literacy, the ethnically divisive character of many societies and, especially, the hostility of African governing elites to local NGO activity.[23] Scoble could identify the existence of only 27 human rights NGOs. A 1994 study by the International Human Rights Internship Program of Washington, D.C. revealed a "remarkable" growth in the NGO movement with the total of NGOs reaching 197 in sub-Saharan Africa.[24] Soon afterwards the scholar, Claude Welch, after examining the roles of NGOs in four representative sub-Saharan African states found them to be, in the main, limited in membership and operating "in harsh social and political climates."[25]

For the very first time in the process leading up to the Vienna World Conference, NGOs could advance their own proposals. Amnesty International formally called for a High Commissioner and the local NGOs responded favorably and enthusiastically. Other NGOs prompted other suggestions. Thus, the International Commission of Jurists placed on the agenda the idea of creating a permanent International Criminal Court. Strikingly, the NGOs appeared to take naturally to the opportunity presented to them. A level of early maturity seemed to be reached. They divided themselves into separate working groups to correspond with the most pressing issues that should be addressed by the regional meeting, and they followed this up with vigorous lobbying. At least 30 NGOs contributed either oral or written statements. Especially significant was the right given them to meet with the crucial drafting committee, a right they had no hesitancy to exploit.

Yet, for all the openings presented to the international and African NGOs, none of their recommendations were accepted by the drafting committee. The relationship between governments and NGOs in Africa was one of an adversarial nature, if not of palpable suspicion and hostility. Besides, African NGOs were a comparatively new phenomenon and their experience was limited. Still, modest strides had been taken and a significant new plateau had been reached.

At the second regional meeting, covering the area of Latin America and the Caribbean, and held in San José, Costa Rica on January 18-22, 1993, the NGOs were more successful. More than 170 organizations attended; 114 of them had their headquarters in the region. Differing interests found expression in the separate organizations: some represented women, others indigenous people, still others ecological and environmental concerns. By the beginning of the eighties, NGOs in Latin America, according to Human Rights Internet, well outdistanced their counterparts in other Third World areas.[26] They numbered 220, as compared with 145 in Asia and 124 in Africa and the Middle East combined. Only a decade later, the number of NGOs in Latin America had more than doubled, reaching 550. What prompted this success, she found, was the pioneering work of a few local NGOs in opposing the Argentine military dictatorship.[27] Careful statistical research by Patrick Ball found a correlation between the emergence of human rights NGOs and the existence in the background of a liberal constitutional tradition confronted suddenly by a repressive military regime using state terror.[28]

A well-known regional research and lobbying group in San José provided a kind of primary headquarters for the NGOs. The Inter-American Institute for Human Rights coordinated NGO participation and scheduled a preliminary meeting where the key issues upon which to lobby were hashed out. Joint declarations later would be prepared reflecting mutual concerns of the NGOs and, like their African colleagues, they won the right to testify before the drafting committee. Their specific perspectives on regional agenda items were made patently evident, not without a certain success.

As in Tunis, NGOs were responsive to the proposal advanced by Amnesty International for a High Commissioner. No special new pleading was needed. It was as if the idea was endemic to NGO concerns. But, unlike the African meeting, the NGO plea found a strong echo on the government level in San José. The host government of the regional meeting, after all, had been the sponsor of the High Commissioner proposal at the UN Commission of Human Rights and the General Assembly in the sixties. As its advocate, Costa Rica had a special stake in promoting the concept to which it could lay a certain claim. And the government succeeded in persuading its colleagues from other Latin American countries to accept, at least partially, the lobbying of the NGOs on this issue.

The regional meeting thus could conclude with a favorable Resolution of partial endorsement: "We propose that the World Conference consider the possibility of asking the General Assembly to study the feasibility of establishing a United Nations Permanent Commissioner for Human Rights."[29] It was hardly a ringing demand. Indeed, the Resolution was distinctly qualified and circumscribed. A study of feasibility was called for, not an appeal for definitely creating an institution. And the reference to a "Permanent Commissioner" rather than to "High Commissioner" reflected unspecified fears of being charged with supporting imperial intervention.

The San José document displayed other positive features, including a recommendation for strengthening the UN Human Rights Centre and appeals for the protection of vulnerable groups in society. What was striking about this significant forward step was that all the positive resolutions that were incorporated into the San José document were prompted and intensively lobbied for by NGOs.

Far more impressive than the NGO achievements at regional meetings in Africa and Latin America were the accomplishments of NGOs at the Asia Pacific Regional Meeting held in Bangkok, Thailand on March 29–April 2, 1993. Some 240 participants from 100 regional NGOs were in attendance along with a number of international NGOs. A keen observer found them to be "the most organized and focussed in their preparations and work" as compared with the NGOs at previous regional meetings.[30]

The level of sophistication and planning among Asian NGOs hardly was accidental. They had already undergone a huge expansion in East Asia, especially in Southeast Asia during the 1980s.[31] Their growth can be traced in part to the availability of funds from donor countries. While the beginnings of the NGO movement can be linked to the remarkable economic growth of the region as a whole that began a decade earlier, the factor that prompted the expansion and early maturation of NGOs was governmental repression. The biggest NGO human rights organizations in the region emerged as a response to political crackdowns resulting in numerous arrests and detentions.

Getting friends and associates out of prison became a paramount objective. This was manifested in Korea following military repression in the mid-seventies, in the Philippines after the government's declaration of martial law in 1972, in Thailand after a 1973 military coup and in Indonesia with the establishment of the Legal Aid Institute in 1970. Even as the NGOs strove to end repression and torture, they took on demands for freedom of expression and organization, thereby demonstrating that interest in civil and political rights was not exclusively a Western preoccupation.

Advocacy of these rights during the same period became linked with other demands that flowed ineluctably from excesses of rapid industrialization. Resource and environmental concerns along with concerns about exploitation of labor, generally, and, woman and child labor, particularly, spawned new groups and new priorities among professional organizations. If individual NGOs took on a particular priority in the humanitarian or environmental area, they nonetheless remained committed to the broad human rights struggle. And, strikingly, they established strong bonds across national borders. A distinctly regional outlook was characteristic of various NGO groups, especially among Thais, Filipinos, Indonesians and Malaysians.[32]

Recognition of shared interests in a human rights field, together with a decade of common experiences, would produce a remarkable and unprecedented NGO document—the Bangkok Declaration. It emerged from a three-day NGO forum held in Bangkok, March 25-28, just prior to the opening of the regional meeting. The conference was extraordinarily comprehensive, examining a broad range of human rights issues extending to women, children and indigenous groups, along with mechanisms for strengthening labor and union rights.

The Declaration expressed a bold and unqualified call for "establishing a UN Special Commissioner for Human Rights as a new high-level political authority to bring a more effective and rapid response, coherence and coordination in the protection of human rights."[33] It was a firm demand for immediate action, not an uncertain appeal for a study of the idea, as proposed at San José. There was firmness, too, in stressing the "universality" and "indivisibility" of human rights and in spelling out a number of specific objectives related to the themes of women, children, labor and indigenous groups. The strengthening of mechanisms dealing with the thematic issues or with human rights broadly also was insisted upon.

Altogether, it was a powerful document that could not easily be dismissed. This was, after all, the voice of numerous Asian citizens speaking. Heretofore, as a leading human rights journal noted, Asian authoritarian governments at the UN Commission on Human Rights "discussed NGO criticisms as concerns of foreigners who do not know their [Asian] cultures."[34] No longer was this possible. As the journal added: "With Asians speaking out so clearly, they [authoritarian governments] will now find that a more difficult defence to adopt."

Nor were the ideas of the NGOs perceived only in the abstract. The surprisingly sophisticated Asian groups vigorously lobbied their governments during the regional meeting and even borrowed from Western human rights activism the need to publicize their views, thus making the proceedings as transparent as possible. Thus, they held press conferences daily. An observer commented upon their impact: "It was evident that Asian governments had not anticipated so many NGOs beating on their doors with their demands."

But, for the time being, the governments were not too responsive. If they accepted NGO statements on women and children's rights and, more importantly, the universality and indivisibility of human rights, they rejected all appeals for strengthening UN implementation machinery, including the establishment of a High Commissioner on Human Rights. This negative outlook on implementation was perfectly consistent with the hostile attitude of these governments toward human rights agitation. Several of the fast-growing Southeast Asian industrial powers were among the most repressive authoritarian regimes in the world, a fact that they rationalized and legitimized in an elaborate manner. Their sophistry, as will be noted later, would be equal to the harshness of their rule.

The toughness of Asian governments, now profoundly aware of the challenge posed by their own NGOs, would assume a fierce determination to prevail. At the fourth and final UN Preparatory Committee meeting held in Geneva on April 19–May 7, 1993, just a few weeks prior to the World Conference sessions, they launched an initiative to sharply limit the NGO role in the forthcoming proceedings. Resistance from Western and African delegations prevented a major retreat. Nonetheless, a compromise between the opposing sides took the form of a setback to traditional UN standards for NGOs set by ECOSOC.

It was agreed that NGOs would be allowed to attend plenary sessions but without speaking. They might make short presentations to the Drafting Committee (initially the Plenary Committee) in its early deliberations. Once, however, the Committee began working in earnest on a draft, NGOs would be required to withdraw. On May 3, the Plenary Committee became the Drafting Committee and NGOs simply were ousted from the room.

In the face of the obdurate stance of mainly Asian regimes, NGO lobbying proved unavailing. The number of NGOs was not very large; there were approximately 60 including international and regional groups. Especially apparent to observers was the ineffectual character of NGO lobbying at this final preparatory meeting where their organization and preparation proved totally inadequate for the occasion.[35] The one exception was the women's groups. Vigorous pressure exerted by these groups succeeded in winning approval of special paragraphs dealing with women's rights.

The stonewalling by the Asian authoritarian governments elsewhere in the Third World later would help trigger a major split in the NGO community. International NGOs, dominant in the so-called Joint

Planning Committee that guided NGO lobbying and general strategy, were seen as indifferent or unresponsive to the local grassroots NGOs. Groups from the Third World regions would conclude that they had not been consulted by the international groups, who appeared to monopolize strategy planning. The stormy three-week session produced a veritable deadlock. Aside from extremely limited progress in the area of women's rights and the rights of indigenous peoples, the offensive initiated at various NGO forums seemed to have collapsed.

Why the apparent collapse occurred is by no means clear. Perhaps, the NGOs felt that since the World Conference was about to begin, it was pointless to waste any energy upon the final Preparatory Committee meeting. If the atmosphere in the world NGO community, for the moment, appeared dismal, there was one encouraging development that was scarcely noticed at the time. It took place in Washington, D.C., not Geneva, but its ramifications ultimately would be felt at the World Conference itself. American human rights NGOs, working in coalition, had persuaded the Clinton Administration, which had come to power only three months earlier (on January 20, 1993), to take a positive attitude toward the idea of a UN High Commissioner for Human Rights. Its Republican predecessors had rejected the need for a High Commissioner on the hardly persuasive grounds that enough high-level UN posts already existed.

Once accepted by the new Administration, the High Commissioner proposal became a focus for Washington's zealous advocacy. At the Preparatory Committee meeting in Geneva, U.S. advocacy did not prevail, although the proposal for a High Commissioner was inserted in brackets, which technically indicated that the language was being considered though not yet accepted. Still, U.S. government activism marked a major turning point. If the NGOs were to resume their previous activism, they would have, on the governmental level, a powerful ally.[36] According to one authority, the key NGO lobbyists in Washington were Holly Burkhalter and "her people" of Human Rights Watch, Joe Eldridge of the Lawyers Committee and Jim O'Dea of Amnesty International–USA. They met regularly with Assistant Secretary of State John Shattuck.[37]

Precisely because the United States was "pushing very heavily" for a High Commissioner, it would enormously ease the task of NGOs, said an informed participant, Reed Brody, the principal lobbyist of the NGO community.[38] Still, from the perspective of a leading expert who was very much involved in the World Conference, Felice Gaer, "as the conference approached, few governments considered that the concept had any chance of survival. . . ."[39]

By the time of the World Conference, held in Vienna on June 14-25, the NGO community had ended its moment of passivity and had become completely energized. NGOs were determined to make their mark on world affairs and they came in droves. Indeed the two-week session would be transformed into grand theater. Never before had the world seen a human rights meeting of such magnitude.

Official figures provide an index of the huge NGO behemoth attending the Vienna meeting at the historic Austria Centre. In attendance as observers were 3,691 representatives from 841 NGO organizations. What had made possible the enormous number of participants was a modification of the access rules. Besides the 900 NGOs formally registered with UN consultative status, an additional 1,004 human rights NGOs without formal UN status also were invited. Thus, the bulk of the representatives in Vienna never had attended a UN meeting before or even were versed in the proceedings of traditional international sessions. Inevitably, impatience with traditional processes would set in among the novices, which might create clashes and cleavages with their colleagues.

The World Conference was preceded by an NGO Forum, June 10-13. In attendance were 2,721 representatives from 1529 organizations. The NGOs varied greatly in character: some were national, others were international; some were multipurpose, others were single issue; some were oriented to gathering information, others were activists; some were from the Third World "South," others were from the developed-world "North." Data on the area breakdown is revealing. The largest group of organizations—numbering 426—was from West Europe; the next in size, not surprisingly, came from Asia, numbering 270, with an additional 38 from Australia/Oceania. Then, in order, were: Latin America—236; Africa—202; East and Central Europe—179 and North America—178.[40]

The Forum was marked by a surprisingly intense cleavage between the Joint Planning Committee (JPC), comprised of a dozen members representing the established international NGOs holding UN consultative status and based in the West (or, rather the "North"), and the vast new national constituencies of the "South." The JPC acted like an Executive Committee. It had made all the arrangements for the Forum, appointed all the Chairmen and Rapporteurs of the Forum's various sessions and programs, selected speakers and finally, acted as liaison with the professionals of the Centre for Human Rights as well as with the major regional government caucuses. From the perspective of the "new kid on the block" the various grassroots groups now beginning to flex their political muscle—the JPC seemed like an elitist group, whose intent was to marginalize them. After all, the NGOs from the South had not been consulted about the agenda, the appointments or the speakers.

Within this heightened tension between establishment and grassroots NGOs, three conflicts appeared that would trigger a stunning insurrection against the JPC and point to a future of less than full harmony between NGOs of the North and NGOs of the South. The first conflict developed around an issue that surfaced on the opening day of the Forum: should NGOs specify or name countries that engage in or support human rights abuses? It was an old and continuing problem at the UN. Apparently, the UN had set as a condition for the convening of the NGO conference that specific countries would not be named.[41] While some international NGOs saw the purpose of the Forum to be one of working with governments in order to strengthen the UN human rights system by creating a North-South consensus, others—especially the grassroots groups—believed that the failure to expose human rights abuses in specific countries would constitute a betrayal of NGO hopes and operations.

The advocates of the openly militant approach carried the day. As reported by the independent organ of the World Conference, *Terra Viva,* the NGOs had thrown down an "extraordinary challenge to governments" on the very eve of the World Conference. A central JPC figure and representative of the Boltzmann Institute, Manfred Nowak, denounced the decision as "provocative and unwise." What added to the conflict was the agreement by the Forum, under UN pressure, to withdraw 5,000 copies of its printed schedule that carried references to specific human rights violations in various countries. As a substitute, the UN printed 2,500 copies of a sanitized version for distribution.

By the next session of the NGO Forum, the groups from the South furiously were demanding that the JPC be ousted and replaced by activists more responsive to the grassroots of the international NGO community.[42] A spokesperson for the revolt, Cecilia Jimenez, declared: "We are protesting against the NGO Forum organisers' efforts to marginalize the South. . . ." An angry Nowak responded that these were "slanderous accusations." The headline in the independent house organ of the World Conference described the session as "Organizational Mayhem."

Adding to the bitterness of the grassroots groups were reports that the Dalai Lama, the Buddhist leader, would not be permitted to address the NGO Forum and even might not be allowed to enter the premises of the Austrian Centre where all the sessions were held. The Dalai Lama had been invited to address the Forum, but China was determined to prevent his appearance by pointing out that the Austrian Centre, for the occasion, was UN territory. Ultimately, a compromise was reached whereby the Dalai Lama could enter the Centre but would not be allowed to speak from the Forum platform itself. Since Amnesty International had invited him to speak to the NGOs at its own tent, nothing fundamental was sacrificed.[43] For the militants, however, protests against the decisions of JPC simply could be linked, even if unwarrantedly, with demonstrations against the restrictions on the Dalai Lama. Thus, when the issue of the Dalai Lama first was raised, a petition was circulated calling upon the JPC to explain its alleged "decision to disinvite His Holiness." An observer characterized the situation as one of "absolute chaos."[44]

The third conflict ended in a grievous and stunning embarrassment that evoked self-examination. The Forum organizers had invited former U.S. President Jimmy Carter to address the closing session since his Administration openly had embraced human rights and his key State Department rights advocate, Patt Derian, had initiated significant major changes in U.S. policy toward Latin America, both directly and through the United Nations. Latin American NGOs immediately expressed "shock" that he was invited and began circulating a petition that he be replaced by the Argentine writer and Nobel Laureate Adolfo Perez Esquivel.[45] The rationale for the anti-Carter fury was that he represented a government that, as one protester put it, was the "biggest violator of human rights on the entire planet." The Forum organizers were said to be lacking in sensitivity in selecting Carter without consulting with the Latin American NGOs.

Iain Guest, the writer of the authoritative study of "disappearances" in Argentina, was covering the Carter appearance as a journalist and could not fail to capture in moving prose what he called "Latin America's Day of Rage" when the former U.S. President began speaking.[46] It began with screaming by Hebe de Bonafini, a leader of the Mothers of the Plaza de Mayo, of the word *asesino* (assassin). She was joined by a whole group of other NGOs from Latin America and other areas, and they almost completely drowned out Carter's speech. What struck Guest was "the irony that was almost overwhelming," for it was Carter's principal human rights official, Patt Derian, who so powerfully had impacted upon the military rulers in Argentina and pushed through the UN the historic breakthrough decision on "disappearances."

In the end, the JPC was forced to disband because it had lost the "legitimacy" of being a leader in the NGO world. Replacing the dissolved

JPC was a newly chosen 30-member NGO Liaison Committee comprising 3 members from each of the major Third World areas—Latin America, Asia and Africa—along with single representatives from a variety of specialized NGOs representing the indigenous, women, children, refugees, youth and the disabled. At the same time, the representation from Europe was sharply cut, from 6 to 2.[47] Accompanying the abdication was a "public apology [by the JPC] for the frustrating organizational chaos" that had prevailed at the Forum.[48]

The veritable insurrection of Third World NGOs, especially in the way it was manifested in the anti-Carter episode, over the long run could not but exert a significant impact upon the NGO movement. As reported in the independent house organ, *Terra Viva,* "NGO delegations here were virtually unanimous that the future of the NGO movement would be grim if this conference were a sign of things to come."[49] What was clearly apparent was that "Southern NGOs have arrived in force" and that "many of them are well-armed, combative and armed with their own agendas." Certainly, their lack of sophistication was evident, as was the need for a greater understanding of the mechanics of both international conferences and diplomacy.

Yet, the international NGOs ineluctably would be compelled to deal with these Third World NGOs in a new way. They were clearly a force with which to contend. At the World Conference, that force effectively was harnessed by those international NGOs who knew their way around governmental and intergovernmental meetings. Especially were the Asian NGOs of critical importance, since the opposition to the primary aims of international NGOs came from the major Asian powers. Besides, one of the world's leading human rights theorists, Professor Philip Alston of Australia, appeared to endorse militancy at the opening day of the Forum. He urged NGOs to be "more confrontational" and less "well-behaved." "Where," he asked, "is the Greenpeace of human rights that gets up the nose of governments?"[50]

The split in NGO leadership did not diminish the determination to prevail on substantive issues. Unity prevailed in adopting strong resolutions on a variety of human rights issues. Typical was the following determined and uncompromising Resolution adopted by the World Conference on the High Commissioner:

> An office of a High Commissioner for Human Rights should be established as a new high level independent authority within the United Nations system, with the capacity to act rapidly in emergency situations of human rights violations and to ensure the coordination of human rights activities

within the United Nations systems and the integration of human rights into all United Nations programs and activities.

Clearly, Amnesty International and other major international NGOs were on the same wavelength as the regional groups of the South.

The united front of the NGO community was of critical importance once the World Conference on Human Rights began its deliberations. While the phalanx of 171 governments in attendance was not unified, a solid core of them, comprised mostly of groups from Asia, was determined to resist all initiatives that might strengthen UN human rights machinery. It would require potent coordinated lobbying by a solidly united NGO community to make inroads, and, even then, uncertainty prevailed.

The transparency of the sharp distinction between government representatives and NGOs was all too evident. The very physical allocation of space illuminated the distinction and reminded the observer of the popular British television series, *Upstairs, Downstairs*. At the mammoth Austria Centre building, the diplomats, correct and formal, sat upstairs. The contrast with the downstairs of NGO stalls and meeting rooms was enormous. Here a beehive of endless public activities was conducted— lectures, films, lobbying, workshops and informational meetings.[51] The coldness of the polished "upstairs" was confronted by angry, hot-blooded NGOs displaying gruesome photos and horror-ridden videos illustrating governmental abuse of human rights.[52] A top veteran staffer of the Geneva Centre for Human Rights recalled his sense of "shock to walk on the lower level just to feel the energy" of the NGOs. "We had struck a gold mine of energy," he added, and it was "our task" to "tap into that energy."[53]

Access was the key procedural issue for the NGOs. Would they be able to attend and participate in Plenary sessions, in the Main Committee and, most importantly, in the Drafting Committee? The procedural question was central to the lobbying effort. Government delegations, especially those from Asia, sought to limit NGO participation generally. Initially, NGOs won a modest victory with respect to the Plenary sessions. They won the right to attend in limited numbers, using special green identification badges and sitting in a separate gallery. Shortly afterward, the restrictions fell by the wayside and any NGO was allowed to attend. Eventually, permission was granted them to speak, although under clear restrictions. In the Main Committee, a total of 550 seats were reserved for NGOs.

It was with reference to the strategically important Drafting Committee that victory was simply unobtainable. Hostile governments were determined to severely curb crucial lobbying in the vital area where fundamental decisions were taken. The U.S. delegation tried to arrange a deal whereby NGOs might sit in the drafting room. Its brokered deal was for a time successful but, unexpectedly, the deal was overruled by the Chairman, a Brazilian, Gilberto Vergne Saboia, on the grounds that some governments would refuse to accept the deal. Assistant Secretary of State John Shattuck vigorously stressed the need for full "NGO participation in the broadest sense" as they "have made extraordinary achievements over the last years that have literally transformed the world."[54] Yet, the Chairman had a point. According to a European source, 80 delegates threatened to walk out if NGOs were permitted to attend the Drafting Committee.[55] For the NGOs, it seemed for the moment a severe setback. Its principal lobbyist with governments, Reed Brody, stated that the refusal of access to NGOs meant that "the real work will be done behind our backs."[56]

Yet, the NGOs were not faced with a blank wall. There were some NGO leaders who also served on official governmental delegations, and they assumed a responsibility to obtain in the Drafting Committee the prevailing status of various draft resolutions and proposals. This timely and crucial information was shared with NGO caucuses, which, in turn, after their own deliberations, would share their views with official delegations through unofficial channels.

Thus, if NGO lobbying was severely handicapped, it was by no means dormant. The contrary was the case. NGOs were everywhere lobbying government delegations, holding press conferences, coordinating their efforts and refusing to give up or abdicate even when the possibility of a significant advance was dim. The Asia/Pacific coordinating group was particularly active. Guided by the Bangkok Declaration, the group would not retreat from pressing all delegations, including particularly the toughest group of all—the Asian powers.

NGO activism in lobbying had its greatest impact in neutralizing the ideological line pursued by a number of major powers in Asia and Africa who stressed cultural "particularities" in response to blunt allegations that they failed to adhere to universal standards. The presence and militancy of the Asian and African NGOs, who refused to accept the theme of cultural distinctiveness and exceptionalism and who insisted upon adherence to universal standards, made a mockery of the "particularities" thesis. In the end, they prevailed. The World Conference stated explicitly that "all human rights are universal, indivisible and interdependent," even if "national and regional particularities . . . must be borne in mind. . . ."

The NGOs' biggest victory, though still a partial one, came on the issue of the High Commissioner. At the beginning of the Conference, few governments thought that the idea had "any chance of survival," as a perceptive participant observed.[57] The predominant view of the Third World was expressed by the Chairman of the Non-Aligned Working Group on Human Rights, Redzuan Kushairi of Malaysia. The group represented the 108 members of the nonaligned movement, which originally had 77 members, and continued to maintain its initial title "Group of 77." Kushairi saw the High Commissioner as an instrument of the West, and asked rhetorically whether it would be "another political exercise to pick and choose Third World nations and humiliate them?"[58]

He wondered aloud and with great skepticism to whether the High Commissioner would "investigate human rights abuses in the United States." Following a tirade against the United States for its treatment of blacks and Hispanics, Kushairi unleashed a blast against Amnesty International for its "open letter" sent to all heads of state that had warned that universal human rights could be undermined in Vienna: "Where is Amnesty International," he asked, "on basic needs such as the right to food, right to education and right to development?" He went on with what was the standard response of authoritarian and totalitarian regimes. "Human rights is not only about individual freedom within the context of political and civil rights but also economic, social and cultural rights."

Only some 40 of the 171 delegations spoke in favor of the High Commissioner concept. These were representatives of states from West Europe, East Europe and North America, as well as Costa Rica and Ecuador from Latin America. The opponents came to recognize that the demand for the new institution could not be halted in Vienna. Pressure from the NGOs, especially from those of Asia and Africa, was too great to be pushed aside totally. So they sought to delay action by calling for "further study." Leaders of this strong initiative were China, Singapore, Indonesia, Malaysia, Cuba, Sudan and Syria.

Hard bargaining in the drafting sessions and in corridors continued until the bitter end. At the eleventh hour, consensus was reached on a compromise formula: "The World Conference on Human Rights recommends to the General Assembly that, when examining the report of the Conference . . . it begin, *as a matter of priority*, consideration of the question of the establishment of a High Commissioner for Human Rights for the promotion and protection of all human rights." [Emphasis added.] The agreement came at 5 A.M., one hour before the close of the

Conference. It was largely a product of continuing U.S. pressure with well-timed strategic assistance provided by Canada and Poland.[59]

Establishment of an office of UN High Commissioner was not within the authority and power of the World Conference. Only the General Assembly could create a new UN institution. A huge obstacle had to be hurdled at the UN session of the General Assembly. There the exercise of state sovereignty could not quickly evaporate. There, too, parliamentary maneuvering moved to the fore and, with the complexity of power relations at the UN where bloc voting is ascendant, postponement of decision-making would not be surprising. Moreover, the unrelenting open pressure of NGOs would be absent from the scene. The staid and correct setting at the UN provided a totally different atmosphere than did the public arena of Vienna.

For the moment, however, NGOs could exult in reaching "a rare, defining moment" in the history of the UN and in the struggle for the protection of human rights. Tribute was paid them in a Resolution adopted at Vienna: "The World Conference on Human Rights recognizes the important role of non-governmental organizations in the promotion of all human rights and in humanitarian activities."[60] It is, nonetheless, significant that at this point the Resolution introduced a series of modifying statements that, in essence, sought to limit the authority of NGOs or to caution them about their conduct. First, it stressed that "the primary responsibility for standard-setting lies with States," and then it went on to say that "the Conference also appreciates the contribution of NGOs to this process." The reality had been otherwise. It was the NGO community that had been in the forefront of the standard-setting process.

Immediately afterward, the Resolution formulation carried a special, although indirect, warning: "NGOs and their members *genuinely involved in the field of human rights* should enjoy rights and freedoms recognized in the Universal Declaration of Human Rights and the protection of national law." [Emphasis added.] The phrasing clearly implied that those not "genuinely involved" might not necessarily be granted rights and the protection of national law. But who is to determine whether individual NGOs are "genuinely involved"? No answer was offered.

The succeeding sentence in the Resolution was also potentially threatening: "These rights and freedoms may not be exercised contrary to the purposes and principles of the United Nations." Again left unsaid was the method for ascertaining whether undefined NGO activities were "contrary" to UN principles and purposes. A concluding sentence constituted yet another cautionary note: "NGOs should be free to carry out their human rights activities, without interference, within the framework of *national law* and the Universal Declaration of Human Rights." [Emphasis added.] The fact is that "national law," in authoritarian and totalitarian regimes, had all too often proved to be notoriously restrictive with respect to rights.

In stark contrast to the language of the Vienna meeting's final document on NGOs was the initial draft that was prepared at the fourth UN Preparatory Committee meeting held in Geneva two months earlier:

> The World Conference pays tribute to the untiring and invaluable efforts of non-governmental organizations in all aspects of human rights and humanitarian activities. . . . Their contributions to standard-setting, monitoring of compliance with existing standards, dissemination of information and the conduct of education, training and research are recognized and their contributions to all human rights activities undertaken by intergovernmental organizations should be facilitated.[61]

Far more glowing in its laudatory comments about NGOs, the much briefer draft carried no confining restrictions or implied any warnings. The reason for this striking difference between the two texts was that the Geneva draft was prepared by members of the UN Secretariat staff, who were keenly aware of the work of NGOs, while the Vienna World Conference document was negotiated by government delegations.

Distrusted by governments in the Third World, NGOs would not have an easy time pressing their demands for a High Commissioner at the forthcoming General Assembly beginning in late September. They would need a friend in court, for only a handful of the major international NGOs had come to UN Headquarters. It was "the usual suspects," as Reed Brody, the spokesperson for the NGO Liaison Committee, wistfully recalled. They were the representatives of the Lawyers Committee for Human Rights, Amnesty International, Human Rights Watch and "principally" Felice Gaer of the Blaustein Institute for the Advancement of Human Rights.[62] Joined by Brody, who also represented the International Human Rights Law Group, they raised some money "to bring other people from the NGO community."[63] In view of travel costs they set their sights mainly on Latin American NGOs.

The American role at the General Assembly was absolutely critical. President Clinton placed the full authority of his new Administration and of the presidential office itself behind the effort in the Assembly to create the post of High Commissioner "soon and with vigor and energy and conviction."[64] Europe solidly supported his determined initiative. Once it was adopted by consensus, U.S. Ambassador to the UN Madeleine Albright could justly claim that the General Assembly action constituted "a major milestone for world human rights."[65] That "milestone," a product of NGO lobbying, ultimately was given reality by the power of determined U.S. diplomacy.

Oddly enough, when the Amnesty International representative at the UN, Andrew Clapham, wrote a scholarly essay relating the "outside story" of the creation of the High Commissioner's office, he all but eliminated the central role played by the United States.[66] When questioned on this point in a later interview, he acknowledged that U.S. lobbying was indispensable for the success of the NGO initiative. This is how Clapham put it: "If the U.S. hadn't been behind it, it wouldn't have happened."[67] He then went on to explain why the U.S. role wasn't given emphasis in his article: "I wouldn't like to give them [the U.S.] the credit for getting it, partly because I think it would damage the [High Commissioner's] office and partly because I don't think it's true." The last point was clarified with the observation that "there were a lot of other countries" that pushed the idea. Moreover, he explained, even when the United States is on the same side as Amnesty on various human rights issues, it has its own agenda—"they've got their own thing going." (Clapham left his Amnesty position in New York in 1997.) Interestingly, former President Jimmy Carter, in an interview in Vienna, sought to tackle the issue of how important the United States is in advancing human rights, in contrast with NGOs. After noting that, as President, "I never met with a head of State when human rights was not on the agenda," Carter then continued: "There is no way that Amnesty International, for all its wonderful work, can play the same role that the President of the United States can play. . . ."[68]

To win consensus, the UN Resolution establishing a High Commissioner was less specific than the proposals of NGOs or supportive governments. Nor did the Resolution urge a militantly activist role for the new international civil servant. Still, by extending to the High Commissioner the authority to "dialogue with all governments . . . with a view to securing respect for human rights," it gave the office plenty of flexibility.[69] Further delineated were a variety of specific responsibilities of the High Commissioner's to make recommendations to UN bodies for the promotion and protection of all human rights; to play "an active role" in the elimination and prevention of violations of human rights everywhere; to provide overall coordination of human rights activities throughout the UN system; to arrange for the rationalization and strengthening of the UN's machinery and mechanisms on human rights and to coordinate the UN's educational and public information programs dealing with human rights. To placate Third World governments and NGOs, the Resolution also added the uncertain and questionable responsibility of promoting "a balanced and sustainable development for all people."

A more potent mandate proposed by the United States that would have enabled the High Commissioner to carry out fact-finding investigations into reported human rights abuses had to be withdrawn.[70] On the other hand, crippling restrictions upon the High Commissioner initially sought by various Asian powers were avoided. A compromise was reached on the issue of where the High Commissioner's office should be located. NGOs had recognized for some time that the move of the human rights secretariat to Geneva from New York in the early seventies had helped undermine the significance and impact of human rights. That the High Commissioner's office should be located in New York at UN Headquarters was strongly argued by Amnesty International "to ensure that human rights are taken seriously at the political level, to secure his or her close involvement in high-level consultations and discussions on all issues with implications for human rights promotion and protection. . . ."[71] It was a view with which most NGOs agreed. In the end, the proponents had to be satisfied with the consensus decision to have the High Commissioner based in Geneva, but with an office in New York.

If the creation of the office of High Commissioner was a monumental achievement, much would depend on who was appointed to the post and how he or she might overcome a host of obstacles and barriers. Two months after the General Assembly decision, the UN Secretary-General appointed Ambassador José Ayala Lasso of Ecuador as High Commissioner. It was clearly a political decision; Ayala Lasso had no experience in the human rights field, nor had he even indicated a special interest in the subject. His professional life was totally involved with diplomacy. He had served at one time as Foreign Minister of Ecuador and in various other diplomatic capacities. What made the choice a not unlikely one was Ayala Lasso's diplomatic role in steering the UN draft resolution to a successful consummation. He had chaired the Working Group of the Assembly's Third Committee that guided the heated debate, resolved the clashing views and finally brought forth a consensus resolution.

Of one thing there could be little doubt, at least at the beginning of his tenure: Ayala Lasso clearly recognized that NGOs were of vital importance to his operation. The very office he occupied was largely a creation of NGOs. He was hoping that their commitment would continue. In a letter to the Chairman of the UN NGO Committee on Human Rights, Harris Schoenberg, written several weeks before his appointment, Ayala Lasso expressed the hope that NGOs would "work closely with the High Commissioner in helping that person confront . . . many challenges. . . ."[72]

Even as NGO initiative and effort were sparking the creation of a landmark institution, developments were unfolding that pointed to the emergence of another milestone for human rights progress at the UN. And again, Amnesty International was involved, at least to some degree. Peacekeeping always had been seen as the primary objective of the United Nations, at least as prescribed in the Charter. During the Cold War, however, peacekeeping could not, except in rare instances, effectively be pursued. With the Cold War's end, peacekeeping increasingly shifted to intrastate conflicts, at times growing out of ethnic or class tensions. No less than 100,000 UN troops had been dispatched by 1994 to handle peacekeeping missions in a half-dozen critical areas including El Salvador, Cambodia, Angola, Mozambique and Rwanda. In several instances, human rights became a significant component of the process, most notably in El Salvador.

Amnesty International monitored these peacekeeping missions in considerable detail. Its report, *Peacekeeping and Human Rights* (1994), offered a detailed analysis of UN missions and outlined several important areas for improvement. Its 15-point list of recommendations also included ensuring that all UN personnel are trained in human rights standards and "instructed that they have a duty to report human rights violations." There were to be "no silent witnesses," too often the case for UN teams. The recommendations further called for the inclusion of human rights language and human rights agreements directly into the negotiated peace agreement. Specifically rejected were preconviction amnesties; instead, human rights abusers were to be prosecuted. Proposed, too, was the creation of governmental institutions for the protection and promotion of human rights, such as an ombudsman's office and/or a National Commission on Human Rights.

While only a few peacekeeping missions—El Salvador, Cambodia, and Haiti—had the distinctive human rights components, the other dozen missions, nonetheless, offered encouraging possibilities in promoting human rights. They operated over long periods of time, extensively involved UN personnel in handling the nuts and bolts of governance and engaged in an elaborate institution-building program. That program has involved the training of civilian police forces, the establishment of judicial and educational systems and the overseeing of prison operations as well as civic facilities. It was precisely these positive features of UN peacekeeping that prompted Amnesty to conclude its survey with the assertion that the features of UN monitoring missions "make these activities potentially very effective."[73] Amnesty's top lobbyist at the UN for peacekeeping told an interviewer that the report drew considerable attention from many in the UN bureaucracy and was taken very seriously by specialists in peacekeeping.[74] He went on to say that his organization's peacekeeping paper "changed the attitudes of a lot of people in the UN toward doing human rights in a peacekeeping context."

In some peacekeeping operations where human rights was not a central element, such as the missions to Mozambique and Liberia, Amnesty intervened directly with the Secretariat of the UN. In those cases, Amnesty succeeded in including, at least, some human rights language in the Secretary-General's implementation plan submitted to the Security Council. However, in dealing with these aspects of the United Nations programs, the process was extremely delicate and difficult. Peacekeeping operations are, of course, delicate in themselves. Moreover, many UN peacekeeping officials were unfamiliar with the organization and, besides, were reluctant to involve NGOs. Because of the secrecy and delicacy of the operation, Amnesty has "never really been able to blow our trumpet," its lobbyist observed, "because people who were devising the [peacekeeping] plan didn't want people to think Amnesty was writing this stuff."[75] So while peacekeeping operations were among the most impressive of this NGO's operations, they were hidden from the general public.

Beyond peacekeeping, Amnesty's presence at the UN steadily has accumulated more authority and influence over the years. As the number of UN instruments and mechanisms increased, the organization's activity as an NGO with consultative status grew. A UN Amnesty office was established in 1977 and a permanent representation was established by 1988.[76] The lobbying work at the UN is overseen by the Legal and International Organisations Programme (LIOP), at Amnesty headquarters in London, which often will call on national sections worldwide to lobby their respective home governments directly.[77] But the amount of work done by LIOP is huge. It makes numerous submissions to UN human rights bodies annually by fax or oral intervention at their various sessions, notably the Commission on Human Rights and its Sub-Commission.[78]

The breakthrough at the UN with respect to peacekeeping was not of a character to excite or even interest the average Amnesty member. It was the organization's public exposures of gross human rights abuses and its advocacy of ending them that had won public attention and popular support in the sixties and seventies. Certainly at Vienna its representatives dramatically presented themselves as activists in various demonstrations. Two years later, its sizable delegation to the UN-sponsored World Conference on Women's Rights, held in Beijing, seized opportune moments to focus media attention on crucial issues.[79] Pierre Sané, the organization's Secretary-General since 1992, was personally involved in these initiatives. Early in September, 1995, Sané participated in a ceremony that handed over a petition signed by one million women demanding rights to the UN High Commissioner for Human Rights. More dramatic and focused was Sané's press conference in mid-September at which he emphasized the crackdown on dissent in Tibet. Petitions on behalf of individual dissenters were delivered by Amnesty officials to the embassies of 11 countries. And, on the last day of the Conference, when the Chinese Foreign Ministry chose to hold a concluding press conference, Amnesty officials sought to present a petition to the Chinese authorities, which they naturally rejected. The rejection hardly could fail to win "massive media coverage," as an Amnesty internal report noted.

The very nature of the organization's rapid growth inevitably sparked problems. Its Secretary-General in the seventies, Martin Ennals, wrote in 1980 that Amnesty's "centre struggled to keep up with the growth of members."[80] By 1993, membership totals reached 1.1 million and the number of countries in which it had sections was 150. Three years later, the membership dropped to just over a million but the number of countries represented had grown to 192. Amnesty was a giant when it came to size and spread of membership. Nothing in the international NGO human rights world equaled such figures. And its budget was commensurate in amount—£17.2 million in 1996.

In its membership spread, the organization is overwhelmingly Western, as it has been since 1980, when Ennals noted that the organization remained very much rooted in the wealthy countries of the North with only tentacles slowly reaching the South. The North/South dilemma is "as much one for Amnesty International as for the rest of the world."[81] Ennals believed that expansion into the forbidding areas outside Western Europe was only a matter of time—a "difficult" but crucial "educational task." In his view, Amnesty's carefully cultivated reputation and methodology can inspire this growth, even in "countries where there is little tradition of non-governmental activity, countries where the political bias of human rights activists is mistrusted, where tension and deprivation result from the low level of economic and social rights, where a one-party-state prevails or where the regime is run by a dictator."[82]

In reality, the picture is distorted, with approximately half of Amnesty's membership to be found in the United States, Britain and Germany. The popularity of the NGO is the greatest in the Netherlands, where it constitutes over 1 percent of the total Dutch population, as compared to .1 percent in the United States.[83] In most developing countries of the South, the membership size is tiny. Pierre Sané, in a recent interview, said that one of his highest priorities was to increase greatly the size of membership in the Third World.[84] Sané noted with sarcasm that Brazil has only 300 Amnesty members and India has but 200. "That is a joke!" he contemptuously observed. The organization, Sané said, was investing significant resources in building a bigger constituency, having selected ten Third World countries upon which to concentrate.

The growth in Amnesty membership has been accompanied by a greater focus upon the activity that had proved to be so stimulating in the early and later years of the organization—writing on behalf of "prisoners of conscience." At the heart of the operation is the so-called Urgent Action Network. The extent of volunteer involvement testifies to the popularity of Amnesty's quick-response system to information on new or pending cases of torture or of prisoners of conscience. The 1977 Amnesty Annual Report cited 208 Urgent Actions issued for the previous year; the cases quadrupled by 1992, reaching 900, and then dropped slightly to 883 in 1996.[85]

In May, 1995, there were approximately 80,000 active participants in 87 countries—12,000 direct participants in the United States alone, not including student groups. Twenty-seven of the 87 countries have "network" offices, and 11 of those are able to respond to emergencies 24 hours a day, 7 days a week. In recent years, the "network" has issued about 1,000 Action Alerts; 600 are new ones, and the rest are usually reissues of previous alerts that have not seen substantial progress.

The work of the network constantly increased as a result of the continuing expansion of Amnesty's mandate. From merely dealing with prisoners of conscience, the organization took on torture, the death penalty, extrajudicial executions, disappearances and "deliberate and arbitrary" killings by governmental entities like paramilitary units.[86] By 1991, its statute would embrace a broad responsibility: Amnesty "opposes grave violations of the right to freedom of expression, the right to freedom from discrimination and the right to physical and mental integrity."[87]

Expansion of the initial Amnesty mandate was, in part, a response to a swiftly growing membership in ever-wider areas. A perceptive Amnesty leader from Canada, David Matas, said in an interview that "Amnesty had become like an old bachelor, set in its ways, comfortable in the pattern it had set for itself, unwilling to change."[88] But through pressure from a sizable membership with diverse interests expressed at International Council Meetings and International Executive Committee Meetings—at times, in opposition to staff thinking—a broader and more nuanced perspective was adopted. At the International Council Meeting in Yokohama, Japan in 1991, the membership pressures for change were especially felt and, as Matas noted, "a typhoon swept through the Amnesty mandate."[89]

A broader mandate has been accompanied by a more diverse staff makeup. People from 70 countries work in the International Secretariat, making it a truly "international staff."[90] Its newest Secretary-General is a Senegalese who previously headed a development center in Ottawa, Canada. Since arriving, Sané has focused especially vigorously on campaigning, rather than research. No doubt, this was a response to the pressures of the broader membership, which wanted faster action on abuses, as well as the broader mandate, which required coverage of additional subjects. What could not be overlooked as a factor was the impressive competition from the newly formed Human Rights Watch. Amnesty was no longer the single most important international NGO sending out missions, studies and reports that attracted world media attention. As will shortly be described, Human Rights Watch had begun spanning the globe in a remarkably aggressive manner and was beginning to gobble up media interest.

In combining the research and campaign departments, Sané hoped to speed up Amnesty's ability to respond to crises and garner more press attention. Encouraging staff, sections and groups to move swiftly to respond to human rights situations around the world became a key objective.

At the same time, criticism arose in some quarters that Amnesty's desire to assure at least minimum coverage of human rights abuses in every part of the world has diverted resources from examining more serious abuses. A survey of the organization's research work noted frequent objections by members for its failure to provide adequate coverage of certain areas and themes. These areas included West Africa, the former USSR, the former Yugoslavia and China. It further was contended that major human rights crises and massive crimes against humanity were insufficiently researched and covered.[91]

At Amnesty's International Council Meeting in Ljubljana in 1995, the adopted Integrated Action Plan called for a reevaluation of media strategies among sections and groups, and particularly for an increased determination to publicize successes—"projecting a more active and dynamic image of AI."[92] This also included moving, in the words of a survey of Amnesty membership, toward producing "shorter, more timely and more lively, readable documents with more visual images" as well as reducing the time between conducting the research and publishing the report.[93] A senior Amnesty official explained to a reporter that the organization's policy had changed from "get it right" to "get it out and fast."[94]

At stake was the quality of the research upon which Amnesty had built an enviable reputation for over 30 years. The issue became especially pronounced when an Amnesty report on the secret rearming by foreign governments of Rwandan Hutus who had fled to Zaire appeared. Not only had the Amnesty report been released after a Human Rights Watch/ Africa study, but also, what was worse, most of the report was "based on secondary sources," according to an article in the New York Times, rather than on Amnesty's own research. This was "a major departure" for Amnesty, the Times article observed; it then revealed that within the organization there had been "opposition" to the release of the report. Sané sarcastically responded that, of course, he would prefer "a nice piece of research where everything is verified to death," but "if that corners us into inaction," he went on, "then what's the point? Amnesty is a campaigning organization."[95]

Several former top Amnesty staffers have claimed that Amnesty's restructuring, designed to make it compete more effectively with the media and campaign successes of Human Right's Watch, has weakened the research review process. The charges have been punctuated with a few costly resignations. Malcolm Smart resigned as Director of Research to become Deputy Director of Article 19; Michael McClintock, a former Deputy Director of Research, moved on to Human Rights Watch to begin installing a rigid review process in Amnesty's biggest rival and Michael Dottridge left the African section to become Director of Research for Anti-Slavery International.[96]

Malcolm Smart was especially revealing in an interview.[97] He had served with Amnesty since 1977, becoming Deputy Director of the research department in 1986 and its Director in 1989. The department was dissolved in March 1994, but it already was apparent by then that the "old values" of the organization, including the quality and accuracy of research, had been radically altered. For him and others, he said, the "ground had shifted," which was found to be "disconcerting." What had prompted the shift from an emphasis on research to emphasis upon campaigning, explained Smart, was pressure from the largest sections of Amnesty, who also provided the largest amount of funding. The U.S. section, he noted, was the largest single source of funds and exerted "the biggest clout." From the perspective of the U.S. section, confronted as it was by a dynamic and aggressive Human Rights Watch organization, Amnesty had to be equally dynamic and quick in releasing reports. If research had to be made secondary, so be it.

Interestingly, the current head of the U.S. Amnesty section, William Schulz, seemed to agree with this assessment. In an interview, he said:

> Human Rights Watch is absolutely superb at its reports, which are well-researched, generally, hard-hitting, provocative. They get excellent attention in the media, and they should, they deserve it. They do in many cases far better than Amnesty does at that kind of thing.[98]

For Sané, neither the criticism nor the resignations would divert him from his purposes of making Amnesty a more dynamic and relevant organization. In an interview, he stressed with considerable emphasis that "we are not a research organization; we are an action or campaigning organization."[99] He added that research was to serve the purposes of action and of bringing about change.

In the meantime, sections have had to struggle through some significant membership reductions. The *Times* article claimed that every national section but the British and Dutch sections had been losing members. The U.S. section, in particular, has fallen on hard times, at least compared with the heady successes of the 1980s. During the four years between 1991 and 1995, the U.S. section lost 120,000 members—a quarter of its membership.[100] The membership figure used in 1996 was 300,000.[101] Besides, only 20 percent of Amnesty's members are under 40, and 24 percent are between 40 and 50, thereby suggesting an aging constituency. Yet an analytical survey of the group's membership stated that Amnesty USA "enjoys at present an almost ideal situation in terms of the characteristics of its current membership base." It lauded Amnesty's members as displaying "one of the most balanced and solid profiles we have seen in our research in recent years."[102] Most members, furthermore, remain confident of Amnesty's strength as an organization but want the group to be more vocal in promoting itself. The survey advised that "Amnesty consider providing members with more images of the organization doing things, speaking out, and making headlines."[103]

That assessment corresponded with the purposes of Pierre Sané. He stressed in an interview that the organization has increased its "campaigning power" and its "field presence" even while displaying a "readiness" to try "new things" and "new techniques." "More aggressive campaigning" was promised, along with a "more confrontational" posture.

Vienna meant "new priorities" for Sané. High among them were women's rights. "We have not paid enough attention" to the "gender-specific" issues, Sané emphasized, noting at the same time that the organization must take on the aims of combating female genital mutilation, which he said, afflicts 6,000 girls every day. He contemplated an elaborate program of educating people through the Amnesty sections in various countries and of sensitizing researchers in the Secretariat throughout Amnesty's London headquarters to deal with the problem.

Another priority for Amnesty emerging from Vienna, Sané said, was to focus more attention upon the poor and to make more visible the connection between poverty and powerlessness. Human rights must not be seen as a marginal phenomenon. Thus, economic and social rights must be given far more attention and a more adequate research methodology must be set in place to respond to the challenges. However, Sané did not spell out how he wanted Amnesty to deal with the new priority and how it should encompass poverty questions within the organization's mandate and the historic focus of human rights NGOs upon civil and political rights.

Sané concluded the interview with the observation that Amnesty is "certainly more realistic" and that its campaigns are "more focussed." There hardly could be any doubt that within the UN system, it remains a principal source of ideas for new human rights institutions and for making human rights relevant to peacekeeping, the UN's basic purpose. Whether the planned dynamic overall campaign will make it equally relevant to its membership is yet to be determined.

CHAPTER THIRTEEN

Genocide and Accountability: Response of the NGO Community

Even while the extraordinary assemblage of NGOs and governmental representatives was congregating in Vienna to advance human rights and make more effective the institutions designed to combat human rights violations, the most heinous of these violations—genocide, the mass destruction of an ethnic, racial or religious community—was being perpetrated in Bosnia, an area not very far away. Indeed, Bosnia once had been part of the old Austro-Hungarian Empire. Oddly, that genocide attracted surprisingly little attention at the Vienna conclave. Only two or three articles dealing with developments in the Former Yugoslavia appeared in the unofficial organ of the World Conference on Human Rights, *Terra Viva*. With the bulk of the NGOs coming from Third World countries, particularly in Asia and Latin America, atrocities in Europe were not seen as urgently consequential.

Nor did it seem that public opinion in the West, of which NGOs were a certain reflection, was clamoring for action against the genocidists. Prime Minister Margaret Thatcher, a year earlier, had urged that NATO, not the UN, threaten "military action" to end Serb aggression against the Bosnians. She frankly acknowledged that the European Community or Union was utterly inadequate for this purpose and that "American leadership" was "indispensable."[1] But her demands found little resonance either in Washington or Brussels. If presidential candidate Bill Clinton was critical in 1992 of the Bush Administration's lethargic approach to

Bosnian genocide, after his inauguration, President Clinton assumed the same posture. And pretty much for the same reason: the Pentagon saw no vital U.S. interest at stake. The commission of genocide elsewhere was not perceived as fitting that category.

And the same perception guided decision-making when genocide in Southeastern Europe was compounded in the spring of 1994 by a massive genocidal assault in Rwanda of Hutus against Tutsis, leaving over a half a million dead in but a couple of months. There was an outcry among NGOs against such atrocities but hardly any marching, demonstrating or lobbying. Nuremberg seemed forgotten, along with the cry of "Never Again!"

The horrors of genocide were certain to prompt some human rights critics to question the effectiveness, if not the usefulness, of human rights organizations. A recent (1996) article in the British journal *Index on Censorship,* pointing to the massive atrocities in Rwanda as well as other "human rights violations . . . occurring today at an overwhelming rate," asked: why are NGOs "achieving very little?"[2] The article took note of the fact that "no other generation has ever known so much, as quickly, so graphically" about human rights violations, and yet the knowledge has had "so little effect." Paradoxically, the cynic might ask whether "more knowledge" has not meant "less action."[3]

Drawing upon the theme, a sociological specialist who held a leadership role in the British-based NGO Africa Rights, Alex de Waal, delivered a blistering broadside in a major British literary organ, singling out Human Rights Watch (HRW).[4] He attacked the "arrogance" of western NGO leaders who "prescribe doses" of human rights and democratization formulas but who, in the face of genocide in Africa, were revealed to be nothing less than "irrelevant or worse." These organizations, he contended, operated on the assumption that "if people knew enough, if the quality of research and reporting was good enough, if the information reached the right people, then action was bound to follow." The assumption proved to be a "failure," de Waal insisted, and the outcome in the case of Rwanda served to disclose NGO "impotence."

The assault, if nasty and brutish—although hardly short—nonetheless could not but hit its mark. Ken Roth, the Executive Director of Human Rights Watch, responded more in sorrow than in anger.[5] Of course, he acknowledged, it is "often not enough to simply expose atrocities or to shame their authors." But if de Waal focuses only upon the exposé reports of Human Rights Watch, he has grievously missed its political and lobbying functions. The process of mobilizing shame has been broadly "transcended," noted Roth. Even if the NGOs were restricted to merely advocacy, to reject such activism because of failure to prevent an episode of genocide would be like "closing down the fire brigade because a building burned down. . . ."

Human Rights Watch, in fact, has been keenly aware of the limitations of the public shaming process from its very origins in 1990 and strenuously has urged the need for the international community to create effective international legal institutions to cope with genocide and other crimes against humanity. At the philosophical core of the proposed legal institutional machinery was the notion of accountability. It was spelled out by an HRW founder, the very creative Aryeh Neier, in an article in February, 1990 that since has been reproduced in an authoritative compilation of scholarly works on the subject.[6] Neier, writing at a time when Soviet totalitarian rule had collapsed in East Europe and dictatorships in Latin America as well as parts of Asia (South Korea, the Philippines, Taiwan and Pakistan) had been swept aside in democratic elections, posed the crucial question: "what to do about the past."

That governments and the international community must hold accountable those who have committed in the past "crimes against humanity" was Neier's fundamental thesis. In his view, accountability for the unspeakable crimes of dictatorships is indispensable for maintaining or promoting democracy and it is essential for upholding a stable society. Equally important is the function of accountability in sustaining the rule of law, the very basis of human rights. The International Covenant on Civil and Political Rights stipulates that states must provide an "effective remedy" for those who suffered abuses. The Geneva Conventions that have been ratified by most states are even more explicit on this matter as it applies to the conduct of states during military conflict. Nations are obligated to search for those who have committed "grave breaches" of human rights principles during wartime; they must be brought to justice whatever their nationality.

One of Neier's colleagues at HRW contributed significantly to detailing the need for distinguishing between two aspects of accountability. Juan Mendes, a legal specialist and former Director of Americas Watch (now serving as the Executive Director of the Inter-American Institute of Human Rights), divided the process of establishing accountability into two phases: the "truth" phase and the "justice" phase.[7] The truth phase comes into play when a government acknowledges the responsibility of a state's former agents in perpetrating such human rights abuses as torture, disappearances, arbitrary and extrajudicial killings and forced detentions. When a government chooses to go beyond the seeking of the truth for past crimes to actual prosecution (and punishment), the process has entered into a separate stage of justice.

While Neier's essay on accountability did not specifically address the subject of genocide, it is clear that international law placed emphasis upon the justice phase. The Convention on the Prevention and Punishment of the Crime of Genocide projected the idea of an international criminal court to punish genocidists. If this was envisioned for an undefined future period, justice and punishment also might be rendered by the national courts of the individual contracting parties to the treaty. Should such courts fail to function because of considerations of state sovereignty, justice still could be rendered by the international community through the United Nations Security Council. The Council was authorized by Article VIII of the Convention—as was any other "competent organ" of the UN—to take appropriate action under the UN Charter to prevent and suppress genocide.

The immediate period after World War II when the Allied powers, prompted by the United States, set up a special international tribunal in Nuremberg to try high Nazi officials for war crimes and "crimes against humanity" offered a precedent for dealing with genocide. The UN General Assembly, again spurred by the United States, adopted the historic resolution making genocide "a crime under international law." Presumably, what the Tribunal and the parallel General Assembly resolution were giving expression to was the popular slogan that would emerge later—"Never Again!" While the phrase arose to commemorate the Holocaust, with its mass destruction of European Jewry, it could just as easily apply to the genocide of others. Yet, when the massive slaughter of ethnic or religious minorities later occurred—at least until 1993—the response of the international community was silence.

An analyst of the history of genocide concludes that "humanity's record in preventing genocide has been nothing short of abysmal."[8] Samuel Totten estimates that during the twentieth century, over 50 million people have perished in genocidal acts, although one source that he cites would more than double that figure. As for the postwar period, two scholars writing in 1988 calculated that the number killed in genocidal episodes since 1945 ranged from 7 to 16 million, which was about equal to the number who perished in all international and civil wars during the same period.[9]

Three examples of substantial genocidal episodes before 1992 illumine the utter absence of accountability: Burundi in 1972, Cambodia in 1975-

79 and Iraq in 1988. These have been selected, in part, because of the availability of detailed studies that document both the genocide and the indifference of the organized international community to it. The study of the genocide in Burundi was conducted by the Carnegie Endowment for International Peace.[10] It found that during the months of April-August, 1972, the Tutsi rulers of Burundi, fearing a coup from the much larger Hutu ethnic group, engaged in a massive slaughter of the Hutu elite. According to documents as well as interviews with U.S. policymakers and knowledgeable State Department officials the genocide was "systematic," with the government seeking "to skim off the cream of the Hutu, to kill every possible Hutu male of distinction over the age of fourteen."[11]

The phrase "selective genocide" appeared in documents of the U.S. embassy in Burundi, in an "Intelligence Memorandum" circulated within the State Department and in various journalistic reports to describe a genocide that was restricted to an educated and elite element of the Hutus. An American Universities Field Staff report defined the victims: all Hutu members of the government's Cabinet, all Hutu officers in the armed services and almost all Hutu soldiers, at least one-half of Burundi's primary school teachers and thousands of Hutu civil servants, bank clerks, and small businessmen. Only a thousand Hutu secondary school students survived. By the end of the summer, estimates placed the number of Hutu victims at a quarter-million from a total population of three million.

Certainly, by mid-May, Western governments knew details of the systematic nature of the mass slaughter. The Prime Minister of Belgium reported to his cabinet on May 19 that what was happening in Burundi was a "veritable genocide." (Burundi, along with Rwanda and the Congo, had been a Belgian colony.) Strikingly, the Organization of African Unity (OAU), which had been encouraged by the United States to intervene, chose to support the Burundi government. In May, the OAU's Secretary-General publicly declared "solidarity" with the Tutsi regime. With most African governments haunted by tribalism, none were inclined to become involved with the strife in member states.

At the UN, the response was a rather modest one. Secretary-General Kurt Waldheim, pressed by his American Deputy, Bradford Morse, took the extraordinary step of flying to the OAU Summit session to recommend a UN observer mission. Two UN missions in late June and late July produced one of the few statements made in the international community about the Burundi carnage. Waldheim, at a press conference in Geneva on July 4, confirmed the mass slaughter found by his first mission. The figure he used for the number of killings was 200,000. Burundi responded with an angry rebuttal while other African states, and the West, greeted the Secretary-General's report with silence. Only Belgium would speak out to condemn the genocide.

No debate took place among policymakers in the United States concerning the Burundi genocide. The Senate still had not provided its required consent for ratification of the Genocide Convention. Nonetheless, an Assistant Legal Adviser for African Affairs in the State Department did prepare a memorandum arguing that under international law, the United States had a binding legal responsibility to uphold human rights so long as there were no "overriding political restraints" against fulfilling this purpose.[12] But, as disclosed by a high-level official, that memorandum was not "taken too seriously." Nor was serious thought given to the idea, advanced in some quarters, to cut off the purchase of Burundi coffee, which could have crippled that country's economy.

The researchers of the Carnegie Endowment summed up a crucial consideration for hesitancy to push for U.S. activism by citing a key comment of a State Department aide during an interview: "Do you know of any official whose career has been advanced because he spoke out for human rights?"[13] The question was simply rhetorical. This was, after all, the era when Kissinger's realpolitik predominated in Washington and human rights took a back seat.

But the most remarkable thing about the Carnegie Endowment study was the absence of any reference to an outcry from the NGO community about genocide in Burundi. Apparently, the major NGOs of the time were not equipped with either African expertise or sources to obtain crucial documentation about genocide in Burundi, especially when that regime made a determined effort to prevent public disclosure of it. Local African NGOs, which might have been relied upon to hunt down and channel critical information to international NGOs or international institutions, were almost nonexistent. And, even when information about the "selected genocide" did seep out through several press accounts or a single UN disclosure, no demand for accountability was made. The slogan "Never Again!" requires NGOs with a keen awareness of the facts and a stubborn determination to press governments to act upon those facts. Otherwise, it remains a mere mantra, not a call to arms.

A much larger and more ruthless example of genocide took place in Cambodia (Kampuchea) during 1975-79, but its extent and character remained almost completely unknown to the civilized world until after a Vietnamese invasion of the area drove Pol Pot and his Khmer Rouge associates from power in Phnom Penh, Cambodia's capital, and into the forests of Thailand. Yet, through the efforts of NGOs as well as scholars since then, extensive documentation of the genocide has been accumulated and, to an extent, recently has been given public exposure on an Internet Web site.[14] Far more significant has been a continuing effort by certain NGOs to end the impunity for the genocidists and achieve some form of accountability. The effort has had the powerful educational effect of raising in some quarters public awareness of the Cambodian genocide.

Estimates of that genocide vary, but the most recent scholarship points to a national death toll of more than 1.5 million, or about 20 percent of the pre-1975 Cambodian population.[15] Genocide, as defined by the Genocide Convention, means the destruction in whole or in part of an ethnic, racial or religious group and, while the massacres conducted by the Khmer Rouge embraced vast numbers of educated Cambodians, there can be little question but that certain ethnic and religious minorities also were specially targeted. Thus, almost the entire population of Buddhist monks—numbering 2,680—was wiped out, and discovered documents show that the elimination of Buddhism and its culture was precisely an objective of the Khmer Rouge.[16]

Similarly, the principal ethnic minorities of Vietnamese, Chinese and Chams were singled out for slaughter—the Vietnamese totally, the Chinese by half and the Moslem Chams by close to half. Nor could there be much doubt that it was the "intent" of the Khmer Rouge to liquidate these groups, as stipulated in the genocide treaty. Documents discovered by researchers point to a chain of command in ordering the killings.[17]

In 1982, the Cambodia Documentation Commission, an NGO comprised of human rights specialists, Cambodian refugees and scholars on Cambodian society was established by David Hawk, the energetic former Director of Amnesty International's U.S. section. Operating under the sponsorship of the Columbia University Center for the Study of Human Rights, Hawk sought to document the monumental nature of the then little-known Cambodian genocide, to raise public consciousness of the horrendous crimes committed by the Khmer Rouge and to seek some form of justice and redress through available international instruments.[18]

The documentation that Hawk assembled, especially audiotaped oral testimony of survivors, photos of newly unearthed mass graves and various archival materials related to Khmer Rouge genocide plans and activities, was significant. It contributed to a 1986 report by a UN Special Rapporteur that characterized the Khmer Rouge killings as genocide.[19]

A major objective of the documentation was to encourage a contracting state party to the genocide treaty to bring the Cambodian case before the International Court of Justice. Arrangement was made for 100 Cambodian survivors to write to the head of government of each contracting party. When accompanied by a press conference, the project could not fail to attract considerable public attention, which served the NGO's consciousness-raising purposes. (Consciousness-raising also was furthered by the use made by Amnesty International of 50 photos and other archival material assembled by the Commission. The photographic exhibit, entitled "Cambodia Witness," toured art galleries and museums in the United States and Europe for five years.) The foreign ministries of Sweden, Australia and Belgium (which, at the time, served as Chairman of the European Community) gave serious consideration to the appeal of the survivors.

The imaginative effort of the Cambodian Commission was unprecedented. Application of the genocide treaty since its coming into force in 1951 never had been undertaken. But the initiative fell prey to the geopolitics of the early 1990s. The Association of Southeast Asian Nations (ASEAN), fearful of the growing power of Vietnam and determined to expel its agents, who dominated Cambodia, felt obliged to support a revived and rearmed Khmer Rouge that could assist in the ouster of the Vietnamese rulers in Phnom Penh. The ASEAN majority hardly would wish to see a judicial indictment of the Khmer Rouge at the moment. And the Western democracies, including the United States, were not inclined to pursue the proposal in the absence of any support from their Southeast Asian allies. Besides, China had been a strong supporter of the Khmer Rouge and hardly anyone was prepared to alienate China in the face of the immediate challenge of Vietnamese expansionism.

The same geopolitical consideration precluded action at the General Assembly and the UN Commission on Human Rights. In these bodies, the Cambodian Commission lobbied intensively for specific condemnation of Cambodian genocide and for the rejection of any return to power of the genocidal Khmer Rouge. The best that it could obtain in these separate UN resolutions was a provision on "non-return to the universally condemned policies and practices of the past." With the resolutions' lack of specificity, accountability for the crime of genocide in Cambodia was absent.

Still, the Cambodian Commission's efforts deepened the awareness of the genocide horrors that had traumatized Cambodia in the middle and late seventies. The Commission also played an important role in winning a range of human rights programs within the settlement agreements arranged by the UN. That agreement authorized Cambodian citizens to actively promote and protect human rights for themselves. It was an idea pressed by the Commission and acknowledged as such by the UN. Once the UN Transitional Authority for Cambodia (UNTAC) began functioning as a peacekeeping operation, the Commission made its services available for human rights education and for the training programs of newly formed indigenous Cambodian human rights NGOs.

The past still remained an open sore. Justice has yet to be rendered. As a report of the Lawyers Committee for Human Rights noted, "the bestiality that roamed at large through Kampuchea [Cambodia] in the 1970s remains unpunished. . . ."[20] The cry for ending the impunity of the Khmer Rouge and for establishing its accountability continues to be sounded. During the course of the past few years, numerous Cambodian leaders have issued calls for an international tribunal to try the principal genocidists. Significantly, polls in Cambodia reveal that the vast majority of the Cambodian public support the idea of such a tribunal.[21] In late April, 1998, the United States began urging the UN Security Council to establish an ad hoc tribunal to try various Khmer Rouge leaders. Pol Pot, a prisoner of his former associates, had died under suspicious circumstances the previous month. With the Khmer Rouge in great disarray and fleeing the Phnom Penh authorities, it seemed possible that some form of justice could be rendered.

A final example of genocide prior to the Bosnian carnage took place in 1987-88 in Iraq against the Kurds. As with the Cambodian case, the deliberate slaughter was hidden from public view by a brutally repressive authoritarian regime in total command of the local media. Access to information by foreign correspondents was nonexistent. Only after the U.S.-led United Nations forces crushed the Iraqi military in 1991, compelling its withdrawal from Kuwait, did circumstances permit the seizure of a vast array of Iraqi documents that brilliantly illuminated the genocide. On the heels of the UN victory, the Kurds revolted and took control of the area of Iraqi Kurdistan. Into their hands fell the files of the Ba'ath Party's all-powerful Northern Bureau and of the regime's local intelligence and security offices.

The files were invaluable for Human Rights Watch/Middle East, which, as early as February, 1990, had focused considerable public attention upon the subject. Through its report, based upon Kurdish exiled sources, Human Rights Watch provided the "smoking gun" of genocide. With the cooperation of the Senate Foreign Relations Committee, this

NGO arranged in May, 1992 for the shipment to the United States of 14 tons of documents, a veritable warehouse of information. Extensive research by key HRW/Middle East staffers followed, accompanied by field research involving oral testimony from over 350 witnesses or survivors. Supplementing the documentary and oral material was critically important forensic evidence obtained through the exhumation of several mass graves near major Kurdish cities. The forensic inquiry was conducted jointly with another important NGO—Physicians for Human Rights.

What emerged from this remarkable firsthand three-year research project was an authoritative volume of analyses and documents published jointly with Yale University Press.[22] The project could lay the foundation for the trial and punishment of numerous officials. An NGO whose Executive Director initially had laid out the basic significance of accountability for horrendous crimes against humanity now occupied a position to validate that thesis. However, political factors intruded to make the validation extremely difficult.

As to the evidence of genocide and of the intention by Iraqi authorities to commit genocide, it was overwhelming. Documents revealed unequivocally the repeated use of chemical weapons against Kurds in 1987 and 1988. The evidence matched in detail the oral and forensic documentation. Key documentary sources include specific instructions by the Secretary-General of the Ba'ath Party's Northern Bureau to kill all inhabitants aged 15-17 in prohibited areas.

The Iraqi military and security authorities used the term Anfal to characterize the mass killings in both internal memoranda and in public pronouncements about the assault upon the Kurds. A total of eight separate Anfals took place during 1988. The documentary record shows a determination to raze Kurdish villages and to deport their populations. It also speaks of mass executions. While no specific figures on killings are provided in the record, an estimate from Kurdish rebels placed the number of disappeared persons in 1988 at 182,000. The chief of the Anfal campaigns and later Defense Minister, Ali Hassan al-Majid, had insisted in anger that it "could not have been more than a hundred thousand."[23]

The care taken by Human Rights Watch to document the case of genocide by Iraq is impressive. In fact, between 1992 and 1994, it published five separate reports on the subject adding new material on the evidence from the varied sources accumulated. One of the reports, *Bureaucracy of Repression: The Iraqi Government in Its Own Words,* released in February, 1994, displayed the basic documents on genocide. The report was included as an Appendix in the Yale University volume.

Two alternative uses of the evidence were contemplated by HRW.[24] The first was the establishment by the UN Security Council of an ad hoc International Tribunal that would hear evidence about genocidal crimes against the Kurds and would be assembled by a specially created international commission of inquiry. The resemblance to what would emerge soon afterward at the UN regarding genocide against Bosnian Muslims is all too apparent. HRW's idea was by no means lost in the long run. And, even in the short run, it had a certain viability. Such a proposal was placed on the agenda of the Security Council by the Clinton Administration in July, 1993. But, as noted by a legal specialist of HRW, it was a "non-starter" in view of the certain opposition of France and Russia.[25]

The second alternative was a variation of the plan advanced by the Cambodian Documentation Commission. One or more contracting parties to the genocide treaty would be encouraged to bring a case against Iraq before the International Court of Justice on grounds that it had breached an international agreement. The Court was authorized under the genocide treaty provisions to resolve disputes between states over violations of the treaty. Geopolitical factors again intruded, just as they had in the Cambodian case. Turkey, a vital element in the NATO structure, a close ally of the United States, and an important—if secular—Moslem state, was hardly enthusiastic about arousing sympathy for the oppressed Kurds of Iraq. Ankara, after all, had its own very serious Kurdish problem and would not wish to see this particular ethnic minority made into a martyred group. Efforts were made by HRW to persuade a significant number of states from a variety of geographical regions to join in bringing the Kurdish case before the court. Only four countries agreed to do so; none were from West Europe, Asia, Africa or South America. The four would not act without a larger coalition and so the idea was placed on the "back burner."

If, in the three examples of genocide, no effort to halt them was made nor, indeed, could have been made, and if the effort, in two cases, to hold the perpetrators accountable failed, a significantly different outcome resulted regarding the policy of "ethnic cleansing" in Bosnia. Even though just five years elapsed between the massacres in Iraq Kurdistan and those in Bosnia, it was almost as if a century or millennium had intervened. What was characteristic of the civil war in Bosnia was a transparency due to the presence of the media that made a total blackout, which had been typical for the authoritarian regimes of Cambodia and Iraq, now inconceivable. Within days or weeks, interviews with neighbors and survivors of slaughterhouses could provide basic documentation.[26]

A second factor distinguishing the genocide in Bosnia from that in Cambodia and Kurdistan was the overriding presence in the first case of a regional grouping—the Conference on Security and Cooperation in Europe (CSCE). This institution, embracing now 53 countries, could not fail to be fully informed of developments in Bosnia.[27]

Even before the horrendous assault by Bosnian Serbs on the newly established independent state of Bosnia-Herzegovina in April, 1992, the Serbian state had launched warfare against first Slovenia and then Croatia to prevent their self-determination aspirations and the breakup of the Former Yugoslavia. By the summer of 1991, some members of the U.S. government and NGO representatives began recommending the creation of a war crimes Tribunal to hold accountable those committing atrocities.[28] As the killings mounted and information about concentration camps became known, talk about a Tribunal grew. As early as October, 1991, CSCE's principal policymaking group, the Committee of Senior Officials, publicly warned that "those responsible for the unprecedented violence against people in Yugoslavia, with its ever-increasing loss of life, should be held personally accountable under international law for their actions." Shortly afterward, the Committee's superior body, CSCE's Council of Foreign Ministers, meeting in Prague on January 31, 1992 handed down an authoritative directive: "all those responsible" for "violations . . . under international law . . . are personally accountable for their actions that are in contravention of the relevant norms of international humanitarian law."[29]

Ineluctably, the UN also would be seized with the issue, especially after Bosnia's declaration of independence in April, 1992, and the violence then unleashed by the Serbs within Bosnia, massively encouraged and aided by Belgrade. The Security Council, taking account of reports of large-scale massacres and the practice of "ethnic cleansing," adopted the historic Resolution 771 in August, 1992. It called upon states and, most significantly, "international humanitarian organizations" to "collate substantiated information. . . relating to the violations of humanitarian law, including grave breaches of the Geneva Convention. . . ."[30] This information the resolution specifically asked to be made "available to the Council."

Clearly, the Council was moving toward implementing the principle of accountability. Equally significant was action taken in the UN Commission on Human Rights. It requested its Chairman to appoint a Special Rapporteur "to investigate firsthand the human rights situation" in Bosnia-Herzegovina. Appointed to that position was the former Prime

Minister of Poland, Tadeusz Mazowiecki.[31] He and his team made two visits to Bosnia, first in August, 1992 and then the following October. The first report gave emphasis to genocide. It noted that "the situation of the Muslim population is particularly tragic: they feel that they are threatened with extermination." Particularly significant was the Special Rapporteur's thesis that "ethnic cleansing does not appear to be the consequences of the war, but rather its goal."[32]

Only two months after the Security Council adopted Resolution 771, it moved a significant step forward, requesting the UN Secretary-General, "as a matter of urgency," to appoint a Commission of Experts to examine and analyze the situation in the Former Yugoslavia and report on the "evidence of grave breaches" of the Geneva Conventions and other violations of international humanitarian law.[33] The Secretary-General appointed a five-member Commission of Experts, headed by the well-known American human rights law professor Cherif Bassiouni of DePaul University. The Commission's finding as reported to the Security Council in May, 1993 was devastating.

Among the "grave breaches" were "ethnic cleansing," mass killings, torture, rape, arbitrary arrests and the destruction of civilian as well as religious and cultural property. Bassiouni later publicly would disclose to a U.S. largely congressional body that his Commission had identified 200,000 dead, mostly civilians, 800 prison camps and detention centers in which more than a 500,000 persons were held and 151 mass grave sites. He further disclosed that he had investigated 1,600 cases of rape and forced impregnation of girls and women of all ages, and that he had received reports alleging thousands of similar cases.[34] The Commission concluded that the creation of an ad hoc International Tribunal was warranted.[35]

The culmination of these steps came in May, 1993 with the Security Council adopting a historic and unprecedented decision: the establishment of an International Tribunal "for the sole purpose of prosecuting persons for serious violations of international humanitarian law" committed in the Former Yugoslavia.[36] While the decision was based upon Chapter VII of the UN Charter, which is geared to the maintenance of peace, the provisions of the Genocide Convention were, nonetheless, a crucial element of it. In the Statute of the International Tribunal, which was adopted at the same time as the vote for its establishment, the prosecution of perpetrators of genocidal acts is specifically noted. That statute had been recommended by the Secretary-General, who called attention to the Convention as embodying rules of international humanitarian law applicable to the Yugoslavia situation.[37]

The potentiality of the ad hoc International Tribunal was considerable. Only a month before the Security Council decision, a ruling of the International Court of Justice revealed that Court's own inadequacy in dealing with genocide. On March 20, 1993, Bosnia-Herzegovina had brought a case before the Court charging that Yugoslavia had breached the Genocide Convention and asking the court to confirm the validity of the allegations. The initial response of the Court was cautious and weak. It refused to rule on whether genocide had been committed. Instead, the Court asked the Federal Republic of Yugoslavia (Serbia) to "ensure" that its military units or those irregulars and paramilitary groups "directed or supported" by it "do not commit any acts of genocide" against Muslims or other ethnic or religious groups.[38]

The Court's early finding on April 8, 1993 demonstrated how it could not serve as an effective judicial body for dealing with genocide. Had the efforts of those who sought to bring the Cambodian and Kurdish genocidal episodes before the International Court of Justice been marked with success, the outcome probably would still have been uncertain. The only redeeming feature of a hearing would have been publicity about the details of genocide. In fact, the pertinent provision of the Genocide Convention indicates that the Court only could rule on disputes between contracting parties to the treaty over "the interpretation, application or fulfillment" of the Convention.

From the very beginning of the UN process that culminated in the creation of an ad hoc International Criminal Tribunal, the role of NGOs was given a certain emphasis, if only by implication. Mazowiecki's first report in August, 1992 stressed the need for "the systematic collection of documentation" on mass human rights violations and on breaches of international law if prosecution is to follow.[39] Security Council Resolution 771 specifically called upon "international humanitarian organizations" to undertake such an initiative. For Human Rights Watch/Helsinki, the invitation could not have been clearer. If genocide in Kurdistan had been given priority attention just a short time earlier, in one branch of Human Rights Watch, now the focus would shift to another branch, one for which it was far better equipped.

It was not only that the Helsinki division of HRW had accumulated some 14 years of experience in field investigations throughout Europe, including Yugoslavia; it had at least one or more staffers present in Bosnia and other parts of Former Yugoslavia throughout all of 1992 and 1993.[40] These virtually full-time representatives of the New York–based NGO had maintained contacts with local human rights activists and a variety of sources within the various levels of governments and media in the area. Interestingly, fledgling human rights groups in Serbia and Croatia also were helped in methodology by the international NGO.

During 1992, Helsinki Watch sent three separate missions to the area. The two initial missions were especially important, the first lasting about six weeks, (March 19–April 28), the other some three weeks (May 29–June 19). A third took place in September-October. The professionals on the mission interviewed victims and witnesses of human rights abuses, refugees and displaced persons, local officials, journalists, medical and relief specialists and UN personnel. An investigation was conducted of detention camps and prisons operated by each of the combatants. A key figure in the investigatory team and author of the reports that followed was Ivana Nizich, who was deeply versed on the subject and would be hired in early 1996 by the International Tribunal for Yugoslavia in The Hague.

What emerged from the continuing investigations on the ground and the various missions was an impressively detailed volume of some 350 pages in the summer of 1992.[41] Almost anticipating the urgent requests of UN bodies, it spelled out how a policy of "ethnic cleansing" conducted mainly by the Serbs in Bosnia (and to a much lesser extent by Croats and Muslims) had resulted in summary executions, disappearances, deportations and forcible displacements of hundreds of thousands purely on the basis of ethnicity or religion. The documentary evidence, as drawn from detailed witnesses' accounts and supplemented by media reportage, overwhelmingly pointed to genocide. Appended to the evidence was a valuable 25-page listing of relevant provisions of international law covering the itemized gross human rights violations.

Strikingly, even as the Helsinki division was fulfilling the requests of the Security Council and of the Special Rapporteur of the UN Commission on Human Rights made precisely the same month, its report called upon the Security Council to take action under the Genocide Convention to suppress the ongoing "acts of genocide."[42] Perhaps more significantly, the report called upon the UN to establish an International Tribunal in order "to prosecute, adjudicate and punish those responsible for war crimes starting with those with the highest level of responsibility for the most egregious crimes."[43] Not until ten months later did the UN Security Council act on this idea. It is noteworthy that in the Acknowledgments of the Nizich report, Aryeh Neier was identified as one of its two editors. His accountability thesis of 1990 now had found a clear-cut expression.

In April, 1993, HRW/Helsinki published a massive second report on genocidal acts in Bosnia.[44] It was far more detailed than the first volume and largely was based upon firsthand oral accounts by witnesses given in interviews carefully arranged to avoid external influence. In deference to the extremely anxious concerns of witnesses, the NGO adopted a policy of using in source identification pseudonyms or initials for all witnesses and deliberately avoiding any reference to time and place of the interviews. These data were kept in secure files outside the Helsinki Watch office and under appropriate safeguards. And, with the agreement of the witnesses, the files were to be made available to the prosecution of the International Tribunal when it eventually would be set up.[45] Nizich, in an interview prior to her leaving HRW for her new position in January, 1996, related how some 30 file boxes were sent by her to the International Tribunal for Yugoslavia once it was established.[46]

During 1993 HRW/Helsinki vigorously pressed for the creation of an International Tribunal by the UN Security Council. While it might urge action by the UN Secretary-General,[47] the NGO was keenly aware that only determined U.S. advocacy of the idea could produce such a breakthrough in the Security Council. A brief, if not clearly detailed, summary in HRW's Annual Report related how it perceived its role:

> Helsinki Watch also continued its traditional efforts to influence the U.S. government to use its leverage to promote human rights. . . .We were successful in urging the U.S. government to take up the call for a war crimes tribunal for the former Yugoslavia and to speak out forcefully against any amnesties for war criminals.[48]

Left unreported was how it accomplished its "successful" effort and whether any other individuals were involved. Certainly, Human Rights Watch/Helsinki was fortunate to have an Administration that was sympathetically inclined to its perspective on the Tribunal, as well as two strong advocates within the State Department: Madeleine K. Albright, then U.S. Ambassador to the UN, and John Shattuck, the Assistant Secretary of State for Human Rights. President Clinton eventually was persuaded that the United States should take the lead within the Security Council to establish the Tribunal and to provide it with adequate funding.

Albright, in another closely related connection, was strongly praised by HRW for a speech she delivered in November, 1993 that sharply rejected any amnesty for war criminals in the former Yugoslavia.[49] The NGO recognized that her speech, formally expressing the Administration viewpoint, was "tremendously important" in that it served to publicly rebuff British and French arguments that amnesty might be useful if only to attain peace and a quick exit for their respective UN troops. Even de Waal, the hostile critic of the United States as well as of Western NGOs, acknowledged that Washington was more responsive to human rights issues than either London or Paris.[50]

The establishment of the International Tribunal for Yugoslavia constituted a milestone in the struggle against genocide.[51] Impunity for this heinous crime no longer would be tolerated. Perpetrators, however high their position in government or society, would be held accountable for their acts of genocide. Amnesty for such crimes was not acceptable. Still, its creation as an institution highlighted two major ironies (which posed two serious problems). First, the Tribunal was established at a moment in time when genocide was by no means diminishing in the Bosnian area and, indeed, would continue for at least two more years. By the middle of 1995, it had assumed a ferociously murderous character. What was the point of the Tribunal's establishment if the crime it was created to try, convict and punish had not been halted?

For the moment, however, more immediate political problems had to be tackled. The selection of the 11 Tribunal judges by the Security Council proved highly contentious and was not quickly completed.[52] A careful geographical balance of appointments was thought essential. Even more politicized was the process of the selection of a Chief Prosecutor. Numerous delays and setbacks, including the appointment for a time of one with scarcely the required high-level legal and human rights credentials— fortunately, he soon withdrew—generated considerable concern. Finally, in July, 1994, the Security Council unanimously named South African Justice Richard J. Goldstone as Chief Prosecutor. He had won a worldwide reputation for his role in heading a South African Commission of Inquiry that revealed police violence and abuses against blacks.

Goldstone's appreciation of the significance of NGOs for the Tribunal's operation later would be recalled in an interview with the author. He said that NGOs had played a "vital role" in the very creation of the Tribunal. That role was defined by him as the "heightening of public opinion in the major countries" to press for early UN Security Council action. Such action, in his personal view, was wholly "unexpected."[53] Justice Goldstone, from the very beginning, was quite aware of the value of NGOs. In the interview, he remembered that he had become interested in NGOs during his student days in South Africa. In his judgment, NGO support for the Tribunal throughout the period of his service as Chief Prosecutor, which continued until October, 1996, remained "vital" in a variety of ways for which he was "very appreciative."

Even prior to his appointment, Human Rights Watch/Helsinki continued to provide the already-established Tribunal in The Hague with a drumbeat of both documentation and a demand for action. In July 1993, it issued a 48-page updated report on "abuses" throughout the Former Yugoslavia. Among the abuses were forced displacement, hostage-taking, summary executions and detentions. Again the reportage was based largely upon eyewitness accounts, taken stenographically or taped.[54]

Several weeks later, HRW/Helsinki released an especially dramatic and powerful 25-page report with a ringing title, *Prosecute Now!* The document focused upon eight cases involving 29 persons.[55] The charges were all spelled out, almost as if it were a lawyer's brief: the names of the alleged offenders were given, each linked to a specific crime and to the pertinent section of international law that had been violated. Each of the eight cases was summarized, together with an elaborate explanation of the type of evidence that could be made available to the prosecution, including the evidence from Helsinki Watch. Among the evidence cited from other sources was the testimony of the important NGO Physicians for Human Rights concerning "a mass execution" at a particular "gravesite" where 200 bodies were found.[56]

The HRW/Helsinki report contended that the eight cases were but "the tip of the iceberg" of a mass of evidence in its file. It said that it had selected the eight from among "the hundreds of cases in its file" because of the supposed "strength" of the selected cases, the availability of the evidence for early prosecution and the diversity of the defendants. Five were Serbs, two were Croats, and one a Bosnian Muslim. The range of crimes of which the accused were charged extended from gang rape to genocide. Equally broad was the rank of targeted persons, who ranged from a mere prison guard to a former Minister of Defense. Significantly, the eight cases selected by Human Rights Watch/Helsinki were among the very first cases the Tribunal's prosecution would investigate— although, it should be emphasized, the prosecution conducted its own independent investigation of each case and relied upon its own findings in the indictment.[57]

There was no let-up in the NGO's pursuit of documentation and clamor for action. Shortly after the release of the eight-case report, HRW/Helsinki issued a useful technical document. At the same time, the NGO pressed for early action. It bitterly complained that the UN had been "all talk" and no action in its preventing genocide and crimes against humanity even in its formally established "safe areas." What was "needed is the political will," the report concluded. The following month saw yet a sixth report, this time concentrated upon "abuses" by Bosnian Croat and Muslim forces.[58]

During 1994 and prior to the Goldstone appointment, Human Rights Watch/Helsinki issued two additional reports.[59] The first, in February, chastised the UN for its failure "to build the rule of law in the region," which was held to be "a necessary foundation for any lasting peace." The report lectured the UN on why an effective Tribunal could bring peace to the area and end the cycle of atrocities. It went on the say that the Tribunal could establish and punish individual guilt and thereby dispel the idea of collective guilt that all too often provided the motivation for endless revenge and the massacres it breeds.

The report then propounded a thesis that HRW/Helsinki later would have a strong reluctance to embrace. Speculating about the possibility that the Tribunal would not be able to arrest and convict alleged war criminals, the NGO argued that it would, nonetheless, "serve a vital function." A detailed indictment would mean that the accused would not be able to set foot outside his country, and this "will constitute punishment in and of itself."[60] The second 1994 report appeared in April and offered a microscopic view of how "ethnic cleansing" operated in a single area.[61] On the basis of eyewitness testimony taken in the course of numerous interviews during the previous summer by a team led in part by Ivana Nizich, HRW/Helsinki was able to identify six war criminals and specify how they blatantly violated international law.

By the summer, Goldstone had been appointed and, as one highly knowledgeable source indicated, he enormously "energized" the entire prosecutorial operation.[62] Without a Chief Prosecutor, the Tribunal simply would not be able to function. The attitude of Russia at the UN slowed the appointment enormously. On July 4, 1994, the President of the Tribunal (a kind of Chief Justice) Antonio Cassese of Italy, put through a phone call to Goldstone and won his assent to the appointment. It was a brilliant political stroke; the Russians hardly could veto a heroic South African jurist who symbolized the struggle against the atrocities of apartheid.[63]

That the newly energized prosecutor's office welcomed the documentation assistance provided by Human Rights Watch/Helsinki and, especially, the research work of Ivana Nizich is illuminated by several letters. On September 7, 1994, Graham Bluett, the Tribunal's Deputy Prosecutor, wrote to Ken Roth of HRW advising that Goldstone and he would be coming the following week to New York and that they would be accompanied by a Tribunal legal adviser, Morten Bergamo. Bluett asked that a separate "practical" meeting be arranged between Bergamo and HRW "researchers" so that he could be advised of "your documentation system" with reference to war crimes in Yugoslavia and, particularly, about "our specific requests for witness information. . . ." The request for a special meeting involving Bergamo was prefaced by the observation that, in connection with the Prosecutor's "on-going investigations . . . we have come across several references to material" held by Human Rights Watch/Helsinki.[64]

What ultimately emerged from a separate Goldstone-Roth meeting was indicated in a letter dated six months later, on March 13, 1995. Sent to Nizich by the Tribunal's External Relations Officer, Donato Kiniger-Passigli, the letter first expressed appreciation "for your personal interest into the activities" of the Tribunal. It then extended a special "thank you on the research work you are conducting on behalf of the Tribunal. . . ." This research was mentioned as an outgrowth of the "agreement" between Roth and Judge Goldstone.

Especially glowing was a letter by Goldstone to Roth on May 17, 1995. He referred to how the Chief of Investigations for the Tribunal "has brought to my attention the excellent cooperation which he has received from Human Rights Watch." Particularly lauded was Ivana Nizich, who "has been very helpful" in providing "testimony and other materials" on violations of humanitarian law. She had agreed, the letter observed, to fulfil "other Tribunal requests" for "additional information." Goldstone continued with an outpouring of unusual praise. He called HRW's help "invaluable."

Even as HRW/Helsinki was making confidential witness material available to the Tribunal, it continued to provide the media and interested parties with a flow of its research findings. In October, 1994, it focused on four areas in the outskirts of Sarajevo, the Bosnian capital that had been the object of endless artillery attacks by the local Serb military and paramilitary units.[65] The report catalogued such abuses as forced labor, detention, rape, forced displacement and armed attacks against civilian targets.

One month later, HRW/Helsinki released a document about abuses in Northern Bosnia.[66] Examined here in some detail were abuses by Muslim political leaders. The abuses were similar to those perpetrated by the Bosnian Serbs. Human Rights Watch was always careful to be evenhanded in its critique, although, of course, the magnitude of the Muslim abuses was tiny as compared with those committed by the Croats and especially the Serbs. When two top *Washington Post* columnists, Stephen Rosenfeld and Charles Krauthammer, suggested that the three principal ethnic groups were equally guilty of genocide, the Executive Director of HRW/Helsinki, Holly Cartner, wrote a "Letter to the Editor" chastising the authors as "imposing an artificial symmetry" on the parties, which she properly considered "dangerous."[67]

Bosnia's torment reached a crescendo-like trauma with the massive assault in July, 1995 by the Serbs on the UN-declared "safe area" of Srebrenica and the deliberate killing of some 7,000 Muslim men and boys. Even as the development stirred the conscience of many, it revealed the utter inadequacy of the UN and the European Union to cope with a deepening crisis. Genocide had become clearly visible to all and mocked the very creation of a Tribunal to hold perpetrators accountable. Without military action to halt the expected Serb drive against the half-dozen other "safe areas," the Tribunal would be transformed into a sham, testimony to a totally hypocritical commitment of the Western world.[68]

At this stage, Human Rights Watch undertook an initiative rare in the annals of the NGO community. Ken Roth invited the representatives of some 40 organizations to attend an "emergency" meeting on July 21 at his headquarters in New York. They agreed to form a coalition of NGOs that would press for "a more effective response by the international community to the atrocities in Bosnia."[69] A "joint statement" to be issued by the coalition at a press conference in Washington was the "first step." A "draft joint policy statement," prepared by Roth, was sent out on July 24 with a covering letter to the invited representatives asking whether their respective organizations would be willing to sign. It was a tough draft, denouncing "the cowardly half-measures and evasions that have character-ized the major powers' response to ethnic slaughter in Bosnia." President Clinton, along with the leaders of the other major countries, was charged with "spinelessness" for failing to stand up to genocide.

The ill-advised personal attack on Clinton and other Western leaders was removed from the final joint policy statement that was signed by 27 organizations and publicly released at a press conference in Washington, D.C. on July 31. Apparently, Felice Gaer of the Blaustein Institute for the Advancement of Human Rights "helped formulate" the new language.[70] The coalition called for "multilateral military action" to halt the massacre of innocent civilians in Bosnia and to "stop genocide." Central to this military effort, the coalition stated, must be "American leadership."

The joint policy statement "urgently" called upon President Clinton and the leaders of the other major powers to undertake the following:

- protect civilians in all Bosnian "safe areas";
- demand immediate access to all detainees from Srebrenica and nearby Zepa;
- ensure the delivery of humanitarian supplies to the "safe areas";
- publicly reveal the names of senior Serb political and military leaders responsible for the atrocities and make the information available to the Tribunal; and
- maintain the sanctions against Serbia until it cooperates fully with the Tribunal.

Certainly, the press conference had a quick and strong media impact. The *Washington Post* gave it prominent attention the next day under the headline, "Coalition Calls for Action in Bosnia."[71] Roth did not neglect the need to tightly link the appeal to the functions of the Tribunal in The Hague. He was quoted in the *Post* account as saying: "Right now there is an assumption of impunity that is driving the slaughter." Only by military forces halting the Serb offensive, he implied, could the Tribunal fulfil the accountability purpose of punishing genocide.

A survey of the signers of the petition is revealing. Fully a quarter (7) of the 27 were major Jewish organizations. The memory of the Holocaust was a driving force for them, as it must have been for some of the other signers. Two were Arab-American groups, no doubt concerned about the brutalities meted out to Muslims in Bosnia. Missing was Amnesty International, whose representative was present at the initial meeting. Its mandate did not provide for recommending the use of military force, whatever the circumstances.

Nor was it an easy decision for Human Rights Watch. Only once before had it publicly welcomed the use of military force. According to the organization's general counsel, in the fall of 1992, HRW had urged humanitarian military intervention to protect the food and medical supplies being shipped to starving civilians in Somalia. A raging civil war between tribal rulers profoundly had interfered with the shipment and HRW vigorously supported the UN initiative, backed by the United States to send in troops.[72]

Since the start of the "ethnic cleansing" campaign by the Serbs in the summer of 1992, Human Rights Watch/Helsinki appeared to be moving in the direction of urging humanitarian intervention, though without specifying the use of military force. In a letter to President George Bush on August 7, 1992, the NGO called upon the United States to take the lead in urging the UN to take action "to prevent and suppress acts of genocide" in Bosnia, as provided for by the Genocide Convention.[73] It was signed by then Executive Director of HRW Aryeh Neier and Helsinki Watch Director Jeri Laber. A somewhat similar letter was sent on August 11 to the UN Secretary-General, Boutros-Ghali. Two years later, in December, 1994, HRW appealed to the leaders of CSCE then meeting at a summit session to protect the UN "safe areas" of Bosnia. The military force implications were evident.

How much of an impact the joint statement had cannot be determined. What is known is that soon thereafter, in August, NATO, with the United States in the lead, launched for the first time, *sustained* bombing attacks upon Serb positions. The neutral posture that had governed UN operations in the area was rejected; the public plea by Margaret Thatcher made three years earlier for a strong NATO response guided by the United States, now was being acted upon. Within the Administration, the voice of U.S. Ambassador to the UN Madeleine Albright would prevail over a hesitant Pentagon, still paralyzed by the Somalia trauma and fearful of breaking with the Powell Doctrine.[74] At the very least, it can be said that Albright and her supporters within the Administration and the State Department were given a solid public base by the action taken on July 31 by HRW and the 26 other national organizations that it had rallied to its side.

The outcome of the tough NATO and U.S. military stance was an agreement on September 8 from the three ethnic Bosnian parties to maintain Bosnia as a single state that would be composed roughly of two entities—a Muslim-Croat federation and a Serb "Republika Srpska." U.S. diplomatic negotiations with Serbia's President and strongman Slobodan Milosevic led to formal talks on November 1 in Dayton, Ohio between the parties. By the end of the year an elaborate peace accord had been reached, a testimony to American power and diplomatic skill that had distinctly maintained the integrity of the Tribunal as a guarantor of accountability.

Not surprisingly, both President Cassese and Prosecutor Goldstone, in a joint statement on November 24, welcomed the agreement and stressed that "justice is an indispensable ingredient of the process of national reconciliation." They emphasized that the parties to the agreement, including the Republika Srpska, "are under a stringent obligation to cooperate with the Tribunal and to render judicial assistance."[75]

The central problem now turned on the apprehension and trial of those accused of genocide, crimes against humanity and war crimes. In June, 1995, Human Rights Watch/Helsinki issued a 45-page study of war crimes trials that already had taken place in Former Yugoslavia, not at the Tribunal in The Hague.[76] Sharply illuminated was the lack of fairness as well as the ineffectiveness of the separate ethnic judicial systems. The study showed that very few trials had taken place in Serbia or in Serbian-controlled areas of Bosnia. In the latter areas, the few trials that had been held were said to have been "rarely prosecuted properly." In Croatia, the trials were found to be "highly politicized" and "seriously lacking in due process." The bulk of the Croatian cases—97 percent—had been brought against Serbs, often "without the presence of the accused."

Overwhelmingly, the evidence documented the significance of the Tribunal in The Hague. Whether it could function effectively was the key question. The President of the Tribunal, Antonio Cassese, underscored the court's total reliance upon the states comprising the UN community in an address to the principal legislative body of the Council of Europe. He characterized the Tribunal as an

> armless and legless giant which needs artificial limbs to act and move. These limbs are the state authorities . . . the national prosecutors, judges and police officers. If state authorities fail to carry out their responsibilities, the giant is paralyzed, no matter how determined its efforts.[77]

Cassese used the same type of description in a meeting six months earlier with Human Rights Watch in New York.[78]

Thus, reliance of the Tribunal upon the authority of the police or military power of states is total. And, thus far, Cassese noted, the experience was hardly encouraging. A disturbing and complete lack of cooperation Serb area in Bosnia, in Serbia and in Croatia was characteristic, in his view. Nor did he expect them to voluntarily cooperate. Distressing, too, was the failure of most UN member states to comply with a Security Council resolution requiring them to adopt legislation that would enable them to apprehend war criminals in their respective areas. Cassese complained that only 12 of the 185 member states had done so. A year later, a top official of the Lawyer's Committee for Human Rights dealing with Tribunal matters, Stefanie Grant, in an address to a leading Latin American assemblage, bitterly commented that "shockingly few" member states had adopted the required legislation and that "in this [Western] hemisphere only the U.S. has formalized its cooperation [with the Tribunal]."[79]

The failure of most states to comply with the legislative obligations set by the Security Council prompted Amnesty International to produce an impressively thorough "Handbook for Government Cooperation" of 109 pages with two extensive Supplements that was sent to every UN member state. By then, the number of states to adopt legislation rose to 20. The documentation was so detailed that no state effectively could argue that it was not fully informed.[80]

The President of the Tribunal pointed out that the two leading culprits, Radovan Karadzic and Ratko Mladic, conceivably could be either pressured or punished by the seizure of their known assets, especially in Swiss and Luxembourg banks, as well as their property in Austria. But the Tribunal in The Hague had no means for accomplishing such a task. With everyone's attention focused upon the Dayton negotiations, it was clear to Cassese that the effectiveness of the Tribunal would have to depend on the peace negotiations and the leverage exerted by the United States upon the various parties to the talks.

A pessimistic outlook characterized the presentation of the Tribunal's President to HRW. He cautioned that the Tribunal might have to close down in one or two years if this unique opportunity for international justice was missed. And, if the Tribunal is compelled to close down, he added, this would kill the idea of a permanent International Criminal Court, which, at the time, was beginning to seem like a realistic option before the end of the century.

The only relief offered from the deepening gloom, in Cassese's judgement, was the pressure that might emanate from NGOs. "We need," he said, "a lot of support from NGOs." He primarily was referring to American-based NGOs, for their role, he made clear, was to exert influence upon American policy so that it could enable the legless giant to function. In response to a question asking what kind of support the NGOs should provide, he referred to a conversation he had had with Tadeusz Mazowiecki, the former Polish Prime Minister and later the UN's Special Rapporteur on Yugoslavia. Mazowiecki had advised him that the Tribunal must rely upon the American government for its very existence and sustenance and, therefore, American public opinion was central to its survival. It was for that reason that NGOs in America had a particular "clout."

It was significant that Cassese chose to brief the leadership of HRW. He was certainly aware of its role in calling for the creation of the Tribunal, in providing it with invaluable firsthand documentation and in urging the United States to use vigorous military force to halt the outrageous atrocities of the Bosnian Serbs. And it was hardly accidental that HRW would respond to Cassese's obvious appeal for assistance in a determined fashion. Following two separate long-term missions to Bosnia in early 1996—January 25–March 26, headed by Ivan Lupis and March 17–April 18, headed by Diane Paul, another research associate— HRW released a powerful critique of NATO and U.S. nonaction with respect to war criminals. The damning 37-page report, "A Failure in the Making," issued in June, 1996, gave expression to the deep concern of Cassese and others:

> If Dayton is to represent anything more than a pause in the fighting, the international community must . . . use all the means at its disposal to see that the commitments made in Dayton are enforced. Persons suspected of war crimes must be arrested and tried, civil authorities and the police must be held accountable for abuses of their power. . . .[81]

But the appeal of the Tribunal's President was by no means restricted to HRW or even to American NGOs. In the first annual report of the Tribunal, which Cassese was required to submit to both the UN Security Council and the General Assembly, NGOs were called upon to provide a variety of forms of assistance. Cassese had sent in that report on August 17, 1994, well over a year before he had spoken to HRW. The report was issued as a UN document a week later.[82] Three forms of assistance were spelled out. The first concerned information: "NGOs can be invaluable in identifying incidents that fall within the jurisdiction of the Tribunal, tracing witnesses and, where possible, providing direct evidence for use by the Prosecutor." Human Rights Watch had assumed that task already. Later, its work would be augmented by the Physicians for Human Rights, whose highly expert cooperation with the Tribunal, including gravesite exhumation and forensic examination of bodies, will be discussed in a separate chapter.

A second form of assistance noted in the first Annual Report was the submission of *amicus curiae* briefs on legal issues of a "highly specialized nature." A number of NGOs, along with several prominent law professors, would submit such briefs. The appeal relating to technical legal expertise also would find expression in documents prepared by the Lawyers Committee for Human Rights on substantive criminal laws and on criminal procedure laws of the former Yugoslav republics.

Even more crucial legal assistance work sponsored by an NGO was outlined by a high official of the Tribunal's Registry, the administrative arm of the court. David Tolbert, a British international law specialist from Cambridge, explained that, through the assistance of the International Commission of Jurists, the judicial chambers of the Tribunal, as well as the Registry, were provided with 22 gifted legal researchers from a variety of countries.[83] They were the equivalent of law clerks to major American justices, he noted. In Tolbert's view, NGOs play a "quite significant role" in relation to the Registry. Aside from filling the core research needs of the judges, NGOs act as "friendly critics" in advising the Tribunal on legal issues and on jurisprudential sources.

A third form of assistance involved the critical matter of "support for victims and witnesses." This type of "practical assistance," whether of a financial or psychological nature, must be made available to victims and witnesses "both before and after trials" and could be better handled, the 1994 Annual Report contended, by skilled NGOs than by "a judicial body" lacking "necessary resources." The Annual Report of 1995 was more precise.[84] It noted that the special "Victims and Witnesses Unit" of the Tribunal had requested "specific organizations with relevant expertise to provide psychological, medical and other support to victims and witnesses. . . ." Even before such technically trained expertise was brought into the picture, NGOs "which are very often the first organizations to be in contact with the victims and witnesses" were asked to help those highly vulnerable persons with all types of material and legal support.

The Coordinator of the Unit, Frans Baudoin, an experienced Dutch judge on leave from his previous and standard judicial work, provided insight into the importance of the problem in the course of an interview at the Tribunal.[85] Many of the victims and witnesses, he noted, had been "traumatized" by their experience and, therefore, were "very nervous" when they arrived at The Hague. More recently, he found, witnesses had become "increasingly reluctant" to appear in court. It was the task of the skilled NGO to help the victims and witnesses "feel at ease"; their needs must be met and satisfied throughout the trip to The Hague, and while they were housed in The Hague.

One particular aspect of the support work for victims and witnesses was of central importance. It dealt with gender-related crimes, a subject new to international law and, of course, not directly dealt with at Nuremberg. The Tribunal had made the subject a key element for prosecution. Goldstone at a conference cosponsored by a women's advocacy group emphasized that "the role of gender-based war crimes . . . is of much greater importance than we originally expected."[86] His successor, Louise Arbour of Canada, at the same conference pledged that gender-based crimes would be "at the center of my attention and . . . I shall deal with it with the sense of priority which it deserves."[87]

Several NGOs were active in promoting the thesis that rape and other gender-specific crimes be accorded special recognition and be treated as a war crime. The Blaustein Institute was in the forefront of this initiative in the United States, inviting top legal specialists on this subject to address two expert consultations it ran at the Yale Club for the UN key budget committee.[88] The result was an increased allocation for this type of investigatory work. The Coordination of Women's Advocacy, based in Switzerland, was especially active on this matter and its conferences at The Hague were extremely well attended by Tribunal personnel, specialists and representatives of women's groups.

Testifying to the significance of gender-specific crimes was the data provided by the Tribunal's senior specialist on gender-specific crimes, Patricia Viseur-Sellers, at the conference sponsored by The Coordination of Women's Advocacy. In the 17 indictments until September, 1996, the Prosecutor charged over 500 counts of criminal activity by the accused. Approximately 130 of such criminal activities concern sexual assaults.[89] Thus one-quarter of the total criminal activity that was being prosecuted by the Tribunal comprised rape and sexual assault which, Viseur-Sellers noted, probably would have not been a focus two years earlier.[90] Incidentally, the Blaustein Institute had urged early on the creation of such a position, a "senior official post."

In the Tribunal's Annual Report of 1995, a fourth role for NGOs was proposed, although with little elaboration. They were called upon to help in "making the Tribunal's activities more widely known."[91] NGOs' earlier activities along these lines were accorded recognition in the report, but it was time to place greater emphasis upon the subject. The reason was obvious: cooperation with the Tribunal from governments, especially those with either pertinence—like Serbia and Croatia—or significant clout was not great. No one has performed that function in the United States as effectively as has the Coalition for International Justice. Headquartered in Washington, D.C., it has brought together regularly the representatives of about two dozen NGOs with particular interest in the Tribunal. Even as it has informed them and the broader public of the critical importance of the Tribunal, the Coalition has served as a vigorous public activist, lobbying Congress and the Administration and drafting legislation related to the purposes of the Tribunal.

The Coalition was founded in September, 1995 by a special branch of the American Bar Association, the Central and East European Law Initiative (CEELI). The ABA action was a far cry from where it had stood on genocide and other international human treaties from 1948 to the mid-seventies. What prompted the extraordinary 1995 initiative is intriguing in itself. According to the Coalition's former Board Chairman, Thomas Warrick, the ABA had been approached by Madeleine Albright, then U.S. Ambassador to the UN; John Shattuck, Assistant Secretary of State; and an official of the State Department's legal office as early as April, 1995. They urged the ABA to create the Coalition.[92] In September, the Coalition formally was created, servicing on its Internet mailing list some 200 activists and embracing some 30-40 NGOs.

Ambassador Albright's characterization of the Coalition testified to the support she and some of her State Department associates extended to the idea:

> The Coalition can tap the energy and expertise of non-governmental organizations and people, helping them make their important contributions to the Tribunal's work. In addition, the Coalition's strong independent voice for justice will help focus international attention and build support for the Tribunal's work.[93]

From the very beginning, the Coalition conceived of its responsibility as encompassing technical and legal assistance in addition to lobbying and advocacy. In November, 1995, it sent to The Hague a U.S. attorney to work full time in the Tribunal's Registry as the Coalition's Liaison.

One of the projects undertaken by the Coalition was particularly important for emphasizing the Tribunal's aim of fairness. Such an image was critical given the nature of ethnic tensions in Bosnia. A training seminar on adversarial trial techniques was organized for members of the legal defense team of a prominent defendant.[94] Goldstone commented: "There is no question that history will judge the Tribunal on the fairness or unfairness of its proceedings and without the intervention of the Coalition, there would be no doubt that the first trial would not have measured up to the test."[95]

Another type of seminar was conducted in March, 1996 for the especially tough-minded UN Advisory Committee on Administrative and Budgetary Questions (ACABQ). The valuable seminar or "consultation" was organized at the Yale University Club by the Blaustein Institute for the Advancement of Human Rights with the cooperation of the Coalition. A similar consultation had been held the previous year and it proved to be a "spectacular success," according to Warrick, in that the UN's budget-cutting for the Tribunal was extremely modest as compared with the heavy across-the-board reductions for all other UN agencies.[96] A memorandum from Felice Gaer related that the March, 1996 consultation for the ACABQ produced a similar result.

But the Coalition's primary task remained advocacy, and its research pointed to the fundamental challenge this NGO as well as the other concerned NGOs faced. As of January, 1997, the Tribunal had indicted 75 persons, and of that number 67 remained at large or not in the Tribunal's custody.[97] Of the 75, 51 were Bosnian Serbs, 18 were Bosnian Croats, 3 were former Yugoslav Army officers and 3 were Bosnian Muslims. A report in April, 1998 noted that over 40 persons indicted by the Tribunal remained at large.

On the anniversary of its founding, the Coalition appealed to President Clinton "to order American and NATO forces to do more to arrest the indicted war criminals and to pressure countries who are protecting them, including Croatia, Serbia and the Bosnian Serb Republic."[98] Soon afterward, the Clinton Administration appeared to move off dead center, where it had been located ever since the Dayton peace agreement. In late June and early July, British forces seized two indictees and killed a third; in October, the United States and the European Union pressured Croatia into surrendering ten indictees; and in December, Dutch forces seized two indicted Bosnian Croats.

While the Administration appeared to become somewhat more responsive, the Coalition and its activist allies struck out on new paths. On the occasion of a meeting in Brussels on January 9-10, 1997 of the European Union and the World Bank to consider the effectiveness of donations for the reconstruction of Bosnia, the Coalition, supported by Human Rights Watch and the European Action Council, urged the conferees to establish new standards related to the handling by states of indicted war criminals.[99] The new standards would require that "additional funds not be sent to countries or entities" that refused to comply with the Dayton peace accords, including the obligation that persons indicted for genocide and war crimes "be turned over to the International Criminal Tribunal" in The Hague.

U.S. action remained the major target of NGO initiatives. On May 6, the Coalition, together with Human Rights Watch, Physicians for Human Rights, the International Human Rights Law Group and the Action Council for Peace in the Balkans wrote to Senator Frank Lautenberg of New Jersey and Senator Patrick Leahy of Vermont commending them on legislation that they would be introducing the next day—"The War Crimes Prosecution Facilitation Act." It would prevent U.S. bilateral economic assistance to countries that harbor indicted war criminals and further would require U.S. Executive Directors at the World Bank and other international financial institutions to vote against multilateral international assistance to those countries. The NGOs promised their "strong support" for the legislation.

Richard Goldstone, prior to leaving his prosecutorial position in October, 1996 and returning to South Africa to resume his position as a justice on the country's highest court, summed up his perspective in a speech on October 3, 1996 in Chicago. It carried the provocative title "Is Genocide Here to Stay?"[100] Goldstone's answer was a qualified "yes." If we don't stop dehumanizing people, he stated, "I'm afraid genocide is here to stay."

But equally important, Goldstone explained, was the need to arrest and prosecute the perpetrators of genocide. "Leaders will only stop giving [genocidal] orders if they fear being caught and fear being punished," he emphasized. Knowing that he was speaking to an American NGO, he stressed that whether genocidists are to be prosecuted and punished is "in the hands of public opinion." He was, of course, keenly aware that public opinion could be shaped by NGOs. And it was precisely that collective group to whom he was addressing his pressing remarks.

Goldstone was even less circumspect when he addressed an NGO conference sponsored in the fall of 1996 by the Norwegian Ministry of Foreign Affairs. The relationship between the Tribunal and NGOs, especially the human rights groups, he said, was of "fundamental" importance. "I have absolutely no doubt," he added, "that without the push from non-governmental organizations in many countries, we would not have either of the international criminal tribunals at all."[101] Goldstone became even more explicit. "If we're to rely solely on the good will of politicians," he maintained, "we would not be in existence very long. . . ." For that reason, pressure from NGOs "needs to be kept up at all times."

By the late spring of 1997, after he had been away from The Hague for some nine months, Goldstone expressed dismay at the failure of the international community to deliver the bulk of the indictees to the Tribunal. With each passing month, he told an interviewer, he had become "more frustrated and more pessimistic."[102] But, at the same time, he refused to relent in his hope that a breakthrough would occur. That hope rested, inevitably, upon the determination of NGOS, especially in the United States, to persist and to prevail. But, it also depended, as in so many other crucial human rights developments, upon the exercise of America's power, whether diplomatic, economic, political or, if necessary, military.

That Madeleine Albright, now Secretary of State, sought a tough U.S. position was made clear at a critical policy meeting at the White House on May 16, 1997, where sharp differences between herself and Secretary of Defense William Cohen were thrashed out.[103] She argued—according to a senior U.S. official—that American credibility was at stake, and that U.S. civilian and military authorities must stop "playing the observer" and assume something of the role of "actor." Moreover, she stressed that "getting the Bosnian piece of the puzzle solved is important to how a unified Europe should look." On May 22, Albright testified before Congress, promising to "renew the momentum" to cope with "the failure of many Bosnian leaders to embrace the political and social integration."[104] She announced that the United States would withhold from Balkan states support for international loans and membership in regional organizations until they surrendered those indicted by the War Crimes Tribunal.[105] Albright's major legal assistant since her UN days, David Scheffer, was nominated as Ambassador at Large to work precisely on the issue of prosecuting war crimes.

It was on the occasion of the fiftieth anniversary of a predecessor's appeal for his Marshall Plan that would provide American leadership for the postwar era that Albright powerfully delineated in a commencement address at Harvard University her own vision of the future and of America's responsibility. The very core of the address dealt with the "ethnic conflict" in Bosnia and how that genocide menaced the civilized world. And, as the late Secretary of State George Marshall had to cope with then immediate dangers, "we, too," she said, "must heed the lessons of the past, accept responsibility and lead."[106]

Her focus ineluctably was upon "full cooperation" with the International War Crimes Tribunal, for it "represents a choice not only for Bosnia and for Rwanda but for the world." The Holocaust was not specifically mentioned in her remarks, but the consciousness of it penetrated a number of key paragraphs. What happened in Bosnia recalled for her the horrors of Hitlerism. She then warned that "we can heed the most searing lesson of this century, which is that evil—when unopposed—will spawn more evil."

CHAPTER FOURTEEN

Overcoming the Crisis of Growth: Human Rights Watch Spans the Globe

In a funding renewal proposal to the Rockefeller Foundation, Human Rights Watch spelled out the nature of its shaming strategy, specifically designed to have an impact on governments. The subject being discussed was unpublicized arms transfers to regimes that were human rights abusers. Governments responsible for the arms transfers, noted the proposal, "are often sensitive to embarrassing publicity and do not want to be stigmatized by the international community. . . ." It is this fact that provides Human Rights Watch with appropriate leverage. By "shining an international spotlight on policies that permit such arms transfers," the NGO noted, it can and does encourage "governments to cut off the arms flow to abusive forces. . . ."[1] The description could just as well have applied to the variety of other projects to which Human Rights Watch has been committed and in which it is involved on a daily basis.

The creation of landmark human rights institutions like the International Tribunal for the Former Yugoslavia was, of course, a central purpose of Human Rights Watch. A major motivation of this group and of other international NGOs was precisely the laying of a permanent institutional foundation for coping with and preventing gross human rights violations and violators. But HRW's stock in trade, the task it pursued on a regular basis, was less institution-building than it was the embarrassment of governments to halt human rights violations. Publicity—pitiless, potent and persistent—has been the continuing and ultimate aim of the organization's numerous projects. And, at this specialty, HRW has developed an expertise unrivaled in the human rights business.

Particularly pertinent were the comments about HRW of Reed Brody, during the course of an interview in February, 1996.[2] Brody had served as Deputy Executive Director of the International Commission of Jurists in Geneva, then as Director of the International Human Rights Law Group in Washington, D.C., from which springboard he acted as the principal lobbyist of the NGO community at the World Conference on Human Rights in Vienna. Later, in 1994-95, he directed the human rights work of the UN's peacekeeping operation in El Salvador, and in 1996, he became an adviser to the government of Haiti to help it prepare the prosecution of the crimes committed by the country's military leaders prior to the restoration of democracy. His knowledge and experience in the field are almost unique. At the time of the interview, he was preparing, at the request of Amnesty International, an evaluation of its program.

Human Rights Watch was considered by Brody to be "the most effective human rights organization. . . ." He then explained that the organization is superior "in terms of having the information that it collects impact on decisions" at the UN, whether in terms of policy or economic aid. Especially impressive, Brody thought, was that the organizations "monitors and reports human rights abuses and then campaigns to have that information have an influence with the real world." Instructive was Brody's comparison of HRW with Amnesty International. Referring to HRW's fact-finding and campaigning, he said, "I think they're doing an incredibly good job at this point, more so than Amnesty." When asked why, he responded that Amnesty has "lost" its earlier preeminence: "I think they haven't been as savvy in the use of their information as Human Rights Watch; I don't think they've put as much effort into lobbying and press work as Human Rights Watch." A full two years later, Brody agreed to become HRW's Advocacy Director.

Brody's judgment in 1996 coincided with that held by a longtime top human rights specialist at the UN. Preferring anonymity, he volunteered, when interviewed at UN Headquarters in New York, that Amnesty had lost its earlier "validity," while HRW very much had assumed that status.[3] The former Director of the UN Division on Human Rights, Theo van Boven, now a professor at the University of Maastricht in the Netherlands, when interviewed in The Hague, was equally laudatory about Human Rights Watch.[4] He called its reports "quite prominent" and compared them most favorably with the International Commission of Jurists (ICJ), on whose policymaking body he sits. In van Boven's view, the ICJ has "diminished" in stature while its staff leadership, he "regrets to say," is "inadequate." As for Amnesty, he only would offer that its reports were "well-researched."

A somewhat similar perspective was expressed by a key staffer of the State Department's human rights bureau, Alex Arriaga, whose function was that of liaison with the NGO community in Washington. She previously had served as coordinator for the congressional caucus on human rights and was well-versed on NGO activities, which she contended were "extremely valuable" to both the caucus and the State Department. In Arriaga's view, the reports of Human Rights Watch were "comprehensive" and especially useful, while Amnesty's "catalogue of abuses" lacked "perspective."[5] At least one HRW official was wildly praised as doing a "fantastic job."[6] No Amnesty official was extended such praise.

HRW's current preeminent global status as an NGO by no means emerged suddenly. On the contrary, when initially formed in 1978 as Helsinki Watch, it had limited horizons. The focus was upon Europe, mainly the Communist half, but with some attention to Turkey. It was started by Robert Bernstein, an activist in publishing circles. While serving as Chairman of the Association of American Publishers, he helped spur the formation of a crucial International Freedom to Publish Committee that vigorously would fight for the rights of foreign authors.

Within the Association, various publishers thought the Freedom to Publish Committee was too aggressive and that, by being less confrontational, the publishers could help infiltrate the Soviet cultural scene and undermine the Iron Curtain. This perspective would find an echo in the repeated controversies in the West about how to deal with human rights violations in totalitarian or authoritarian societies. In recent years, the resonance has been especially loud in debates about strategy related to China: should it involve "critical engagement" or should it be more confrontational? Bernstein remained consistent. In December, 1995, he told a university audience:

> I am in favor of making contacts, but I am against shaping one's talking points at meetings with high officials, and thereby papering over issues that ought to be discussed just for the sake of convening meetings.

To avoid the split in the publishers' Association, Bernstein formed in 1964 the Fund for Free Expression, which embraced publishers, editors, authors and columnists who were determined to challenge the Kremlin and its minions on the crucial right to publish. That Fund would become the channel for Ford Foundation money when Bernstein was targeted by Bundy to organize and lead Helsinki Watch in 1978. Interestingly, the Fund remains today a valuable, although small, part of the elaborate Human Rights Watch structure.

Only three years after Helsinki Watch was established, Bernstein, together with the Executive Director of Helsinki Watch, Aryeh Neier, created Americas Watch. It was prompted by the reaction in various liberal circles to President Ronald Reagan's policy of support for Latin American right wing military dictatorships. From Bernstein's perspective, the view of Jean Kirkpatrick, who was an architect of Reagan's policy, was "a disaster."[7] Her famous article in *Commentary* that had distinguished between totalitarian and authoritarian regimes and found the latter more responsive to democratic pressure was utterly distasteful to him.

The initial expansion of Helsinki Watch to include Americas Watch was not seen by Bernstein as a major step in broadening the scope of human rights activity. "We saw ourselves as an American human rights organization," he recalled.[8] It never seemed to him at the time that extending the area of Helsinki Watch's operation constituted a step in global direction and, therefore, represented a challenge to Amnesty International's monopoly of the global human rights arena.

As perceived by Bernstein, a primary preoccupation of Americas Watch was to subject the State Department's annual Country Reports to close and critical scrutiny. The initial scrutiny was done in cooperation with the Lawyers Committee for Human Rights. The purpose, he later stated, was the correction of "all the lies" that went into the official Country Reports.[9] "We made them clean up that [country] report," Bernstein proudly recalled. In his view, referring to Americas Watch reportage with respect to El Salvador, Guatemala, Honduras and Nicaragua, the role of his broadened organization was that of "investigative journalists." Newspapers, he believed, simply were not performing this function. Reportage of Latin America was not the only target; he noted, too, that Turkey, a NATO ally, was handled too gently with respect to gross human rights violations. So awkward had this become, observed Bernstein, that "I remember Jeri [Laber] rewriting the whole Turkish section [of the State Department's Country Report] one year."[10]

Asia Watch was added in 1985, then Africa Watch in 1986 and Middle-East Watch in 1989. For Bernstein, the broadening of the initial Helsinki Watch structure was by no means seen as something planned, envisioned and ultimately consummated as Human Rights Watch. On the contrary, it was a kind of happenstance, similar to the way he had extended Random House by adding Knopf, Pantheon, Ballantine and Modern Library.

Beyond the regional areas was the incorporation of special project areas like the Women's Rights Project and the rather remarkable Arms Project. How the latter came about, in the recollection of Bernstein, is intriguing. He called the initial proposal and how it unfolded "a particularly tricky one, because we were offered a million dollars by [the] Rockefeller [Foundation] which we really wanted, and yet we didn't want to go into nuclear arms." Apparently, Bernstein believed, the Rockefeller Foundation focused heavily upon the nuclear arms issue, which he considered "a whole other business." According to Bernstein, it was Aryeh Neier who offered, as often was the case, an ingenious, as well as historic solution:

> So Aryeh devised a system of how arms related to human rights, which was arms that affected civilian populations, like land mines, poison gas, and so forth. And so we told Rockefeller we wouldn't take a million, we would only take half a million, which we did.

But, even as Helsinki Watch grew into a major human rights operation, focusing upon abuses in broad segments of the globe, Bernstein's perception of it remained distinctly American, preeminently U.S.-centered. Comparing his NGO with Amnesty, he explained: "We're much more involved with the United States government. We're in all parts of it."

Aryeh Neier's perception of how Helsinki Watch grew into Human Rights Watch is sharply different and very much reflects the views of a professional political science analyst, in which he had been trained.[11] The emergence of Human Rights Watch was not happenstance, nor was it accidental. From the very beginning, he "always had in mind becoming global. . . ." In the late seventies, he said, he was "always wanting to do that." However, he failed to set down his global vision on paper, although he said he shared it with very close colleagues. It is, nonetheless, odd and puzzling that Neier, a prolific writer, chose not to give verbal expression to an early global vision for HRW.

In Neier's opinion, "we didn't become global right away," but rather "took on region after region," because that was "the only way you could do effective human rights work. . . ." He explained that the organization had "to pay attention to a single area" and "stay with it as long as was necessary." Neier contended that "you couldn't hop, skip and jump from one part of the world to another and be effective in promoting human rights."

Building on a regional basis enabled an organization to establish credibility, which would permit a new regional division to link itself with the already-existing and recognized division. This had been an aspect of his organizational strategy. Thus, the creation of Helsinki Watch "established certain credentials" and, had it "not already established a reputation, we would have had great difficulty doing battle with the Reagan Administration" over its Latin American policy. "The credibility that the Helsinki Watch gave us turned out to be crucial," Neier emphasized.

When asked whether the intention to operate globally did not directly challenge the effectiveness of Amnesty International as well as its authority and power, Neier was inclined to stress Amnesty's limitations with respect to the mandates that governed it. If Amnesty did "a superb job" with respect to people being detained or imprisoned or tortured or killed, it nonetheless didn't deal with a host of highly relevant issues involving freedom of the media or other matters "which seemed to be enormously important to the human rights cause." A particular example of neglect by Amnesty concerned transgressions in the context of armed conflict. Such limitations enabled the various divisions and projects of HRW to fill a vacuum in the human rights field created by Amnesty's strict adherence to its mandate system.

Of equal, if not greater significance in Neier's pressing for a global agenda was the use of American power throughout the world. Since HRW was an American-based institution, its regional divisions could and did seek to influence American human rights policies with respect to other regions. Neier, like Bernstein, did not shun emphasizing the organization's American connections; nor did he attempt to stress its international focus at the expense of its geographical base. He appeared to take pride in asserting that "we were a national organization. . . ." And, he was similarly blunt in highlighting his organization's special focus upon the United States:

> . . . as an American organization, we could focus significantly on U.S. policy, and U.S. policy was so significant on a worldwide basis, that our impact would derive from our relationship to U.S. policy.[12]

Neier disclosed that he actually went to the trouble of talking with Amnesty officials about their failure to place a greater emphasis upon influencing American policy. Among the persons with whom he met were the former Secretaries-General of Amnesty, Thomas Hammarberg and Ian Martin, as well as Amnesty USA officials. How they responded to his initiative—as he related it—was revealing. Amnesty officials told him that "as an international organization, they felt that they could not focus significantly on the foreign policy of any one country, because they had to have an even-handed approach in their efforts worldwide." This reported attitude was consistent with how Amnesty's UN representative played down and, by implication, distorted America's role in creating a UN High Commissioner of Human Rights.

Where Amnesty's neglect was especially pronounced was in relation to the crucial Helsinki process, which had contributed greatly to transforming Europe in 1989-90. Amnesty hardly was involved in that process and its representatives avoided showing up at its various and historic follow-up meetings and special conferences. Neier observed that this related to "that sense of themselves as an organization that has to operate the same way in every part of the world." Since a counterpart to the Helsinki process did not exist in other global areas, therefore, Amnesty "wouldn't devote special resources to the Helsinki process." His judgment was pointed, if understated: "I think it's carrying the notion of consistency to a very foolish extreme."

That Neier was the prime builder of HRW into a giant human rights organization second only to Amnesty International in size is self-evident.[13] Bernstein, today hardly an enthusiastic partisan of Neier's talents, admits that "in the building of the [HRW] organization, he was wonderful."[14] He went on to say that Neier was "particularly good at bringing in people. . . . He brought in a lot of good people."

An independent management study group that carefully examined the operations of HRW in 1993 was especially impressed by "the quality of the staff."[15] It was this that gave the organization its "greatest strength." The typical staff member was found to be a "true human rights professional—intelligent, creative, articulate, principled and courageous . . . [with] an extraordinary commitment to making a difference and to upholding the standards of excellence."[16] So overwhelmed were the management study authors by the staff as well as the HRW volunteers in leadership positions that their language was almost gushing: "The quality of the people associated with this organization is outstanding; we have rarely encountered such a uniformly impressive collection of staff and volunteers."

The selection of principal staff officers was largely Neier's work. But he also was responsible for the high degree of their motivation. The management study found that he made HRW "an enormously exciting and creative place to work."[17] His intellectual leadership set standards for excellence that were high and demanding. Additional stimulation of a rather profound nature was extended by Neier's inclination to push the boundaries of the human rights field and to frequently remain on the cutting edge. This especially will be noted with respect to human rights in armed conflict, an area that Neier virtually invented. The "adventurous and pioneering nature" of HRW augmented the sense of independence that the decentralized style had granted. The result was a sizable human rights organization distinguished more by "agility and flexibility" than by "rigid mandates," to which Amnesty was prone.

Unusually impressive was the youthfulness of the staff. According to an age breakdown in April, 1996 provided by the then Associate Director of HRW, Gara LaMarche, 75 percent of the staff were under forty years of age, with some two-thirds in their thirties.[18] Only 2 of the staff were in their sixties and 4 in their fifties. The bulk of the senior staff were in their thirties and forties. A significant degree of gender, racial and cultural diversity also characterized the staff. As of the last month of 1995, two-thirds of the staff were female and one-third were nonwhite.

Perhaps the most salient feature of the organization, as the management study indicated, was "the impeccable reliability of HRW's information." From the very beginning of Helsinki Watch to the unfolding of a global Human Rights Watch, Neier understood that the organization's influence depended in large part on the credibility of its research findings. A commitment to "absolute accuracy" was fundamental to the organization, along with fairness and neutrality in the gathering and dissemination of the researched information.[19] In the judgment of the Management Assistance Group, HRW, under Neier, built and maintained "a remarkable reputation for even-handedness, objectivity and dependability." The credibility was to prove of central importance in impacting upon the media. Ultimately, the major press organs would come to trust and rely upon the reports and studies of HRW and its various divisions.

Inevitably, errors would creep into the most meticulously researched reports. What HRW was determined to do, especially after the management study was completed, was to check and recheck initial reports to reduce the possibility of mistakes. An elaborate review procedure was established, headed by especially knowledgeable and experienced senior staff researchers, to weed out the uncertain or speculative. As noted by Bernstein, "the secret of our success has been our tremendous care in not making too many errors." It also lay, he added, in "our willingness, if we find . . . [an error] to immediately admit it and change it and not try to defend it."[20] He had been particularly upset, he recalled, when an Amnesty report about Kuwait was shown to be erroneous.[21]

Beyond precision in accuracy was another feature of HRW that requires emphasis. Carefully researched information was at the very heart of its reputation, but the research simply could end up on a shelf of unnoticed reports. Early on, Helsinki Watch had realized that a method was needed to make certain that the research would get attention. As remembered by Bernstein, Helsinki Watch became "very conscious . . . of never doing a report where we didn't know how we were going to use it when it was finished." Over the years, he noted, "we've gotten better and better at planning how to use our material, and that I think had a real effect on the world."

The extraordinary growth of the organization in the course of a mere decade from simply a European (Helsinki)—focused operation to one that embraced global human rights issues exposed grave inadequacies and liabilities that plunged it into a serious crisis. This was the principal finding of the management survey. It was as if a Hegelian or Marxist dialectic had been in operation: the very success of the Human Rights Watch had produced contradictions that threatened its very survival.[22]

For one thing, the expansion of the various regional divisions and thematic projects meant a significant enlargement of staff, and, in the absence of any centralized bureaucratic procedure, the exercise of an effective kind of oversight and review seriously declined. The positive consequences of autonomy now turned into the threatened danger of fragmentation. A creeping confusion had set in in the outside world. For the public or the media, accustomed to the dealing with the research and reports of individual regions, it was difficult to conceive of a unified organization. For the donors of the organization, the fragmentation was especially perplexing. To whom was the grant being given? Many of the potential financial supporters of the organization, noted the management study, were under the "misimpression that there are several, separate Watch Committees rather than one big organization. . . ."[23]

What aggravated the emergent tensions and internal conflicts was the leadership style of Neier. According to the management study, his "rather authoritarian manner" in allocating funds spurred conflict among the staff, while his "tendency to inadequately consult" with prominent volunteer members of the Executive Committee led to a sense on their part that they no longer could perform a useful role.[24] The tensions reached a "peak" at the "now infamous retreat" in late 1992 that apparently involved both staff and volunteers. Precisely what happened at the retreat was not recorded in the management study except for the reference that the angry complaints contributed to "Aryeh's decision to leave the organization." Bernstein, in his first interview, reported that Neier had become more prickly and irascible, with the result that troubles with the staff had prompted a revolt at the retreat.[25]

As the Ford Foundation had been since 1978 the principal donor of the organization, the internal crisis ineluctably became an issue for the Foundation. Bernstein related that he sought to bring Neier to a meeting of the Foundation in order to resolve the crisis. Neier responded, according to Bernstein, that this was unnecessary, since he had decided to resign in order to take a position with the Soros Foundation.[26] An irritated Bernstein commented that either Neier had been "romancing" Soros for some time or "they him." The HRW Chairman went on to complain that Neier refused to talk to him. Bernstein found Neier's anger mystifying.

Neier's explanation for his resignation from HRW ran along a different track. He contended that it resulted from "a peculiarity about the way the organization developed." The "peculiarity," he explained, was that "the more successful the organization was, the less interesting my own job got." He meant that as HRW expanded, he found himself running faster and harder to obtain the funds to operate an organization that had no constituency to guarantee a steady income flow. "As time went on, I was spending the bulk of my time raising money . . . [and] doing less and less of the work that I enjoyed. . . ."[27]

The internal crisis was certain to be compounded by Neier's resignation. On the one hand, as the management study pointed out, he was one of the organization's two main fundraisers.[28] On the other hand, he was, in the words of the study, "the oracle whom everyone consulted" on policy and strategy, as well as "the glue that held HRW's many parts together." How would it function without him? The depth of the crisis undoubtedly prompted the Ford Foundation to strongly recommend a management study, and it probably advised which group ought to do the study. A letter from Ken Roth, Neier's successor, to Shepard Forman, a top Ford Foundation official, dated June 16, 1995, spelled out several institutional changes in HRW and expressed "appreciation for the pivotal role played by the Ford Foundation in bringing about the MAG [Management Assistance Group] process that had led to these . . . reforms."[29]

From the perspective of the authors of the management study, Neier's departure was by no means a calamity. On the contrary, it was a "mixed blessing." For one thing, the operational procedure and structure had to be radically altered. HRW simply had overgrown its previous structure. The study stressed that "the time when everyone could sit in a room together on Wednesday mornings and make policy had long since passed."

Nor could a sizable organization permit the Chairman and Executive Director to arbitrarily assume a multiplicity of leadership tasks and reach key administrative and policy decisions without consultation. Bernstein remembered that well into the eighties, he would meet weekly with Neier, "maybe for an hour and a half every week, or two hours, trying to hold things together. . . ."[30] By then Bernstein already had turned over Helsinki Watch to someone else.[31] And he was increasingly less involved in policy discussions than he had been. He thought that he would move his previous Helsinki expertise to Chinese issues. But overall policy issues were handled by the two of them.

What made this possible was Neier's ability to maintain a central control in his own person. No other senior staffer was essential to the high-level, informal deliberations in which "Aryeh would have had everything in his hands," recalled Bernstein. "He could sit down for two hours and tell you everything that was going on." Bernstein contrasted this procedure with the way Ken Roth operated. It was now far more formal, far more structured, far more bureaucratized. (Bernstein remained as Chairman of HRW until his retirement in early 1998.)

The Management Assistance Group proposed a system for effecting a much higher level of unity and coherence in leadership, strategy and governance, which in turn, required a sharply delineated central structure and "clearly defined central processes for reviewing work and approving important decisions."[32] Coherence through a clearly defined senior administrative team would provide the organization with a clear identity that would prevent and eliminate confused perceptions of the organization as well as balkanization tendencies.

Centralization must not mean, however, depriving HRW's "strong staff" of "a great deal of latitude" within a unified policy framework. Especially important was the need to provide the regional divisions as much autonomy as possible—within, of course, central guidelines—for their work "is both the heart and backbone" of HRW's program.[33] The new type of management structure would be able to set priorities enabling the organization to concentrate on fewer matters and cover in depth fewer countries. Priority-setting necessarily meant focusing more on advocacy than previously, without, however, "compromising the quality of its research."[34] With increasing professionalization of the organization, clearly demarcated lines separating staff from volunteers were essential. The lay leadership no longer should be directly involved in operational activity; "equal partners in the running of HRW is gone."

About one critically important issue, the management study chose not to offer an answer, but rather to pose pointedly a question concerning the organization's identity. Was it to remain primarily an American institution, or should it become an international organization, a direction in which it appeared to be moving? The authors, on the one hand, cited those who believed that HRW's "main strength and unique niche" lay in its ability to press the U.S. government and U.S.-based institutions to adopt policies that promote human rights. This view would entail concentrating and capitalizing upon the American connection and seeking to build a strong, broad-based American constituency.

At the same time, the authors took note of recent, new trends in HRW strategies in which the focus was largely non-American, including the creation of a UN operation and the establishment of a European-oriented office and apparatus based in Brussels.[35] Should HRW continue to pursue the internationalization of its strategies and, therefore, focus more upon influencing the policies of non-U.S. governments and institutions? This, said the authors, was a "key question which HRW needs to resolve."[36]

The management study impacted heavily upon Human Rights Watch, as the June 16, 1995 letter from its new Executive Director spelled out to the Ford Foundation. Initially, the study was shared with every member of the HRW staff and board, and this was followed by a series of three-hour meetings in which the authors of the study could respond directly to questions from staff and volunteers. Early in 1994, separate all-day retreats for senior staff and for board members were held. According to Roth, there was "broad acceptance" of the "diagnosis" provided by the management study, although, apparently, there also were some undefined "small exceptions."

In keeping with the study's major recommendation, HRW was given a clearly defined public identity in 1995, with the various regional components linked closely to the central body partly through new names such as HRW/Helsinki and HRW/Asia, which enhanced the sense of interdependence and coherence. The structural changes were more crucial, including the creation of the post of Program Director who, together with a highly experienced Deputy, would provide increased coordination and oversight of regional and project research activities. Advocacy also was to be centralized with a new position of Advocacy

Director located in Washington, D.C.[37] A new position of General Counsel would oversee coordination of policy and legal questions. Overall media efforts would be handled by a Central Communications Director. As noted by Roth, "we are well on our way toward achieving the structural changes" recommended by the management study.

On the key question of the future identity and direction of HRW, Roth indicated that the staff's consensus pointed to a process, already underway, "to internationalize our strategies for wielding leverage to combat abuses" in the human rights area. He referred to "expanded work" at the UN, in Europe and in Japan. He noted that attention was being given to the translation of HRW's reports as well as their distribution to other countries. And, of particular importance, he observed that HRW was expanding its relationships with local human rights groups around the world.

The first step in the process of internationalization was to acquire consultative status with ECOSOC at the UN. Strangely enough, Human Rights Watch made no effort to secure such status until 1991 even though, by then, its reach had become global in scope. A *New York Times* report suggested that it had not sought accreditation until then "because it assumed such efforts would be blocked."[38] But, according to a former Ford Foundation program official who dealt with HRW, the reason was to be found in the contempt that Neier held for the UN. He thought the institution to be useless as a mechanism for raising human rights issues, let alone for doing something about them.[39] Apparently Neier changed his mind when the UN played a valuable role in securing an end to the raging civil war in El Salvador and in the early nineties also providing the mediation process with a strong human rights component. Clearly overlooked by Neier and his associates were the extraordinary developments at the UN during the eighties that involved the unprecedented creation of a host of mechanisms to highlight human rights abuses. The failure to note such opportunities is not easily explicable.

At a meeting of ECOSOC's 19-member Committee on Non-Governmental Organizations on January 22, 1991, it already was clear that HRW would become a convenient target of various totalitarian and authoritarian regimes. The Cuba representative, for example, wanted to know why HRW "focussed primarily on African and Latin American countries."[40] Ken Roth, HRW's Deputy Director at the time, found the query puzzling since "a wide range of countries was covered" by his organization, including "prison conditions in the United Kingdom" as well as immigration issues on the Mexican-U.S. border.[41]

It was Cuba's delegate that led the fight against HRW, accusing it of "acting as a kind of international prosecutor" and denouncing its criticism of China's crackdown on student dissidents as "irreverent."[42] The Cuban was supported by the Sudanese delegate on the Committee, who contended that HRW's report on his country "contains lies." Openly bigoted were the remarks of the Iraqi delegate. After rhetorically asking: "What is the religious and political background of the staff and board of Human Rights Watch?" he later answered that the organization was of "a certain kind—we are all aware of the nature of that membership."[43]

One had to reach back two decades to recall an earlier UN era of NGO witch-hunting with its language of bigotry. When asked now by the *Times* UN reporter what the Iraqi meant, Roth responded that the remarks "probably allude to the fact that I'm Jewish, as are our chairman, Robert R. Bernstein, and our executive director, Aryeh Neier." Still, some things had changed radically. In the sixties and seventies, the principal enemies of the NGOs were the Soviet Union and its East European allies. Now the USSR, under Gorbachev, strenuously supported HRW. Its Committee delegate praised the organization as "serious-minded," while Romania's representative characterized HRW as "good for society."

The principal UN obstacle to Human Rights Watch in the early nineties was a technical one: a consensus now was required in the UN Committee for approval of consultative status. Even were an NGO to have a solid majority in support of it, any strong opposition from an individual country or group of countries could prevent positive action. A group of six countries—Cuba, Syria, Iraq, Sudan, Libya and Algeria—insisted upon deferment of action and carried the day. The episode prompted a sharp editorial in the *New York Times*, which commented that "no finer compliment has been paid Human Rights Watch" than the opposition of "six flagrant human rights abusers. . . ."[44]

Cuba's effort's to stymie the admission of HRW to consultative status were in vain. By 1993, the consensus device was dropped and the second largest human rights organization in the world quickly was admitted. Soon, under the direction of Joanna Weschler, a former spokesperson of Poland's Solidarity in the United States during the eighties, HRW's UN office, established in November, 1994 moved quickly to become a leading human rights advocate and lobbyist in the various organs of the international body. Nothing can illustrate better the prominent role that HRW would play than two reports by the UN Secretary-General to the Security Council, one in late November, 1995, the other in the form of a letter to the President of the Council in January, 1996.

The first report dealt with violations of international humanitarian law by Bosnian Serbs in Srebrenica, Zepa, Banja Luka and Sanski. Detailed documentation of the horrendous violations was provided in this 16-page report which also identified the specific military officials responsible for the outrages.[45] The Secretary-General's report concluded with a powerful and moving appeal:

> The moral responsibility of the international community is heavy indeed. The world surely must not allow such acts to go unpunished, wherever and by whoever they are committed. If it does, these and similar crimes will happen again.[46]

If the language recalled formulations of Human Rights Watch/Helsinki in its various reports following Srebrenica, what was unusually striking about the UN document was its specific reference to reportage by this NGO.[47] It was the only NGO source to whom reference was made. All the other sources were UN bodies or firsthand press accounts. At one point, the Secretary-General's report noted that HRW/Helsinki had collected evidence pointing to a certain site as an execution area. In a second instance, the UN cited specific interviews conducted by the same NGO that pointed to the involvement of Serb paramilitary forces in the mass killings. That an official Security Council document carried reference to any NGO was extremely rare, perhaps even unique.

On January 26, 1996, the UN Secretary-General wrote a lengthy letter to the President of the Security Council summarizing the reports of the International Commission of Inquiry, which had been examining reports about the sale and supply of arms and related military materiel to the former Rwandan government forces that had perpetrated the genocide against the Tutsis.[48] The Commission had been set up by the Secretary-General in response to a Security Council request of September 7, 1995 that was designated "a matter of urgency." According to the Secretary-General's letter, the Commission of Inquiry had received "detailed and voluminous information" about arms deliveries made to Goma airport in Zaire for the use of the former Rwandan government forces, which was in violation of a Security Council embargo imposed in May, 1994.

After noting the "detailed and voluminous information," the Secretary-General recorded that:

> This information came primarily from the NGO Human Rights Watch Arms Project, whose report was based on four months of field investigation

in Central Africa, and whose researchers interviewed, among others, several officers of the former Rwandan government forces, including those of the highest ranks.

It was the first time that the HRW Arms Project was given attention by the world body, an endorsement that would seem to be unprecedented in UN annals. The letter appeared to commend the thoroughness of HRW's researcher. He was said to have interviewed, besides former Rwandan government military officers, Zairian officers as well as Goma airport staff and local businessmen. He further was reported to have cited numerous incidents with dates that explicitly demonstrated that "the perpetrators of the Rwandan genocide have rebuilt their military infra-structure, largely in Zaire, and are rebuilding themselves in preparation for a violent return to Rwanda."

Then, in a further unexpected turn, the UN letter commented that "the Human Rights Watch report was subsequently confirmed by Amnesty International." For the two principal human rights agencies to be mentioned in an official letter of the highest UN agent was nothing short of spectacular, especially since one was treated as confirming the research of the other. An amusing if indirect comment followed that appeared to affirm the NGOs' findings and the significance of this achievement: "The Commission would note . . . that rumours of persistent embargo violations seem to have greatly diminished following the publication of the Human Rights Watch and Amnesty International reports and the accompanying media attention." Clearly, NGO disclo-sures had a positive consequence, a result that impressed even the highest level officials of the world organization.

The Security Council was an infrequent focus of HRW attention. The bulk of its communications were addressed to the Commission on Human Rights. HRW's UN Director, in an interview, related how she would advise the organization's division and project heads about what was on the Commission's six-week agenda each spring. Should any of them have special items of interest or concern that warranted consider-ation by the Commission, Weschler then would help shape a submission to the UN body.[49]

Two reports to the 1995 Commission session illustrate the wide-spread involvement of HRW in that UN body's work. One submitted on January 31, 1995 dealt with the rights of women and took as its point of departure two developments: (1) the appointment in 1994 of the first UN Special Rapporteur on violence against women, Radhika Coomaraswamy; and (2) the forthcoming World Conference on Women, scheduled for the fall in Beijing.[50] The submission covered domestic violence against women migrant workers in Asia—a subject that carefully had been researched and reported upon by HRW. The HRW document concluded with an appeal to the Commission "to strengthen mechanisms of accountability" so that governments will take steps to end discrimination against women and punish perpetrators of violence against them.

A second HRW report, while addressing the subject of torture, gave special attention to how some governments extend various forms of assistance, including military assistance, to regimes or armed groups that engage in torture.[51] It was a hard-hitting document, showing how Myanmar (Burma) receives extensive economic assistance and military supplies from China, how France provides considerable help to abusive francophone regimes in Africa and how the United States extends a huge amount of military assistance to Turkey, where torture apparently is a common phenomenon. HRW cited Turkish human rights groups for an allegation that 90 percent of Turkish political detainees are tortured. HRW called upon the international community to deprive governments that practice torture of "assistance and support."

HRW did not restrict itself only to the submission of documentation to the UN summarizing human rights violations and calling for action; it also actively and vigorously lobbied members of the Commission on Human Rights. Weschler spelled out in an interview how, during the 1995 session of the Commission in Geneva, she and her colleagues lobbied unsuccessfully to get adoption of a Special Rapporteur on Nigeria, one of the world's worst human rights violators, as well as a Special Rapporteur on Colombia, another human rights abuser.[52] Concerning China and the effort to win a Commission resolution condemning its human rights practices, HRW conducted a "major campaign."[53] Lobbying was directed at the European Union in Brussels to persuade it and its leading members to join with the United States in achieving a breakthrough. In addition, HRW wrote letters to some 25 members of the Commission urging a resolution.[54]

China countered with an intense diplomatic effort in 1995 to weaken Western unity and solidify support among Third World countries. By a single vote it succeeded in killing the initiative by HRW. Still, the closeness of the vote testified to the fact that no longer was even a major country certain of avoiding a critical UN resolution. The intensity of the Chinese diplomatic effort revealed, too, the lengths to which major powers would go to avoid being shamed or embarrassed on the international stage. A country's image remained a greatly prized item in measuring the national interests of any country, a reality that NGOs always had understood. For HRW, the shaming device remained an especially valued instrument.

In the course of just three years since HRW had acquired consultative status, it clearly had left a strong mark on the world organization. There was no greater evidence of its impact than the reaction of Secretary-General Boutros-Ghali to HRW's critical remarks about his failings in its annual report. The Secretary-General was chastised for having "grievously failed" to uphold the UN Charter's principles of promoting respect for human rights through his unwillingness "to offend powerful governments."[55] Specifically noted was his refusal to publicly criticize China for "brazenly flouting the rights of free speech and association" of those attending the UN-sponsored Conference on Women in Beijing. Also angrily noted was Boutros-Ghali's response of "no comment" to a question from reporters about the butchery by the Russian army in Chechnya.

The Secretary-General, through his spokesman, on December 7, 1995 chose to immediately respond to HRW's press release that very day by asserting that he "spends an extraordinary amount of his time and energy in the campaign against human rights abuses around the world."[56] With respect to the Beijing Conference on Women, Boutros-Ghali was said to have "engaged in long but quiet diplomacy" with the Chinese regime to ensure the success of the Conference and to facilitate a parallel NGO meeting. As for Chechnya, the Secretary-General "expressed his great personal anguish over the fighting" but stated that "the UN had no mandate to intervene."

Clearly, the UN Secretary-General was deeply concerned about criticism emanating from HRW. It is striking that once Kofi Annan was chosen to replace Boutros-Ghali, Roth and Weschler, in a joint letter, wrote to him on January 13, 1997 urging a series of specific steps so that "under your leadership . . . human rights can be given a far more central role at the United Nations." Human rights concerns, stated the letter, "should be more fully integrated" into the Secretariat's political and peacekeeping operations.[57] What followed were several recommendations concerning the High Commissioner for Human Rights, a subject that will be discussed in a subsequent chapter. Especially pronounced was an HRW proposal to have the human rights mechanisms now headquartered in Geneva be given "more visibility and impact at the political center of the [UN] Organization, in New York."

In the new international reach of HRW, as important as the UN operation, if not more so—although, at the same time, less visible publicly in the United States—was the Brussels office, created in May, 1994 to serve a variety of purposes. It was to be the link to a host of European institutions associated with the European Union. It was also a short distance from the Council of Europe in Strasbourg and the Organization of Security and Cooperation in Europe (OSCE), based in Vienna but with a human rights operation in Warsaw, the Office of Democratic Institutions and Human Rights (ODIHR). Heading up the Brussels office was an extremely knowledgeable and versatile Danish lawyer, Lotte Leicht, who previously had directed the Vienna-based International Helsinki Federation.

Leicht's task was not easy. Europe had not shown leadership in the struggle for human rights. In 1995, the Brussels office made its presence felt. Its primary concern was the mass slaughter of Chechens by Russian military forces in Grozny and other cities in Chechnya. The indiscriminate bombing and shelling of civilians stood in violation of the Geneva Conventions and of the rules of OSCE as well as of the UN, as adopted in 1969. The nature of the violations and the details of the horrors imposed on the Chechens were spelled out in four HRW reports, based upon a firsthand fact-finding mission to areas near Chechnya.[58]

Alone among international NGOs, HRW had assumed the burden of responsibility for highlighting the Chechen tragedy. Amnesty International made no attempt at an investigation, since the subject was not within its mandate. The Brussels office mailed out the reports to virtually every European institution of the EU, OSCE and Council of Europe, as well as to Foreign Ministers and desk officers dealing with Russia in every European country.[59] When the UN Commission on Human Rights met in Geneva in March, Leicht made sure that its members received copies of the report.

A fundamental obstacle to European activism was America's reluctance to take a vigorous stand. The Clinton Administration, while issuing mild calls for Russian restraint, characterized the conflict as "an internal matter." The earlier relationship between Europe and the United States regarding human rights issues now was reversed, with European institutions taking strong initiatives. To some extent, Leicht legitimately could claim credit. She had appealed to the Council of Europe, particularly its Political Affairs Committee, to suspend consideration of Russia's request for membership in that body. It was a status for which the Yeltsin regime had been pressing during the previous two years.

The Council of Europe did act to hold up action on the Russian request. Leicht also urged the European Commission of the European Union (EU) to suspend its interim trade agreement with Russia. At the same time, she pressed the European Parliament in Strasbourg to freeze ratification of a permanent "partnership and cooperation" agreement between the European Communities and Russia. In these various initiatives, she found a favorable response. During an interview, she called the various European actions "important small successes for us."[60] She was hopeful that these decisions might find an echo in the OSCE and the UN Commission on Human Rights.

They did, partly in response to HRW pressure. In April, 1995, the OSCE sent a mission to Grozny with a mandate to monitor human rights, along with other security concerns. The mission, however, did not meet with Russian human rights groups and failed to deal with the issues of accountability. Leicht continued the pressure and was accorded an unprecedented privilege of being permitted to address OSCE's policymaking body—the Permanent Council. Later, she and her colleague from HRW's Moscow office, Rachel Denber, again addressed the Council. Meanwhile, in Geneva, the Chairman of the UN Commission on Human Rights, in a formal statement, expressed the Commission's "deep concern over the disproportionate use of force by the Russian Armed Forces" in Chechnya. It was obvious that the Brussels office already had left its mark upon several European or European-based institutions.

Sensitizing and getting the European Union to respond to the atrocities in Chechnya was but one of several responsibilities assumed by Lotte Leicht in 1995. On behalf of HRW/Asia, she raised with the European Commission of the EU the issue of bonded labor in Pakistan, a subject to which the International Confederation of Free Trade Unions (ICFTU) already had called attention. The issue had considerable relevance, as Pakistan's trade status with Europe could be deleteriously affected.

An overall objective set by HRW that Leicht pursued on trade issues generally was a code of conduct for businesses. The same type of issue was raised with respect to trade with Nigeria. Irresponsibility or non-responsibility were to be eschewed. Some officials of the European Union had complained to Leicht that she and her HRW associates were becoming "picky," even a "pain in the neck." But after only one year, she took special pride that "we had put ourselves on the map." "They take us seriously," she noted in the interview.[61]

By the following spring, Leicht's staff had increased to five persons, including a full-time and highly experienced press officer, Jean-Paul Marthoz. HRW quickly would be receiving a surprising degree of attention in the West European media, although not anywhere near the coverage it received in the U.S. media.[62] An example of HRW's new media impact was the international explosion of reportage concerning HRW/Asia's disclosure of the China orphanage story in January, 1996. It revealed how China orphanages in major centers deliberately had neglected the health of girl children, thus facilitating an extraordinarily high mortality rate among them. The European press gave this story as much play as the U.S. media did. The top leaders of the European Union were sufficiently affected that, when visiting Beijing on official business, they raised the issue.

Leicht saw the orphanage story as providing the backdrop for HRW's major campaign to obtain a critical resolution on China at the UN Commission of Human Rights in late March or April in Geneva. This was communicated in an interview in New York in May when Leicht summarized the various steps she had taken in connection with a Commission session the previous month.[63] But what was far more instructive was a memo she wrote in July, 1996, to the head of HRW/Asia in New York. It revealed details of the major role she had played—considerably greater than that of HRW's UN office—in seeking to win support from the European Union.[64] A host of representatives of West European countries and of key European Union figures directly were contacted by her. Especially striking was how many officials, carefully not identified, leaked information to her, while others kept her abreast of what was happening behind the scenes.

Most impressive was Leicht's effort, supported by her New York colleagues, to get the European Parliament, meeting in Strasbourg on April 18, to adopt a resolution by an overwhelming vote calling for action by the Human Rights Commission on a resolution critical of China's human rights abuses. The irritated Chinese delegation attending the Strasbourg session walked out. The July memorandum was also striking in the way Leicht showed how and why the European Union commitment to press for a strong resolution had disintegrated. She pointed to a big Airbus Industrie deal with China consummated by the consortium of France's Aerospatiale, British Aerospace, Germany's Daimler-Benz and Spain's CASA, a leading airline company. Discussion of China's planned purchase of several Airbus planes took place on March 1-2 during a Bangkok summit of Chinese Premier Li Peng with Germany's Chancellor Helmut Kohl and French President Jacques Chirac. "This was the moment when things started to go wrong," she wrote.

China clearly had mobilized considerable economic power to prevent a hostile resolution. While HRW's campaign did not succeed, it hardly could be considered a failure. Many in Europe had been sensitized to the human rights abuses of China, as demonstrated by the vote in the European Parliament. Beijing was surely aware that its domestic human rights policy carried a cost, even a burdensome one, which was precisely HRW's objective. The energetic Leicht functioned on a variety of levels.[65] She helped raise funds for the Brussels operation from European sources. The internationalization of HRW obviously had been extended to fundraising. She was engaged in the serious humanitarian purpose of quietly encouraging EU governments to admit some 50 young Chinese dissidents who had fled to Hong Kong after the Tiananmen massacre. Their lives were in jeopardy if they remained hidden in Hong Kong.

Even as Leicht handled these special tasks, she was performing as HRW's agent with respect to Bosnia, pressing for postponement by the OSCE of municipal elections and urging apprehension of the indicted war criminals. She also pressed for action on banning land mines and blinding lasers. Her Brussels office remained a key player in making the EU react effectively with respect to the products of bonded child labor in India. Under its General System of Preferences (GSP), the EU's trade agreement with India carries a human rights clause banning imports of goods produced by bonded child labor.

With reference to the last concern, a visitor accompanied Leicht on October 9 when she met with the Principal Administrator of the European Parliament's Foreign Affairs Committee. In her lobbying with this key official with whom she had an obvious good working relationship, she asked for a favorable resolution by Parliament on bonded child labor in India. Discussion also centered on EU relations with Kazakstan and Uzbekistan, and on EU attitudes to a forthcoming land mine conference in Ottawa, Canada. For the visitor, who had had considerable experience in lobbying administrators, Leicht's performance was impressive.[66]

A third facet of the internationalization of HRW had a different dimension—reaching out to NGOs specifically in Asia and establishing a close and continuing relationship with them. In January 1995, HRW/Asia created a new position. As spelled out in its Annual World Report, a newly appointed professional who had been a longtime researcher with the organization, Jeannine Guthrie, would seek fulltime to "understand their [Asian NGOs'] priorities and facilitate exchanges of information." Her job also would aid researchers in New York to "formulate more effective strategies for working with local partners on human rights concerns."[67]

That the idea for the new position probably was sparked by the Ford Foundation was suggested in an interview with Larry Cox, the Foundation's human rights program officer. He emphasized that local NGOs were "the thrust for the future" and that a relationship between them and international NGOs was "the key to their future operation."[68] But if the future meant local groups, why the exclusive concentration of the HRW liaison upon Asian NGOs? Guthrie provided the answer in an interview. She said that in the course of the decade since 1985, "thousands and thousands of national NGOs, perhaps hundreds of thousands" of NGOs had sprung up in Asia.[69] How she functioned in her new position will be discussed later.

Ever since the management study of HRW was completed in November, 1993, raising at the end the question of HRW's future identity, it had moved forward with giant strides toward a new image. In its Annual World Report for 1994, it recorded that during that year, "we took significant steps to internationalize our strategies for change."[70] If, until then, "our advocacy had been centered on Washington and the U.S. press," now "we recognize the need to extend the scope of our advocacy to other foreign and major powers." Besides the UN and Brussels operations, the Annual World Report took note of the fact that the Moscow office of HRW had been transformed "from a center for launching field investigations to one that also addressed Russian foreign policy."[71] Offices also had been added in that year in Dushanbe, Tajikistan and Rio de Janeiro, Brazil. Already in existence was a London office, one of whose professionals played a prominent part on arms trade issues in Africa; a smaller office in Sarajevo and, of course, the major listening post in Hong Kong. The possibility of an office in Japan also was projected. When Ken Roth, HRW's Executive Director, was interviewed in June, 1995, he took great pride in stressing how HRW had moved the "center" of its "geopolitical" work away from Washington.[72] These multiple centers, he felt, enabled HRW to "react much more quickly" to outside concerns.

Even with the thrust toward internationalization, HRW still was rooted in the American scene and utilized its connections with the American power structure to affect other governments on human rights issues. Thus, three important, always bipartisan congressional groups that it helped to create and continues to advise closely perform valuable functions when activated, as is done from time to time, by HRW. It is a typically American phenomenon that is not likely to be structured anywhere else.[73] Members of these groups write critical letters to governments engaging in human rights violations. Such letters from important Senators and Congressmen help pressure foreign governments to halt their abuses. Copies of these letters are sent to U.S. Ambassadors in the specified countries, a tactic that could prompt their involvement. Copies also are sent to the local press in the targeted countries, which could help focus public attention upon the abuses and the reaction to the abuses by American legislators.

Contacts developed over the years with the White House and the executive branch also enable HRW to play a decisive part on various human rights issues. Thus, Roth related how in a meeting with an important National Security Council aide in April, 1994, HRW vigorously criticized the United States for its repatriation of Haitian refugees then fleeing the Haitian military dictatorship.[74] When the aide asked Roth what he would want done, the latter spelled out three initiatives, including the halting of repatriation. All were adopted the very next day. The same aide was of central importance in bringing about a change in America's policy of indifference, if not opposition, to the proposed International Criminal Court then being debated at the UN.

Not surprisingly, the government aide was quite close to the top staff of HRW in New York, hardly a situation that could be replicated by various HRW offices abroad. More important still was the power that the United States could exert in the international arena; no other major country could come close to the United States in exercise of power for human rights purposes. Were HRW able to impact upon American decision-making, it would have a potent lever to be internationally applied. The big problem, however, was that HRW lacked a formidable mass constituency in the United States and, therefore, as observed by the highly perceptive John Shattuck in the State Department, it could not "bring matters to a climax."[75]

Shattuck explained that while HRW could bring an issue to the U.S. Congress, it could not bring about a successful vote on that issue. HRW was "the best" at promoting a human rights cause but, lacking a constituency, (i.e., a mass lobbying force), it was "the worst" at not achieving "closure." Not that Amnesty was much better for this purpose, he held, even though it did have a sizable constituency in the United States. According to Shattuck, it simply was unable to deliver that constituency in terms of public pressure upon Congress or the Administration.

If the management survey of November, 1993 helped HRW push in new directions, both structurally and geographically toward centralization and internationalization, about one aspect of the operation—the regional divisions and projects—it firmly urged little change. These basically research (as well as advocacy) sections were perceived as the heart of the organization, which should be kept intact and given the maximum autonomy and encouragement. Of the five regional divisions, the former Helsinki Watch—the oldest—continued to play a starring role, especially since it was seized with the continuing Bosnian crisis and the International Criminal Tribunal for the Former Yugoslavia in The Hague. Moving up quickly to occupy an increasingly important place in the organization was Asia Watch, with an extremely talented Director at its helm, Sidney Jones. That division will be dealt with separately.

The former Americas Watch declined in significance with the emergence of a number of democratic states in Latin America, the end of the Cold War and the related diminution of civil strife in Central America. But the division, largely operating out of the Washington, D.C. office of HRW, still retained importance. The newest regional groups— Africa and the Middle East—after having to cope with some leadership problems, were beginning to hit their stride.

A solid basis of public attention, aside from the regional divisions, were several special project operations, particularly the Arms Project, initiated in 1992. It was an idea that Aryeh Neier took particular pride in having promoted.[76] Even earlier he had succeeded, as he would note, in the "focussing of a significant part of the human rights movement on the laws of war." The Project entailed seeking a ban on weapons systems that can be classified as "inherently indiscriminate or as cruel and inhuman under international humanitarian law."[77] A second purpose carried a conflict prevention aspect. It would oppose the flow of weapons or military assistance, including the training of forces, to those regimes or insurgents that had a proven record of violating human rights and international humanitarian law.

Land mines were targeted early and HRW quickly became a key NGO in the International Campaign to Ban Landmines.[78] HRW was one of six members of the Campaign's key steering committee. One of the first substantive publications on the subject was prepared by Human Rights Watch, together with Physicians for Human Rights.[79] Another among the early principal initiatives that the Arms Project undertook was the urging of a ban on blinding laser weapons as devices "inherently" cruel and inhumane. These weapons, already planned in 1995 for the military arsenal of the United States and other countries, were perceived as particularly dangerous because the injury they inflicted was irreversible and struck at a vital body part. HRW disclosures about the new weapons attracted extensive media attention in the United States and Europe, including in military publications. The media reports were followed up with meetings that the HRW/Arms Project arranged with U.S. officials and with officials of major European governments.

The effort had a telling effect upon a major international conference in Vienna in September-October 1995 that reviewed a treaty prohibiting or restricting certain types of dangerous weapons. There, a new Protocol to the treaty was adopted banning the use of blinding laser weapons, an action that the International Committee of the Red Cross (ICRC) appropriately called a "great advance for civilization."[80] What a representative of the International Committee of the Red Cross had to say about the role of HRW as conveyed in a letter to the organization was lavish:

> I should now like to express our profound appreciation for the decisive support which you . . . gave to this effort. We are convinced it is thanks to your support and enormous efforts in the U.S. that this Protocol was able to be adopted. This wonderful success is thanks to you.

It was signed by a top official of ICRC, Yves Sandoz. Indirect praise also came from the European Parliament, which referred to the Arms Project in a report attached to a resolution that the legislative body adopted in June, 1995 calling for a ban.[81]

With respect to arms transfer, the Project already has demonstrated a certain effectiveness. The UN Secretary-General, citing a study of a special Commission of Inquiry, noted how HRW disclosures in the case of arms transfers from major countries to Rwandan refugee military forces in Zaire had brought a significant diminution of the transfer. Equally successful, although on a quite different level, was the Arms Project's attempt to halt the sale by a U.S. company of some 500 deadly cluster bombs to Turkey. The Project in December, 1994 prepared a report about the nature of such bombs.[82] It sent the report to Secretary of State Warren Christopher, together with a letter urging the United States to deny an export license approval of the transfer.

The grounds for the action were in part rooted in human rights. Turkey's human rights record was hardly up to Western standards and the organization appropriately expressed concern that Ankara would use such weapons indiscriminately in its ruthless struggle against the Kurdish insurgents in southeast Turkey. But HRW's opposition also was based on the lethal antipersonnel capabilities of the advanced cluster bombs. News coverage of the report was extensive. Ultimately, the sale was canceled, no doubt in great part due to the disclosures, which evoked considerable national and congressional concern.[83] Since then, HRW has pressed the

United States, as well as the European Union, to set guidelines for arms transfers to Turkey that would require assurances that the arms would not be used to commit human rights abuses or violations of the laws of war.[84]

Two other full-time and impressive thematic projects were adopted by HRW in the mid-nineties—Women's Rights and Children's Rights. These themes constituted new emphases, although hardly radical departures for the traditional human rights organizations. The output of the regional divisions and of the projects—at times, they appeared in joint publications—is simply staggering. A catalog published in 1995 shows the total number of HRW publications in the form of reports or books, reaching back to 1986, was 556, numbering 30,433 pages.[85] The number of new publications released annually was estimated in July, 1997 to be about 70. The then Communications Director, Susan Osnos, anticipated that this figure will decrease as HRW focused more upon advocacy rather than on research alone.

HRW's country-by-country sections in annual reports appear more analytical, with an attempt made to examine the causes of a government's conduct and how pivotal abuses developed. Moreover, despite its cultivation of an internationalist image, HRW delineates in each country analysis the role that the United States has played in coping with abuses or how international institutions have dealt with them. Of particular importance is a section devoted to the manner in which HRW or an appropriate division of the organization has dealt with an abuse or sought to cope with it.

From the perspective of HRW, its annual *World Report* is used as a potent public relations weapon to call attention to trends in human rights abuses during the previous year and to the failures of the United States as well as international institutions to respond to these trends. At the same time, of course, the annual report calls attention to the organization itself. Press coverage is usually extensive and cannot fail to focus interest on the value of HRW. Recognizing the importance of the annual report, the staff leadership organize an intense concentrated effort, beginning in early October, to have each regional division and thematic project complete a full report by the beginning of the following month. A month is given over for the printing of a rather handsome paperback along with the preparation of press releases and the mailing out of copies to the media commentator and key officials.

Timing is absolutely critical. The date chosen for the public release is in early December, close to the anniversary of the Universal Declaration of Human Rights—December 10. The contrast with the publication of Amnesty's annual report could not be greater. Amnesty's report usually appears in June, not less than six months after the year has ended. Clearly timeliness is not a guideline for Amnesty. In fact, if the text is ready at the end of the year, it is turned over to translators for translation into a half-dozen languages.[86] Unlike HRW's annual reports, which receive extensive coverage in the media, Amnesty receives little, if any, attention.

Research, howsoever important—and has been central to the organization's prominence—has been linked increasingly to advocacy and publicity. Over the course of the past ten years, according to Susan Osnos—now HRW's Associate Director—HRW has focused more and more on packaging the research output and, therefore, on its timeliness and relevance.[87] One of the veterans of the organization, this very knowledgeable editor and executive explained that a careful public relations strategy, prepared almost on a daily basis, is worked out for every story HRW sends out. Account is taken of how the release will impact on policymakers, the public and the media. Public relations, Osnos emphasized, is approached "much more aggressively" than was the case in the past.

Osnos estimated that HRW sends out ten releases per week, eight of which are responsive to specific events that are taking place or have just taken place. And two releases are related to articles or studies that just have been completed by one or another regional or thematic division of HRW, most often HRW/Asia or HRW/Helsinki. Thus, over the year, several hundred releases go out. Osnos calculates that the number of releases has been increasing by 20 percent annually.

Every two weeks, HRW assembles clips from the press throughout the world in which its officials are cited commenting on one or another human rights issue. Or the clip could be an op-ed piece written by an HRW staffer, a long, analytical article in a popular or scholarly journal quoting an HRW finding or an interview with an HRW official. The number of such clips is mind-boggling—seventy per week, several thousand over the year. Citations in the major journals and papers, like the *New York Times,* are quite frequent, sometimes occurring several times a week.

Of course, human rights was hardly a commonplace phrase when Helsinki Watch began. Certainly, foreign correspondents did not consider the issue essential; rather, as Osnos put it, human rights was but the "soft underbelly of foreign policy."[88] But as HRW's reputation grew, with a concomitant increase in media attention to human rights, the subject became a critical part of the "beat" of a foreign correspondent. Osnos disclosed to an interviewer that it is "common for reporters on new foreign assignments to come here [to HRW offices] for briefings."[89] At the same time, and significantly, more and more of the foreign press, including the major newspapers in London, Paris, Germany, Japan and in Latin America, will carry stories originating in HRW.

Osnos still regards Amnesty International as "dean of the corps" when it comes to media recognition. However, that NGO, she notes, has found it difficult to adjust to the new and broader international human rights interests that extend far beyond "prisoners of conscience," the traditional concern of Amnesty. "At the moment," she added, "it is not as effective as we are." One reason she offered was the more aggressive character of HRW's public relations. But that inevitably was rooted in hard-hitting advocacy based upon solid research. The reorganization of 1994, prompted by the management study six months earlier, clearly has proved to be a marked success.

CHAPTER FIFTEEN

The "Diplomatic Approach" vs. the "Human Rights Approach"

The High Commissioner for Human Rights, and the Blaustein Institute

No grander vision for an effective functioning human rights institution was conceived than that of the UN High Commissioner for Human Rights, established in 1994 after being dreamed about for some 30 years. Madeleine Albright, then the U.S. Ambassador to the UN, articulated that vision in an address to a well-known NGO just one month before the vote in the UN General Assembly establishing the institution. The High Commissioner may "not be able to wave any magic wands," she said, but he would be able "to elevate, legitimize, publicize and coordinate the response of the international community to crises affecting basic human rights."[1]

The verbs characterizing the institution hardly could be stronger: "elevate," "legitimize," "publicize." Albright went further: the High Commissioner was "to call the world's attention to significant human rights violations wherever and whenever they might occur." In short, he was to tackle the key human rights issues and act as the conscience of the international community. Albright's vision was shared by others. Six of the most prominent NGOs, in a joint statement just a few weeks before her speech, projected the image of an institution that would transform a "marginalized subject" of the world body into a "central, system-wide priority" for all UN activities. The High Commissioner "would bring both moral and political stature" to UN bodies seeking to ameliorate human rights abuses and ensure accountability.[2]

Agreeing with the NGOs was a leading human rights authority at UN Headquarters, B. G. Ramcharan, who had held a number of major Secretariat posts in the world body. Writing in an important scholarly journal, Ramcharan declared that "above all else, the international community expects that the High Commissioner will make a positive difference when it comes to preventing and stopping human rights violations."[3] And that difference would involve public diplomacy. He would have the High Commissioner submit monthly reports to the Security Council advising it of all situations involving human rights violations that relate to the maintenance of peace and security. "Where necessary," he added, the High Commissioner should submit "urgent fact-finding reports."

But, supposing the occupant of the post of High Commissioner viewed his or her function quite differently from that expressed in the grand vision, what then? Supposing the person selected for the task was someone who had little or no background in human rights? Reed Brody, who was the principal lobbyist at the UN General Assembly on behalf of the NGOs, reflected the widespread dismay in the NGO community when the former Foreign Minister of Ecuador, José Ayala Lasso, was appointed: "Ayala Lasso has never conducted a human rights investigation or even written a major article on human rights."[4] A *New York Times* story on the appointment carried a subhead in the article which read: "Critics Say the UN Nominee Will Need On-the-Job Training."[5]

The dapper Ayala Lasso, the very model of a diplomat, could not fail to recognize that this new institution was, in large part, the result of the intense and determined lobbying by nongovernmental organizations. And, in his early statements after his selection, he appeared to go out of his way to indicate that he held a high regard for NGOs and that he expected to work closely with them. The very first formal UN report, which he issued in November, 1994, specifically referred to the need for NGO cooperation in implementing the Vienna Declaration.[6] Yet, he kept a certain distance from the NGOs. Ayala Lasso's references to NGOs, initially, largely were focused upon how they could help implement human rights aims or upon their cooperation with respect to development and human rights education. If he noted that his office maintained "close contacts" with NGOs in Geneva, he avoided details on such questions as "with whom," specifically, and "about what."

Certainly, on the critical issue of his first formal visits to countries, he chose not to consult with international NGOs. The first two countries that he visited were Austria and Switzerland, hardly places where human rights issues were at the center of international discourse. He later explained that his mandate called for "dialogues" with governments and he wanted to build up a reservoir of governmental support and goodwill. But one of his next visits, to Cuba, evoked considerable concern from the NGO community. He sought no advice from international NGOs as to whether he should go or how he should handle his visit, whom he ought to seek to visit and what statements might be issued before, during or after the visit.

Moreover, Cuba was not Austria. On the contrary, it was regarded in the NGO community as a notorious violator of human rights that had incarcerated thousands of political prisoners. This record had prompted the UN Commission on Human Rights to establish a country-specific Special Rapporteur. Compounding its negative human rights reputation, the Castro regime for several years had refused permission for the Special Rapporteur, Carl-Johan Groth, a prominent Swedish diplomat, to enter the country for official fact-finding. Despite this record, and without consulting the Special Rapporteur, Ayala Lasso went to Cuba. What prompted him, he said later, was that he visits countries to which he has been invited and where he believes he might achieve results. He obviously had been invited by the Castro government.

"Quiet diplomacy" is, of course, the standard form of foreign office professionals and Ayala Lasso held to this device religiously. No public comments were made by him during his visit to Cuba or afterward, although he did meet privately with some local NGOs in the country. What irritated many NGOs was his failure to ask the authorities to meet with political prisoners. However, he did seek to obtain the release of a number of these prisoners. From a list of nearly 50 persons which he had given to the authorities, some 20 were released.

But through the bypassing of the Special Rapporteur, the High Commissioner permitted the Cuban regime to play one part of the UN machinery against another and, at the same time, to derive the benefit of a kind of tacit approval from the UN's highest authority on human rights. If Ayala Lasso thought he had made some progress, the attitude of Special Rapporteur Groth was summed up in a statement he made to an interviewer. The High Commissioner, he said, was "naive."[7] Amnesty

International took special note of the political maneuvering. While it regarded the visit of the High Commissioner as "an important step," at the same time it emphasized that the visit could not be considered a "substitute for the government reversing its policy of non-cooperation with the Commission's recommendation . . . [and] particularly with their refusal to allow the Special Rapporteur to visit."[8]

Cuba was not the only egregious misstep. Shortly after the trip to Havana, Ayala Lasso went on an official visit to Colombia without consulting international or local NGOs. More disturbingly, he failed to consult with or seek the advice of two Special Rapporteurs of the Commission, one on torture, the other on extrajudicial executions. They had just returned from a joint official mission to the country. The anger in the NGO community was intense, resulting in a sharply critical letter to the High Commissioner from several organizations. One former NGO official wrote a paper whose subtitle aptly characterized the sentiment in the nongovernmental community: "One Step Forward or Two Steps Back?"[9]

Ayala Lasso's inclination to "quiet diplomacy" was seen by some NGOs as an abdication of moral responsibility and a self-denial of the High Commissioner's great potential leverage. It was not only about his visit to Cuba that the High Commissioner refrained from public comment. He also visited Rwanda, Burundi, India and East Timor, and his silence about human rights abuses in these areas was more than obvious. HRW commented that "his voice was not heard on the major human rights questions of the day. . . ."[10] Yet, from his perspective, "quiet diplomacy" and not "public diplomacy" was the route to take, even if it made him and his office, as Aryeh Neier later would observe, "virtually invisible."[11] He frankly acknowledged that he differed sharply with those advocating public diplomacy. In a meeting with 20 Canadian NGOs in March, 1995, Ayala Lasso said: "I do not share the approach of NGOs to human rights issues, but I do respect the approach."[12]

But, if the High Commissioner was silent in the public arena about human rights abuses, he did move quickly, although not very effectively, to deal with massive killings of genocidal proportions in Rwanda. He took office on April 5, 1994; on the next day the plane carrying the Presidents of both Rwanda and Burundi from a regional summit to Kigali, Rwanda was shot down and destroyed, resulting in the organized mass slaughter of Tutsis by Hutu extremists. Ayala Lasso undertook a personal mission to Rwanda the next month and, on an emergency basis, arranged for a small monitoring group to be stationed there. It later would be enlarged to some

100 members who were to collect evidence on genocide and prevent human rights violations. It was a significant step in laying the foundation for field operations by the Centre for Human Rights, which was supposed to function under his overall direction. The problem was that the Centre did not possess the basic logistical capacities to provide support for a standby specialized field operation.

The Centre's deficiencies and their deleterious impact upon Rwanda were exposed by the report of an experienced British lawyer who had served the UN in various field capacities and who spent three months in the Rwanda field operation from September to December, 1994.[13] The first monitors were without office space, vehicles, radio or guidance. It was as if they were to function as commandos living off the land and making do with what was available. Stung by this report, the Centre responded by acknowledging that it had faced a "daunting" and difficult task but, nonetheless, had succeeded in deploying 119 human rights monitors and already was promoting a broad-based program of activities in the field of human rights.[14]

At least one NGO recognized both the enormous difficulties faced by the High Commissioner, already burdened by a set of professional habits of thought and action, as well as by the great potentialities of his task were he to be encouraged to slough off some of those habits. Felice Gaer, Director of the Jacob Blaustein Institute, had spent a lifetime mastering the intricacies of the UN human rights system, and she was equally adept at seeking to affect behavioral habits in the human rights field. She undertook the extraordinary job of bringing together Ayala Lasso with a dozen human rights NGO officials as well as some independent experts both in and out of the UN. It would be an off-the-record discussion running for two days— June 4-6, 1995. Cohosting this unprecedented initiative was the Atlanta-based Carter Center for Human Rights, headed by Harry Barnes, formerly a high Foreign Service official in the State Department. Significantly, Ayala Lasso had requested the "consultation" with the NGOs.[15]

Gaer had a special interest in the subject since the Institute, which she directed, took its name from one who could claim a certain degree of intellectual responsibility for the very idea of a High Commissioner for Human Rights. Her presentation at the unique assemblage was a model of frankness oriented to sparking an exchange that might prove productive for all concerned.[16] At the beginning, she stressed that it is in the nature of NGOs to be frustrated and this feeling can serve the positive purpose of driving human rights action. Then she shifted to an analytical presentation of the contrast between the "diplomatic approach" to human rights issues and what she chose to call the "human rights approach." The contrast was by no means narrow, limited or easy to traverse; rather, it was really quite profound.

What followed in her words had the remarkable ring of candor. The diplomatic approach was held to be mainly nonjudgmental while the human rights approach was nothing if not judgmental. The diplomatic approach normally was focused and oriented toward process; the human rights approach always was oriented toward outcome. The diplomatic approach normally was geared to confidentiality and low visibility while the human rights approach was focused on transparency, accountability and high visibility. The diplomatic approach usually would contend that publicity complicates matters while the human rights approach would contend that publicity works. The diplomatic approach often would seek the political support of states; the human rights approach would seek mainly the political support of world public opinion. The diplomatic approach would pursue goodwill missions to open contacts; the human rights approach would require missions to resolve grievances—if possible, immediately. The diplomatic approach would aspire to promote dialogue; the human rights approach would aim to promote compliance with international law or standards.

After this general cataloguing of tour de force proportions, Gaer turned to the concrete concerns of the NGO world. Particularly noted was the undertaking by the High Commissioner of country visits. She clearly was referring to the Cuban visit. The "invisibility" of the results of the visit and the "invisibility" of any follow-up could not but undermine the trust of NGOs who inevitably felt uninformed and uninvolved in a development in which a dissident's security could be jeopardized. But her concern about invisibility concerned the entire question of the High Commissioner's operation. An entire year had passed, she observed, and the sense of NGOs was that his very presence was missing, his operation had a "lack of visibility." She strongly advised that "public action" was indispensable to maintain linkage with NGOs.

Especially, she believed, that "presence" must be felt in New York, the headquarters of the UN itself. No doubt Gaer was thinking of the city serving as a headquarters for major international NGOs, far more so than Geneva. Besides, New York served as the headquarters of major international press organs. Most important, it was at UN Headquarters where the Security Council functioned and, increasingly, it was this organ that assumed responsibility, even if only indirectly, for human rights concerns. The absence of the High Commissioner in New York in order to impact upon the deliberations of the Security Council, or, for that matter, upon the UN Secretariat, along with the General Assembly, was "deeply troubling" to her.

Yet, even as Gaer posed sharply worded questions for the High Commissioner, reflecting the broad concerns and criticisms of the NGOs about the veritable silence of his operation, she was too perceptive and analytical an NGO representative not to also take note of significant contributions that Ayala Lasso had made. Indeed, even before embarking upon a critique of his concrete acts perceived as mistakes, she chose to applaud him for establishing a field operation in Rwanda that she saw as "revolutionary and extremely important." She wondered aloud whether it could be applied elsewhere, for example to Chechnya, Bosnia or Haiti. Only those NGOs who were aware of the various UN instruments and their growing contemporary function would have appreciated Gaer's attention to what was not ordinarily an emotional issue for NGOs.

While the High Commissioner found her comparison of the two "approaches" perceptive, he registered his own disagreement with it. At the same time, he was reported to have been "attentive, responsive and pleased" with the proceedings.[17] At a Wednesday meeting of HRW on June 14, some eight days after the Atlanta session, Ken Roth reported that the discussion with the High Commissioner had been a "useful exchange," but he recognized that Ayala Lasso's world was hardly one that would or could dramatize concern about human rights. Rather, Ayala Lasso was described as the "master of the unquotable phrase." Gaer observed that Ayala Lasso had acknowledged in Atlanta that he had a problem communicating with the public and had stated that he would try to make appropriate changes, presumably in style.

A statement hammered out by the participants at the end of the two-day session deliberately was designed to be positive and encouraging. After all, only 14 months had elapsed since Ayala Lasso had taken office, and it was Gaer's hope as well as the hope of most NGOs that the off-the-record meeting could prove beneficial to the High Commissioner. The three-page statement appropriately was entitled "The Promises of the United Nations High Commissioner for Human Rights."[18]

The statement began by recognizing that the office of the High Commissioner constituted "a great breakthrough" for international human rights and that, in its first year, it had begun "important innovations in the areas of emergency response to human rights violations, field monitoring and preventive activities." The High Commissioner was called upon to consolidate and further develop these innovations. Criticism followed, but was expressed quite gently and most indirectly:

> Participants expressed the great hopes they have in the office of the High Commissioner, expecting the High Commissioner to be the champion of human rights globally, to be the standard bearer of the universality, [and] indivisibility . . . of international human rights norms, to launch bold new initiatives for the global protection and promotion of human rights. . . .

After all, his office was, in a real sense, their creation. How could they abandon it, at this stage? Rather, the intention of the statement was one of encouragement, but with the clear implication that the NGOs sought high visibility and public activity.

Only his country visits were subjected to a certain implied negative commentary, but again with the lightest of touches. The High Commissioner was cautioned to avoid maneuvers by governments "responsible for violations of human rights" to play him off against efforts of UN Working Groups and Special Rapporteurs. More specifically, he was urged to consult with NGOs, particularly those with expertise on a particular country when a visit to that country was planned.

Special attention in the statement was given over to women's rights, since two months after the Atlanta meeting the Fourth World Conference on Women would be held in Beijing, China. The High Commissioner was urged to "use his authority and influence to prevent any regression" from the emphasis on women's rights in the Vienna Declaration and Program of Action. NGOs in Atlanta underscored the need for protection of women's rights to be among "the core strategies for entrenching a universal culture of human rights."

Ayala Lasso obviously was affected in a positive manner by the NGO meeting. In his next report to the UN Commission on Human Rights, prepared one month later, he almost gushingly embraced the NGOs. Their "active presence," he said, "has become a prerequisite of efficient action in the field of human rights."[19] Suddenly, the NGOs were declared to be the "natural partners of the High Commissioner." He desired, he said, "close cooperation with them," and he planned to have "regular meetings and consultations with NGOs. . . ." Such intimate and ongoing contacts, he believed, "have become an important component of the activities of the High Commissioner."

Two weeks later, Felice Gaer, joined by Ken Roth of HRW, decided to send a letter that she drafted to the High Commissioner offering their assistance in fulfilling his mandate and spelling out in a lengthy attached memorandum three specific proposals.[20] The letter suggested considerable optimism on the part of the two NGOs that he would be able to remedy the well-known bureaucratic inadequacies of the Centre for Human Rights and seize the moment to achieve "more action-oriented and coordinated human rights initiatives, including preventive diplomacy and establishment of human rights components of peace-keeping operations."

First and foremost, the letter stated, was the need for him to elaborate a clear "statement of mission" that recognized "the prevention and protection against violations of humans as a core purpose" of his responsibility. The statement would need to be precise and concrete even as it specified priorities. The second proposal related to structure—and, particularly, to the structure of the Centre. What was indispensable for effective operation of the body was "a regional and country specific focus," which would enable it to have "a capacity to analyze conditions and make recommendations for specific countries."

Finally, the letter called for "a strong New York presence by the High Commissioner. . . ." If, as the Vienna Declaration suggests, he is to be the center of a system wide human rights operation, then he must interrelate with peacekeeping and peacemaking, along with UN programs involving women's rights, children's rights, election monitoring and humanitarian aid. Access on a continuing basis to the Secretary-General as well as the Security Council is "essential to effective functioning of the High Commissioner and the UN's human rights programs." The Secretary-General's "cabinet" of Under-Secretaries, most notably the one handling political affairs, should have the continuing input of the High Commissioner. If the High Commissioner's office cannot be located in New York, then he should have "a substantial presence" at UN Headquarters "with adequate staffing."

The advice was excellent, but it required a forceful and determined personality to carry it out. In reality, none of the three proposals ever were implemented by Ayala Lasso, although he did establish a rather modest branch office in New York. He was especially reluctant to attempt to involve himself in Security Council matters. At a presentation to Human Rights Watch in December, 1995, Ayala Lasso declared that the Security Council was quite unreceptive to such an idea and, therefore, human rights intervention would prove "unproductive."

In preparation of his own role for the Beijing Conference, he obviously took to heart the recommendations of the Atlanta meeting. Several NGO participants at that session had provided him with detailed proposals and suggestions. The High Commissioner prepared a statement for Beijing reaffirming the universality of human rights and closely linking it to women's rights.[21] His statement was most helpful in the Beijing deliberations and was cited by numerous delegates. In Felice Gaer's judgment, Ayala Lasso at Beijing had demonstrated his ability to act "in cooperation with NGOs" thereby "advancing the credibility of his office. . . ."[22]

Still, the High Commissioner at Beijing could not overcome diplomatic cautiousness in responding to a journalist's query concerning a separate human rights issue. The Chinese authorities had detained some journalists, not an unusual action on the part of a totalitarian regime. When queried on the subject by a reporter at a press conference, Ayala Lasso, in the words of Human Rights Watch, "ducked the opportunity to criticize this clear human rights violation by saying he would have to investigate the circumstances."[23]

Encouraging to some degree was the way the High Commissioner in 1995 handled the question of visits to certain countries. Invitations to him to visit Iran, Iraq and Sudan were deferred. Each, a notorious practitioner of human rights violations, deliberately had refused admission to the UN Special Rapporteur who had been authorized to investigate human rights conditions in the country.[24] The lesson of the Cuba visit had been learned. Particularly welcomed by HRW/Americas was the initiative shown by the High Commissioner in sending a delegation to Colombia for purposes of determining whether to open a permanent human rights office in that country.[25]

Toward the end of 1995, Ayala Lasso in an interview in New York made it clear that while he regarded the approach of NGOs as "valid" and "fruitful," it was not the "*only* valid and fruitful approach."[26] He stressed that he chose to "work in a different way." But during 1996, Ayala Lasso once again was stressing his relationship with NGOs. In his report to the Human Rights Commission in March, he spoke about how he had given "high priority to enhancing cooperation with the NGO community. . . ."[27] In a long interview in his Geneva office two days after his report, he maintained that he had "frequent meetings" with NGOs.[28] Their "input," he went on, had been "critical" and he explained that whenever he traveled, he made certain to consult with local NGOs. As an example he pointed to a visit he recently had made to Cambodia, where, after such consultations, he pressed for and won an agreement from the government to sign a memorandum providing for his Centre's training of the country's judiciary, police and educators.

Even as Ayala Lasso reached out to NGOs, lauding them, seeking their advice and assistance and following a variety of guidelines that had been agreed upon in Atlanta, he could not shed the "diplomatic approach," with its emphasis upon "quiet diplomacy." Human Rights Watch summed up his accomplishments in 1996 as a "painfully low-key approach to human rights."[29] It was perhaps gratuitous and unfair but, as a voice of the international conscience, which often required a high-key approach, Ayala Lasso's cautious diplomatic tactfulness left something to be desired.

Ayala Lasso, in his final 1996 report, went to some lengths to credit NGOs for being the primary sources of information for the UN. "Various UN organs and bodies recognize that they would not have been in a position to appropriately cope with their tasks, without *data* provided by non-governmental organizations," he wrote.[30] But, it was precisely such NGOs like HRW and the Lawyers Committee for Human Rights who were deeply critical of his "quiet diplomacy" strategy.

Among the UN organs to which Ayala Lasso made special reference were the implementing organs of the various UN human rights treaties. Also strongly emphasized was how NGOs had demonstrated their "importance" in the functioning of the UN Sub-Commission's working groups on indigenous populations and on minorities. Strikingly, the High Commissioner, for the very first time, used the term "violators" in the context of discussions about human rights abridgements and the role of NGOs. He said that he had been conducting "close consultations" with NGOs in "reaction to human rights violations." That crucial term had not been included by the General Assembly in his mandate when it created his office. He, accordingly, was reluctant to use it lest it offend one or another power. But it was precisely that word which was central to the vocabulary of many NGOs, including the most important ones. Highlighting and publicly reacting to human rights violations was their primary purpose; clearly, it hadn't been his, but at least Ayala Lasso now was able to mouth it.

Of far greater interest to the High Commissioner precisely because it made no obvious target for the states and the diplomatic world was the quiet, though valuable, work in creating a series of 9 field offices and the stationing of several hundred human rights field officers in them, as well as elsewhere. The first offices to be established were in Malawi, Bosnia, Rwanda, Cambodia and Zaire, with one scheduled for Colombia.[31] Among the 289 field workers and consultants that Ayala Lasso placed in 18 locations, 174 were in Rwanda, 50 in Cambodia, 31 in Burundi and

19 in 4 states of the former Yugoslavia. It was not an unimpressive accomplishment, as Felice Gaer recognized. She called it "surely . . . the single most important achievement" of Ayala Lasso.[32]

In the creation of these field offices and the stationing of human rights specialists, Ayala Lasso stressed that he worked closely with NGOs.[33] Local NGOs, he pointed out, provided him assistance "in the form of training courses on human rights . . . and [other] appropriate projects. . . ." NGOs generally, including international NGOs, helped in developing training materials for "capacity building." What turned out to be Ayala Lasso's last report, on February 24, 1997, constituted, in part, a paean to NGOs. He called NGOs "one of the pillars of the UN human rights programme."[34] But the rhetorical embrace of what now were called "pillars" of the UN human program was too late. In fact, he never really had embraced their approach to activist public diplomacy.

A leading and popular foreign affairs British journal soon would characterize Ayala Lasso's personality as "bland" and describe him as one who "set out to please rather than make waves."[35] No sooner was Kofi Annan selected as Secretary-General than the biggest international NGOs sensed the opportunity to press for a change, especially since Annan's first speech to the General Assembly vigorously stressed the need for working together with people to meaningfully advance human rights objectives. Human Rights Watch was in the forefront of this initiative.

On January 13, 1997, Roth and Joanna Weschler wrote to Kofi Annan, commending him on his acceptance speech, which recognizes that the "roots of many political and military conflicts lie in intolerance, injustice and oppression."[36] The letter expressed the hope that Annan would be "particularly sensitive to the need for addressing human rights issues in seeking most political solutions." As he assumed his new position, they expected that "protection and promotion of human rights can be given a far more central role at the United Nations." Focusing upon the blandness of Ayala Lasso, they asked the Secretary-General to encourage him to "take a more activist approach and become a leading public voice and moral authority on human rights issues worldwide."

Activism should entail, they emphasized, more visibility and impact at the political center of the UN in New York. This had been a major point made at the Atlanta meeting but had been implemented in a manner that was barely apparent, if at all. Roth was more precise in an interview with the *New York Times*'s UN correspondent. Ayala Lasso's preference for quiet diplomacy resulted, said Roth, in his being silent about war crimes in the Balkans and in his failure to draw the Security

Council to serious human rights violations.[37] In their letter to Annan, Roth and Wechsler complained that UN peacekeeping operations generally had failed to report on human rights violations, thereby becoming "silent witnesses" to serious abuse.

But it wasn't only HRW that was pointedly critical. Amnesty International, in a report to the UN Commission on Human Rights, urged the High Commissioner to take a stronger stand on human rights violations in Colombia. As he was planning a field office in that country, Amnesty asked him to have the field office monitor and publicize human rights abuses. Regrettably, publicity of such abuses was meticulously eschewed by Ayala Lasso.

Amnesty's growing irritation would become apparent two months later, in April, 1997. Its published report at the time sharply attacked the High Commissioner's "role as traveling diplomat," which highlighted "a chasm between the expectations and the delivery."[38] His public statements in the countries he visited, Amnesty observed, "seemed simply to praise the governments' efforts and bury the human rights violations." In Amnesty's report, the "silence" of the High Commissioner on "ongoing human rights violations" could not but be regarded by violators and NGOs as "weakness."

Ayala Lasso may have suspected that his time had run out and that he no longer enjoyed the confidence even of his previous supporters among NGOs or of the United States Government, one of whose prominent diplomats openly hinted to NGOs that the High Commissioner's usefulness was at an end.[39] When he once again was offered the position of Foreign Minister in Ecuador, he announced his resignation suddenly on February 21, 1997 while on a trip to Rwanda that was supposed to spur investigations into the killing of five field workers there.[40] Amnesty issued a press release on that day referring to "the reported resignation" of Ayala Lasso and urging the UN Secretary-General to "choose a successor who will confront those responsible for gross human rights violations."

It is a kind of eloquent, if nonetheless ironic, commentary on Ayala Lasso's hasty resignation that it received no coverage in major press organs. Hardly a line appeared in the *New York Times* or other leading newspapers. Had anyone else in such a high UN position decided to suddenly resign, it certainly would have attracted at least a modicum of public attention. But the silence in which he enveloped himself and his operation made him what his critics called the "invisible" man. Reed Brody, who was the chief NGO lobbyist for a High Commissioner, welcomed his resignation in the *International Herald Tribune*.[41] Ayala Lasso's "lackluster performance," Brody wrote, "disappointed human rights advocates." In a field in which "publicity and the marshaling of shame" are among the "few weapons in his arsenal," he chose—Brody observed—not to "use his visibility" and "become the conscience of humanity."

Clearly, the gulf between the "diplomatic approach" and the "human rights approach" that Felice Gaer brilliantly had defined at the Atlanta meeting could not be bridged by Ayala Lasso; his entire diplomatic career had moved him in one direction that apparently could not be balanced by human rights NGO contacts or advice. Yet, if much of the NGO community could heave a sigh of relief with Ayala Lasso's resignation, it was Gaer herself, recognizing all his inadequacies, who publicly commended his achievement of initiating field office operations, most notably the one in Rwanda.[42] Brody, too, commended Ayala Lasso for his "bold" and "important new initiatives" in Rwanda and other countries where he established field operations, but he contended that the High Commissioner only acted in this way "when it did not require him to openly displease powerful states."[43]

Gaer could understand, even if she was critical, why Ayala Lasso was so reluctant to speak out: "His position is delicate because countries are so sensitive to charges of abuse," she noted.[44] What Gaer meant was that his "diplomatic approach" disinclined him from raising sensitive human rights issues. That she was capable of comprehending, even if entirely disagreeing with, Ayala Lasso's "diplomatic approach," was undoubtedly a product of her own experience. Gaer was one of the very few in the human rights community who not infrequently functioned on two levels: as part of the U.S. government's official delegation to UN conferences and as an independent human rights lobbyist or activist. While serving as Director of the Blaustein Institute, she, at the same time, participated as a public member of U.S. delegations to: the World Conference on Human Rights in Vienna, the Women's Rights Conference in Beijing and five sessions of the UN Commission on Human Rights in Geneva during 1994-98.

Needless to say, Gaer at times felt internally conflicted. She recalled in an interview: "And there are moments in each of those [occasions when she served on a delegation] where I've had that same feeling of 'I was more effective on outside; oh, my God, what am I doing here?'"[45] The head of the U.S. delegation to the UN Commission on Human Rights in 1995-96, Geraldine Ferraro, would tell her: "Felice, you have to jump across the table, now look at it from the inside." Ferraro was convinced that she could be "more effective inside than outside." As Gaer saw it, "the challenge is to find ways to do that."

Gaer's basic outlook was the promotion of human rights. She had been doing that for over two decades: at the Ford Foundation, at the International League for Human Rights, at the UNA and finally, at the Blaustein Institute. Could she be more effective on the inside? Could she serve on an official delegation without compromising her fundamental human rights principles? Her answer:

> I would argue that I was probably more effective outside at the time of the World Conference on Human Rights than inside; but by the time of the Beijing Conference, I was more effective inside because I knew how to use the inside and the outside. I knew the players better and I had the confidence of both sides.[46]

Gaer vividly recalled that at the World Conference, the State Department representatives "went so far as to keep cables and [other] information from her and other public members of the delegation." She recognized "very quickly" that the Washington career officers thought "that I'd be great to talk to NGOs, but not to get in their [the career officers'] way." Only after some time elapsed did the head of the U.S. delegation come to realize how useful she and other public members might be in promoting the mutual human rights objectives of the NGOs and the Clinton Administration. Only then did the career officers provide her with the "access and involvement" that were essential for maximizing her effectiveness.

It was, of course, helpful in resolving potential personal conflicts that the official delegation and its Chairperson were, in general, on the same human rights wavelength as Gaer. This happened to be the case in the various delegations on which she served as a public member. Prior to Vienna and Beijing, she was able to ascertain, by her lobbying as an NGO representative prior to these meetings, that her views ran on the same track as those shaping policy in the State Department. Reed Brody remembered her NGO activism in Washington prior to Vienna and later at the UN General Assembly and found it invaluable in pushing the official policy line on human rights.

But, if the official delegation found Gaer's advice useful and helpful, what was the reaction of various NGOs? Her answer: "I think they trust me. I think they recognize that I'm trying to do what's in our mutual interests."[47] Especially was this the case at Beijing. The women's human rights groups, with whom she worked in close tandem, thought her to be— she believed—"wonderful." That was hardly accidental, since Gaer made it her business to be steeped in all aspects of women's rights issues. Except for the High Commissioner matter, nothing prompted a keener interest on her part.

The attitude of various NGOs to Felice Gaer and the Blaustein Institute also was suggested by the decision of the leading and most powerful NGOs to involve her in the so-called Directors' Group and to seek her assistance in the drafting and signing of joint letters to key U.S. or UN officials. The Directors' Group, established by Mike Posner, head of the Lawyers Committee for Human Rights, embraced on an informal basis the heads of the major NGOs. The group would hold from time to time off-the-record, informal meetings aimed at keeping each other abreast of common concerns.

The selection of Gaer and the Blaustein Institute was rather anomalous. The Institute was a two-person operation—Gaer and an assistant—while the other Directors headed staffs that ranged from a dozen or so persons to quite sizable organizations like Human Rights Watch, the Carter Center or Amnesty USA. Certainly, the Institute was not a mass-membership body, nor did it serve a professional constituency of, say, lawyers, physicians or civil libertarians. Rather, it was a small grant-awarding foundation under the umbrella of the American Jewish Committee that, for over 25 years, had doled out modest funds for advancing human rights research studies and deliberations. Under her direction, the Institute funding was directed, as she said in an interview, "more towards making things happen, taking a leadership role. . . ."[48] Awarding grants was to be a process of human rights activism, particularly in cutting-edge areas.

Her expertise about UN human rights issues was rare. Very few scholars or practitioners grasped the factual and historical details of these matters as well as the scope and depth of the issues involved, or the strategic problems that required solving, as thoroughly as did Gaer. A comment offered by Ken Roth of Human Rights Watch on the occasion of the Blaustein Institute's twenty-fifth anniversary in May, 1997 captured, in a definitive manner, the significance of her work:

> The Institute has become no less than the nucleus around which the U.S.-based human rights movement works out its strategy on major UN issues, not to mention as a unique source of inside information and activist ideas based on extraordinary access to serious officials.[49]

Roth rarely was given to extending such extravagant praise. After indicating the unique centrality of the Institute's function in the NGO world, he went on to describe how it had organized "an extraordinarily valuable in-depth seminar" of NGOs with Ayala Lasso in June, 1995. But, in addition, the influential HRW Director contended that the Institute also had been "an important source of 'glue' holding the human rights movement together and initiating joint actions where our singular voices would be less effective." With the resignation of Ayala Lasso, Gaer was prepared to offer advice on how the High Commissioner should operate even before she knew who the Secretary-General would select to fill this vital post. In a perceptive analytical article written in April, 1997 for the Carter Center's International Human Rights Council Project, she described in outline form what the priorities of the High Commissioner ought to be.[50] Not surprisingly, her first recommendation was that the High Commissioner must create "effective institutionalized channels for greater NGO input into decision-making" in a variety of areas. These channels should not be concentrated in a single office, which Ayala Lasso had proposed, but rather "should permeate [all] the programs of the Centre for Human Rights. . . ."

Gaer always was championing the role of the NGO in making things happen. In her second recommendation, she stressed how NGOs could be invaluable in preserving norms, advising on country visits, suggesting responses to emergencies and crises and helping build more effective national human rights systems. Most of the next recommendations already had been advanced in the Gaer-Roth joint letter to Ayala Lasso of July, 1995 that she had drafted. Especially stressed was a proposal that "the High Commissioner's office and principal residence should be in New York, at the center of UN decision-making. . . ." The idea never had been put as sharply as it was now. A key reason that Gaer offered for the move was that it would "ensure that the High Commissioner has greater access to a wide range of NGOs. . . ."

Gaer was not the only one producing recommendations for a new High Commissioner. Amnesty International hastened to prepare, also in April, an "Agenda" for this office.[51] It offered almost a dozen recommendations, with particular attention to strengthening field offices, restructuring the Centre for Human Rights and speaking out publicly against rights violators. But the "Agenda" said nothing about establishing the primary residence and operation of the office in New York at UN Headquarters. This may not be altogether surprising. Amnesty had not been a determined opponent of the move of the UN's human rights operation to Geneva in the seventies. Nor had it ever urged that the primary locus for the High Commissioner's operation be New York.

B. G. Ramcharan, who had prepared as early as 1994 the priorities for the new High Commissioner, once again returned to the subject. In an unpublished manuscript, this highly experienced UN official urged the High Commissioner to prepare an annual human rights report on the human rights situation in every UN member state.[52] The document would serve a variety of purposes, including its use as a lever to bring about change. And, the report also would recommend "achievable steps a state might take and the assistance that the Centre can give." Ramcharan considered of particular importance the idea of the High Commissioner reporting directly to the Secretary-General and, at least on a quarterly basis, to the Security Council. Reportage to the latter would serve, he said, an "early-warning" function.

Reed Brody, too, advanced proposals in his *International Herald Tribune* essay.[53] Like Gaer, he was very much in favor of a strong High Commissioner presence in New York. In criticizing Ayala Lasso, Brody emphasized that "he proved unable . . . to inject human rights concerns *where they really count*—on the agenda of top UN officials and the Security Council. . . ." [Emphasis added.] It is at UN Headquarters in New York, he added, "where officials set long-term strategy, respond to crises and deploy peacekeeping operations."

On June 12, 1997, Secretary-General Annan appointed Ireland's President, Mary Robinson, as High Commissioner. More than most other top government officials, she typified the personality who could conduct a human rights approach rather than a "diplomatic approach" to problems of abuse. Professionally, she was a human rights lawyer and a constitutional scholar who fought against Irish laws banning divorce and abortion and campaigned against antihomosexual legislation.[54] Clearly an activist, she would be expected to speak out against human rights abuses and, thereby, articulate the moral conscience of the international community. Amnesty had warned as early as February 21 when it learned of Ayala Lasso's planned resignation that "lessons must be drawn from . . . the past three years to make sure this crucial post is the beacon for human rights in the world."[55]

Robinson was the candidate pushed by the United States and Britain.[56] But her candidacy also was strongly backed by various human rights NGOs, including HRW and the Lawyers Committee for Human Rights. According to Susan Osnos, HRW worked vigorously behind the scenes in order to support her nomination.[57] As soon as her appointment was announced, HRW publicly hailed the choice as a move toward achieving the "great potential" of the High Commissioner's post.[58]

The Blaustein Institute, under Gaer, was without question an activist NGO. But it also by charter and choice was a financial supporter of research projects and conferences, particularly those that ventured onto the cutting edge of new ideas and proposals. Even before Gaer's arrival in 1993 it had sponsored in 1972 in Uppsala, Sweden a colloquium on the right to leave a country that had a significant impact on the struggle for emigration of Soviet Jews. The document drafted by 70 scholars and human rights experts provided a legal basis for the assault upon restrictions of the free international movement of people.[59] A decade later, the Institute sponsored an important study of the right to know one's rights, which had significant legal ramifications. Later, the analysis and recommendations would be a crucial link to a recently adopted UN Declaration to protect the rights of human rights defenders.

Numerous other cutting-edge studies and conferences were funded by the Blaustein Institute in recent years, of which two are especially striking. The Institute helped jump-start in 1994 a research institute in The Hague, the Foundation for Inter-Ethnic Relations, which would provide a vital OSCE institution, the High Commissioner on National Minorities, with essential advice and source material. In late 1996, the Institute sponsored a workshop and study of new human rights protection strategies for field personnel of international organizations and institutions, an extremely sensitive topic growing out of contemporary genocidal conflicts in southeast Europe, Asia and Africa.[60] Raoul Wallenberg's strategies in Budapest, Hungary in 1944 served as an inspiration for the workshop organizer, Diane Paul.

Perhaps the Institute's most significant contribution, aside from its work in connection with the High Commissioner, came in the area of women's rights, particularly in steps leading up to and in active involvement with the historic Beijing Fourth World Conference on Women in September, 1995. The subject was made an Institute "priority" in 1993, which enabled Gaer to be involved in an extraordinary amount of lobbying, the drafting of a large number of joint NGO letters to U.S. and UN officials, personal engagement on a leadership level at international conferences, and the preparation of the only detailed historical survey of the evolution of the women's rights movement culminating in the Beijing Conference.[61]

The central figure in the women's rights movement was Charlotte Bunch, Executive Director of the Center for Women's Global

Leadership at Rutgers University, who coordinated the Global Campaign for Women's Human Rights at the 1993 Vienna World Conference as well as women's human rights activities at the Beijing assemblage. In a recent essay published by UNICEF, she perceptively captured the nature of the women's rights issue as it seized hold of the international imagination during the last decade of the twentieth century.[62] Statistical data, presented in bulletlike fashion, illuminated the literally monumental scope of the problem: roughly 60 million women who should be alive today are "missing" because of gender discrimination, predominantly in South and West Asia, China and North Africa; in the United States where overall violent crime against women has been growing in the past quarter-century, a women is physically abused by her intimate partner every 9 seconds; in India, more than 5,000 women are killed each year because their in-laws consider their dowries inadequate; rape as a weapon of war has been documented in 7 countries in recent years; about 2 million girls each year, or 6,000 every day, are genitally mutilated, with the total number being 130 million in 28 countries; and more than 1 million children, overwhelmingly female, are forced into prostitution every year, the majority in Asia.

Gender violence, mainly at home, according to Bunch, has come to be recognized only in the 1990s as a human rights issue. She cited a World Bank analysis of 35 recent studies from industrialized and developing countries showing that between one-quarter to one-half of all women have suffered physical abuse from an intimate partner. In the United States, only 1 in 100 battered women even reports the abuse. Statistics on rape in industrialized and developing countries reveal similar patterns: between 1 in 5 and 1 in 7 women will be victims of rape in their lifetime. The figures on rape become huge in circumstances of ethnic violence and genocide: 20,000 women have been raped in Bosnia and more than 15,000 in Rwanda.

It was at the World Conference at Vienna in 1993 that "women's rights as human rights" formally entered into international discourse. The breakthrough was as significant as the breakthroughs on recognizing the "universality and indivisibility" of human rights and on the formal call for a High Commissioner for Human Rights. And, as with the other milestones realized at Vienna, it was NGOs, with women's NGOs in the lead, who pressed for according women's rights the full status of human rights.[63]

As early as 1991, the Center for Women's Global Leadership launched what would become the Global Campaign for Women's Human Rights. With violence against women as a focal point, the campaign would assume a coordinated character, having human rights as a framework with which to link the women's struggle.[64] Soon, it would become apparent to the Center that the Vienna World Conference, already scheduled by the UN General Assembly in December, 1990, should be the occasion that warranted an all-out effort to connect women's rights to human rights.

Meetings of women's groups in various regions of the globe began taking up the issue. At the 1992 conference on the environment in Rio de Janeiro, women activists acquired the know-how to deal with UN-sponsored meetings. The know-how was reinforced in Latin America, where the Inter-American Institute for Human Rights in San José offered intellectual and organizational leadership training along with financial resources. Initial planning further was advanced at the regional preparatory meetings before Vienna. These meetings were preceded by NGO conferences at which women's groups could urge government representatives to place women's rights on the agenda at Vienna.

The Asian NGO Forum, preceding the Bangkok preparatory meeting, was especially noteworthy in revealing the intellectual and emotional gulf between NGOs and governmental representatives on women's issues. The NGO declaration stressed that "women's rights are human rights" and that "crimes against women are crimes against humanity." Such strong language was missing from the regional governmental document.

At the Vienna World Conference a genuine watershed was reached on focusing international attention on women's rights. Charlotte Bunch, joined by Florence Butegwa of Uganda, would present a statement to the World Conference that constituted a ringing declaration:

> Abuses of women have too long been dismissed as private, family, cultural or religious matters. Today, we demand that they be seen for what they are: fundamental violations of the "right to life, liberty and security of the person," as guaranteed by the Universal Declaration of Human Rights.[65]

Bunch and her associates were to prevail, a striking demonstration of the newfound power of women's NGOs supported by NGOs in general. Rarely before were women's groups so visible on specifically women's human rights issues.

The reasons were not hidden. Of the total number of 2,721 NGOs in attendance at the NGO Forum, 49.4 percent were women's NGOs.[66] A large double room called "The Rights Place for Women" was set up in the NGO area of the Conference center. The women brought with them hundreds of thousands of signed petitions, which they were to present to governmental representatives at the conference.

Greatly reinforcing the highly visible participation was a well-organized, professionally staffed media campaign, which was located right next to the double room headquarters. A team from the Center for Women's Global Leadership and from the so-called Communications Consortium Media Center briefed reporters on their issues and made available to them diverse expert voices. In advance of the Conference, the team prepared and distributed 3,000 sophisticated press kits with background fact sheets on 13 key women's rights issues and sent press advisers to some 3,400 U.S. reporters and 1,200 editorial page editors. During the World Conference, professional women journalists arranged for numerous interviews and press releases of specific interest to women. The impact was enormous. More than a thousand stories in the U.S. press during June, 1993 referred specifically to women's rights topics.

The "defining moment" of the phenomenal women's NGO campaign at Vienna, according to Bunch, came at the so-called Global Tribunal on Violations of Women's Human Rights.[67] It was "theater" rather than a formal courtroom and the dramatic impact was powerful. For an entire day, 33 women offered what turned out to be "riveting personal testimony" about the abuses they had suffered. The abuses fell into five categories: human rights abuse in the family, war crimes against women, violations of women's bodily integrity, socioeconomic violations of women's human rights and gender-based political persecution and discrimination.[68] The staging included four "judges" who were knowledgeable officials from the UN or human rights groups. They ruled that the outcry of the witnesses must be "investigated and sanctioned, and the violations of their human rights must be redressed."

The Tribunal was an outgrowth of the petition drive conducted by women NGOs and the various regional NGO hearings in preparation for the Vienna World Conference. Its aim was to demonstrate "the failure of existing human rights mechanisms to promote and protect the human rights of women."[69] Bunch pointed to the "rapt attention" of the audience to conclude: "The Tribunal marked an official end to the centuries-old cover-up of these atrocities and it awakened many women and men to the international community's responsibility to protect women from such abuse."[70] Supported by 270,000 signatures from a massive petition drive started in April, the activists, quite impressively organized, helped achieve the aim of making women's rights issues highly visible.

Violence against women specifically was condemned for the first time in an international document—the Vienna Declaration and Programme of Action. Violence against women in armed conflict situations was defined as a violation of human rights and of humanitarian laws. Women's rights were held to be integral to the universality of human rights. Indeed, on the action level, the Conference called for women's rights to be integrated into all UN human rights activities. In this context, the Conference proposed that the UN Convention on the Elimination of All Forms of Discrimination Against Women (CEDAW), adopted in 1979, be strengthened with an optional protocol for individual petitions.

The impact of the pressure that women's NGOs placed upon the Vienna meeting was felt shortly afterward in UN bodies. In December, 1993, the General Assembly adopted a formal Declaration on the Elimination of Violence Against Women. The Declaration, in effect, was an extension of CEDAW, which never mentioned violence against women. Of greater significance was the decision taken at the Commission on Human Rights in 1994 to appoint a Special Rapporteur on Violence Against Women. Bunch was correct in observing that "few social movements have registered as great an impact in so short a time—and with such remarkably peaceful methods."[71]

Gaer, of course, as a member of the U.S. delegation, was helpful in advising informally key women's NGOs on the political situation in various delegations. Since the Blaustein Institute had given women's rights "priority" attention, it hardly was unexpected that she would devote at least some time to this subject. But, at Vienna, she principally was preoccupied with the major issues concerning universality of rights and the creation of a High Commissioner and, thus, her assistance focused on the major national and international NGOs.

That the subject of women's rights however would resonate loudly in Gaer's myriad human rights activities afterward was certain, particularly as events moved from Vienna to the Beijing conference in the fall of 1995. Beginning in March, 1994, at meetings of the Commission on Human Rights in Geneva, where Gaer served on the U.S. delegation, she saw herself as "a watchdog on the [Commission's] resolutions," making certain they included "concern over violence against women."[72] She urged the State Department to broaden the scope of strategy planning for the Beijing meeting to encompass the theme of violence against women. At the same time, Gaer helped create a special lobbying group in Washington—the Washington Working Group on the Human Rights of Women—whose key representatives were Lea Browning of the American Bar Association and Anne Goldstein of Georgetown University.[73] This group, together with Bunch's Center, Gaer wrote, "were to play the central role in keeping pressure" upon Western governments as Beijing approached.

An initial focus of the emerging Washington group was a document produced by the Economic Commission of Europe (ECE). It was designed for the European regional preparatory meeting, scheduled for Vienna in October, 1994, which, along with other regional meetings, would culminate in the worldwide Conference in Beijing. Not unnaturally, the document carried an economic frame of reference, with attention concentrated upon women's economic empowerment. Women's rights activists in Washington were shocked by the failure of the ECE report to deal meaningfully with the broad gamut of discrimination and violence against women. A detailed, blistering critique was prepared in which Gaer was involved, seeking to alert the State Department to the need for protecting the achievements of Vienna and building upon them for Beijing.[74]

The inadequacy of the ECE document was but one concern of women activists. There was also a growing fear that a number of countries were seeking to weaken or undermine the Vienna achievement of integrating women's rights into the UN human rights system.[75] According to Bunch, China was a "silent partner" in these downgrading initiatives.[76] Indeed, at the March, 1995 Commission on Human Rights, China effectively prevented adoption of language in a resolution that specifically called for the human rights of women to be on the agenda of the Beijing Conference.

A reflection of the reversal tendencies was the emergence of initiatives to restrict NGO participation. The UN Secretariat had decided not to recommend 493 NGOs that formally had applied for NGO status at the Beijing Conference. At this point, a coalition of 24 NGOs—women's groups and general human rights groups—signed a letter dated January 9, 1995, and sent it to U.S. Secretary of State Warren Christopher, urging that the State Department to "use its influence publicly and privately to intervene with the Chinese Government and the UN to ensure that they adhere strictly" to established rules. These rules would permit all NGOs meeting the standard UN criteria to attend the NGO Forum that would run prior to the Beijing Conference. And such rules also required the host government—China—to issue visas to all accredited participants.[77] The joint letter was drafted by Felice Gaer.[78] The United States and the West were effective in realizing greater "transparency" and in enlarging to a considerable extent NGO accreditation.

What greatly complicated the NGO issue was the decision by China to move the planned NGO Forum from Beijing's outskirts to Hairou, an hour away from the Conference. The question of adequate personal facilities, as well as facilities for NGO meetings and functions, of transportation to the main conference center, of provisions for media and other burning issues were vigorously raised by the NGOs, including the Blaustein Institute, and prompted the Chinese government to agree to a number of concessions.

To preclude the threat of repression, which even had penetrated into the draft Beijing Platform for Action, NGOs chose to urge High Commissioner Ayala Lasso to address the issue as if he were the UN's formal defender of established norms. On July 16, 1995, the head of the International Women's Human Rights Law Clinic at City University, Rhonda Copelon, and Gaer sent him a detailed fax outlining ten major principles and commitments on the human rights of women adopted at Vienna that they held were undermined by formulations in the draft Beijing Platform for Action.[79] The fax stressed his "responsibility under the [Vienna] mandate" to act to preserve the prevailing norms. He did follow through, which prompted Copelon and Gaer to write him on August 18, congratulating him on his "authoritative and compelling critique" of the draft Platform for Action that already had had a salutory effect.[80]

Especially emphasized in the letter to Ayala Lasso was the fact that his emphasis "on the priority of human rights over religious and cultural claims to the contrary" was of "particular importance" for the Beijing Conference. Opposition to the integration of women's rights to human rights came from regimes of Asia and Africa which argued that particular religious and cultural patterns limited or transcended general human rights.

By the time the Beijing Conference opened in September, 1995 women's rights NGOs, supported by general human rights NGOs, had laid the groundwork for moving beyond Vienna to a new plateau, in the sense of concretizing a section of the final Vienna statement that read, "the human rights of women are an inalienable, integral and indivisible part of human rights." The NGO movement now was to impose its own much simplified formulation as the prevailing theme: "women's rights are human rights"—period. A well-organized campaign had pressed the United States to assume a major leadership role in the West and throughout the world. Women turned out to be remarkably effective as part of delegations from the Third World.

At the largest women's and NGO conference ever, with 35,000 in attendance and with emotions already at an exultant level, Hillary

Rodham Clinton would electrify the huge audience with a powerful speech demanding that "it is time for us to break our silence . . . to say here in Beijing . . . that it is no longer acceptable to discuss women's rights as separate from human rights."[81] The First Lady brought the audience to its feet as she orated in a kind of mantra-like style that each of the following is a violation of human rights: "when babies are denied food, or drowned, or suffocated . . . because they are born girls"; "when women and girls are sold into the slavery of prostitution"; "when women are doused with gasoline, set on fire and burned to death because their marriage dowries are too small. . . ." The list went on in this dramatic fashion to include individual rape and mass rape in military conflict, domestic violence against women, genital mutilation, forced abortion and forced sterilization. To everyone, she drove home the principal message that emerged from this conference: "human rights are women's rights . . . and women's rights are human rights."[82]

It was a moment of unparalleled excitement, as recorded by Gaer. For the women's rights movement would reach a milestone in UN and world history. Even as she chronicled the history of that movement, she privately would convey to a colleague that she "was heavily involved all the way through" Beijing on a variety of matters, including such "specific issues" as religion, language, universality and inheritance.[83] On the one hand, she served in a crucial advisory capacity to the Vice-Chairman of the U.S. delegation, Geraldine Ferraro. On the other, she met frequently with NGOs offering information, suggestions, assistance and recommendations. She was functioning on two separate but interrelated tracks at Beijing. No one else did or could have performed such a role.

Involvement with women's rights issues did not come to an end with Beijing. Two months later, Gaer was organizing an effort related to the Dayton accords but with special concentration on Bosnian women and the prosecution of rape. Entirely at her initiative, a letter together with a lengthy Annex entitled "Women and the Bosnian Peace Process: Preliminary Questions on Ten Issues of Concern" was prepared for the attention of Ambassador Madeleine Albright. Twenty other women leaders and activists from NGOs signed the letter. The principal point of the letter was in its third paragraph: "Strikingly, women were invisible in Dayton." The Annex was devoted to acquainting Albright with those issues related to women's concerns.

In a conference call with the signers, Albright promised to take up the issues raised in the Annex with the State Department and officials in Bosnia. It was followed by a second conference call with Albright. Later,

Ferraro and Gaer shared the letter with the commander of NATO forces in Sarajevo. The joint letter soon would find a wider reach. At the suggestion of a State Department contact, a variation of the communication to Albright, but with a concentration upon the issues discussed in the Annex, was sent on February 21, 1996 to Jock Covey, who was Chief of Staff at the Office of the High Representative of the Peace Implementation Conference in Sarajevo.[84]

Joint letters on other human rights subjects frequently were initiated by Gaer and at times drafted by her. They covered such subjects as the failure by the International Criminal Tribunal on Rwanda to deal with rape in the indictment. The new Chief Prosecutor, Louise Arbour, promised an American official that the indictment would be appropriately modified.

In these joint letters, memos and conference calls, as well as incessant lobbying, Gaer constantly was seeking to give life to institutions, instruments, resolutions, platforms and accords. John Shattuck, the U.S. Assistant Secretary of State for Democracy, Human Rights and Labor caught the significance of NGOs when he observed that without them, these institutions and accords "would be lifeless words on a page." When he uttered these words, he made it explicit that he was thinking of "the work of extraordinary people like . . . Felice Gaer." It is "their energy and ideas," he added, "[that] bring these documents to life."[85]

CHAPTER SIXTEEN

"Uncharted Terrain": Minority Rights, Ethnic Tensions and Conflict Prevention

That among the cutting edge issues of the nineties, minority rights, generally, and the tensions between the various ethnic groups in society, specifically, would emerge as crucial, if not transcendent, was apparent, at least in Europe. But once they were recognized as preeminent concerns, it was to be expected that NGOs soon would be seized with these subjects. Indeed, an NGO would be specially created in Europe in a unique way to focus exclusively on this cutting-edge issue. Another European NGO, Minority Rights Group, had been wrestling with the subject on a worldwide basis for some time, but its work inevitably received far less attention during the Cold War than did the efforts of NGOs who concentrated upon individual rights and the gross violations that targeted individuals. Acts of genocide, of course, were the exception although, until the nineties, there was too little known about such episodes as to concentrate the public mind.

The end of the eighties in Europe and in the West was marked by a distinctive euphoria. The democratic revolutions that engulfed the countries of East Europe in 1989, together with the radical transformation of Soviet society under Mikhail Gorbachev ending totalitarian rule, and climaxed by the collapse of the Berlin Wall, were believed to have ushered in a new era. It was a moment of exultation for the West, with one prominent policy analyst asserting that the "end of history" had been reached through the victory of Western democracy over Soviet totalitarianism.[1] President George Bush spoke of a "new world order" while his Secretary of State, James Baker, declared that "the Western vision of freedom, peace and democracy had prevailed."[2]

Adoption of the Charter for a New Europe at the November, 1990 Paris Summit of the national leaders comprising the Conference on Security and Cooperation in Europe (CSCE) was perceived as the crowning achievement of the new democratic order. It elaborated in considerable detail traditional individual human rights and provided them with formal assurances. Recognized, too, was a detailed listing of minority rights that had been unprecedently accepted by the CSCE the previous June in Copenhagen. Prime Minister Margaret Thatcher, at the Paris Summit, compared the Paris Charter to the Magna Carta of 1215 A.D., noting that human rights now were fully "enshrine[d] for every European citizen...."[3] Her view was echoed by Soviet President Mikhail Gorbachev, who observed that a world of "new dimensions" had appeared on the horizon "in which universal human values are shared by all the people...."[4]

A far more skeptical view was articulated by the distinguished philosopher of history Sir Isaiah Berlin. Not democracy, he wrote, but rather racism and nationalism "are the most powerful movements in the world today." These forces had "never died," even if many considered that they had only now, and suddenly, become "resurgent."[5] Sir Isaiah would reiterate his thesis in especially vigorous fashion in an interview with *The New York Review of Books* at the end of 1991.[6] He was particularly careful to stress that the phenomenon of racism and nationalism was not restricted only to Europe; these movements, he said, are "cutting across many social systems."

Sir Isaiah Berlin was not alone in sensing the racist and ethnic vibrations beneath the surface of society that would soon explode in Yugoslavia and the USSR, rupturing these multinational states, while elsewhere in East Europe, the furies of nationalism would produce dangerous fissures in the state structures. The French scholar and policy analyst Dominique Moïsi expressed concern that people would be "fatally attracted by dark temptations of xenophobia, racism and jingoism."[7] Poland's prominent anti-Communist dissident, Adam Michnik, creatively observed that post-totalitarian societies very well may breed the dangers of racism, anti-Semitism and xenophobia.[8]

Michnik's observation was especially perceptive and soon came to be recognized as the explanation for the suddenness of the violence in

East Europe. Totalitarian controls kept ancient ethnic attitudes, grievances and hostilities from being expressed. For totalitarian rulers, unregulated and unchanneled ethnic hostility could produce anarchic consequences, always dangerous to the state. Once these controls were lifted, acts of ethnic hostility, extending even to secession, could assume a burgeoning character. A specialist on nationality issues in East Europe, writing in an prominent German international affairs journal in 1991, found that, in this geographical area, excluding the USSR, "the reservoir of conflicts . . . is immense."[9] His research disclosed that each of the various ethnic groups inhabiting the non-Soviet region considered that the "borders" encompassing them were "unjust."

Of far greater significance, the various ethnic groups taught and propagated the theme of ethnic injustice in the schools and universities as well as in the media that were under their respective control. Ineluctably, the psychological "component" of ethnicity in East Europe took on a distinctly "politic-territorial aspect." Revisionism of borders or secession, legitimized as self-determination, became the order of the day. The drive was reinforced by limited historical experience; most of the borders of East Europe were not demarcated until the twentieth century. This diminished adaptation to or acceptance of existing borders.

In addition, historical memory and collective myths in the area acted as powerful sources for identifying the ancient and traditional "enemy." Equally important, the memory and myths inevitably projected a romanticized utopian past onto the future. Multinational Yugoslavia was especially prone to an ethnic explosion once a popular will was allowed to express itself after the lifting of the totalitarian regime's arbitrary and repressive controls. But the hostility of groups extended beyond Yugoslavia to encompass Czechoslovakia, Hungary, Romania, Bulgaria, Greece and Albania.

The huge monolith of the USSR was itself a hidden laboratory of ethnic stresses and strains that could not fail to impact ultimately upon existing borders. Researchers at the Institute of Geography of the Soviet Academy of Sciences calculated that, as of August, 1991—only four months before the empire disintegrated—most of its internal union-republic borders were contested by the various ethnic or national groups inhabiting them, or inhabiting a nearby area. Only 3 of the 23 borders surrounding the 15 union-republics were unchallenged. And the total number of territorial conflicts in the USSR, including the numerous nationalities of the Russian Republic itself, was estimated to be a staggering 75.[10] Enormously complicating this picture was the presence of the Russian nationality, numerically dominant in the USSR, but also appearing in fairly large numbers in various union-republics, where they took the form of a minority, often resented and sometimes hated.

Racism and xenophobia in Europe had another dimension, unrelated to borders. The targets could be a dispersed minority, such as Jews or Gypsies, historically scapegoats for economic difficulties or social dislocations. A new target was a distinctive immigrant group from Asia, Africa or southeastern Europe. Anti-Semitism was recognized at the CSCE Copenhagen meeting and later at the Paris Summit as a threatening and dangerous phenomenon. At Copenhagen, the Czechoslovak Foreign Minister, Jiri Dienstbier, warned that it, along with xenophobia in general, could "jeopardize European security."[11]

The big Jewish community of Russia especially felt threatened by a variety of virulent and anti-Semitic nationalist organizations, especially one called Pamyat, as well as the failure of government officials in the Gorbachev regime to speak out against the threat. An unprecedented Congress of Jewish Organizations comprising delegates from 126 Jewish cultural organizations in 70 cities was held in Moscow at the beginning of 1990 and spoke out in opposition to the "sharp upsurge of public anti-Semitism."[12] B'nai B'rith, along with other Jewish organizations, played a leading role in calling world attention to this serious threat of a revived popular Soviet anti-Semitism.[13] Soviet Jewish fears triggered during 1990-91 the biggest mass exodus to Israel and the West in history. Elsewhere in East Europe, the new post–Cold War freedom produced intense nationalist fervor which, in turn, stimulated or reinforced older anti-Semitic attitudes and actions.

Bigotry against Gypsies was far more intense. A study conducted by Freedom House and the American Jewish Committee found public hostility to be overwhelming. Eighty percent of the respondents in Poland, Czechoslovakia and Hungary said they would not want a Gypsy "to move into their neighborhood."[14] A very recent study in the particularly enlightened country of the Czech Republic where the Gypsy (or Roma) minority is quite sizable, numbering 200,000, shows considerable evidence of bigotry. Statistics of reported incidents of violence against Gypsies have increased six times over between 1994 and 1996.[15]

At the important CSCE meeting in Copenhagen in June, 1990, the governmental representatives appeared to recognize the need to undertake two fundamental responsibilities: (1) to grant and assure minorities a host of basic rights; and (2) to combat bigotry and xenophobia. What emerged was a remarkably impressive document, "the most far-reaching international statement on the subject [of minority rights] to date."[16] More than a dozen detailed provisions on minority rights were adopted. In contrast, the UN Covenant on Civil and Political Rights devoted only one article to the subject and the Helsinki Final Act extended merely a brief paragraph to it.

In the Copenhagen meeting's concluding document, members of minorities were assured of the right to express and develop their "ethnic, cultural, linguistic, or religious identity" and to "develop their culture in all its aspects."[17] Spelled out was the right to use one's mother tongue in public, the right to establish autonomous or independent educational, cultural and religious institutions and the right to maintain contact with other members of the same minority, both within and outside the state in which they lived. Group rights were *not* the primary objective of the document. Rather, the focus was upon individual rights and the "free choice" of an individual "to belong to a national minority." Discrimination against an individual from a minority or against the minority as a whole was sharply repudiated. The values of the minority culture were underscored. CSCE member states were called upon "to take account of the history and the culture of national minorities" in the general education system and to "promote a climate of mutual respect, understanding, cooperation and solidarity. . . ."

The most far-reaching paragraph of the minority rights section dealt with ethnic hatred, a subject never before treated in an international document. Implicit in this statement was the obligation of each CSCE government to speak out strongly and clearly against ethnic hatred and xenophobia. In essence, heads of governments were called upon to assure that their offices would be used, in the language of President Theodore Roosevelt, as a "bully pulpit." Ambassador Max Kampelman of the United States, who had more to do with the adoption of the Copenhagen document than anyone else, summed up the obligations of leadership: "The time calls for vigorous, systematic and public condemnation of such prejudices by the highest authorities of government. There is no substitute for vigorous moral leadership."[18]

Left unexamined at Copenhagen, and at the subsequent summit in Paris, was the question, how far does one carry minority rights? Does a resurgence of nationalism in a multinational state ineluctably lead to self-determination, a basic recognized principle in international law and, if so, how is self-determination to be defined? Does it mean secession? Few recognized at the time that the nationalism (and racism) referred to by Sir Isaiah Berlin could rupture the established order of peace. Self-determination was a fundamental principle of the Helsinki Final Act, just as it was a fundamental principle of the Universal Declaration of Human Rights and the International Covenant on Civil and Political Rights. But, sharing that status of a fundamental principle in the Helsinki Final Act on an equal basis was the principle of "inviolability of borders." The two principles, unless handled in a prudential manner, stood in sharp conflict with one another. Secession, inescapably, sunders borders. Moreover, secession in one multinational state can serve as an incentive to encourage additional breakaways by other national groups in the same state, thereby igniting violence and even chaos. The stimulus even might extend to other multinational states, adding to the potential of violence.

At a time when clear and careful strategic thinking and planning were necessary to deal with an emerging thrust of nationalism among Slovenians and Croatians, specifically, driving toward secession in Yugoslavia, the United States withdrew from an active leadership role in dealing with the brewing Yugoslav crisis in CSCE. According to testimony of a key State Department official to both the (Helsinki) Commission on the Security and Cooperation in Europe and to the Senate Foreign Relations Committee in October, 1991, the United States had turned over principal responsibility with respect to Yugoslavia to the European Community.[19] The State Department contended that America's trade and investment relationship with Yugoslavia was insignificant as compared with that of the European Community. It was an extraordinary explanation for a department that was obligated to deal not only with economic issues but also with strategic and political concerns. For the very first time since 1977-78, America had abdicated its leadership role in the Helsinki process.

European Community leadership was Hamlet-like, paralyzed by sharp differences over how to proceed. Only the newly unified Germany pursued a clearly defined specific goal of active support for the secessionist drives of Slovenia and Croatia. That support had two dangerous consequences: (1) a full-scale revolt of the Serb minority in Croatia promoted by the intensely nationalist regime of Slobodan Milosevic in Serbia; and (2) the spread of secessionist sentiment to Bosnia and Macedonia, both embracing various ethnic groups. Europe now faced open war for the first time since 1945; ironically, this situation came on the heels of a successful Helsinki-sponsored peaceful democratic revolution throughout East Europe.

An architect of CSCE's historic achievement of the 1989-90 democratic revolution, Max Kampelman, has written a perceptive and scholarly analysis of the application of self-determination that challenges the absoluteness of the principle.[20] He emphasized that the principle of "inviolability of borders" in the Helsinki Final Act requires respect because it is "necessary for peace and stability." If borders are unjust, they can appropriately be changed "by mutual agreement, through negotiation, public opinion, moral argument, practical appeal and political pressure." If self-determination is carried to an extreme in multinational societies, there can be no logical end to the clamor for secession. The exercise of prudence and the application of pragmatic considerations, Kampelman stressed, are indispensable for a modern-day interpretation of Woodrow Wilson's historic principle of self-determination.

The distinction between self-determination and secession had been made clear by the leading drafter of the Universal Declaration of Human Rights, Eleanor Roosevelt. Speaking before the General Assembly in 1952, she posed a series of rhetorical questions that carried a self-evident conclusion: "Does self-determination mean the right of secession? Does self-determination constitute a right of fragmentation or a justification for the fragmentation of nations?" Her conclusion: "Obviously not."[21] Boutros Boutros-Ghali came to a similar conclusion. In his *Agenda for Peace,* issued on June 17, 1992, the Secretary-General said: "if every ethnic, religious or linguistic group claimed statehood, there would be no limit to fragmentation. . . ."[22] Such fragmentation would make more difficult the achievement of peace and security, as well as economic progress. Boutros-Ghali recognized that to avoid secession, it is necessary to focus upon and respond sensitively to human rights problems, especially those of minorities, be they ethnic, religious or linguistic.

Especially costly was the price paid by the Helsinki process for the imprudent use of the self-determination principle. One of the leading participants in that process from the beginning, Ambassador Hans Meesman of the Netherlands, in a careful examination in 1995 of the history of the Helsinki Final Act, called the secessions in Yugoslavia "a clear and significant deviation from the Helsinki principles" and "the severest blow to CSCE."[23] Meesman placed the major blame for the deviation from Helsinki principles upon German insistence and pressure. But he also criticized the United States for contending that "you had a European problem and it was for the Europeans to come up with a solution." But this "first and premature exercise" of a common European foreign and security policy, he stressed, "ended in a fiasco."

CSCE found itself unable to cope either with the secessionist phenomenon or its primal sources of ethnic hostility and hate. The Paris

Summit had urged a special meeting of experts devoted to minority rights, which was held in Geneva in July, 1991. While the Geneva meeting expressed concern about "the proliferation of acts of racial, ethnic and religious hatred [and] anti-Semitism," it offered little beyond a verbal commitment to "take measures to promote tolerance, under-standing, equality, and good relations between individuals of different origins within their country."[24] The Geneva experts, in a concluding statement, agreed that "issues concerning national minorities . . . are matters of legitimate international concern and consequently do not constitute exclusively an internal affair of the respective state." It had been the USSR that ferociously had opposed the notion that human rights, in any of its forms, was not a domestic matter. However, once the August 19-21, 1991 attempted coup against Gorbachev by right-wing forces took place and failed, the newly chastised Soviet regime became an ardent supporter of international intervention on human rights issues that went beyond even Geneva. Moscow accepted a new ruling whereby the CSCE members "categorically and irrevocably declare that the commitments in the field of the human dimension . . . are matters of direct and legitimate concern to all participating states. . . ."[25]

Several months earlier, and even prior to the CSCE meeting of experts on minorities, the UN Security Council itself reached a decision similar to the one taken by CSCE. In doing so, it shattered a UN tradition that precluded intervention for the protection of human rights. After the UN military forces, under U.S. leadership, had defeated Iraq and forced it to retreat from its occupation of Kuwait, the Kurds in the north of Iraq rose in revolt. Baghdad sought to crush the Kurdish revolt, which prompted the Security Council to adopt a landmark resolution. It condemned "the repression of the Iraqi civilian population . . . including most recently in Kurdish populated areas, the consequences of which threaten international peace and security in the region."[26]

The phrases "conflict prevention" and "crisis management" had entered into CSCE discourse in a major way. As early as the Paris Summit, CSCE had created a Conflict Prevention Center to be headquartered in Vienna. By the end of 1993, a total of some 13 missions were dispatched, mainly to tension-ridden areas in the Former Yugoslavia, and the balance to the regions of ethnic conflict in the former Soviet Union. Especially noteworthy were missions in late 1992 to Kosovo, Vojvodina and the Sandzak—all parts of Serbia. Each was a hot spot of great ethnic tension: the first was inhabited largely by an oppressed Albanian population, the second by Hungarians and other ethnic minorities and the last by a significant number of Bosnian Muslims. Another important mission was sent to Macedonia, a country inhabited mainly by Slavs but with a big Albanian minority and several small ethnic groups.[27]

Independent observers agreed that the missions in Serbia performed remarkably well, maintaining a certain calmness in high tension areas. The very presence of a modest number of observers—some 20 in each Serbian area—prevented more serious and vicious forms of repression while offering some hope for the non-Serbian ethnic groups inhabiting the region.[28] But the Serbian government rather quickly ended this effort at conflict prevention. In July, 1993, it simply refused to renew the visas of the missions' observers, bringing a halt to the experiment. The headline in a Reuters news dispatch told the tale: "Yugoslavia Refuses New Mandate for CSCE Missions."[29] The mission to Macedonia, in sharp contrast, was not plagued by such arbitrariness. Embracing several hundred observers from a number of West European countries and the United States, the mission has proved successful in keeping tensions under some form of control, although, of course, it did not attempt to deal with the question of reducing tensions.

If the CSCE mechanisms were unproductive and the mission initiatives were scarcely great successes, one new institutional device adopted by CSCE in July, 1992, at its important meeting in Helsinki proved to be unusually effective—the High Commissioner on National Minorities.[30] He was to provide the Council of Ministers of CSCE and its Committee of Senior Officials (CSO) with "early warning" about minority problems that might threaten peace or undermine regional stability. The explosive ethnic violence by Serbs in April, 1992 following Bosnia's secession from Yugoslavia unexpectedly had rocked the West and prompted the creation of this "early warning" device. The very perceptive analysis of the Helsinki process by Hans Meesman later would conclude that from a process that had been "a major catalyst of liberalisation and democratisation," it had become a mere "modest accessory"; only the High Commissioner "has turned out to be a welcome addition."[31]

Appointed to the post of High Commissioner was the former Dutch foreign minister, Max van der Stoel, who had considerable UN and CSCE experience in dealing with human rights questions. He assumed the new post in January, 1993. For the UN Commission on Human Rights, he had served and continued to serve as Special Rapporteur on Iraq, providing the UN organ with valuable and informed reports. With this rich diplomatic and rights background, van der Stoel nonetheless was hobbled by the absence of a budget and staff. He recalled in an interview that all that was made available to him—and this by the Dutch government, not by CSCE—were rooms for an office and funds for traveling.[32] Visits to areas of ethnic tension in East Europe were of course vital to his new operation. As of 1997, he reported, his diplomatic visits as High Commissioner consumed 150 days for the previous 12 months, an extraordinarily large amount of time for any international functionary.[33]

And, the traveling was generally to approximately ten tension areas in East Europe. Repeated visits were inevitable given the "especially difficult and complicated minority issues which need continued attention," he explained in a report to OSCE.[34] Van der Stoel was keenly aware that societies in transition in formerly multinational and authoritarian structures, whose value systems were very different from West European democratic values, faced grueling problems.

What the High Commissioner recognized from the very beginning was that in no conceivable way could he perform his task without expertise provided by specialists and without continuing research on minority issues in specific areas. As he noted in an interview, he required a "think tank" to provide him with information, documentation and advice.[35] Each time that he returned from an official visit, he would be able to offer the think tank a host of new projects to research.

Out of this need, there emerged in 1993 a unique NGO—the Foundation on Inter-Ethnic Relations. The Dutch government legally could authorize its establishment, thereby permitting the think tank to obtain the necessary financial support for sustaining a top-level research and consulting operation. The Foundation's *1996 Annual Report* noted that funding had been provided by the Ford Foundation, the Charles Stewart Mott Foundation and the Open Society Fund as well as by the governments of Canada, Finland, the Netherlands, Norway, Sweden, Switzerland and the USA. Other contributors included the Council of Europe and the European Commission.[36]

Initially, however, the office of the High Commissioner in its early stage had to rely upon assistance rendered by Konrad Huber and several other researchers made available on a temporary basis by a friendly government. Huber, the acting Director of the Foundation, was known as an "assistant" to the High Commissioner.[37] Huber's work was financed by the Blaustein Institute on Human Rights in New York, which correctly saw the High Commissioner's responsibility as a vital cutting-edge task. Another early funder was the Marshall Foundation.[38] By 1997, the various funding sources brought in one to one and a half million dollars. This supported a staff of six persons, almost every one a specialist.[39]

The Foundation's first formal Director, Professor Arie Bloed, in an interview, stressed that the Foundation was an unprecedented creation and that "no other NGO in the world" was quite like it.[40] Most telling was its nonadvocacy character. Unlike the bulk of human rights NGOs, it was not engaged in lobbying institutions or in affecting broad public attitudes. Rather, it served the "political needs" of the High Commissioner, and these needs "determined policy." But, to the extent that the High Commissioner was a "conflict prevention instrument" who, inexorably, must be "flexible and dynamic," so, too the Foundation, even as it served as a continuous source of documentation and consultation, had to be "very pragmatic." In the last analysis, even as its research was independent and "must satisfy the funders," at the same time, no document by the Foundation could be released without the "full consent of the High Commissioner." The Foundation and he were like "Siamese twins," observed Bloed in the interview.

The Foundation is governed by a *private* Board of Directors numbering only a handful, but most of them are Dutch government functionaries. The Chairman is a very prominent human rights legal specialist, Pieter van Dijk, who is a member of the Netherlands Court of Human Rights.[41] An impressive 12-member International Council services the Foundation with unusual expertise in the fields of conflict prevention and minority rights. Included is Professor Thomas Buergenthal of the United States. On a project-by-project basis, the Foundation has collaborated with a half-dozen prominent NGOs in a variety of countries, including several in Latvia and Estonia. At the same time, the Foundation has called regularly upon "experts and officials from the OSCE, the Council of Europe, and the United Nations agencies . . . in the realization of the Foundation's projects, both as external advisers and direct participants."[42]

Almost from the beginning, the work of the High Commissioner on National Minorities was highly and enthusiastically regarded by the CSCE (later OSCE), his mentor in Vienna. Toward the end of 1993, his report submitted to the Council of Ministers, meeting in Rome, was acknowledged as one of CSCE's main "success stories."[43] Indeed, the Council was so pleased that it enhanced the status and authority of the High Commissioner.[44]

In July, 1992, there was considerable uncertainty at the Helsinki meeting as to whether the minority problems could be handled at all effectively by peaceful means. Indeed, many feared that the very establishment of the new institution would encourage minorities to oppose the prevailing regimes in their respective areas.[45]

It was assumed by various leadership elements among the regimes of East Europe that a High Commissioner would be inclined to favor minorities, which only would exacerbate ethnic tensions and provoke violence. Precisely because of such fears, the initial mandate for the office was made rather weak and his title would specifically read "High Commissioner *on* National Minorities," rather than "*for* National Minorities" [emphasis added]. In contradistinction, the office of UN High Commissioner for Human Rights, which was pushed through at the General Assembly in December, 1993, was expected to be a partisan proponent of human rights.

Given the prevailing fears, a carefully researched analysis showed that the primary goal of the High Commissioner was "the de-escalation of tensions through promotion of dialogue, confidence and cooperation" among the concerned parties, which usually were a government and an ethnic minority seeking the fulfillment of certain rights.[46] The nature of geographical as well as historical patterns in East Europe often led to a situation in which the government was dominated by one ethnic group, usually the largest, which had monopoly control over the instruments of power and force. The High Commissioner, recognizing this reality, was to act as a mediator or adviser and, therefore, in a strictly "non-coercive" manner. To enable him to function effectively in a potentially tense or actively tense situation, he was required to maintain a position of total independence and impartiality. Absolutely essential for keeping the confidence of both sides to a conflict was the confidentiality of the office, in any of its reportage activities.

Conflict *prevention* was the essence of the High Commissioner's task. Precluded was his involvement should violence break out unless the CSO permitted it. Rather, his mission was two-fold. As officially described, he was "first, to try to contain and de-escalate tensions, and second, to act as a 'tripwire,' meaning that he should alert the OSCE whenever such tensions threaten to develop to a level at which he cannot contain them with the means at his disposal."[47] The "tripwire" term was in fact a formulation designed to more concretely characterize the "early warning/early action" purpose of the High Commissioner's mandate.

The "tripwire" or "early warning" function has never, as yet, been brought into play. From the perspective of the Foundation on Inter-Ethnic Relations, this demonstrated that the "conflict prevention tools at his disposal have been relatively effective."[48] Indeed, the Foundation holds that the High Commissioner's regular work is, in fact, "early action."[49] An analyst of the High Commissioner's office quotes van der Stoel as often saying "that he would consider his efforts to have failed should he feel obligated to issue an early warning notice."[50] It is precisely the High Commissioner's "flexible interpretation of his mandate," as it focuses on conflict prevention, that maximizes his effectiveness.[51]

Flexibility and diplomatic tactfulness are at the heart of van der Stoel's operation. A perceptive observer found that the High Commissioner's "immediate task" in the case of ethnic tensions is to "prevent acute escalation of the tensions"; after that, and over "the longer term," he must "help set in motion a process of dialogue that will . . . deal with the root causes of the tensions."[52] What make the two interrelated steps possible and, indeed, are "essential" to his functioning "as an instrument of conflict prevention," are precisely the following: confidentiality and discretion, noncoercion and cooperation, independence and accountability and constant, ongoing involvement.[53]

The primary concern of the High Commissioner and the Foundation in 1993 was the tension situation in Estonia between native Estonians and Russians. Other specific ethnic tension situations requiring their attention were in Latvia, Slovakia, Romania, Macedonia and Albania. What made Estonia a priority was the presence on its border of the huge Russian state, which was intensely anxious about the condition of a half million of their Russian kinsmen that had inhabited that area since World War II. Were the internal tensions not to diminish, they could spill over borders, sparking possibly external conflict and worse. It was a characteristic feature of many East European ethnic conflict situations that they bordered on areas in which the kinsmen of a minority dominated the neighboring state.

Huber, the initial acting head of the Foundation and the High Commissioner's Assistant, has described the problem as it emerged in 1993 and as it was perceived by CSCE.[54] That Estonian independence would carry a distinctly anti-Russian bias once it was free of the repressive Soviet empire was hardly unexpected.[55] Nor was it altogether surprising that that national bias would be reflected in attitudes toward the Russians within Estonia, who were seen as intruders. The Estonian Parliament enacted in 1993 a new citizenship, or aliens, law that was distinctly anti-Russian in character. While citizenship automatically was granted to Estonians, sharp restrictions with respect to language facility and residency were imposed upon Russians seeking citizenship, which only stirred an angry burgeoning response among Russians in the country, particularly in areas where they constituted a majority or close to a majority.

The priority aim of the High Commissioner, noted Huber, was with the "Estonian government's willingness (or lack thereof) to take visible steps toward the integration" of the non-Estonians.[56] Van der Stoel coordinated his efforts of mediation with the CSCE's long-term mission to Estonia, but he brought into play "personal and professional qualities" that were "an incalculable contribution" to the success of his efforts. Repeated trips to the area were necessary in order to meet with government officials, on the one hand, and activists among the minority, on the other. He would present options and help the disputants to "explore [those] options" in a way as "to de-escalate tensions and have their [respective] needs adequately met."[57] Van der Stoel, in his interview, stressed that always upon a return from one of his visits, he would pose questions that the Foundation would research in order to proceed ahead.[58]

Conflict prevention could not be seen as a "one-shot deal," as Huber quite rightly described the "standard international fact-finding mission."[59] Rather, tensions required continuing nursing, and, therefore, must be "low key and exploratory." A concomitant of that approach is secrecy and even-handedness. With the building of trust on both sides, the High Commissioner was in a position to offer criticism that would find some receptivity since the source would be seen as fair and objective. Thus, van der Stoel was able to write a letter to government officials identifying "various shortcomings and ambiguities" in the initial draft of the law on aliens and the Estonian government would be encouraged to return the legislation to the parliament for appropriate improvements.

Of fundamental importance to the process of conflict prevention was the willingness of both parties to accept a continuing dialogue with each other. Arie Bloed gave particular emphasis to this point, contending that once the Foundation finds that the two sides are talking, "we can offer expertise" for a solution.[60] Getting the sides to engage in dialogue was a key objective of the High Commissioner. In his view, it only can be achieved if the minority agrees to be an "integral part of the society and the state . . . on whose territory they live."[61] At the same time, the state must be willing to protect and preserve the ethnic, cultural, religious and linguistic identity of the minorities living within its territory.

What stood at the core of the Foundation's function and the highly developed diplomatic skill of the High Commissioner was the transcendent importance of peace and stability. Huber put it this way: "CSCE is primarily interested in preventing the development of additional conflicts that would threaten peace, stability or relations between states in the region."[62] It is not justice in the abstract that is pursued; for justice, as seen from the perspective of the minority, potentially could be disruptive to stability and, therewith, trigger a conflagration. Yet, what is recognized as basic to the process is the indisputable fact that peace and stability in a region rests upon the satisfaction at least to some extent, of minority rights. An "Expert Consultation" held by the Foundation toward the end of 1993 concluded that "a process of dialogue and cooperation" is essential in reaching "constructive policy approaches to minority issues. . . ."[63]

Precisely because the two sides had accepted fundamental commitments, the High Commissioner could follow up the return of the aliens legislation to the Estonian Parliament. Van der Stoel would engage in a rarely used device of holding a press conference in which he commended both sides for reiterating their assurances that, above all, they were committed to peace and cooperation.[64] It was the Foundation's Acting Director, Konrad Huber, who was convinced that only as a result of the High Commissioner's efforts was "a disaster in Estonia's inter-ethnic relations . . . narrowly averted."[65]

Even with positive responses, there still remained the uncertainty as to whether adherence to or fulfillment of commitments would follow. From the perspective of the High Commissioner and the Foundation, a crucial consideration was the internal nature of the state. Huber contended that "the successful management of societal differences . . . requires democratic institutions and full respect for the rule of law." Both features characterized Estonian society and, to the extent that Russia was an omnipresent external factor, its political system was also favorable, although virulent nationalism already had made a disturbing appearance there.

The features of democratic institutions and the rule of law contributed significantly to a practice that the High Commissioner and the Foundation would recommend and implement—creation by the government of a "round-table" at which its representatives would sit with representatives of the minority to air complaints and consider options. The procedure would become "customary practice" in the various conflict prevention pursuits in which the High Commissioner and the Foundation were involved. From their perspective, the "round-table" not only served the purposes of dialogue but also, equally important, it enabled the High Commissioner to provide guidance in creating laws and policies that were favorable to the minority.[66] In this sense, his role was a positive one with respect to minority rights.

What Huber was stressing was an upbeat approach to conflict prevention. The High Commissioner's intervention in the Estonian crisis even as it was becoming increasingly heated contributed to the cooling of tensions. And, as tempers cooled, new devices were added to keep discussions going until agreements eventually could be reached or at least considered while a certain pragmatic modus vivendi tentatively prevailed. That which required rejection was the prevalent notion that "with each progression [toward conflict] there is less that outsiders can do to prevent the coming violence, if indeed there was even anything they could have done from the start."[67]

Estonia, of course, was but one of several areas targeted for detailed consideration by the High Commissioner. In an Appendix to the report on the "Expert Consultation" concerning national minorities run by the Foundation in November, 1993, Huber and a colleague, Susanna Terstal, offered details on van der Stoel's other activities.[68] In his almost bimonthly visits to Estonia—January, March, June, September and October—the High Commissioner made certain that he also visited Latvia, where the Russian population was even larger, percentage-wise, than the one in Estonia, and where the Latvian government was imposing upon the local Russians a certain diminution in citizenship rights somewhat similar to what had been attempted in Estonia.[69]

The High Commissioner, no doubt with the encouragement of the Foundation, proposed creating in Latvia a special, permanent institution such as an "ombudsman," a "Commission on Ethnic and Language Questions" and a "round-table for minorities."[70] The proposed institutions were to help give effect to "necessary changes in substantive policies toward the Russophone communities." Such changes were the crux of a solution for the diminution of tensions and the prevention of conflict.[71]

The Foundation staff, in the Appendix, also took note of the minority language complaints of the Hungarians living in Slovakia. A proposal that the High Commissioner advanced, apparently with the purpose of appearing even-handed, would have the Slovak and Hungarian governments agree to a formula whereby a team of "neutral minority experts" would visit each country and then offer policy recommendations relating to the teaching and use of the language of the respective minority. In Romania, several minorities, most especially the Hungarians in Transylvania, were primarily concerned with language and education issues. At the recommendation of the High Commissioner, the Bucharest regime created in April, 1993 a Council for Ethnic Minorities in which the Foundation's purpose of dialogue and consideration of options for satisfying minority needs would be pursued.

Finally, the Foundation staff reported on the Albanian minority in Macedonia (of the Former Yugoslavia), which was principally anxious about education, language and its status under the country's constitution. The High Commissioner had yet to offer recommendations, which would be advanced only after several more visits. In Albania, the principal minority were the Greeks. Once again the focus was upon education and the High Commissioner recommended to the Tirana government that it give "priority to legislation in the educational field," which would include the establishment of "complaint procedures" to which the minority could have "recourse for their grievances."[72] Restitution of Greek Orthodox church property also was recommended by him. (Regrettably, the Foundation could not undertake conflict prevention on the very egregious Albanian condition in the Serbian-ruled province of Kosovo. The Albanians there constituted no less than ninety percent of the population but, since 1989, the province had been deprived by Slobodan Milosevic of its autonomy. Brutal cultural repression of this ethnic group has characterized Serb rule ever since. Once overt resistance by militant Albanians made its appearance in early 1998, the ruthless military hand of the oppressor was applied extending by the middle of the year to the destruction of houses and villages on the border with Albania. With thousands of ethnic Albanians fleeing Kosovo, it recalled early stages of the "ethnic cleansing" in Bosnia during 1994-95. While President Clinton and Secretary of State Albright made clear that another "Bosnia" would not be tolerated, effective conflict prevention was not easy to achieve without the willingness of the U.S. and NATO to bring to bear the full weight of their economic and military power.)

Toward the end of its first year of operation, the Foundation brought in a variety of outside nationality and conflict prevention experts to "analyze" the various minority situations in East Europe, "to reflect on possible policy approaches" and "to identify possible lacunae in the current understanding of and action on such issues."[73] Based upon the experts' conclusion that communication between the opposing sides of government and minority leaders was poor among various different situations in East Europe, the Foundation concluded that "the most that might be reasonably expected, even under ideal conditions, may be the *managing* of ethnic tensions and not their final resolution."[74] It would become apparent that this point was to serve as a major guideline for the High Commissioner and the Foundation.

The Foundation also ascertained from the initial year's evaluation that to be effective with minorities, a government must institute within its structure "the visible functioning of a well-supported minority-related authority. . . ."[75] Another policy recommendation was to provide for some form of "self-rule" or "autonomy" or "arrangements for devolving power to sub-national levels." What would loom especially large in subsequent years was a proposal to press for bilateral treaties between neighboring countries in which the kin of the dominant ethnic group in one state is a minority across the border and vice versa. Such treaties should contain specific border and minority-related provisions.

As a final recommendation, the experts emphasized that since each situation in East Europe was unique, even if certain common characteristics were applicable to all or most, "policy approaches" should have a "design" that is "specific to the situation concerned" and takes fully into account "the communities affected." Clearly, the consultation had provided a large order of fundamentals in conflict prevention that the Foundation had, in any case, been absorbing for almost a year. But it went beyond the substantive recommendation to urge the Foundation, as a means of remaining the primary supporter of the High Commissioner, to develop continuing partnerships with individual scholars and specialists, universities and think tanks abroad. This basic thesis was, in part, already being implemented during 1993; it would be fully applied in subsequent years.

The Foundation's initial year also was marked by the release of a fairly extensive report by the High Commissioner on Roma (or Gypsies). CSCE's Committee of Senior Officials (CSO) had asked the High Commissioner on April 26-28, 1993, "to study the social, economic and humanitarian problems relating to the Roma population" as well as to examine "the relevance of these problems to the mandate of the High Commissioner. . . ."[76] The study undoubtedly was prepared for the High Commissioner by the Foundation, though, meticulously, no reference was made to the latter. It was submitted to the CSO at its meeting, on September 21-23, 1993.

The report was by no means an original investigation of the topic, in whole or even in part. Rather, the researchers relied on secondary sources and offered only an "overview of significant Roma-related issues. . . ."[77] That the broad facts about the Roma were included is evident. The 7-8 million Gypsies in countries of the CSCE, the report noted, have been and continue to be confronted by "grave challenges to the enjoyment of basic rights and to full participation in the social, economic and political life of countries in the region."[78] Moreover, because of a variety of "complex factors including historical discrimination against them, the vast majority of Roma could be regarded as occupying an extremely vulnerable position in the societies . . . of the region."

That extreme vulnerability was not hidden, although neither was it presented in detail with appropriate documentation. As broadly sketched by the researchers, "the overall condition manifests itself in widespread and acute poverty, unemployment, illiteracy, lack of formal education [and] substandard housing. . . ." Worse still, the anti-Roma prejudice has found "renewed expression in the collective scape-goating of the Roma for the ills of society-at-large." The consequence has been "numerous attacks against Roma and their property in recent years."

Carefully avoided were references to individual countries and how each treated the Roma. That might have contributed to "shaming" various CSCE states and, thereby, potentially mobilizing the forces for social change. But this would have launched the High Commissioner onto the path of advocacy, which he was determined to shun. After all, his mandate was conflict prevention and not human rights or minority rights advocacy. Moreover, the condition of the Roma, howsoever abused or oppressed, did not constitute a threat to peace or stability. It was in vain that the Copenhagen document had gone out of its way to highlight the plight of the Gypsies and demand an end to the abuse.

The recommendations of the High Commissioner were as vague and nonspecific as his analysis had been. CSCE countries were to be "encouraged to devise and implement constructive policies for addressing the serious social, economic and humanitarian problems of the Roma, including attacks and discrimination against them."[79] As for the High Commissioner, the report made it clear that his office "should become involved in only those [Roma] situations which meet the criteria of the mandate," which meant noninvolvement unless, of course, their condition produced such instability that violence might occur.[80]

Still, on one occasion, the High Commissioner did speak out in a clear manner regarding human rights. He told an OSCE seminar in Warsaw in 1994 that "in no case should new citizenship laws be drafted and implemented in such a way as to discriminate against legitimate claimants for citizenship. . . ." He clearly was referring here to the plight of Roma in the Czech Republic but he carefully avoided naming that country. Discriminatory legislation he said, would "greatly undermine" the "long-term interests of the state" by tearing at the "loyal bond" between the state and its inhabitants. He urged that "appropriate changes" be made in the legislation.[81]

If the High Commissioner had failed to specifically identify and document the egregious conduct of what seemed to be the most democratic state that had emerged from the revolutions of 1989 and the collapse of the Soviet empire, another far more modest instrument of OSCE did so. On the basis of information obtained from NGOs and the Council of Europe, OSCE's Office of Democratic Institutions and Human Rights (ODIHR) in Warsaw reported that the Czech Citizenship Law No. 40/1992 had imposed "burdensome conditions for citizenship."[82] Numerous Roma were "classified as Slovaks or have become stateless as a result of the law." The NGO that had provided the most detailed information on the law was the so-called Tolerance Foundation, which operated in Prague.[83] The valuable material of this NGO would be effectively used by the U.S. Commission on Security and Cooperation in Europe to demand that the Prague government correct a gross human rights abridgement.[84] In April 1996, Prague adopted an amendment to the citizenship law easing some restrictions but leaving in place its fundamentally exclusionary approach to Roma.[85]

Aside from the Roma issue, the Office of High Commissioner, with the research and expert consultative assistance rendered his office by the Foundation, had made significant advances in its maiden year of 1993 in dealing with ethnic tension. Konrad Huber, in reporting to the Foundation's funder, the Blaustein Institute, in 1994, correctly concluded that the relationship had "developed an effective practice of preventive diplomacy in situations of ethnic tension, hitherto uncharted terrain not only for the CSCE but for multilateral institutions in general."[86] It certainly was a trailblazing development upon which to build. Huber anticipated that, in the following year, tensions in Latvia and Macedonia would emerge as "top priorities" in the East European region.[87] But the Foundation also planned visits to the Romanian Council for National Minorities and, as part of an expanded program, both geographically and substantively, expert consultations on minority issues in Ukraine and Kazakstan, which had international ramifications.

But it was upon the long run that the Foundation now focused. It recognized that a central factor for ethnic tensions exploding into violence and war was the role of a "kin-state," i.e., a nearby state in which the kin of one of the contending ethnic groups controls the machinery of state power. Everyone understood how the presence of the Serbian state decisively affected the course of developments in Bosnia in 1992-93 through armed assistance rendered to Bosnian Serbs. Similarly, the presence of Croatia crucially had impacted upon the Muslim-Croatian tensions in Bosnia. The Foundation sought to figure out ways to reverse such outcomes and determine how the kin-state might be encouraged to play a constructive role with respect to neighboring minority situations. A project prospectus was developed in August, 1994 that anticipated for the Foundation an integrated program involving research and seminars to attain this objective.[88] It was hoped that the Foundation's work would have the effect of "maximizing the constructive—de-escalatory role for such actors"—and minimizing their potentially negative role with respect to tensions involving their ethnic kin.

Among the Foundation's planned half-dozen research projects, several concerned kin-state activities, including bilateral treaties containing minority-related provisions. Others would focus on mechanisms for dialogue, minority-related measures with respect to the media and targeted economic assistance for minorities.[89] A specific consideration of the Foundation dealt with education for the Greek minority in Albania. Because relations between the two ethnic groups were tense, the Foundation sought to avoid leaving the impression that it favored the Greek minority. Instead, the NGO chose to define the assistance as "multicultural" and as focusing on "curriculum development, teacher training and management aspects of minority education."[90]

By 1995, the High Commissioner was accorded almost universal recognition in OSCE circles as contributing significantly to the reduction of tensions. He unanimously was reelected for a second three-year term. His success story in bringing about a significant change in the application of the Estonian aliens law was especially impressive even though key Estonian officials were critical, in private, about his intrusiveness.[91] With the High Commissioner's work so strongly endorsed, the Foundation could appropriately bask in the refracted enthusiasm, and more staff could be hired in order to service him more effectively.[92]

"In-country projects" became a primary focus of Foundation activity in that year.[93] In Macedonia, the Foundation developed a pilot project on both government-minority cooperation and curriculum development. In Romania, where the state had enacted a new education law, an important seminar was conducted on minority education. Seminars also were arranged to "provide a forum where officials and minority leaders could consider constructive approaches to specific ethnic issues." These were held in Kazakstan, Kyrgyzstan, Estonia and Romania. A training workshop was conducted for the professional staff of the Council for National Minorities in Romania.

The in-country projects were supplemented on the outside by a useful "expert consultation" concerning "the role of bilateral treaties with minority-related provisions in moderating ethnic tensions and improving bilateral relations."[94] The consultation, together with the Foundation's own research, led to the conclusion that minority clauses in bilateral treaties were valuable provided there was good faith on both sides and that basic democratic institutions prevailed in each country. What was also essential was that the clauses carried reference to the principles of international law.[95] The recommendations would assist in the drafting of treaties between Hungary and Slovakia covering their respective Slovak and Hungarian minorities, and between Hungary and Romania covering the Hungarian minority in Romania. The treaties, a product of the High Commissioner's encouragement, marked a seminal development in East Europe. The consultation was typical of Foundation initiatives: it "focused on a concrete situation that the High Commissioner faces" with the aim of providing him with "expert information, analysis and advice directly relevant to his work."

One seminar merits special attention, since it enabled the Foundation director, Arie Bloed, to present a fundamental overview of the minority rights problem. It was held in Kyrgyzstan, a republic that had a distance to go with respect to modernization; nonetheless the Asian republic had expressed a strong interest in the work of the High Commissioner and, as early as 1994, invited him to visit.[96] Its minorities of Russians, Uzbeks and Chinese, with their radically different cultural characteristics, made for an uncertain future.

Bloed's address, "International Norms and Practices in the Field of Minorities," constituted a veritable background primer for multiethnic successor states of collapsed empires.[97] While focusing upon "major achievements" in the area of international protection of national minorities, he stressed that "the norms on minority protection agreed upon in the framework of the OSCE are *clearly unparalleled* in international relations." [Emphasis added.] He summarized OCSE's monitoring systems, its human dimension mechanisms and its missions. Then he turned to the creation of the High Commissioner's office, which, he correctly observed, "reflected the conviction that much better results could be achieved by activities aimed at the prevention of conflicts, involving national minorities, than by the much more burdensome activities aimed at the solution of actual conflicts once they have occurred." It was as thoughtful a rationale for the Office of High Commissioner, as well as for Bloed's own work, as one could find in OSCE literature.

The seminar, involving both government leaders and minority representatives, concluded with various theses that carried the implication for specific action. First, kin-state support for ethnic minorities can be most useful, but it also can lead to difficulties if there is no formal bilateral treaty with the state in which the minority lives. Second, there is an urgent need in Kyrgyzstan (and, presumably, elsewhere) for legislation specifically banning discrimination against minorities, and this antidiscriminatory legislation must be perceived as such by and be accessible to minorities. Third, government-controlled media can be dangerous, since "biased reporting of ethnic issues can severely divide groups and create enormous distrust and animosity between them." Fourth, governments, in cooperation with minority representatives, should fund the establishment of cultural centers, "as a means for developing [various] groups' unique identities through publications, festivals, and the like." Finally, especially useful would be the creation within the local government of a special minority body that can aid the local authorities in allocating financial resources to the minority and in serving as a provider of jobs and services relating to the minority.

During 1995, the Foundation branched out in a major way in making the results of its research and consultations available to the scholarly world as well as the general public.[98] The published studies, some edited by Bloed, others prepared under his guidance, provided important insights for specialists in the growing field of conflict prevention. That his NGO operation was doing landmark, even if limited, work could hardly be questioned.

In the following years, the Foundation focused upon minority education issues, which increasingly were seen as central to the reduction of ethnic tensions. For the first time, it sponsored a regionwide seminar on the subject in October, 1996 at which the staff formally submitted for discussion and consideration "The Hague Recommendations Regarding the Education Rights of National Minorities."[99] From the perspective of the Foundation, the "Recommendations" were based upon the assumption that "the ultimate object of all human rights is the full development of the individual human personality in conditions of equality."[100] The region-wide seminar was an obvious effort to showcase the "Recommendations" and have them distributed en masse to OSCE member states in the region and all other NGOs as well.[101]

The "Recommendations" covered public and private institutions and focused upon specific minority education requirements at primary, secondary and tertiary levels as well as in vocational schools. Examined, too, was the area of curriculum development as it related to minority education and the training of teachers.[102]

At a special seminar that the Foundation held in Riga, Latvia in May, emphasis was placed upon the need for governments to ensure that minorities can use their own language in schools and, at the same time, learn the official state language. A formal pledge was made for bilingual schools with teachers of high quality in Latvia.[103] At the beginning of 1997, the Foundation promised to "support the establishment of in-service teacher training centres" in Albania.[104] A similar promise was made for Macedonia and for Ukraine. With reference to the latter, the Foundation planned a seminar on creating low-cost textbooks on minority education.[105]

Concentration upon education did not mean the exclusion of traditional Foundation activities. Mechanisms for facilitating dialogue remained an important goal. During 1996, the Foundation ran seminars in Croatia, Estonia, Kazakstan, Latvia, Macedonia, Slovakia and Ukraine.[106] Special attention was given over to a seminar in Riga that had, as co-hosts, local and even regional NGOs and university sponsors. Latvia was important, since the Russian-speaking minority constituted perhaps nearly 48 percent of its total population. What made the Riga seminar particularly significant were the comments of van der Stoel in his opening address. He emphasized that the Copenhagen document required a dual and mutual responsibility upon the part of minorities and governments. While governments vigorously must oppose discrimination and forced assimilation of minorities, minorities must make a determined effort to integrate themselves into the larger society and respect the laws of the country in which they live.[107] The relevance of the High Commissioner's advice to a country in which the minority was numerically fairly close in size to the predominant nationality hardly can be obscured. It illuminated how the High Commissioner worked and underscored his commitment to stability, rather than to self-determination, let alone secession.

At the same time, the High Commissioner could and did effectively pursue fulfillment of minority rights once a government had committed itself to fulfilling them. An example of how he functioned can be seen in a letter of his dated August 13, 1996 to the Minister for Foreign Affairs of Slovakia, Juraj Schenk. One of the concerns in his letter was fair treatment for the large Hungarian minority of some 600,000 in Slovakia. He stressed that persons belonging to a national minority should have the right to set up and manage their own private educational and training establishments.

After referring to several documents establishing standards for minorities, he vigorously inquired into whether a particular Pedagogical University was training "a sufficient number of Hungarian teachers. . . ." He also sought assurances that Hungarian educators in Slovakia would be able to arrange for "the publication of Hungarian textbooks."[108]

Other subtle questions on education and cultural policy were raised by the High Commissioner. Noting that a considerable number of persons in the education sector had been dismissed over the past two years, van der Stoel wondered why the percentage of Hungarians dismissed was higher than their percentage in the total population would warrant. He asked for "an explanation of this phenomenon." He also asked why only 13 percent of projects submitted by Hungarian cultural organizations were approved, whereas almost 75 percent of projects submitted by other minorities were approved. With information obviously obtained by Foundation researchers, he noted that cultural organizations of the other minorities received five times as much in subsidies than did the Hungarian cultural organization, even though the other minorities, taken together, constituted but 3.6 percent of the total Slovakian population, while the Hungarians constituted 10.7 percent. That he would insist upon "greater transparency of the system of public funds" in reference to culture was not unexpected.

Schenk's response suggests that the authorities did seek to be as forthcoming as possible on the education issues that were raised and that, on the funding of Hungarian minority cultural organizations, the prevailing system that the High Commissioner had criticized "will be reconsidered with a view of its improvement." Schenk added that the Slovak Minister of Culture "promised to consider your recommendations and to utilize them to the extent necessary. . . ."[109]

Another example of the High Commissioner's tough-mindedness as well as his even-handedness was the way he dealt with the Serbian minority in Croatia while on a visit to Zagreb and the region of Eastern Slavonia in late January, 1997. As recorded in the *OSCE Newsletter,* he discussed with the local authorities the "measures to be taken by the Croatian Government in order to create a feeling of security and trust among Serbs in the region. . . ." At the same time, he "appealed to Serbs to take full part in the local elections and to stay in the regions."[110] Later developments suggested that van der Stoel was not very successful in easing tensions in the East Slavonian area.

Overall, however, his achievement has been remarkably positive. An official State Department report in 1997 on OSCE called the office of the High Commissioner "one of OSCE's most effective diplomatic instruments."[111] In any assessment, attention must be paid to the NGO that was so closely linked to van der Stoel's operation that the two were called by Arie Bloed "Siamese twins." The Foundation on Inter-Ethnic Relations had charted new paths in conflict prevention on the difficult terrain of minority rights and ethnic tensions. The groundwork it had laid was certain to have favorable and important repercussions.

CHAPTER SEVENTEEN

The "Unexplored Continent" of Physician Involvement in Human Rights

In July, 1997, official Washington was apprised of disturbing firsthand testimony about massive human rights violations by the forces of Laurent Kabila and his military supporters from the Rwanda army, in their revolutionary sweep to power in the Congo. Presenting that testimony to the important International Relations Committee of the House of Representatives were specialists from the Boston-based Physicians for Human Rights (PHR). The specialists impressed key Congressmen, a fact that ultimately would exert a certain impact upon policymakers in the Administration.

The report was based upon careful investigation by a three-member team assembled by Physicians for Human Rights. It was headed by Dr. Jennifer Leaning from Harvard Medical School and Brigham and Women's Hospital, who spent two weeks in the eastern Congo and western Rwanda, June 20–July 2, 1997. Its 18-page report, based upon extensive interviews with international human rights and humanitarian groups and local human rights activists, as well as witnesses and victims of gross human rights abuses, was released on July 16. The occasion for the release was Dr. Leaning's testimony to the Committee.[1]

The report, summarized in Dr. Leaning's testimony, recorded that Rwandan soldiers were "often identified as perpetrators" of "killing of Rwandan refugees" in the Congo. Rwandan soldiers also were implicated in the killing of Congolese villagers in eastern Zaire. Finally, in western

Rwanda, the counterinsurgency campaign of the Rwandan army was said to have killed 2-3,000 civilians during the previous three months. While the data and accounts hardly were suggestive of the massive genocide of Tutsis in 1994, they warranted the characterization of "gross abuses." Particularly disturbing to the investigators was the information they gleaned that U.S. military trainers and advisors were used by the Rwandan forces in their counterinsurgency campaign.

Dr. Leaning was shocked that the attitude of the U.S. Embassy in Kigali "turned out to be hostile to and contemptuous of human rights concerns." She reported to the House Committee that a top member of the Embassy staff told her colleague: "I defy you to identify a single human rights violation in Rwanda." This attitude she found to be incredible given the fact that "thousands of civilians [in Rwanda] have been killed by the army and 100,000 languish in jail without charge or trial." She urged Congress to look into "the role of the U.S. military trainers and advisers in this extremely abusive campaign."

According to Holly Burkhalter, PHR's legislative representative, the response of the House Committee members was strong and positive. Committee Chairman Benjamin Gilman was "very helpful," while Congressman Christopher Smith was "terrific."[2] They and other members had been briefed in advance and Smith went to the trouble of reading aloud—and, therefore, into the formal record—information from the PHR report. More importantly, Smith, who also served as co-chairman of the U.S. Helsinki Commission, quickly drafted a letter to the Administration asking for an accounting of its military aid program to Kabila's forces. From the perspective of the PHR lobbyist, what had happened here was the very essence of democracy, a congressional challenge to an administration's accountability, with the challenge resulting from NGO fact-finding and advocacy. She compared it to the Democratic Congress's challenge a decade earlier to the Reagan Administration's policy in Central America. A "critical Congress," she emphasized, was essential for advancing human rights objectives.

It is fairly clear that the Administration, in fact, had established a certain unpublicized military training relationship with Rwanda's military force. A month after the release of the PHR document and testimony, the *Washington Post* obtained an internal Defense Department report showing that the military role of the United States was considerably larger than was previously known.[3] Interestingly, the Defense Department report, as yet unpublished, was said by the *Post* to be a "response to congressional questions about the U.S. military role in Rwanda."

Some in Congress may have been surprised that a physicians' NGO had taken the lead in uncovering the gross human rights violations of the Kabila revolution and America's military involvement with the Rwandan forces. Traditionally, it has been lawyers' groups that have preoccupied themselves with human rights. And, among the leadership of general human rights NGOs, lawyers play a central role. After all, a fundamental theme of the human rights movement has been the need to establish or uphold the rule of law.

Yet, for those members of Congress concerned with human rights issues, Physicians for Human Rights (PHR) as an NGO was hardly unknown. The group had appeared before congressional committees several times, and their reputation for integrity and accuracy was accorded appropriate recognition. Still, the physicians were very much the "new kid on the block," having only been formed in June, 1986. Human Rights Watch may have been started several years later, but its various constituent parts had been functioning for some time. PHR was almost brand new and now, in 1997, with a top-level Advocacy Director in Washington, it already was making waves on the political scene in that city and well beyond.

How the organization got started is very much the story of a single individual, not dissimilar from the way Amnesty International had begun. Dr. Jonathan Fine, who was PHR's founder and would become its first Executive Director, was described by a colleague, in an interview, as passionate, determined, single-minded, and forceful in his convictions.[4] A telephone call to him in 1981 had propelled him into a human rights career through a special expedition abroad.

As recorded in the *Harvard Medical Alumni Bulletin*, Fine, while working at a health center in the north end of Boston, was called by a Harvard history professor, John Womack, who inquired whether Fine knew of a Spanish-speaking physician who could go to Santiago, Chile on an emergency mission. It was June, 1981, and three Chilean physicians were reported by Womack to have disappeared during the era of the Pinochet dictatorship. It was feared that the doctors had been tortured and perhaps murdered. Dr. Fine dropped everything; within a week he himself undertook the assignment and was in Santiago, Chile.[5]

The visit to the ruthless military regime that had accumulated a record of horrendous human rights abuses was an eye-opening experience for the Harvard doctor. He founded the American Committee for Human Rights (ACHR), which included high-level professionals from several fields. All were dedicated to human rights advocacy. During the subsequent three years, various ACHR members focused their attention on the need for an organization that would become preoccupied solely with medical or health care issues.

Several factors were uppermost in the thinking of Fine and his colleagues. Doctors were in the best position, it was contended, to advise on the consequences to public health of indiscriminate use of gases to dissipate riots. At the time, the technique was used on a mass scale in South Korea to break up student disturbances and dissident demonstrations. On other military and police tactics, doctors also could be helpful in evaluating the nature of the harm that was perpetrated on targets or victims. Finally, it was thought—and probably correctly so—that America's doctors generally were held in high esteem abroad and, therefore, they could be "particularly effective in influencing world opinion" on such matters.

By June, 1986, a watershed in ACHR thinking had been reached. Dr. Fine later was reported by the *Harvard Medical Alumni Bulletin* to have declared that month that ACHR was "standing on the frontier of a huge unexplored continent of physician involvement in human rights." The leaders chose to dissolve the organization and to form a new group— the Physicians for Human Rights. The backyard of a Boston condominium was the actual scene where the new NGO was born. Present were a half-dozen mainly medical professionals with a keen commitment to human rights.[6]

The hostess was Dr. Jane Schaller, who was Chief of Pediatrics at Boston's North East Medical Center and would become the group's first President. In attendance, besides Fine, were Dr. Robert Lawrence of Harvard's Department of Internal Medicine, Dr. Carola Eisenberg, a prominent psychiatrist who was Dean of Students at Harvard and Dr. Jack Geiger, also of Harvard, who already had shown himself to be a strong supporter of human rights advocacy through his involvement in Physicians for Social Responsibility. An invited guest was Professor Philip Alston, the prominent legal authority on international human rights who was visiting from Australia and teaching at the Fletcher School of International Affairs at Tufts University in Boston. On technical human rights advice, few could be his equal.

A small national board was created, largely composed of doctors from the various Boston medical school facilities. With an investment by Dr. Fine of $400,000 of his own money, as well as his own time as the group's first Executive Director, Physicians for Human Rights was on its way to exploring a "new frontier." Soon recruited was Eric Stover, who had served on the staff of the American Association for the

Advancement of Science (AAAS). A writer who had pioneered in applying to human rights the key new field of forensic sciences, Stover set the group's initial sights on three abusive regimes upon whom the United States could exercise some deterrent influence—Chile, the Philippines and South Korea. Also recruited as Associate Director the following year was Susannah Sirkin, who would become the organization's principal professional. She had worked for Amnesty in the United States, specializing in building membership from the legal and medical fields. Fine's visionary zealousness, when matched with the experienced and pragmatic Sirkin, could not fail to make an early impact upon the human rights scene. What helped make possible her hiring as well as the organization's initial outlays was a $50,000 grant from the Ford Foundation. The Foundation would continue to be a major donor for this NGO as it has been for numerous other human rights NGOs.

In creating a structure and staff, the NGO also would accept an agenda "put forward" by its first president, Dr. Schaller. It would provide medical documentation on human rights violations, support medical colleagues who face difficulties while defending human rights, denounce health professionals who participate in abuses, develop a human rights curriculum for the medical profession and build a network of support for the organization. The agenda later would be described by PHR as "a set of goals that would be the organization's guiding principles for the next ten years."[7]

Almost from its inception and even before PHR hired staff, the organization embarked upon its first formal investigatory mission abroad. The triumphant results of that mission would resonate for a long time afterward and lay the groundwork for future exploratory expeditions, numbering no less than 70 over a ten-year period to some 40 countries—a rather extraordinary achievement.[8] The first mission in August, 1986 was to Chile and was made—as would be so many others— at the request of a local group, in this case the Colegio Medico de Chile, the country's medical organization.

There was a general reason for the request, but it was augmented by a specific plea that necessitated quick and early action by PHR. As known and already anticipated by ACHR, many Chilean doctors were being imprisoned by Pinochet's regime because they had refused to cooperate with the torture of prisoners. But what triggered the mission was the arrest of the two top officials of the Colegio Medico—its President and Secretary-General. They were accused of organizing a national strike against the regime in early July. Founding members Carola Eisenberg and Robert

Lawrence, both of Harvard Medical School, flew to Santiago to intervene on behalf of medical professionals and, in the words of the *Boston Globe*, to express support for distant colleagues doing "battle with a beast" and, therewith, bringing "a special dimension to their profession."[9]

The distinguished Harvard medical specialists also decided to look into the status of three other cases that encompassed their responsibility as doctors: (1) health workers in a Catholic organization who had been jailed for treating a man the military government had said was a terrorist; (2) two young persons who reportedly had been burned by soldiers during a strike and (3) a physician who illegally had returned from an imposed 1974 exile abroad and promptly was arrested after he reported his presence to the authorities.[10]

But only recently established, Physicians for Human Rights quickly won its spurs. One month after the Eisenberg-Lawrence visit—followed, incredibly, by a quick visit by Dr. Fine to treat a surviving burn victim— the Chilean military regime released from jail many of its political prisoners, including the President and Secretary General of the Colegio Medico, most of the Catholic organization workers and the physician who had returned from exile. From Dr. Fine's perspective, the reason for the government's humanitarian gesture was a clear result of "the effort of physicians around the world to bring attention to these cases." He added that "such attention threatened to weaken support for the Pinochet government from international economic institutions."[11] Dr. Fine perceptively had grasped the significance of the leverage offered by international economic institutions in which the United States exercised a powerful influence. A key State Department official on Latin America, Assistant Secretary Elliott Abrams, told a House of Representatives panel in late July, 1986 that the United States would vote against new loans to Chile totaling $250 million from the World Bank to "protest persistent human rights abuses and failure to move toward democracy."[12] It was scarcely typical of the Reagan Administration's posture on Latin America.

PHR's involvement with Chilean repression, while a maiden voyage, laid the foundation for PHR prominence and effectiveness in the human rights field. Its officers had made seven trips to that country in two years, including a trip to Santiago by its President, Dr. Jane Schaller, in April, 1988, to observe the delayed court trials of the Chilean medical organization officials.[13] A detailed report documenting its concern and, more importantly, its evidence was published in 1988, entitled *Sowing Fear: The Uses of Torture and Psychological Abuse in Chile*, it received considerable attention in the media.[14]

The unique medical expertise of PHR, in its initial years, also was tested in South Korea and in Iraqi Kurdistan. In 1987, it sent an epidemiologist to the former to evaluate the effect of tear gas, which the military rulers were using against demonstrators.[15] The PHR specialist found that the extensive use of the gas produced a health hazard and that it resembled the category of "excessive use of force." A new area of investigatory work had opened for the organization.

During the following year, the focal point of medical inquiry came to center on the Kurds of Iraq. PHR sent a team of scientists to Kurdish refugee camps who ascertained that Baghdad had used poison gas. The Boston NGO created a Working Group on Chemical and Biological Weapons, whose findings led to the publication of an important work by the organization: *Winds of Death: Iraq's Use of Poison Gas Against Its Kurdish Population.* In testimony before a Senate committee, PHR urged Congress to "reintroduce legislation against Iraq for its breach of the international agreement banning uses of chemical weapons and for its gross violation of human rights."

Especially impressed by PHR's work, Aryeh Neier of Human Rights Watch had initiated a collaborative effort between the two groups.[16] Jointly, they later would have specialists in forensic medicine examine mass graves to ascertain genocidal intent and practice of the Iraqis. In 1992 a PHR team collected soil samples that, after chemical examination, enabled the group to demonstrate that Baghdad was using lethal nerve agents against Kurdish villagers.

The most significant contribution of PHR came during the "ethnic cleansing" campaign by Serbs against Bosnian Muslims beginning in 1992. Its pioneering work in forensic medicine and the exhumation of grave sites would attract authoritative attention and lead to a special, indeed unique, relationship with the International Criminal Tribunal in The Hague. What made this kind of work critical to the human rights field in general, and to the specific problem of accountability, later would be made clear by a PHR staff official, Barbara Ayotte, who was in charge of programming and communication. Forensic evidence, she said, was "the most powerful weapon to be used in our mission to ensure personal responsibility when prosecuting." She went on to observe that "bodies don't lie . . . and physical evidence is a lot harder to refute than [oral or written] testimony."[17]

As early as 1990, PHR had become aware of Yugoslavia's ethnic problems and the ruthlessness of the Milosevic regime in responding particularly to the Albanian minority. In that year, 11 Serbian prison guards were charged with abusing Albanian prison inmates. PHR sent a delegation to observe the trials.[18]

The forensic team that PHR assembled was impressive. The Director of the program was Dr. Robert Kirschner. A top-level associate was William Haglund, who was a forensic anthropologist specializing in developing legal evidence from human bones. The team also included John Fitzpatrick, a leading expert on forensic radiology, and Clyde Snow, who had collaborated with Kirschner in identifying victims in a famous case involving a serial killer. The new top PHR professional, Eric Stover, played a central role. A medical writer, Stover had succeeded Jonathan Fine as Executive Director of the organization in 1993, a position he would hold until 1996. Stover had worked with Kirschner in the mid-eighties investigating the earlier killings of dissidents in Argentina by the previous military rulers. Their evidence helped convict eight top-level military officers for mass murder.[19]

The exhumation of graves and the gathering of evidence at the site by experts was of vital importance to the prosecution at the Tribunal in The Hague. Professor Cherif Bassiouni, the Chairman of the UN Commission of Experts, emphasized the significance of forensic evidence in a report to the American Bar Association. It would be able to pinpoint the precise location of the grave sites, and it could help identify the bodies of the victims and determine whether they were combatants or civilians.[20] Bassiouni also believed that the digging up of mass graves could be a means of "bring[ing] the two [opposing] parties together to establish some form of cooperation and eventual reconciliation." The vision was more than a bit optimistic. Ken Roth of HRW, whose training had been in prosecutorial legal work, called the forensic investigation "actually a revolutionary moment in the history of the human rights movement."[21]

What made forensic science especially valuable from a legal viewpoint was that, in part, it relied on statistical probability. The forensic scientists need but prove that a random sample of the exhumed bodies were shot and it could be legally demonstrated that all the bodies were shot. While the human rights movement and the NGOs comprising it relied upon the imposition of moral and economic pressures on murderous governments, with forensic science, the evidence could assure that those responsible might very well be brought before a court. In March, 1996, PHR's forensic labors helped indict 3 senior Serbian army officers for the mass killing of 261 wounded soldiers and civilians, along with hospital staff and others.[22] But the NGO's work was still only beginning. During that year PHR teams were busy exhuming mass grave sites in the

Former Yugoslavia, most notably at the notorious Srebrenica site. Recognition by its colleagues in the medical profession had reached a high point; the popular medical journal, *Lancet,* noted in May, 1996 that local physicians may be reluctant to raise or provide evidence of abuses lest they themselves be confronted by the threat of torture or death. It went on to add that the work of PHR "in coordinating investigations by teams from outside" can fulfill a scientific obligation while, at the same time, providing support for "doctors and others who wish to examine in closer detail episodes of violence or extrajudicial execution. . . ."[23]

It was at The Hague that appreciation was the greatest. The Tribunal's Chief Prosecutor, Richard Goldstone, commented on PHR forensic work in this way: "An investigation of this nature, when performed by highly qualified experts of the caliber used by PHR, will yield supporting evidence that will be of considerable value to the prosecution." Perhaps not surprisingly, PHR was the only American-based NGO to be singled out for mention in the Tribunal's annual report to the UN Security Council. The other NGO mentioned was a Norwegian group.

PHR forensic experts, as they gathered evidence in the field, had to cope with the often ferocious anger of local Bosnian Serbs. Frequently, an observer noted, they had to be "escorted by a bustling contingent of NATO troops" while NATO aircraft "buzzed overhead to deter any attack. . . ."[24] In some cases, the NATO military forces in Bosnia were reluctant to guard the grave sites or remove surrounding mines "so investigators can search for evidence."[25]

The ethnic cleansing in Bosnia in 1992-96 soon would find an echo in the genocide of the Rwandan Tutsis by the Hutus in the spring of 1994, and PHR was called upon by the International Criminal Tribunal for Rwanda to investigate. No other NGO was equipped with the expertise and experience of PHR. In December, 1995, it sent a team headed by Kirschner and Haglund and including 15 other experts. They gathered evidence from mass graves containing over 500 bodies. Included in their investigation was the largest mass grave exhumation ever conducted. More than half of the victims were under the age of 18.[26] The governor of the area was quoted as saying "killing with impunity has been part of the tradition in this country . . . We have to eradicate this culture. . . ."[27]

The evidence accumulated by PHR was able to document the premise that the mass killings of Tutsis by the Hutu leadership constituted genocide, rather than being merely the results of civil war. From the forensic evidence, it was clear that the victims offered no resistance. The team found, in fact, that the legs of many of the victims had been hacked by machetes in order to immobilize them until the genocidists could return to finish them off. Most victims in Rwanda were killed either by machetes or clubs. So vast was the genocide—over one-half million—that PHR did not expect to identify more than 10 percent of the bodies as compared with an expected 50 percent in the Former Yugoslavia.[28]

Even while preoccupied with genocide, the PHR leadership and staff already were preparing the organization's three-year program plan for the years 1994-97. Though only started in 1986, it had acquired an impressive amount of experience that would help in determining the direction it wished to go and the priorities it should assume. The plan, published in April, 1994 set forth several "precepts" that would guide its "program priorities."[29] Strikingly, the plan emphasized as the top priority "medical and forensic fact-finding missions" that were considered to be "the driving force" of the organization. Coincidentally, that same month the genocide in Rwanda was launched, which would rather quickly, at the behest of the Tribunal, bring PHR into the picture.

The other "program priorities" of the plan included a general human rights one for establishing "accountability" for abuses and advocating measures to "prevent future abuses." More specific to the organization's character was a proposed program requiring it to "assist medical organizations to investigate abuses in their own countries." Finally, the plan stressed education, or rather "training" activities, by which it meant the training of medical personnel to assume various human rights functions.

In listing these priorities, the plan at the same time stressed that certain types of abuses would be a primary concern of the organization, such as extrajudicial executions, torture, and cruel and inhuman or degrading punishment—traditional concerns of human rights NGOs. But of special interest would be violations of medical neutrality and the use of antipersonnel land mines. These were regarded as particularly relevant to a physicians' NGO. At the same time, it was recognized, no listing of priorities can substitute for the objective reality of the outside world. "PHR's program priorities," the plan read, "have been largely dictated by its response to . . . crises around the world."[30] And so it would be in the future. The organization took special pride in having "developed a reputation [as a group] that responded quickly to emergencies." That sense of pride would continue to be actively cultivated.

A leading priority concern of PHR from the early nineties was land mines.[31] Together with Asia Watch, in 1991 a PHR team went to Cambodia and reported that this Southeast Asian country had an extraordinary number of amputee victims from land mines—about 36,000. The two organizations presented their findings to the U.S. Congress, which had begun to draft foreign aid legislation that would link economic aid to the removal of land mines.[32] The findings became the basis for an article in a specialized journal of the American College of Surgeons that could not but focus broad attention of the medical profession upon PHR.[33]

During the following year a PHR team visited Somalia and learned about the existence of 1,500,000 land mines with few prostheses available and the training for carrying out amputations minimal.[34] In 1994, PHR experts were in Mozambique, documenting the extensive character of land mine injuries that affected civilians, not those engaged in fighting the internal civil war. Three-quarters of the afflicted were civilians and 60 percent of them were without prostheses. The team estimated that it would cost $30 million annually for the next ten years to locate and remove the mines in Mozambique.[35]

PHR's technical and scientific expertise became an invaluable asset to the worldwide campaign to ban land mines that began in 1992. No other organization could involve the medical world in the struggle in the way PHR could through key articles in medical journals. Two examples are illustrative. One, in *Lancet,* documented the extent of damage done by land mines in Mozambique.[36] The second appeared in a highly technical orthopedics journal.[37] While the HRW/Arms Project, as noted earlier, occupied a central leadership role in that campaign, PHR also played a vital part. Together, they published in 1993 *Landmines: A Deadly Legacy,* which summarized the evidence compiled in missions to Cambodia, Angola, Mozambique, Somalia and Iraqi Kurdistan. Alone, PHR prepared the information brochure and media kit for the campaign's first major international conference, held in 1994.[38] Within the United States, during 1995, it lobbied intensively through letter-writing and petitions on behalf of the Landmines Use Moratorium Act, which was adopted that year by Congress as part of the Foreign Operations Appropriation Bill.[39]

As an organization that worked very closely with the Steering Committee of the International Campaign to Ban Landmines, it fulfilled an early priority obligation. And it accomplished this task in the distinctive manner of scientists who amassed data, which lent credibility to the campaign. PHR's ultimate objective was made clear by one of its staff officials, Barbara Ayotte, who told the *Boston Globe* that it sought to "make [the] use of personnel mines a war crime."[40] Efforts by PHR and others to prevail upon the Clinton Administration to join in an international treaty to ban land mines were unsuccessful. The group publicly chastised the Administration in September, 1997 for being "in the unpleasant company of such landmine abusers as India, China and Russia who also refuse to sign [the treaty]."[41]

Turkey in the nineties came to be of special concern. The military in that regime had acquired a notoriety for involving physicians in torture. A study published by the Boston NGO in August 1996, the results of which were carried in the leading American medical journal, underscored the validity of the negative reputation.[42] Interviews in the survey were conducted with physicians who had examined those subjected to torture in Turkey. Also interviewed were those who had been tortured. Medical reports of the latter were examined as well. The results strongly suggested that Turkish physicians who had examined prisoners were forced to ignore, misrepresent or omit evidence of torture. Surveys of this type were not likely to have a legal impact upon the Ankara government. The authorities contended that, since Turkey had not signed a Geneva Protocol covering this issue, it had no obligation to become involved.[43] On the other had, press coverage of the PHR study could not fail to exert a moral impact. The image of Turkey was certain to be affected.

Mistreatment of doctors, whether in Chile or Turkey, is a matter of constant PHR attention. The organization's membership is regularly informed by "Medical Alerts" about these cases that appear in its monthly house organ. Intervention by key members or specialists or prominent medical bodies may follow and prove productive.

In the case of Ankara, PHR found an ally in the Turkish Medical Association, which diligently had labored to document physician involvement in torture. The Association also provided forensic training for doctors.[44] That function also was undertaken by PHR itself in Turkey in 1995.[45]

The scientific skill of PHR members could be called upon for other purposes that served the interests of the United Nations. The international organization, which had been directly involved in ending the ferocious civil war in El Salvador, was seeking assistance for a humanitarian purpose. During the civil war, many children had been taken from their peasant families and had been subsequently adopted or placed in an orphanage. When a particular mother believed she had located her son, PHR was asked to do DNA testing, which resulted in a happy outcome.[46] PHR's Dr. Robert Kirschner characterized this testing as one of the organization's special talents. In dealing with poor countries, he said, it "makes up for the lack of official birth records and footprints for children separated from their parents at a very early age."[47]

Even while assuming an activist role in the international human rights field, PHR places great emphasis upon education. It regards one of its prime missions to be the holding of "educational and training projects for health professionals, members of the judiciary, and human rights advocates on the application of medical and forensic skills in the investigation of violations of human rights."[48] Its *Annual Report* of 1994 noted that every year, PHR officials and members gave some 40 presentations at universities, medical schools, or scientific conferences both in the United States and in foreign countries.[49] Specifically noted in that report was that PHR had convened a conference in Turkey on forensic methods of investigating torture and organized a seminar in Cambodia for prison health officials. Particularly important was a seminar in The Hague, which covered the medico-legal investigation of war crimes as well as the psychological aspects of working with victims and witnesses of human rights abuses.

The teaching even would have a Boston base. The 1994 report noted that the organization had helped develop at Harvard Medical School a course entitled "Human Rights and Medicine," covering torture and land mines, along with refugee health and political asylum. No doubt, the addition of the new course could be facilitated by the presence at Harvard of several key officials of PHR.

From its base in the prominent medical complex of Boston universities, PHR has considerably expanded, numbering close to 5,000 members by 1997. Two-thirds of the membership were doctors, the rest being scientists and other professionals.[50] With a budget of $1.4 million (in 1995), a staff of 12, and branches in the United Kingdom, Denmark, Israel and the Netherlands, PHR considers itself as still in a growing stage. Work has begun on establishing chapters in Asia and Africa. Under its recently chosen executive director, Leonard Rubenstein, a lawyer who had headed a center for mental health in Washington, D.C., the organization has been planning a significant expansion of its membership as well as income.[51]

Membership growth is crucial. Currently 25 percent of PHR's income comes from its members. PHR believes, in order to become "financially stable," at least 50 percent of its annual income must come from membership dues and individual member donations. Major foundations, in addition to Ford, have provided the NGO with funding. These include the MacArthur Foundation, John Merck Fund, Open

Society, Reebok and Joyce Mertz-Gilmore. Clearly, the reputation it already has established augurs well for the future.

What made the organization especially critical was its role in connection with war crimes Tribunals, particularly the one dealing with the Former Yugoslavia. Eric Stover explained why: "It's easy to call for war crimes trials and justice, but without specific evidence of specific crimes by specific commands, we'll never bring criminals to justice."[52] And much of the crucial evidence was provided by the forensic expertise of PHR. Yet, remarkably little public attention was paid to PHR's forensic work in Rwanda in contrast to its similar role in Bosnia. Indeed, the genocide of the Tutsis in Rwanda evoked little public concern in general. Even in the black community, oddly enough, no apparent impact publicly was felt. The seeming lack of interest aroused fears among several of the leading human rights advocacy groups, including PHR, that support on behalf of the International Criminal Tribunal for Rwanda, whether in the United States or elsewhere, could dissipate at the expense of accountability for the crime of genocide.

To correct this anomaly, the Coalition for International Justice, of which PHR was a key member, undertook a special responsibility.[53] An unusual briefing was presented by the Coalition on the Rwanda Tribunal case to a joint meeting of the Congressional Human Rights Caucus and the Congressional Black Caucus held on June 6, 1996. Written by the Coalition's Director, John Heffernan, although delivered by Nasser Ega-Musa, the testimony sought to emphasize the need "to bring international justice to Africa."[54]

The testimony stressed that the very existence of the Tribunal, based in Arusha, Tanzania, with the Prosecutor's office located in Kigali, Rwanda, would "send a message to the people of Africa that there is hope for redress" for those victimized by murderous regimes engaged in genocidal attacks on people because of their ethnicity or religion. After taking particular note of the "brutal wars ravaging the African continent from Liberia to Somalia and from Sudan to Burundi, the witness drove home the point that "the success of the Rwandan Tribunal has far-reaching implications." Current and future African leaders, *at long last,* would learn that there are "consequences to committing crimes against humanity."

For the Tribunal to even begin to achieve its purpose, according to the testimony, the "world needs to know that it exists." Lack of public attention in the United States "can only lead to the common perception that it has taken a back seat to the Yugoslav Tribunal" and to the "misleading conclusion" that "maintaining the rule of law" in Africa is "less important" than "maintaining it" in Europe. That public indifference in the United States could subvert the rule of law and, thereby, encourage further barbarities in Africa was underscored. Heffernan pointed out that many of the so-called "Big Fish" who had organized or led the genocidal attacks had fled to Zaire and Kenya, where "they appear to be welcome."

Consequently, it was "imperative" to have those nations harboring alleged war criminals understand how they seriously could be affected by their "disregard" of "international obligations." The reference here was to the U.S. Foreign Operations Appropriation Act of 1996, which denied bilateral U.S. economic aid and required the United States to veto aid from international financial institutions to those countries granting sanctuary to indicted war criminals. Congress was called upon to insist that the Clinton Administration enforce this provision. The legislative body also was asked to include the provision in the 1997 appropriations bill and to make clear to the UN that "full and adequate funding" for the Tribunal was "imperative."

What made the testimony unusually striking was its inclusion of basic information that apparently had not previously registered. For example, it contended that over 800,000 people systematically were killed in the course of 100 days during 1994, a rate "nearly three times the rate of those killed during the Holocaust." The staggering numbers meant that the carnage of World War II inevitably "pales in comparison to the genocide in Rwanda." Unless the world grasped the horrors of that genocide and assisted the Tribunal in its "precedent setting" task, it was "in danger of being relegated to a mere footnote in history."

Other statistical data in the testimony also were helpful in communicating the extent of the problem. Of some 400 successful leading genocidists, few if any were in the hands of the Tribunal. Only 11 had, as yet, been indicted; a handful of others were being held in custody in Europe or elsewhere. Rwanda itself was said to hold 70,000 persons in prison awaiting trial. With its legal system virtually in tatters—since so many judges, jurists and lawyers were victims of the genocide—it was difficult to conceive of a significant or meaningful resolution of the legal crisis.

The Coalition vigorously would pursue its determination to "raise the issue" of the Rwandan profile, as Heffernan explained in an interview.[55] The initial focus was upon the black community in the United States. Aside from addressing the Congressional Black Caucus, Heffernan wrote a letter on June 25, 1996 to the 135 members of the National Bar Association who served in its International Law Section.[56]

The letter was suggested by Beverly Baker-Kelly, the Chair of the International Law Section.[57] After describing the Coalition's general function, Heffernan concentrated upon the Rwanda Tribunal and the hope it encouraged to "break the cycle of violence and retribution that has fueled waves of genocide in Rwanda."

Heffernan frankly acknowledged that he sought the assistance of black specialists in international law in "raising the profile of the Rwandan Tribunal." He noted that "the world focuses its attention on The Hague," where Bosnian crimes are targeted, while "the equally historic proceedings occurring in Arusha, Tanzania are being ignored." If the Rwanda Tribunal represented "a radical advancement in the rule of law in Africa," he appealed to the professionals in the African American legal community to "assume a personal responsibility for the advancement of the cause of justice in Africa." He invited them to volunteer their services for the Tribunal and to seek out ways to educate and inform the American black community on the significance of the Tribunal.

In a closing comment, Heffernan stressed that the Tribunal was crucial for advancing the rule of law and the search for justice "in a part of the world where these concepts have long been mere promises." How much of an impact Heffernan's appeal had is not known, but he was committed to involving, if possible, the black community of the United States and, therewith, pressing Washington to be as forthcoming as possible on the Arusha Tribunal. Heffernan may very well have been thinking of the key role played by the black civil rights movement in energizing the antiapartheid campaign of the seventies and eighties. He chose to go beyond addressing black lawyers and send a direct message to the black community. Several weeks after the testimony to black Congressmen and lawyers, Heffernan wrote a special op-ed essay for the largest black newspaper in the United States, the *New York Amsterdam News*.[58] It was a moving piece, describing in a very personalized way the terrible character of the atrocities in Rwanda and how "justice for war criminals in Rwanda" might stay "the hand of the next warlord or despot." The need for public attention and support for the Arusha Tribunal was given strong emphasis, for it could reinforce the slogan of "Never Again!" and even possibly "change the world."

The Coalition's Update of its *Annual Report* issued on July 21, 1997 took note of an effort to give exposure to the documentary film *The Devil's Children,* which examined the systematic rape of women of all ages in Rwanda by the Hutus. The film, which was found "compelling," was sponsored by Human Rights Watch.[59] More importantly, the

Update recounted how the Coalition and its constituents had pressed Congress to approve, despite Administration opposition, The War Crimes Prosecution Facilitation Act, which conditions nonhumanitarian aid to countries on their compliance with the Tribunal's requirement that war criminals be apprehended and turned over to the Tribunal.[60]

Precisely because little was known about the structure and function of the Tribunal for Rwanda and how it differed from the one on Yugoslavia, in the fall of 1997, the Coalition prepared a special fact sheet on the subject that was widely distributed, especially among legislators, lawyers and human rights activists.[61] Especially noted was the fact that both Tribunals share the same Chief Prosecutor and a five-judge appellate chamber, but they have different administrative officers—called Registrars—and Deputy Prosecutors. The Tribunal of Rwanda has, as its President—the equivalent of a Chief Justice—an African, Laity Kama of Senegal.

At the time the fact sheet was prepared the Rwanda Tribunal had indicted 23 persons, 14 of whom were being held in custody in the Tribunal's facility in Arusha. The apprehended included 3 officials of the previous Hutu government accused of having masterminded the genocide of the Tutsis. That record of apprehension was quite good as compared with the Yugoslav Tribunal. At the same time, the Rwanda Tribunal was plagued by financial and administrative difficulties. Rwanda itself, in contrast to Arusha, was to handle the lesser war criminals. A staggering total of 90,000 were in jail awaiting trial. As of March 1, 1997, 11 were sentenced to death and 16 to life imprisonment. Rendering justice here hardly was expected to be easy.

The administrative difficulties to which the update report referred were partly due to the inexperience as well as the less than adequate facilities in Arusha. But the principal problem, as the Coalition recognized early on and complained about, lay in the lack of skill, integrity and professionalism of top-level personnel.[62] The report of an extensive investigation of the Tribunal by the Office of International Oversight Services, released by the UN Secretary-General on February 6, 1997, was devastating.[63] It found "serious operational deficiencies in the management of the Tribunal." Spelled out were a host of such deficiencies including the fact that "personnel in key positions did not have the required qualifications."

Not only was the administrative apparatus—the Registrar and his staff—severely criticized, but also the Office of the Prosecutor in Kigali was accused of "administrative, leadership and operational problems," including "lack of experienced staff." In addition, the respective offices of Registrar and Prosecutor were "characterized by tension rather than cooperation."

The report concluded that if the UN means "to keep its promises to the Rwandan victims of genocide," then the Secretary-General must assume the "task of ensuring that the body established to bring to justice the persons responsible for such grievous crimes becomes fully functional."

For the Coalition, as well as for Physicians for Human Rights, Human Rights Watch and the International Human Rights Law Group, the report was considered invaluable. They joined in a letter to Secretary-General Kofi Annan on February 20, 1997 calling for "urgent action" on his part, including "the replacement of senior officials with qualified, competent personnel."[64] The letter stressed that the UN's crucial judicial function "will have failed if effective measures are not taken to ensure that the Tribunal is able to bring to justice those responsible for the Rwanda genocide." In a separate release the same day, the Coalition and the other three groups specifically called for the "firing" of the Tribunal's Administrator and Deputy Prosecutor.[65] Six days later, Secretary-General Annan fired the two.[66]

Other matters related to the efficiency and effectiveness of the Rwanda Tribunal also troubled the Coalition and its constituent groups. One especially concerned PHR, whose forensic scientists were made available gratis the UN. A formal report by the Secretary-General to the General Assembly that addressed the subject of reform called for the phasing out over time of the use of "gratis personnel." In a letter addressed to Kofi Annan on August 7, 1997, the Coalition and its constituents pointed out "that the unique nature of the Tribunals makes the use of gratis personnel particularly critical to their survival and success."[67]

The letter went on to explain that the Tribunal requires "very highly-specialized personnel" at proper levels of seniority and, at the same time, cannot offer permanent UN posts to such personnel. A General Assembly resolution was cited in the letter to the effect that "without the early infusion of gratis personnel, the Tribunals might not have survived."[68] On the same day—August 7, 1997—the Coalition prepared for a key House of Representatives figure, Congressman Donald Payne, a strong resolution calling upon the Administration to provide various types of support for the Tribunal. Two demands stand out: that the President of the United States should instruct the U.S. representative to the UN to use America's power in the Security Council to "ensure that . . . indicted individuals are apprehended and prosecuted"; and that the United States should oppose all international institution loans to those countries failing "to apprehend indicted persons and otherwise cooperate with the Tribunal."

The relationship between the Coalition and the Administration became closer when its Chairman, Thomas Warrick, took a position as deputy to the recently appointed Ambassador-at-Large on War Crimes, David Scheffer. The new and unprecedented ambassadorship was the creation of Madeleine Albright and indicated her strong commitment to making accountability work in preventing genocide and other crimes against humanity. Scheffer had been Albright's legal adviser while she served as Ambassador to the UN. Now his office in the State Department was put on the seventh floor, near Albright's own office, testifying to the priority concern of the Secretary of State. In September, 1997, Scheffer made certain that what he and his boss stood for would be implanted on the Rwandan mind as well as upon the world's conscience.

He deliberately visited a hillside where a field of crosses defined the site of the mass slaughter of Tutsis by Hutus. A front-page story in the *New York Times* with the headline "Making Sure War Crimes Aren't Forgotten" gave poignancy to the U.S. commitment.[69] Scheffer was challenged by a prominent Rwandan radio broadcaster about American intent with respect to punishing those responsible. "I think there is a lack of moral commitment by the U.S.," said the broadcaster. Scheffer, acknowledging that he had to cope with allegations of irrelevance, told the *Times* correspondent: "It is my responsibility to demonstrate this is more than symbolic."

While PHR was in the forefront of the joint NGO initiative of keeping the issue of accountability for genocide in Rwanda on the international agenda, it would not retreat from its determination also to focus U.S. and world attention upon the massacres perpetrated by Kabila's armies and their allies. UN agencies continued to report that 120,000 refugees from Rwanda were missing. PHR's documentation was augmented in October, 1997 by a detailed investigative report presented publicly by Human Rights Watch/Africa and the International Federation of Human Rights Leagues, based in Paris, which obliged authorities to take notice.[70]

During a six-week mission, the two organizations collected what their joint release called "irrefutable physical evidence of massacres of refugees" by Kabila's troops, including his Rwandan military units. The investigators were able to photograph mass graves and the decomposing remains of civilian refugees in a remote region of the Congo. Another critical finding of the mission was documentation of "concerted efforts to conceal the evidence of civilian killings." This was part of a major campaign by Kabila's forces "to cover up" civilian killings throughout Congo, largely through the physical cleansing of massacre sites and by the intimidation of witnesses.[71]

Besides the disclosure of the damning evidence, the study carefully reviewed what the UN and United States did and did not do about the reports of the massacres. The review was fairly objective in characterizing the difficulties confronting, for example, the United States in shaping policy. "Torn between concerns for the stability and territorial integrity of Congo," the United States, with a desire to resolve the refugee problem, "long remained silent on the massacres and obfuscated important questions. . . ."[72] What the evidence seemed to show was that the United States provided backing for Kabila's forces, a conclusion "strongly reinforced by revelations of U.S. military aid to Rwanda." In this connection, it cited the testimony of Physicians for Human Rights before the House International Relations Committee on July 16, 1997.

In the end, the United States the study showed, took a positive role in publicly informing Kabila that his failing to act "in a credible and a humanitarian way with respect to the proposed investigatory mission by the UN could damage his standing in the international community." Delays by Kabila would not be tolerated. Ambassador-at-Large for War Crimes David Scheffer warned that U.S. aid to the Congo was "contingent on [its] cooperation with the U.N. investigating team."[73]

By the middle of 1998, it was not clear how and whether accountability could be achieved with respect to the gross, perhaps genocidal, abuses of Kabila's insurgents. Kofi Annan has withdrawn the UN investigatory team because of Kabila's harassment of its members and his resistance to the investigation. What was clear was that an initial inquiry by Physicians for Human Rights that was limited to the atrocities committed by Kabila's troops, including supporting elements from Rwanda, had opened up questions that had yet to be answered. One thing was certain: the attitude and conduct of the U.S. Embassy in Kigali was certain to be changed. It was PHR that first disclosed in a testimony to Congress how that Embassy rejected any information about the reported atrocities and, generally, engaged in a whitewash. The NGO community considered the Embassy's conduct unacceptable and intolerable, a view it communicated to Secretary of State Albright and several of her top associates, including Undersecretary Thomas Pickering. The meeting at which this information was disclosed took place on November 5, 1997 and the response of both Albright and Pickering to the report on the Kigali Embassy was one of surprise and dismay. It was the only time during the 70-minute meeting that the embarrassment flowing from ignorance was registered. To the NGOs, it was an encouraging indication of human rights sensitivity.

Mrs. Roosevelt's NGO Takes on New Dimensions: Freedom House's Changing Priorities

Religious freedom long had been a concern of the NGO community, and disclosures of religious discrimination and religious oppression always had appeared in their annual reports and specialized studies. But the subject was never the touchstone of how a society was measured, nor was it seen as a priority issue on their respective human rights agendas. In mid-1997, by an extraordinary—if totally unexpected—development, it was catapulted onto center stage at least in the United States, which meant that, inevitably, the subject would become an international concern. The Clinton Administration was fully preoccupied with the issue, Congress was seized with the preparation of draft legislation, often controversial, which was intended to combat religious repression and the NGO community found itself playing "catch-up" in sometimes embarrassing and frequently conflicting ways. How this remarkable series of developments occurred and promised to reach an even higher priority level in the future was largely the work of Freedom House, America's oldest human rights NGO.

Its reputation lay elsewhere—not in human rights advocacy but rather in the promotion of freedom and free societies, in combating totalitarianism and in helping build institutions that were central to freedom, particularly freedom of the press. From its very beginning, the organization held aloft its name—Freedom House—and rarely used the phrase "human rights," although it regarded civil rights and political rights to be at the core of freedom.

Freedom House was born on October 31, 1941 during the dark days of World War II when Nazi totalitarianism and its Fascist Italian partner already had swept democracy from much of Europe and were threatening to conquer the Soviet Union, while their ally in Asia, Imperial Japan, was engaged in destroying the colonial empires of Britain and France even as it sought to subdue all of China. If the Administration of Franklin D. Roosevelt was providing essential help to the bastion of freedom in England, it was confronted by the serious internal problem of isolationism that threatened to subvert America's activism on behalf of freedom.

The establishment of Freedom House was a response to that threat and, indeed, it was prompted by President Roosevelt himself. As recalled by a former Executive Director of Freedom House, Leonard Sussman, the President had called to the White House the leaders of two separate organizations comprised of prominent citizens, created in the late thirties to oppose Nazi aggression, Fight For Freedom and the Committee to Defend America by Aiding the Allies.[1] Apparently, the President wanted to see the two united in order to more effectively provide "citizen support for his troubled efforts to bring America into effective opposition to Nazism and Fascism." Roosevelt, Sussman confided, was "winking knowingly" when he pleaded for "citizen support." The message was clear. "Freedom House was created to provide that support," said Sussman. Thus was born the oldest American-based NGO dealing at least in part with human rights. Not until the following year—1942— was the International League for the Rights of Man established.

For the principal founders of Freedom House—columnist Dorothy Thompson, publisher Herbert Agar and its first Executive Director, George Field—nothing was more compelling than the struggle against totalitarianism, support of Britain in its lonely fight against the Axis and a greater involvement of the United States in the fight for democracy. Combating isolationism and promoting an activist foreign policy on behalf of democracy would remain central to its very existence from its birth to the present. Further, it was to act as "a headquarters and clearinghouse for organizations enlisted in the fight for freedom, whether at home or abroad," and to serve as "a coordinating center . . . to make the symbolism of Freedom House plain to the world."[2]

Pressure for Lend-Lease assistance to Britain accompanied the call for greater American participation in the struggle against the Berlin-Rome-

Tokyo Axis. After Pearl Harbor, of course, the initial purpose of promoting the war effort was greatly eased. Freedom House now would be engaged in a massive information and education campaign unique for an NGO at the time. It sponsored a vast number of booklets, speeches, broadcasts and manifestos written by the country's leading authors—Archibald MacLeish, Pearl Buck, Walter Lippman, Norman Cousins, Stephen Vincent Benet and Lewis Mumford.[3] In 1942 alone, the NGO arranged more than 180 broadcasts. Still, the founders of Freedom House already were looking beyond the war. Mindful of the outcome of World War I, they planned for a postwar effort to foster democracy in Europe.

On the occasion of the organization's fiftieth anniversary, its Board Chairman, Max Kampelman, recalled that, at its founding, "in the dark days" when "the very concept of democracy" was "under attack," Freedom House "immediately became a lively participant in the titanic struggles of this century."[4] Among these struggles with which it was involved, besides the Marshall Plan, were support of the Truman Doctrine, support of NATO and support of the United Nations. Americans were not alone in according praise for Freedom House's efforts on behalf of the Western Allies. Winston Churchill and Charles de Gaulle expressed support for its initiatives.[5]

Significantly, the Honorary Chair of Freedom House from the moment of its founding was Eleanor Roosevelt. It was the only NGO in which she occupied an official post, even if honorary. That she was very much cognizant of the organization's activity was clear, as was her willingness to share with it her problems at the UN Commission on Human Rights.[6] When Freedom House presented its annual award to Bernard Baruch for his atomic control plan, Mrs. Roosevelt made the formal presentation. Similarly, a balance between business and trade unions was brought onto the Board, along with leaders from the media, academia and the community at large. Prestigious, if small in numbers, the elite leadership would carry weight with the public and the government. That balance of interest groups would be continued into the present.

The Roosevelt influence at its origin did not mean that the organization was designed as a Democratic Party instrument. From its very beginning, Freedom House sought to have a 50-50 split between Democrats and Republicans on its Board. Thus Wendell Willkie, Roosevelt's challenger for President, served as a prominent member of the organization's leadership.

In 1947, while working at the UN Commission for the draft of the Universal Declaration of Human Rights, Mrs. Roosevelt told a Freedom

House forum that Soviet strategists were using negative reports about racial discrimination in the United States to disparage American human rights advocacy at the UN.[7] Indeed, the Soviets were planning at the time, she said, to introduce a specific clause in the Declaration condemning racial discrimination in the expectation that it would be opposed by the United States. This information may have prompted Freedom House to step up its domestic activities to oppose discrimination within the United States. Already, during the war, the organization had called for an end to discrimination within the defense industry and within the armed forces.

When Freedom House opened its new building, the Willkie Memorial Building, it chose to invite organizations that were fighting for the "elimination of racial and religious antagonism [and] advancement of the Negro people" to use its premises.[8] Thus, the offices of the National Association for the Advancement of Colored People (NAACP) and the National Council on Civil Rights came to be housed in the Willkie headquarters of Freedom House. In 1949, Freedom House gave the racial discrimination issue a high priority on its agenda with a five-point program calling upon Congress to enact legislation banning lynching and providing for equal opportunity in education and employment.

With the onset of the Cold War, Freedom House's principal target became crystal clear: the Soviet Union and its satellites in East Europe. The contrast between freedom and totalitarianism was sharply defined. The phrase "human rights" was much less the focus of its attention as was the term "freedom." That America would be seen as the bulwark against totalitarianism was unavoidable. The organization's function was perceived as acting as a kind of moral compass for the government, a vote of conscience that continued to support or urge U.S. intervention to promote democracy and freedom. In this connection, it should be noted that Freedom House, "from its very inception, rejected all forms of pacifism" and that, faced with a choice between peace and freedom, it would choose the latter.[9]

In the struggle against totalitarianism, Freedom House created one of its most valuable institutions, which has continued until today to be a basic source—if not the basic source—of information about the political character of individual countries throughout the globe. In 1955, the "Balance Sheet of Freedom" was established. It was designed to serve as an annual review of gains and losses in the area of freedom during the previous year. By the sixties, the annual survey of the progress of freedom assumed the name *Freedom in the World; The Annual Survey of Political Rights and Civil Liberties.*

Of the survey's significance, there could be little doubt. It was the first attempt to establish a single standard for the measurement and rating of freedom and civil liberties in all nations. Publicizing the disparities in freedom could not fail to focus public attention upon the countries that ranked low and to spur their citizenry to become more activist in order to correct or improve poor ratings. The surveys measured not the form of government, not the constitution nor the basic laws that prevailed in a country, but rather the actual or real situation that existed in any given country.

Survey editors defined "freedom" as involving real-life institutions that, in fact, "enable people to participate freely in the political process." What is measured is whether a "system is genuinely free or democratic to the extent that people have a choice in determining the nature of the system and its leaders." Civil liberties were defined as "the freedoms to develop views, institutions and personal autonomy apart from the state." The definitions included language that John Stuart Mill would have recognized. A checklist of indicators for these rights and liberties was and is used to determine the degree of freedom present in each country. Each country is then rated as "free," "partly free," or "not free." The survey today covers 191 countries and 59 dependent territories. For much of the year, Freedom House employs its several regional or geographic specialists, along with outside experts, to prepare the annual review.

With every Communist country ranked in the lowest category of freedom and civil liberties, it was hardly surprising that the survey would serve until the late eighties as a powerful propaganda weapon against the Soviet Union and its satellites. Indeed, the survey had value above and beyond the struggle against communism. It could serve as a basis for judgment about individual non-Communist countries, particularly those in the Third World. Such judgments had special relevance for analysts seeking to evaluate attitudes of governmental representatives at the UN or in other international organs. Scholars and human rights activists made extensive use of the survey. A sympathetic reviewer in *Journal of Democracy* called the survey "impressively accurate and objective."[10]

The basic findings of the survey were and are given considerable attention every year in Freedom House's principal bimonthly organ, *Freedom Review,* which initially was called *Freedom at Issue.* The current President of the organization, Adrian Karatnycky, used the occasion of the publication of the 1996 volume to analyze global and regional trends of freedom, as revealed in the survey, and to identify the 18 worst-rated countries and 5 worst-rated territories.[11] Significantly, top policymakers in the U.S. Administration make extensive use of the data. Deputy Secretary of State Strobe Talbott, in an authoritative article in *Foreign Affairs,* cited the 1996 Freedom House survey in order to demonstrate how the "American ideal" of democracy had so spread in the last quarter-century that, "for the first time in history a slim but clear majority of the world's population —54 percent—lives under democracy."[12] President Clinton, himself, later would use the data in his historic address to the UN General Assembly in September, 1997. He said: "For the first time in history, more than half of all people represented in this Assembly freely choose their own government."[13]

Still, when focused largely upon free elections, the observed trend could prove quite misleading. The managing editor of *Foreign Affairs,* Fareed Zakaria, drawing upon the Freedom House survey of 1996-97, concluded that half of the "democratizing" countries of the world were "illiberal democracies" with limited civil liberties. In reaching this conclusion, he had examined the Freedom House data of those countries that lie between confirmed dictatorship and consolidated democracy, and he found that 56 percent of them "do better on political liberties than on civil ones."[14] After demonstrating that there is a growing trend within new democracies of restrictions upon liberties, the foreign affairs analyst concluded that while elections are important, economic, civil and religious liberties "are at the core of human autonomy and dignity." Nonetheless, the editor of *Foreign Affairs* agreed that "elections are an important virtue of governance" and he found the data of Freedom House invaluable for revealing the limitations of elections alone.

For Freedom House, nothing is or was more important than press freedom. The free flow of information is seen as standing at the heart of a free society. The subject was and is the special personal preserve of its previous Executive Director, Leonard Sussman, who headed the organization from 1967 to 1988. A scholar on the subject, he launched, in 1979, an annual survey of the free flow of information through the print and broadcast media. The media of 187 countries are monitored and evaluated in terms of advances and setbacks.[15] Widespread interest by the media usually gives the survey extensive attention when it is annually released on May 3—the UN World Press Freedom Day.

The point of departure for the survey is Article 19 of the Universal Declaration of Human Rights, which emphasizes the right "to seek, receive and impart information and ideas through any media regardless of frontiers." The Freedom House survey makes its clear that neither cultural distinction nor economic underdevelopment ever can justify government "control of the *content* of news and information. . . ."[16] There can be no ideological deviation from the precise obligation spelled out in the Declaration. At the same time, the survey always seeks to examine not the constitutional provisions of a particular state dealing with freedom of information—which all too often are observed in the breach—but "the *reality* in daily practice."[17]

In the 1997 survey, Sussman called attention to the fact that, notwithstanding constitutional provisions, no less than 43 countries already were discussing new press laws that were, in large part, restrictive, even though they were presented as regularizing press freedom. Sussman cautioned that "such restrictions by legislation are violations of human rights and should be restricted."[18] Thus, the survey avoids the issue of "press responsibility" or even of the ethics of the media. Rather, it is guided by the way the U.S. Supreme Court has dealt with the issue of press freedom: the press need not be fair or even truthful; it need only be free.[19] When, during the seventies and eighties, UNESCO sought to establish guidelines for a responsible press that implicitly or explicitly justified government control of the media, Sussman vigorously fought this intrusion into the free flow of information.[20]

Surveys on civil liberties and freedom of information were vital parts of Freedom House's confrontation with communism and the Soviet empire. Its journal, *Freedom at Issue,* carried a host of articles on the subject. Among them were special essays written by dissidents from East Europe that had been smuggled out of their respective countries. Of particular importance was the journal *Samizdat,* which Freedom House initiated for the publication of numerous articles by democratic activists in the USSR or by advocates among the various nationalities or minorities comprising the Soviet Union. The West was provided with an insight about unofficial opinion, as reflected in material often secretly brought out.

This work was greatly stepped up with the signing of the Helsinki accord in August, 1975. Freedom House stood in the forefront of efforts to promote the human rights provisions of the Helsinki Final Act and of the debates at the Helsinki forums sponsored by CSCE that addressed discrimination and repression in Communist states. Indeed, Freedom House was the first to use the phrase "Helsinki Watch," designed to alert Western leaders of the need to expose all assaults upon freedom.

Anticommunism found particular expression in the Caribbean areas. Cuba was given considerable attention in Freedom House studies and publications, as were the Sandinistas in Nicaragua and the revolutionary movement in El Salvador. The organization created a Center for

Caribbean and Central American Studies, which gave exposure to abuses of the Miskito Indians by the Sandinista regime, as well as to refugee problems in the area and the need for the United States to adopt a humanitarian attitude toward them. Among these refugee problems, Freedom House gave some positive attention to the boat people fleeing the military dictatorship in Haiti.[21]

Cuba remained a priority concern after the Cold War was ended. Indeed it took on a wider, if more relaxed, dimension. Headed by Frank Calzon, the organization's Cuba program operates the Free Cuba Center, which provides moral, material and humanitarian support to Cuban dissenters, as well as information about the Communist regime to the rest of the world. Humanitarian aid is fairly large-scale and includes emergency cash assistance and medicine to the families of political prisoners along with much-needed typewriters and computers for journalists and prode-mocracy organizations.[22] Current emphasis is upon nonviolent change in Cuba rather than upon proposals for the country's isolation. To achieve this aim, the Freedom House program disseminates literature on democ-racy, civil society (in contrast to totalitarian society) and free markets. The program even sponsors travel to Cuba by persons who are familiar with the institutions of a free society and by those who are specialists on transitions to democracy and market economies elsewhere on the globe. An outreach aspect of the program is designed to inform NGOs and the public in general about developments within Cuba.

While Cuba is a holdover from the Cold War period, Freedom House largely has moved from the negative to the positive in its general programmatic efforts. Institution-building was and is now seen as the heart of its objectives.[23] Karatnycky stressed that Freedom House sees democratic institutions as the "best lasting instrument for protecting human rights." In developing democratic institutions, nothing occupies a higher priority than a system of elections. Freedom House's primary and oldest purpose, as reflected in its survey, was oriented largely to evaluating whether and how democracy works through elections. Civil liberties observance was, of course, a second consideration.

Election monitoring, as well as related procedures associated with elections, played a key part in the functioning of the organization. Indeed, its monitoring tradition goes back to 1979, when it engaged in observing early election practices in Cambodia. Similar monitoring took place in several Latin American countries as well as in Kashmir and in Haiti. Since, however, the Carter Center in Atlanta made electoral monitoring a priority of its operation extending to the process trained staff and expertise, Freedom House has chosen to limit its involvement with the process in most areas, offering, instead, its cooperation and consultation.[24]

The Carter Center's operation with respect to the electoral process was restricted geographically. It did not involve itself with the former Soviet Union, which was a preeminent concern of Freedom House. Having served in the forefront of the struggle against the Kremlin and Communist ideology, Freedom House was certain to consider the transition to democracy in the area a rather high priority. Ukraine was the first site. In March, 1994, Freedom House launched a comprehensive, multifaceted "Voter Awareness Program" that concentrated upon the Ukrainian parliamentary elections and the expected subsequent runoffs.[25]

"Voter awareness" meant sensitizing people who had no experience in choosing among candidates to appreciate the significance of choice. Under the Soviet system, the Communist Party simply selected the candidates for public office and compelled everyone to cast a vote. Overcoming the cynicism that the system had wrought required considerable effort. For Freedom House, the aim was nothing short of a get-out-the-vote campaign that educated potential voters as well as candidates about all aspects of political campaigns as they are conducted in democratic countries. Thus, the program sponsored TV debates on the issues of the elections and created an information center and press service to act as a clearinghouse for information about the candidates and the issues. The program also engaged in monitoring how the media reported on the campaign.

On the heels of this fairly impressive educational initiative, Freedom House decided to open a Ukraine Bureau in Kiev, its first office abroad. The Bureau helps administer a so-called Habits of the Heart program that seeks to promote democratic change and human rights through a collaborative working relationship with Ukrainian public policy research institutions and local NGOs.[26] Funding for this operation is provided largely by a U.S. government agency—Agency for International Development (AID)—demonstrating Washington's special interest in the project, which it also has for several other Freedom House projects.

A second overseas Freedom House office was opened the following year, in February, 1995, in Moscow, the capital of the Russian Federation. Building democracy and promoting human rights are the office's primary objectives. Thus, it has been involved in a critical way with the Chechnya crisis, observing Russian elections, developing exchange programs for Russian journalists and propagating ideas about democracy through a partnership with the major TV network, Ostankino Television.[27]

Among the most important projects of the Moscow office is the administration of The Sakharov Center for Peace, Progress and Human Rights, which was opened on May 20, 1996, by Yelena Bonner, Andrei Sakharov's wife. It houses the archives of the great Nobel Laureate humanist and scientist—manuscripts, books, personal correspondence and memorabilia. Situated in the center is a museum that chronicles the massive repressions of Soviet totalitarianism. Especially pertinent is the Center's role in hosting meetings and seminars of Russian NGOs and in advancing human rights aims.[28]

Russia and Ukraine constituted but a part of Freedom House's high priority objective of assisting what it called "nations in transit"—the 25 countries of the former Soviet empire—in Central and East Europe as well as the former USSR itself. Besides the regional offices in Ukraine and Russia, Freedom House opened offices in Budapest, Hungary and Bucharest, Romania. A survey, funded by the Agency for International Development (AID), has been conducted annually since 1995 by Freedom House to ascertain progress in advancing from totalitarianism to democracy. Several key areas are evaluated and measured: the political process, including free and fair elections; the evolution of civil society; the status of independent media; the rule of law; constitutional and criminal law reform; governance and public administration and economic reform. Based upon the variables, the survey rates, on a comparative basis, the various nations. The 1997 survey, a fairly sizable volume, concluded that democratic institutions are central for advancing economic reform and achieving a successful outcome.[29] Stressed, too, was the importance of U.S. aid and America's general engagement with individual countries.[30] In a concluding statement, the survey contended that "in many cases foreign assistance has empowered indigenous forces and created a basis for a future democratic transition." American engagement, it added, has contributed to the emergence of "a large number of articulate voices for democratic change. . . ."

But if Freedom House has concentrated upon the countries comprising the former Soviet Union and the former Soviet-dominated area in East Europe, it has not neglected other parts of the globe, especially those states that have established some democratic institutions or are seeking to strengthen them. An extensive exchange program conducted by the organization has brought human rights NGO activists from East Asia, South Asia and sub-Saharan Africa to New York and Washington to meet and share ideas with their counterparts in the United States. Among the subjects covered in the bilateral discussions have been freedom of expression, freedom of the press and civil rights. The visitors are expected to study how NGOs operate in the United States. Other information activities also are pursued. In 1997, for example, Freedom House brought nine women's rights activists from South Asia to visit Washington and the Midwest and to meet especially with women candidates for Congress. The exchange program, in addition to NGOs, also has involved journalists.[31] That the U.S. government would have a special interest in the exchange programs is self-evident and, indeed, the U.S. Information Agency (USIA) funds them.[32]

Corresponding to the shift in overseas programmatic emphasis with clear and obvious links to U.S. government assistance, Freedom House has moved the center of its operation and staff to Washington, D.C. Karatnycky already was based there, commuting to New York for several days a week. On August 1, 1997, Freedom House enlarged the Washington office through a merger with the National Forum Foundation, whose function had been the promotion of political and economic freedom in East Europe.[33] The latter also engaged in leadership training programs to advance democratic governance. Freedom House, with a staff now numbering about 40 and an annual budget totaling some $5 million, had become one of the largest human rights NGOs.[34] But it still remained Board-driven in terms of policy. The Board remained the "big tent" it had been at the time of its founding, embracing equally major personages of both political parties, as well as of business, labor, media, academia and the community. Especially impressive was the roster of former high officials from the foreign policy establishment. Freedom House could count on leverage to affect policy.

While the principal projects of Freedom House focus upon democracy-building, especially for "nations in transit," under Karatnycky the organization has branched out into being a human rights advocacy partisan on certain selected themes. As early as 1994, it initiated a Children at Risk program that focuses upon child welfare issues worldwide such as child prostitution, child labor, street children and militarized children in ethnic warfare. The program, as yet, does not involve firsthand investigation followed by publicized disclosures, as practiced by Amnesty or Human Rights Watch or the Anti-Slavery International. Instead, the project tends to follow a pattern characteristic of Freedom House.

What is being contemplated instead is a new survey that would evaluate the condition of children around the world using a specific single set of indices. Included in the indices are the effects of warfare and ethnic conflict upon children; levels of poverty and malnutrition; participation rates in primary schooling; prevalence of disease and access to health services. Even if largely educational, and not necessarily advocacy-oriented, the documentation, when appropriately interpreted, could lead to direct advocacy. Interwoven into the comprehensive survey are planned public forums and expert panels. Such forums and panels in the United States, it is expected, would have as topics, refugee children, education, health care and resettlement.[35]

Linked to the planned survey aspects of the Children at Risk program was an aspect of the new Freedom House thrust: exchange programs that involved NGO training features. In April-May, 1996, Charles Brown, the program's Director of Training, traveled to India, Pakistan, Bangladesh, Sri Lanka and Nepal to meet with children rights activists. Again, it was sponsored by USIA to assist NGO activists in Asia. Several months later, in August-September 1996, Freedom House hosted the Asian NGO children rights activists and conducted a training program on relevant issues. Arrangements were made for three weeks of training visits with American NGOs and with government officials in New York, Washington, Baltimore and smaller communities.[36] One internal impact of the new program became apparent: the annual Freedom in the World Survey began paying more attention to children's rights.

Advocacy of a kind that required a linkage between domestic and international purposes characterized Freedom House strategy in 1993 with respect to the Radio Free Europe and Radio Liberty. These two media instruments, which had played an extraordinarily important role in keeping alive the ideas of freedom and civil liberties during the seventies and eighties in East Europe and the former Soviet Union, were about to be axed by the new Administration. Yet, these congressionally funded institutions, each with a certain autonomy in policy formation and implementation, were seen by their supporters as potentially valuable in promoting democratic practices. Freedom House, already embarked upon a program of institution-building, recognized in Radio Free Europe and Radio Liberty strong allies in advancing the importance of elections and human rights as part of the democratic process. It intensely lobbied both Congress and the Administration, using such public devices as advertisements carrying the names of prominent intellectuals and human rights advocates. In the end, it prevailed in maintaining the two media instruments, although with a much reduced staff and budget.[37]

A more typical example of Freedom House's advocacy took place in connection with the Chinese-American human rights activist Harry Wu, who had been arrested by Beijing in the summer of 1995 for illegally entering China. He had been instrumental in bringing the U.S. public's attention to the vast use and abuse of prison labor for producing export commodities. Together with the Puebla Institute, headed by Nina Shea, Freedom House took up the cudgels on behalf of Wu, urging his release. Shea and Karatnycky met with President Clinton's National Security Adviser, Anthony Lake, and Under Secretary of State Tim Wirth.[38]

Shea formulated a tactical line in dealing with the problem that would carry considerable political weight. In an article written for the *Wall Street Journal*—which also was published in its Asian edition—she called for the United States to refuse to participate in the UN-sponsored Women's Conference to be held in Beijing in the fall of 1995 unless Wu was released.[39] While Shea, joined by Karatnycky, lobbied Congress, she also met on her own with Senate Majority Leader Bob Dole. The outcome of the lobbying was a letter by the Senate and House leadership on July 13, 1995 to the Administration linking American participation in the Beijing conference to Wu's release. Shea's lobbying included numerous interview appearances on television and radio, and she extended it to the UN in Geneva, which she visited accompanied by Wu's wife, Ching Lee, and where UN officials were informed of the human rights situation in China. In August, Wu was expelled from China after an initial procedure of imposing a judicial sentence. The push for a boycott of Beijing was dropped, although no one was certain what might have happened had Wu not been released.[40]

The collaborative relationship of Puebla Institute and Freedom House was formalized in September, 1995 with the Institute's Project on Religious Freedom becoming absorbed into Freedom House's general lobbying operation. Advocacy on behalf of religious freedom, during the following three years, would emerge as one of Freedom House's top priorities, attracting an extraordinary amount of public interest. Indeed, Freedom House, with Shea playing a leadership role, would transform the human rights subject of religious freedom from one of modest concern to one occupying almost a central place in the rights firmament.

Puebla Institute had been founded by Nicaraguan democrat Humberto Belli in 1995. Devoted to the promotion and protection specifically of religious liberty, it shifted its primary focus from Nicaragua to China and Southeast Asia, although it continued to investigate and publish reports on every area where religious repression was found. A major breakthrough on the subject came on January 23, 1996 when Puebla Institute, now part of Freedom House, held a conference entitled "Global Persecution of Christians." The title had a certain shock characteristic;

no one ever had suggested formulating the problem in this dramatic fashion. In attendance were over 100 key Christian leaders, mainly fundamentalist, rather than from the major established churches.[41]

A major theme of the conference dealt with strategies for ending the indifference of the West regarding Christian persecution. What was sparked was a genuinely revolutionary movement to concentrate public attention on repression and discrimination against Christians, whether in China or in Moslem countries. Strikingly, after the Institute conference, the U.S. Congress held four hearings at which testimony was presented on Christian persecution and the State Department was criticized for giving short shrift to the issue. A key House panel, the Subcommittee on International Operations and Human Rights, held an unprecedented session, never before undertaken, devoted exclusively to the persecution of Christians abroad.[42]

With the clamor for documentation of the dramatic charges of persecution certain to emerge, Freedom House's Puebla program released in the fall of 1997 a book, *In the Lion's Den,* written by Shea, which gave coverage to the subject.[43] The release date was designed to appeal to a specific constituency—the evangelical Christians—whose churches, numbering in the thousands, would be commemorating on September 29 the "International Day of Prayer for the Persecuted Church." The book's basic appeal was to evangelical Christians, urging them to demand action by the U.S. government to take action against religious persecution.

According to *In the Lion's Den,* Communist countries and militant Islamic states are the sources of the most egregious human rights violations of religious freedom; it also states that "Christians are the chief victims of this religious persecution around the world today."[44] It profiles persecution of Christians in the following Islamic countries: Nigeria, Sudan, Egypt, Saudi Arabia, Kuwait, Pakistan and Uzbekistan. The persecuting Communist countries that then are identified include: China, North Korea, Cuba, Vietnam and Laos. Highlighted is the alleged failure in U.S. foreign policy to protect religious freedom, whether in its bilateral relations or in its policy at the United Nations. A concluding chapter, "A Call to Action," encourages Christians to continue their grassroots educational and lobbying programs.

The language of Shea carried a razor-edge sharpness clearly designed to motivate her readers to vigorous public action. An example: "The most egregious human rights atrocities are being committed against Christians living in Communist and militant Islamic societies solely because of their religious beliefs and activities."[45] A listing of the atrocities follows that can't fail to prick the conscience and arouse furious anger: "torture, enslavement, rape, imprisonment, forcible separation of children from parents, killings and massacres. . . ." The listing is accompanied by the prediction that the abuses "threaten the very survival of entire Christian communities, many of which have existed for hundreds or even a thousand years. . . ." Even as they threaten to destroy entire communities, the abuses are said to intimidate others from following "their conscience toward Christ."

A prime target, of course, was China. According to Shea, "there are more Christians in prison [in China] because of religious activities than in any other nation in the world."[46] Specifically noted was the way Protestants continued to be arrested and tortured for holding prayer meetings without approval for preaching and for distributing Bibles again without authorization. Imprisoned, too, were Roman Catholic bishops and priests when they, in the absence of official approval, celebrated mass or administered the sacraments. In testimony before a congressional panel, Shea observed that in China, religious activities of any kind must be registered with the government's Religious Affairs Bureau and, thereby, become subject to strict official regulations.[47] Her estimate was that between 60 and 100 million Christians in China have refused to register with the government religious bureau and thereby risk their lives and liberty to worship freely in underground "house-churches." During 1996, the Beijing regime cracked down on the underground churches, resulting in the arrest or beatings of Christians.

What disturbed and irritated the Freedom House specialist on religious freedom was the American public's ignorance of the Chinese persecution practices. In her congressional testimony, she bitterly complained that "the level of knowledge [in the U.S.] about Christian persecution in China is abysmal." She went on to demand that "our political leaders and envoys must become informed themselves and wage an aggressive education campaign so that everyone can do his part to augment freedom for not only Christians, but for all Chinese citizens." It was more than apparent that Shea's greatest interest was in Chinese abuses. Her comment about extending freedom to all citizens, not merely religious observers, was not made about any other country engaged in violations of religious freedom.

In fact, Shea and Freedom House already were actively involved in cracking the silence barrier in the United States about which she had complained. After her conference of Christian leaders in January, 1996 that called for holding an International Day of Prayer for the Persecuted Church on September 29, 1996, the National Association of Evangelicals, with its very large constituency, issued a *Statement of Conscience and Call to Action* that pledged to fight the persecution and appealed to the U.S. government to take a stand in protecting religious freedom.[48] The Day of Prayer of this conservative activist mass group was not lost upon the U.S. Congress.

Both the Senate and the House in the fall of 1996 adopted parallel resolutions that encouraged the Clinton Administration to expand and invigorate its international advocacy on behalf of persecuted Christians. At the same time, the resolutions recommended the creation by the Administration of an advisory committee that would report to the Secretary of State on religious freedom abroad. That these resolutions were products of the initiative, energy and determination of Freedom House's Puebla Institute openly was claimed by the latter. In its journal, it pointed out how the resolutions drew from the Institute's documentation and were an outgrowth of its January, 1996 conference.[49] The power of the new conservative constituency quickly was demonstrated at the executive level of government. In November, 1996, the Administration created a State Department Advisory Committee on Religious Freedom to which Nina Shea was named.[50]

Having produced significant political achievements within the time frame of but one year, Freedom House hardly was resting on its laurels. Puebla Institute's newsletter, *The First Freedom,* a twice-yearly publication, besides updating reports on Christian persecution around the world, spelled out for its growing constituency a strategy of continuing lobbying and application of pressure in the public arena. A flow of letters to Congress was urged, together with op-ed pieces for local media. Even more potent political action was proposed through the enactment of local ordinances or legislation restricting business dealings with regimes abusing religious freedom. Not to be neglected, as Freedom House could not fail to be cognizant of its newfound constituency, was a recommendation for formal prayer on behalf of persecuted Christians.[51]

Even while mobilizing support through Puebla Institute's home organ, Nina Shea was continuing her effort to lobby Congress. During early 1997, she briefed the Congressional Human Rights Caucus concerning Christians in China and also provided testimony to a panel of the Senate Committee on Foreign Relations. Especially intriguing was her testimony before the Select Committee on the New York City Council, which strongly had endorsed a bill by the Speaker of the Council, Peter Vallone, that would have prohibited the city from awarding contracts to companies that did business with China and 14 other countries in which Christians were persecuted. The bill also would have required that the city remove its investment funds from banks dealing with the same regimes.[52]

The very tough economic proposal echoed the tactics pressed by NGOs during the seventies and eighties against the apartheid regime of South Africa. It suggested that, with the new constituency, the remarkable effect against apartheid could be replicated. It was not to be. No doubt, powerful business concerns made it clear to Vallone that economic interests of the city—and its major businesses and banks—could be seriously hurt by this tactic. Vallone later would withdraw his initiative. Shea persisted, in any case, to give the Christian issue in China the strongest possible political punch, which carried threats of political intimidation. Thus, on April 3, 1997, after disclosing that Beijing had arrested eight of the most important Protestant leaders of China's underground "house-church" movement, including the head of a "church" embracing four million persons, Shea commented:

> Last week Vice President Gore—in toasting China's Premier Li Peng over commercial agreements while failing to forcefully assert America's concern for religious freedom—gave the message that the U.S. government is willing to avert its eyes from the ongoing crackdown against Chinese Christians.[53]

The warning to the Administration was clear.

Persecution of Christians in China and Islamic countries and the work of Shea and Freedom House, were given powerful resonance in the columns of A. M. Rosenthal on the Op-Ed page of the *New York Times*. Beginning in February, 1997, the subject became a principal theme of this former Executive Editor of the *Times*, who published no less than 16 columns on the subject until mid-October.[54] His series began on February 11 with a column entitled "Persecuting the Christians" that cited extensively from Shea's book, *In the Lion's Den*.[55] Not only was the Shea program at Freedom House given great emphasis, but also the book directly was promoted, with a listing of the publisher's telephone number. Rosenthal openly called upon organizations and Congressmen to study the Soviet Jewry movement and apply its techniques for ending persecution. And he specifically called upon certain Senators and Congressmen to assume the lead in the proposed struggle. Two would: Senator Arlen Specter of Pennsylvania and Congressman Frank Wolf of Virginia.

Six weeks later, the Specter-Wolf legislation would be introduced. It would create a new office within the White House to monitor the treatment of religious minorities around the world, especially Christians in China and some Moslem countries, Buddhists in Tibet and Bahais in Iran. It would require economic sanctions against those countries that abuse their citizens on the basis of religion. The sanctions would include the cutting off of direct U.S. economic aid and opposition to granting multilateral aid. The bill would extend U.S. asylum priority to those fleeing religious persecution.

In introducing the legislation in the House on May 21, 1997 Congressman Wolf outlined the principal features of the proposed statute, taking special note of religious repression in China, Sudan and Iran. Emphasizing that it was a bipartisan bill, with Democrats joining Republicans as sponsors, Wolf made a somewhat startling point: "the persecution of people of faith is the great untold human rights story of this decade [of the nineties]."[56] Not mass ethnic genocide in Bosnia and in Rwanda nor the burgeoning ethnic tensions elsewhere in the world that promote slaughter and threaten peace, but rather, religious repression was held to be the essence of the human rights problem of the decade. Curiously, not even the massacre of Tiananmen Square demonstrators in 1989 that involved the issue of free speech and democracy was perceived as defining the era's human rights problem.

Wolf's remarks carried a second distinctive feature. He compared his draft legislation to the Jackson-Vanik statute that had played a vital part in the Soviet Jewry movement in facilitating emigration. "Jackson-Vanik," he observed, "was the movement that crystallized concern for those suffering persecution in the Soviet Union." What followed was an indication of how he viewed the significance of his role or rather how he would want history to characterize his role: "I am hoping that this bill will be its [Jackson-Vanik's] counterpart for the 1990's."[57] Others, too, would compare the legislation with Jackson-Vanik.

In fact, the purpose and nature of Jackson-Vanik was very different. It did not seek the end of repression of Soviet Jews, as this bill sought to end Christian persecution. Rather, Jackson-Vanik assumed that Soviet repression would not or could not be ended and, therefore, the bill's objective was to persuade the Kremlin to let Soviet Jews emigrate. Political reform, which stands at the heart of Specter-Wolf, was utterly alien to Senator Henry Jackson's legislation.

In a crucial respect, Wolf-Specter would take on a certain similarity to Jackson-Vanik. A powerful broad-based public constituency would emerge demanding legislative action. During the year, prompted by the Freedom House–Puebla Institute conference of January, 1996, the National Association of Evangelicals, the Southern Baptist Convention and the Family Research Council conducted a quiet, but vigorous, grassroots campaign pressuring the Administration and Congress. Use was made of denominational newsletters and broadcasts on Christian radio and television stations.[58] Later, the Christian Coalition would join in the massive grassroots lobbying. Nina Shea commented that "this is a new lobby that is emerging" to replace the human rights movement that "fell apart" at the grassroots level after the collapse of the Soviet Union and the end of apartheid in South Africa.[59]

The first reflection of the power of the grassroots campaign came on July 22, 1997 in a State Department report on persecution of Christians throughout the world. It was the first comprehensive review of the subject by the Department, even though its annual country reports do deal with the problem as part of the evaluation of each country's human rights record for the year. The report was prepared at the behest of Congress, which, in 1996, had demanded "a detailed summary of United States policies designed to reduce and eliminate today's mounting persecution of Christians throughout the world."[60] Seventy-eight countries were surveyed, with the focus almost exclusively upon a range of difficulties confronting Christians. To a limited extent, others, like Buddhists in Tibet or animists and non-Islam believers in Sudan, were examined. In addition to reviewing anti-Christian acts, the report concentrated upon what the United States was doing to promote religious freedom and to "eliminate religious discrimination, intolerance, and persecution throughout the world, with a particular focus on the situation for Christians, as requested by Congress."

With respect to China, the prime target of the Republican-dominated Congress, the report openly acknowledged the continuing violations of the religious freedom that had been promised in the Beijing Constitution. In response to these violations, according to the report, the United States had raised its concern with Chinese officials at every opportunity, at bilateral meetings and on various levels. Nina Shea, the leading advocate for producing the report, welcomed it as "a very good thing" that "underscores a serious human rights issue that has been overlooked."[61]

Yet, the pressure tactics of the grassroots campaign hardly had been in vain. The report itself was given remarkable press coverage. The State Department had assumed a new sensitivity, with Secretary of State Albright instructing American embassies to give more attention to questions of religious freedom and to keep more closely in touch with leading religious figures, whether or not those leaders are likely targets for discrimination.[62]

Newsweek, the popular national weekly, caught the new atmosphere in the nation's capital, noting in an article subhead in August, 1997 that "Nina Shea is making Christian persecution Washington's hottest cause."[63] Human rights officials rarely, if ever, got that kind of attention. A top congressional official on human rights issues, Representative Christopher Smith of New Jersey, was quoted as saying that Shea "has been the prime fighter on religious issues." Smith was Chairman of the key House Subcommittee on International Operations and Human Rights and also Co-Chairman of the U.S. Helsinki Commission. At his House Subcommittee, Shea was identified by *Newsweek,* "as a favorite witness."

The central feature of Shea's advocacy was her claim that "more Christians have died for their faith in the 20th century than in the previous 19 centuries."[64] It was a stunning statistic that was treated skeptically by experts, according to *Newsweek*. Shea, while offering no precise documentation, said that she got the figures from an unnamed encyclopedia on Christians produced by a religious group in Virginia. Howsoever accurate or inaccurate her dramatic statement may be, she is convinced and effectively has convinced others that anti-Christian persecution "is massive and vastly unreported."[65] She told *Newsweek* that while "everyone focussed on the human rights of journalists, of political dissidents, of Jews . . . Christians have been ignored."

The implication was clear—mainstream human rights NGOs have avoided the issue. A long article in the liberal journal *The New Republic,* in July, 1997 made precisely that argument, alleging that Human Rights Watch, for example, had maintained a "conspicuous silence" on the persecution of Christians in China.[66] In contrast, Shea's Puebla Institute, with its Global Persecution of Christians conference, became the starting point for the emergence of public attention to the issue. The article in *The New Republic* cited an interview in a New York weekly with Ken Roth of HRW, who was reported to have called the attention given to Christian persecution as "special pleading" and "an effort to privilege certain classes of victims." Shea, in the same weekly, was quoted as saying: "I don't think he's familiar with the issue. They're playing catch-up. They need to minimize the problem because they missed it."[67]

That HRW had been silent about persecution in China was totally without foundation. In its *World Report 1997,* HRW provided considerable details about how "unofficial Christian and Catholic communities were targeted by the [Beijing] government during 1996."[68] Indeed, the details presented in the *World Report 1997* were remarkably similar to the Freedom House's disclosures of April 3, 1997 about China's stepped-up arrests of Christian leaders. As for the persecution of Buddhist monks in Tibet, the same HRW report offered pertinent information.[69] Besides the *World Report,* an examination of HRW publications over the last few years showed an extensive amount of attention to religious discrimination generally, and to religious discrimination in China, specifically. Still, there could be little question that Freedom House had succeeded in giving the issue a high priority. Significant segments of the public that never had been concerned with human rights matters had become very much involved. The Southern Baptist Convention alone numbers 15.6 million members. No one questions that the Christian Coalition comprises a vast, multimillion-member constituency and when it formally declared, in August, 1997, that ending religious persecution around the world was its "top legislative priority," Washington was bound to take notice.[70]

Adrian Karatnycky acknowledged, in an interview, that the subject of Christian persecution had become one of Freedom House's "most significant priorities."[71] Explaining how the organization had moved in this direction, he contended that the United States, in the early 1990s, suffered from "post–Cold War indifference" concerning foreign policy matters. To address this problem, Freedom House decided to look for ways to interest new constituencies in foreign policy, in human rights and in democracy. While speaking to specific groups about specific interests that concerned them, he hoped that Freedom House could draw their attention to more general issues and broader themes. Karatnycky was pleased that the issue of Christian persecution had proved quite successful in tapping into the deep concerns of a number of groups that traditionally had not been involved in human rights issues.

Inevitably, the differences between NGOs on how much emphasis to place upon religious repression rested on how each rated the problem in its scheme of values. Nina Shea, indirectly, made her own preference clear when she observed that "there's a bias among some of our political elites, that if you are willing to die for the Bible, you're a fanatic, but if you die in front of a tank, you're a hero."[72] What was suggested here was that the ruthless military repression at Tiananmen Square was not to be regarded as more significant and consequential than murderous religious repression. Shea's next comment suggested, although again indirectly, that she believed the struggle for religious freedom was more important than the clamor for other freedoms:

> The great lesson absorbed by the tyrants of the world from the collapse of the Soviet empire is that it was the churches that contributed to the democratization and collapse of the empire. So you see a pattern of persecution in places like China and Saudi Arabia.

In fact, the East European churches, except for those in Poland, and, to a much lesser degree, in East Germany, had virtually nothing to do with the collapse of the Soviet empire. Nor were the Orthodox churches in Russian moving forces for democratization in that country.

The thesis that religious freedom and its converse—religious repression—warrant priority attention was provided with a powerful underpinning by a new academic study that was published, coincidentally, at the very moment when the issue had surfaced in a major way in the NGO community. *Freedom of Religion and Belief: A World Report* was an unprecedented attempt by two leading human rights scholars at the University of Essex's Human Rights Center to examine how nearly 60 countries of the globe, representative of all major religious and cultural perceptions, observe the demands of international law concerning religious rights and freedom.[73]

The very Introduction to the volume makes the telling point that "religious persecution of minority faiths—the proscribing of belief and pervasive discrimination, killings and torture are daily occurrences at the end of the twentieth century."[74] Yet, interestingly, a flyer from the publisher promoting the book identified Human Rights Watch, Amnesty International and other major human rights centers as "contributing research material to the project." Freedom House was not mentioned.

What Freedom House and Nina Shea had done was translate the new sense of urgency about widespread and growing religious repression into political action that might affect abuser regimes through American economic pressure. And this achievement was accomplished by tapping anxieties and concerns in a widespread conservative religious constituency. What was pointedly, perhaps painfully, exposed was the lack of a constituency, or of an effective constituency of other human rights groups. HRW had been publishing critical material on religious repression, including repression of Christianity, for some time, but it stirred so little interest that some would conclude—utterly mistakenly—that it was silent on the problem.

The question that arose among the established NGOs was: how would they respond to the new conservative constituency that never had been involved or interested in human rights? And, on such issues that were dear to the general human rights community, like women's rights—especially reproductive rights—or gay rights or even broad civil rights matters, like affirmative action, that constituency scarcely could be considered friendly.

William Schulz, the head of Amnesty International USA, in the organization's newsletter, welcomed the involvement of "those who genuinely care about human suffering no matter what their views of God or the state." At the same time, he asked: Is it right for Christians to limit their outrage to violations against Christians?[75] Strikingly, on the eve of the Jiang-Clinton summit in Washington—October 23, 1997—Amnesty USA joined a protest panel that included as sponsors Freedom House, the AFL-CIO and the Christian Coalition.[76]

Even more significant was the attitude of Holly Burkhalter, the former longtime Advocacy Director of HRW and its lobbyist in Washington, who had switched in 1997 to the liberal Physicians for Human Rights. She thought the new constituency was a positive development that might produce breakthroughs on the legislative scene in Washington.[77] Always realistic, the tough-minded human rights advocate could not fail to recognize that the Republican leadership in Congress was pressing for human rights legislation that was distinctly confrontational with both China and the Clinton Administration. For the human rights NGOs in Washington who long had demanded a tough stance against totalitarian Beijing, only to be repeatedly frustrated, this was no small development.

What still remained unanswered was the question: how much of a priority should religious freedom be? Was it more important than ethnic genocide or mass killings, torture or free speech, press, assembly? And should religious freedom be restricted only to some religions? The response came in a letter sent on September 9, 1997 to Congressman Benjamin Gilman, Chairman of the House International Relations Committee, then considering the Specter-Wolf draft bill. The signers were Ken Roth, William Schulz, Felice Gaer and Leonard Rubenstein, Director of Physicians for Human Rights and two other groups.[78]

After announcing their strong support for the goals of the Freedom from Religious Persecution Act and specifically for its aim of "putting pressure on the authorities to end religious repression," the signers offered several suggestions that could "better achieve" the intended goal. The suggestions were instructive. A key recommendation was to list all "vulnerable religious communities" so that "the bill will have more universal resonance" and to include the "other forms of discrimination and intolerance" besides the extreme form of persecution. Equally rejected was the notion that "special preference . . . over other victims of persecution" be given. They recommended that the number of refugee slots be expanded so that "no one currently eligible [for asylum] will be denied entry."

A final criticism dealt with the imposition of sanctions. The NGOs took note of the fact that there already existed human rights law prohibiting bilateral aid and requiring U.S. opposition to multilateral aid to countries engaged in a consistent pattern of human rights violations. Certainly, religious persecution would fall within this category, and those laws would assure the imposition of sanctions immediately. The proposed draft, in contrast, only would require acts of religious persecution that were "widespread and ongoing," a less precise formulation. As a matter of fact, the entire question of sanctions evoked considerable questioning. Freedom House, itself, refused to take a position on sanctions, since its Board was split on the subject.[79] Max Kampelman expressed uncertainty, saying in an interview that he saw sanctions "as a tool to be used, not a principle to be exercised."[80]

Significantly, the House International Relations Committee had invited Jerry Goodman, the former Executive Director of the National Conference on Soviet Jewry, to testify on the draft. It was hoped that he could offer advice on the legislation, as a Congressman questioning him put it: "This Bill . . . is based on the admirable movement you helped lead."[81] In his testimony and in response to questions, Goodman was hesitant about supporting sanctions until all other options proved ineffective. He spoke about "a collaborative approach" being applied, which would be interwoven with "quiet diplomacy." Only when all else had failed in persuading the Kremlin to permit emigration, he said, was Congress then urged to focus upon "linking trade benefits to the Soviet Union with the right to leave."[82] It will be noticed that Goodman used the term "trade benefits" to characterize the Jackson-Vanik leverage. This was a crucial point. The granting of most-favored-nation tariff treatment as well as low interest credits from the U.S. Export-Import Bank were benefits. To refuse to grant them was not in the same category as the cutting off of economic aid.

However different in character, purpose and form Specter-Wolf was from Jackson-Vanik, Goodman enthusiastically welcomed the new proposed legislation, as did most of the representatives of Jewish organizations in Washington. Freedom House had succeeded powerfully in placing religious persecution as a burning human rights concern upon the agendas of the Administration, Congress and the human rights NGO community.[83]

In May 1998, the House of Representatives, by a huge majority of 375 to 41, adopted the legislation providing for suspension of most aid to countries engaging in religious persecution. Restrictions were also placed on trade with them and opposition to loans for them from international financial institutions. Difficulties, however, arose in the Senate where major business and farm interests strongly opposed any restrictions on trade. On July 23, a milder version of the House bill failed to win approval of the Senate Foreign Relations Committee. But the issue is by no means dead. On October 9 the full Senate unanimously endorsed a more flexible form of the legislation. This version is fairly certain to be enacted in the very near future.

CHAPTER NINETEEN

"Asian Values" vs. The Universal Declaration of Human Rights

On the eve of the UN's planning for the year-long fiftieth anniversary ceremonies of the Universal Declaration of Human Rights, suddenly the United States and the West found themselves challenged by a Southeast Asian bloc of states. "Asian values" or the "Asian concept of human rights" were the phrases that were used to characterize the challenge. The challengers called into question the validity and universality of the Declaration even as they demanded a fundamental revision of its essential character. The assault carried with it some ugly overtones that echoed themes utterly rejected by the international community after World War II. Whether the challenge will hold up in the face of the collapse of the Southeast Asian economies at the end of 1997 is uncertain. It would be naive to assume that a basic outlook of the elite leadership on human rights will be discarded. At the same time, revolutionary developments in May 1998 in Indonesia, a leader in "Asian values" advocacy, all but indicated that the rights incorporated in the Universal Declaration were what the broad public demanded and to an extent won.

"Asian values," as counterposed to the Universal Declaration of Human Rights, reached a climactic moment in late July, 1997 at the annual meeting of ASEAN, the nine-member Association of Southeast Asian Nations, held in Kuala Lumpur, Malaysia. The confrontation between Asian leaders—of which the host country Prime Minister, Mahathir Mohamad, acted as the leading spokesman—and the West was a profoundly disturbing one, with the United States finding it necessary to sharply challenge in public its Asian allies. ASEAN had actually been a creation of U.S. diplomacy to resist the encroachment of communism in Asia. And now, for the first time since the ideological exchanges of the Cold War, the United States found itself engaged in angry verbal blasts carrying distinct ideological components.

Interwoven into the fabric of the ideological and cultural confrontation was the emergence of a vital and dynamic element in numerous Asian societies of popular NGOs involving thousands of members. These elements were assisted by the leading international NGOs, headquartered in London and New York. How and in what way these national and international NGOs related to the issue of Asian values and the Universal Declaration stands at the heart of the struggle for human rights in Asia and beyond.

Three issues were involved in the confrontations: (1) what was to be done about Myanmar (Burma) in relation to ASEAN? (2) how was the deepening currency crisis that had afflicted major Asian "Tigers"—Thailand, Indonesia, Malaysia—and particularly their markets and banking systems to be explained? and (3) was the time not appropriate for a revision of the Universal Declaration of Human Rights, by taking account of "Asian values"? Certainly, there was awareness at the ASEAN meeting that 1998 would mark the fiftieth anniversary of the Universal Declaration and considerable public attention would focus upon the Declaration during the anniversary year. The three issues, seemingly so unrelated, were very much interrelated, at least in the minds of some key Asian spokesmen at the meeting in Kuala Lumpur.[1]

Prior to the ASEAN meeting, the United States, urged on by American-based international NGOs, like Human Rights Watch, strongly had pressed its leading friends in the area to resist admitting Myanmar into the conference. This country's human rights record after the military's suppression of the election of 1990, which would have brought Daw Aung San Suu Kyi and her democratic party to power, was outrageous. Ruthless repression of the democrats and her isolation was characteristic of the military regime. Legislation in Congress, supported by the Administration, called for strong economic sanctions to be imposed upon Myanmar. Yet U.S. diplomacy to prevent its seating in ASEAN was unsuccessful. Democracy and human rights, after all, were hardly major priorities of most ASEAN members.

Having defeated the United States on this diplomatic concern, the ASEAN host moved to an offensive. Malaysian Prime Minister Mahathir, in a speech, chose to indirectly attack American policy even as he privately unleashed to his listeners anti-American statements. But what was especially startling was his assault upon a prominent American financier and philanthropist, George Soros, as the source of the recent wild fluctuations of Asian currencies that significantly had diminished their value. Mahathir saw it as a conspiracy, "a well-planned effort to undermine the economies of all the Asian countries by destabilizing their currencies." The reason for Soros's manipulation of the currencies of ASEAN countries was self-evident in the conspiracy theorizing. Knowing that the American financier was a vigorous advocate of human rights, Mahathir charged that Soros deliberately was seeking "to block Myanmar's admission into ASEAN." But Soros's presumed motivation was only one part of the conspiracy theory.

For over a decade, Mahathir had made the Jew or Zionist the scapegoat of any political or economic problem faced by Malaysia. The fact that Soros was Jewish had not gone unnoticed in this perception of reality. Back on August 20, 1986, addressing Malaysian journalists, Mahathir strongly complained that most Western newspapers were controlled by Jews and, therefore, the media "have to bow to Zionist interests."[2] One month later, the Prime Minister returned to his anti-Semitic vituperation, only this time overt censorship action was taken against the Western media. On September 26, 1986, he banned for three months the Asian edition of the *Wall Street Journal*, which had run articles critical of the government's economic practices. The *Journal*, according to Mahathir, was controlled by Jews and was part of a "Zionist" plot to control Malaysia.[3]

The suggestion that the collapse of Southeast Asian currencies in July, 1997 was a result of manipulation by Soros or other "Zionist influences" was of course absurd. It only echoed themes of the infamous "Protocols of the Elders of Zion" that frequently had been repeated by professional hatemongers. Only when the bigoted allegations were repeated by the Malaysian Foreign Minister, Abdullah Ahmad Badawi, did the United States finally decide to snap back. Under Secretary of State Stuart Eizenstat, with Albright's approval, tartly rejected Malaysia's conspiracy theories. Currency fluctuations, he sought to explain, stem from judgments about the economy by "markets as a whole" and not by speculators, who, at best, may only take advantage of the market situation. The lesson in the basics of business economics made little impact upon Mahathir. Six months later, a *Times* columnist traveling through the Southeast Asian area at the height of the financial and banking crash noted that "Malaysia's leader is still blaming Jews and currency traders for his woes."[4]

Far more ideologically confrontational were Mahathir's comments about the Universal Declaration of Human Rights, which appeared to win considerable support from his ASEAN colleagues. He called for a "review" of the veritably sacred Universal Declaration of Human Rights on grounds that the document, which traditionally was understood as "a common standard of achievement," in Eleanor Roosevelt's words, supposedly was "formulated by the superpowers which did not understand the needs of poor countries." The Malaysian newspapers trumpeted the demands of Mahathir with a headline in the *New Straits Times* reading: "U.N. Review Necessary Says Dr. M."[5]

The "review" proposal marked a renewal of the debate during the World Conference on Human Rights in Vienna in 1993. Now that it had resurfaced, Indonesian Foreign Minister Ali Alatas joined in. He reminded his listeners that the Universal Declaration was approved by only the 51 members that comprised the UN at the time in 1948; since then, 120 new states had joined the UN. A review would serve "to create a better balance that responds to the new situation in the world," said the Indonesian.[6] According to Alatas: "Everybody knows that human rights does not consist of individual political and civil rights." He went on to say that "people are now much more aware that economic rights, cultural rights, social rights are just as important."

If the United States offered little in the way of a response on the Burmese issue or the conspiracy theories of Mahathir, it decided to take on the political attempt to review and revise the Universal Declaration. Not only was that pride and joy of a former American First Lady who also happened to be the idol of Mrs. Hillary Clinton, but also the idea of "universality" was one for which the United States bitterly had fought at Vienna in 1993. To permit "Asian values" to rebound and reverse the victory at Vienna would have meant capitulation to the benighted forces of yesteryear that continued to be a genuine threat to human rights and democracy. The State Department spokesman, Nicholas Burns, quoted Albright as saying: "It would be a great mistake to consider these principles of the [Universal Declaration as] imposed by the West." It was Eizenstat who joined the issue by launching a counterattack against the "Asian values" group, the bulk of whom were present. He called it "remarkable" that anyone would want to challenge and review the basic human rights charter.[7] He caustically observed: "Universal values don't know a time period."[8]

The Southeast Asian outburst calling for review of the Universal Declaration of Human Rights only months before the opening of celebratory ceremonies of the Declaration's fiftieth anniversary was not entirely new. Even before Vienna, in 1991, the Indonesian Foreign Minister at an ASEAN–European Community Ministerial Meeting in Luxembourg had argued that economic development must precede the full unfolding of political and civil rights, that Asians place greater value on the harmony of the community than on individual freedoms and that the interpretation of international standards on human rights should be left to individual states.[9] In the same year—1991—China issued a "White Paper" entitled "Human Rights in China" that was sharply critical of reports in the West— whether on a governmental level or on an NGO level—attacking the country's human rights activity. The official Chinese position was similar to that articulated by the Indonesian Foreign Minister: economic development must precede the advance of political and civil rights.

A somewhat different critique of Western human rights approaches was taken by the former Prime Minister of Singapore, Lee Kuan Yew. In an interview with the journal *Foreign Affairs,* he upheld the perspective of the good society to which various freedoms must be subordinated. His perspective on America and its freedoms was characteristic:

> The expansion of the right of the individual to behave or misbehave as he pleases has come at the expense of orderly society. In the East, the main object is to have a well-ordered society so that everybody can have maximum enjoyment of his freedoms.[10]

The most elaborate initial statement on "Asian values" that, at the same time, openly denounced and repudiated Western criticism of Asian countries was made by a high official of the authoritarian regime in Singapore, Bilahari Kausikan, in the pages of *Foreign Policy.*[11] He, like others articulating the "Asian values" theme, contended that all international action regarding the promotion of human rights is "shaped by and deployed as an ideological instrument," even among well-meaning human rights advocates. Promotion of human rights therefore is seen as part of a prolonged, historic effort by the West to assert its hegemony over Asia by imposing alien values and cultural standards, especially in its promotion of civil and political rights over economic, social, and cultural rights. In the interest of international consensus and understanding, it is argued, the Asian experience must be included: "That experience sees order and stability as preconditions for economic growth, and growth as the necessary foundation of any political order that claims to advance human dignity."[12]

Underlying the "Asian concept of human rights" are two assumptions: first, that cultural or religious traditions justify the abrogation of certain rights that Westerners consider universal; second, that as a nation's economy grows one can expect greater adherence to some of the rights of its people. The Asian tradition, Kausikan and others claim, is less confrontational and more consensus-seeking, less concerned with checks against the power of the state (rights) and more with obligations toward society and community. "Many East and Southeast Asians tend to look askance at the starkly individualistic ethos of the West," Kausikan observed.

Asian human rights advocates, while quick to denounce the arguments of Singaporean, Chinese, and Indonesian officials regarding human rights standards as self-serving, nonetheless might agree that Asia has special needs. Some Asian NGOs, particularly those belonging to popular movements, emphasized various development-oriented rights like the right to form trade unions, the right to live on one's ancestral land and the right to a decent standard of living. Furthermore, many Asian NGOs share the belief that Western human rights advocates have ulterior motives, and therefore are cautious or even hostile in their interactions with American or European groups. Mistrust of American involvement is palpable in any interaction, including those on an NGO level. When attending Asian conferences of NGOs, Jeannine Guthrie of HRW/Asia explained, her tactic was to agree as much as possible with criticism of American international NGOs for as long as two or three days.[13] From there, she could "begin a conversation."

The mistrust stems from the intimidating presence of American politics and foreign policy, which is seen as impacting upon American NGOs. When American labor unions bring complaints about labor practices to international bodies, some Asian NGOs believe the motivation is the protection of an American standard of living at the cost of international growth. America's propensity to link trade sanctions with any number of issues—human rights practices, nuclear proliferation, intellectual property rights—only deepens their cynicism. Western-born institutions like the World Bank, which funds development projects that are perceived as harmful, and the International Monetary Fund, which imposes austerity measures as conditions for loans, only serve to heighten animosity toward the West.[14]

Many Asian human rights advocates and academics agree that Asia has a separate identity from that of the West.[15] They trace this separate identity to economic, geopolitical, historical and cultural factors. Human rights violations in Asia more frequently are challenged on a group or class basis rather than by individuals.[16] And, whether from cultural traditions or from the nature of the most common human rights abuses in Asia, the focus of many human rights organizations is on group-based or "associational" rights. Indeed, the Bangkok NGO Conference clearly was not distinguished by the civil liberties groups that attended but by the populist groups, particularly women's and indigenous peoples' groups. The latter groups have stressed the right of communities to their ancestral domain, as recognized in the constitution of the Philippines.[17] At a recent conference organized by the Carnegie Council on Ethics and International Affairs, a Philippine human rights advocate argued that the foundation of popular support for human rights standards would be stronger if the standards were grounded in particular local cultures and traditions.[18]

The Human Rights Initiative of the Carnegie Council on Ethics and International Affairs, entitled "The Growth of East Asia and Its Impact on Human Rights," is a project created to address the continuing East-West debate over human rights issues. Few scholars in the dialogue, Western or Asian, were willing to question the universality of human rights; but many—again, both Asian and Western—believe that human rights arguments ought to be grounded in a cultural context. Many contributors to the dialogue have begun by questioning a generalization made by most advocates of the "Asian concept of human rights" that Western societies are primarily individualistic, Asian ones primarily communal. Nor do many believe that human rights concepts are inherently part of the Western tradition, or absent from Asian thought.

NGOs similarly have responded to the conceptual human rights challenge implicit in the "Asian values" thesis. In September, 1992, Human Rights Watch published "Indivisible Human Rights: The Relationship of Political and Civil Rights to Survival, Subsistence, and Poverty."[19] Echoing the arguments of many scholars (including the works of Amartya Sen), the paper described the need for basic political and civil rights in order to assure a stable social and business environment, free and open debate over the wisest allocation of resources, and a constitutionally based rule of law to ensure rights to property, work and consumption.

Elsewhere, Human Rights Watch directly has confronted the proponents of an "Asian concept of human rights." Examples include Aryeh Neier's rebuttal in *Foreign Policy*[20] or Sidney Jones's "The Impact of Asian Economic Growth on Human Rights," published by the Council on Foreign Relations. Human Rights Watch's approach has been to point out the inconsistencies in the "Asian values" argument. Neier charged that in the authoritarian states of Asia, where societies are alleged to be defined by their appreciation of consensus, the norm is hardly "consensus-seeking" but rather "consensus-imposing."[21] He also pointed out that though proponents like Kausikan ostensibly demand freedom to violate only a few rights relating to freedom of expression, in fact, the most ardent supporters of relativistic arguments tend to be the grossest violators of human rights. Jones, pointing to the rising numbers of human rights organizations throughout the region, claimed that "to think that concern over political and civil rights is a Western conceit is to do an enormous disservice to the efforts of many Asians who oppose abuse of state power."[22] She pointed out that much of the Asian reaction to human rights activism

> is not over different principles . . . it is over the tone, style, and means used to address political and civil human rights violations; the often inconsistent use of aid and trade conditionality in the battle for human rights; and the tendency to equate human rights and democracy with the implicit and sometimes explicit attacks on non-democratic political systems that that equation entails.[23]

Of considerable worry to human rights groups everywhere is the "growth-first" or "modernization" theory raised in opposition to human rights advocacy. According to Jones, the argument frequently is not supported by the facts. Citing the cases of Indonesia, Malaysia and China, where the overriding concerns of the substantial and growing middle class were with the maintenance of their business interests, Jones disputed the inherent existence of democratic urges among the middle classes of Asia.[24]

That Asian NGOs found the theme of "Asian values," at least as articulated by their respective government officials, as little more than a deliberate attempt by their elites to obfuscate human rights norms, confuse the issues and prevent international action for rights protection was made patently evident at Bangkok in 1993.[25] Their *Voice*—as defined by the title of the volume they produced, *Our Voice: Reports of the Asia-Pacific Conference on Human Rights*—angrily demanded why the governmental representatives at the official Bangkok meeting consciously deleted all references to torture, freedom of expression and the rule of law in the final draft of the Bangkok Declaration.

Nor did it go unnoticed that for all the talk about the precedence of economic and social rights by the partisans of "Asian values," none of them—neither Malaysia, nor Singapore, nor Indonesia, nor China (until

October, 1997)—had ratified the International Covenant on Economic, Social and Cultural Rights.[26] (China finally signed it in October, 1997, but has yet to ratify it.) Asian NGOs increasingly have been attacking their governments for their failure to uphold the economic and social rights of indigenous peoples, migrant workers, ethnic minorities and women. Nor are these NGOs certain that development policies will have positive consequences over the long term. Specifically, they are fearful of such development consequences as pollution, environmental degradation and reduction in access to land and water resources. Particularly uncertain have been the results of economic growth on the conditions of work and the right of everyone to form and join trade unions. Violations of these rights are reported as "rampant throughout the region."[27]

How the Asian human rights NGOs entered into the mainstream of the international NGO movement merits special attention. Nowhere has the worldwide NGO movement, which by now has established itself in every region of the world and in almost every country of the world, seen such dramatic growth as in Asia. Nowhere has such growth needed to draw so little support form the West, where the biggest international NGOs reside and where they enjoy their widest financial and political support. Human rights campaigns and organizations in Asia are independent, relatively self-sustaining and increasingly powerful in regional and national politics.

Three major groups characterize the Asian NGO phenomenon.[28] The first and often the oldest are the civil liberties groups such as the Indonesian Legal Aid Foundation and the Union for Civil Liberty of Thailand. The second are the development-oriented groups—peasants' organizations, trade unions, women's organizations and various groups struggling for the protection of the culture and land of indigenous populations. The third are the charity and religious organizations.

Human rights activism has a rather recent, almost current, history in Asia. Few groups can trace their roots farther back than a few decades, most of them locating their origins in the democratic revolutions or democratic movements of the 1970s, 80s and 90s. The vast number of Asian NGOs today is mind-boggling. The Philippines, which once had no NGOs whatsoever, today ranks among the world leaders in the number of human rights NGOs,[29] perhaps amounting to tens of thousands.[30] NGOs in the Philippines and elsewhere developed through the democratic movement that emerged in response to 13 years of dictatorship.

According to a compilation of Asian human rights NGOs made by Human Rights Internet, human rights groups exist in virtually every country in Asia except Afghanistan, Brunei, the Maldives, Bhutan and Myanmar.[31] A few even exist in such surprising places as Laos, China, North Korea, Singapore and Vietnam, but these are clearly for international show, either to obfuscate international scrutiny by addressing issues that do not clearly fall into the Western definition of human rights, or to impugn the ideological motives of human rights advocates. Many human rights organizations take international solidarity links very seriously, enthusiastically attending intergovernmental meetings and cooperating with other NGOs in the region.

In an interview, Jeannine Guthrie of Human Rights Watch used the case of India to describe the scope and significance of NGO growth in Asia.[32] Unlike U.S. NGOs, which are composed of professionals inspired by "post-Nuremberg and Cold War" developments, India's NGOs grew out of independence and post-independence movements as well as charitable and social justice motivations. Guthrie claimed that in the case of most social justice groups, the human rights focus is somewhat superficial and is seen as merely a useful instrument. NGO membership is more male than female overall, although there are far more women in NGO work than in any other "professional" occupation. The age of the membership is mostly in the range of 40-50 years, with a few older true believers and a small group of younger college-educated members as well. Funding comes from either of two sources: wealthy, educated elites inspired by a modern vision of secular society; or activist, leftist groups— such as rural poverty groups—working on behalf of disadvantaged castes, groups or minorities and adopting a more political orientation.

Overall, however, the social elites have been the main source of human rights activism. In Indonesia and Malaysia, for instance, mass membership groups were more likely to meet with government repression, while lawyers' groups dedicated to the rule of law were considered useful for the modernization of society.[33] For this reason, Indonesia's leading human rights organization, the Legal Aid Institute (LBH), which began in 1970, has survived and expanded over the years.

The expanding network of NGOs increasingly is able to make use of international and national contacts and support both for protection and for progress. In India in 1992 and 1993, peasant groups, environmentalists and civil liberties groups joined to bring pressure against the Narmada Dam Project, which resulted in the cancelation of a World Bank loan for the project. The civil liberties–oriented Indonesian Legal Aid Institute has brought class-action suits against polluters on behalf of peasants whose land has been damaged.[34] The local NGOs also have cultivated the assistance of official and nongovernmental international bodies concerned with human rights in their countries, and the relationship is increasingly symbiotic.

Economic growth has meant rapid computerization for nongovernmental entities like universities and businesses, and Asia quickly is increasing its presence on the Internet. Most countries in the region have e-mail connections and other basic services. Asians and Asian NGOs are using the Internet as a means of communicating and making contacts with the West, and Westerners in turn increasingly are able to find information about Asian human rights issues produced by Asian themselves. For human rights advocates in the West and in Asia, this aspect of economic growth is probably the most promising development. Worldwide, there are more than 40 million people with access to e-mail, the most basic Internet service, and this figure is increasing at about 10 percent a year.[35] In China, use of the Internet has been available for almost three years and commercial Internet accounts are available, albeit at high cost. In June, 1995, China's Telecommunications Minister stated that "as a sovereign state, China will exercise control of the information" entering China through the Internet. He went on to say: "By linking with the Internet, we do not mean absolute freedom of information."[36] Despite such concerns, which also have been expressed by other authoritarian regimes, there is little government ministries can do to stem the flow of information over the Internet.

Agitation for constitutional democracy, for the rule of law, for an independent judiciary and for protection against the worst abuses—torture, extrajudicial executions, and detention without trial—have been the foremost occupations of the most established and respected NGOs throughout Asia. Even in some of the most inhospitable environments, human rights NGOs are making progress. In Malaysia, the Malaysian Bar Council has vowed to win an independent judiciary. In 1995, following questionable verdicts in celebrated trials, the press gave widespread attention to the Bar Council's condemnations of unfair trials.[37] In Cambodia, the growth of NGOs has been spectacular even by the high growth standards of Asian NGOs in general; before the 1992 peace agreement was signed, Cambodia had no human rights NGOs and no history of NGOs. Today, the State Department country reports refer to over 40 active major human rights NGOs in that country.

In Pakistan, the Human Rights Commission of Pakistan, an NGO, is extremely active; its annual report, *State of Human Rights in Pakistan*, is a glossy, well-written and detailed account of conditions on a broad variety of rights across the country. Founded only in 1987, the group had by 1995 organized over 20 fact-finding missions across the country, released 12 publications (several of them in both Urdu and English), directed at least a dozen seminars and workshops and continued extensive public education efforts, including a new project to publicize The Convention on the Elimination of Discrimination Against Women (CEDAW).[38] In Indonesia, at the urging of the United Nations Human Rights Centre, the government created an Indonesian National Commission on Human Rights (NCHR). It was established by a presidential decree in 1993 that directed a former Chief Justice of the Supreme Court to appoint the members. It can and does receive direct petitions from citizens—thousands yearly—on everything from disappearances to farmland evictions. Almost immediately, the NCHR demonstrated unexpected independence; it proposed that Indonesia adopt several major international human rights agreements including the Convention on the Elimination of All Forms of Racial Discrimination and the Convention Against Torture. During and after the popular uprising in April, 1998 that led to the resignation of President Suharto, it played an important role.

Human rights NGOs, despite their growth and challenges to authoritarian regimes, obviously exist in an uncomfortable position in most parts of Asia. As their efforts increase, NGOs are meeting more effective and subtler forms of repression. Crackdowns and threats of crackdown are not uncommon. Government repression in Indonesia until the 1998 uprising was subtle but powerful. Closure of three popular newspapers in the early nineties had meant reduced publicity for human rights groups. Reporters still attended press conferences but did not publish stories about them. At one press conference in 1994, a human rights group member encouraged the press to attend: "Just take notes. Maybe you can print this next year."[39] A new era would dawn in the spring of 1998.

Mushrooming local NGO influence can count on cooperation from major international NGOs. For Human Rights Watch, Asia is a priority concern, the number of its publications devoted to that area running just behind the number of its reports on Europe. Most significantly, HRW employs a skilled and knowledgeable staffer to working full time with local Asian NGOs. No other geographical region of HRW has such a staffer and no other international NGO carries on its staff such a distinctive position. An obvious objective is to help protect the tenuous independence and political space reserved for local Asian human rights NGOs.

Besides focusing on China, HRW/Asia has concentrated recently on Myanmar, Indonesia, India, Sri Lanka, Pakistan and Cambodia. In addition to civil liberties, it has focused on communal violence, violations of the laws of war, bonded labor and repression of trade unions and forced prostitution. Human Rights Watch especially has attended to the circumstances faced by local human rights groups, and has helped distribute, translate and publicize the reports and publications of some local groups, such as the Indonesian Legal Aid Foundation and the Bonded Labour Liberation Front of India.

Myanmar's gross human rights violations have been a major target of the U.S. trade sanctions strategy, culminating in the passage of American legislation in July, 1997 that placed restrictions on economic and military trade and assistance. HRW/Asia joined in the effort to pass the legislation. As early as May, 1990, it had begun publicizing the crackdown on Daw Aung San Suu Kyi and her democratic party and pressing their case both in the United States and the United Nations.[40] Japan was a key element in the organization's strategy. HRW/Asia officials met with Japanese trade and foreign ministry officials to discuss how to use Tokyo's considerable foreign aid expenditures to promote human rights in Myanmar.[41]

Indonesian human rights violations prior to the uprising had been another prime HRW/Asia target. According to the *New York Times* columnist Thomas Friedman, citing an Indonesian editor in July, 1997: "The Indonesian Government is a police state about six hours a day. The other 18 hours you can negotiate with it, bribe it, ignore it, or go around it."[42] Nevertheless, HRW/Asia never has been hesitant to criticize Indonesia or to cooperate with Indonesian NGOs. Keenly aware that Indonesia is the fourth most populous country in the world and a key power in Asia, the organization regularly has focused on Indonesia's repressive policies toward the formation and maintenance of NGOs like trade unions and human rights and legal defense groups.

If American government attention to the human rights situation in Indonesia prior to the spring of 1998 was never very great, HRW/Asia has compensated by working through congressional avenues, directly appealing to Senators and Representatives, utilizing especially the Congressional Friends of Human Rights Monitors that it had created.[43] While in the mid-1980s Congress rarely, if ever, held hearings on human or labor rights issues concerning Indonesia, by the early 1990s these hearings became more common, in part due to HRW/Asia's pressure. HRW also has pressed for continued attention to Indonesia's repression in East Timor.[44] That HRW's efforts, with respect to the U.S. Congress, joined to the vigorous activities of local NGOs, have been productive was noted by a traveling *New York Times* columnist in 1997. He reported that local groups insisted that pressure from the American Congress had resulted in improvements in the rights of workers and of the inhabitants of East Timor.[45]

No greater challenge on the world scene to the Universal Declaration of Human Rights exists than China. With its enormous population of 1.2 billion and a huge, if uneven, economy marked by very sizable annual percentage increases of productivity and income, China has been in a position to champion the ideas of "Asian values," particularly the rejection of Western insistence upon adherence to the Universal Declaration. International human rights NGOs barely have made a dent in the practices of one of the world's most notorious human rights violators. In fact, China's violations have proceeded apace. The massacre at Tiananmen Square in June, 1989 has been accompanied and followed by arbitrary detentions and arrests of government critics and human rights advocates. A constant feature of the Chinese scene is the harassment of religious and ethnic minorities. Confronted by serious setbacks with respect to limiting economic trade or winning a condemnation vote at the UN, NGOs, more recently, have been engaged in reevaluating their tactics and reconsidering how to cope with this formidable and rising power. Only in the case of preventing China from becoming the site of the Olympic Games could an NGO claim a modest success.

Today, human rights groups may be preoccupied with the People's Republic of China (PRC), but it wasn't always this way. During the first two decades of the Communist regime in China, almost all international human rights organizations failed to address the massive human rights abuses that took place in that country. For those who look upon the international NGO community as the great lever for exposure of human rights abuses, the stunning reality of that community's conduct with respect to China during and after the Mao Tse-tung period is simply dismaying. During the epoch of the Cultural Revolution in the mid-sixties and extending into the early seventies, when hundreds of thousands were killed or imprisoned and starved, silence engulfed the NGO world. The extraordinary early record of failure of NGOs to ascertain the terrible truths about China was documented in 1988 by Roberta Cohen.

The reasons for silence were many. Numerous Western intellectuals were prepared, following the much-awaited granting of entrance visas, to award China greater indulgence as an ideological alternative to Soviet communism, which disillusioned leftists already had abandoned. Of course, many eventually were made aware of the terrible loss of life that had occurred during two and a half decades of Mao's rule, but the Communists' public affirmation of those abuses (in contrast to post-Stalinist secrecy in the Soviet Union), and the assurances by China's new "paramount leader," Deng Xiaoping, that all victims would be rehabilitated, prompted many Westerners to believe that Deng's ascent meant the beginning of a new, more democratic age. Finally, many Westerners thought more of China's value as America's ally against the Soviet Union; human rights issues took second billing to that aim.[46]

Even more decisive was the impenetrable fortress that Chinese society had become under Communist rule. Add to all this the efficiency of the government's Public Security Bureau, whose offices were able to oversee virtually every area of life and whose *laogai* or "reform through labor" camps effectively silenced hundreds of thousands of voices.

Human rights NGOs awoke to China's abuses slowly, led by Chinese students studying in the West and by Amnesty International, which began a "research project" in 1976, at about the time of Mao's death. Other groups, such as Freedom House, began direct interventions on behalf of prisoners arrested for political reasons in 1979, directly confronting Chinese officials and presenting lists of banned publications and prisoners.[47] Freedom House also published an account of a prisoner's experiences in a labor camp. In 1978, Amnesty released the first detailed report by a human rights NGO on China. It noted the continuing use of mass public trials and unlimited pretrial detention. Amnesty added to its list of prisoners of conscience the names of 20 editors and contributors to unofficial journals and 5 Catholic priests, along with those of democracy activists and Tibetans.

Amnesty's information was gathered from Chinese and Hong Kong newspapers, government reports and statistics, accounts of former prisoners and refugees and presumably contacts inside the country. From these disparate sources it was able to compile enough information to produce a fairly extensive 1984 report entitled "China: Violations of Human Rights," which contained a wealth of detail and new criticisms of constitutional provisions and law codes restricting rights of citizens or various sections of the population. It also contained sketches of prisons, texts of law and trial verdicts and profiles and photographs of prisoners. To coincide with the report, Amnesty launched a campaign to publicize Chinese human rights abuses. The campaign lasted several months and produced substantial press attention.

Human Rights Watch/Asia was strangely quiet on Chinese human rights abuses, publishing two reports in 1985 that absolved Chinese leaders of culpability on the grounds that "the lack of intellectual freedom in China today is perceived as a problem by only a tiny minority of the Chinese people." The authors incorrectly regarded the prevailing Communist attitude toward religion as a "slightly disapproving neutrality" and further stated that "those whose rights are being violated most conspicuously today are not 'dissidents' at all, but those charged with ordinary crimes." Until the Tiananmen massacre, HRW/Asia's main work with regard to China dealt with its occupation of Tibet and the abuses of Tibetans by the Public Security Bureau.[48]

Human Rights Watch's response to the Beijing massacre appears to have been the most dramatic reversal of strategy among the human rights NGOs. It released several reports a year and began funding and supporting Chinese human rights activists who had started the expatriate organization Human Rights in China. This organization had provided HRW with the internal resources it had lacked. HRW also met with U.S. Customs Service officials to discuss the use of prison labor in Chinese exports to the United States and began making appearances at many of the ever-increasing number of congressional hearings on China. Along with the hearings, it briefed legislators and their staffs and prepared seminars for Congressional Research Service staff.

Even as the Tiananmen massacre faded from memory, Chinese human rights abuses continued, this time with more aggressive analysis on the part of international NGOs and a more sensitized Western press. Within a few years, NGOs had documented in great detail countless abuses, including suppression of political dissent; repression of religious and cultural practices; violations of internationally accepted norms of criminal procedure; torture and abuse of prison inmates and forced labor and denial of medical care for inmates; forced resettlement of various populations; violations of the environment in connection with projects like the Three Gorges Dam and controversial charges of abuses stemming from population planning policies, including forced abortions, sterilization and "fatal neglect" at state-run orphanages.[49]

During the period from 1990 to late 1993, human rights NGOs benefited from a public consensus that demanded vigorous action on the part of the Bush and early Clinton Administrations. The Chinese leadership was somewhat responsive to human rights matters. The government released 881 prisoners related to the Tiananmen uprising and other well-known dissidents like Wang Juntao, Han Dongfang, Wei Jingsheng, Chen Ziming and Wang Dan; it also permitted Fang Lizhi to leave China from his refuge at the U.S. Embassy and go into exile. The largest group of releases (573 people) was announced in January, 1990, days before Congress was to vote on legislation to protect the more than 40,000 students studying in the United States against involuntary return to China.

The 1992 *World Report* of Human Rights Watch emphasized that "Asia Watch devoted more time and resources to work on China and Tibet than on any other country or region in Asia."[50] In late 1990 and through 1991, the organization successfully pushed to expand the State Department's official list of political dissidents from 150 to over 800.

The most important success of Human Rights Watch involved its lobbying against the selection of Beijing as the site of the Olympic Games for the year 2000. It came during a high point of the international community's scrutiny of human rights matters in China and was largely the achievement of Richard Dicker, an important staffer in the Asia section of HRW who also served as the organization's Assistant General Counsel. The Chairman of the organization, Bob Bernstein, had an especially keen interest in the project and a number of staff members participated in the preparation of a novel strategy.

The original impetus for the formulation of a special strategy came in February, 1991, when China sentenced several leaders of the Tiananmen demonstrators to long prison sentences. Dicker said in an interview:

> I think several people at this organization, and particularly Bob Bernstein, realized, looking back at the experience of the movement that developed in the 70s and 80s on behalf of individual dissidents in the Soviet Union, that one of the things that was lacking in helping make the plight and persecution of Chinese democracy and human rights activists real was, in this country, a personalization of the issues. In the Soviet experience, Andrei Sakharov became a real human being to many, many active-minded people here in the United States, as did Anatoly Shcharansky and Yuri Orlov.[51]

To overcome this failing, HRW, together with the Robert F. Kennedy Memorial Center for Human Rights, in mid-1991 formed a Committee to End the Chinese Gulag, whose Co-Chairs included Bernstein, Cyrus Vance, Chinese physicist and dissident Fang Lizhi, Chinese journalist and dissident Lui Binyang, and Yuri Orlov. The Committee embraced important individuals in the arts and sciences from Beverly Sills to Arthur Miller. Dicker was made Director. It resurrected strategies developed during the seventies to dramatize and expose Soviet brutalities.

Dicker met with members of various professional associations and urged them to take up the cause of Chinese dissidents somehow associated with their profession. This was an effective technique of the seventies in dealing with the Kremlin. The case of Liu Gang, a student leader at Tiananmen who was studying physics at the time, was taken up by a number of Nobel Laureates in letters to the PRC government. Dicker co-wrote, with Fang Lizhi, articles on human rights that were published in scientific journals and magazines. The original aim was to direct pressure on the Bush Administration as well as on the PRC leadership, but this strategy soon was dropped when, in February, 1992, the International Olympic Committee (IOC) announced that Beijing was chosen as one of five finalists for the 2000 Olympics.[52] The stakes now had become extremely high, both for the IOC and Beijing. Though Sydney, Australia, was the frontrunner among athletes, Beijing was the favorite among politicians.[53] Beijing, for its part, craved the international exposure and dramatic symbolism the Olympics can bring to a country, and was lobbying intensively to be chosen.[54]

The Committee to End the Chinese Gulag and HRW itself aggressively began lobbying IOC voting members in anticipation of the September, 1993 vote. They pointed out that the head of Beijing's bid committee was the mayor of Beijing during the 1989 crackdown and had ordered martial law in the weeks preceding the massacre. Besides meeting with IOC members and encouraging editorials in leading newspapers, they lobbied sportswriters from major newspapers in America and Europe. "Slowly but surely," Dicker said, "there began to appear in sports columns and sports articles, questions and commentary about Beijing hosting the 2000 Olympics."[55]

In June, Dicker attended the opening of the Olympic History Museum in Switzerland, where sports delegations and IOC members had gathered and where a large number of European sportswriters assembled. The next month, he testified before the Senate, urging Congress to take a position against Beijing's Olympic bid. At the end of September, when the five finalists were to make their final presentations at the IOC's meeting in Monte Carlo, Dicker arrived to represent Human Rights Watch; in striking contrast, 200 lobbyists came to represent China.

Financial considerations appeared to dominate the meetings in Monte Carlo prior to the vote on September 23. Some in the IOC leadership pushed hard for China, claiming that television networks would be able to charge higher rates and get more viewers because of Beijing's exotic locale and the historic drama of having a new China host the games. "There was all kinds of positioning and maneuvering going on," Dicker said, and "the word in the hotel lobbies and the cafes was that it was a done deal on behalf of Beijing." In the end, the vote was about as close as it could get—45 votes for Sydney, 43 for Beijing. Dicker observed: "IOC members looked over the edge, so to speak, saw the kinds of problems that a government with a human rights record like China's could bring about, in terms of bad PR, for the Olympic Games and the IOC, and enough of them stepped back." This quote appeared in dozens of major newspapers around the world. In an interview, he added, the decision put "the Chinese leadership on notice that they will pay a price for the continued abuse of their own citizens."[56]

After this astonishing success, what would follow turned out to be a grave disappointment. Within the United States, a debate on the question of granting most-favored-nation (MFN) tariff treatment to China had become heated by the time of the IOC vote. It culminated in President Clinton's "de-linking" of human rights and MFN status, signaling to Chinese officials that China could proceed with arrests and repression of dissenters without significant international reprisals. The debate also signaled the arrival of the private business sector as an important player in human rights matters far more influential than sportswriters. Human Rights Watch would be overwhelmed by the lobbying efforts of American corporations with a financial stake in trade with China. The result was a devastating failure for HRW and its allies. Out of the confrontation with formidable business adversaries, HRW would seek to develop a new tactical line directed at lobbying businesses and finding ways of using commercial partners of China to promote human rights.

HRW had continued to push for refusing China its MFN status until Clinton officially "de-linked" MFN status and human rights in 1994. In the opinion of HRW staffers, the very debate on MFN status for China lent credibility to the notion of a possible cut-off of trade benefits, which prompted Beijing to respond with some human rights concessions including the release of several prisoners. But once Clinton's decision had been made, according to Sidney Jones, HRW's top Asian strategist, two lessons were learned: "The business community is an extremely powerful lobby. And if you don't make a threat credible, you may as well forget it."

The MFN debate with American business awakened HRW not only to its differences with commercial interests, but also to possible common agendas. This realization was dramatized in a discussion Jones had with an AT&T official, who argued that getting the Chinese government to open up its system on the control and dissemination of information would free up cellular phone channels to foreign competitors. "That, more than anything else," Jones said, "demonstrated to me that what we've got to be looking for if we're going to use the business community as allies are the points of intersection so that we're appealing to the common interests of the business community and the human rights community."[57]

Human Rights Watch also has begun concerted efforts at confronting corporations and commercial interests that obstruct Western pro–human rights efforts. It continues to advocate linking acceptance of China into the World Trade Organization with its human rights behavior. It also would link loans to China from the World Bank, the International Monetary Fund and the U.S. Export-Import Bank to appropriate human rights conduct. HRW also has sought partnerships with "progressive" Western corporations with operations in China.[58]

President Jiang Zemin's visit to the United States in November, 1997 constituted a significant test of the Clinton Administration's use of "constructive engagement" as the centerpiece of policy toward China. The visit garnered major press attention, particularly due to Jiang's nationwide tour of historical sites, during which human rights groups made careful use of the opportunity. At every stop Jiang encountered demonstrations criticizing China's occupation of Tibet, suppression of religious and political movements, use of prison labor and labor rights violations. But the highlight of his visit was a "kitchen debate"–style press conference at the White House between Jiang and Clinton.

Responding to a question regarding the meaning of the Tiananmen massacre, Jiang claimed that the crackdown was the "correct conclusion" and that "the facts have also proved that if a country with over 1.2 billion population does not enjoy social and political stability, it cannot possibly have the situation of reform and opening-up that we are having today." Clinton responded that "we have a very different view of the meaning of the events at Tiananmen Square. . . . I believe that what happened . . . and the continuing reluctance to tolerate political dissent has kept China from politically developing the level of support in the rest of the world. . . ." Jiang in turn claimed that "concepts on democracy, on human rights and on freedoms are relative and specific ones. And they are to be determined by the specific national situation of different countries." Clinton got the last word: "On this issue, we believe the policy of the [Chinese] government is on the wrong side of history. There is, after all, now a Universal Declaration of Human Rights."[59]

Shortly before leaving for Hawaii, Jiang said in a news conference in Beijing that China soon would sign the UN Covenant on Economic, Social, and Cultural Rights.[60] In the United States, Clinton, under pressure from many sides, pledged to bring up human rights in his discussion with Jiang. The pressure was unusually strong. Demonstrations outside the White House and at almost every stop in Jiang's tour contained Chinese dissidents in exile, Tibetan monks, labor leaders, members of Congress, representatives of human rights organizations and Hollywood stars. Organizations included the RFK Memorial Center for Human Rights, the AFL-CIO, Gary Bauer's right-wing Family Research Council and the International Campaign for Tibet.[61] An audience at the National Press Club, where human rights protestors also were criticizing the PRC, heard from Zhang Lin, a newly escaped dissident and labor organizer who served three separate jail terms following efforts that began in 1989. There Zhang argued that support from human rights groups, including Human Rights in China, saved his life by forcing his jailers to relax his schedule of regular beatings and to generally improve the conditions of his imprisonment.[62]

Clinton's confrontation with Jiang was dismissed by many human rights groups, including HRW, as window-dressing for a policy that relies preeminently on commerce and business relationships to which human rights must be subordinated. Jiang's attitude toward public demonstrations was flippant, referring to them once in a press conference by saying, "noises came into my ears."[63] Yet, soon after his return to China, he did provide a significant gesture: he released Wei Jingsheng. From the perspective of NGOs, the release of Wei was hardly a major victory; still it was an achievement that was in large part a result of their agitation. Human Rights Watch, Amnesty and other groups ultimately won his release by making him a person of almost heroic proportions known everywhere. In March, 1998, Beijing offered a similar gesture by releasing and exiling Wang Dan, a student leader at Tiananmen. It was an obvious response to the decision of the United States to withdraw its co-sponsorship of a resolution criticizing China at the UN Commission on Human Rights. China, in another concession, agreed to ratify the Covenant on Civil and Political Rights.

The exchange between the Chinese and American leaders once again served to illuminate the sharply different perspective of the two on the validity, legitimacy and moral supremacy of the Universal Declaration of Human Rights. While Jiang was giving "Asian values" an ideological underpinning by insisting that human rights are "relative" and vary according to "specific national" circumstances of particular countries, Clinton, without using the term "universality," made it clear that there is only one standard for human rights, the Universal Declaration, from which there can be no deviation on grounds of relativity and specificity. The same theme would be reiterated by Clinton during his official state visit to China in late June, 1998 at a press conference in Beijing and in a lecture to university students. On June 29, he told the students that personal freedom is the "mandate of the new century" and that certain basic human rights are "universal." China was "on the wrong side of history," in Clinton's view, as were, by implication, the other proponents of "Asian values"—Malaysia, Singapore, and Indonesia.

No more moving and powerful endorsement of the principle of universality has been articulated than that made by UN Secretary-General Kofi Annan just a couple of months before the beginning of the fiftieth-anniversary celebration of the Universal Declaration of Human Rights. Speaking at a dinner in New York on October 14, 1997, Annan took note of transformations in his own continent, Africa, which are pushing toward greater democracy and more human rights. Some Africans, he observed, view "the concern of human rights as a rich man's luxury for which Africa is not ready, or even as a conspiracy, imposed by the industrialized West." The argument simply echoed that made by China or Singapore or Indonesia. Annan found such thinking "demeaning" to every African.

And then, paraphrasing that great oration in Shakespeare's *The Merchant of Venice,* Annan asked: "Do not African mothers weep when their sons and daughters are killed or tortured by agents of oppressive rule? Do not African fathers suffer when their children are unjustly sent to jail? Is not Africa as a whole the poorer when one of its voices is silenced?" Annan's response to these rhetorical questions merits permanent inscription in a hallowed place:

> Human rights are African rights. They are also Asian rights, they are European rights. They are American rights. They belong to no government, they are limited to no continent, for they are fundamental to humankind itself.[64]

Certainly, that was how the international and national NGOs perceived the issue. And, significantly, that was precisely the goal of the Indonesian university students and their supporters during their seizure of the Parliament building in Jakarta in May 1998. Just as they demanded an end to cronyism, corruption and nepotism that had characterized the Suharto regime, they also called for free elections, free expression and the release of political prisoners. The slogan of "Asian values" of the military elite, at least in Indonesia, was all but interred for the time being. The Universal Declaration of Human Rights was clearly the unexpressed goal of the popular uprising in a state whose elite leadership was a major champion of its opposite. Not surprisingly, Suharto's successor, B. J. Habibie, related that, on his first day in office, he was "negotiating about human rights." Whether the Indonesian example will spread elsewhere in Asia cannot, of course, be ascertained. But that the military and political elites will seek to cling to the formulation of "Asian values" or its variation elsewhere in the Third World, can be expected if only as a means for ideologically justifying their arbitrary rule and maintaining their power.

Yet, in China, Clinton virtually echoed the thesis and language of Kofi Annan:

> But we are convinced that certain rights are universal, not American rights or European rights or rights for developed nations but the birthright of people everywhere, now enshrined in the United Nations Declaration of Human Rights.[65]

CHAPTER TWENTY

Lobbying for the Rule of Law

When the new UN High Commissioner for Human Rights, Mary Robinson, made her very first speech in the United States, it was to the Lawyers Committee for Human Rights on October 8, 1997. The occasion was the Committee's annual dinner, where she was presented with its 1997 Human Rights Award. The affair was less an honor for the High Commissioner than it was for the Committee, upon whom a special bestowal of recognition was made by the international organization's highest human rights official. After all, she had been in office only a short time, hardly enough to have earned distinction, although she earlier had established a reputation in the human rights field. Other NGOs were anxious for her to address them or to use their platform for significant pronouncements on her plans and programs. Mary Robinson's selection of the Lawyers Committee gave it a kind of pride of place in America's human rights firmament.

And, indeed, her opening remarks—seemingly off-the-cuff—appeared to point in this direction.[1] She recalled that on her first visit to the United States in 1992 while President of Ireland, it was suggested to her that she "have a meeting with somebody called Mike Posner," who is the Executive Director of the Committee. Paying respect to the persuasive powers of Posner, Robinson recalled that he wanted to tell her what the Committee was doing generally and, specifically, with respect to Northern Ireland. She then added: "and I sat and I listened like we all do when Mike gets us into a corner, by and large he gets his way. . . ."

Besides the praise for Posner and "the very important and very thoughtful and insightful and sensitive work that is being done" by the Lawyers Committee particularly in the context of Northern Ireland, the High Commissioner singled out his Director of Policy and Programming, Stefanie Grant. Robinson recalled that the very first "working paper"—presumably on human rights—that came across her desk in Dublin after she was approved in her new post was from this Committee official, who offered to be "helpful" in this "very difficult" job Robinson had undertaken.

What followed in Robinson's presentation was a listing of the Lawyers Committee's quite impressive "asylum program," its special efforts to assure the independence of lawyers and judges in various countries, its unusual success in encouraging prominent corporate attorneys to provide pro bono work in the human rights arena, its especially distinctive "lawyer-to-lawyer network" and, finally, its "very detailed . . . very analytical" critique of U.S. foreign policy in the organization's Quadrennial Report. The itemized outline very well could serve an outside observer as a point of departure for characterizing the Committee's achievements. Only one or two important priorities were surprisingly, if regrettably, not noted.

When Robinson concluded her speech, she acknowledged that the problems her office would face "continue to be very serious" and that she had "a great deal to absorb." To illustrate, she related her experience of finding the right UN elevator to enter in order to push the right button that would take her to the floor she was seeking. It was by no means easy; on the contrary, uncertainty and confusion plagued the novice at UN Headquarters. Robinson hoped that "the kind of gifted thinking that Stefanie Grant gave" would be available to assist her in coping with the problems. Of Grant's and the Lawyers Committee's assistance, she need have had little doubt.

The Lawyers Committee, from its very beginning, has sought to be helpful to those needing human rights assistance. As its name indicates, it is "the largest and most influential American lawyers organization dedicated to human rights. . . ."[2] It was founded in 1978 as an outgrowth of the International League for Human Rights and the Council of New York Law Associates.[3] The Council was a New York–based group that provided pro bono opportunities for lawyers and was seeking to expand this special pursuit into the international field. Funding was provided by the Ford Foundation and the Rockefeller Brothers' Fund, enabling the Lawyers Committee to come into an independent existence, although it continued technically to be a part of the League until 1980.

Initially, the Committee saw itself as being based upon the mold of Amnesty International, engaged in monitoring human rights abuses using established international human rights standards as a guideline and approaching its subject in a cautious manner. In more recent years, the Committee moved away from what a staffer called "the business of monitoring."[4] Two reasons were the basis of the change. Firstly, the Committee was a far smaller organization than Amnesty. Lacking the latter's extensive research manpower and facilities, it seemed fruitless to try to replicate their research methods. Besides, soon afterward, Human Rights Watch would begin spanning the globe and the logic for yet another monitoring body quickly would dissipate.

One further consideration was involved and would prove critical in the thinking of the Committee. Local or national NGOs were beginning to emerge in the late seventies and eighties that themselves were engaged in monitoring human rights abuses.[5] Instead of replicating the efforts of local NGOs, it would be far more productive to become a "facilitating and networking organization" vis-à-vis these groups, a role that the Committee would champion.

"Selective" was how a staffer defined the Committee's function. He meant that the Committee was selective in its determination of which issues to take up and in what ways to become involved. Posner, in an interview, elaborated upon this theme. While the Amnesty or HRW models were still valuable, he explained, there was a fundamental difference in how the Committee perceived the issues. In some ways the Lawyers Committee's view was quite distinctive from the other two. Instead of getting the "facts of what is wrong . . . the most useful contribution" the Committee could make would be to take "a new look at how to approach these issues."[6] For one thing, emphasis would be placed upon international and national legal standards. That made perfect sense for a law-oriented body. The Committee naturally was determined to "figure out how to use international and national law standards to advance rights."

What the new High Commissioner for Human Rights recalled first among the various programs of the Lawyers Committee that impressed her—the asylum project—was, in fact, closely tied to refugee protection, one of its earliest, if not the earliest, operations. Posner recalled that the first person he hired was Arthur Helton, who would be in charge of immigration-related activities. The date Posner gave was 1980-81, which coincided with the beginning of the Lawyers Committee itself.[7] Helton remained for more than a dozen years, building up an operation that impacted greatly on America's humanitarian image. As a leading Committee staffer recalled, the new program was "based on the idea that refugees were people, too, and have human rights."[8] At the time, the idea, he said, "was quite revolutionary." Now, the Lawyers Committee need no longer feel like a "revolutionary." In a recent *Annual Report,* it took special pride in noting that it is the "only international legal human rights group to include refugee protection as an integral part of its wider human rights work."[9]

The gratification is neither misplaced nor unwarranted. For the desperate, fleeing persecution or the threat of it and clinging to the hope of survival, the refugee and asylum programs of the Lawyers Committee cannot be easily replicated. The 1996 asylum representation caseload was quite huge—900 clients from over 70 countries.[10] And the expertise of the Committee can assure a fairly high degree of success—85 percent—hardly inconsequential when measured against other types of caseloads. Much of the work done by the Committee is accomplished by volunteers, often from major law firms providing service on a pro bono basis. An estimate in 1996 placed the number of hours of voluntary service as being 45,000—the equivalent of $6.5 million.

The Lawyers Committee has an elaborate program for recruiting, training and supervising lawyers for asylum representation. A video training library is available for the preparation of asylum applications and for judicial review. The library tapes also provide reviews of human rights conditions in various countries of the world, thereby giving insight into motivations for seeking asylum. A typical volunteer might donate up to 500 hours on a particular case, extending as long as three years.[11] According to a Committee staffer, the asylum program is "the most successful program involving our volunteer lawyers."[12]

As part of its immigration reform strategies or even with respect to special cases, the Committee employs its Washington office personnel to lobby Congress and the Administration on behalf of asylum-seekers and immigrants. An early *Annual Report* stressed that the Committee would monitor "legislative developments and administrative rule-making that potentially could threaten the due process rights of refugees."[13] The monitoring process is done in a rather precise manner and numerous columnists of major newspapers have often called attention to these cases, no doubt after prompting by Committee specialists. An *Annual Report* frankly admitted that the Committee certainly would pursue "litigation in selected cases of potential national significance."[14]

An example of the Committee's legislative activity can be found in the fight it put up to prevent enactment of legislation introduced in 1995 that would impede the ability of genuine refugees to seek asylum in the United States. Refugees arriving in the United States without valid travel documents immediately would be deported unless they were able to prove a "credible fear of persecution." But, not infrequently, a refugee could be a dissident or an opponent of a repressive regime and was hardly in a position to seek official travel documents. Or his threatened circumstances may have compelled him to resort to false travel documents. Since the proposed legislation in the House of Representatives would leave little time for proving that the asylum-seeker faced torture or persecution at home, the Committee sent out a "Call to Action" to members of the legal profession, stating that the House measure would "fundamentally change the U.S. asylum system from one that is designed to protect refugees to one that will return them directly to their persecutors."

While the Lawyers Committee could not kill the legislation that imposed new "harsh restrictions on asylum seekers," it was able to help win acceptance of the more lenient Senate version that changed the filing deadline for application submission from 30 days to one year. In a Committee publication, a Washington office staffer thanked the volunteer lawyers whose phone calls and letters helped the Committee "influence" the congressional decision.

It is not only the refugee problem in the United States that concerns the Lawyers Committee. World refugee issues are a continuing subject in which the organization is very much involved. The office of the UN High Commissioner for Refugees (UNHCR) is a major international agency with which it has a relationship and the Committee is frequently engaged in "commenting on the limitations and problems with the UNHCR's approach."[15] For the Committee, the primary refugee problem has been located in Africa. After a close examination of the refugee question in seven African countries, which had involved considerable research, the study concluded that Africa's "refugee crisis" could not be addressed without determining what motivated the refugees to flee their homelands. "Overwhelmingly," the reasons prompting the flight "were connected with abuse of human rights."[16] Committee investigators found that "it is clear that most of the worst abuses of refugee rights would be overcome if governments simply complied with the international standards which they have, in most cases, already ratified."

African governments were called upon to ratify the Convention on Refugees of the Organization of African Unity (OAU), as well as the UN Convention Relating to the Status of Refugees. Ratification was not enough. The study asked African governments to establish training programs for those dealing with refugees and to create independent mechanisms to receive and investigate complaints by refugees. Anticipating the later Congo and Rwanda refugee traumas in 1995-97, the Committee urged African governments to "prohibit armed activity by those purporting to be refugees."[17] Also, they were asked to "prosecute those alleged to be responsible for gross violations of human rights." The OAU itself was urged to "establish a network of national human rights NGOs," and the UNHCR was called upon to openly criticize "governments that seriously fail to meet their obligations to protect refugees."[18]

Whether these recommendations were expected to be responded to or acted upon was hardly likely. OAU was the weakest of all regional institutions, especially when it came to human rights. And UNHCR, as an international agency dependent upon the UN and donor countries, was unlikely to challenge sources of its influence and funding. Still, the report and the workshop that followed it in Senegal in 1995 was useful. The workshop provided legal training for the participants and offered guidelines on how to proceed further. Present at the Senegal workshop were 18 NGOs from 11 countries in Africa, as well as representatives of UNHCR and of refugee organizations. For African human rights NGOs, it marked a step forward into the international limelight.

An especially high priority objective of the Lawyers Committee in recent years has been assistance to NGO groups, especially in developing countries. Entitled the NGO Partnership Program, it is designed to "support the work of local human rights activists [who are] essential to human rights protection around the world."[19] No other international NGO has had this special orientation to local NGOs, although Human Rights Watch/Asia, as noted previously, has had a distinctive relationship with Asian NGOs. For the Lawyers Committee, local NGOs are "key operational partners in all [our] programs." Indeed, as characterized by a top staffer, "our central obligation" is "the protection of these advocates and the creation of a legal environment in which they can operate freely. . . ."[20]

The special interest in local NGOs is an outgrowth of the Committee's analysis of the fundamental shifts in NGO human rights advocacy.[21] As perceived by Posner and a colleague who served as Coordinator of NGO and UN programs, Candy Whittome, the first phase in NGO advocacy came with the creation and development of internationally focused NGOs, which corresponded in time with the establishment of the UN, the adoption of its basic international covenants and the establishment of international enforcement mechanisms and procedures. The second phase of NGO advocacy involved the proliferation of national human rights monitoring and advocacy groups in all regions of the world. If international NGOs were and are "vitally important," they "can never be a substitute for local advocacy efforts."

Posner and Whittome went on to say that "effective domestic implementation by human rights law depends in large part on the development, institutional strength and independence of local human rights organizations." Local NGOs are critical for the emergence of civil society, and they are indispensable for assisting societies in transition from authoritarian to more participatory forms of government. Besides holding governments accountable, they provide an important educational function, advising groups in society of their rights and of governments' obligation to respect them.

An especially creative project used in conjunction with its NGO Partnership operation was the Lawyers Committee's so-called Witness Program. Begun in 1992, it enabled NGOs in developing countries, and especially those that were isolated from the mainstream of international society, to be able to report fully and accurately on human rights violations and transgressions. They would be equipped with hand-held video cameras and later with fax machines. These basic instruments of communication would allow the isolated NGOs to record and immediately report details of repression by an abusive authoritarian regime.[22]

How the program got started involved a significant brush with the entertainment world as well as some imaginative thinking by a former Amnesty International staffer. Also critical was the willingness of a major corporation to invest substantially in a modest human rights initiative. In 1987-88, the famous rock-and-roll singer Peter Gabriel was on a world tour for Amnesty International, spreading human rights ideas. He had brought along a hand-held video camera to record his own impression of the different countries that he was visiting. In conversations with human rights–oriented persons in India or Zimbabwe, he was asked: "Where did you get the camera? We're working here in isolation. Nobody knows what we do."[23]

Gabriel talked to the Lawyers Committee and together they approached the Reebok Foundation. As described by a Lawyers Committee report, the Witness Program gives technical support to local NGOs "by training them and equipping them with hand-held video cameras and fax machines."[24] In this manner, they are enabled to "communicate more effectively with [NGOs in] their own countries and with the international community." More than anything, the idea was a living expression of what Eleanor Roosevelt was saying some 45 years earlier about the "curious grapevine." In charge of this program at first was Mary Bailey, who once had worked for Amnesty as a press representative but came over to the Committee to handle special projects.[25]

The Witness Program under her coordination was hardly systematic; it was done in an ad hoc manner. In 1993, 50 cameras and fax machines were given to 50 groups in 36 countries. But by 1995, Posner emphasized, it had become an "organizational priority." The Committee provided an interviewer with a listing of 40 countries in which 64 organizations (deliberately not identified for security reasons) used the equipment.[26] What made the videotape footage extremely valuable was that it could be utilized not only for TV media coverage but as direct evidence in courts and UN human rights bodies. Thus, the Lawyers Committee shared footage of mass graves in Croatia with Physicians for Human Rights, who submitted it to the UN Commission of Experts. It was a valuable piece of evidence for demanding an International Criminal Tribunal for the Former Yugoslavia. And, indeed, footage later would be used by the Tribunal.

Precisely because of their work in defending people against infringement of their fundamental rights as incorporated in the Universal Declaration of Human Rights, the Covenant and other instruments, local NGOs inevitably are regarded with suspicion by their own governments, especially if those governments are known as abusers and violators of human rights. Independent NGOs often are seen as antigovernmental, rather than nongovernmental and, more disturbingly, as a threat to security and stability.

Especially are local NGOs in need of assistance when one or another international NGO targets a particular abusive regime in which local NGOs operate. A Lawyers Committee staffer observed that "local groups are on the sharp end of [retaliation] when the government is offended by a report" that an international NGO has issued. "They don't arrest us," he caustically, if sympathetically, commented, "they arrest them [local NGOs]."[27] Targeting an NGO as scapegoat is a traditional, if irrational, technique for responding to criticism. The staffer pointedly commented that international NGOs must recognize "a responsibility we have to bear, we have to think of the consequences of our work on the people who we very closely identify with in the country."

Frequently, however, the local NGO is targeted because it publicly has spoken out against human rights abuses. When subjected to one or another form of repression, the local NGO may want to consider this, said the staffer, as a "backhanded compliment since it shows that the government is taking notice because the criticism hurts them." Whether as scapegoats or as hostile critics, local NGOs, perceptively observed the Committee staffer, "are held hostage by the government."[28] In recognizing the dangers these NGOs face of being incarcerated or threatened as a "hostage," the Lawyers Committee engages in a number of activities to provide "protection of these advocates."

The 1996 *Annual Report* of the Committee outlined various protection devices, including "legal and regional expertise; [and] technical assistance." Especially important was to extend the threatened NGO with "international credibility," which meant submitting action recommendations to various legislatures calling for the release of an NGO, lobbying officials, appearing in court as trial observers if the "hostage" was subjected to trial and, most important, helping "to orchestrate at the international level [an appropriate protest]."[29]

Numerous examples of governmental restrictions imposed upon NGOs were detailed in a volume produced by the Lawyers Committee— *Shackling the Defenders*—that provided an almost authoritative account of problems confronting "independent human rights advocacy worldwide."[30] The Posner-Whittome article in the Columbia law journal highlighted and summarized examples of the major forms of governmental restrictions.[31] Chinese law is illustrative of the means used to prevent the emergence of independent human rights monitors. Political dissent simply is regarded as an attempt to undermine the Communist political system. Until recently, dissent was treated as "counterrevolutionary" and was seen as "sabotage" of the "people's democratic dictatorship."

In March, 1997, the National People's Congress of China dropped the category of "counterrevolutionary crimes." However, in its place there was substituted the category of "crimes endangering state security." For the Lawyers Committee, the legislative modifications constituted "mere cosmetic change."

A second example of the total suppression of monitoring human rights groups was to be found in Singapore. An interrelated legal and administrative system resembling *Catch-22* prevents human rights NGOs from existing: a so-called Societies Act grants the government authority, through the "Registrar of Societies," to refuse or to cancel the registration of a group. All groups of more than ten members are required to register. Denial of registration under the law is very much part of the government's powers, and an applicant need not be told why its application has been denied. An appeal hardly would be possible, since the constitution of Singapore grants its parliament the authority to impose "restrictions on the right to form associations."[32]

Egypt provided an example of how a government may not prevent the operation of an NGO but, rather, by law, may limit its operation by licensing procedures. All NGOs must be authorized by the government to operate freely. Even when it grants such permission, the Egyptian Ministry of Social Affairs holds the power to prohibit the approved NGO from affiliating with outside groups. If refused licensing for whatever reasons, the NGO can appeal through various court levels. One of the most prominent Egyptian human rights groups—Egyptian Organization for Human Rights (EOHR)—for a long time, through appeals, after first being rejected—has lived an existence of suspended animation, always uncertain about its future.

The legal restrictions are but a mild illustration of the obstacles confronting human rights monitors in authoritarian societies. More dangerous and more formidable are the use of torture, disappearances, killings and arbitrary detentions to intimidate or frighten the monitors. A particularly disturbing facet of this process of intimidation has to do with the defenders of human rights monitors. Specifically, lawyers and judges who have acted as counselors for or defenders of the rights of activists have been targeted as enemies of the state and subjected to attacks and threats. In 1993 alone, the Lawyers Committee documented over 250 cases of attacks on lawyers and judges, involving some 450 people in 50 countries.[33]

In all of the Lawyers Committee's programs, whether dealing with refugee and asylum cases, NGO Partnership relations or aspects of multifaceted UN operations, volunteers of the legal profession stand at its core. The Lawyers Committee takes open pride in its purpose of both educating and mobilizing "U.S. lawyers in human rights advocacy."[34] In an interview, Posner emphasized that what "distinguished" the work of the Lawyers Committee from that of other leading U.S. based human rights groups was precisely its "legal skills" and its "established and expanding roots in the U.S. legal community."[35] Tapping those roots and utilizing the legal connections and skills was and is a mainstay of the Lawyers Committee operation.

A Lawyer-to-Lawyer Network, established in 1986, is the core instrument for mobilizing the more activist segments of the American legal community to become involved and to act. The proposed action has a certain sectarian quality, although there is absolutely nothing wrong with initially being preoccupied with the members of one's own profession. Besides, very frequently the defense of attorneys under attack cannot but have a spillover effect in protecting human rights activists whose defenders often are legal activists. Posner and the Chairman of the Committee, Norman Dorsen, succinctly characterized the "defining purpose of the Lawyers Committee" as being "to protect human rights lawyers and uphold their legitimate role as front-line defenders of rights within their own communities."[36]

Monthly appeals are issued on the most urgent cases of abuses against lawyers. Ordinarily an appeal provides a one-page description of the case and is sent to 9,000 members of the international bar in 134 countries, each of whom is encouraged to write to the offending government. Also receiving copies of the appeal are members of Congress, diplomats, U.S. State Department officials and the news media. In addition, the Committee sends out an "Advocacy Alert" that focuses, usually in the form of a three-page summary, on a particular issue, such as the introduction of legislation that might undermine or weaken human rights work. Members are urged to write governments opposing the threatening legislation.

Each year, the Committee publishes *In Defense of Rights,* a digest of attacks on lawyers and judges. The 1992 edition included 324 cases in 54 countries, among which were 23 lawyers who were murdered.[37] The Lawyer-to-Lawyer Network embraces some 1,000 members. Since 1987, it has sought to help more than 200 legal professionals around the world.[38]

An example of how the Network functions was a communication sent out concerning Colombia in December, 1997. The viciously repressive apparatus of the country's military, through paramilitary instrumentalities, had been a major concern of the Lawyers Committee for some time. It already had highlighted the abuses by the military to the UN Human Rights Committee as well as in op-ed articles in major press organs. Especially disturbing developments affecting the legal profession surfaced toward the end of the year. The Network communication revealed that at least four Colombian human rights lawyers faced criminal prosecution and other threats as a result of accusations contained in a series of military reports submitted to prosecutors. One of the lawyers who defends victims of human rights violations was accused by the military of being "dedicated to having bandits held in various jails declared 'political prisoners.'" A "human rights collective" embracing 15 organizations had been dubbed by a military intelligence report as a "subversive front organization." Criminal cases against several members of the organization, including two lawyers, already had been initiated.

The Lawyers Committee's focus was upon the urgent need to protect lawyers. It stressed that "the military's accusations improperly equate the attorneys who provide representation for those charged with participation in insurgency with the insurgents themselves." Again, the Network communication pointed to the Basic Principles on the Role of Lawyers adopted by the UN in 1990. One of the key Principles cited specifies that "lawyers shall not be identified with their clients or their client's cases as a result of discharging their functions." In addition, the intimidating threat of trials for human rights lawyers was compounded, noted the Network commentary, by the possibility of physical violence being used against them.

Recipients were urged to "write politely worded letters" to Colombia's Prosecutor-General outlining the concerns under international law raised by these cases. The letters should cite as a point of departure the International Covenant on Civil and Political Rights, since the Colombian government expressly had given its commitment to comply with recommendations of the Covenant's implementing organ, the Human Rights Committee. What was to be requested was an immediate review of the cases involving human rights lawyers and the termination of the investigation if the allegations were without foundation.

Also suggested were letters to the UN Office of the High Commissioner for Human Rights in Bogota, urging the office's legal specialists to formally request information from Colombian authorities about why the investigations of these cases had been initiated. Copies of the appeals were asked to be sent to specific high-level government officials in Bogota and to Colombia's Embassy in Washington and to the U.S. Ambassador in Bogota. Communications from prominent American attorneys, it was hoped, would not go completely unnoticed, especially when they were reinforced by similar appeals from attorneys in Europe or Latin America and when copies of the appeal appeared in the hands of influential diplomatic and political officials.

At times, the intervention might take a more direct form, through a visitation, rather than by mail. A dramatic example was provided when the Human Rights Foundation of Turkey—the 1994 recipient of a very prized Committee award, the Roger Baldwin Medal of Liberty—had nine of its Board members hauled before a court in Ankara on grounds of "publicly insulting the laws of the Turkish Republic." When the Foundation requested help, the Committee was obligated to respond, as it would in every case involving a Baldwin Medal winner. An emergency Committee delegation was sent to Ankara to "observe" the trial. Their presence may have had the required effect; the nine Foundation Board members were acquitted of all charges.[39]

A final subject of the Lawyers Committee that impressed Mary Robinson was its Quadrennial Report on Human Rights and U.S.

Foreign Policy. The subject had been, in fact, a priority concern of the Committee almost from its earliest years, when it prepared, with the cooperation of Human Rights Watch, strong and effective critiques of the State Department's annual Country Reports on Human Rights Practices. It was probably because of the embarrassing disclosures made in these critiques that the later State Department Country Reports became unusually accurate. Still the Committee continued to demonstrate the need for precisely accurate information and documentation by closely reviewing each year the State Department Country Reports and, as a recent critique noted, "correcting and supplementing them."[40] With a certain degree of legitimate pride, the Committee called its critique "an indispensable companion volume to the State Department reports."[41]

A fundamental thesis of the Lawyers Committee as it deals with American foreign policy is that U.S. human rights policy should be guided by internationally recognized laws and norms and by a uniform application of universal standards. Moreover, the Committee holds as its basic tenet that the promotion of human rights policy is in the national interest of the United States. In applying these theses to specific policy matters, the Committee gives great attention to U.S. economic aid programs. The linkage of U.S. foreign assistance programs to human rights was pursued in an important work by the Committee entitled *Human Rights and U.S. Foreign Policy*. Especially examined was the role legislation could offer by linking aid programs to human rights.[42]

As an organization for which international law must have a binding and universal character, the Committee would want to have the United States drop its "reservations" to the International Covenant on Civil and Political Rights.[43] The Committee has not been reluctant to advise a UN body—the Human Rights Committee—that U.S. law and practices in certain matters do not meet the required standards of the International Covenant on Civil and Political Rights. At a briefing for members of the Human Rights Committee in March, 1995, the Lawyers Committee itemized several examples of a lower U.S. standard: the expansion of capital punishment, poor prison conditions and racial discrimination.[44]

Every four years since 1988, the Lawyers Committee has conducted a broad survey of human rights aspects of U.S. foreign policy. Thus, when the value of incorporating human rights as a component of American foreign policy was challenged in a leading foreign policy journal in 1994-95, it was only natural that the Committee's Director was asked to respond. The trenchant criticism was delivered by Alan Tonelson, a former staff editor at *Foreign Policy*.[45] In an elaborate assault upon official American human rights policy as a total failure, he traced its origin at the foreign policy level of government to the Cold War. With the end of the Cold War, Tonelson insisted, human rights as "a systematic, dedicated policy" was certain to collapse.

In Tonelson's vision of the international scene, U.S. human rights policy had resulted in little improvement in the internal situation of abusive regimes. What was worse, Washington policy was either alienating its allies and friends or was motivating them to consciously subvert that policy. In Asia, America's human rights policy, he said, was seen as an "arrogant effort to impose Western values. . . ." Symptomatic of the failure was the Clinton Administration's "zig-zag record on numerous human rights fronts."

For Posner, the argument was so flawed with inaccuracies that he found it unnecessary to be excessively irritated. Human rights had not begun with the Cold War; only the uninformed or misinformed would not have known that the end of World War II, largely in consequence of the searing Holocaust trauma, saw a blossoming of human rights purposes, inscribed in the UN Charter, evoked in the Nuremberg Tribunal, spelled out in the Universal Declaration of Human Rights and made legally binding in the genocide treaty and subsequent human rights conventions.[46]

Then, taking up the question of whether human rights advocacy had been effective, Posner showed how human rights issues are at the center of public attention almost everywhere and that most governments greatly fear being stigmatized as an abuser state. And with the emergence of human rights as a throbbing issue on the world agenda, a huge number of NGO human rights activists dot the political landscape everywhere, especially in East Asia, where they, not their rulers, are winning the battle on the universality of the human rights movement.

It was the most recent Quadrennial Report that attracted the attention of the UN High Commissioner for Human Rights. The study's main point was that "the consistent pursuit of human rights is in the long run, not only quite compatible with but likely to enhance other U.S. national interests."[47] Significantly, the report found that while human rights in U.S. foreign policy was better than it ever had been earlier, it nonetheless still occupied a rather minor and modest place.

Two examples pointed to the severe limitations of the human rights aspects of U.S. foreign policy. When Energy Secretary Hazel O'Leary visited China in late 1994, she was asked whether she intended to "leave the issue of human rights to the other departments of government that are charged with that responsibility." The question obviously referred to the State Department Bureau of Democracy, Human Rights and Labor.

O'Leary replied that this was "a very fair interpretation of her position." Similarly at the UN World Conference on Human Settlements (Habitat), held in Istanbul in 1996, the U.S. delegation was instructed by the State Department to "make clear for the record that the U.S. does not recognize the international right to housing," despite reference to this point in the Covenant on Economic, Social and Cultural Rights.[48]

Four major themes stand out in the Quadrennial Report. The most important theme is that despite Clinton's support for human rights, the government was "lacking a coherent, consistent and coordinated approach to implementing human rights policy across the board."[49] Secondly, multilateral actions are far preferable to individual state actions in moving human rights forward, for they offer "an effective means of helping to contain or resolve conflicts that could turn more deadly."[50] Thirdly, the strength or weakness of a UN peace operation stands in direct proportion to the success or failure "in putting human rights concerns in the forefront." Fourth, the U.S. government and business community must come to recognize that "their long-term interests are best served by governments that are founded on the rule of law and accept internationally agreed upon standards of conduct."[51]

An example of how the Committee would advise on decision-making with respect to a single country was provided in a letter by Posner to President Clinton on June 16, 1997.[52] He began by warning that the President's policy of "comprehensive engagement" with China would not have "domestic support" unless Congress and the American people perceive that the United States has a "coherent and effective strategy for promoting China's respect for internationally recognized human rights." That strategy must be geared to "insistence on the rule of law, based on international standards...." What Clinton was urged to do was to engage in a "persistent, principled critique of Chinese law and practice" including the encouragement of "systemic [legal] reform in key areas."

The letter was consciously nonprovocative. While it urged the Administration to press China on taking "immediate steps" to improve its human rights record, including the release of "prisoners of conscience," its basic thrust was in signaling the Chinese leadership that Washington "recognizes the significance and complexity of the reform process within China" and that it "appreciates the positive role played by Chinese advocates of rule of law." A key aim of the United States should be reinforcement of "the efforts of Chinese legal reformers...." The Lawyers Committee was probably the only human rights agency that called attention to these "legal reformers." If these "reformers" constituted a substantial and influential group, the Committee's recommendation could prove particularly productive. For the time being, the rule of law proposal carried overtones of valuable symbolism without constituting a serious challenge to the Chinese-American relationship.

A *New York Times* foreign affairs columnist, Thomas Friedman, recognized the letter's significance.[53] Urging the Chinese to move to a more law-based society would be far less abrasive than asking them to become "a democracy tomorrow." The rule of law would be welcomed by those seeking permanent business relationships or accountability; it was at the heart of modern social relationships and of the stability they required. Certainly, for an NGO of lawyers, the Committee's advocacy was perfectly reasonable. Not everyone was convinced, however, that it provided an opening wedge for advancing human rights in China.

That the Committee would focus upon American foreign policy rather than upon international affairs in general was and is a distinctive feature of this NGO. It issues no World Report, does not identify itself as an international NGO and, except in special instances, deliberately has chosen to avoid monitoring abuses in other countries, leaving that to Amnesty International and Human Rights Watch. It claims no offices abroad; nor does it aspire to have any. And it takes particular pride in noting that it is American-based, as distinct from the International Commission of Jurists, which, Posner emphasized, is Geneva-based and has "a European focus."[54]

Still, it is one of the most important human rights NGOs, with a staff that increased enormously from its 1978-80 beginning, reaching 35 by 1993 and 42 by 1996. It is expected to reach about 50 within the next few years.[55] Similarly, its budget jumped from a mere $50,000 when the Committee was first launched to $750,000 in the mid-eighties, mostly from foundations, to $3.4 million in 1996.[56] But that relatively high figure does not reflect the pro bono voluntary contributions of the U.S. legal community, "valued at more than $8,000,000. . . ."[57] Of the $3.4 million, 60 percent came from 25 foundation grants. Yet a significant amount came from 150 law firms, 12 law schools, 8 public interest/legal service groups and numerous individuals.[58] The members of its Rule of Law Council are drawn from influential segments of law schools, universities, leading law firms and corporations.

Within the spectrum of NGOs on the American scene, the Lawyers Committee occupies an unusually prominent place, even if the size of its staff and its budget are much smaller than those of either Human Rights Watch or Amnesty, and even if references to its activities in the media are insignificant as compared to those of the NGO giants. Highlighting the Committee's prominence is its role as coordinator of the so-called Directors' meetings of some ten key U.S.-based human rights organizations. The idea of a regular, although infrequent, meeting of the staff heads of leading NGO groups was an idea of Posner's, for which he has taken special pride.[59] The meetings were seen by him as a means of communicating between the organizations on the major issues confronting the human rights community. It was his hope to have the process of exchanges institutionalized and, to a considerable extent, the process has moved in that direction.

Oddly, while Mary Robinson ticked off in summary fashion the various areas in which the Lawyers Committee had acquired recognition, she said nothing about the Committee's role at the United Nations and its various agencies, particularly the World Bank, where the Committee's role had been of a pioneer character.

For the Lawyers Committee, the subject of the defense of monitors was of central importance. That it would become one of the strongest protagonists of a proposed UN Declaration to deal with the subject would be very much expected. In 1992, the UN Commission on Human Rights considered the adoption of an instrument with a title as awkward as it was imposing: Declaration on the Right and Responsibility of Individuals, Groups and Organs of Society to Promote and Protect Universally Recognized Human Rights and Fundamental Freedoms.[60] It explicitly elaborated on the rights of individuals and NGOs to know and act upon their rights. A fundamental assumption of the draft Declaration was akin to what East European NGOs fought for at the various forums of the Helsinki Final Act. In April, 1998, after numerous delays, the Declaration finally was adopted.

That the Lawyers Committee would consider a strong UN text on rights defenders a high priority is self-evident. Interestingly, the Committee was not accorded consultative status at the UN until 1991. Unlike Human Rights Watch, which had been totally uninterested in consultative status until the early nineties—and, indeed, was negative toward the UN generally—the Lawyers Committee already saw its potential quite early and, throughout the eighties, it sought consultative status. A full decade was consumed in applications. The process was described by Posner in an interview:

> Yes, we were ten years in the process . . . we were denied. . . .We had probably had over time fifteen or twenty countries that opposed us. The Soviets were out front, but Cuba in the end stopped us. And the [NGO]

Committee had a rule that any country in this committee could veto. One year, we offended the Yugoslav government, Chile, one year; Kenya, Pakistan, Libya. . . . It was ridiculous.[61]

"Ridiculous," it certainly was. Even with its consultative status, the Lawyers Committee carefully husbands its resources. If Amnesty and Human Rights Watch undertake dozens of responsibilities at the UN on various levels and especially at the Commission on Human Rights, the Lawyers Committee restricts itself to just two or three matters, particularly when they have distinctly focused legal aspects. The Commission meeting itself does have a representative from the Lawyers group but, as noted by Posner, "we've decided to spend less attention on the Commission."[62] He went on to explain: "basically, we decided that there are a couple of things in particular we want to do and do well with regard to the UN."

One of the things they decided they could do well related to the Human Rights Committee, the implementing instrument of the International Covenant on Civil and Political Rights. It was a Lawyers Committee leader, Professor Lou Henkin, formerly a distinguished constitutional expert at Columbia University Law School, who pushed the Committee in this direction. Concentrating upon legal obligations of the Covenant made considerable sense, even if the focus was narrow and public interest nonexistent. As noted elsewhere, the Committee's work with the 18-member UN body was unequaled by any other NGO and served to make that organ a model for the instruments of other UN treaty bodies. Posner recalled that: "The feedback we got was very positive." In fact, he said, "they were thrilled with it."[63] Since the briefing went over so well, the Lawyers Committee decided to link it through its Witness Program into a major video education program.

Another UN area of special interest for the Lawyers Committee was the effectiveness of the human rights component of various UN peacekeeping operations, notably the ones in Cambodia, El Salvador and Haiti. According to Posner, the Committee was "centrally involved" in preparing the Aspen Institute's report on those peacekeeping operations. Besides the overall report, he related that the Committee had done its own report on El Salvador and was planning to do an analysis of the Guatemala peacekeeping program administered by the UN. From the perspective of the Committee, these peacekeeping operations have an important "potential," and it would be in consonance with the group's purpose to "strengthen" the human rights component of the operation. The Committee arranged for the heads of the three human rights components who wrote the various segments of the Aspen book to meet with the top UN officials, especially those involved in peacekeeping. The outcome, in terms of making the UN peacekeeping officials aware of and responsive to human rights factors, was seen to be positive.

That the Committee would venture into areas of El Salvador and Haiti is not too surprising given the special history of the Committee in these two areas. As far back as 1980, the Lawyers Committee had been monitoring El Salvador and had published over a dozen reports on the area. Among those reports were four on the traumatic murder of Jesuit priests in 1989, which were published in 1991. Again in 1993, it published two studies, one of which dealt with proposed reforms to the judicial system.[64] Its most recent contribution, made in April, 1998, was especially significant. Two of its staffers, in interviewing a former National Guard member convicted of murdering three nuns, were told that he had acted on the basis of orders from higher military officials. For a long time, the two highest former El Salvador military officials were suspected of being involved with this crime. They are reported to be currently living in Florida.

As for Haiti, the Committee, throughout the early nineties, worked "intensively to restore the rule of law."[65] Especially striking was the establishment "clandestinely" of an "international fax network" in order to reach the local human rights advocates, thereby providing them with a "lifeline." Not accidentally, the Committee's Deputy Director, Bill O'Neill, was appointed Legal Director of the UN's human rights monitoring mission in Haiti.[66]

Among the Committee's UN priorities, the Tribunals at The Hague and Arusha occupy a prominent place. And it has done considerable advocacy work on behalf of a permanent international criminal court. Such effort could hardly be otherwise given the nature of an organization committed to the rule of law. A central figure in this involvement is the Director of Program and Policy, Stefanie Grant. In a remarkably perceptive speech at the end of 1996 to the Organization of American States (OAS), she traced the evolution of the struggle against genocide, highlighting the unique role of Raphael Lemkin, in the creation of the ad hoc Tribunal in The Hague. More than anyone, she caught the future significance of the Tribunal in a pungent observation: "for almost 50 years, it was a self-evident truth that the greater the atrocity, the greater the impunity enjoyed by the perpetrator under international criminal law."[67]

Precisely because of the indispensable need for the cooperation by all governments in apprehending indicted war criminals, Grant chastised her OAS audience because "few—shockingly few" countries have enacted legislation to arrest and extradite to the Tribunals indicted war criminals. And, in the Western hemisphere, only the United States has enacted such legislation, she noted. Yet, every government was obligated to do so by virtue of the decision of the Security Council requiring all governments to cooperate with the Tribunals. She went out of her way to praise the United States for being the only state of both North and South America to have "formalised its cooperation" with the Tribunals, and she specifically pointed to the arrest by the FBI on September 26, 1996 of Elizphan Ntakirutimana, indicted for genocide against Tutsis in Rwanda. He had been a pastor of a church in Rwanda to which hundreds of victims had fled for sanctuary. He was charged with bringing a force of Hutu killers to the church to carry out a large-scale massacre. After the victory of the Tutsi army, he had fled to Laredo, Texas to live with his son.[68]

Grant is optimistic that an international criminal court probably will be in existence "by the next century." The crucial issue is whether that court will be "effective," which will depend on how governments and NGOs respond to the challenge of cooperating with the Tribunal in The Hague dealing with Bosnia and Rwanda. Only then, she concluded, will everyone know "whether historians will judge the last years of this savage century a time of progress."[69]

Perhaps the most significant achievement of the Lawyers Committee relates to its role with respect to the World Bank. What the Committee accomplished was in the nature of a breakthrough in strategy for NGOs in dealing with the question of leverage. Leverage always had preoccupied strategists in the human rights field seeking change. Not too many levers to promote change existed for NGOs; after all, they were lacking control of economic or political machinery at the disposal of a state.

There was, of course, Section 701 of the International Financial Institutions Act, adopted by the U.S. Congress in the late seventies, which required U.S. Executive Directors to the World Bank (and other multilateral donor banks) to oppose loans and other technical or financial assistance to countries that were gross human rights violators. This always had been a potentially powerful lever for an NGO persuasive enough to press Washington to utilize the statutory lever, or to persuade the World Bank that the United States, which was, after all, the Bank's largest shareholder, was intent upon using the lever. The Lawyers Committee was among the first of the major human rights NGOs to recognize its potential. It was certainly the only NGO that was prepared to invest the necessary capital in terms of staff to exploit this potentiality. Significantly, it hired the very economically sophisticated and knowledgeable Patricia Armstrong to head up a permanent staff coordinating operations dealing with the Bank.

Early on, Armstrong recognized the potentiality of Section 701. But her interest inevitably deepened with the end of the Cold War, the consequent reduction in bilateral aid by the United States and, most importantly, the World Bank's emerging recognition that what it called "governance concerns" were "profoundly relevant."[70] From the perspective of the Lawyers Committee, "effective and sustainable development" projects in which the Bank provides assistance, would only be "possible in an environment where basic human rights are respected."[71] It was only at the point when the World Bank began to look at issues outside of its traditional and exclusive economic guidelines, into areas related to environmental and women's rights issues, that it became feasible to think in terms of "good governance" as a category meriting special attention in the decision-making process of the Bank.

What brought a change in the Bank's projects, according to Armstrong, was a series of failed development projects in countries such as Zaire where human rights abuses were endemic to society. The Bank had come to recognize, she said, that if you don't have an accountable, responsible government, "all the money in the world isn't going to make any difference." She then stressed her major point: "And to get an accountable, responsible government, human rights are important." The traditional guideline for the Bank was that it had, in fact, excluded civil and political rights, although economic and social rights were taken into consideration in development strategies that aimed in part at job creation. A publicly announced shift to civil rights first came in 1988 by the Bank's general counsel:

> Civil rights are also basic to human development and happiness. No balanced development can be achieved in my view, without the realization of a minimum degree of all human rights, material or otherwise in an environment that allows each people to preserve their culture. . . .[72]

Five years later, at the World Conference on Human Rights, the Bank's sister agency announced its willingness to "take into account the measure by which massive infringement of political and social rights directly derails economic programs."[73] The Bank could justify its new stance, using "good governance" as a guideline, by claiming that such practice was essential for maximizing the effectiveness of its aid programs. Precisely because "a crisis of governance" was held to be responsible for the failure of many development programs, the Bank would be willing to undertake initiatives increasing accountability as well as legal reform in developing nations without being transformed into a politically oriented instrument, which might contradict its historic purpose and image.[74]

As part of its new orientation, the World Bank has begun to stress legal reform and even has created a special unit, the Legal Reform and Advisory Services Department. And, at the end of 1993, it approved the very first loan devoted exclusively to judicial reform. It was to be for Venezuela. Since then, many other Bank projects have included judicial and legal reform components into their loans. Among the countries receiving loans involving such components were China, Bolivia, Argentina, Ecuador and Poland.[75] Besides judicial reform, the World Bank also has moved to affirm the importance of a free press.[76]

In addition, the Bank has stressed less authoritarian modes of decision-making in development projects, including the involvement of local participating groups. The new orientation has proved especially beneficial for environmental and development NGOs. "Good governance" is not seen as in any way alien to the historic purposes of the World Bank but rather as a contributory factor to economic performance. The Bank carefully has eschewed the question of whether "good governance" is or should be an important factor in its own right. Rather, legal reform is stressed for the resolution of economic disputes, promotion of trade and investments and the maintenance of a stable economic environment.

Changes in the Bank's perspective were welcomed by the Lawyers Committee Director. He told an interviewer: "You don't want to be giving money for technical assistance without holding governments to some kind of test."[77] Yet, it would be premature to expect applause. If the Bank finally incorporated "good governance" in its considerations, the Committee thought that it was slow to act upon this frame of reference.[78] The Committee's specialist, Patricia Armstrong, commented that the Bank has articulated "an awful lot of good rhetoric," but what remains is "the problem of translating the rhetoric into the operation of the Bank."[79]

Armstrong went to on observe that even the rhetoric is not continuous nor even consistent. Rather, she found it to be "very ad hoc." Not only was the rhetoric found wanting, but also the very use of the phrase "human rights" in Bank literature was found by the Committee to be "rare" and "seen only in connection with the Bank's distinction between economic and social rights," which it says it embraces on the one hand, and civil and political rights, which it says it does not, on the other.[80]

A joint study by the Committee and an Indonesian NGO concluded that "while the World Bank has acknowledged the relevance of [human] rights concerns in its work, its performance has yet to match its rhetoric."[81] In the opinion of the two NGOs, human rights should be considered on the same level as a country's monetary policy, its trade imbalances and its exchange rate. The absence of specific human rights considerations, according to the Committee, cannot but mean that "respect for human rights as well as development effectiveness will be undermined."[82]

If human rights is less than endemic to the World Bank's vocabulary, it does not mean that the institution has been indifferent to NGOs. The contrary is the case, provided the NGOs are geared to environmental or, better still, developmental matters. It generally is agreed that environmental groups have been successful in compelling the World Bank to take account of environmental factors in decision-making.

The Lawyers Committee, through Armstrong, closely has followed this development and actively has sought assistance from environmental and development NGOs. Advising the Committee is a group of representatives from such organizations as Bread for the World and the National Wildfire Federation. With the help of the advisory group, the Lawyers Committee will seek to make certain that human rights considerations play a role in decisions dealing with the development process and that the benefits of economic growth are funneled to the poor.

By modeling itself on the strategy of environmental NGOs, the Committee has moved its lobbying away from the "high policy levels" of the Bank to the "technical policy level" or the "project design and implementation level." It is at these lower levels that human rights can more effectively be integrated into the operational activities of the Bank. As early as 1993, the Lawyers Committee had set for itself the task of "integrating human rights concerns into the decisions of international financial institutions such as the World Bank."[83]

A fundamental assumption of the Lawyers Committee was that an "effective and sustainable development is only possible in an environment where basic human rights are respected."[84] It carefully avoided pressing the tactic of "conditional lending," whereby the Bank only would support a loan if the recipient took positive human rights initiatives. While other NGOs might pursue this technique, from the Committee's perspective, conditionality would not likely produce significant results. It is the Committee's view that the World Bank is important as a potentially powerful tool for promoting global economic growth as well as alleviating poverty.

In keeping with the objective of deepening Bank awareness of human rights concerns, the Committee organized workshops for Bank officials and encouraged the establishment of procedural guidelines for certain judicial reform projects planned for Peru and Argentina, while, at the same time, urging consultation with local NGOs.[85] Of particular importance were case studies it undertook and published on World Bank projects in Indonesia and in Venezuela. The Indonesian study involved two Bank-financed programs: (1) the construction of a dam in central Java that brought about the displacement of over 30,000 persons; and (2) strategies for introducing population control devices.[86]

The Committee study underscored the human rights abuses in both aspects. Land was appropriated from villagers through coercive and intimidating means. Those who refused to give up their land became targets of official criminal investigations. What was apparent to the researchers was that the World Bank made no attempt to monitor or supervise the resettlement activities of the Indonesian regime and only learned about the harsh human rights abuses after local Indonesian NGOs mounted an international campaign two years after the project had begun. With respect to population control, the report also called attention to the use of coercion by the Indonesian military to obtain responsiveness from Indonesians rather than winning them over through participatory engagement techniques. Once again, the Bank was chastised for delegating authority to the military rather than independently monitoring the program.

The report concluded with an observation intended to identify the more universal problem that the dam and population control issues represented. More specifically, the study was designed to demonstrate the certain and inevitable link between the observance of human rights standards and the success of the project. As characterized by the Committee, "the human rights environment in which development activities take place supports or undermines the development process, the degree to which the objectives of the project are met and the Bank's ability to monitor both."[87] What the report seemed to drive home was that the Bank must assume a direct responsibility to insure that the project implementators do not carry out the projects in an "abusive manner."

On a deeper level, the Committee report had a further and critical lesson to teach. The scope of World Bank projects ineluctably has to be widened to encompass active and cooperative citizens and NGO participation. The outcome represented a major step forward by the Committee in an area that offers the potential for considerable progress in the future, even if it is quite limited on the current scene. The Venezuelan project of the Bank had a totally unique dimension and the Lawyers Committee critique was obliged to assume a very different character from that exercised in the Indonesian project. The Bank project on Venezuela was an unprecedented one for the financial institution and probably was a kind of response to NGO criticism that the Bank had concentrated on large infrastructure projects and macroeconomic structural reform assistance to the neglect of the broader issues in which the rule of law is essential. The World Bank provided a $30 million loan to the Venezuelan government devoted exclusively to judicial reform. The assumption for the loan was that the maintenance of a stable legal environment was essential for progress and that an independent judiciary to assure that the rules are clear was prerequisite for long-term growth.[88]

From the perspective of the Committee and a Caracas-based NGO, the loan, if carried out with proper instructions and guidelines, could serve as a model for similar loans to other countries and, thereby, serve broad human rights objectives. The two NGOs, after examining the loan and its conditions, recommended that it not be an operation restricted to the Bank and the Justice Ministry but, rather, that it involve the participation of all groups affected by the reform—judges, bar associations, lawyers and law-oriented NGOs. Further, they recommended that judicial independence should be underscored as more important than modernization, for without such independence, the credibility and fairness of the legal system would be placed in jeopardy.[89]

Scrutiny, from the perspective of wider human rights objectives, inevitably found the Venezuela project wanting. Yet, the study nonetheless could prove valuable. One important outgrowth of it was the convening of a policy forum in Caracas in June, 1996 to discuss the implications of the study. The two-day workshop, entitled "Judicial Reform in Latin America: The Role of Multinational Banks," included representatives from the World Bank and the Inter-American Development Bank. Among the topics addressed at the workshop were: What does judicial reform encompass and what does it seek to accomplish? And, what is the role of NGOs in the judicial reform?

If on World Bank projects in Indonesia and Venezuela, the Lawyers Committee actions carried an educational purpose oriented to the future, on a third major project with which it was involved, the Committee's examination of the issue had immediate ramifications. In India, a massive dam—Sardar Sarovar—was to be constructed on the Narmada River; this project was to be funded in part by a $450 million World Bank loan. Over one-half million persons would be forced to resettle by the flooding of the area and by the emerging canal and irrigation system. The areas that were to be flooded were inhabited by tribal Indians whose very culture and way of life was threatened by their resettlement as required by the project.

Precisely because of the project's expected adverse socioeconomic and environmental impact, local NGOs mounted a serious challenge to the project. The Lawyers Committee came to their support with an investigatory mission in March, 1993, which found that the Indian authorities had unlawfully arrested, detained and tortured the opponents of the dam. Its findings documenting the abuses were published as *India's Sardar Sarovar Project and Violations of Human Rights.* The report principally was directed to the World Bank. It was but the opening shot across the bow when the Indian government sharply criticized the Lawyers Committee report. A group of activist environmental organizations mounted a large-scale campaign, supported by the Lawyers Committee, aimed at killing the project. Advertisements were placed in major newspapers specifying the human rights and environmental abuses of the dam project. The resulting international uproar had the effect of bringing about cancelation of the project.[90]

Ordinarily, however, the Committee is most hesitant about either weakening the Bank with excessive criticism or attaching conditions to its operation that would jeopardize its role as an important lending institution. From the point of view of Patricia Armstrong, the Bank as an instrument promoting global economic growth and combating poverty is important in itself. Equally important as a consideration is the attitude of local NGOs with whom the Committee maintains or seeks a close working relationship.[91] Since many local NGOs would be opposed to find the flow of development assistance to their countries reduced, and, on the contrary, would argue for both more assistance and a greater role for NGOs in the implementation of loan projects, they would resent and resist an effort by international NGOs to attach conditions. Of course, when local NGOs take the lead in opposing Bank loans, as in the case of the Indian dam project, the Lawyers Committee will provide them with all the appropriate international legal assistance.

In 1993, it became possible for the Lawyers Committee to publish its first report on the Bank, entitled *The World Bank: Governance and Human Rights.* Two years later, it was updated, becoming a comprehensive treatment of the relatively recent inclusion of governance in the Bank's decision-making process. If the Bank's decisions remain predominantly based upon economic factors, it nonetheless has acknowledged that the observance of human rights is an indicator of stability.

What was not anticipated when the Committee moved into the field was the selection in 1995 of James Wolfensohn as the new Bank President, who brought far greater sensitivity to these issues. In instructions that Wolfensohn sent out, he spoke about the need for increased contact and coordination with NGOs, which cannot but lead to a greater degree of accessibility to the institutions.

In dealing with the UN and UN agencies, the Committee kept a close watch on the role of the High Commissioner for Human Rights ever since the creation of the office. Of the NGOs, Posner was the most critical of Ayala Lasso, terming him "a pretty weak guy . . . not a fighter" and calling him "risk averse."[92] Like others, Posner noted that Ayala Lasso had "spent too much time in a diplomatic world" and, therefore, "he's not going to stick his neck out or push the limits. . . ." Posner was especially furious with the two country visits—to Cuba and Colombia—that Ayala Lasso made without consulting the appropriate Special Rapporteurs: "who gave him the right to make this decision?" he sharply asked.

By inviting Mary Robinson to be the recipient of its special award, the Lawyers Committee must have hoped that she would assume a strong, vigorous leadership of the office and that the Committee might help guide her decision-making. Indeed, she all but indicated that she would want their advice because: "I am new to this job in the real sense of having a great deal to learn. . . ."[93] Her speech did reflect the changed political and bureaucratic situation at the UN. Under the "reform" package of the new Secretary-General Kofi Annan, which she called a "quantum leap" for human rights, the status of her office and of human rights generally at the UN had been greatly raised.[94] She declared that human rights was now "mainstreamed" and given a "cross-cutting value throughout the UN itself." What she was referring to was a decision by the Secretary-General to have her serve as a member of four separate Executive Committees covering key operational areas of the Secretariat, most notably, peacekeeping and development. With the augmented power of her office, there could be little doubt that the Committee and other NGOs would respond favorably to her request for assistance.

Indeed, that relationship was very much in evidence at a two-day briefing session for the High Commissioner held by NGOs on May 7-8, 1998 at the Carter Center in Atlanta and sponsored by the Center and the Blaustein Institute (they had held a similar session for Robinson's predecessor a couple of years earlier.) The focus in Atlanta was largely upon strengthening the special UN human rights mechanisms, but it ranged well beyond that critical subject to winning higher allocations for human rights purposes and augmenting national and regional institutions in order to prevent and halt gross human rights violations. The nearly two dozen NGO leaders "greatly appreciated" what they held to be "her active involvement in the discussions." It remains to be seen how the NGO relationship with the High Commissioner will unfold and whether the unsatisfactory "diplomatic approach" of Ayala Lasso will be superseded by a genuine "human rights approach."

CHAPTER TWENTY-ONE

Recapturing the Spirit of Nuremberg

When the recent President of the ad hoc International Criminal Tribunal in The Hague, Antonio Cassese, in his 1997 annual report to the UN, chose to define and characterize the Tribunal's overall "mission," he referred back to the Nuremberg Tribunal and to the words of a then young and obscure American prosecutor, Benjamin Ferencz: "If these men be immune, then law has lost its meaning and man must live in fear."[1] The no-longer young and obscure Ferencz had made it his life's mission to create a permanent International Criminal Court so that law has meaning and man need no longer "live in fear."

President Cassese's choice was hardly accidental. He had set forth as the International Criminal Tribunal's mission "to hear and record for posterity the stories of those who have suffered in the camps and killing fields . . . and to dispense justice on that account in the name of the international community."[2] The worst nightmares of the victims at Auschwitz and at the other Nazi concentration camps was that once they were free, people would not listen to the horrors they had suffered or would be indifferent or disbelieving. Like the Nuremberg Tribunal, thought Cassese, the International Criminal Tribunal forever would document and illuminate the horrors so that all can see and know. There was yet a second mission, noted the Italian jurist and scholar: to achieve "Justice's cathartic effects." He noted that witnesses before the Tribunal at The Hague reported "great relief" after their testimony. In Cassese's view, this catharsis promises "hope for recovery and reconciliation" for society.

It was just a bit more than a half-century earlier, on September 29, 1947, when Ferencz made the opening statement for the prosecution of

Nazism's most notorious killers—the Einsatzgruppen.[3] The 22 defendants were on trial for the deliberate slaughter of men, women and children; in Ferencz's words, theirs was "the tragic fulfillment of a program of intolerance and arrogance." The sentences that followed were to provide the basic theme of Ferencz's writings since then:

> We ask this court to affirm by international action man's right to live in peace and dignity regardless of his race or creed. The case we present is a plea of humanity to law.[4]

It was the last sentence that illuminated the language that would become central to Nuremberg and the Tribunals on the Former Yugoslavia and on Rwanda—"crimes against humanity."

At the end of Ferencz's "opening statement" came the phrase that Cassese cited. It was preceded by Ferencz's charge to the court that the defendants had written "the blackest page in human history." On April 10, 1948, all 22 defendants were convicted, with 13 sentenced to death by hanging. The court's judgement was a mere prologue for the prosecutor to eventually launch a writing and teaching career devoted to the establishment of a permanent International Criminal Court, which, mainly through the incessant and determined lobbying of NGOs, would acquire a solid foundation. Scheduled for the summer of 1998 was a plenipotentiaries conference in Rome that was to create the Statute for the International Criminal Court.

An authoritative account by Ferencz of what the future Tribunal would look like and how it might operate was published in 1980 in two volumes.[5] In explaining why he had written the new work, he used language that echoed the words from his opening prosecution statement at Nuremberg 33 years earlier. Ferencz said that he sought in the two volumes to preserve "the most fundamental of all human rights," which was "to live in peace and dignity without the constant fear and threat of imminent extinction."

On the eve of the UN Security Council's decision to create an ad hoc Tribunal for the genocide and crimes against humanity perpetrated in the Former Yugoslavia, Ferencz had written a new work, *New Legal Foundation for Global Survival*, which incorporated and updated the earlier themes on the International Criminal Court.[6] In the "Author's Preface," Ferencz indicated that his goal "cannot be attained quickly or easily." "Quite the contrary," he added, noting that "it will take patience, determination and great efforts."[7]

The timeframe for the fulfillment of Ferencz's dream altered dramatically once the ad hoc Tribunals on Bosnia and Rwanda were beginning to function. In June, 1997, UN Secretary-General Kofi Annan wrote to Ferencz, calling his book "remarkable" and saying that he attached "great importance" to the chapter on the International Criminal Court.[8] Two months after the Annan letter, a British newspaper columnist caught Ferencz at an "extraordinary gathering" on Capitol Hill in Washington seeking to energize a major lobbying effort for U.S. backing of a permanent International Criminal Tribunal.[9] The now 77-year-old former Nuremberg prosecutor "thundered" at his Washington audience: "We thought it was 'Never Again,' but it has been again and again—over and over again—ever since." Ferencz went on to say: "Ever since Nuremberg, the innocent have been massacred and the perpetrators have walked away scot free."

The Capitol Hill assemblage was determined, said the journalist, to "end the cycle of impunity." One of the principal speakers was Judge Gabrielle McDonald, the American member on the 11-member ad hoc Tribunal at The Hague, who would become its President in 1998. She stressed that whether a permanent court was created and enabled to function would depend upon "the influence and prestige and power of the U.S., and the assertion of its leadership role."[10] That was the reason for the Washington, D.C. meeting. Everyone recognized that the U.S. role was a decisive consideration. Without American support, the entire initiative would founder. Ferencz reminded the audience that it took the United States 40 years to ratify the Genocide Convention.

Ferencz's reference to the Genocide Convention could not fail to recall the lobbying work of Raphael Lemkin, the father of the genocide treaty who so intensely had pressed for U.S. ratification and leadership in preventing genocide. Ferencz reminds one of the fierceness and zealotry of Lemkin. His closing remarks in Washington were described as "explosive" in their challenge to the audience:

> It depends what kind of a world you want. If you want a world in which people like those we prosecuted at Nuremberg can do it again and again with impunity, then fine. Go home. Do nothing. And just pray to God they never get round to you.

That lobbying of Congress, of legislatures everywhere and of UN delegations was the task of the moment, Ferencz recognized. In that recognition, he was following in Lemkin's footsteps.

It was precisely such political will that had been missing earlier. Actually, the idea for an International Criminal Court has been around for over a century, even if it has been little-known. In 1870, Gustav Moynier, one of the founders of the International Committee of the Red Cross, proposed an international court to enforce the Geneva Convention of 1864 concerning the treatment of wounded soldiers.[11] Moynier's proposal almost unanimously was rejected by leading international lawyers of the day.

The Versailles Peace Conference of 1919 offered another opportunity. A commission of inquiry that had been set up recommended the establishment of an ad hoc International Criminal Tribunal with jurisdiction over war crimes. But the Peace Conference failed to act upon it. In 1920, a Committee of Jurists, appointed by the League of Nations and dominated by Elihu Root, a former U.S. Secretary of State and Secretary of War who also had served as a U.S. Senator from New York, proposed that an International Criminal Court be established "to try crimes constituting a breach of international public order or against the universal law of nations."[12] The advice of these international jurists politely was brushed aside by professional diplomats.

For the first time in the early twenties, several of the NGOs of the day made a historical appearance to champion the idea of an International Criminal Court. They included the International Law Association, the International Congress of Penal Law and the Inter-Parliamentary Union. Their various proposals, however, were unable to mobilize public support and the court idea ceased to be articulated.

Various proposals were advanced during World War II but eventually were abandoned in favor of the historic, although ad hoc, Nuremberg and Tokyo Tribunals. The movement in favor of a permanent International Criminal Court (ICC) was revived again after the Second World War with the establishment of the United Nations. The International Law Commission (ILC) of the UN was mandated to codify the Nuremberg principles and to prepare a draft statute for the establishment of an International Criminal Court with stronger guarantees of the right to fair trial. The ILC studied the issue at its 1949 and 1950 sessions, concluding that such a court was "desirable" and "possible." The endeavor essentially was sidelined by the Cold War. When the Cold War finally ended, however, there emerged renewed interest and opportunity for the establishment of the ICC.[13]

While the General Assembly finally agreed upon a definition of aggression in 1974 and the ILC made real progress in drafting a code of crimes under international law between 1982 and 1991, the most significant headway came in the late 1980s.[14] In 1989, the Prime Minister of Trinidad and Tobago, A. N. R. Robinson, in a major move, reintroduced the idea of a permanent court to the General Assembly. The important development was prompted by the realization that the Caribbean was being devastated by international criminal activity, mostly in the form of drug trafficking.[15] Genocide or crimes against humanity may not have been the source of the proposal, but the idea of a permanent court now began to take on a life of its own. The circumstances were appropriate. In 1992, "ethnic cleansing" in Yugoslavia was shocking the international community.

The Assembly again requested that the ILC prepare a draft statute for a permanent ICC.[16] While the ILC was deliberating about a permanent court, the Security Council moved ahead to establish two ad hoc Tribunals, one for the Former Yugoslavia and the other for Rwanda. These statutes helped expedite the ILC deliberations while, at the same time, they generated favorable international sentiments regarding the ICC.[17]

An Amnesty International report contended that a permanent Tribunal was far more important than the ad hoc bodies. The General Assembly gave the idea some support and asked the ILC to complete its work on the draft statute of an International Criminal Court "as a matter of priority" by July, 1994.

When the draft statute finally came before the General Assembly in the summer of 1994, the ILC recommended that a conference of plenipotentiaries be called to draw up a treaty to enact the statute for the permanent court. However, this proposal was defeated in the Sixth Committee of the Assembly. Instead a special ad hoc committee, established to review the draft statute, met in two two-week sessions in 1995. Although a majority of nations in the Sixth or Legal Committee of the Assembly favored calling for a conference of plenipotentiaries, a powerful minority that included the United States, the United Kingdom, China and India insisted upon further discussions before agreeing to a date for a diplomatic conference.

A compromise decision was reached in December, 1995. The UN General Assembly agreed to create a Preparatory Committee that would meet twice in 1996 and would have as its purpose the preparation of a "consolidated text" for a treaty that would constitute the "next step towards consideration by a conference" of diplomatic plenipotentiaries.[18]

At the end of 1996, the UN instructed the Preparatory Committee to hold four sessions of up to nine weeks during 1997 and 1998 "in order to complete the drafting of a widely acceptable consolidated text of a convention, to be submitted to the diplomatic conference." That conference of plenipotentiaries would meet in 1998, to finalize and adopt a treaty establishing an International Criminal Court. It was the expectation of Amnesty International that "with sufficient political will," the diplomatic conference would adopt a treaty containing the statute of a permanent International Criminal Court in the summer of 1998 and that "the court will be established before the end of the century."

A critical factor in the fixing of a firm date for the holding of a treaty conference was the decision of the White House to support an International Criminal Court. Until 1996, there had been no indication that Washington would favor such a court. At the end of the UN session the previous year, U.S. representatives joined other major powers in opposing a plenipotentiaries conference. On October 15, 1996, in remarks at the opening of the commemoration of "50 Years After Nuremberg: Human Rights and the Rule of Law" at the University of Connecticut, President Clinton, for the first time, endorsed a permanent ICC as a way to "send a strong signal to those who would use the cover of war to commit terrible atrocities that they cannot escape the consequences of such actions."[19]

Clinton's speech was at the dedication of the Thomas J. Dodd Research Center, a new archive at the University of Connecticut. The late Thomas Dodd had served on the prosecutorial team at Nuremberg and later was elected Senator from Connecticut. Human Rights Watch played a critical role here. After Clinton's statement, a date finally was set for a treaty conference and no other government opposed it.[20]

The final decision of the UN to hold a Rome session to draft a Statute on the Court was reached on December 17, 1996. The plenipotentiary Rome ICC Treaty Conference was scheduled to be held from June 15, 1998 to July 17, 1998. The five-week meeting was expected to have several hundred NGOs in attendance, most of them, because of costs, for but brief periods.[21] The coordinator of the NGO campaign on behalf of the International Criminal Court, William Pace, reacted in an enthusiastic manner to the UN resolution calling for the special Rome meeting to establish the treaty conference:

> The adoption of this resolution represents an extraordinary achievement for those governments and NGOs who have been the strongest supporters of the establishment of an ICC, and who believed that setting the date at this General Assembly was a critical test in maintaining the level of commitment and momentum for this truly historic initiative.[22]

Pace's emphasis on the unprecedented and historic nature of the expected Rome proceedings was in keeping with NGO activism and anticipation. Throughout much of the UN deliberative process, both in UN corridors and in foreign office hallways, during the prior four-year period, nongovernmental organizations had played a significant role in bringing the ICC to an eventual reality, at least on paper. Significant NGO involvement was begun in 1994. Until then, Pace explained in an interview, "the ICC was not taken seriously among NGOs." Prior to 1994, he said, only a few NGOs were involved, such as Amnesty International. It was the failure of the General Assembly in December, 1994 to establish a diplomatic conference that acted as "a kind of wake up call to the NGO community."

Pace represented in New York the World Federalist Movement (WFM), not a major NGO and certainly not one given to human rights issues. But it was militantly supportive of peace and, while most NGOs—including human rights NGOs—were paying little attention to the idea of an International Criminal Court, it was one of the few NGOs that "responded strongly in favor of Prime Minister Robinson's appeal for an ICC in 1989" and was one of three NGOs present in 1994 when the ILC presented the first draft Statute to the General Assembly.[23] The World Federalist Movement, which is an advocate of a strengthened United Nations, is an international NGO citizens organization dedicated to a just world order. It has a membership in some 40 countries with active groups in 19 countries.[24]

How Pace and the World Federalists Movement became the coordinator of NGO lobbying is intriguing. In early 1995, Amnesty International contacted Pace, asking his group to convene a meeting of NGOs at the UN in order to discuss the upcoming UN meetings on the draft ICC Statute prepared by the ILC. As he later explained in an interview, Amnesty had asked the WFM to engage in the initial organizing endeavor because "Amnesty International doesn't do networking."[25] What was meant here was that Amnesty as an NGO may collaborate with other NGOs but doesn't itself organize collective action. While Amnesty long had been involved in researching the subject of an International Criminal Court and had gone beyond research to active support for the idea, it recognized that to win support for such an institution, a major NGO collaborative and lobbying activity would be necessary.

Amnesty, of course, would continue to attend UN General Assembly meetings on the subject and prepare a series of background reports and analyses. In the meantime, Pace could be relied upon, from

Amnesty's perspective, to assemble an informal coalition of NGOs for purposes of extensive and broad lobbying.[26] Another consideration, as noted by Pace, was the very smallness of the World Federalist Movement, which employed but a couple of persons in its New York office. Its size and leverage was too limited to challenge or threaten the big NGOs like Amnesty or Human Rights Watch.

The WFM convened the first meeting on February 10, 1995, in cooperation with Amnesty International and the Italian NGO, No Peace Without Justice. More than a dozen NGOs were present at the strategy meeting. Besides, every major NGO group and numerous smaller ones were present. Besides, members of task groups of the American Bar Association and the American Society of International Law were present without officially representing their respective organizations. Some could not attend but expressed their desire to be included in the coalition's work.[27]

It was agreed to form a coalition in which the WFM would serve as the Secretariat with Pace as the convenor. A fundamental consideration agreed upon was that the NGO community must do everything possible to ensure the effectiveness and success of the ad hoc Tribunals in order to demonstrate that an international criminal jurisdiction is not an impossible goal. Agreement also was reached on the principle that even if various NGOs had differences of opinion concerning various parts of the ILC draft Statute of the Court, they would cooperate in supporting the establishment of a just, fair and effective International Criminal Court. A fax and e-mail list was compiled and all NGOs agreed to forward information to the network. It was decided to reach out beyond the legal and human rights communities to involve peace, civil rights, women's issues and environmental groups.[28]

One of the crucial considerations of the strategy session involved the attitude of many African nations. While they were for the creation of an ICC, they were afraid that it might become a tool of Western states and be used only against the Third World. The NGO community agreed to seek to persuade these nations that the crimes under the jurisdiction of the ICC are crimes that all nations must oppose regardless of who commits them.[29] The Coalition for an International Criminal Court was established on an informal basis.

Since its initial meeting in 1995, the NGO Coalition for an International Criminal Court has grown to include over 300 participating organizations. Membership requirements are fairly simple and self-evident. To be an affiliate of the Coalition, an NGO must (1) endorse in principle the creation of a just and effective International Criminal Court and (2) wish to be involved at some level in the effort to create an ICC. No membership fee is required; only a commitment to support the ICC in whatever way seems possible and feasible by each group. To serve its educational mission, the Coalition produced a newsletter, *The International Criminal Court Monitor,* and provided media advisories, reviews and papers on a World Wide Web site and through e-mail lists.

The Coalition also agreed to convene working groups on funding and on information/media as well as a special group dealing with influencing the United States. The Steering Committee of the Coalition was to meet regularly about once a month, and would consist of Amnesty International, the European Law Students Association, Federation Internationale des Ligues des Droits de l'Homme, Human Rights Watch, the International Commission of Jurists, the Lawyers Committee for Human Rights, No Peace Without Justice (IRP), Parliamentarians for Global Action, the Women's Caucus for Gender Justice in the ICC and the World Federalist Movement.[30]

Pace, in an interview, offered a broad overview of the Coalition's strategy. As its primary purpose was "to start dialogue with governments," he described the benefit of a broad-based coalition that had the flexibility and hence the ability to meet with as many different governments as possible. NGO groups that were asked to meet with a specific country would be tailored to have at least a certain affinity with that country. For example, "China will not meet with Human Rights Watch so Human Rights Watch will not be in the room when the Coalition meets with China," Pace observed.[31] The Coalition he stressed, was more effective in dealing with governments that "don't want to meet separately with each group."

The Coalition made it its business to meet with national and regional delegations at every UN Preparatory Committee meeting dealing with the ICC. At every arranged meeting, the Coalition would include five of its constituent members. The Coalition, at the same time, sought to arrange for lobbying in individual capitals. A half-dozen specific NGOs were asked to focus on one or another national or regional targets. Thus, the Human Rights Watch group in Brussels focused on the European Parliament and the European Union. In Rome, Amnesty International would collaborate with No Peace Without Justice. The Amnesty International branch in the United Kingdom would concentrate on London-based groups. Others were asked to undertake tasks in Africa and Asia, the governments of which were thought to be especially difficult to persuade. Latin American NGOs, with funding from the Soros Foundation, were expected to bring regional experts to Coalition meetings and then return to their home countries for additional networking. A special NGO, the DePaul Institute, was thought to be particularly active with respect to Latin America.

Initially, the Coalition worked on a very limited budget. Its member organizations gave "very modest contributions, mostly with mailings, or contributions in kind."[32] Pace put it this way: "I can say with some confidence, that perhaps until very recently, virtually no government or NGO, except the WFM on behalf of the Coalition, has had anyone working on the ICC full time." He acknowledged that he, personally, spent between half to three quarters of his time on the Coalition. Meanwhile, the Coalition's financial base has grown considerably since 1995. In its first year, the Coalition was in debt, but serious funding from the Ford Foundation eased that problem. What made possible the Ford grant, according to Pace, was "Amnesty International and Human Rights Watch support." In 1995, the Coalition's budget was only $40-50,000 but in 1996, it jumped to between $200,000 and $300,000. During 1997, it again increased, this time to between $500,000 and $600,000. Besides the Ford Foundation, the MacArthur Foundation was reported as a generous contributor.

Since the Coalition was comprised of various NGOs who hold a variety of opinions and positions on differing specific legal technical and political considerations relating to the establishment of the International Criminal Court, Pace stressed that it must not take positions on these various issues. Neutrality on the technical issues nonetheless was seen as crucial:

> By remaining "neutral" the Coalition gives those governments and UN officers the greatest ability to argue for the principles supporting the participation of non-state experts in this historic process and negotiation. If the Coalition itself took positions against and campaigned in opposition to those of a particular government or governments, it would be very difficult to oppose those governments' efforts to exclude the NGOs from the negotiating process. Thus, by remaining "neutral," the Coalition actually increases the political space and strengthens the capacity of all NGOs to argue their positions.[33]

That the Coalition of NGOs played a highly significant role in the extraordinary progress made in just a few years to achieve an International Criminal Court is evident. Without the Coalition, the coordinated efforts of NGOs would have been difficult, if not impossible. And the same would have applied to obtaining the support of so many nations. One particularly active observer, the Holy See representative, told Pace privately that, during his tenure at the UN, the issue of the International Criminal Court had become "the most important issue before the General Assembly."[34]

Speaking before an audience of NGOs in Montevideo, the coordinator related that an "important government delegation representative" had called the NGO Coalition the "largest and most powerful delegation in the negotiations" for the court. Pace then commented that this observation was "surely an overstatement." Still, he added: "that we are a major 'player' in the process cannot be denied." The leading authority on the International Criminal Court, Benjamin Ferencz, who had kept the issue active ever since Nuremberg, recognized that without the lobbying of NGOs, the historic breakthrough of a Statute for a permanent court never would have been possible.[35] Their work was "vital and decisive," he said. "Political will" was essential to overturn governmental narrowness, and it was the "human will" provided by the NGOs through their lobbying that turned the tide in favor of international law.

What particularly caught Ferencz's fancy was the European Law Students Association (ELAS). Its members, from a variety of European law schools, were extremely well-versed on the technical aspects of the subject and were found by him to have exerted an enormous impact upon the UN delegations at the Preparatory Committee sessions. The diplomats simply could not fail to be "tremendously impressed" by their dynamism, commitment and unbreakable determination, he said. With their stay in New York funded by the European Union, their numbers, noted Ferencz, "jammed" the public seats at all the UN preparatory sessions. When not at the sessions, they maintained a continuing lobbying stance at all working hours. As for NGOs from Third World countries, Ferencz found their impact much less, although as a result of their general lobbying initiatives, "nobody dared speak against the court idea."

Ferencz recognized that Christopher Hall of Amnesty International was a "very good" point man in the NGO community in dealing with the court issue. At the same time, he considered the Coalition "a very effective" instrument in maximizing NGO lobbying. The bringing together of "like-minded groups" who would "act in concert" performed an invaluable service. That NGOs couldn't receive everything they fought for was hardly unexpected. The major powers, including the United States, would not agree to a key objective of the NGO community that would permit the Chief Prosecutor of the permanent court to initiate and pursue investigations of alleged criminal acts without regard for the views of the Security Council.

For Ferencz, the technical discussion of a basically political issue was not as critical as getting agreement on a Statute. Yet the NGOs won vital support from the Chief Prosecutor of the Tribunal at The Hague, Louise Arbour, who, while in New York on the final days of deliberations in December, 1997, strongly expressed herself in favor of the independent authority of the court's Chief Prosecutor to launch investigations. A compromise proposal advanced by Singapore offered a way out of the dilemma. While the Chief Prosecutor can trigger the procedure for investigation, the Security Council temporarily can halt the investigation if the case already is being dealt with as a security issue by the Security Council. The compromise was endorsed by Britain, thereby rupturing the unity and solidarity of the major powers.[36] From the perspective of the NGOs, the British decision was "extremely important," as a spokesperson for the Lawyers Committee for Human Rights noted. That NGO commented that "it has loosened the Security Council's ranks" and, thereby, was certain to facilitate the expected compromise.

But when the plenipotentiaries assembled in Rome for a five-week session on June 15, 1998, the compromise was found to be inadequate. The United States, prompted by Pentagon concerns, insisted that prosecution of a citizen of a state that has not signed or ratified the Statute be barred unless the state provided its consent. The United States was concerned that, as a superpower with military forces around the work, its troops might become the target of politically-motivated and frivolous prosecution. Even when additional compromises were extended, the United States stood firm on the principle that a targeted state must consent to the prosecution. When a vote was taken on the Statute on July 17, the United States found itself in a tiny minority of seven in opposition. One hundred-twenty countries voted in favor of the Statute while twenty-one abstained. Clearly NGO pressures on the U.S. Administration and delegation, mainly from HRW and the Lawyers Committee, could not overcome the Pentagon and its security considerations.

Still for Ferencz, the decision in Rome was a "historic and remarkable achievement" in advancing the rule of law. That the United States will not sign or ratify the Statute, he thought, does not reduce the significance of the Rome decision. He reminded observers that it took Washington 40 years to ratify the Genocide Convention. He hoped that the United States would ultimately come to accept the ICC Statute. A similar view was expressed by America's friend in Rome. Thus, Canadian Foreign Minister Lloyd Axworthy, a leading advocate of the Statute, expressed the "hope that the U.S. will someday decide to join."

Adoption of the Statute on the International Criminal Court by no means completes the process. Even the signing of the treaty by numerous states, while encouraging, is hardly the end of the story. Ratification by 60 states will be essential to bring the treaty into force and make it operational. In an essay in September, 1997, Ferencz was extremely hesitant about offering a guess about the future. "How long it will take before nations will ratify such a treaty is an open question," he stated.[37] Of one thing, Ferencz was absolutely certain. Without NGOs pressing for ratification by prodding and lobbying governments, nothing will happen. He put it somewhat differently: "In the last analysis, everything depends upon the will of the public and its ability to communicate its desires to willing politicians and diplomats who have the courage to seize the moment in order to save the future." For the former Nuremberg prosecutor, the "will of the public" only can be transmitted by NGOs. The "curious grapevine" has yet a major institutional function to perform for the international community.

Were the moment seized, and the Statute of the court to command a significant number of ratifications, bringing it into being and making it operational, it would be, in the words of Boutros Boutros-Ghali, "a monumental advance." This was how the former Secretary-General characterized such a future development when he projected "An Agenda for Democratization" on December 20, 1996.[38] The very establishment of an International Criminal Court, thought the Secretary-General, would produce "manifold" benefits for human rights, most notably "deterring" the "commission" of "grave international crimes." His successor, Kofi Annan, held to a similar view. At the beginning of the Conference on June 15, he said that the establishment of an International Criminal Court would be a "bulwark against evil."

Upon completing his prosecution work at Nuremberg and before undertaking initiatives that would significantly help in "developing effective world law"—as he put it—to prevent another Holocaust, Benjamin Ferencz steeped himself in a related task of obtaining restitution for those victims of the Nazi genocidal program who had managed to survive. Accountability for mass murder not only means punishment for those who organized and conducted the carnage, but also means compensation and reparations for the families of victims and for survivors. Ferencz served in the Federal Republic of Germany as the director of postwar restitution programs and helped fashion and implement laws providing compensation. Later, in the United States, he acted as a legal adviser for the Conference of Jewish Materials Claims Against Germany, helping win billions of dollars in compensation from the West German government.

A major 1993 study for the UN Sub-Commission on Prevention of Discrimination and Protection of Minorities by Professor Theo van Boven, the former Director of the UN's Division on Human Rights, solidly established the "right to restitution, reparation and rehabilitation for victims of gross human rights violations." Van Boven served as Special Rapporteur of the Sub-Commission in the preparation of this trailblazing work.[39] Van Boven called compensation and reparation "an imperative norm of justice" that regularly has been ignored by government practitioners of gross human rights violations.[40]

He pointed out how international human rights bodies have established specific standards in this area, including a "coherent and consistent line of action . . . [for] the facts, the bringing to justice persons found to be responsible, ensuring reparation to the victims." This policy specifically has been outlined on numerous occasions by the Human Rights Committee, the Inter-American Commission on UN Human Rights and the Inter-American Court of Human Rights.[41] The Sub-Commission study stressed that "under international law, the violation of any human rights gives rise to a right of reparation for the victim . . . for the purpose of relieving the suffering of and affording justice to victims." Those who possess this right include the victims themselves, and their families in the event of their death.[42] And no statute of limitations can be considered as applicable for compensation to the victims and survivors of gross crimes against humanity.

A significant illustration of how an NGO has worked to achieve compensation for certain types of victims and survivors of the Nazi epoch was provided by the World Jewish Congress (WJC) with respect to Switzerland. A not insignificant number of German Jews had deposited savings into Swiss banks to prevent the Nazis from seizing their money. Some apparently had asked third parties to open the accounts for them for fear they would be tortured or otherwise coerced into signing power of attorney agreements that would allow Nazi agents to pilfer their accounts. After the war, Swiss banks refused families of Jewish victims and survivors who sought to regain their savings. And they resisted returning the gold Germany had looted from conquered nations and Jews.

Following Germany's surrender, the Allies negotiated the "Washington Agreement" with Switzerland for the return of 250 million Swiss francs, a mere 12 percent of the alleged value of looted gold sold by Germany to Swiss banks. Pressure also arose to force Swiss banks to relinquish monies stored in accounts opened by Jewish victims of the Holocaust, and in 1962, a new Swiss law forced banks to review their records.[43] This resulted in almost 10 million Swiss francs being identified; 7.5 million in 961 accounts were made available for claim and another 2 million provided to Swiss Jewish organizations and a nondenominational Swiss refugee organization. As the WJC later pointed out, this was a tiny fraction of the amounts still believed to be held by Swiss banks. It emphasized that the 1962 law had not required independent review or public oversight.[44] In 1985, an abridged report was released by the Swiss National Bank acknowledging its purchase during the war of 1.2 billion Swiss francs' worth of looted gold.[45] But public outcry continued, and in 1987 the Union Bank of Switzerland donated $40 million to the International Red Cross—an organization, the WJC noted, that inexcusably had failed to acknowledge and resist the Holocaust. Israel Singer, the WJC Secretary-General, called the donation "a gift of money from those who did not own it to those who did not deserve it."[46]

It was in the context of continued Swiss resistance to acknowledging the truth about the past and failure to account for Jewish holdings that Edgar Bronfman, President of the WJC, launched a public "shaming" campaign in 1995 to force the banks to open their records.[47] The campaign was part of the WJC's rapidly expanding activity in pressing for justice for the Jewish victims of Nazi atrocities. In 1992, the WJC, along with B'nai B'rith, the Joint Distribution Committee, the Jewish Agency and Holocaust survivors' groups formed the World Jewish Restitution Organization (WJRO). Bronfman was made Chairman, and the Israeli Minister of Finance agreed to cooperate in seeking the return of "communal property and the transfer of heirless holdings to the Jewish People."[48]

Bronfman enlisted the support of the tough-minded New York Senator Alfonse D'Amato, who was Chairman of the Senate Banking Committee. The WJC and D'Amato aides pored over thousands of pages of declassified documents in the National Archives to establish Swiss complicity in the Nazi war effort. Their findings made news headlines every week around the world, particularly in leading financial magazines; the *Financial Times,* the *Wall Street Journal* and *Business Week.*[49] Ten thousand survivors or their heirs have filed suit against the banks. Bronfman encouraged American investors and New York City Comptroller Alan Hevesi to threaten financial retaliation against Swiss banks if they remained uncooperative. The Clinton Administration joined in the effort with a study coordinated by Stuart E. Eizenstat, then Under Secretary of Commerce and later Under Secretary of State. It produced a scathing report exposing Nazi-Swiss cooperation and the "Operation Safehaven" scandal, in which before the war's end German business leaders and Swiss banks cooperated in preparing postwar Germany's growth.[50]

Swiss authorities grudgingly responded to the pressure. Stating that Swiss banks held over $32 million dollars in unclaimed accounts, they offered a portion of those funds to settle the matter. Bronfman was indignant: "They didn't understand that what we want is a proper accounting, not a payoff."[51] Finally, in September, 1996, the Swiss Bankers' Association signed an agreement with the WJC and WJRO to establish an Independent Committee of Eminent Persons to be chaired by Paul Volcker, the former head of the U.S. Federal Reserve Board, to perform a "thorough and transparent audit."[52] Switzerland's parliament had approved legislation forcing this action and established its own Truth Commission to carry out a broad investigation into Swiss policies during the war.[53]

World and Swiss public opinion finally turned against the banks once a security guard caught officials of the Union Bank of Switzerland shredding thousands of documents and then acted to save many of them. The destruction of records was being carried out in violation of a recent Swiss law. The WJC promptly brought public attention to the plight of the guard, who had been suspended and then fired for saving the records, and the Anti-Defamation League of B'nai B'rith donated funds to pay his legal costs.

In the wake of the public outcry across Europe, even from Switzerland's conservative newspapers, the Swiss Bankers Association acceded to Bronfman's demand for an "interim fund" of $200 million dollars to provide immediate reparations to Jewish victims while further investigations by the Volcker committee and others proceeded. "I'm in a hurry," Bronfman said, "the survivors are dying."[54] Many, poverty-stricken, were in East Europe and had not received earlier reparations from the Federal Republic of Germany. Later, the Swiss government, stung by documentation revealing profound moral hypocrisy during and immediately after the war, planned to set up a $4.7 billion foundation that was to benefit death-camp survivors.

The ultimate positive response to the World Jewish Congress pressure was by no means automatically achieved. Swiss banking officials regularly accused Jewish organizations of conducting an anti-Swiss conspiracy to "destabilize and compromise" Switzerland and warned that some Swiss, as a result, might exhibit "negative and anti-Semitic reactions."[55] If Swiss officials eventually capitulated, a *New York Times* correspondent suggested, it was because they were certain that American Jewish groups would organize boycotts of Swiss financial institutions and stage demonstrations in front of Swiss banks.[56]

In short, what was feared was a possible repetition of the strategy of the antiapartheid movement among NGOs in the United States and Britain in the seventies and eighties that helped bring down the apartheid regime in South Africa. Already, Swiss banks were facing three class-action suits in New York courts asking payments totaling $20 billion in compensation for their wartime and postwar behavior. In addition, sanctions might be imposed by several state and local authorities.

Ultimately, the Swiss-created international panel of historians issued a report on May 24, 1998 which documented how Swiss bank officials were fully aware that they were recipients of gold taken by the Nazis from Jews sent to death camps. The looted gold included wedding bands, jewelry, coins and even teeth fillings. A week later, on June 2, 1998, U.S. government historians released its own study which showed that the Swiss Government's central bank carried and transmitted $300 million of Nazi looted gold—worth $2.6 billion today—to pay for Germany's war purchases from neutral countries. When the principal Swiss commercial banks finally agreed to a class-action compensation settlement for $1.25 billion on August 12, 1998, the threat of sanctions was withdrawn.

Clearly, the stigmatization of Switzerland by the World Jewish Congress before the bar of world public opinion proved to be a remarkably successful achievement and underscored the historic value of the shaming process to which NGOs have been committed. It helped, of course, that important politicians on various levels of government were encouraged to facilitate and reinforce the stigmatization procedure and to assist in the negotiations once they had begun. The personal involvement of the organization's President, Edgar Bronfman, was of vital importance. Through his personal political connections—as one of his top staffers noted in an interview—on a single day in the spring of 1996, he gave testimony to the Senate Banking Committee, chaired by D'Amato, and then went to the White House to meet with President Clinton.[57]

The successful outcome was a climactic moment for the organization whose previous Secretary-General, Gerhart Riegner, had been the first to alert the world from his office in neutral Geneva during World War II about the Holocaust. The same organization several decades later would reveal that Kurt Waldheim, the former UN Secretary-General, had served as an intelligence officer for the Nazi army in the Balkans and effectively had covered up this past.

However, the WJC had yet to complete its task. With a modest-sized staff in eight international offices and a budget of over $5.5 million, it coordinates the international affairs work of Jewish communal structures in numerous countries.[58] It is not a membership organization, like B'nai B'rith, but it is able to tap grassroots support through communal structures in various countries outside the United States and through a number of constituent organizations within the United States. The central coordinating character of WJC has enabled it to arrange meetings for Bronfman with officials in a number of countries—such as Sweden, Norway, Hungary, Poland, Romania and Slovakia—to pursue the crucial issues of restitution for survivors. An agreement similar to the one reached with Swiss banks was signed with the banks of Sweden.[59] And the organization takes pride in noting that about a dozen countries have established commissions to examine their respective roles toward Jews during the Nazi era.[60]

Prompted by the Holocaust and the Nuremberg Tribunal, the striving for a permanent International Criminal Court was a distinguishing feature of the last half-century, particularly during its final decade. But it was not the only aim of those who sought accountability for crimes against humanity. At times, effective justice could not be rendered because that which brought an end to such crimes and to gross violations of human rights was an agreement with the very military that had perpetrated abuses or an election that replaced arbitrary military rule with democracy but that did not fundamentally diminish the power of the military.

In wrestling with the problem of establishing at least a certain accountability, some pressed for Truth Commissions, which would reveal to the public the truth of what happened. In this way, the aggrieved might ascertain what happened to those who had been tortured or disappeared or killed. Revelations also might bring answers to questions of how and why. Truth would constitute a kind of closure for relatives and friends of the abused. And, to the extent that accountability was taking place after a fierce struggle for power in which great class or ethnic interests were at stake, truth about what occurred might begin the process of reconciliation between bitterly hostile and antagonistic elements in society and thereby possibly lay the foundation over the long run for a unified community.

Aryeh Neier, the creative head of Human Rights Watch, had already in 1990, in an important essay, carefully distinguished between truth and justice in establishing accountability.[61] Minimally, he noted, by revealing the truth about gross abuses and crimes against humanity, the perpetrators do bring upon themselves a certain limited form of justice as the revelations "mark them with a public stigma that is a punishment in itself. . . ."[62] At the same time, for perpetrators to identify "the victims and how they were tortured and killed, is a way of acknowledging their worth and dignity."

Perhaps the most pointed argument for a truth commission rather than a Nuremberg-style Tribunal came recently in a study by a South African Professor of Human Rights Law, Kader Asmal.[63] He grasped very quickly the distinctiveness of Nuremberg and how it differed in fundamental ways with what the South Africa of Nelson Mandela was seeking to do through its Truth and Reconciliation statute, or more precisely "The Promotion of National Unity and Reconciliation Act."

Nuremberg inevitably meant, observed Asmal, "the triumphant approach of victors' justice," which, however circumscribed by all the basic rules of a democratic judicial system, could not have been established without the total military victory of the United Nations.[64] In contrast, the end of the apartheid system was consummated by an agreement with those who had governed on the basis of and through an apartheid system. Thus, it was seen in part as having the purpose of "nation-building and reconciliation between the oppressors and the previously oppressed," while at the very same time revealing to all the utterly horrendous evils of the apartheid system and the atrocities committed in its name.

Moreover, Nuremberg, at best, meted out justice to only a relatively few perpetrators of gross abuses. Ordinary Germans could escape any sense of guilt and responsibility for the Nazi outrages simply by the "demonisation of the few in the dock."[65] Kader brings in Daniel Goldhagen's book, *Hitler's Willing Executioners,* to demonstrate how "ordinary" Germany embraced the Nazi system and fully collaborated in it.[66] In contrast, the South African parliament "deliberately decided upon a non-judicial forum that would allow the country to confront and renounce its past. . . ."[67] The hearings of the Truth and Reconciliation Commission were to serve as a "cathartic experience," one that can be realized fairly quickly and not through the "time-consuming and expensive process" of facing the past through a judicial system.

In order to obtain full disclosure of how the apartheid system operated in all its brutal and gory details, the option of possible amnesty for those providing such admissions was decided upon. Details of the gross and inhuman outrages that have shocked the international community, when provided by former apartheid officials seeking amnesty, could not very likely have come to light—and certainly not as quickly and fully—without the availability of the option.

To the extent that Truth Commissions appeared on the human rights agenda as a method for dealing with accountability in general and, particularly, when a country was moving from authoritarianism or military dictatorship or apartheid to democracy, it was evident that NGOs would be very much involved, in at least the most important ones. A specialist on the subject counted 15 examples of Truth Commissions.[68] The focus here will be upon those Commissions in which NGOs played an active and sometimes significant role.

In 1983, Argentina's President Raul Alfonsin, reasserting democratic rule following the humiliation of the Falklands War, was pressured by human rights NGOs to create a Truth Commission similar to one which had been created the previous year in Bolivia, entitled the National Commission of Inquiry Into Disappearances. The Bolivian effort was a failure; after three years, it disbanded without publishing a report.[69] Significantly, Alfonsin selected internationally respected figures to the National Commission on the Disappeared, which also included figures appointed by both houses of congress. It was chaired by Ernesto Sabato, Argentina's most respected author. The powers and resources of this Truth Commission were considerably greater than that of Bolivia's.

Some testimony, which was taken outside the country, was broadcast on national television; the Commission enjoyed national prominence and close contacts with local human rights NGOs and the press. Its final report, *Nunca Mas* ("Never Again") documented cases of some 9,000 disappeared persons and in book form was a best seller. Argentina's Commission was the most successful effort in Latin America at bringing justice for victims of gross human rights violations during periods of repressive rule.[70]

In 1990 Chilean President Patricio Aylwin formed a National Truth and Reconciliation Commission, bowing to the pressure of local NGOs. The Commission was headed by former Senator Raul Rettig and included prominent representatives of various groups. Some of the commissioners, like Jaime Castillo and José Zalaquett, were respected human rights advocates and had been exiled by Augusto Pinochet before he stepped down.[71] Records of trials and investigations into disappearances by authorities also were handed over to the Commission. Approximately 3,400 cases were brought before it, and the Commission decided to conduct detailed investigations of 2,920 of them. The Truth

Commission benefited from over 60 staffers, the detailed records kept by conscientious lawyers and law enforcement authorities and NGOs, and considerable public and political support. NGOs provided important information on specific cases and background to the Commission,[72] planned extensive efforts to disseminate the report and planned to institute national days of reflection and organize community gatherings commemorating the victims.[73]

The Commission on the Truth for El Salvador formally was established on July 15, 1992, as part of the peace accords negotiated over three years between the government and rebel forces. It was allotted six months—later extended for two more—to report on human rights violations carried out by both sides in the twelve-year civil war, with the "overarching aim" being the "promotion of national reconciliation."[74] Though it analyzed many specific cases in detail, its primary function was to survey overall patterns of abuse and compile statistics on the tens of thousands of cases it uncovered. It was funded and staffed by the United Nations as an impartial third party in the peace process, the first such Commission sponsored by the UN. Financial support was provided through a UN-managed fund furnished by the United States, the European Community, the Netherlands and the Scandinavian countries. The Commission consisted of 15 staffers, several administrators and 3 Commissioners—Professor Thomas Buergenthal, former President of Colombia Belisario Betancur and former Foreign Minister of Venezuela Reinaldo Figueredo Planchart. For purposes of neutrality, none were Salvadoran. The final report (titled "From Madness to Hope") listed over 40 names of people found to be responsible for widespread human rights violations; most were government figures. The Commission recommended removing all of these individuals from power, permanently barring them from military or security positions, and barring them from official positions for ten years.[75]

The commission also benefited from substantial American congressional and NGO support, including international human rights groups. The so-called National Security Archive, an organization that compiles U.S. documents for purposes of studying American foreign policy, was helpful.[76] Local human rights organizations were "surprisingly unprepared to assist the Commission," but the already-published reports of international human rights NGOs, particularly HRW/Americas and the Lawyers Committee for Human Rights, "provided useful background information and served as guideposts for the Commission's investigation," said Buergenthal.

Finally, the Commission benefited from two external factors: first, the election of Bill Clinton as President and the ensuing, though incomplete, release of U.S. documents; second, the dramatic release of the report by a domestic Ad Hoc Commission composed of three "distinguished Salvadoran civilians." These two developments drove previously unwilling witnesses and suspects into the waiting arms of the Truth Commission. As Buergenthal's efforts to collect U.S. documentary evidence of human rights violations began to succeed, military officials with more acceptable human rights records began to talk.

And the report of the Ad Hoc Commission, which eventually was leaked to the press, slammed the military for its poor human rights record and included the names of more than 100 officers, including the Minister and Deputy Minister of Defense and the Chief of the General Staff. Because the Truth Commission had the power to make recommendations regarding prosecutions and amnesties, suddenly speaking truthfully to the UN Commission held out the possibility of job security and the evasion of prison.

The most prominent Truth Commission was the one in South Africa. While providing the same benefits that such commissions did in Latin America did, South Africa's Truth and Reconciliation Commission, headed by Nobel Laureate Archbishop Desmond Tutu, was more ambitious. It was a product of Mandela's desire for inclusion and healing, but it also was intended as an instrument, however modest and incomplete, of justice. The South African Commission was the first and only Truth Commission to have subpoena powers and the first to grant amnesty on a case-by-case basis. Its ability to grant amnesty (provided that the applicant tells everything he knows) has relieved strains on already overwhelmed prosecutors and brought out evidence that high-level officials knew of and participated in some of the most heinous crimes, including assassinations, bombings and poisonings. The Commission succeeded in proving beyond doubt the patterns of violence and repression that had characterized the apartheid regime. The freedom of applicants to testify without fear of rigorous cross-examination and the built-in incentive to make sure that all their crimes were aired offered South Africans the advantage of getting far more information than they would have in ordinary court proceedings.

Among the episodes exposed by the commission were the torture and killing by police officers of Black Consciousness leader Stephen Biko, the assassinations of various high-level African National Congress (ANC) officials, bombings and murders conducted by several death squads attached to the military and police forces, and the complicity of national officials like former President P. W. Botha.

The Commission, sworn into office in December of 1995, began slowly. During its first half-year, most of its hearings covered relatively well-known episodes; most of its witnesses already were convicted of crimes and had applied for amnesty after being sentenced. The Commission's arguably more effective work came in 1997, since the possibility of prosecution pressured many low-level participants in the apartheid regime to apply for amnesty with the Commission. Its hearings were televised and captured the country's attention. Thousands of applications for amnesty were received, many from current or former police officials. And, since the Commission also dealt with murders, assassinations, bombings and torture committed by those in the antiapartheid movement, various high-ranking officials of the African National Congress and the Inkatha Freedom Party also made application for amnesty.

The total number of applications for amnesty, submitted before the May 10 deadline, was eight thousand.[77] In one early episode, a former Minister of Law and Order, Adriaan Vlok, claimed that Botha told him to bomb the headquarters of the South African Council of Churches, a symbol of nonviolent resistance to apartheid, because it had become a "house of evil." Vlok also claimed responsibility for falsely accusing an antiapartheid activist of carrying out the bombing; he further provided details about other bombings of a trade union headquarters, church groups, movie theaters planning to show the movie "Cry Freedom" (about Stephen Biko) and other antiapartheid organizations.[78]

Unofficial support for the Commission was considered important. Prior to the passage of legislation, the Justice Minister called for contributions from "individuals, organizations, [and] religious bodies" regarding the mandate and powers of the commission.[79] Some organizations provided support for victims who testified before the Commission, including counseling services and medical clinics.[80] But some international NGOs were not very enthusiastic about the Truth Commission.

Amnesty, in a statement provided to the Select Committee on Justice of the South African legislature, pointed out the requirement laid out in various human rights agreements to which South Africa was a signatory: "victims of such serious violations as torture, extralegal executions or enforced 'disappearance' and/or their families have an international recognized right to have their complaints fully investigated and to obtain redress and compensation." The overall objective of Truth Commissions, Amnesty concluded, is "reconciliation by providing victims with some measures of justice."[81] Amnesty objected to the Commission's failure to consider enforced disappearances, torture, extralegal executions and detentions of individuals with nonpolitical motivation.

Amnesty International also objected to the broad powers of amnesty granted the Commission. It argued that pardons ought only be granted *after* successful convictions of human rights abusers:

> The interests of national reconciliation after a period of political violence or turmoil may be served by measures of clemency. . . . Amnesty International takes no position on such measures, but it does insist that the truth is revealed and the judicial process completed. We do not believe that justice should constitute a form of vengeance, but rather is an essential component of reconciliation and lasting peace.[82]

The Truth and Reconciliation Commission's Committee on Amnesty, whose powers were relatively broad and whose hearings were held in secret, came under particular criticism from Amnesty International, which asked that the Committee's hearings be open to victims and/or families of victims.

In fact, general amnesty was not applied and was not at issue; only specific amnesty was granted in exchange for full disclosure of the truth. Archbishop Desmond Tutu explained in a British television interview what was at the heart of his Commission's purpose:

> . . . experience worldwide shows that if you do not deal with a dark past, it is going, as sure as anything, to come back and haunt you horrendously. We need to deal with this past as quickly as possible, then *close the door on it and concentrate on the present and future*. [Emphasis added.][83]

Clearly, Tutu, like Asmal, was looking for reconciliation and closure. In his view and that of his supporters, "knowing is enough," and "if there was no amnesty, then we would have had justice and ashes."

For the central figure in the El Salvador Truth Commission, Professor Thomas Buergenthal, "the most important function" of such an institution "is to tell the truth" rather than to be preoccupied with national reconciliation.[84] Certainly reconciliation is important, but only through unearthing and revealing the truth about the past, Buergenthal contended, can a nation acknowledge "the wrongs that have been committed in its name" and, therewith, "successfully embark on the arduous task of cementing trust between former adversaries . . . which is a prerequisite for national reconciliation." Without the airing of "the basic truth" about the past, reconciliation will be difficult to achieve and, indeed, past wounds will "fester," endangering the social peace.

Precisely because of the importance of having the past stand fully revealed, international and national NGOs have been supportive of the creation of Truth Commissions, even if in specific instances, some may have objections to the use of amnesty for purposes of obtaining disclosures. According to Priscilla Hayner, who carefully has studied the various Commissions, NGO contributions to their creation and operation has been considerable, especially in the collection of evidence and background information on crimes.[85] She explained that NGOs were a principal source of documentation. In the case of South Africa, they assumed the task of interviewing the victims of abuses and making their statements available to the Commission. In the case of El Salvador, NGOs provided the Truth Commission with their files, totaling 14,000 cases, including confidential submissions by the Lawyers Committee for Human Rights and Human Rights Watch/Americas.

In some instances, local NGOs helped in the staffing of the Commissions, notably in Argentina and Chile. Elsewhere, they advised the Commissions where to look for evidence. At times NGOs assisted in providing training to the Commissions' staffs in the carrying out of their functions. They also have been helpful in aiding witnesses whose testimony was essential. Especially important, NGOs have played a pivotal role in publicizing the work and reports of the various Truth Commissions.

It is perhaps not accidental that Buergenthal, a champion of Truth Commissions and of the all-consuming need to bare the facts about gross human rights violations, was, himself, a strong supporter of NGOs. When he served as a judge on the Inter-American Court of Human Rights in San José, Costa Rica, he actually helped found an NGO that would promote research and education in the human rights field. This was done at a time in the late seventies when it was dangerous to discuss human rights issues in broad areas of the Americas where rightist military dictatorships exercised power. At Buergenthal's initiative, the Inter-American Institute on Human Rights, a Costa Rica–based independent NGO, was founded and has played a remarkable role in advancing human rights programs and free elections throughout the Americas.[86] Besides the Institute, Buergenthal has served on the boards of various other NGOs, including the Blaustein Institute.

Nor is it accidental that Buergenthal, while an academic, jurist and public official, considers an activist struggle against racism and discrimination a personal obligation.[87] He is a survivor of the Holocaust, having spent four of the first ten years of his life in the Nazi concentration camps of Auschwitz and Sachsenhausen. The pain and suffering of those years and especially of the profoundly traumatic Death March out of Birkenau in January, 1945 forever have been imprinted in his memory and briefly sketched in a human rights journal.[88] For the survivors, he has stressed, remembrance means an obligation to act to prevent similar horrors from being perpetrated.

The Holocaust, for Buergenthal, was a seminal event, but its lessons are universal. When genocide was being practiced against Bosnian Muslims in 1993 and the European democracies were responding with inaction or indifference, he bitterly responded in testimony to the U.S. Helsinki Commission:

> I am outraged—all humanity should be outraged—by the inaction of the same governments which in the 1930s tried to appease Hitler and which for many months have done the same with the murderers and rapists in the former Yugoslavia.[89]

The closing words in the form of a rhetorical question summed up his fury: "Have we learned nothing from the Holocaust?"

It was a fury that would be transmuted by NGO activists into demands for a permanent International Criminal Court, for reparations to the victims and survivors of genocide, for Truth Commissions and for standards and institutions to hold abusers accountable. Beyond the specific demand for accountability, the Holocaust would trigger an NGO advocacy program urging compliance with the Universal Declaration of Human Rights. After 50 years, it remains an unfulfilled task and obligation of "the curious grapevine."

NOTES

INTRODUCTION

1. Cited in Ambassador Madeleine K. Albright, "Human Rights Near the Turn of the Century" (address made to the 52nd Session of the United Nations Commission on Human Rights, Geneva, March 20, 1996).

2. Daniel J. Goldhagen, *Hitler's Willing Executioners: Ordinary Germans and the Holocaust* (New York: Alfred A. Knopf, 1996).

3. Karin Ryan and Laurie Wiseberg, "ECOSOC Resolution 1996/31: The End Result of the ECOSOC Review Process of Rules Governing Relations with the United Nations," in *Human Rights, the United Nations, and Nongovernmental Organizations* (Atlanta: The Carter Center, 1997), 9.

4. Jessica T. Mathews, "Power Shift," *Foreign Affairs* (January-February, 1997), 52-54. According to Laurie Wiseberg, who has followed closely the extraordinary expansion of NGOs, no scientific data has been accumulated to warrant using any broad estimates. She conveyed this information to the author in a telephone conversation in October, 1997.

5. Hans J. Morgenthau, *Politics Among Nations: The Struggle for Power and Peace,* 5th ed. (New York: Alfred A. Knopf, 1973). Previous editions of this classic and standard work were published in 1948, 1954, 1960 and 1967.

6. Hans J. Morgenthau and Kenneth W. Thompson, *Politics Among Nations: The Struggle for Power and Peace,* 6th ed. (New York: Alfred A. Knopf, 1985), 274-78. The book cover notes that the book was "Revised by Kenneth W. Thompson" of the University of Virginia. In his preface, Thompson notes that he drew upon Morgenthau's papers, letters and essays for any additions.

7. A very useful frame of reference, although modified by the author, is J. D. Tolbert, *International Non-Governmental Organizations (NGOs) and The Changing Nature of International Law: An Examination of the Emerging Role of NGOs in Human Rights and Environmental Law* (Ph.D. diss., University of Nottingham, 1990), 42-52.

8. Harry J. Steiner, *Diverse Partners: Non-Governmental Organizations in the Human Rights Movement—The Report of a Retreat of Human Rights Activists* (Cambridge: Harvard Law School, 1991), 28-34, 41-44.

9. From a memorandum by Ken Roth to all Human Rights Watch (HRW) Advisory Committee Members dated September 30, 1996. That memo refers to cultural rights as well, since it specifically refers to the Covenant on Economic, Social and Cultural Rights.

10. The "International Bill" is comprised of the Universal Declaration, the twin Covenants on Civil and Political Rights and on Economic, Social and Cultural Rights, as well as the measures of implementation that are part of the "Optional Protocol" to the Covenant on Civil and Political Rights.

11. Felix Ermacora, "Non-Governmental Organizations as Promoters of Human Rights," in Franz Matscher and Herbert Petzold, eds. *Protecting Human Rights: The European Dimension* (Køln: Carl Heymanns Verlag KG, 1988), 180.

12. Tolbert, op. cit., 51.

13. "A Human Rights Agenda for the Clinton Administration," unpublished document, 12 pp. A mimeographed copy of the typescript is in the author's possession. An oral report of the meeting with Albright was provided to the author by a participant.

14. *Speech of Gay McDougall on Human Rights Day, 1997,* December 9, 1997.

15. Peter Baker, "Clinton Calls Human Rights a 'Pillar' of Foreign Policy," *Washington Post,* December 10, 1997. For the text see The White House Office of the Press Secretary, *Remarks of the President in Honor of Human Rights Day,* December 9, 1997. The speech was delivered in New York.

16. *Human Rights Watch World Report 1998* (New York: Human Rights Watch, December 4, 1997), xix-xxiv.

17. Mathews, op. cit., 50-66.

18. The four-page fact-sheet was entitled "Human Rights in China." It was distributed at a press conference for Wei Jiangsheng on November 21, 1997 at the New York Public Library.

19. Mathews, op. cit., 54.

20. Ibid.

21. Stanley Cohen, *Denial and Acknowledgment: The Impact of Information About Human Rights Violations* (Jerusalem: Hebrew University, 1995), Mimeo, iv.

22. Ibid., 8-9.

23. Ibid., 179, 183.

24. *The International Council on Human Rights Policy,* May 1997, 4. The Council was established in Switzerland by a grant from the Ford Foundation which provided the author with this report.

25. Ibid., 9.

26. Anthony DePalma, "As U.S. Looks On, 120 Nations Sign Treaty Banning Land Mines," the *New York Times,* December 4, 1997.

CHAPTER 1

1. Cited in *To Reaffirm Faith in Fundamental Human Rights: The UN and Human Rights, 1945-95* (New York: The Jacob Blaustein Institute for the Advancement of Human Rights, 1995), 1. The booklet carried a speech by Blaustein's daughter, Barbara Hirschhorn, delivered on June 22, 1995.

2. John P. Humphrey, "The UN Charter and the Universal Declaration of Human Rights," in *The International Protection of Human Rights,* ed. Evan Luard (New York: Praeger, 1967), 39-40.

3. Ibid.

4. The text is in Clark M. Eichelberger, *UN: The First Twenty-Five Years* (New York: Harper & Row, 1970), 70.

5. Dorothy B. Robins, *Experiment in Democracy: The Story of U.S. Citizen Organizations in Forging the Charter of the United Nations* (New York: Parkside Press, 1971), 100-101.

6. Ibid., 102.

7. *Report to the President on the Results of the San Francisco Conference; Department of State Publication No. 2349, Conference Series 71* (Washington, D.C.: U.S. Government Printing Office, 1945), 27.

8. Robins, op. cit., 104.

9. Cited in Ibid.

10. Ibid., 122-23.

11. Ibid., 127.

12. Sidney Liskofsky, *NGOs and Human Rights,* (New York: July, 1974), 31. (Unpublished paper. The American Jewish Committee was the organization for which Liskofsky worked.)

13. "Tribute by James Shotwell," *A World Charter for Human Rights* (New York: American Jewish Committee, n.d.)

14. This section is drawn from the initial draft of a speech on the fiftieth anniversary of the UN prepared by Felice Gaer, Director of the Committee's Blaustein Institute for the Advancement of Human Rights. While undated, the draft was written in 1995.

15. *A World Charter for Human Rights,* op. cit.

16. *To Reaffirm Faith,* op. cit., 5.

17. Liskofsky op. cit., 32.

18. O. Frederick Nolde, *Freedom's Charter: The Universal Declaration of Human Rights,* Headline Series No. 76 (New York: Foreign Policy Association, July-August, 1949), 12.

19. Ibid., 10.

20. *To Reaffirm Faith,* op. cit., 6.

21. Eichelberger, op. cit., 269; Joseph Proskauer, "A New Birth of Freedom" (speech to the Carnegie Endowment, April 26, 1958).

22. Joseph M. Proskauer, *A Segment of My Times* (New York: Farrar, Straus and Co., 1950) 225.

23. Ibid.

24. Robins, op. cit., 132. In Stettinius's official report to President Harry Truman, he candidly acknowledged the significant impact of the NGOs. See Theo van Boven, "The Role of Non-governmental Organizations in International Human Rights Standard-Setting: A Prerequisite of Democracy," *California Western International Law Journal* 20 (1990): 210.

25. Ibid.

26. Humphrey, op. cit., 40.

27. The proposals sent to Stettinius can be found in Proskauer, *A Segment of My Times,* 221-23.

28. Ibid., 226.

29. Ibid., 223.

30. Humphrey, op. cit., 46.

31. Ibid., 47. Also U.S. Department of State Bulletin, Vol. XII, No. 314, 5.

32. William Korey, "Eleanor Roosevelt and the Universal Declaration of Human Rights," in *Eleanor Roosevelt, Her Day: A Personal Album,* A. David Gurewitsch, ed. (New York: Interchange Foundation, 1968), 12.

33. Ibid., 15.

34. Liskofsky, op. cit., 45.

35. René Cassin, "Twenty Years of NGO Effort on Behalf of Human Rights," in *Human Rights: Final Report of the International NGO Conference* (Paris: UNESCO, September, 1968), 20.

36. UN Doc., SG/SM 999 (1968), 2.

37. David Weissbrodt, "The Contribution of International Nongovernmental Organizations to the Protection of Human Rights," in *Human Rights in International Law: Legal and Policy Issues,* Theodor Meron, ed. (New York: Oxford University Press, 1984), 429.

38. The observations of Mrs. Roosevelt were made in her introduction to Nolde, op. cit., 3.

39. Van Boven, op. cit., 211.

40. Nolde, op. cit., 22; Korey, op. cit., 17.

41. *New York Times,* December 8, 1948.

42. UN General Assembly Official Records (GAOR): 3rd Sess., Part 1, 3rd Comtee., 92nd Mtg., 2 October 1948, 61; and 89th Mtg., September 30, 1948, 32.

43. Egon Schwelb, *Human Rights and the International Community* (Chicago: Quadrangle Books, 1964), 48-49.

44. Economic and Social Council Official Records (ESCOR): 34 Sess., 1962, Suppl. No. 8 (E/3616/Rev.1), para.105.

45. *Montreal Statement* (Montreal: Assembly for Human Rights, 1968).

46. Cassin, op. cit., 21.

47. Ibid.

CHAPTER 2

1. Economic and Social Council (ECOSOC) Res. 75(V), 5 August 1947.

2. Liskofsky, *NGOs and Human Rights* (New York: July 1974), 51.

3. UN Doc. E/CN, 4/AC.21/L.1, December, 1966, 50-4.

4. ESCOR: 26th Sess., Suppl. No. 8 (E/3088), para. 194.

5. UN Doc. A/CONF. 32/6, 20 June 1967, 68-9.

6. Sir Samuel Hoare, "The UN Commission on Human Rights," in *The International Protection of Human Rights*, E. Luard, ed. (New York: Frederick Praeger, Inc., 1967), 90.

7. "Report of the [Nuclear] Commission on Human Rights," ESCOR: 2nd Sess., 1946, Annex 4 (E/38), 228.

8. ECOSOC Res. 2/9, 21 June 1946.

9. U.S. Mission to the UN, Press Release USUN-27, 12 March 1967.

10. UN Doc. A/CONF. 32/L.3, 15 February, 1968, 19-20.

11. UN Doc. E/CN.4/154, 24 June 1948.

12. John P. Humphrey, *Human Rights and the United Nations: A Great Adventure*, (Dobbs Ferry: Transnational Publishers, 1984), 296-300.

13. See Richard N. Gardner, foreword in Roger S. Clark, *The United Nations High Commissioner for Human Rights* (The Hague: Martinius Nijhoff, 1972), xii.

14. ESCOR: 39th Sess., 1965, Suppl. No. 8 (E/4024), para. 16. Also see UN Doc. E/CN.4/887, 18 March 1965.

15. UN Doc. E/CN.4/SR 881, 21 June 1966.

16. UN Doc. E/CN.4/934, 8 February 1967.

17. ESCOR: 42nd Sess., 1967, Suppl. No. 6 (E/4322), para. 492.

18. Commission on Human Rights Res. 14 (XXIII), 22 March 1967.

19. See R. St. J. MacDonald, "The United Nations High Commission for Human Rights," *The Canadian Yearbook of International Law* (1967), 84-117. Also see William Korey, "A Global Ombudsman," *Saturday Review*, August 12, 1967, 20.

20. UN Doc. E/CN.4/501/Rev.1, 18 May 1950.

21. ESCOR: 22nd Sess., 1956, Suppl. No. 3(E/2844), 4-7.

22. ESCOR: 34th Sess., 1962, Suppl. No. 8(E/3616/Rev.1), 9-13.

23. William Korey, "The Key to Human Rights—Implementation," *International Conciliation*, no. 570 (November, 1968), 26-7.

24. Ben Ami, *Between Hammer and Sickle* (New York: Signet Books, 1967), 295-96. The author originally used a pseudonym, but it was known that he was a well-placed Israeli official, Arie Eliav.

25. *American Jewish Yearbook 1961* (Philadelphia: The American Jewish Committee and the Jewish Publication Society of America, 1962), 369.

26. See William Korey, *The Soviet Cage: Anti-Semitism in Russia* (New York: Viking, 1973), 4-82.

27. *Memorandum on Discrimination in the Matter of the Right of Everyone to Leave Any Country Including His Own and to Return to His Country* (New York: Coordinating Board of Jewish Organizations, 1960).

28. José D. Inglés, *Study of Discrimination in Respect of the Right of Everyone to Leave Any Country, Including His Own, And to Return to His Country* (New York: United Nations, 1963).

29. Arkady N. Shevchenko, *Breaking with Moscow* (New York: Random House, 1985), 315-20.

30. UN Doc. E/CN.4/Sub.2/SR.382, 6-7, and UN Doc. E/CN.4/Sub.2/SR.385, 11-2.

31. See Alan Dowty, *Closed Borders* (New Haven: Yale University Press, 1987), 135.

32. Ronald I. Rubin, "Soviet Jewry and the United Nations: The Politics of Non-Governmental Organizations," *Jewish Social Studies* 29, 3 (July, 1967): 152.

33. Rubin, op. cit., 147.

34. See *Petitions, Letters and Appeals from Soviet Jews* (Jerusalem: Hebrew University, 1979), vols. IX and X.

35. See Korey, *The Soviet Cage*, 80-81.

36. See Richard N. Gardner, *In Pursuit of World Order* (New York: Praeger, 1964), 257-59.

37. Rubin, op. cit., 150.

38. ECOSOC Res. 1102 (XL), 4 March 1966.

39. Commission on Human Rights, Res 2 (XXII), 25 March 1966.

40. John Carey, "Procedures for International Protection Human Rights," *Iowa Law Review*, (October 1967): 307-11.

41. For the Commission's discussions and various draft Resolutions, see ESCOR: 44th Sess., 1968, Suppl. No. 4(E/4475), 58-79.

42. See William Korey, "The Key to Human Rights—Implementation," *International Conciliation* no. 570, (November 1968): 65.

43. See United Nations Public Sales No. E.68.XIV. 2 (A/CONF.32/41), September 1968.

44. Richard Bilder, "Rethinking International Human Rights: Some Basic Questions," *Wisconsin Law Review* (1969).

45. Thomas Buergenthal, *International Human Rights in a Nutshell*, 2nd. ed. (St. Paul: West Publishing Co., 1995), 66.

46. Cassin, op. cit., 21.

47. Buergenthal, op. cit., 49.

48. Ibid.

CHAPTER 3

1. UN Doc. E/CN.4/930, 27 January 1967, 79-81.

2. The Special Rapporteur's document and the episode accompanying it are described in William Korey, "The Key to Human Rights—Implementation," *International Conciliation* no. 570 (November 1968): 27-28. The author had access to the document and was present during the discussion of it.

3. See ibid., 23-24.

4. Sidney Liskofsky, "The U.N. Reviews Its NGO System," *Reports on the Foreign Scene* no. 10 (January 1970): 4.

5. Ibid.

6. William Korey, "We, The Peoples," *Vista* 5, no. 6 (May-June 1970): 29.

7. Ibid.

8. Liskofsky, op. cit.

9. Cited in Korey, "We, The Peoples," op. cit.

10. *Boston Sunday Globe,* April 20, 1969.
11. *New York Post,* May 22, 1969.
12. Cited in Harris Schoenberg, *The Mandate for Terror: The United Nations and the PLO* (New York: Shapolsky Publishers Inc., 1989), 303.
13. Liskofsky, op. cit., 12.
14. Jerome J. Shestack, "Sisyphus Endures: The International Human Rights NGO," *The New York Law School Law Review* 24 (1978): 114.
15. Homer Jack, "The Human Rights Commission at Geneva," *World Conference on Religion and Peace Report,* March 7, 1975.
16. Shestack, op. cit., 115.
17. *New York Post,* May 4, 1977.
18. Goronwy Rees, "Zionism," *Encounter* 46 (January 1976): 29-31. For a detailed review of the episode see Schoenberg, op. cit., 309, 327.
19. Cited in Daniel Patrick Moynihan, *A Dangerous Place* (Boston: Little, Brown, 1978), 191.
20. Paul Johnson, *Modern Times* (New York: Weidenfeld and Nicolson, 1983), 690.
21. William Korey, *Russian Anti-Semitism, Pamyat, and the Demonology of Zionism* (Jerusalem: Harwood Academic Publishers, 1995), 30-45.
22. Moynihan, op. cit., 198-99.

CHAPTER 4

1. Interview with E. S. Reddy, May 8, 1996.
2. Ibid.
3. E. S. Reddy, ed., *Anti-Apartheid Movement and the United Nations: Statement and Papers of Abdul S. Minty* (New Delhi: 1994), 11.
4. E. S. Reddy, "Contribution of Non-Governmental Organizations" (paper presented at the Symposium on "World Peace and the Liberation of South Africa and Namibia," Geneva, June 11-13, 1986). The author was provided a copy of the paper.
5. Ibid.
6. Ibid.
7. E. S. Reddy interview.
8. Ibid.
9. Ibid.
10. UN Doc., E/CN.4/AC.22/SR.1, 14 July 1967, 4.
11. UN Doc. E/CN.4/AC.22/SR.24, 22 September 1968, 20.
12. *United Nations Action in the Field of Human Rights,* UN. Doc.ST/HR/2//Rev.2 U.N. Sales No. E. 83.XIV.2 (1983), 10-11.
13. See Richard Schifter, "Human Rights at the United Nations: The South African Precedent," *The American University Journal of International Law and Policy* 8, nos. 2 & 3 (winter/spring 1992/1993): 365.
14. Ibid., 366.
15. The decision was taken on April 1, 1960 in Security Council Resolution 134.
16. UN General Assembly Resolution, A/RES/31/6 K, 9 November 1976.
17. Laurie S. Wiseberg and Harry M. Scoble, "The International League for Human Rights: The Strategy of a Human Rights NGO," *The Georgia Journal of International and Comparative Law* 7 (1977): 296.
18. Ibid.
19. International League for Human Rights, *ILHR Human Rights Bulletin* (winter/spring 1995): 2.
20. Laurie S. Wiseberg and Harry M. Scoble, "Human Rights as an International League," *Society* (November 1977): 71.

21. Oral History Project (Columbia University), Roger Baldwin, 1954, 627.
22. Ibid., 626.
23. Ibid., 628.
24. Ibid., 11.
25. Ibid., 113.
26. Ibid., 115.
27. Ibid., 117.
28. Ibid., 120-21.
29. Ibid., 135-36.
30. Les de Villiers, *In Sight of Surrender: The U.S. Sanctions Campaign Against South Africa, 1946-1993* (Westport, CT: Praeger, 1995). The preface of the book provides a brief sketch of the author's work.
31. Ibid., xiv-xv of the preface.
32. Interview with George Houser, February 22, 1996, conducted in B'nai B'rith Building.
33. George M. Houser, *No One Can Stop the Rain: Glimpses of Africa's Liberation Struggle* (New York: The Pilgrim Press, 1982), 7.
34. De Villiers, op. cit., xv.
35. Houser interview.
36. Houser, *No One Can Stop the Rain,* 63.
37. For details, see the lengthy historical document, "The International Impact of the South African Struggle for Liberation," prepared by George Houser for the UN Centre Against Apartheid, No. 2/82, January 1982, 11. It was extraordinarily significant that a NGO was asked to do a study for a UN unit. This was not the case with the UN Human Rights Division.
38. Ibid., 17.
39. De Villiers, op. cit., 23.
40. Ibid.
41. Houser interview.
42. Cited in de Villiers, op. cit., 7.
43. Interview with Vela Pillay, June 15, 1995, conducted by Clarity Educational Productions, Inc. of Berkeley, California. A copy was presented to the author.
44. Ibid.
45. See George W. Shepherd, Jr., *Anti-Apartheid: Transnational Conflict and Western Policy in the Liberation of South Africa* (Westport, CT: Greenwood Press, 1977), 150-51.
46. Houser, "The International Impact of the South African Struggle for Liberation," op. cit., 21.
47. De Villiers, op. cit., 24.
48. Houser interview.
49. Houser, "International Impact of the South African Struggle for Liberation," op. cit., 26.
50. De Villiers, op. cit., 55.
51. Ibid.
52. Ibid., 29.
53. Ibid.
54. Ibid., 125.
55. Ibid.
56. *Time Magazine,* June 14, 1993.
57. The thesis is developed in the de Villiers volume.
58. Houser interview.
59. Shepherd, Jr., op. cit., 228.
60. E. S. Reddy, *Struggle for Freedom in Southern Africa: Its International Significance* (New Delhi, 1987), 31, 36.

61. *Non-Governmental Organizations, Action Against Apartheid* (New York: United Nations Centre Against Apartheid, 1978).

62. Ralston Deffenbaugh, Jr., "The Southern Africa Project for the Lawyers' Committee for Civil Rights under Law," in *Global Human Rights: Public Policies Comparative Measures and NGO Strategies,* Ved P. Nanda, James P. Scarritt and George W. Shepherd, eds., (Boulder, CO: Westview Press, 1981), 289-301.

63. Ibid., 296-97.

64. For details, see Tim Wells, "Witnessing Freedom," *The Washington Lawyer* (September/October 1994): 22-32, 57-58.

65. Ibid., 26.

66. Ibid., 23.

67. Ibid., 58.

68. *The United Nations Blue Book Series, Volume I: The United Nations and Apartheid, 1948-1994* (New York: UN Department of Public Information, 1995). See especially Documents # 49, 52, 92, 103, 100, 111, 124, 127, 128, 129, 142, 148, 198, 199, 214, 216.

69. See de Villiers, op. cit., 194.

CHAPTER 5

1. *Annual Report of the Anti-Slavery Society,* 1977-78 (London), 3.

2. Peter Archer, "Action by Unofficial Organizations on Human Rights," in *The International Protection of Human Rights,* Evan Luard, ed. (New York: Praeger, 1967), 162.

3. Ibid.

4. Frederick B. Artz, *Reaction and Revolution, 1814-1832* (New York: Harper, 1934), 112.

5. Ibid.

6. Roger Sawyer, *Slavery in the Twentieth Century* (London: Routledge & Kegan Paul, 1986), 217.

7. See Archer, op. cit., 169 and Sawyer, op. cit., 219.

8. Baldwin Robertson, *Anti-Slavery International for the Protection of Human Rights,* (New York, 1996), 3. This essay was prepared for the author's use.

9. *Reporter* (November 1976): 24.

10. It was carried in full later in the *Reporter* (June 1960): 55-61.

11. The full text of the Convention is in the *Reporter* (February 1957): 4-8.

12. Ibid., 4.

13. Lord Hailey's speech, "A New Phase in Colonial Policy," was published as a pamphlet, *Address to the Annual Meeting,* July 24, 1952.

14. *Reporter* (April 1949): 15.

15. Sawyer, op. cit., 107.

16. *Reporter* (January 23, 1958): 44-45.

17. *Reporter* (January 1963): 33-37.

18. Montgomery's handwritten report on these developments, entitled "Is Slavery Important?" was made available to the author by the Anti-Slavery Society.

19. *Annual Report of the Anti-Slavery Society, 1975* (London).

20. As reported in Robertson, op. cit., 19.

21. *Reporter* (December 1981): 20.

22. Robertson, op. cit., 22.

23. *Reporter* (November 1980).

24. *Reporter* (November 1979): 18-19.

25. *Reporter* (November 1980): 37-40.

26. Sidney Liskofsky, *NGOs and Human Rights* (New York, 1974), 60. Unpublished.
27. Ibid., 64.
28. Cited in Robertson, op. cit., 26.
29. Liskofsky, op. cit., 64.
30. Ibid.
31. The episode is detailed in the *Reporter* (1990): 51.
32. Ibid.
33. See Sawyer, op. cit., 28-31.
34. *Reporter* (1987): 53-55.
35. Robertson, op. cit., 21.
36. *Reporter* (1987): 37-42.
37. *Reporter* (1994): 42.
38. Ibid. Berger now works for the UN in the same field.
39. *Oral Intervention of Patrick Montgomery, August 29, 1979 at the Sub-Commission, Agenda Item 11.* Cited in Robertson, op. cit., 29.
40. According to Andrew Gray, an anthropologist with the Society in a report entitled "Work on Indigenous Peoples from 1983-9," made available to the author.
41. *Annual Report 1990/1991,* (London: Anti-Slavery Society), 5.
42. The typed "Personal Comments" of Ms. Roberts are in the author's possession.
43. Ibid.
44. Interview with Lesley Roberts, London, October 19, 1995.
45. Interview with Mike Dottridge, October 19, 1995.
46. Roberts interview.
47. *Newsweek, International Edition,* May 4, 1992, 8-15.
48. "No Protection for Human Rights in Sudan," *Human Rights Watch/Africa Press Release,* May 29, 1996; "Sudan: Progress on Public Relations?" *Amnesty International Summary,* May 29, 1996.
49. For details, see Steven A. Holmes, "Slavery is an Issue Again as U.S. Looks to Sudan," *New York Times,* March 24, 1996.
50. Nat Hentoff, "Farrakhan and the Slave Masters," *The Village Voice,* December 12, 1995. An earlier essay on the same subject by Nat Hentoff was "Slavery and The Million Man March," *Washington Post,* November 28, 1995.
51. The developments have been described in some detail by a member of the Society, Lilian Passmore Sanderson, an authority on the subject in *Reporter* (February 1992): 41-51. Her article is entitled, "The Role of Anti-Slavery International in the Work for the Ultimate Elimination of All Forms of Female Genital Mutilation."
52. Ibid., 48-50.
53. Barbara Crossette, "What Modern Slavery Is, and Isn't," *New York Times,* July 27, 1997, Section 4, 1,3.
54. *Contemporary Forms of Slavery in Pakistan* (New York: Human Rights Watch/Asia, 1995), 3., fn.6.
55. This was communicated to the author in a personal letter from Mike Dottridge dated June 22, 1997.

CHAPTER 6

1. Sidney Liskofsky, *NGOs and Human Rights* (New York: 1974), 65.
2. Interview with Felice Gaer, December 13, 1995. Mrs. Gaer had been the Executive Director of the League in the eighties.
3. Interview with Roberta Cohen, December 7, 1995.
4. International League for Human Rights (ILHR), *Annual Report,* 1973, 1.
5. *New York Times,* February 26, 1974.

6. Laurie S. Wiseberg and Harry M. Scoble, "The International League for Human Rights: The Strategy of a Human Rights NGO," *The Georgia Journal of International & Comparative Law* 7, no. 289 (1977): 303.

7. *Times* (London), May 21, 1974.

8. Ibid.

9. Commission on Human Rights, *Report to the Thirty-first Session,* 3 February–7 March 1975, 58. Cited in Wiseberg and Scoble, op. cit., 304.

10. Ibid.

11. Ibid.

12. Wiseberg and Scoble, op. cit., 305.

13. Cohen interview.

14. Gaer interview.

15. Cited in Wiseberg and Scoble, op. cit., 291.

16. Ibid., 306-307.

17. Undated, signed memo in the files of Roberta Cohen.

18. Ibid. Further clarification about the allegation of "communist domination" and how the League succeeded in getting the allegation removed is missing from the note.

19. Harrison Salisbury, ed., *Sakharov Speaks* (New York: Alfred A. Knopf 1974), 19-20; Andrei Sakharov, *Memoirs* (New York: Alfred A. Knopf, 1990), 320-21.

20. William Korey, *The Soviet Cage: Anti-Semitism in Russia* (New York: Viking Press, 1973), 60-63, 282-95.

21. Gaer interview.

22. Wiseberg and Scoble, op. cit., 307.

23. Amnesty International, *Annual Report, 1974-75,* 119.

24. *ILHR Human Rights Bulletin,* summer, 1985, 2.

25. *ILHR Human Rights Bulletin,* November 1973, 2.

26. *ILHR Annual Review 1976-77,* 7.

27. *New York Post,* May 3, 1977.

28. Ibid.

29. Gaer interview.

30. United Nations Working Group on Forced or Involuntary Disappearances, June 5, 1984. Testimony by Jerome J. Shestack on behalf of the International League for Human Rights.

31. Gaer interview.

32. Ibid.

33. *ILHR Human Rights Bulletin,* summer, 1985, 4.

34. *ILHR Human Rights Bulletin,* November 1972, 1. The League's formal complaint on the trial was one of the very few petitions accepted by the Working Group of the UN Subcommission under the 1503 procedure. Significantly, the Chairman of the League at the time helped draft the rules for the Working Group. He resigned from the League in August, 1971, to become an alternate expert member of the Subcommission.

35. Jerome J. Shestack, "Sisyphus Endures: The International Human Rights NGO," *New York Law School Review* 24 (1978): 114.

36. See John Melithoniote, "A Profile of the Three Organizations," *Ethos,* December 6, 1973, 24; and Baldwin Robertson, *The International League for Human Rights,* (1996), 18.

37. *ILHR Bulletin,* September 1974, 9.

38. *ILHR Annual Report, 1975-1977,* 3.

39. *ILHR Bulletin,* winter 1980-81, 8.

40. *ILHR Bulletin,* summer 1985, 1.

41. It would assume the form of a volume. See Richard Arens, ed., *Genocide in Paraguay* (Philadelphia: Temple University Press, 1976).

42. *ILHR Bulletin,* September 1974, 6.

43. *ILHR Bulletin,* April 1975, 2.
44. Cited in *ILHR Bulletin,* April 1978, 1-5.
45. Shestack, op. cit., 113-14.
46. *New York Times,* February 28, 1977.
47. Ibid.
48. Ibid.
49. The advice took the form of a major policy paper, "Recommendations for U.S. Policy at the U.N. in the Human Rights Field." It was presented by Roberta Cohen to a group of human rights NGOs associated with the United Nations Association of the USA on March 31, 1977. Though the paper was read orally to the group, mimeographed copies were made also available.
50. A copy of the April 3 missive from the files of the League was made available to the author.
51. Wiseberg and Scoble, op. cit., 309.
52. See ibid., 308-309.
53. Ibid.
54. Gaer interview.
55. The "granddaddy" description was used by Felice Gaer in her interview.

CHAPTER 7

1. *New York Times,* October 11, 1977.
2. The text was incorporated in *AI Index NWS 06/02/79,* January 8, 1979.
3. *First Annual Report 1961-1962* (London: Amnesty International, 1962).
4. Cited in Jonathan Power, *Amnesty International: The Human Rights Story* (London: Fontana Paperbacks, 1981), 2.
5. The *First Annual Report 1961-1962* provides their names, See, especially, page 4.
6. See William Korey, "Eleanor Roosevelt and the Universal Declaration of Human Rights," in A. David Gurewitsch, *Eleanor Roosevelt, Her Day: A Personal Album* (New York: Interchange Foundation, 1968), 27.
7. Ibid., 29.
8. *First Annual Report 1961-1962,* op. cit., 2.
9. *First Annual Report 1961-62,* op. cit. Also, see *Amnesty International Handbook* (London: Amnesty International Publications, 1983), 5.
10. Power, op. cit., 3.
11. Ibid., 5.
12. Ibne Hassan, *Amnesty International as a Human Rights Organization,* (Ph.D. diss., New York University, 1977), 222.
13. Ibid.
14. Power, op. cit., 36.
15. *New York Times,* October 11, 1977.
16. Ibid.
17. *Guardian,* (London), October 11, 1977.
18. For background and discussion, see Iain Guest, *Behind the Disappearances: Argentina's Dirty War Against Human Rights and the United Nations* (Philadelphia: University of Pennsylvania Press, 1990), 78.
19. Martin Ennals, "Amnesty International and Human Rights," in *Pressure Groups in the Global System: The Transnational Relations of Issue-Oriented Non-Governmental Organizations,* ed. Peter Willetts, (London: Frances Pinter Publishers, 1982), 78.
20. Ibid.
21. David Matas, *No More: The Battle Against Human Rights Violations* (Toronto: Dundurn Press Limited, 1994), 192-93.

22. Ennals, op. cit., p. 72.
23. David Ottaway, "The Growing Lobby for Human Rights," *Washington Post,* December 17, 1976.
24. Ennals, op. cit., 72-73.
25. Ibid., 73.
26. Ramesh Thakur, "Human Rights: Amnesty International and the United Nations," *Journal of Peace Research,* 31, no. 2 (1994): 150.
27. The episode is related in Harry M. Scoble and Laurie S. Wiseberg, "Human Rights and Amnesty International," *The Annals of the American Academy of Political and Social Science* (May 1974): 18.
28. Ottaway, op. cit.
29. Ibid.
30. Ibid.
31. Ennals, op. cit., 81.
32. Scoble and Wiseberg, op. cit., 23.
33. Ibid., 14.
34. *Annual Report 1980,* (London: Amnesty International, 1981), 8.
35. Ennals, op. cit., 68.
36. Annual Report 1972-1973 (London: Amnesty International, 1973), 15.
37. Nehemiah Robinson, *The Universal Declaration of Human Rights—Its Origin, Significance, Application and Interpretation* (New York: World Jewish Congress, 1958), 108.
38. *Report on Torture* (London: Amnesty International, 1973).
39. Power, op. cit., 61.
40. Details were provided to the author by Nigel Rodley, in an interview on December 2, 1996 in Washington, D.C.
41. Helena Cook, "Amnesty International at the United Nations," in Peter Willetts, ed., *The Conscience of the World: The Influence of Non-Governmental Organizations in the UN System,* (Washington, D.C.: Brookings Institution, 1996), 181-213. 42. UN General Assembly Resolution 3059 (XXVIII), 2 November 1973.
42. Cook, op. cit.
43. *Annual Report 1974-75* (London: Amnesty International, 1976), 18.
44. Ibid.
45. Nigel Rodley, *The Treatment of Prisoners under International Law* (New York: Oxford University Press,1987), 23.
46. *Annual Report 1974-1975,* op. cit., 21.
47. Cook op. cit.
48. Rodley interview.
49. Virginia Leary, "A New Role for Non-Governmental Organizations in Human Rights: A Case Study of Non-Governmental Participation in the Development of International Norms of Torture," in *UN Law/Fundamental Rights,* ed. Antonio Cassese (Netherlands: Sitjhoff & Noordhoff, 1979), 197-210. 51. Ibid., 202-203.
50. Rodley, op. cit., 33.
51. UN General Assembly Resolution 3452(XXX).
52. Leary, op. cit., 204.
53. Power, op. cit., 65.
54. *Annual Report 1975-76,* (London: Amnesty International, 1976) 24-28.
55. Ibid.
56. Leary, op. cit., 206.
57. *Annual Report 1975-76,* op. cit., 49.
58. Leary, op. cit., 206.
59. Ibid.
60. Ibid.
61. Rodley, op. cit.

62. Ibid., 41.
63. Iain Guest, *Behind the Disappearances: Argentina's Dirty War Against Human Rights and the United Nations* (Philadelphia: University of Pennsylvania Press, 1990), 40.
64. Ibid., 40.
65. Jacobo Timerman, *Prisoner Without A Name, Cell Without A Number* (New York: Alfred A. Knopf, 1981). The author was involved in obtaining the release of this journalist.
66. Guest, op. cit., 31-2.
67. Ibid., 85.
68. Ibid., 80-6.
69. Ibid., 85.
70. The citations are from the internal files of Amnesty, *AI Index, NWS 01/01/77* November 23, 1977.
71. *New York Times*, October 11, 1977.
72. *Amnesty International Newsletter*, Vol. VII, No. 11, November, 1977.
73. Rodley, interview.

CHAPTER 8

1. *Human Rights in the World Community: A Call for World Leadership, Report of the Subcommittee on International Organizations and Movements of the Committee on Foreign Affairs, House of Representatives* (Washington, D.C.: U.S. Government Printing Office, 1974), 53pp. The actual hearings were published separately as: *International Protection of Human Rights: The Work of International Organizations and the Role of U.S. Foreign Policy,* Foreign Affairs Committee, Subcommittee on International Organizations and Movements, 93rd Congress, 1st Session (Washington, D.C.: U.S. Government Printing Office, 1974).
2. *Human Rights in the World Community,* op. cit., 9.
3. Ibid., 50.
4. See, especially, Sandy Vogelgesang, *American Dream, Global Nightmare: The Dilemma of U.S. Human Rights Policy* (New York: W.W. Norton & Company, 1980), 110-57.
5. Cited in ibid., 80.
6. Peter Berger, "Are Human Rights Universal?" *Commentary* (September 1977): 60-63.
7. David P. Forsythe, *Human Rights and World Politics* (Lincoln: University of Nebraska Press, 1989), 92.
8. Henry Kissinger, *White House Years* (Boston: Little, Brown and Company, 1979); and Henry Kissinger, *Years of Upheaval* (Boston: Little, Brown and Company, 1983).
9. *Human Rights in the World Community,* op. cit., 3.
10. *Washington Post*, December 12, 1976. The article was entitled "The Growing Lobby for Human Rights."
11. Vogelgesang, op. cit., 144.
12. Ibid., 145.
13. Ibid., 147.
14. Interview with Joseph Eldridge, July 10, 1996. At the time of the interview, he was Director of the Washington Office of the Lawyers Committee for Human Rights.
15. Ibid. The group included Edward Koch, later Mayor of New York City. According to Eldridge, he was a "champion" of human rights in Latin America.
16. Forsythe, op. cit., 141.
17. Ibid., 145.

18. Ibid., 140.

19. Interview with Patricia Derian, July 9, 1996, conducted at her home in Alexandria, Virginia.

20. A copy of the "Evaluation" is in the author's possession. While undated, it evidently was written in 1979.

21. The memo is in the author's possession.

22. This "Evaluation" too is in author's possession.

23. Forsythe, op. cit., 105.

24. Ibid., 153.

25. Alan Dowty, *Closed Borders* (New Haven: Yale University Press and the Twentieth Century Fund, 1987), 231.

26. Andrei Sakharov, *An Open Letter to the U.S. Congress,* September 14, 1973. A copy is in the author's possession.

27. See *Congressional Record, Senate,* March 15, 1973, Vol. 119, No. 41, 8071.

28. The bulk of this section running to the end of the chapter is drawn from the author's detailed and close analysis of the Jewish conflict with the Nixon Administration that appears in two separate *American Jewish Yearbook* volumes: William Korey, "The Struggle over Jackson-Mills-Vanik," *The American Jewish Year Book, 1974-75* (Philadelphia: American Jewish Committee and Jewish Publication Society of America, 1976), 149-245; William Korey, "The Struggle Over Jackson Amendment," *The American Jewish Year Book, 1976* (Philadelphia: American Jewish Committee and Jewish Publication Society of America, 1976), 160-70. These analyses were based on personal observations, interviews with all the principal Jewish leaders, the *Daily Bulletin* of the Jewish Telegraphic Agency and general press accounts. Various other essays of the author deal with aspects of Jackson-Vanik. See William Korey, "Jackson-Vanik and Soviet Jewry," *Washington Quarterly* (Winter 1984): 116-28; William Korey, "The Future of Soviet Jewry," *Foreign Affairs* 58, no. 1 (fall, 1979): 67-81; and William Korey, "Jackson-Vanik and Its Myths," *Midstream* (August-September, 1989): 7-11.

29. In a speech to an audience of the American foreign policy elite, invited and hosted by Vice President Al Gore, on September 27, 1994, Yeltsin referred to the new White House decision on the application of Jackson-Vanik and observed that "every Russian school child" knows the meaning and significance of that amendment. The episode was disclosed to the author by Mark Levin, Director of the National Conference on Soviet Jewry, who was an invited guest.

CHAPTER 9

1. The statement was made in a letter to the U.S. Embassy in The Hague. See Michael Dobbs, "War Crimes Prosecutor Says U.S. Information Insufficient," *Washington Post,* November 7, 1995.

2. William Korey, "The Embarrassed American," *Saturday Review,* October 31, 1964.

3. Churchill's comment was made in a speech on August 24, 1941.

4. Raphael Lemkin, *Autobiography* (Lemkin Archive, New York Public Library), n.d.

5. *New York Times,* December 4, 1983.

6. Cited in William Korey, "Human Rights Treaties: Why is the U.S. Stalling?" *Foreign Affairs* 45, no. 3 (April 1967): 416.

7. Ibid., 416-17.

8. Ibid.

9. Ibid.

10. Stephen H. Klitzman, Craig H. Baab and Brian C. Murray, "Ratification of the Genocide Convention: From the Ashes of 'Shoah' Past the Shoals of the Senate," *Federal Bar News and Journal* 33, no. 6 (July-August, 1986): 258.

11. Korey, "Human Rights Treaties," 417.

12. Ibid., 418.

13. William Korey, "America's Shame: The Unratified Genocide Treaty," *Midstream* (March, 1981): 10.

14. William Korey, "Lemkin and Trifa: Memory and Justice," *Christian Science Monitor*, August 30, 1984.

15. Steven Schnur, "Unofficial Man: The Rise and Fall of Raphael Lemkin," *Reform Judaism*, Fall 1982, 45.

16. See *National Jewish Post*, December 11, 1953. The amount was $100 per month. The group was closely linked to the International Ladies Garment Workers Union and the Amalgamated Clothing Workers.

17. Korey, "America's Shame," op. cit., 11.

18. Information provided to the author by Betty Kaye Taylor, former Secretary of the Committee.

19. The mimeographed statement of Gardner, running 12 pages, was released on March 8 by the Ad Hoc Committee on Human Rights and Genocide Treaties, together with a press statement summarizing its contents. The documentation is in the author's possession.

20. See Korey, "The Embarrassed American."

21. Korey, "Human Rights Treaties: Why is the U.S. Stalling?" Korey, who represented B'nai B'rith, was an active member of the Ad Hoc Committee's inner group.

22. See Jack Donnelly, *Human Rights and U.S. Foreign Policy: Forty Years of Thinking* (Chapel Hill, fall 1987): 3. Mimeo, privately produced.

23. William Korey, "Sin of Omission," *Foreign Policy* no. 39 (summer 1980): 172-75.

24. *Statement by the AFL-CIO Executive Council,* February 23, 1968.

25. *New York Times,* April 29, 1967.

26. Ibid.

27. *Honolulu Advertiser,* August 10, 1967.

28. The letter, dated November 30, 1967, is in the possession of the author.

29. The Fulbright letter is dated December 13, 1967 and is from the Ad Hoc Committee files.

30. Ibid.

31. The Taylor letter, dated December 5, 1967, is in the Ad Hoc Committee files.

32. See President Nixon to Reverend Herschel Halbert letter, dated February 27, 1970, for special reference to this transmittal. The letter is from the files of the Ad Hoc Committee.

33. Ibid.

34. The above citations were excerpted from *American Bar News* 14, no. 12 (December 1969), and are to be found in the files of the Ad Hoc Committee. The Committee made it available to the author under the heading, "Section Seeks Endorsement of Genocide Convention."

35. For details of the meeting, see the *New York Times,* February 24, 1970.

36. Jerome J. Shestack, "Sisyphus Endures: The International Human Rights NGO," *New York Law School Law Review* 24 (1978): 89-123.

37. *Congressional Record, Senate,* June 10, 1970, S8720.

38. *Washington Post,* April 26, 1971.

39. *Congressional Record, Senate,* Vol. 118, No. 24, February 22, 1972, S2254.

40. Arthur J. Goldberg and Richard N. Gardner, "The Genocide Convention," *New York Times,* March 28, 1972. The original article is Arthur J. Goldberg and Richard N. Gardner, "Time to Act on the Genocide Convention," *American Bar Association Journal* 58 (February 1972): 141-45.

41. From the files of the Ad Hoc Committee, made available to the author.

42. Information about this was recorded by Betty Taylor and is in the files of the Ad Hoc Committee.

43. The citation is from the files of the Ad Hoc Committee.

44. Details are in the *Congressional Record, Senate,* Vol. 118, No. 159, October 5, 1972.

45. Ibid.

46. William Korey, "The Genocide Convention: Time to Sign," *New York Times,* Op-Ed Page, December 8, 1973.

47. *New York Times,* February 7, 1974.

48. The Taylor letter is from the Ad Hoc Committee files.

49. The testimony is from the files of the Ad Hoc Committee.

50. From the files of the Ad Hoc Committee.

51. His testimony is in the files of the Ad Hoc Committee and was made available to the author.

52. *New York Times,* December 4, 1983. Dr. Gregorian's comment in the *Times* was appropriate: "I'm also personally interested in the genocide treaty, as an Armenian." For other details on the exhibit, see *Jewish Week* (New York), December 2, 1983.

53. This appeared in "The Genocide Treaty: Unratified 35 Years," *New York Times* on June 23, 1984. Additional op-ed pieces came later: William Korey, "Inertia on the Genocide Pact," *New York Times,* Op-Ed page, May 19, 1987; and William Korey, "Seal and Deliver the Genocide Pact," *New York Times,* Op-Ed page, April 2, 1988. Other op-ed articles of his appeared in the *Wall Street Journal,* the *Chicago Tribune,* the *Baltimore Sun* and the *Christian Science Monitor.* In a lead editorial—"Ratify the Genocide Treaty," *Washington Post,* September 7, 1984—reference was made to the author's essays.

54. B'nai B'rith had encouraged both candidates to address the genocide treaty. Mondale's key public relations staffer was most sympathetic to the idea but could not prevail.

55. *New York Times,* September 6, 1984. The *Washington Post* commented in a lead editorial, "Ratify the Genocide Treaty," the next day, September 7, 1984.

56. Cited in Jewish Telegraphic Agency (JTA), *Daily News Bulletin,* December 23, 1985, 4.

57. JTA, *Daily News Bulletin,* February 12, 1986.

58. *New York Times,* October 15, 1988.

59. See the *New York Times,* October 29, 1988.

60. *New York Times,* November 5, 1988.

CHAPTER 10

1. For details of the Helsinki Final Act, See William Korey, *The Promises We Keep: Human Rights, The Helsinki Process, and American Foreign Policy* (New York: St. Martin's Press, 1993), 1-19.

2. Stephen Rosenfeld, "A Timely Warning," *Washington Post,* November 30, 1990.

3. William Korey, "A New Charter for Helsinki," *The New Leader* (August 6-20, 1990): 11-13.

4. For details, see William Korey, "On Scrapping Individual Rights," *International Herald Tribune* (Paris), Op-Ed page, January 17, 1978. The article initially had appeared as an Op-Ed piece in the *Washington Post,* January 11, 1978.

5. Korey, *The Promises We Keep,* 6-8.

6. For details, see Ludmilla Alexeyeva, *Soviet Dissent: Contemporary Movements for National Religious and Human Rights* (Middletown, CT: Wesleyan University Press, 1985).

7. Ibid., 336.

8. For Orlov's views, see Paul Goldberg, *The Final Act: The Dramatic Revealing Story of the Moscow Helsinki Watch Group* (New York: William Morrow and Co., 1988), 33-6. Also see Yuri Orlov, *Dangerous Thoughts: Memoirs of a Russian Life* (New York: William Morrow and Co., 1991), 188-89.

9. Goldberg, op. cit., 36-7.

10. See U.S. Commission on Security and Cooperation in Europe, *Documents of the Helsinki Monitoring Groups in the USSR and Lithuania, 1975-1986,* Vols. 1 and 2 (Washington, D.C.: U.S. Government Printing Office, 1986).

11. *Dissent in Poland: Reports and Documents in Translation, December 1975-July 1977* (London: Association of Polish Students and Graduates in Exile, 1979) 12-5.

12. For details, see Jan Jozef Lipski, *KOR: A History of the Workers' Defense Committee in Poland, 1976-81* (Berkeley: University of California Press, 1985).

13. Lech Walesa, *A Way of Hope* (New York: Henry Holt and Co., 1987), 97.

14. *Prologue to Gdansk: A Report on Human Rights by the Polish Helsinki Watch Committee* (New York: U.S. Helsinki Watch Committee, 1980); and *Human Rights in Poland since December 1981: A Report by the Polish Helsinki Committee to the Human Rights Experts Meeting in Ottawa, May 1985* (New York: U.S. Helsinki Watch Committee, 1985).

15. U.S. Commission on Security and Cooperation in Europe, *Human Rights in Czechoslovakia: The Documents of Charter 77, 1977-1982* (Washington, D.C.: U.S. Government Printing Office, 1982).

16. Ibid., 14-15.

17. *Toward Civil Society: Independent Initiatives in Czechoslovakia* (New York: U.S. Helsinki Watch Committee, 1989). Also see Timothy Garton Ash, *The Magic Lantern: The Revolution of 1989* (New York: Vintage Books, 1990).

18. Donald R. Shanor, *Behind the Scenes: The Private War Against Soviet Censorship* (New York: St. Martin's Press, 1985), 160-61.

19. Ibid., 146-47.

20. Ibid.

21. *Annual Report of RFE/RL Media and Opinion Research* (Munich: RFE/RL Research Institute, 1980). Also see the subsequent *Annual Reports.*

22. Shanor, op. cit., 132.

23. Orlov, op. cit., 195.

24. Walesa's observation is to be found in *The Failure of Communism: The Western Response* (Washington, D.C.: Radio Free Europe/Radio Liberty, November, 1989), 47. The booklet carried the proceedings of an international conference held in Washington on November 15, 1989. It was sponsored by RFE/RL.

25. Ernst Kux, "Revolution in Eastern Europe—Revolution in the West?" *Problems of Communism* 40 (May-June, 1991): 1-13.

26. Korey, *The Promises We Keep,* 22-24.

27. Goldberg, op. cit., 36-37.

28. Madeleine Albright and Alfred Friendly, *Executive-Legislative Cooperation and East-West Relations: The Birth of the Helsinki Commission* (Washington, D.C.: December 1984), 16. Later, the paper was published as a chapter in Edmund Muskie, Kenneth Rush and Kenneth Thompson, eds., *The President, the Congress, and Foreign Policy: A Joint Policy Project of the Association of Formers Members of Congress and the Atlantic Council of the United States* (Lanham: University Press of America, 1986).

29. Korey, *The Promises We Keep,* pp. 259-60.

30. *Proceedings of the 84th Annual Meeting, "Human Rights: The Helsinki Process"* (Washington, D.C.: The American Society of International Law, 1990).

31. Orlov, op. cit., 194.

32. Background information was provided in interviews with Jeri Laber of U.S. Helsinki Watch; Stephen Marks, a former Ford Foundation Program Officer and Frank Sutton, a retired high Ford Foundation official.

33. Ford Foundation Archives, Appendix A.

34. Details are to be found Ibid.

35. Interview with Jeri Laber, April 14, 1994.

36. The information is drawn from a diary of Laber provided to the author.

37. Jeri Laber, "Moscow vs. Rights," *New York Times*, Op-Ed page, July 31, 1980.

38. Jeri Laber, "The Moscow Book Fair: But Where Are the Writers?" *Washington Post*, Op-Ed page, May 6, 1981.

39. Jeri Laber, "The Dreams That Died," *The Village Voice*, December 23-29, 1981.

40. Gara LaMarche, "Jeri Laber: From Cold Wars to Hot Ones, She Makes Countries Live Up to Their Human Rights Commitments," *Human Rights Watch Quarterly Newsletter* (Summer 1993): 6.

41. *Le Monde*, (Paris) November 12, 1980.

42. Freedom House hosted a sizable number of Soviet dissenters and had arranged to bring Andrei Amalrik to Madrid, but he was killed in an automobile accident while on his way. See *Freedom at Issue* (January-February, 1981): 39.

43. For details on the repression, see Peter Reddaway, *Soviet Policies on Dissent and Emigration: The Radical Change of Course Since 1979* (Washington, D.C., August 28, 1984). Also see Korey, *The Promises We Keep*, 115-18.

44. William Korey, "Minority Rights After Helsinki," *Ethics and International Affairs* 8 (1994): 135.

45. *Document of the Copenhagen Meeting* (Washington, D.C.: Commission on Security and Cooperation in Europe, June 1990), 19.

46. Laber interview.

47. Interview with Lotte Leicht, April 14, 1944.

48. *Program of Events, CSCE Seminar of Experts on Democratic Institutions* (Oslo: CSCE, November 4-5, 1991), 4.

49. Stefan Lehne, *The Vienna Meeting of the Conference on Security and Cooperation in Europe, 1986-1989; A Turning Point in East-West Relations* (Boulder: Westview Press, 1991), 292.

50. See *Charter of Paris for a New Europe* (Paris: U.S. Commission on Security and Cooperation in Europe, 1990).

51. Ritva Grönick. "The CSCE and Non-Governmental Organizations," in Michael R. Lucas, *The CSCE in the 1990s: Constructing European Security and Cooperation* (Baden-Baden: Nomosverlagsgesellschaft, 1993), 227-48.

52. Ibid.

53. Ibid.

54. Amnesty International, *News Release*, July 9, 1992.

55. CSCE Office for Democratic Institutions and Human Rights, *Press Release*, October 14, 1993. See Annex.

56. Ibid.

57. *Budapest Document 1994: Towards a Genuine Partnership in a New Era* (Budapest: CSCE, 1994), 44 pp. At this review meeting, CSCE was changed to OSCE—Organization for Security and Cooperation in Europe. The titles of several CSCE organs also were changed and, in a couple of cases, their functions were modified.

58. This section has drawn mainly on the *OSCE Handbook* (Vienna: Secretariat of the Organization for Security and Cooperation in Europe, 1996), 88-90.

CHAPTER 11

1. Nigel S. Rodley, "Monitoring Human Rights Violations in the 1980s," in *Enhancing Global Human Rights*, ed. Jorge I. Dominguez (New York: McGraw-Hill, 1979), 119-51, esp. 123.

2. Iain Guest, *Behind the Disappearances: Argentina's Dirty War Against Human Rights and the United Nations* (Philadelphia: University of Pennsylvania Press, 1990), 153.

3. The position was first called Coordinator and later Assistant Secretary of State for Human Rights and Humanitarian Affairs.

4. Interview with Patt Derian, May 9, 1996.

5. Guest, op. cit., 155.

6. Ibid., 161.

7. Ibid.

8. UN Resolution 1979/38, 10 May 1979.

9. *Testimony on Secret Detention Camps in Argentina* (London: Amnesty International, 1980). Cited in Guest, op. cit., 194.

10. The episode is described in Felice Gaer, "Reality Check: Human Rights Non-Governmental Organizations Confront Governments at the United Nations," *Third World Quarterly* 16, no. 3 (1995): 392-93.

11. Guest, op. cit., 196.

12. David Weissbrodt and David Kramer, "The 1980 U.N. Human Rights Commission and The Disappeared," *Human Rights Quarterly* 3, no. 1. (1981): 18. Cited in Guest, op. cit., 198-99.

13. UN Resolution 20 (XXXVI).

14. Gaer, op. cit., 393.

15. UN Resolution 35/195, 15 December 1980.

16. Nigel Rodley, *The Treatment of Prisoners Under International Law* (New York: Oxford University Press, 1987), 209.

17. Ibid., 215.

18. Ibid., 217. Rodley may not have earlier anticipated how such international mechanisms might be established, but once in existence, no one was more competent in analyzing their effectiveness than he.

19. Barbara Crossette, "U.N. Reports Latin America Suffers Fewer 'Disappearances,'" *New York Times*, May 24, 1997, 5.

20. Cited in Guest, op. cit., 125.

21. *Political Killings by Governments* (London: Amnesty International, 1983).

22. Rodley, *The Treatment of Prisoners*, 158.

23. Ibid., 12.

24. Ibid., 160.

25. UN Doc. E/CN. 4/1984/SR.63, para. 48.

26. *Torture in the Eighties* (London: Amnesty International, 1984).

27. Rodley, *The Treatment of Prisoners*, 121.

28. Ibid., 124.

29. Tom J. Farer and Felice Gaer, "The UN and Human Rights in the Beginning," in *United Nations, Divided World: The UN's Roles in International Relations*, 2nd. ed., eds. Adam Roberts and Benedict Kingsbury (Oxford: Clarendon Press, 1993), 240-96.

30. World Conference on Human Rights, Preparatory Committee, A/CONF. 157/PC/60/Add.6, 1 April 1993, 16. The study was prepared by Nigel Rodley.

31. UN Doc. E/CN.4/1995/5, para. 26(h). The conference was held in June, 1994.

32. UN Doc. E/CN.4/1995/47, 12. The report on 1994 was prepared the following year.

33. Ibid.

34. See ECOSOC Doc. E/CN.4/1994/42, 14 February 1994, 15.

35. Interview with Georg Maurtner-Markhof, March 13, 1996, conducted in Geneva.

36. Ibid.

37. Helena Cook, "Amnesty International at the United Nations," *"The Conscience of the World": The Influence of Non-Governmental Organizations in the UN System*, ed. Peter Willetts, (Washington, D.C.: Brookings Institution, 1996), 181-83.

38. Diego Garcia-Sayan, "Non-Governmental Organizations and the Human Rights Movement in Latin America," *UN Bulletin of Human Rights* 90/1 (1991): 39.

39. For a detailed discussion of 1235 and 1503, see UN Doc. E/CN.4/1994/42, February 14, 1994, 13-5.

40. UN Doc. E/CN.4/1975/SR.45.

41. See Farer and Gaer, op. cit., 281, fn. 91.

42. The experts, Frank Newman and David Weissbrodt, were cited in ibid.

43. World Conference on Human Rights, UN Doc. A/CONF.157/ PC/60/Add.6, 1 April 1993, 16.

44. For a description of how the Special Procedures section operates and how it would channel communications into appropriate mechanisms, see UN Doc. E/CN.4/ 1994/42, X February 14, 1994, 21-6.

45. For an analysis of the difference, see World Conference on Human Rights, UN Doc. A/CONF. 157/PC/60 Add. 6, 19.

46. Interview with Carl-Johan Groth, November 18, 1996, conducted by telephone.

47. They were listed in UN Doc. A/51/460, 7 October 1996, 3.

48. Ibid., 15.

49. UN Doc. E/CN 4/1997, 7-10 January 1997. The Special Rapporteur was Nigel Rodley.

50. Ibid., 49, 51.

51. Ibid., 8.

52. Ibid., 23.

53. Ibid.

54. UN Doc., E/CN.4/1997/95/Add.1, 17 February 1997. The Special Rapporteur was Mrs. Ofelia Calcetas-Santos. In this addendum, she focused on the Czech Republic as well as on the abuse as it extended across the border with Germany.

55. Ibid., 3-17.

56. Ibid., 12-14.

57. UN Doc., E/CN.4/1997/64, 6 February 1997. The Special Rapporteur was Rajsmoor Lallah.

58. Ibid., 5.

59. Ibid., 19.

60. UN Doc. E/CN.4/1997/57, 21 February 1997. Van der Stoel is also the High Commissioner on Minority Rights for OSCE.

61. Statement of Mr. Max van der Stoel to the Fifty-Third Session of the Commission on Human Rights, April 11, 1997, 2.

62. Interview with Max van der Stoel, May 16, 1997, conducted in The Hague.

63. Farer and Gaer, op. cit., 288.

64. UN Doc. E/CN.4/1995/5/Add.1.

65. Farer and Gaer, op. cit., 288.

66. Buergenthal, *International Human Rights in a Nutshell*, 2nd ed. (St. Paul: West Publishing Co., 1993), 85.

67. Ibid., 66.

68. Ibid., 75.

69. UN Doc. A/CONF./157/PC/62/Add.11/Rev.1, 22 April 1993, 5.

70. Ibid., 6.

71. UN Doc. A/CONF.157/PC/62/Add.11/Rev.1, 22 April 1993, 22.

72. UN Doc. E/CN.4/1992/30, para. 645.

73. UN Doc. E/CN.4/1993/26, para. 594.

74. Interview with Helga Klein, March 13, 1996.

75. Gaer, op. cit., 294.

76. Interview with Thomas Buergenthal, December 8, 1995, conducted in Washington, D.C.

77. UN Doc. A/49/537, 19 October 1994, para. 41.

78. Klein interview.
79. See UN Doc./CCPR/C/103/Add.3, 8 October, 1996. This 132-page report by Colombia covered its alleged fulfillment of obligations under the International Covenant on Civil and Political Rights.
80. *The Americas: Comments Relating to the Fourth Periodic Report on Colombia before the UN Human Rights Committee* (New York: Lawyers Committee for Human Rights, March 1997), 35pp.
81. Robert Weiner, "War by Other Means: Colombia's Faceless Courts," *NACLA Report on the Americas* 30, no. 2 (Sept./Oct. 1996): 35.
82. Diana Jean Schemo, "Rightist Avengers Become the Terror of Colombia," *New York Times*, March 26, 1997, 1, 8.
83. UN press releases summarizing the Committee's daily deliberations offer a detailed picture of what transpired. See UN Press Release HR/CT/484, 31 March 1997; Press Release HR/CT/485, 31 March 1997; Press Release HR/CT/486, 1 April 1997 and Press Release HR/CT, 487, 1 April 1997.
84. UN Press Release HR/CT/487, 1 April 1997, 1.
85. For details, see Theo van Boven, "The Role of Non-Governmental Organizations in International Human Rights Standard-Setting: A Prerequisite of Democracy," *The California Western International Law Journal* 20 (1990): 215.
86. Interview with Tom McCarthy, March 27, 1996, conducted in Geneva.

CHAPTER 12

1. For the Secretary-General's speech at Vienna, see *World Conference on Human Rights: The Vienna Declaration and Programme Action* (New York: United Nations, 1993), 5-21.
2. Boutros Boutros-Ghali, "Democracy is a Guarantor of Human Rights, " *Washington Post*, June 9, 1993.
3. See Boutros-Ghali's speech in *World Conference on Human Rights,* op. cit., 5.
4. The calculations were based upon Freedom House data of 1995-96. The data and calculations by Shai Franklin were made available to the author.
5. UN Doc. E/CN.4/1992/18, para. 4, 19.
6. UN Doc., E/CN.4/1992/30, para. 616.
7. UN Doc. E/CN.4/1992/17, paras. 6, 228.
8. *World Conference on Human Rights, Facing Up to the Failures: Proposals for Improving the Protection of Human Rights by the United Nations* (London: Amnesty International, December 1992), 3.
9. *World Conference on Human Rights,* op. cit., 8.
10. Obinna Anyadike, "A Question of Money," *Terra Viva* no. 10, (June 22, 1993), 12.
11. Ibid.
12. Ibid.
13. UN Doc. A/CONF.157/PC/60/Add.6, 1 April 1993, 31.
14. Ibid., 7.
15. Ibid., 44.
16. Andrew Clapham, "Creating the High Commissioner for Human Rights," *European Journal of International Law* 5, no. 4 (1994): 560.
17. Fateh Azzam, "Non-Governmental Organizations and the UN World Conference on Human Rights," *The Review* (International Commission of Jurists) no. 50 (1993): 89-105.
18. Ibid., 90.
19. Ibid., 90-91.
20. Ibid., 91.

21. *World Conference on Human Rights, Facing Up to the Failures,* op. cit., 5-20.

22. The information about the regional preparatory meetings was taken from Azzam, op. cit., 89-105.

23. Harry M. Scoble, "Human Rights Non-Governmental Organizations in Black Africa: Their Problems and Prospects in the Wake of the Banjul Charter," in Claude E. Welch, Jr. and Robert I. Meltzer, eds., *Human Rights and Development in Africa* (Albany: State University of New York Press, 1984), 185-90.

24. *The Status of Human Rights Organizations in Sub-Saharan Africa* (Stockholm and Washington, D.C.: The Swedish NGO Foundation for Human Rights and the International Human Rights Internship Program, Institute of International Education, 1994), 1-6, 185-204.

25. Claude E. Welch, Jr. *Protecting Human Rights in Africa* (Philadelphia: University of Pennsylvania Press, 1995), 74. Also see pp. 286-97.

26. Cited in Margaret Keck and Kathryn Sikkink, "Transnational Issue Network in International Politics," *Activists Without Borders, Paper Series, No. 8* (Ann Arbor: International Institute, University of Michigan, 1995).

27. Kathryn Sikkink, "Human Rights, Principled Issue-Networks and Sovereignty in Latin America," *International Organization* 47, no. 3 (summer, 1993): 419-28.

28. Patrick Ball, "Human Rights Organizations in Global Perspective: Constitutional Rights, State Terror and International Differences," *Advanced Study Center, 1995-96, Working Paper Series, No. 10* (Ann Arbor: International Institute, University of Michigan, 1996), 1.

29. Clapham, op. cit., 559., fn. 12.

30. Azzam, op. cit., 93.

31. See Sidney Jones, *The Impact of Asian Economic Growth on Human Rights* (New York: Council on Foreign Relations, January 1995), 22-24. Jones headed Human Rights Watch/Asia.

32. Ibid.

33. *Bangkok NGO Declaration on Human Rights* (Bangkok, March 27, 1993), 19.

34. *Human Rights Monitor* no. 21 (May, 1993): 21.

35. Azzam, op. cit., 95.

36. Felice Gaer, "Reality Check," *Third World Quarterly,* 398.

37. Interview with Reed Brody, February 13, 1996.

38. Ibid.

39. Gaer, op. cit., 398.

40. The data is from the Ludwig Boltzmann Institute of Human Rights, "World Conference on Human Rights," *NGO-Newsletter* no. 4, cited in Gaer, op. cit., 396.

41. See the discussion of the issue in "NGOs Rebuff UN, Rights Conference," *Terra Viva* no. 1 (June 11, 1993): 16.

42. Lucy Johnson and Peter da Costa, "Organizational Mayhem Sparks NGO Coup Move," *Terra Viva* no. 2 (June 12, 1993): 1.

43. For details, see "Dalai Lama Diplomacy Wins Out," *Terra Viva* no. 4 (June 15, 1993): 1.

44. Pauline Comeau, "NGO Forum Disintegrates: Protest to Highlight Complaints," *Terra Viva* no. 2. (June 12, 1993): 12.

45. "Latin NGOs: Carter Shouldn't Speak," *Terra Viva* no. 2 (June 12, 1993): 11.

46. Iain Guest, "Latin America's Day of Rage," *Terra Viva* no. 4 (June 15, 1993): 13.

47. Peter da Costa and Lucy Johnson, "NGO Infighting Gives Way to Patch-Work Compromise," *Terra Viva* no. 3 (June 14, 1993): 8.

48. Pauline Comeau, "NGO JPC Disbanded," *Terra Viva* no. 3 (June 14, 1993): 12.

49. Ramon Isberto, "Southern NGOs Tilt the Balance in United Nations Meetings," *Terra Viva* no. 13 (June 25, 1993): 24.

50. "NGOs Rebuff UN Rights Conference," *Terra Viva* no. 1. (June 11, 1993): 16.

51. Azzam, op. cit., 96.

52. Gaer, op. cit., 397.

53. Interview with Tom McCarthy, March 27, 1996.

54. Laurie S. Wiseberg, "Access to Drafting Committee Key Concern," *Terra Viva* no. 2 (June 12, 1993): 11.

55. Peter da Costa and Lucy Johnson, "NGO Monitors Excluded," *Terra Viva* no. 6 (June 17, 1993): 1.

56. "NGOs Still Denied Fixed Presence in Drafting," *Terra Viva* no. 5 (June 16, 1993): 9.

57. Gaer, op. cit., 398.

58. Thalif Deen, "Non-Aligned Nations Support Rights Chief," *Terra Viva* no. 1 (June 11, 1993): 16.

59. *25 Years on the Cutting Edge of Human Rights: JBI's 25th Anniversary Review* (New York: The American Jewish Committee, 1997), 7.

60. *Vienna Declaration and Program of Action, World Conference on Human Rights,* June 1993, para. 38.

61. UN Doc., A/CONF. 157/PC/82, Fourth Preparatory Committee, World Conference on Human Rights, April 1993, Principle 25.

62. Interview with Reed Brody, March 27, 1996. The stress he placed upon Gaer's role was related to her close relationship with the American delegation at the UN along with her extensive technical familiarity with the issues.

63. Ibid.

64. Cited in Gaer, op. cit., 399.

65. Trevor Rowe, "U.N. Creates High Post for Human Rights," *The Interdependent* (winter 1993/1994): 1.

66. Clapham, op. cit., 556-68.

67. Interview with Andrew Clapham, July 19, 1995.

68. The interview, conducted by Jonathan Power, who had written a work on Amnesty, and Ramon Isberto, is in *Terra Viva* no. 3 (June 14, 1993): 5.

69. UN Doc. A/48/632/Add.4, p. 14. The resolution, as adopted and recommended by the Third Committee of the Assembly, was entitled "High Commissioner for the Promotion and Protection of All Human Rights." It formally was approved by consensus on December 12, 1993.

70. Paul Lewis, "UN Agrees to Create Human Rights Commissioner," *New York Times,* December 14, 1993, 7.

71. *World Conference on Human Rights, Facing Up to the Failures,* op. cit., 9.

72. The letter, which Dr. Schoenberg shared with the author, was dated January 24, 1994.

73. Ibid., 2.

74. Clapham interview.

75. Ibid.

76. Cook, op. cit., 185.

77. Clapham interview.

78. Cook, op. cit., 203.

79. *Evaluation of Campaign on Women and Human Rights* (London: Amnesty International, n.d. [probably 1996]), 3. This was identified as an "internal draft" prepared for "internal" purposes. A copy was made available to the author. The rest of the paragraph about activities at the Beijing Conference is drawn from the same "internal draft."

80. *Annual Report, 1980* (London: Amnesty International, 1980), 8. This section of the annual report was written by Ennals.

81. Ibid. The later membership figures in the balance of the paragraph are drawn from the subsequent annual reports of the organization.

82. Ibid., 9.

83. Raymond Bonner, "Defining and Proving Rights Abuses: Debate Splits Amnesty International," *New York Times,* July 26, 1995.

84. Interview with Pierre Sané, October 18, 1996, conducted in London.

85. These figures are drawn from the annual reports of Amnesty.

86. *Killings in Armed Conflicts: Review of Current Policy and Outline of Future Options* (London: Amnesty International, 1995), 1.

87. Interview with David Matas, March 5, 1998. Matas, a high official in the Amnesty lay structure, emphasized this point in interview with the author.

88. Ibid.

89. Ibid. In his fascinating book, Matas, a Canadian, called attention to the fact that Amnesty was moving from a "prisoner [of conscience] organization to a general human rights organization." See Matas, op. cit., 187.

90. Clapham interview.

91. *Final Report: Review of Amnesty International's Research* (London: Amnesty International, 1993), 7.

92. *Amnesty International's Ljubljana Action Plan* (London: Amnesty International): 48.

93. *Final Report: Review of Amnesty International Research,* op. cit., 13.

94. Bonner, op. cit.

95. Ibid.

96. Ibid.

97. Interview with Malcolm Smart, October 20, 1995, conducted in London.

98. Interview with William Schulz, January 30, 1996, conducted in New York.

99. Interview with Pierre Sané, October 18, 1996, conducted in London.

100. Ibid.

101. Schulz interview.

102. *Key Findings for a Membership Study* (New York: Peter Hart Research Associates, 1995), 3.

103. Ibid., 15.

CHAPTER 13

1. *New York Times,* August 6, 1992.

2. Caroline Moorehead and Ursula Owen, "Time to Think Again," *Index on Censorship* 1(1996): 53.

3. Ibid.

4. Alex de Waal, "Becoming Shameless," *Times Literary Supplement* (London) February 21, 1997, 3-4.

5. Ken Roth, "Human Rights Abuses in Rwanda," *Times Literary Supplement* (London), March 14, 1997.

6. Aryeh Neier, "What Should be Done About the Guilty," *The New York Review of Books,* February 1, 1990, 32-35. The volume of essays is in Neil J. Kritz, ed., *Transitional Justice: How Emerging Democracies Reckon with Former Regimes.* (Washington, D.C.: U.S. Institute of Peace, 1995), Vol. 1.

7. *Truth and Political Justice* (Washington, D.C.: Americas Watch, 1987).

8. Samuel Totten, "Non-Governmental Organizations Working on the Issue of Genocide," in *The Widening Circle of Genocide,* ed. Israel Charny, Vol. 3, *Genocide: A Critical Bibliographic Review* (New Brunswick: Transaction Press, 1994), Chapter 15, fn. 5.

9. Barbara Harff and Ted Robert Gurr, "Toward Empirical Theory of Genocides and Patricides: Identification and Measurement of Cases Since 1945," *International Studies Quarterly* 32 (1988): 359-71.

10. Michael Bowen, Gary Freeman and Kay Miller, *Passing By: The United States and Genocide in Burundi, 1972* (Washington, D.C.: The Carnegie Endowment for International Peace, n.d.), 49 pp.

11. Ibid., 5.

12. Ibid., 17.

13. Ibid., 25.

14. See Tina Rosenberg, "Editorial Notebook: Cambodia's Blinding Genocide," *New York Times,* April 21, 1997.

15. See Ben Kiernan, "The Cambodian Genocide: Issues and Responses," in *Genocide: Conceptual and Historical Dimensions* ed. George J. Andreopoulos (Philadelphia: University of Pennsylvania Press, 1994), 191-93.

16. Ibid., 187.

17. Rosenberg, op. cit. 18. Material on the genocide is drawn from mimeographed Annual Reports of the Commission, various papers, studies and reports prepared by David Hawk, and his article, "Toul Sieng Extermination Centre (Cambodia)," *Index on Censorship* 15, no. 1,(January 1986): 25-32. A particularly useful document was his "Draft Summary" of the Commission's work from 1982 to 1994.

18. The UN report was entitled "Revised and Updated Report on the Question of the Prevention and Punishment of the Crime of Genocide."

19. Cited in Kiernan, op. cit., 215.

20. Rosenberg, op. cit.

21. Human Rights Watch/Middle East, *Iraq's Crime of Genocide: The Anfal Campaign Against the Kurds* (New Haven: Yale University Press and Human Rights Watch Books, 1995). It initially was published in a different form by Human Rights Watch in July, 1993.

22. Cited in ibid., Preface, xxi.

23. This is briefly discussed in ibid., xvii-xix.

24. Interview with Richard Dicker, May 5, 1997. Dicker was the key staffer in that operation.

25. Ibid.

26. The vivid reporting of Roy Gutman of *Newsday,* John Burns of the *New York Times* and David Rohde of the *Christian Science Monitor* was especially effective.

27. See William Korey, *The Promises We Keep: Human Rights, The Helsinki Process and American Foreign Policy* (New York: St. Martin's Press, 1993), 433-36.

28. *Prosecuting War Crimes in the Former Yugoslavia: An Update* (Commission on Security and Cooperation in Europe, June 1995), 2.

29. Cited in Korey, op. cit. 434.

30. UN Department of Public Information, *The United Nations and the Situation in the Former Yugoslavia,* S/RES.771, 31 August 1992, 38.

31. George J. Andreopoulos, "Introduction: The Calculus of Genocide," in *Genocide: Conceptual and Historical Dimensions,* op. cit., 20-21.

32. UN Doc. A/47/635/S24766, 6 November 1992.

33. UN Security Council Resolution 780, 6 October 1992.

34. *Prosecuting War Crimes in the Former Yugoslavia,* op. cit.

35. It was perhaps not accidental that Bassiouni was dismissed by his old Egyptian friend, Boutros-Ghali. The UN Secretary-General was both morally neutral about Bosnia and strikingly indifferent. See David Rieff, *Slaughterhouse: Bosnia and the Failure of the West* (New York: Simon & Schuster, 1995), 24. Also see David Rieff, "The Institution that Saw No Evil," *The New Republic,* February 12, 1996, 23-24.

36. UN Security Council Resolution 808, 25 May 1993.

37. For the basic features of the Statute as well as its background, see the mimeographed fact-sheet, *The International Criminal Tribunal for the Former Yugoslavia,* prepared by the Coalition for International Justice on March 19, 1997. An informal consultant in the drafting of the Statute was Benjamin Ferencz, who had served as Telford Taylor's deputy at the Nuremberg proceedings.

38. For details, see Andreopoulos, op. cit., 27-28, fn 84.

39. UN Doc. A/47/418 S/24516, 3 September 1992.

40. *Human Rights Watch Report 1993: Events of 1992* (New York: Human Rights Watch, December, 1992), 274; and *Human Rights Watch Report 1994: Events of 1993* (New York: Human Rights Watch, December 1993), 257.

41. *War Crimes in Bosnia-Hercegovina* (New York: Human Rights Watch, August 1992). The spelling of Hercegovina was that of HRW/Helsinki. Most spelled the word with a "z," not a "c."

42. Ibid., 2.

43. Ibid., 5.

44. *War Crimes in Bosnia-Hercegovina,* Vol. II (New York: Helsinki Watch, April 1993), 422pp.

45. Ibid., 5.

46. Interview with Ivana Nizich, December 20, 1995.

47. See *War Crimes in Bosnia-Hercegovina,* Vol. II, op. cit., 2.

48. *Human Rights Watch Report 1994: Events of 1993,* op. cit., 193.

49. Ibid., Introduction, xxiv.

50. De Waal, op. cit., 3.

51. For a detailed chronology of the Tribunal's evolution, see Iain Guest, *On Trial: The United Nations, War Crimes and the Former Yugoslavia* (Washington D.C.: Refugee Policy Group, September, 1995), 185 pp.

52. The judges are divided into two trial chambers and one appeals chamber. Five sit in the latter, and three each in the former. Presiding over the appeals chamber is the President of the Tribunal—a kind of Chief Justice.

53. Interview with Justice Richard J. Goldstone, May 9, 1997. The interview, prearranged by the author with the Coalition for International Justice, was conducted by long-distance telephone.

54. *Abuses Continue in the Former Yugoslavia: Serbia, Montenegro and Bosnia-Hercegovina* (New York: Human Rights Watch/Helsinki, July 1993), Vol. 5, Issue 11, 48 pp.

55. *Prosecute Now! Helsinki Watch Releases Eight Cases for War Crimes Tribunal on Former Yugoslavia* (New York: Human Rights Watch/Helsinki, August 1, 1993), Vol. 5, Issue 12, 25 pp.

56. See ibid., 8, fn. 13. The reference is to the testimony of the then Executive Director of the Physicians for Human Rights, Eric Stover, to the U.S. Commission on Security and Cooperation in Europe on January 19, 1993. Stover's testimony covered the group's forensic exploration of a mass grave site in Vukovar.

57. Interview with Gavin Ruxton, May 13, 1997, conducted at The Hague. Ruxton was the senior prosecution official at the Tribunal.

58. *Bosnia Hercegovina, Abuses by Bosnian Croat and Muslim Forces in Central and Southwestern Bosnia-Hercegovina* (New York: Human Rights Watch/Helsinki, September 1993), Vol. 5, Issue 18, 17 pp.

59. *The War Crimes Tribunal: One Year Later* (New York: Human Rights Watch/Helsinki, February, 1994), Vol. 6, Issue 3, 26 pp.

60. Ibid., 2.

61. *War Crimes in Bosnia-Hercegovina: Bosanki Samac, Six War Criminals Named by Victims of Ethnic Cleansing* (New York: Human Rights Watch/Helsinki, April 1994), Vol. 6, no. 5, 18 pp.

62. Interview with Thomas Warrick, November 13, 1996. Warrick had served as counsel to the Bassiouni UN Commission of Experts and later became Chairman of the Coalition for International Justice.

63. The episode was related in ibid.

64. The letter from the files of Human Rights Watch/Helsinki was made available to the author. Bluett, it should be noted, was a prosecutor from Australia.

65. *Bosnia-Hercegovina: Sarajevo* (New York: Human Rights Watch/Helsinki, October 1994), Vol. 6, No. 15, 31 pp.

66. *Bosnia-Hercegovina: "Ethnic Cleansing" Continues in Northern Bosnia* (New York: Human Rights Watch/Helsinki, November 1994) Vol. 6, No. 16, 36 pp.

67. The Op-Ed columns appeared in the *Washington Post,* August 11, 1995. Cartner's letter was carried in the *Washington Post,* August 18, 1995.

68. For a detailed examination of the Srebrenica horrors, see David Rohde, *Endgame: The Betrayal and Fall of Srebrenica, Europe's Worst Massacre Since World War II* (New York: Farrar, Straus and Giroux, 1997).

69. See the letter signed by him and officials from Physicians for Human Rights—Susannah Sirkin and Dr. Jane Schaller—and sent to the participants on July 24.

70. This was noted in a letter to the author sent out by Gaer's assistant, Ann Eisenberg, on August 15.

71. August 1, 1995.

72. Interview with Juan Mendes, August 29, 1995.

73. The letter from the files of HRW was made available to the author by Juan Mendes.

74. Named after General Colin Powell, who had counseled against U.S. involvement unless a clear American interest was at stake. Moreover, he stressed that any involvement must have the full backing of the American public and must take the form of the application of overwhelming military power.

75. *Bulletin of the International Criminal Tribunal for the Former Yugoslavia,* No. 1, XII, 1995, 5.

76. *Former Yugoslavia: War Crimes Trials in the Former Yugoslavia* (New York: Human Rights Watch/Helsinki, June 1995), Vol. 7, No. 10, 45pp.

77. *Statement by A. Cassese, President of ICTFY to the Parliamentary Assembly of the Council of Europe,* 25 April 1996.

78. The meeting was held on November 8, 1995.

79. Stefanie Grant, "Human Rights: Challenge for the XXI Century," 10 December 1996.

80. See *International Criminal Tribunals: Handbook for Government Cooperation* (London: Amnesty International, August 1996). Supplements One and Two came out the same time.

81. *Bosnia-Hercegovina: A Failure in the Making: Human Rights and the Dayton Agreement* (New York: Human Rights Watch, June 1996), Vol. 8, No. 8 (D), 37 pp.

82. UN Doc. A/49/342, S/1994/1007 29 August 1994. See, particularly 29-30.

83. Interview with David Tolbert, May 13, 1997, conducted at The Hague.

84. UN Doc. A/50/365, S/1995/72, 23 August 1995, 36.

85. Interview with Frans Baudoin, May 13, 1997, conducted at The Hague.

86. *Witness Protection: Third Consultative Working Group on Gender-Specific War Crimes Between the International Criminal Tribunal and The Coordination of Women's Advocacy* (Geneva: The Coordination of Women's Advocacy, January 1997), 12. The document carried the printed proceedings of the Conference, held on September 18-20, 1996.

87. Ibid., 13.

88. *25 Years on the Cutting Edge of Human Rights: JBIs 25th Anniversary Review* (New York: American Jewish Committee, May 1997), 8.

89. *Witness Protection: Third Consultative Working Group on Gender-Specific War Crimes,* op. cit., 40. 90. Ibid.

90. Ibid.

91. UN Doc. A/50/365, S/1995/728, 23 August 1995, 35.

92. Details were provided in an interview with Thomas Warrick, November 13, 1996.

93. Flyer for the Coalition for International Justice, produced in 1996.

94. See the article, "Coalition for International Justice Marks One Year Anniversary," *CEELI Update* 6, no. 4 (winter 1996): 11. The journal was published by ABA's Central and East European Law Initiative.

95. Flyer of the Coalition, 1996.

96. Thomas Warrick interview.

97. The data was provided in a fact-sheet, *The International Criminal Tribunal for the Former Yugoslavia,* produced by the Coalition on March 19, 1997.

98. "Coalition for International Justice Marks One Year Anniversary," *CEELI Update,* op. cit. The appeal also was signed by Human Rights Watch and Amnesty-USA.

99. See their Press Release: "Human Rights Groups Call upon the European Union and World Bank to Promote Compliance with the Dayton Peace Accords Through Effective Conditionality." It was dated January 9, 1997.

100. Citations from the address are in *The Jewish Monthly,* (December 1996–January 1997): 27. The monthly is the organ of B'nai B'rith International, which ran the Drabinsky lecture series at which Goldstone spoke.

101. *Non-Governmental Organizations and the Tribunals: A New Partnership* (Oslo: The Royal Norwegian Ministry of Foreign Affairs, 1996), 108. The reference to the plural "Tribunals" refers to the Rwanda Tribunal, along with the Yugoslav one.

102. Interview with Richard Goldstone, May 19, 1997.

103. See Steven Erlanger, "How Bosnia Policy Set Stage for Albright-Cohen Conflict," *New York Times,* June 12, 1997, 1. The disclosures, based upon reliable sources, have not been challenged.

104. Steven Lee Myers, "Albright Outlines Moves to 'Renew Momentum' in Bosnia," *New York Times,* May 23, 1997.

105. See the editorial, "Not Giving Up on Bosnia," *New York Times,* May 25, 1997.

106. Excerpts from the text of the Albright address were published in the *New York Times,* June 6, 1997, 8.

CHAPTER 14

1. *The Human Rights Watch Arms Project: Funding Renewal Proposal to the Rockefeller Foundation, Fourth Year, 1995-96.* Unpublished document. (New York: Human Rights Watch, September 7, 1995), p. 7.

2. Interview with Reed Brody, February 13, 1996.

3. Interview with UN official, February 19, 1996, conducted in New York.

4. Interview with Theo van Boven, May 13, 1997, conducted in The Hague.

5. Interview with Alex Arriaga, May 10, 1995, conducted in Washington, D.C. Arriaga said that she had communicated such criticism to Amnesty.

6. She was referring to Holly Burkhalter, who was, at the time, HRW's Advocacy Director in Washington, D.C.

7. Interview with Robert Bernstein, January 2, 1996.

8. Interview with Robert Bernstein, January 20, 1996. Jeri Laber was present at his request during this interview, and participated in several responses.

9. Bernstein interview, January 2, 1996.

10. Bernstein interview, January 20, 1996.

11. Interview with Aryeh Neier, February 13, 1996.

12. Ibid.

13. While Amnesty, with 300 employees in its London headquarters, may be more than twice as large as Human Rights Watch, the latter is increasing at a rapid rate. During the past four years, its staff increased from 92 to 135 with an additional 50 consultants, and its budget jumped to about $14 million per annum.

14. Bernstein interview, January 20, 1996.

15. Susan Gross and Michael Clark, *Discussion Paper Regarding the Structure, Management and Organization Development of Human Rights Watch* (Washington, D.C.: Management Assistance Group, November 5, 1993), 1.

16. Such a rave review was echoed in comments by Robert Bernstein in his interview of January 20, 1996. The author of this book, after attending many of HRW's "Joint Public Meetings" every other Wednesday and interviewing numerous staff members, would agree with many of the accolades.

17. Ibid., 3.

18. The author is in the possession of this data. Gara left HRW in late 19 96 to join Neier at the Open Society, founded by George Soros.

19. Gross and Clark, op. cit., 2-3.

20. Ibid.

21. What Bernstein was referring to was an embarrassing error that somehow cropped up in Amnesty's research in 1990. In releases to the press on December 18-19, 1990, Amnesty, while cataloguing the torture of Kuwaitis by Iraqi occupation forces, charged that the latter had cut off 300 premature babies from hospital incubators, resulting in their deaths. The allegation was revealed to be a 'myth' by *The Nation* in February, 1991.

22. Gross and Clark, op. cit., 4-5.

23. Ibid., 6.

24. Ibid.

25. January 2, 1996.

26. Ibid.

27. Neier interview.

28. Gross and Clark, op. cit., 9.

29. A copy of the letter is in the author's possession.

30. Bernstein interview, January 20, 1996.

31. Jonathan Fanton, President of the New School for Social Research, was his successor.

32. Gross and Clark, op. cit., 11.

33. Ibid.

34. Ibid., 14.

35. Consideration also was given to creating a professional center in Japan.

36. Ibid., 15.

37. It later shifted to New York.

38. Paul Lewis, "Faction in U.N. Panel Blocks a Rights Group," *New York Times*, February 3, 1991.

39. Interview with Stephen Marks, May 1, 1996. Marks sought in various ways to persuade HRW officials about the value and significance of the UN connection.

40. *United Nations Press Release*, NGO/191, 22 January 1991, 7.

41. Ibid.

42. Lewis, op. cit.

43. Ibid.

44. "A Gang of Six at the U.N.," *New York Times*, February 9, 1991.

45. UN Security Council, S/1995/988, 27 November 1995.

46. Ibid., 16.

47. See ibid., 3, 8.

48. 808 SG to SC, 26 January 1996.

49. Interview with Joanna Weschler, February 22, 1996.

50. UN Doc. E/CN.4/1995/NGO/5, 31 January 1995.

51. UN Doc. E/CN.4/1995/NGO/6, 31 January 1995.

52. Weschler interview.

53. *Human Rights Watch World Report 1996,* (New York: Human Rights Watch, December 1995), 147.

54. Report by Joanna Weschler to HRW, April 5, 1995.

55. *Human Rights Watch World Report, 1996,* op. cit., xxvii.

56. A copy of the official "Statement" released by the "Spokesman" on December 7, 1995 is in the author's possession.

57. A copy of the letter to Kofi Annan is in the author's possession.

58. *Russia's War in Chechnya: Victims Speak Out* (New York: Human Rights Watch/ Helsinki, January 1995), Vol. 7, No. 1, 8 pp.; *Russia, War in Chechnya: New Report from the Field* (New York: Human Rights Watch/Helsinki, January 1995), Vol. 7, No. 2, 14 pp.; *Russia: Three Months of War in Chechnya* (New York: Human Rights Watch/Helsinki, May 1995), Vol. 7, No. 6, 26 pp.; and *Russia: Partisan War in Chechnya, On the Eve of the WWII Commemoration* (New York: Human Rights Watch/Helsinki, May 1995), Vol. 7, No. 8, 19 pp.

59. Interview with Lotte Leicht, September 28, 1995, conducted in New York.

60. Ibid.

61. Ibid.

62. Interview with Lotte Leicht, May 2, 1996.

63. Ibid.

64. A copy of the memorandum was shared with the author when he met with Leicht in Brussels, October 7-10, 1996.

65. This is drawn from interviews the author had with Lotte Leicht, October 7-10, 1996, conducted in Brussels.

66. The author was the one who accompanied Leicht on her lobbying mission.

67. *Human Rights Watch World Report 1996,* op. cit., 127.

68. Interview with Larry Cox, January 2, 1996. Cox was deeply versed in NGO matters, having served as a high-level professional with Amnesty International, both in London and in its U.S. section.

69. Interview with Jeannine Guthrie, January 2, 1996.

70. *Human Rights Watch World Report 1995* (New York: Human Rights Watch, December 1994), xxvi.

71. Ibid.

72. Interview with Ken Roth, June 22, 1995.

73. For a discussion of this operation, see *Human Rights Watch World Report 1997* (New York: Human Rights Watch, December 1996), 374.

74. Interview with Ken Roth, June 22, 1995.

75. Interview with John Shattuck, February 29, 1996, conducted in Washington, D.C.

76. Neier interview.

77. *The Human Rights Arms Project: Funding Renewal Proposal,* op. cit., 2.

78. Ibid., 5.

79. *Landmines: A Deadly Legacy* (New York and Boston: Human Rights Watch and Physicians for Human Rights, 1993).

80. The comment was in a letter to HRW from the International Committee of the Red Cross (ICRC) in Geneva dated November 14, 1995. The letter was addressed to Ann Peters of the London office of HRW/Arms Project. A copy was made available to the author.

81. Details of the Arms Project lobbying in Vienna on both landmines and blinding lasers were provided by their London office experts. Interview with Alex Vines, October 18, 1995; and interview with Ann Peters, October 18, 1995.

82. *U.S. Cluster Bombs for Turkey?* (New York: Human Rights Watch Arms Project, 1994).

83. For details, see *The Human Rights Watch Arms Project Funding Renewal Proposal,* op. cit., 8-9.

84. Details on this and other aspects of the Arms Project were provided to the author by its Director, Joost Hilterman, in an interview in Washington, D.C., May 10, 1996.

85. *Human Rights Watch Publications Catalog* (New York: May 1995).

86. A former high-level Amnesty researcher, Mike McClintock, now with HRW in a crucial supervisory capacity, expressed some amusement at the utterly untimely way Amnesty prepared its annual reports. Interview with Mike McClintock, October 5, 1995.

87. Interview with Susan Osnos, December 29, 1995.

88. Ibid.

89. Ibid.

CHAPTER 15

1. It was in her address on November 2, 1993 to the International Rescue Committee. See USUN (U.S. Mission to the United Nations) Press Release, 182-93. The release was issued by the USUN.

2. The Statement, "A High Commissioner for Human Rights," was signed by Amnesty International, Human Rights Watch, the International Human Rights Law Group, the International League for Human Rights, the Jacob Blaustein Institute for Human Rights and the Lawyers Committee for Human Rights. The mimeographed document is undated, but one of the signers, the Blaustein Institute's Felice Gaer, dates it as October, 1993. See her *Non-Governmental Organizations and the UN High Commissioner for Human Rights,* April 1997. The paper was prepared for the Carter Center's International Human Rights Council Project.

3. B. G. Ramcharan, "Reforming the United Nations to Secure Human Rights," *Transnational Law & Contemporary Problems: A Journal of the University of Iowa College of Law* 4, no. 2 (Fall 1994): 516-17.

4. Pauline Comeau, "First Human Rights Commissioner Appointment Disappoints NGOs," *Human Rights Tribune* 2, no. 3 (March-April, 1994): 13, 14.

5. See "Ecuadorean is Nominated to Head UN's New Human Rights Post," *New York Times,* February 2, 1994.

6. UN Doc. A/49/36, para. 11, 115-16.

7. Interview with Carl-Johan Groth, November 18, 1996.

8. *AI's Concerns at the 51st Commission on Human Rights,* (London: Amnesty International, December, 1994).

9. Most of the above is taken from Helena Cook, *The Role of the High Commissioner for Human Rights: One Step Forward or Two Steps Back?* Unpublished memorandum, (London), p. 3.

10. Ibid.

11. Aryeh Neier, "The New Double Standard," *Foreign Policy* no. 105 (winter 1996-1997).

12. M. Logan, "UN Rights Commissioner Has Advice for NGOs," *Human Rights Tribune* (June-July 1995).

13. Adam Stapleton, "Amateurs Posing as Professionals," *Human Rights Tribune* (June-July 1995), 13-15.

14. "HRFOR Faces a Daunting Task, Say Officials at the UN," *Human Rights Tribune* (June-July 1995), 16-17. HRFOR stood for Human Rights Field Operations in Rwanda.

15. This was reported in a June 6, 1995 memo by the Chairman of the Blaustein Institute, David Squire, to its Administrative Council. A copy is in the author's possession.

16. The author drew upon notes compiled by an observer.

17. See ibid. The quotes are from David Squire's memo of June 6 to the Administrative Council of the Blaustein Institute.

18. A copy of this document, prepared following the June 4-6, 1995 meeting in Atlanta, Georgia, was made available to the author.

19. UN Doc. E/CN.4/1995/112, 14 July 1995, para. 12.

20. The letter was dated July 27, 1995, and the memorandum was entitled "Priorities in Restructuring the United Nations Centre for Human Rights." Both are in the author's possession.

21. Felice Gaer, *Non-Governmental Organizations and the UN High Commissioner for Human Rights* (New York: Carter Center, April 1997), 10. The essay was prepared for the Carter Center's International Human Rights Council.

22. Ibid.

23. *Human Rights Watch World Report 1996* (New York: Human Rights Watch, December 1995), xviii.

24. Ibid., xix.

25. Ibid., 84.

26. Interview with José Ayala Lasso, November 21, 1995.

27. UN Doc. E/CN.4/1996/103, 18 March 1996, paras. 25-26.

28. Interview with José Ayala Lasso, March 20, 1996.

29. *Human Rights Watch World Report 1997* (New York: Human Rights Watch, December 1996), xxv.

30. Ibid.

31. *Agenda for New UN High Commissioner for Human Rights* (London: Amnesty International, 1997), 6.

32. Gaer, *Non-Governmental Organizations and the UN High Commissioner for Human Rights*, op. cit., 15.

33. UN Doc. A/51/36, 18 October 1996, para. 31.

34. UN Doc. E/CN.4/1997/11, 24 February 1997, para. 45.

35. "Human Rights: Politics Aside. . . ." *The Economist,* March 29, 1997, 48.

36. A copy of the letter is in the author's possession.

37. Paul Lewis, "U.N. and U.S. Pressed on Rights Stance," *New York Times,* February 2, 1997.

38. *Agenda for a New UN High Commissioner for Human Rights,* op. cit., 2-3.

39. This was conveyed to the author by a knowledgeable NGO who preferred anonymity on this issue.

40. "Human Rights: Politics Aside. . . ." op. cit., 48.

41. Reed Brody, "Give the World a Clear Voice for Human Rights," *International Herald Tribune,* March 6, 1997.

42. Lewis, op. cit.

43. Brody, op. cit.

44. Ibid.

45. Interview with Felice Gaer, December 13, 1995.

46. Ibid.

47. Ibid.

48. Ibid.

49. *Comments by Kenneth Roth, Executive Director, Human Rights Watch.* These were undelivered remarks at the Institute's 25th Anniversary at the Capitol Hilton Hotel in Washington, D.C. on May 7, 1997. A copy is in the author's possession.

50. Gaer, *Non-Governmental Organizations and the UN High Commissioner for Human Rights,* op. cit., 16-18.

51. *Agenda for a New United Nations High Commissioner for Human Rights,* op. cit.
52. The outline was entitled *The Protection Conception of the United Nations High Commissioner for Human Rights,* 16pp.
53. Brody, op. cit.
54. "Irish President Favored for U.N. Rights Post," *New York Times,* May 19, 1997.
55. *Amnesty International News Release,* February 21, 1997.
56. Evelyn Leopold, "Ireland's Robinson campaigns for UN Rights Post," *Reuters,* May 23, 1997.
57. Interview with Susan Osnos, July 31, 1997.
58. *HRW Press Release,* June 12, 1997.
59. For background on this and other examples, see *25 Years on the Cutting Edge of Human Rights: JBI's 25th Anniversary Review* (New York: The American Jewish Committee, 1997), 16pp.
60. See Diane Paul, *Beyond Monitoring and Reporting: Strategies for Field-Level Protection of Civilians Under Threat* (New York: The Jacob Blaustein Institute for Human Rights and the Center for the Study of Societies in Crisis, 1996), 86pp.
61. *25 Years on the Cutting Edge of Human Rights,* op. cit., 4.
62. Charlotte Bunch, "The Intolerable Status Quo: Violence Against Women and Girls," in *The Progress of Nations* (New York: UNICEF, July 1997), 41-49.
63. Felice D. Gaer, *And Never the Twain Shall Meet? The Struggle to Establish Women's Rights as International Human Rights at the United Nations* (Draft), October 4, 1997, 1. The draft was intended for publication later in a book. Gaer made it available to the author.
64. Ibid., 66-67.
65. Cited in ibid., 75.
66. Boltzmann Institute of Human Rights, *NGO Newsletter* No. 4 (July 1993).
67. Bunch, op. cit., 45.
68. Gaer, *And Never the Twain Shall Meet?,* op. cit., 84-85.
69. Ibid., 84.
70. Bunch, op. cit., 45.
71. Ibid., 45.
72. Felice Gaer, letter written to the author on August 1, 1997.
73. Ibid.
74. *Comments on the ECE Draft Document for the High Level Preparatory Meeting for the Fourth World Conference on Women.* The *Comments* were an outgrowth of the conference in Washington on September 8, 1994 that was sponsored by the Blaustein Institute and the International League for Human Rights. Browning and Goldstein were key figures in preparing the *Comments.* The document was published by the sponsoring organizations.
75. See Gaer, *And Never the Twain Shall Meet?,* op. cit., 93, 112.
76. Ibid., 112.
77. A copy of this letter is in the author's possession.
78. Prior to the letter and on the same issue, Gaer had prepared a questionnaire to be used by women's NGOs in challenging government delegates at the preparatory regional meeting in Vienna in October. It was sharp and pointed. A copy is in the author's possession.
79. A copy of the fax is in the author's possession.
80. The letter is in the author's possession.
81. Hillary Rodham Clinton, *Remarks for the United Nations Fourth World Conference on Women,* Beijing, China, September 5, 1995, 4-5.
82. Gaer, *And Never the Twain Shall Meet?,* op. cit., 61.
83. Letter to the author, undated, but probably August 1, 1997.
84. A copy of the letter is in the author's possession.

85. From an address by John Shattuck, "Building International Human Rights Institutions," at the 25th Anniversary Dinner of The Jacob Blaustein Institute for the Advancement of Human Rights, Washington, D.C., May 7, 1997, 7.

CHAPTER 16

1. Francis Fukuyama, "The End of History," *The National Interest* no. 16 (summer, 1989).
2. Department of State, Bureau of Public Affairs, "Secretary [James] Baker: Power for Good, American Foreign Policy in the New Era," *Current Policy*, No. 1162, 1-4.
3. *Statement by Margaret Thatcher at the Paris CSCE Summit Meeting*, November 19, 1990.
4. *Statement by Mikhail S. Gorbachev at the Paris CSCE Summit Meeting*, November 19, 1990.
5. The Berlin article appeared in the fall 1991 issue of *New Perspectives Quarterly*. It was cited in Anthony Lewis, "Hate Against Hate," *New York Times*, November 15, 1991.
6. Cited in William Korey, *The Promises We Keep: Human Rights, the Helsinki Process and American Foreign Policy*, (New York: St. Martin's Press, 1993), 419.
7. Dominique Moïsi, "A Spectre is Haunting Europe: Its Past," *New York Times*, Op-Ed page, May 29, 1990.
8. Adam Michnik, "Why I Won't Vote for Lech Walesa," *New York Times*, Op-Ed page, November 23, 1990.
9. Magarditsch Hatschikjan, "Eastern Europe Nationalist Pandemonium," *Aussenpolitik* 42 (1991): 213.
10. The data of the Institute of Geography were published in a leading London journal. See John Lloyd and Leyla Boulton, "The Soviet Union: Myriad Territorial Disputes Set to Take Center Stage," *Financial Times*, August 28, 1991.
11. *Statement by Foreign Minister Jiri Dienstbier to the Copenhagen Meeting of the Conference on the Human Dimension*, June 4, 1990.
12. William Korey, "A Fear of Pogroms Haunts Soviet Jews," *New York Times*, Op-Ed page, January 25, 1990.
13. William Korey, *Glasnost and Soviet Anti-Semitism* (New York: American Jewish Committee, 1993), 16-19.
14. Renee Cohen and Jennifer L. Golub, *Attitudes Toward Jews in Poland, Hungary and Czechoslovakia* (New York: American Jewish Committee, 1991). See, especially tables 19 and 20, on 19-20.
15. Institute for Jewish Policy Research and American Jewish Committee, *Anti-Semitism: World Report, 1997* (London: Chandlers Printers Ltd., 1997), 128-29.
16. Thomas Buergenthal, "The Copenhagen CSCE Meeting: A New Public Order for Europe," *Human Rights Law Journal* 11 (1990): 20.
17. *Document of the Copenhagen Meeting of the Human Dimension of the CSCE* (Washington, D.C.: CSCE, June, 1990).
18. *Statement by Max M. Kampelman, Head of the U.S. Delegation to the Copenhagen CSCE Meeting*, June 11, 1990.
19. See the testimony of Ralph R. Johnson, the Principal Deputy Assistant Secretary of State for European and Canadian Affairs, in *Hearing on the Conflict in Europe* (Washington, D.C.: CSCE, October 31, 1991); his testimony to the Senate Foreign Relations Committee on October 16, 1991 is in Department of State, *Dispatch* 2, No. 42.

20. Max M. Kampelman, "Secession and the Right of Self-Determination: An Urgent Need to Harmonize Principle With Pragmatism," *The Washington Quarterly* (summer, 1993): 5-12.

21. Eleanor Roosevelt, "The Universal Validity of Man's Right to Self-Determination," *Department of State Bulletin* 27 (1952), 917, 919. Cited in Kampelman, op. cit.

22. See paragraphs 17-19 in Boutros-Ghali's *Agenda*.

23. Hans Meesman, "From CSCE to OSCE: The Helsinki Final Act 1975-95, From Catalyst to Modest Accessory," *International Spectator* (September 1995). The article appeared in Dutch. A translation of it was sent to the author. The journal is a monthly publication of the Netherlands Society for International Affairs.

24. *Report of the CSCE Meeting of Experts on National Minorities* (Geneva: CSCE, July 1991).

25. *The Moscow Meeting of the Conference on the Human Dimension (CSCE), September 10–October 4, 1991* (Washington, D.C.: CSCE, 1991), 42.

26. UN Security Council Resolution 688 (1991), 5 April 1991.

27. For details on the missions and their effectiveness see David Shorr, "Preventive Diplomacy," *Government Executive* (April 1993): 22-24.

28. Ibid.

29. *Reuters*, July 2, 1993.

30. For the decisions taken at Helsinki that ran from March to July, see *Helsinki Decisions* (Helsinki: CSCE, 1992.)

31. Meesman, op. cit.

32. Interview with Max van der Stoel, May 16, 1997, conducted in The Hague.

33. Ibid.

34. *Report by Max van der Stoel, OSCE High Commissioner on National Minorities* (Vienna: Organization on Security and Cooperation in Europe, November 4, 1996), 4.

35. Interview with Max van der Stoel, May 16, 1997.

36. *The Foundation on Inter-Ethnic Relations 1996 Annual Report* (The Hague: The Foundation on Inter-Ethnic Relations, March, 1997).

37. See Konrad J. Huber, *Fourth (Final) Quarterly Report* (March 1, 1994): 1-2. The Report covered the period November 1, 1993 through February 1, 1994. It was sent to the Blaustein Institute, the funder of the Huber operation. The Report was made available by Felice Gaer to the author.

38. Details were provided in an interview with Arie Bloed, May 16, 1997. Following Huber's temporary occupancy of the post, Professor Bloed became the Director of the Foundation from 1993 to June 1997, when he left to take a position with the Open Society in Budapest. On leave from the University of Utrecht Law Faculty, he is a top-level specialist on OSCE matters.

39. Ibid. The staff was listed in the Foundation's *1996 Annual Report* (The Hague: Foundation on Inter-Ethnic Relations, 1996), 36.

40. Bloed interview.

41. *1996 Annual Report,* op. cit., 3607.

42. The Foundation on Inter-Ethnic Relations, March 1996: A Fact Sheet.

43. Huber, *Fourth (Final) Quarterly Report,* op. cit., 1-2.

44. *CSCE and the New Europe: Our Security is Indivisible* (Rome: CSCE, December 1, 1993), 3-4.

45. Rob Zaagman and Hannie Zaal, "The CSCE High Commissioner on National Minorities: Prehistory and Negotiations," in *The Challenges of Change: The Helsinki Summit of the CSCE and the Aftermath,* ed. Arie Bloed, (Dordrecht: Martinus Nijhoff, 1994) 105-109. This is a revised and expanded version of an article written by Hannie Zaal for the *Helsinki Monitor* no. 4 (1992): 33-37.

46. Katherine Birmingham, *OSCE and Minority Issues* (The Hague: Foundation on Inter-Ethnic Relations, November, 1995), 29.

47. *OSCE HCNM Fact Sheet,* 2. HCNM stands for High Commissioner on National Minorities.

48. Birmingham, op. cit., 30.

49. *Bibliography on the OSCE High Commissioner on National Minorities: Documents, Speeches and Related Publications* (The Hague: Foundation on Inter-Ethnic Relations, 1997), 5.

50. Diana Chigas, "Bridging the Gap Between Theory and Practice: The CSCE High Commissioner on National Minorities," *Helsinki Monitor* no. 3 (1994): 28-29.

51. Ibid.

52. Ibid., 30.

53. Ibid., 31-37.

54. Konrad J. Huber, *Averting Inter-Ethnic Conflict: An Analysis of the CSCE HCNM in Estonia, January-July, 1993* (Atlanta: The Carter Center of Emory University, Conflict Resolution Program, April 1994), Vol. 1, No. 2, Working Paper Series. The background is described in 1-11.

55. Soviet demographic policy encouraged Russians to move to Estonia and, thus, the ethnic Estonian population dropped from 88 percent in 1939 to 61 percent by 1988. See Erika B. Schlager, "The Right to Have Rights," *Helsinki Monitor* 8, no. 1 (1997): 25.

56. Ibid., 11.

57. Ibid., 4.

58. Van der Stoel interview.

59. Huber, *Averting Inter-Ethnic Conflict,* op. cit., 14-15.

60. Bloed interview.

61. *Report by Max van der Stoel,* op. cit., 5.

62. Huber, *Averting Inter-Ethnic Conflict,* op. cit., 27.

63. *Report on an Expert Consultation in Connection with the Activities of the CSCE High Commissioner on National Minorities* (Bentveld, Netherlands: The Foundation on Inter-Ethnic Relations, November 5-7, 1993), 1.

64. Huber, *Averting Inter-Ethnic Conflict,* op. cit., 19.

65. Ibid., 1.

66. 66 Ibid., 24.

67. Ibid.

68. Susanna Terstal and Konrad Huber, *Appendix C: Background Notes on the Functioning of the High Commissioner on National Minorities* (The Hague: Foundation on Inter-Ethnic Relations, 1993), 3-6.

69. Due to Soviet demographic policy, ethnic Latvians dropped from 75.5 percent in 1935 to 52 percent in 1991. See Schlager, op. cit., 25.

70. Terstal and Huber, op. cit., 3-4.

71. Latvia, under pressure from a variety of sources, including the High Commissioner, reduced the residency requirement from 16 years to 5 years. See Schlager, op. cit., 27, fn. 22.

72. Terstal and Huber, op. cit., 6.

73. *Report on an Expert Consultation,* op. cit., 1.

74. Ibid., 4.

75. Ibid., 7.

76. *Roma (Gypsies) in the CSCE Region: Report of the High Commissioner on National Minorities.* It was prepared for the Conference on Security and Cooperation in Europe and released at a Meeting of its Committee of Senior Officials (CSO) on September 21-23, 1993, 19pp.

77. Ibid., i.

78. Ibid.

79. Ibid., ii.

80. Ibid., 13.

81. Statement of Max van der Stoel, OSCE High Commissioner on National Minorities at the Seminar on Roma jointly convened by the Council of Europe and the OSCE in Warsaw, September, 1994.

82. *Situation of Roma and Sinti in the OSCE Region: Background Material for the Review Conference* (Warsaw: Office of Democratic Institutions and Human Rights, October 1, 1996), 16. The document's reference number is REF. RM/35/96/Add.1 22 October 1996.

83. See its *Report on the Czech Citizenship Law* (Prague: Tolerance Foundation, May 1994), 44pp.

84. A most devastating legal indictment of Czech conduct is to be found in Schlager, op. cit., 33-35. Schlager is an international legal specialist with the U.S. Commission.

85. Ibid., 33.

86. Huber, Fourth (Final) Quarterly Report, op. cit., 4.

87. Ibid., 2-3.

88. *Defining a Constructive Role for the Kin-State Actors in Minority Situations: An Integrated Program of Research Policy Analysis and Seminars.* (The Hague: Foundation on Inter-Ethnic Relations, August, 1994).

89. *Integrated Program in Support of the CSCE High Commissioner on National Minorities* (The Hague: Foundation on Inter-Ethnic Relations, August 1994).

90. *Project Concerning Minority Education in Albania* (The Hague: Foundation for Inter-Ethnic Relations, August 1994). This was an internal Foundation document.

91. This was communicated to the author by a highly knowledgeable American source who preferred anonymity. The source indicated that the criticism was known by most insiders.

92. *Year Report 1995* (The Hague: The Foundation on Inter-Ethnic Relations, 1995), 2.

93. Ibid., 5-8.

94. Ibid., 4.

95. *Conclusions and Recommendations: Conclusion of Bilateral Treaties Project,* November 1995. Typescript. This apparently was an internal Foundation document.

96. *Report of the Seminar on Inter-Ethnic Relations and Regional Cooperation* (Bishkek, Kyrgyzstan: Foundation on Inter-Ethnic Relations, May 17-18, 1995).

97. Ibid., 33-38.

98. See *Year Report 1995,* op. cit., 5.

99. For details, see *The Hague Recommendations Regarding the Education Rights of National Minorities and Explanatory Note* (The Hague: Foundation on Inter-Ethnic Relations, October, 1996).

100. Ibid., 3.

101. *1996 Annual Report* (The Hague: Foundation on Inter-Ethnic Rights, March 1997), 19-22.

102. *The Hague Recommendations,* op. cit., 18.

103. *Report from the Seminar on Minority Rights and Mechanisms: Facilitating Government-Minority Dialogue* (Riga, Latvia: Foundation on Inter-Ethnic Relations, May 16, 1996), 6-7.

104. *Specialized Programmes in Support of the High Commissioner on National Minorities of the OSCE* (The Hague: Foundation on Inter-Ethnic Relations, January, 1997), 6.

105. Ibid., 10-11.

106. *1996 Annual Report,* op. cit., 13-18.

107. Ibid., 1.

108. The letter was part of a communication from OSCE to its member state delegations. OSCE, REF.HC/12/96, 25 October 1996.

109. The Schenk letter is also in ibid.

110. *OSCE Newsletter* 4, no. 1 (January 1997): 6.

111. *Department of State, OSCE Implementation Report, 1997* (Washington, D.C.: Bureau of European and Canadian Affairs, August 1997), Mimeo., 11.

CHAPTER 17

1. See *Investigations in Eastern Congo and Western Rwanda* (Boston: Physicians for Human Rights, July 16, 1997), 18 pp.; and *Human Rights in the Democratic Republic of Congo and Rwanda: Testimony of Dr. Jennifer Leaning for Physicians for Human Rights,* 5pp. The testimony was given to the House International Relations Committee, July 16, 1997.

2. Interview with Holly Burkhalter, September 24, 1997, conducted by telephone.

3. Lynne Duke, "U.S. Military Role in Rwanda Greater Than Disclosed," *Washington Post,* August 16, 1997.

4. Interview with Susannah Sirkin, November 26, 1996. Sirkin is Associate Director of PHR in Boston.

5. Debra J. Trione, "Universal Accountability: Physician Activism in Human Rights," *Harvard Medical Alumni Bulletin* 61, no. 4 (Spring 1988): 24-25.

6. Sirkin interview.

7. *10-Year Report, 1986-1996* (Boston: Physicians for Human Rights, 1996), 7.

8. *PHR Missions and Investigations 1986-1996.* This was an internal PHR document without author or date.

9. *Boston Globe,* August 8, 1986.

10. Harris Meyer, "U.S. MDs Monitor Jailing of Chilean Leaders," *American Medical News,* (August 22/29, 1986).

11. Harris Meyer, "Chile Frees Two Leaders of National MD Group," *American Medical News,* (September 19, 1986).

12. Mary McGrory, "Acts of Commitment," *Washington Post,* July 31, 1986.

13. Jane Green Schaller, "In Chile a Doctor's Duty Can Make Him a Criminal," *International Herald-Tribune,* April 8, 1987.

14. See, for example, the *San Francisco Chronicle,* September 27, 1988.

15. Sirkin interview.

16. Ibid.

17. Daniel Vasquez, "Forensic Anthropologists Solve War Crimes Mystery," *Post-Standard,* July 31, 1996. The *Post-Standard* is published in Syracuse, N.Y. and is part of the Knight-Ridder chain.

18. Barend A. J. Cohen, "Prisoner Abuse Cited in Yugoslav Trial," *PHR's The Record* 3, no. 1 (winter/spring 1990): 1. The Record is a publication of PHR.

19. Eric Stover, "War Crimes in Balkans," *PHR's The Record* 7 (winter/spring 1994): 41-42. Also see, Mike O'Connor, "Harvesting Evidence in Bosnia's Killing Fields," *New York Times,* April 7, 1996.

20. American Bar Association, Section of Individual Rights and Responsibilities, "Giving a Voice to the Dead: Forensic Scientists Join World-wide Human Rights Investigations to Uncover the Truth," *Human Rights* 22, no. 1 (winter, 1995): 28-29, 47-48.

21. Cited in O'Connor, op. cit.

22. H. Jack Geiger, "Balkan War Crimes indictment," *The Lancet* 347 (March 1, 1996): 672.

23. "The Truth of Torture," *The Lancet* 347, nos. 9012, 1345 (May 18, 1996).

24. Elizabeth Neuffer, "A Gruesome Search Concludes in Bosnia," *Boston Sunday Globe,* April 14, 1996.

25. Elizabeth Neuffer, "For Women of Srebrenica, Gravesites Hold Few Answers," *Boston Globe,* July 30, 1996.

26. "Remains from Rwandan Mass Graves Echo Witness Testimonies of Slaughter," *PHR's The Record* (spring, 1996): 1, 7.

27. Thomas Friedman, "Where Beauty Stops: The Dilemma of War Crimes in Rwanda," *New York Times,* February 4, 1996.

28. Richard A. Knox, "Doctors Work to Document Horror—and Prevent It," *Boston Globe,* May 6, 1996.

29. *A Three Year Plan for Physicians for Human Rights* (Boston: Physicians for Human Rights, April 1994), 6-7.

30. Ibid., 5.

31. Sirkin interview.

32. "Land Mines: Cambodia's Hidden Menace," *PHR's The Record* (summer/fall, 1991): 1, 4-5.

33. James C. Cobey, "Medical Complications of Anti-Personnel Land Mines," *Bulletin of the American College of Surgeons* 81, no. 8 (1992): 9-11. The article carried the illuminating comparative data that one out of 235 civilians in Cambodia was missing a limb due to landmine injuries as compared to one in 22,000 in the U.S.

34. "Somaliland: Thousand Maimed by Land Mines," *PHR's The Record* (spring, 1992): 7-8.

35. Paul Epstein and Adrienne Epstein, "Mozambique: Study Finds Landmine Injuries Widespread," *PHR's The Record* (summer, 1994): 3. Excerpts from the article appeared as an Op-Ed piece in the *Boston Globe,* June 2, 1994.

36. "Death and Injuries Carried by Land Mines in Mozambique," *The Lancet* 346, no. 8977 (September 16, 1995): 723.

37. James C. Cobey, Eric Stover, and Jonathan Fine, "Civilian Injuries due to War Mines," *Techniques in Orthopaedics* 10, no. 3 (1995): 259-64.

38. *1994 Physicians for Human Rights Annual Report,* (Boston: PHR, 1994), 8.

39. "Landmines Update: Several Advances in the Campaign," *PHR's The Record* (summer, 1995): 14. The law would become operational in 1998.

40. Colin Nickerson, "Mine Ban Gains Ground: Canada Destroys Weapons, Seek Global Action," *Boston Globe,* March 7, 1997.

41. "Rights Group Appeal for U.S. Support of Landmines Treaty," *PHR Press Release,* September 18, 1997.

42. Vincent Iacopina, et.al., "Physicians Complicity in Misrepresentation and Omission of Evidence of Torture in Post detention Medical Examination in Turkey," *Journal of the American Medical Association* 276, no. 5 (August 7, 1996): 401. The four authors of the article included Dr. Robert Kirschner. All were associated with PHR.

43. M. Gregg Bloche, "The Turkish Army's New Target for Destruction: The Health Care System," *Boston Globe,* March 21, 1995.

44. Iacopina, et.al., op. cit., 397.

45. *1995 Physicians for Human Rights Annual Report,* (Boston: PHR, 1995), 11.

46. Barbara Crossette, "DNA Testing Reunites Salvadoran Mother and Child," *New York Times,* January 21, 1995.

47. Daniel Alder, "Missing Children Turning Up in El Salvador," *San Francisco Chronicle,* July 10, 1995.

48. *10-Year Report, 1986-1996,* op. cit., inside back cover.

49. *1994 Physicians for Human Rights Annual Report,* p. 9.

50. Sirkin interview.

51. See *A Three Year Plan for Physicians for Human Rights,* op. cit., 5-22.

52. Eric Stover, "War Crimes in Balkans," *PHR's The Record* 7, no. 1 (winter/spring 1994).

53. Interview with John Heffernan, September 26, 1997.

54. *Members Briefing on the International War Crimes Tribunal for Rwanda: Congressional Human Rights Caucus, Congressional Black Caucus* (Washington, D.C.: Coalition for International Justice, June 6, 1996), 4pp. Nasser Ega-Musa was an American of African descent who had witnessed, firsthand, the "results of the atrocities committed in Rwanda. . . ."
55. John Heffernan interview.
56. The NBA was the black lawyers' organization.
57. A copy of the letter is in the author's possession.
58. John W. Heffernan, "Demand Justice for War Criminals in Rwanda," *The New York Amsterdam News,* July 20, 1996.
59. *Update to 1995-1996 Annual Report* (Washington, D.C.: Coalition for International Justice, July 21, 1997), 3.
60. Ibid., 4.
61. *The International Criminal Tribunal for Rwanda* (Washington, D.C., September 16, 1997), 5pp.
62. Heffernan interview.
63. See UN Doc., A/51/789 6 February 1997, 25pp. This is the *Report of the Secretary General on the Activities of the Office of Internal Oversight Services.* The citations are from the "Summary" of the *Report,* 2-3.
64. A copy of the letter is in the author's possession.
65. *Coalition for International Justice, Groups Supporting U.N. War Crimes Tribunal for Rwanda Call for the Firing of Tribunal's Administrator, Deputy Prosecutor,* February 20, 1997.
66. "Two Dismissed from Tribunal on Rwanda," *New York Times,* February 27, 1997.
67. The letter is in the author's possession.
68. UN Doc. A/51/688, para.10.
69. See Steven Lee Myers, "Making Sure War Crimes Aren't Forgotten," *New York Times,* September 22, 1997.
70. *Democratic Republic of the Congo: What Kabila is Hiding* (New York: Human Rights Watch/Africa, Fédération Internationale des Ligues des Droits de L'Homme, October 1997), Vol. 9, No. 5(A), 41pp.
71. Ibid., 25.
72. Ibid., 34.
73. Ibid., 37.

CHAPTER 18

1. Leonard R. Sussman, *NGOs and the Promotion of Human Rights at the UN* (New York: September 11, 1997), 7 pp. This paper was an address to the fiftieth DPI/NGO Annual Conference on "Building Partnerships." DPI was the UN Department of Public Information.
2. Aaron Levenstein, *Freedom's Advocate: A Twenty-Five Year Chronicle* (New York: The Viking Press, 1965), 21.
3. *Freedom House Golden Anniversary 1991* (New York: Freedom House, 1991), 8.
4. Ibid., 1.
5. Ibid., 3, 7.
6. This information was provided to the author in a letter from Leonard Sussman, dated October 4, 1997.
7. Ibid.
8. Ibid.
9. Levenstein, op. cit., 83.

10. *Journal of Democracy* 4 (1993): 127-29. The *Journal* is published by the National Endowment for Democracy.

11. Adrian Karatnycky, "Democracy and Despotism: Bipolarism Removed?" Freedom Review 27, no. 1 (January-February, 1996): 5-15.

12. Strobe Talbott, "Democracy and the National Interest," *Foreign Affairs* 75, no. 6 (November/December 1996): 3. The citation is to the Karatnycky article in ibid.

13. *White House Press Release: Remarks by the President to the 52nd Session of the United Nations General Assembly,* September 22, 1997.

14. Fareed Zakaria, "Democracies That Take Liberties," *New York Times,* Op-Ed page, November 2, 1997.

15. For the most recent information on the survey, see *Freedom Monitor* 10, no. 1 (summer 1994): 7; *Freedom Monitor* 11, no. 2 (Fall 1995): 2; and *Freedom Monitor* 12, no. 1 (spring 1996): 7.

16. Leonard Sussman, *NGOs and the Promotion of Human Rights at the UN,* op. cit., 5.

17. Ibid.

18. Sussman, "Survey's Method," op. cit., 15.

19. See Leonard R. Sussman, "Can a Free Press Be Responsible? To Whom?" In *De La Liberté Aux Libertes: Federico Mayor; Amicorum Liber,* Vol. 2 (Brussels: Bruylant, 1995), 723-24. For his own role, see particularly the starred note on page 759.

20. Interview with Leonard Sussman, April 17, 1996. Also see Lowell Livezy, *Nongovernmental Organizations and the Idea of Human Rights* (New Jersey: Center for International Studies—Princeton University, 1988), 46.

21. "Promoting Human Rights and Democracy in Cuba," *Freedom Monitor* 13, no. 1 (winter 1997): 1, 11.

22. Ibid.

23. Interview with Adrian Karatnycky, October 9, 1997. 24.

24. Ibid.

25. "Freedom House Launches Ukraine Program," *Freedom Monitor* 10, no. 1 (summer 1994): 3.

26. "Freedom House in Ukraine," *Freedom Monitor* 13, no. 1 (winter 1997): 4.

27. "Russia-Strengthening Democratic Values," *Freedom Monitor* II, no. 1 (spring 1995): 3.

28. "Sakharov's Museum and Center Opens," *Freedom Monitor* 13, no. 1 (Winter 1997): 3.

29. Adrian Karatnycky, Alexander Motyl and Boris Shor, eds., *Nations in Transit 1997* (New Brunswick: Transaction Publishers, 1997), 5.

30. Ibid., 15.

31. "Freedom House Profile," *Freedom House News,* 2.

32. "Exchange Programs," *Freedom Monitor* 13, no. 1 (winter 1997): 8.

33. "Freedom House and the National Forum Foundation Join Forces," *Freedom House News,* August 1, 1997. The former head of the Forum Foundation, Jim Denton, would assume the task of Executive Director of the merged organization but Karatnycky would remain as President of the merged group.

34. Karatnycky interview.

35. "Works in Progress," *Freedom Monitor* 10, no. 1 (summer 1994): 6.

36. "Exchange Programs," op. cit., 8.

37. "Freedom House Campaigns for RFE/RL," *Freedom Monitor* 9, no. 2-3 (winter/spring 1993): 1.

38. "Puebla Institute, Freedom House, Combine Forces," *Freedom Monitor* 2, no. 2 (fall 1995): 4.

39. Nina Shea, "Free Harry Wu," *Wall Street Journal,* Op-Ed page, July 3, 1995.

40. See "Freeing Harry Wu," *Freedom Monitor* 2, no. 2 (fall, 1995): 1, 11.

41. "Puebla Holds Historic Conference on Christian Persecution," *The First Freedom* (January-June 1996): 4. *The First Freedom* is the organ of the Puebla Institute.

42. Ibid.

43. "Puebla Program Releases 'In the Lion's Den,'" *Freedom Monitor* 13, no. 1 (winter, 1997): 5. The book initially was prepared as a report that Shea had edited. It later was published in an expanded version that she had prepared.

44. Nina Shea, *In the Lion's Den* (Nashville: Broadman and Holman, Publishers, 1997), 5.

45. Ibid., 2.

46. Ibid., 58.

47. *Testimony of Nina Shea Before the House Committee on International Relations Subcommittee on International Operations and Human Rights,* December 18, 1996.

48. This is described in Shea, op. cit., 8-11.

49. "Congress Adopts Resolutions Condemning the Persecution of Christians," *The First Freedom* (July-December, 1996): 6.

50. "Puebla Director Named to State Department Advisory Committee on Religious Freedom," *Freedom Monitor* 13, no. 1 (winter 1997): 5.

51. "Action Points," *The First Freedom* (January-June, 1997): 7.

52. See "Puebla in the News," *The First Freedom* (January-June 1997): 2; and "New York City Council Targets Persecution of Christians," *The First Freedom* (January-June, 1997): 4.

53. "China Detains Key Christian Leaders," *Freedom House News,* April 3, 1997.

54. The author has collected all these columns. Significantly, the coverage of the subject in the *Times'* news stories until July, 1997 was negligible.

55. A. M. Rosenthal, "Persecuting the Christians," *New York Times,* Op-Ed page, February 11, 1997.

56. For Frank Wolf's remarks in introducing his legislation, see *Congressional Record-Extension of Remarks,* E 996 and E 997, May 21, 1997. Exactly the same bill was introduced the same day in the Senate by Arlen Specter.

57. Ibid.

58. For some details, see Steven A. Holmes, "G.O.P. Leaders Back Bill on Religious Persecution," *New York Times,* September 11, 1997.

59. Ibid.

60. Department of State, *U.S. Policies in Support of Religious Freedom: Focus on Christians* (Washington, D.C., July 22, 1997).

61. Steven Erlanger, "U.S. Assails China Over Suppression of Religious Life," *New York Times,* July 22, 1997.

62. Ibid.

63. Carroll Bogert, "Facing the Lions," *Newsweek,* August 25, 1997.

64. Shea, op. cit., 4.

65. Erlanger, op. cit.

66. Jacob Heilbrunn, "Christian Rights," *The New Republic,* July 7, 1997, 24.

67. Ibid., 23-24. The New York weekly cited was *New York Magazine,* March 31, 1997.

68. *Human Rights Watch World Report 1997* (New York: Human Rights Watch, December 1997), 152.

69. Ibid., 151.

70. Holmes, op. cit.

71. Karatnycky interview.

72. Erlanger, op. cit.

73. Kevin Boyle and Juliet Sheen, eds., *Freedom of Religion and Belief: A World Report* (Florence, KY.: Routledge, 1997). Boyle is Professor of Law and a teacher at the Human Rights Center at the University of Essex. He at one time headed the NGO Article XIX, in London. Sheen is a Fellow of the Center who specializes on freedom of religion and belief.

74. Ibid., 1.

75. Holmes, op. cit.

76. Karatnycky interview.

77. Interview with Holly Burkhalter, September 24, 1997.

78. A copy of the letter is in the author's possession. The two letter signers were the Directors respectively of The Robert F. Kennedy Center and the Minnesota Advocates for Human Rights.

79. Karatnycky interview.

80. Interview with Max Kampelman, September 23, 1997, conducted by telephone.

81. The remarks were taken from the stenographic record of the Committee and sent to Jerry Goodman on October 6, 1997. Goodman shared the text with the author.

82. *Statement by Jerry Goodman, Founding Executive Director, National Conference on Soviet Jewry before the House Committee on International Relations,* September 10, 1997.

83. Because the Specter-Wolf legislation had been introduced late in the legislative session, it was not acted upon by the time Congress adjourned in November, 1997. But, as Congressman Wolf wrote in a letter to a proponent, he intended to "redouble our efforts to make sure it receives early action next year [1998] when Congress returns." The letter, addressed to Jerry Goodman on November 13, 1997, was made available to the author.

CHAPTER 19

1. For details on the confrontation, see Steven Erlanger, "Asians Are Cool to Albright on Cambodians and Burmese," *New York Times,* July 28, 1997; Steven Erlanger, "Malaysia's Conspiracy Theory Draws Criticism from Albright," *New York Times,* July 29, 1997; and Keith B. Richburg, "Asians, West Clash Over Human Rights," *Washington Post,* July 30, 1997.

2. The story was filed by Agence-France Press on August 21 from Kuala Lumpur. It appeared in *Arab News,* August 22, 1986. The headline of the article was "Western Media Controlled by Zionists, Mahathir Says. " *Arab News* was published in Saudi Arabia.

3. "Malaysia: 'Zionist' Plot to Control Malaysia," *The Economist,* October 4, 1986; also see "Malaysia Misses the Point," (Editorial) *Washington Post,* October 3, 1986. The two *Wall Street Journal* correspondents were ousted from Malaysia.

4. Thomas L. Friedman, "The Thai Bind," *New York Times,* December 11, 1997.

5. Cited in Erlanger, "Malaysia's Conspiracy Theory Draws Criticism from Albright," op. cit.

6. Richburg, op. cit.

7. Ibid.

8. Ibid.

9. Jones, *The Impact of Asian Economic Growth on Human Rights* (New York: Council on Foreign Relations, 1995), 3. fn. 3.

10. Fareed Zakaria, "Culture is Destiny: A Conversation with Lee Kuan Yew," *Foreign Affairs* (March/April 1994): 111.

11. Bilahari Kausikan, "Asia's Different Standard," *Foreign Policy* (fall, 1993): 24-41.

12. Ibid., 35.

13. Interview with Jeannine Guthrie, January 2, 1996.

14. Yash Ghai, "Human Rights and Governance: The Asia Debate," *Occasional Paper No. 1, Center for Asian Pacific Affairs* (Asia Foundation, November 1994), 22pp.

15. Christine Loh, "The Rights Stuff," *Far Eastern Economic Review* 156, no. 27 (July 8, 1993): 15.

16. Ghai, op. cit., 13.

17. Joanne Bauer, "International Human Rights and Asian Commitment," *Human Rights Dialogue* 3 (December 1995): 4.

18. Joanne Bauer, "Human Rights in the Post–Cold War Era: The Cases of North Korea, China, and Burma—A Conference Report," *Human Rights Dialogue* 1 (May 1994): 4.

19. *Indivisible Human Rights: The Relationship of Political and Civil Rights to Survival, Subsistence and Poverty* (New York: Human Rights Watch, September 1992), 82pp.

20. Aryeh Neier, "Asia's Unacceptable Standard," *Foreign Policy* (fall, 1993): 42-51.

21. Ibid., 43.

22. Jones, *The Impact of Asian Economic Growth,* op. cit., 23.

23. Ibid., 10.

24. Ibid., 7-9.

25. Asia-Pacific NGO Conference on Human Rights, Coordinating Committee for Follow-Up, *Our Voice: Reports of the Asia-Pacific Conference on Human Rights and NGOs' Statements to Asia Regional Meeting* (Bangkok: Asian Cultural Forum on Development, 1993), 253.

26. Jones, *The Impact of Economic Growth,* op. cit., 10.

27. Ibid., 12.

28. Interview with Clarence Dias, April 1996; also see Manuel Guzman, *Asia,* CUSHRID Conference Paper. Part of a Report on the November 3-5, 1994 CUSHRID Net Inaugural Meeting at the American Association for the Advancement of Science. AAAS Science and Human Rights Program.

29. Guzman, op. cit.

30. Jones, *The Impact of Asian Economic Growth,* op. cit., 22.

31. *Human Rights Internet Reporter,* 15 Supplement Master List 1994.

32. Interview with Jeannine Guthrie, January 2, 1996.

33. Daniel S. Lev, "Human Rights NGOs in Indonesia and Malaysia," in *Asian Perspectives on Human Rights,* eds. Claude E. Welch, Jr. and Virginia A. Leary, (Boulder: Westview Press, 1990), 142-61.

34. Sidney Jones, "The Organic Growth: Asian NGOs Have Come Into Their Own," *Far Eastern Economic Review* (June 17, 1993): 23.

35. Katie Hatner and John Lyon, "Talking Headers," *Washington Post Magazine,* August 4, 1996, 9-13, 21-28.

36. Robert Kimzey, "The Potential Impact of Global Computer Networks on the Protection and Evolution of Human Rights." Part of a Report on the November 3-5, 1994 CUSHRID Net Inaugural Meeting at The American Association for the Advancement of Science.

37. U.S. Department of State, *Country Reports on Human Rights Practices for 1995* (Washington, D.C.: U.S. Government Printing Office), p. 664.

38. *State of Human Rights in Pakistan in 1995* (Lahore: Human Rights Commission of Pakistan, 1995).

39. Margot Cohen, "High Anxiety: Government Proposal Could Crimp NGO Activities," *Far Eastern Economic Review* 157, no. 39 (September 28, 1994): 32.

40. *World Report 1990* (New York: Human Rights Watch, 1990), 264-66.

41. *World Report 1992* (New York: Human Rights Watch, 1992), 353.

42. Thomas L. Friedman, "Living Dangerously," *New York Times,* July 10, 1997.

43. *Annual Report 1987* (New York: Human Rights Watch, 1987), 38.

44. Ibid., 39-40.

45. Thomas L. Friedman, "The Globalutionaries," *New York Times,* July 24, 1997.

46. Roberta Cohen, "People's Republic of China: The Human Rights Exception," *Occasional Papers/Reprint Series in Contemporary Asian Studies* (Baltimore: University of Maryland School of Law, 1988), 25-27.

47. Ibid., 56.

48. *Annual Report 1987,* op. cit., 46; and *Annual Report 1988* (New York: Human Rights Watch, 1988), 41-42.
49. Andrew Nathan, "China: Getting Human Rights Right," *The Washington Quarterly* 20, no. 2 (spring 1997): 138-39.
50. *World Report 1992,* op. cit., 394.
51. Interview with Richard Dicker, April 17, 1996.
52. Ibid.
53. Randy Harvey, "Sydney is Chosen for 2000 Olympics," *Los Angeles Times,* September 24, 1993.
54. Alan Riding, "2000 Olympics Go to Sydney in Surprise Setback for China," *New York Times,* September 24, 1993.
55. Dicker interview.
56. Ibid.
57. Interview with Sidney Jones, May 23, 1996.
58. Ibid.
59. "Transcript of Clinton-Jiang Conference," *Washington Post,* October 30, 1997.
60. Steven Mufson, "Jiang Says China to Sign UN Charter on Rights," *Washington Post,* October 25, 1997.
61. Lena H. Sun and Cindy Loose, "Diverse Crowd Joins Ranks for Rights Protest," *Washington Post,* October 30, 1997.
62. Lena H. Sun, "A World of Difference," *Washington Post,* October 30, 1997.
63. "Transcript of Clinton-Jiang Conference," op. cit.
64. *Press Release,* SG/SM/6359, 15 October 1997.
65. John M. Broder, "President Terms Certain Rights 'Universal,'" *New York Times,* June 30, 1997.

CHAPTER 20

1. A transcription of her speech was made available to the author by the Lawyers Committee.
2. "A Letter from the Executive Director and Chairman" [Michael Posner and Norman Dorsen], *1996 Annual Report* (New York: Lawyers Committee for Human Rights, 1996), 3.
3. Interview with Michael Posner, June 22, 1995.
4. Interview with Neal Hicks, August 23, 1995.
5. Ibid.
6. Posner interview.
7. Ibid.
8. Hicks interview.
9. *1996 Annual Report,* op. cit., 16.
10. Ibid., 15.
11. *1989 Annual Report* (New York: Lawyers Committee for Human Rights, 1989), 14.
12. Hicks interview.
13. *1987 Annual Report* (New York: Lawyers Committee for Human Rights, 1987), 16.
14. *1989 Annual Report,* op. cit., 16.
15. Hicks interview.
16. *African Exodus: Refugee Crisis, Human Rights and the 1969 OAU Convention. A Report of the Lawyers Committee for Human Rights* (New York: Lawyers Committee for Human Rights, June 1995), 16.
17. Ibid., 197.
18. Ibid., 197-99.

19. Hicks interview. Hicks is a high official of the Committee, working especially on Middle East countries.

20. Ibid.

21. For this analysis see, Michael H. Posner and Candy Whittome, "The Status of Human Rights NGOs," *Columbia Human Rights Law Review* 25 (1994): 269-72.

22. *1993 Annual Report* (New York: Lawyers Committee on Human Rights, 1993), 25.

23. Posner interview.

24. *1993 Annual Report,* op. cit., 18.

25. Posner interview.

26. A copy was made available to the author. 27. Hicks interview.

27. Ibid.

28. *1996 Annual Report,* op. cit., 7.

29. *Shackling the Defenders: Legal Restrictions on Independent Human Rights Advocacy Worldwide* (New York: Lawyers Committee for Human Rights, 1994).

30. Posner and Whittome, op. cit., 276-81.

31. Ibid., 277.

32. Ibid. 274.

33. *1993 Annual Report,* op. cit. See particularly, the inside cover.

34. Posner interview.

35. *1996 Annual Report,* op. cit., 3. It was in the form of a letter sent to the recipients of the *Annual Report.*

36. 1993 Annual Report, op. cit., 17.

37. Ibid., 7.

38. *1996 Annual Report,* op. cit., 8.

39. *1993 Annual Report,* op. cit., 4.

40. Ibid.

41. *1991 Annual Report* (New York: Lawyers Committee for Human Rights, 1991), 17.

42. The "reservations" adopted by Senators in the treaty-ratifying process, in effect, nullify the application of a particular provision of the Covenant to the United States.

43. *Lawyers Committee for Human Rights General Support Proposal: Submitted to the Ford Foundation,* June 30, 1995, 28.

44. Alan Tonelson, "Jettison the Policy," *Foreign Policy* no. 97 (winter 1994-95): 121-32.

45. Michael Posner, "Rally Round Human Rights," *Foreign Policy* no. 97 (winter 1994-95): 133-39.

46. *In the National Interest: 1996 Quadrennial Report on Human Rights and U.S. Foreign Policy* (New York: Lawyers Committee for Human Rights, 1996), vii-viii.

47. Ibid.

48. Ibid., xiv-xv.

49. Ibid., x.

50. Ibid., xi-xii.

51. A copy of the letter is in the author's possession.

52. Thomas L. Friedman, "Elephants Can't Fly," *New York Times,* November 3, 1997.

53. Posner interview.

54. The figures are drawn from interviews with Michael Posner and Neal Hicks in the summer of 1995.

55. *1996 Annual Report,* op. cit., 28-29.

56. Ibid.

57. Ibid., 26-27.

58. Posner interview.

59. UN Doc. E/CN.4/1992/53, 1992.

60. Posner interview.

61. Ibid.

62. Ibid.

63. *1993 Annual Report,* op. cit., 11.

64. *1991 Annual Report,* op. cit., 9.

65. *1993 Annual Report,* op. cit., 13.

66. Stefanie Grant, *Human Rights: Challenge for the XXI Century.* Address given at the Organization of American States (OAS) on December 10, 1996, 1-2. A copy is in the author's possession.

67. For Grant, and her associates, it must have come as a dismaying shock that on December 17, 1997, a local magistrate released Ntakirutimana on grounds that the distinctive congressional legislation of 1996 authorizing the U.S. Government to turn over fugitives from the Rwandan Tribunal was unconstitutional since the U.S. has no extradition treaty with the Tribunals. A *New York Times* editorial stressed that the Constitution did not require an extradition treaty to surrender an international fugitive and that a Supreme Court ruling of 1936 had noted that an act of Congress was sufficient. The episode testified to how fragile the exercise of justice and accountability can be in the case of international law.

68. Grant, op. cit., 6.

69. Interview with Patricia Armstrong, September 12, 1995.

70. *1993 Annual Report,* op. cit., 3.

71. "The World Bank and Human Rights," *The Bank's World (1989)* cited in Peter Fidler, *The Lawyers Committee for Human Rights and the Shifting Route of Governance at the World Bank* (New York, July, 1996), 12. Fidler, a student of the World Bank, prepared the study for the author.

72. Cited in ibid., 13.

73. Ibid.

74. Ibid.

75. The Bank's 1994 report referring to its experience with "governance" makes this point. Cited in ibid.

76. Posner interview.

77. *1993 Annual Report,* op. cit., 3.

78. Armstrong interview.

79. *In the Name of Development: Human Rights and the World Bank in Indonesia, A Joint Report of the Lawyers Committee for Human Rights and the Institute for Policy Research and Advocacy (ELSAM),* 1995, 1.

80. Ibid.

81. Ibid., 11.

82. *1993 Annual Report,* op. cit., 3.

83. Ibid.

84. *1993 Annual Report,* op. cit., 3.

85. *In the Name of Development,* op. cit.

86. Ibid., 10.

87. The material here is drawn from the Fidler essay.

88. The unpublished draft of the findings was examined and reported upon in the Fidler essay. The study by the Lawyers Committee and the Programma Venezolano de Educacion-Accion en Derechos Humanos was entitled *The World Bank and Judicial Reform in Venezuela: A Case Study,* 1996.

89. See *1993 Annual Report,* op. cit., 9. Fidler's essay provides further details.

90. Interview with Patricia Armstrong, July 3, 1996, conducted by Peter Fidler.

91. Ibid.

92. Posner interview.

93. From the transcript of Mary Robinson's speech on October 8, 1997.

94. Annan was present as a Committee guest when she made her speech.

CHAPTER 21

1. *Report of the International Tribunal for the Prosecution of Persons Responsible for Serious Violations of International Humanitarian Law Committed in the Territory of the Former Yugoslavia*, U.N. Doc. A/52/375 and S/1997/729, 18 September 1997, 46, para. 193. Cassese was replaced as President in 1998 by Judge Gabrielle McDonald of the United States.

2. Ibid., para. 192.

3. *Trials of War Criminals Before the Nuremberg Military Tribunals*, Vol. IV, "The *Einsatzgruppen* Case" (Washington, D.C.: U.S. Government Printing Office, 1949).

4. Ibid., 30.

5. Benjamin B. Ferencz, *An International Criminal Court: A Step Toward World Peace* (Dobbs Ferry, NY: Oceana Publications Inc., 1980), 2 vols.

6. Benjamin B. Ferencz, *New Legal Foundations for Global Survival: Security Through the Security Council* (Dobbs Ferry, NY: Oceana Publications, Inc., 1993). See, especially, Chapter Two, pages 67-78.

7. Ibid., vi.

8. The letter from Annan to Ferencz is dated June 24, 1997. A copy is in the author's possession.

9. Ed Vulliamy, "Why We Still Need a Nuremberg Court," *Guardian* (London), August 5, 1997.

10. Ibid.

11. The historical background has been spelled out in an illuminating article by a top Amnesty International lobbyist, Christopher Keith Hall, "Origins of the ICC Concept (1872-1945)," *The International Criminal Court Monitor* Issue 6 (November 1997): 6.

12. Benjamin B. Ferencz, "At Liberty: A Guest Column," *Constitution* (1993): 80. The journal was published by the Foundation for the United States Constitution.

13. Interview with William Pace, October 24, 1997.

14. *The International Criminal Court: Making the Right Choices*, Part I (London: Amnesty International, January 1997).

15. Pace interview.

16. "ABCs of the ICC," *The International Criminal Court Monitor* no. 1 (July/August, 1996): 1.

17. "About the Coalition," *Coalition for an International Criminal Court*, October 1, 1996, 1.

18. "ABCs of the ICC," op. cit., 7.

19. *Remarks by the President at the Opening of the Commemoration of "50 Years After Nuremberg: Human Rights and the Rule of Law*," October 15, 1996.

20. Pace interview.

21. "ICC Treaty Conference," *Monitor* no. 6 (November 1997): 7.

22. Ibid.

23. Ibid.

24. "World Federalist Movement," World Federalist Home Page, NTTP://www.allifi/ -JEF/WFM/November 5, 1997.

25. Pace interview.

26. Ibid.

27. *NGO Strategy Meeting on the International Criminal Court*. The paper and list of attendees was provided by the World Federalist Movement.

28. Ibid.

29. Ibid. Details were provided by World Federalist Movement.

30. For details see "About the NGO Coalition for an ICC," *Monitor* no. 6 (November 1997): 2, 12.

31. Pace interview.
32. Ibid.
33. Ibid.
34. Ibid.
35. Interview with Benjamin Ferencz, December 11, 1997.
36. Barbara Crossette, "Legal Experts Agree on an Outline for a Global Criminal Court," *New York Times,* December 14, 1997.
37. Benjamin B. Ferencz, "Courting an International Criminal Court," *Journal of the Nuclear Age Peace Foundation* (summer, 1997): 7.
38. See ibid. for the quotation.
39. Theo van Boven, *Study Concerning the Right to Restitution, Compensation, and Rehabilitation for Victims of Gross Violations of Human Rights and Fundamental Freedoms.* UN Doc. E/CN.4/Sub.2/1993/8, 2 July 1993, 65pp. The document was prepared for the Subcommission on Prevention of Discrimination and Protection of Minorities.
40. Ibid., 53.
41. Ibid. The principle was also accepted at the Rome Conference of plenipotentiaries that approved the Statute for the ICC.
42. Ibid., 56.
43. Alan Cowell, "Switzerland's Wartime Blood Money," *Foreign Policy* (summer 1997): 136-37.
44. World Jewish Congress, "The Sinister Face of 'Neutrality': The Role of Swiss Financial Institutions in the Plunder of European Jewry," *Policy Forum, No. 13* (Jerusalem: Institute of the World Jewish Congress, 1996), 6.
45. Cowell, op. cit., 136-37.
46. *The Sinister Face of "Neutrality,"* op. cit., 6.
47. Cowell, op. cit., 136-7.
48. *The Sinister Face of "Neutrality,"* op. cit., 14.
49. Ann Louise Bardach, "Edgar's List," *Vanity Fair,* March 1997, 269.
50. *U.S. and Allied Efforts to Recover and Restore Gold and Other Assets Stolen or Hidden by Germany During World War II. Preliminary Study* (Washington, D.C., May 1997). The study was coordinated by Stuart E. Eizenstat, Under Secretary of Commerce and prepared by William Slany, the Historian of the Department of State.
51. Bardach, op. cit., 256.
52. Ibid.
53. Ibid.
54. Ibid., 269.
55. Alan Cowell, "How Swiss Strategy on Holocaust Fund Unraveled," *New York Times,* January 26, 1997.
56. Ibid.
57. Interview with Elan Steinberg, September 15, 1997.
58. Ibid.
59. Ibid.
60. Ibid.
61. Aryeh Neier, "What Should Be Done about the Guilty," *The New York Review of Books,* February 1, 1990, 32-5.
62. Ibid., 34.
63. Kader Asmal, *Reconciliation Through Truth* (Cape Town: David Philip, 1996). Asmal, who taught at the University of the Western Cape, has lectured movingly on the subject of reparations for victims and survivors.
64. Ibid., 18.
65. Ibid.
66. Ibid., 144.

67. Ibid., 19.

68. Priscilla Hayner, "Fifteen Truth Commissions—1974 to 1994: a Comparative Study," *Human Rights Quarterly* 16 (1994): 597-655.

69. Ibid., 612-13.

70. Ibid., 614-15.

71. Ibid.

72. Ibid., 621.

73. Priscilla Hayner, "Commissioning the Truth: Further Research Questions," *Third World Quarterly* 17, no. 1 (1996): 28.

74. Thomas Buergenthal, "The United Nations Truth Commission for El Salvador," *Vanderbilt Journal of Transnational Law* 27, no. 3 (October, 1994): 498-500.

75. Hayner, "Fifteen Truth Commissions—1974 to 1994," op. cit., 649.

76. Buergenthal, "The United Nations Truth Commission, op. cit., 507.

77. This was reported in the international press in mid-1997.

78. Suzanne Daley, "Testimony in South Africa Ties Ex-Leader to Bombing," *New York Times,* June 21, 1997.

79. Hayner, "Fifteen Truth Commissions—1974 to 1994," op. cit., 639.

80. Suzanne Daley, "In Apartheid Inquiry, Agony is Relived but Not Put to Rest," *New York Times,* July 17, 1997.

81. *Memorandum to the Select Committee on Justice: Comments and Recommendations by Amnesty International on Promotion of Unity and Reconciliation Bill* (Amnesty International, January 13, 1993), 5.

82. Ibid., 13.

83. "Two Views: Finding Peace Without Justice," *World Press Review* (February, 1997): 8.

84. Buergenthal, "The United Nations Truth Commission," op. cit., 544.

85. Information about her research findings as it pertained to NGOs has been made available to the author during several interviews, notably on May 21, 1996; October 30, 1996 and April 30, 1997.

86. For details on the Institute and Buergenthal's role, see Jo M. Pasqualucci, "Thomas Buergenthal: Holocaust Survivor to Human Rights Advocate," *Human Rights Quarterly* 18 (1996): 984.

87. Ibid., 898.

88. Thomas Buergenthal, "Remembering the Auschwitz Death March," *Human Rights Quarterly* 18 (1996): 874-75. The article was drawn from a talk he delivered the previous year at the U.S. Holocaust Museum.

89. William Korey, "Minority Rights After Helsinki," *Ethics and International Affairs* 8 (1994): 138.

BIBLIOGRAPHY

BOOKS

Fouad Ajami, ed., *Human Rights and World Order Politics* (New York: Institute for World Order, 1978).

Ludmilla Alexeyeva, *Soviet Dissent: Contemporary Movements for National Religious and Human Rights* (Middletown, CT: Wesleyan University Press, 1985).

American Jewish Committee, *25 years on the Cutting Edge: JBI's 25th Anniversary Review* (New York: American Jewish Committee, 1997).

Richard Arens, ed., *Genocide in Paraguay* (Philadelphia: Temple University Press, 1976).

Frederick B. Artz, *Reaction and Revolution, 1814-1832* (New York: Harper, 1934).

Timothy Garton Ash, *The Magic Lantern: The Revolution of 1989* (New York: Vintage Books, 1990).

Asia-Pacific NGO Conference on Human Rights, Coordinating Committee for Follow-Up, *Our Voice: Reports of the Asia-Pacific Conference on Human Rights and NGOs' Statements to Asia Regional Meeting* (Bangkok: Asian Cultural Forum on Development, 1993).

Kader Asmal, *Reconciliation through Truth* (Capetown: David Philip, 1996).

Association of Polish Students and Graduates in Exile, *Dissent in Poland: Reports and Documents in Translation, December 1975—July 1977* (London, 1979).

Lewis Baldwin, *Toward the Beloved Community: Martin Luther King and South Africa* (New York: Pilgrim Press, 1995).

John Bierman, *Righteous Gentile: The Story of Raoul Wallenberg, Missing Hero of the Holocaust* (New York: Viking Press, 1971).

Katherine Birmingham, *OSCE and Minority Issues* (The Hague: Foundation on Inter-Ethnic Relations, November 1995).

Kevin Boyle and Juliet Sheen, *Freedom of Religion and Belief: A World Report* (Florence, KY: Routledge Press, 1997).

Thomas Buergenthal, *Human Rights, International Law and the Helsinki Accord* (Montclair, NJ: Allanheld, Osmun, 1978).

Thomas Buergenthal, *International Human Rights in a Nutshell,* 2nd ed. (St. Paul: West Publishing Co., 1995).

The Carter Center, *Waging Peace Around the World: The Carter Center 1992-1993* (Atlanta, GA: The Carter Center, 1993).

Antonio Cassese, *UN Law, Fundamental Rights: Two Topics in International Law* (Alphen aan den Rijn: Sijthoff & Noordoff, 1979).

Israel W. Charny, *How Can We Commit the Unthinkable? Genocide: The Human Cancer* (Boulder, CO: Westview Press, 1982).

Chiang Pei-heng, *Non-Governmental Organizations at the United Nations: Identity, Role, and Function* (New York: Praeger, 1981).

Roger S. Clark, *The United Nations Crime Prevention and Criminal Justice Program: Formulation of Standards and Efforts at Their Implementation* (Philadelphia: University of Pennsylvania Press, 1994).

Richard P. Claude and Burns Weston, *Human Rights in the World Community: Issues and Action,* 2nd. ed. (Philadelphia: University of Pennsylvania Press, 1992).

Bernard C. Cohen, *The Influence of Non-Governmental Groups on Foreign Policy-Making* (Boston: World Peace Foundation, 1959).

Stanley Cohen, *Denial and Acknowledgement: The Impact of Information about Human Rights Violations* (Jerusalem: Hebrew University, 1995).

Commission to Study the Organization at Peace, *The United Nations and Human Rights* (Dobbs Ferry, NY: Oceana, 1968).

Carol Ann Cosgrove and Kenneth Twitchett, *The New International Actors* (New York: St. Martin's Press, 1970).

Irwin Cotler and F. Pearl Eliadis, *International Human Rights Law: Theory and Practice* (Montreal: Canadian Human Rights Foundation, 1992).

Les De Villiers, *In Sight of Surrender: US Sanctions Against South Africa* (New York: Praeger, 1994).

Jorge I. Dominguez, ed., *Enhancing Global Human Rights* (New York: McGraw-Hill, 1979).

Alan Dowty, *Closed Borders* (New Haven: Yale University Press, 1987).

Jan Egelman and Thomas Kerks, eds., *Third World Organizational Development: A Comparison of NGO Strategies* (Geneva: Henry Dunant Institute, 1987).

Clark M. Eichelberger, *UN: the First Twenty-Five Years* (New York: Harper & Row, 1970).

Arie L. Eliav, *Between Hammer and Sickle* (New York: New American Library, 1969).

Werner J. Feld, *Non-Governmental Forces and World Politics: A Study of Business, Labor, and Political Groups* (New York: Praeger, 1972).

Benjamin B. Ferencz, *Less than Slaves* (Cambridge: Harvard University Press, 1979).

Benjamin B. Ferencz, *An International Criminal Court: A Step Toward World Peace* (Dobbs Ferry, NY: Oceana Publications, 1980).

Benjamin B. Ferencz, *New Legal Foundations for Global Survival: Security Through the Security Council* (Dobbs Ferry, NY: Oceana Publications, 1993).

David P. Forsythe, *Human Rights and World Politics* (Lincoln: University of Nebraska Press, 1989).

Thomas Franck and Edward Weisband, *Foreign Policy by Congress* (New York: Oxford University Press, 1979).

Richard N. Gardner, *In Pursuit of World Order* (New York: Praeger, 1964).

Raymond D. Gastil, *Freedom in the World: Political and Civil Liberties* (New York: Freedom House, 1978).

Paul Goldberg, *The Final Act: The Dramatic Revealing Story of the Moscow Helsinki Watch Group* (New York: William Morrow and Co., 1988).

Daniel J. Goldhagen, *Hitler's Willing Executioners: Ordinary Germans and the Holocaust* (New York: Alfred A. Knopf, 1996).

Iain Guest, *Behind the Disappearances: Argentina's Dirty War Against Human Rights and the United Nations* (Philadelphia: University of Pennsylvania Press, 1990).

Iain Guest, *On Trial: The United Nations, War Crimes, and the Former Yugoslavia.* Mimeo, (Washington, DC: Refugee Policy Group, September 1995).

Hurst Hannum, ed., *Guide to International Human Rights Practice* (Philadelphia: University of Pennsylvania Press, 1984).

Louis Henkin, *The Rights of Man Today* (Boulder, CO: Westview Press, 1978).

Louis Henkin and John L. Hargrove, *Human Rights: An Agenda for the Next Century* (Washington, DC: American Society for International Law, 1994).

Natalie K. Hevener, ed., *Dynamics of Human Rights in US Foreign Policy and the Pursuit of International Human Rights* (New Brunswick, NJ: Transaction Books, 1981).

Donald Horowitz, *Ethnic Groups in Conflict* (Berkeley: University of California Press, 1985).

George M. Houser, *No One Can Stop the Rain: Glimpses of Africa's Liberation Struggle* (New York: Pilgrim Press, 1989).

Konrad J. Huber, *Averting Inter-Ethnic Conflict: An Analysis of the CSCE HCNM in Estonia, January-July 1993* (Atlanta, GA: The Carter Center, Conflict Resolution Program, April 1994). Working Paper series: Vol. 1, No. 2.

Human Rights Watch/Middle East, *Iraq's Crime of Genocide: The Anfal Campaign Against the Kurds* (New Haven: Yale University Press and Human Rights Watch Books, 1995). [Initially published in a different form in July 1993.]

John P. Humphrey, *Human Rights and the United Nations: A Great Adventure* (Dobbs Ferry, NY: Transnational Publishers, 1984).

Leon Hurwitz, *The State as Defendant: Governmental Accountability and the Redress of Individual Grievances* (Westport, CT: Greenwood Press, 1981).

José D. Inglés, *Study of Discrimination in Respect of the Right of Everyone to Leave Any Country, Including His Own, And to Return to His Country* (New York: United Nations, 1963).

Institute for Jewish Policy Research and the American Jewish Committee, *Anti-Semitism: World Report 1997* (London: Chandlers Printers, 1997).

International Human Rights Internship Program and the Swedish NGO Foundation for Human Rights, *The Status of Human Rights Organizations in Sub-Saharan Africa* (Washington, DC: International Human Rights Internship Program, September 1994).

International League for Human Rights, *Report of the Conference on Implementing a Human Rights Commitment in United States Foreign Policy* (New York: International League for Human Rights, 1975).

Thomas Jabine and Richard Claude, *Human Rights and Statistics: Getting the Record Straight* (Philadelphia: University of Pennsylvania Press, 1991).

Paul Johnson, *Modern Times* (New York: Weidenfeld and Nicolson, 1983).

James Avery Joyce, *The New Politics of Human Rights* (London: Macmillan, 1978).

Adrian Karatnycky, Alexander Motyl, and Boris Shor, eds., *Nations in Transition* (New Brunswick, NJ: Transaction Publishers, 1997).

Henry Kissinger, *White House Years* (Boston: Little, Brown, and Co., 1979).

Henry Kissinger, *Years of Upheaval* (Boston: Little, Brown, and Co., 1983).

Henry Kissinger, *Diplomacy* (New York: Simon & Schuster, 1994).

Donald P. Kommers and Gilburt D. Loescher, eds., *Human Rights and American Foreign Policy* (Notre Dame: University of Notre Dame Press, 1979).

William Korey, *The Soviet Cage: Anti-Semitism in Russia* (New York: Viking, 1973).

William Korey, *The Promises We Keep: Human Rights, the Helsinki Process, and American Foreign Policy* (New York: St. Martin's Press, 1993).

William Korey, *Russian Anti-Semitism, Pamyat, and the Demonology of Zionism* (Jerusalem: Harwood Academic Publishers, 1995).

Neil J. Kriz, *Transitional Justice: How Emerging Democracies Reckon with Former Regimes* (Washington, DC: US Institute of Peace, 1995).

J. Josef Lador-Lederer, *International Non-Governmental Organizations* (Brussels: Union of International Associations, 1957).

Egon Larson, *A Flame In Barbed Wire: The Story of Amnesty International* (New York: W. W. Norton, 1979).

Hersch Lauterpacht, *An International Bill of the Rights of Man* (New York: Columbia University Press, 1945).

Stefan Lehne, *The Vienna Meeting of the Conference on Security and Cooperation in Europe, 1986-1989; A Turning Point in East-West Relations* (Boulder, CO: Westview Press, 1991).

Aaron Levenstein, *Escape to Freedom: the Story of the International Rescue Committee* (Westport, CT: Greenwood Press, 1983).

Aaron Levenstein, *Freedom's Advocate: A Twenty-five Year Chronicle* (New York: Viking Press, 1965).

Richard Lillich, ed., *International Human Rights: Problems of Law, Policy, and Practice*, 2nd. ed. (Boston: Little, Brown, and Co., 1991).

Richard Lillich, ed., *Fact-Finding Before International Tribunals* (Ardsley-Hudson, NY: Transnational Publishers, 1992).

Jan Josef Lipski, *KOR: A History of the Workers' Defense Committee in Poland, 1976-81* (Berkeley: University of California Press, 1985).

Lowell Livezey, *Nongovernmental Organizations and the Idea of Human Rights* (Princeton, NJ: Center for International Studies, Princeton University, 1988).

Evan Luard, ed., *The International Protection of Human Rights* (New York: Praeger, 1967).

Ellen L. Lutz, Hurst Hannum, and Kathryn J. Burke, eds., *New Directions in Human Rights* (Philadelphia: University of Pennsylvania Press, 1989).

David Mason, *Public and Political Change in Poland, 1980-1982* (Cambridge: Cambridge University Press, 1985).

David Matas, *No More: The Battle Against Human Rights Violations* (Toronto: Dundurn Press Ltd, 1994).

Michael McClintock, *Instruments of Statecraft: US Guerrilla Warfare, Counter-insurgency, Counter-terrorism, 1940-1990* (New York: Pantheon Books, 1992).

Theodor Meron, *Human Rights in International Law: Legal and Policy Issues* (New York: Oxford University Press, 1984), 2 vols.

Hans J. Morgenthau, *Politics Among Nations: The Struggle for Power and Peace*, 5th ed. (New York: Alfred A. Knopf, 1973).

Hans J. Morgenthau and Kenneth W. Thompson, *Politics Among Nations: The Struggle for Power and Peace*, 6th ed. (New York: Alfred A. Knopf, 1985).

Moses Moscovitz, *The Politics and Dynamics of Human Rights* (Dobbs Ferry, NY: Oceana, 1968).

Daniel Patrick Moynihan, *A Dangerous Place* (Boston: Little, Brown & Co., 1978).

Daniel Patrick Moynihan, *Pandaemonium: Ethnicity in International Affairs* (New York: Oxford University Press, 1993).

Joshua Muravchik, *The Uncertain Crusade: Jimmy Carter and the Dilemmas of Human Rights Policy* (Lanham, MD: Hamilton Press, 1986).

Ved P. Nanda, James R. Scarritt, and George W. Shepherd, eds., *Global Human Rights: Public Policies, Comparative Measures, and NGO Strategies* (Boulder, CO: Westview Press, 1981).

Paul Nelson, *The World Bank and Non-Governmental Organizations: The Limits of Apolitical Development* (New York: St. Martin's Press, 1995).

Frank C. Newman and David Weissbrodt, eds., *International Human Rights: Law, Policy, and Process* (Cincinnati: Anderson Publishing Co., 1990).

O. Frederick Nolde, *Freedom's Charter: The Universal Declaration of Human Rights*, Headline Series No. 76 (New York: Foreign Policy Association, July-August, 1949).

Non-Governmental Organizations and the Tribunals: A New Partnership (Oslo: The Royal Norwegian Ministry of Foreign Affairs, 1996).

Yuri Orlov, *Dangerous Thoughts: Memoirs of a Russian Life* (New York: William Morrow and Co., 1991).

Jonathan Power, *Against Oblivion: Amnesty International's Fight for Human Rights* (London: Fontana Paperbacks, 1981).

Joseph Proskauer, *A Segment of My Times* (New York: Farrar, Straus and Co., 1950).

Tom Quigley et al., *U.S. Policy on Human Rights in Latin America (Southern Cone) A Congressional Conference on Capitol Hill* (New York: Fund for New Priorities in American Foreign Policy, 1978).

B. G. Ramcharan, ed., *Human Rights: Thirty Years After the Universal Declaration* (Boston: Martinus Nijhoff [Kluwer], 1979).

E. S. Reddy, ed., *Anti-Apartheid Movement and the United Nations: Statement and Papers of Abdul S. Minty* (New Delhi, 1994).

RFE/RL Research Institute, *The Failure of Communism: The Western Response* (Washington, DC: RFE/RL, November 1989).

David Rieff, *Slaughterhouse: Bosnia and the Failure of the West* (New York: Simon & Schuster, 1995).

Adam Roberts and Benedict Kingsbury, eds., *United Nations, Divided World: The UN's Roles in International Relations*, 2nd ed. (Oxford: Clarendon Press, 1993).

Dorothy B. Robins, *Experiment in Democracy: The Story of US Citizen Organizations in Forging the Charter of the United Nations* (New York: Parkside Press, 1971).

Nehemiah Robinson, *The Universal Declaration of Human Rights—Its Origin, Significance, Application and Interpretation* (New York: World Jewish Congress, 1958).

Nigel Rodley, *The Treatment of Prisoners Under International Law* (New York: Oxford University Press, 1987).

David Rohde, *Endgame: The Betrayal and Fall of Srebrenica, Europe's Worst Massacre Since World War II* (New York: Farrar, Straus and Giroux, 1997).

Peter Rohn, *Relations Between the Council of Europe and International Non-Governmental Organizations* (Brussels: Union of International Associations, 1957).

Barry M. Rubin, and Elizabeth P Spiro, eds., *Human Rights and United States Foreign Policy* (Boulder, CO: Westview Press, 1979).

Abdul Aziz Said, *Human Rights and World Order* (New York: Praeger, 1978).

Andrei Sakharov, *Memoirs* (New York: Alfred A. Knopf, 1990).

Harrison Salisbury, ed., *Sakharov Speaks* (New York: Alfred A. Knopf, 1974).

Roger Sawyer, *Slavery in the Twentieth Century* (London and New York: Routledge & Kegan Paul, 1986).

James R. Scarritt, ed., *Analyzing Political Change in Africa* (Boulder, CO: Westview Press, 1980).

Harris Schoenberg, *The Mandate for Terror: The United Nations and the PLO* (New York: Shapolsky Publisher Inc., 1989).

Lars Schoultz, *Human Rights and United States Policy Toward Latin America* (Princeton, NJ: Princeton University Press, 1981).

Egon Schwelb, *Human Rights and the International Community* (Chicago: Quadrangle Books, 1964).

Donald R. Shanor, *Behind the Scenes: The Private War Against Soviet Censorship* (New York: St. Martin's Press, 1985).

Nina Shea, *In the Lion's Den* (Nashville: Broadman and Holman Publishers, 1997).

George W. Shepherd, *Anti-Apartheid: Transnational Conflict and Western Policy in the Liberation of South Africa* (Westport, CT: Greenwood Press, 1977).

Arkady N. Shevchenko, *Breaking with Moscow* (New York: Random House, 1985).

Henry J. Steiner, *Diverse Partners: Non-Governmental Organizations in the Human Rights Movement* (Cambridge, MA: Harvard Law School Human Rights Program and Human Rights Internet, 1991).

Hans Thoolen and Berth Verstappen, *Human Rights Mission: A Study of the Fact-finding Practice of Non-Governmental Organizations* (Boston: Martinus Nijhoff, 1986).

Jacobo Timerman, *Prisoner Without a Name, Cell Without a Number* (New York: Alfred A. Knopf, 1981).

Howard B. Tolley, *The International Commission of Jurists: Global Advocates for Human Rights* (Philadelphia: University of Pennsylvania Press, 1994).

United Nations Association of the USA, *Inalienable Rights, Fundamental Freedoms: A U.N. Agenda for Advancing Human Rights in the World Community* (New York: United Nations Association, 1996).

Berth Verstappen, ed., *Human Rights Reports: An Annotated Bibliography of Fact-Finding Missions* (New York: Hans Zell, 1987).

Sandy Vogelgesang, *American Dream, Global Nightmare: The Dilemma of US Human Rights Policy* (New York: W.W. Norton & Co., 1980).

Lech Walesa, *A Way of Hope* (New York: Henry Holt & Co., 1987).

Claude E. Welch, Jr., *Protecting Human Rights in Africa* (Philadelphia: University of Pennsylvania Press, 1995).

Claude E. Welch and Ronald I. Meltzer, eds., *Human Rights and Development in Africa* (Albany: State University of New York Press, 1984).

Thomas G. Weiss and Leon Gordenker, eds., *NGOs, the UN, and Global Governance* (Boulder, CO: Lynne Rienner, 1996).

Lyman C. White, *International Non-governmental Organizations: Their Purposes, Methods, and Accomplishments* (New Brunswick, NJ: Rutgers University Press, 1951).

Peter Willetts, ed., *Pressure Groups in the Global System* (London: F. Pinter, 1982).

Peter Willetts, ed., *"The Conscience of the World": The Influence of Non-Governmental Organisations in the U.N. System* (Washington, DC: Brookings Institution, 1996).

Laurie Wiseberg, *Defending Human Rights Defenders: The Importance of Freedom of Association for Human Rights NGOs* (Montreal: International Centre for Human Rights and Democratic Development, 1993).

BOOKLETS

Patrick Ball, *Human Rights Organizations in Global Perspective: Constitutional Rights, State Terror, and International Differences*, Advanced Study Center Working Paper Series No. 10 (Ann Arbor: International Institute, University of Michigan, April 12, 1996).

Renée Cohen and Jennifer Golub, *Attitudes Toward Jews in Poland, Hungary, and Czechoslovakia* (New York: American Jewish Committee, 1991).

Jennifer L. Golub, *German Attitudes Toward Jews: What Recent Survey Data Reveal* (New York: American Jewish Committee, 1991).

Jacob Blaustein Institute and the International League for Human Rights, *Comments on the ECE Draft Document for the High Level Preparatory Meeting for the Fourth World Conference on Women* (New York: Jacob Blaustein Institute and the International League for Human Rights, 1994).

Margaret Keck and Kathryn Sikkink, "Transnational Issue Networks in International Politics," in *Activists Without Borders: Transnational Issue Networks in International Politics*, Working Paper Series No. 8 (Ann Arbor: International Institute, University of Michigan, 1995).

William Korey, *Glasnost and Soviet Anti-Semitism* (New York: American Jewish Committee, 1993).

United Nations Association, *A Global Agenda: Issues Before the 50th General Assembly of the United Nations* (New York: United Nations Association, 1995).

SCHOLARLY ARTICLES

Kenneth P. Adler and Davis Bobrow, "Interest and Influence in Foreign Affairs," *Public Opinion Quarterly* 20 (Spring 1956).

Ozong Agborsangaya, "Human Rights NGOs and Human Rights Components of Peacekeeping Operations," in The Carter Center, *Human Rights, the United Nations, and Non-Governmental Organizations* (Atlanta, GA: Carter Center, 1997).

American Bar Association, Section on Individuals Rights and Responsibilities, "Giving a Voice to the Dead: Forensic Scientists Join World-Wide Human Rights Investigations to Uncover the Truth," *Human Rights* 22, No. 1 (winter, 1995).

George Andreopoulos, "Introduction: The Calculus of Genocide," in George Andreopoulos, ed., *Genocide: Conceptual and Historical Dimensions* (Philadelphia: University of Pennsylvania Press, 1994).

Peter Archer, "Action by Unofficial Organizations on Human Rights," in Evan Luard, ed., *The International Protection of Human Rights* (London: Thames & Hudson, 1967).

J. D. Armstrong, "Non-Governmental Organizations," in R. J. Vincent, ed., *Foreign Policy and Human Rights: Issues and Responses* (Cambridge, UK: Cambridge University Press, 1986).

Timothy Garton Ash, "True Confessions," *New York Review of Books* (July 17, 1997).

Fateh Azzam, "Non-Governmental Organizations and the UN World Conference on Human Rights," *Review of the International Commission of Jurists* 50 (1993).

R. B. Ballinger, "UN Action on Human Rights in South Africa," in Evan Luard, ed., *The International Protection of Human Rights* (New York: Frederick A. Praeger, Inc., 1967).

Ann-Louise Bardach, "Edgar's List," *Vanity Fair* (March, 1997).

Peter Berger, "Are Human Rights Universal?" *Commentary* (September, 1977).

Richard Bilder, "Rethinking International Human Rights: Some Basic Questions," *Wisconsin Law Review* (1969).

Donald Blaisdell, "Pressure Groups, Foreign Politics, and International Politics," *Annals of the Academy of Political and Social Science* 319 (September 1958).

Andrew Blane, "The Individual in the Cell: A Rebuttal to 'Politics and Amnesty International,'" *Matchbox* (winter 1979).

Arthur Blaser, "How to Advance Human Rights Without Really Trying: An Analysis of Non-Governmental Tribunals," *Human Rights Quarterly* 14 (August 1992).

Arthur Blaser, "Human Rights in the Third World and Development of International Non-Governmental Organizations," in Ved P. Nanda and George W. Shepherd, Jr., eds., *Human Rights and Third World Development* (Westport, CT: Greenwood Press, 1985).

Michael Bowen, Gary Freeman, and Kay Miller, *Passing By: The United States and Genocide in Burundi, 1972* (Washington, DC: Carnegie Endowment for International Peace, n.d.).

Thomas Buergenthal, "The Copenhagen CSCE Meeting: A New Public Order for Europe," *Human Rights Law Journal* 11 (1990).

Thomas Buergenthal, "The United Nations Truth Commission for El Salvador," *Vanderbilt Journal of Transnational Law* 27, no. 3 (October 1994).

Thomas Buergenthal, "Remembering the Auschwitz Death March," *Human Rights Quarterly* 18 (1996).

Charlotte Bunch, "The Intolerable Status Quo: Violence Against Women and Girls," in UNICEF, *The Progress of Nations* (New York: UNICEF, July 1997).

Holly J. Burkhalter, "The Question of Genocide: The Clinton Administration and Rwanda," *World Policy Journal* 11, no. 4 (winter 1994).

John Carey, "Procedures for the International Protection of Human Rights," *Iowa Law Review* (October 1967).

Carnegie Endowment for International Peace, "The United Nations and Non-Self-Governing Territories," *International Conciliation* No. 432 (November, 1947).

Thomas Carothers, "Democracy Promotion Under Clinton," *Washington Quarterly* 18, no. 3 (autumn 1995).

Antonio Cassese, "How Could Non-Governmental Organizations Use U.N. Bodies More Effectively?" *Universal Human Rights* 1, no. 4 (October-December, 1979).

Antonio Cassese, "Progressive Transnational Promotion of Human Rights," in B. G. Ramcharan, ed., *International Law and Fact Finding in the Field of Human Rights* (The Hague: Martinus Nijhoff, 1982).

René Cassin, "Twenty Years of NGO Effort on Behalf of Human Rights," in *Human Rights: Final Report of the International NGO Conference* (Paris: UNESCO, September, 1968).

Diana Chigas, "Bridging the Gap Between Theory and Practice: The CSCE High Commissioner on National Minorities," *Helsinki Monitor* no. 3 (1994).

Andrew Clapham, "Creating the High Commissioner for Human Rights," *European Journal of International Law* 5, no. 4 (1994).

Roger S. Clark, "The International League for Human Rights and South West Africa 1947-1957: The Human Rights NGO as Catalyst in the International Legal Process," *Human Rights Quarterly* 3 (1981).

Inis Claude, "Collective Legitimization as a Political Function of the United Nations," in *International Organization* 20 (summer 1966).

James C. Cobey, "Medical Complications of Anti-Personnel Land Mines," *Bulletin of the American College of Surgeons* 81, no. 8.

Roberta Cohen, "Human Rights Diplomacy in the Communist Heartland," in David D. Newsom, ed., *The Diplomacy of Human Rights* (Washington, DC: Institute for the Study of Diplomacy and University Press of America, 1986).

Roberta Cohen, "People's Republic of China: The Human Rights Exception," *Occasional Papers/Reprint Series in Contemporary Asian Studies* No. 3 (86) (Baltimore: University of Maryland School of Law, 1988).

Helena Cook, "Amnesty International at the United Nations," in Peter Willetts, ed., *"The Conscience of the World": The Influence of Non-Governmental Organizations in the UN System* (Washington, DC: Brookings Institution, 1996).

Irwin Cotler, "Human Rights Advocacy and the NGO Agenda" in Irwin Cotler and F. Pearl Eliadis, eds., *International Human Rights Law: Theory and Practice* (Montreal: Canadian Human Rights Foundation, 1992).

Alan Cowell, "Switzerland's Wartime Blood Money," *Foreign Policy* (Summer 1997).

Richard Dean, "Non-Governmental Organizations: The Foundation of Western Support for the Human Rights Movement in the Soviet Union," in Richard P. Claude and Burns H. Weston, eds., *Human Rights in the World*

Community: Issues and Action (Philadelphia: University of Pennsylvania Press, 1989).

Ralston Deffenbaugh, "The Southern Africa Project for the Lawyers' Committee for Civil Rights Under Law," in Ved P. Nanda, James R. Scarritt, and George W. Shepherd, eds. *Global Human Rights: Public Policies, Comparative Measures, and NGO Strategies* (Boulder, CO: Westview Press, 1981).

Norman Dorsen and Michael Posner, "Call to Action," *Advisor* 1, No. 3 (Spring 1997).

Martin Ennals, "Amnesty International and Human Rights," in Peter Willetts, ed., *Pressure Groups in the Global System: The Transnational Relations of Issue-Oriented Non-Governmental Organizations* (London: Frances Pinter Publications, 1982).

Felix Ermacora, "Non-Governmental Organizations as Promoters of Human Rights," in Franz Matscher and Herbert Petzold, eds., *Protecting Human Rights: The European Dimension* (Köln: Carl Heymanns Verlag KG, 1988).

Tom Farer and Felice Gaer, "The UN and Human Rights at the Beginning," in Adam Roberts and Benedict Kingsbury, eds. *United Nations, Divided World: The UN's Roles in International Relations* (Oxford: Clarendon Press, 1993).

Werner J. Feld, "Non-Governmental Entities and the International System: A Preliminary Quantitative Overview," *Orbis* 15 (fall 1971).

Benjamin B. Ferencz, "Courting an International Criminal Court," *Journal of the Nuclear Age Peace Foundation* (summer 1997).

Benjamin B. Ferencz, "At Liberty: A Guest Column," *Constitution* (1993).

Thomas M. Franck, and H. Scott Fairley, "Procedural Due Process in Human Rights Fact-Finding by International Agencies," *American Journal of International Law* 74 (1980).

Francis Fukuyama, "The End of History," *The National Interest* no. 16 (summer, 1989).

Felice Gaer, "Reality Check: Human Rights Non-Governmental Organizations Confront Governments at the United Nations," *Third World Quarterly* 16, no. 3 (1995).

Diego Garcia-Sayan, "Non-Governmental Organizations and the Human Rights Movement in Latin America," *UN Bulletin of Human Rights* 90/1 (1991).

Diego Garcia-Sayan, "The Experience of ONUSAL in El Salvador," in Alice H. Henkin, ed., *Honoring Human Rights and Keeping the Peace* (Washington, DC: Aspen Institute, 1995).

Richard N. Gardner, foreword, in Roger S. Clark, *The United Nations High Commissioner for Human Rights* (The Hague: Martinus Nijhoff, 1972).

H. Jack Geiger and Robert Cook-Deegan, "The Role of Physicians in Conflicts and Humanitarian Cases," *Journal of the American Medical Association* 270, no. 5 (August 4, 1993).

Yash Ghai, "Human Rights and Governance: The Asia Debate," *Occasional Paper No. 1 of the Center for Asian Pacific Affairs* (New York: The Asia Foundation, November 1994)

Paul Ghils, "International Civil Society: International Non-Governmental Organizations in the International System," *UNESCO International Social Science Journal* 44 (1992).

Arthur J. Goldberg and Richard N. Gardner, "Time to Act on the Genocide Convention," *American Bar Association Journal* 58 (February, 1972).

J. F. Green, "NGOs," in Abdul Aziz Said, ed., *Human Rights and World Order* (New York: Praeger, 1978).

Rita Grönick, "The CSCE and Non-Governmental Organizations," in Michael R. Lucas, *The CSCE in the 1990s: Constructing European Security and Cooperation* (Baden-Baden: Nomosverlagsgesellschaft, 1993).

Barbara Harff, and Ted Robert Gurr, "Toward an Empirical Theory of Genocides and Politicides: Identification and Measurement of Cases Since 1945," *International Studies Quarterly* 32 (1988).

Magarditsch Hatschikjan, "Eastern Europe Nationalist Pandemonium," *Aussenpolitik* 42 (1991).

David Hawk, "Toul Sieng Extermination Centre (Cambodia)," *Index on Censorship* 15, No. 1 (January 1986).

Priscilla Hayner, "Fifteen Truth Commissions—1974 to 1994: A Comparative Study," *Human Rights Quarterly* 16 (1994).

Priscilla Hayner, "Commissioning the truth: further research questions," *Third World Quarterly* 17, no. 1 (1996).

Vladimir Hercik, "The Worldwide Dimension of the NGOs," *Transnational Associations* 11 (1980).

Sir Samuel Hoare, "The UN Commission on Human Rights," in Evan Luard, ed., *The International Protection of Human Rights* (New York: Praeger, 1967).

Darril Hudson, "A Case Study of an International Pressure Group," *International Associations* 6 (1968).

John P. Humphrey, "The UN Charter and the Universal Declaration of Human Rights," in Evan Luard, ed., *The International Protection of Human Rights* (New York: Praeger, 1967).

Samuel Huntington, "Transnational Organizations in World Politics," *World Politics* 25 (April 1973): 333-68.

Vincent Iacopina, et. al., "Physicians Complicity in Misrepresentation and Omission of Evidence of Torture in Post-Detention Medical Examination in Turkey," *Journal of the American Medical Association* 276, no. 5 (August 7, 1996).

Michael Ignatieff, "How Can Past Sins be Absolved?" *World Press Review* (February 1997).

Homer Jack, "The Human Rights Commission at Geneva," *World Conference on Religion and Peace Report* (March 7, 1975).

Cecilia E. Jimenez, "The Proliferation of National Human Rights Institutions: For Other Ends?" *Human Rights Forum* 4 (1994).

Sidney Jones, "The Impact of Asian Economic Growth on Human Rights," *Council on Foreign Relations Working Paper* (New York: January 1995).

Max M. Kampelman, "Secession and the Right of Self-Determination: An Urgent Need to Harmonize Principle With Pragmatism," *Washington Quarterly* 16, no. 2 (summer 1993).

Edy Kaufman and Patricia Weiss Fagan, "Extrajudicial Executions: An Insight in the Global Dimension of Human Rights Violations," *Human Rights Quarterly* 3, no. 4 (fall, 1981).

Bilahari Kausikan, "Asia's Different Standard," *Foreign Policy* 92 (fall 1993).

Ben Kiernan, "The Cambodian Genocide: Issues and Responses," in George J. Andreopoulos, ed., *Genocide: Conceptual and Historical Dimensions* (Philadelphia: University of Pennsylvania Press, 1994).

Jeanne Kirkpatrick, "Dictatorships and Double Standards," *Commentary* 68, no. 5 (November 1979).

Stephen H. Klitzman, Craig H. Baab and Brian C. Murray, "Ratification of the Genocide Convention: From the Ashes of 'Shoah' Past the Shoals of the Senate," *Federal Bar News Journal* 33, no. 6 (July-August 1986).

Juliano Kokott, "Indonesian National Commission on Human Rights," *Human Rights Law Journal* 16 (December 1995).

William Korey, "The Embarassed American," *Saturday Review,* October 31, 1964.

William Korey, "Human Rights Treaties: Why is the US Stalling?" *Foreign Affairs* 45, no. 3 (April, 1967).

William Korey, "A Global Ombudsman," *Saturday Review,* August 12, 1967.

William Korey, "Eleanor Roosevelt and the Universal Declaration of Human Rights," in A. David Gurewitsch, *Eleanor Roosevelt, Her Day: A Personal Album* (New York: Interchange Foundation, 1968).

William Korey, "The Key to Human Rights—Implementation," *International Conciliation* 570 (November, 1968).

William Korey, "We, the Peoples," *Vista* 5, no. 6 (May-June 1970).

William Korey, "The Struggle over Jackson-Mills-Vanik," *American Jewish Yearbook, 1974-5* 75 (Philadelphia: American Jewish Committee and Jewish Publication Society of America, 1976).

William Korey, "The Struggle over the Jackson Amendment," *American Jewish Yearbook, 1976* (Philadelphia: American Jewish Committee and Jewish Publication Society of America, 1976).

William Korey, "The Future of Soviet Jewry," *Foreign Affairs* 58, no. 1 (Fall, 1979).

William Korey, "Sin of Omission," *Foreign Policy* no. 39 (summer 1980).

William Korey, "Jackson-Vanik and Soviet Jewry," *Washington Quarterly* 6, no. 4 (winter 1984): 116-28.

William Korey, "Genocide Treaty Ratification," in Warren F. Kimball, ed., *America Unbound: World War II and the Making of a Superpower* (New York: St. Martin's Press, 1992).

William Korey, "Minority Rights After Helsinki," *Ethics and International Affairs* 8 (1994).

Louis Kriesberg, "International Non-Governmental Organizations and Transnational Integration," *International Associations* 24 (1972).

Ernst Kux, "Revolution in Eastern Europe – Revolution in West?" *Problems of Communism* 40 (May-June 1991).

Virginia Leary, "A New Role for NGOs in Human Rights: A Case Study of Non-Governmental Participation in the Development of International Norms of Torture," in Antonio Cassese, ed., *UN Law, Fundamental Rights: Two*

Topics in International Law (Alphen aan den Rijn: Sijthoff & Noordoff, 1979).

Daniel Lev, "Human Rights NGOs in Indonesia and Malaysia," in Claude E. Welch, Jr. and Virginia Leary, eds., *Asian Perspectives on Human Rights* (Boulder, CO: Westview Press, 1990).

Sidney Liskofsky, "The UN Reviews Its NGO System," *Reports on the Foreign Scene* no. 10 (January 1970).

Evan Luard, "Conclusions," in Evan Luard, ed., *The International Protection of Human Rights* (New York: Praeger, 1967).

R. St. J. MacDonald, "The United Nations High Commissioner for Human Rights," *The Canadian Yearbook of International Law* (1967).

Ian Martin, "Paper versus Steel: The First Phase of the International Civilian Mission in Haiti," in Alice H. Henkin, ed., *Honoring Human Rights and Keeping the Peace* (Washington, DC: Aspen Institute, 1995).

Jessica Mathews, "Power Shift," *Foreign Affairs* (January/February, 1997).

John Melithoniote, "A Profile of the Three Organizations," *Ethos* (December 6, 1973).

Harris Meyer, "US MDs Monitor Jailing of Chilean Leaders," *American Medical News* (August 22-29, 1986).

Harris Meyer, "Chile Frees Two Leaders of National MD Group," *American Medical News* (September 19, 1986).

Stephen Miller, "Politics and Amnesty International, *Commentary* (March, 1978).

Caroline Moorhead and Ursula Owen, "Time to Think Again," *Index on Censorship* 25, no. 1 (January/February 1996).

Andrew Nathan, "China: Getting Human Rights Right," *Washington Quarterly* 20, no. 2 (Spring 1997).

Aryeh Neier, "Watching Rights," *The Nation* (November 19, 1990).

Aryeh Neier, "What Should Be Done About the Guilty?" *New York Review of Books* (February 1, 1990). Also appears in Neil J. Kriz, *Transitional Justice: How Emerging Democracies Reckon with Former Regimes* (Washington, DC: US Institute of Peace, 1995).

Aryeh Neier, "Asia's Unacceptable Standard," *Foreign Policy* 92 (fall 1993): 42-51

Aryeh Neier, "The New Double Standard," *Foreign Policy* no. 105 (winter 1996-1997).

Diane Orentlicher, "The Responsibility to Arrest," *Tribunal* No. 8 (April/May 1997). [A publication of the Institute for War & Peace Reporting.]

Diane Orentlicher, "Bearing Witness : the Art and Science of Human Rights Fact-Finding," in *Harvard Human Rights Journal* 3 (Spring 1990): 83-135.

Jo M. Pasqualucci, "Thomas Buergenthal: Holocaust Survivor to Human Rights Advocate," *Human Rights Quarterly* 18 (1996).

Michael Posner and Candy Whittome, "The Status of Human Rights NGOs," *Columbia Human Rights Law Review* 25 (1994).

Michael Posner, "Rally Round Human Rights," *Foreign Policy* No. 97 (winter 1994-1995).

B.G. Ramcharan, "Reforming the United Nations to Secure Human Rights," *Transnational Law & Contemporary Problems: A Journal of the University of Iowa College of Law* 4, no. 2 (fall, 1994).

Philip L. Ray, Jr. and J. Sherrod Taylor, "The Role of Nongovernmental Organizations in Implementing Human Rights in Latin America," *Georgia Journal of International & Comparative Law* 7, supp. (summer 1977).

Goronwy Rees, "Zionism," *Encounter* 46 (January, 1976).

Randy B. Reiter, M. V. Xunzunegui, and Jose Quiroga, "Guidelines for Field Reporting of Basic Human Rights Violations," *Human Rights Quarterly* 8, no. 4 (1986).

Nigel Rodley, "Monitoring Human Rights by the UN System and Nongovernmental Organizations," in Donald P. Kommers and Gilburt D. Loescher, eds., *Human Rights and American Foreign Policy* (Goshen, IN: University of Notre Dame Press, 1979).

Nigel Rodley, "Monitoring Human Rights Violations in the 1980s," in Jorge I. Dominguez, ed., *Enhancing Global Human Rights* (New York: McGraw-Hill, 1979).

Stephen Roth, "CSCE Outlaws Anti-Semitism," *Institute of Jewish Affairs Research Report,* No. 6 (October 1990).

Trevor Rowe, "UN Creates High Post for Human Rights," *The Interdependent* (winter 1993-1994).

Ronald I. Rubin, "Soviet Jewry and the United Nations: The Politics of Non-Governmental Organizations," *Jewish Social Studies* 29, no. 3 (July, 1967).

Karin Ryan and Laurie Wiseberg, "ECOSOC Resolution 1996/31: The End Result of the ECOSOC Review Process of Rules Governing Relations with the United Nations," in The Carter Center, *Human Rights, the United Nations, and Nongovernmental Organizations* (Atlanta, GA: The Carter Center, 1997).

John Salzberg, "UN Prevention of Human Rights Violations: The Bangladesh Case," *International Organizations* 27 (winter 1973).

John Salzberg and D.P. Young, "Parliamentary Roles in Implementing International Human Rights," *Texas International Law Journal* (spring/summer 1977).

Lillian Passmore Sanderson, "The Role of Anti-Slavery International in the Work for the Ultimate Elimination of All Forms of Female Genital Mutilation," *Anti-Slavery Reporter* (February 1992).

Oscar Schachter, "The Nature and Process of Legal Development in International Society," in R. MacDonald and D. Johnston, eds., *The Structure and Process of International Law* (Dordrecht: Martinus Nijhoff, 1983).

Richard Schifter, "Human Rights at the United Nations: The South African Precedent," *American University Journal of International Law & Policy* 8, nos. 2 & 3 (winter/spring 1992-93).

Erika B. Schlager, "The Right to Have Rights: Citizenship in Newly Independent OSCE Countries," *Helsinki Monitor* 8, no. 1 (1997).

Arthur M. Schlesinger, Jr., "Human Rights and the American Tradition," *Foreign Affairs* (Special issue, 1978).

Steven Schnur, "The Unofficial Man: The Rise and Fall of Raphael Lemkin," *Reform Judaism* (fall, 1982).

Harry M. Scoble, "Human Rights Non-Governmental Organizations in Black Africa: Their Problems and Prospects in the Wake of the Banjul Charter," in Claude E. Welch and Ronald I. Meltzer, eds., *Human Rights and Development in Africa* (Albany: State University of New York Press, 1984).

Harry M. Scoble & Laurie Wiseberg, "Human Rights and Amnesty International," *Annals of Academy of Political and Social Science* 413 (1974).

Harry M. Scoble & Laurie Wiseberg, "The International League for Human Rights: The Strategy of a Human Rights NGO," *Georgia Journal of International and Comparative Law* 7 (1977).

Harry M. Scoble & Laurie Wiseberg, "Human Rights NGOs: Notes Toward Comparative Analysis," *Human Rights* 9, no. 4 (winter 1976).

Albert W. Sherer, Jr., "Goldberg's Variations," *Foreign Policy* no. 39 (summer 1980).

Carroll Sherer, "Breakdown at Belgrade," *Washington Quarterly* 1, no. 3 (autumn, 1978).

Jerome J. Shestack, "Sisyphus Endures: The International Human Rights NGO," *New York Law School Law Review* 24 (1978).

David Shorr, "Preventive Diplomacy," *Government Executive* (Washington, DC: April, 1993).

James Shotwell, "A Tribute by James Shotwell," in American Jewish Committee, *A World Charter for Human Rights* (New York: American Jewish Committee, n.d.).

Kathryn Sikkink, "Human Rights, Principles Issue—Networks and Sovereignty in Latin America," *International Organization* 47, no. 3 (summer 1993).

Kjell Skjelsbaek, "The Growth of International Non-Governmental Organizations in the 20th Century," *International Organizations* 25 (summer 1971).

Gino Strada, "The Horror of Landmines," *Scientific American* (May 1996).

Leonard Sussman, "Can a Free Press be Responsible? To Whom?" in *De La Liberté Aux Libertés: Fédérico Mayor; Amicorum Liber* Vol. II (Brussels: Bruylant, 1995).

Strobe Talbott, "Democracy and the National Interest," *Foreign Affairs* 75, no. 6 (November/December 1996).

Susanna Terstal and Konrad Huber with Christopher Kamp, "The Functioning of the CSCE High Commissioner on National Minorities," *New Community* 20, no. 3 (April 1994).

Ramesh Thakur, "Human Rights: Amnesty International and the United Nations," *Journal of Peace Research* 31, no. 2 (1994).

David Tolbert, "Global Climate Change and the Role of International Non-Governmental Organizations," in Robin Churchill and David Freestone, eds., *International Law and Global Climate Change* (London: Graham and Trotman, 1991).

Samuel Totten, "Non-Governmental Organizations Working on the Issue of Genocide," in Israel W. Charny, ed., *The Widening Circle of Genocide* (New Brunswick, NJ: Transaction Publishers, 1994).

Debra J. Trione, "Universal Accountability: Physician Activism in Human Rights," *Harvard Medical Alumni Bulletin* 61, no. 4 (spring 1988).

Theo van Boven, "The Role of Non-Governmental Organizations in International Human Rights Standard-Setting: A Prerequisite of Democracy," *California Western International Law Journal* 20 (1990).

Robert Weiner, "War by Other Means: Colombia's Faceless Courts," *NACLA Report on the Americas* XXX, No. 2 (Sep/Oct 1996).

David Weissbrodt, "Role of International Non-Governmental Organizations in the Implementation of Human Rights," *Texas International Law Journal* 12 (1977).

David Weissbrodt, "Human Rights Implementation and Fact-Finding by International Organizations," *Proceedings of the American Society of International Law* (1980).

David Weissbrodt, "The Influence of Interest Groups on the Development of United States Human Rights Policies," in Natalie K. Hevener, ed., *Dynamics of Human Rights in US Foreign Policy and the Pursuit of International Human Rights* (New Brunswick, NJ: Transaction Books, 1981).

David Weissbrodt, "Strategies for the Selection and Pursuit of International Human Rights Objectives," *Yale Journal of World Public Order* 8 (1981).

David Weissbrodt and James McCarthy, "Fact-Finding by International Non-Governmental Human Rights Organizations," *Virginia Journal of International Law* 22, no. 1 (1981).

David Weissbrodt and David Kramer, "The 1980 UN Human Rights Commission and the Disappeared," *Human Rights Quarterly* 3, no. 1 (1981).

David Weissbrodt, "The Contribution of International NGOs to the Promotion of Human Rights," in Theodor Meron, *Human Rights in International Law: Legal and Policy Issues* 2 vols. (New York: Oxford University Press, 1984).

David Weissbrodt, "International Fact-Finding in Regard to Torture," *Nordic Journal of International Law* 57 (1988).

David Weissbrodt, "The Role of International Organizations in the Implementation of Human Rights and Humanitarian Law in Situations of Armed Conflict," *Vanderbilt Journal of Transnational Law* 21 (1988).

Laurie S. Wiseberg, "Monitoring Human Rights Violations: The Role of NGOs," in Donald P. Kommers and Gilburt D. Loescher, eds., *Human Rights and American Foreign Policy* (Goshen, IN: University of Notre Dame Press, 1979).

Laurie S. Wiseberg, "Human Rights and Soviet-American Relations: The Role of NGOs," in Richard Melanson, ed., *Neither Cold War Nor Detente* (Charlottesville: University of Virginia Press, 1982).

Laurie S. Wiseberg, "The Role of Non-Governmental Organizations," in Richard P. Claude, and Burns Weston, eds., *Human Rights in the World Community: Issues and Action* 2nd. ed. (Philadelphia: University of Pennsylvania Press, 1992).

Laurie S. Wiseberg and Harry M. Scoble, "The International League for Human Rights: The Strategy of a Human Rights NGO," *Georgia Journal of International & Comparative Law* 7 (1977).

Laurie S. Wiseberg and Harry M. Scoble, "Human Rights as an International League," *Society* (November, 1977).

Laurie S. Wiseberg and Harry M. Scoble, "Recent Trends in the Expanding Universe of NGOs Dedicated to the Protection of Human Rights," in Ved P. Nanda, James R. Scarritt, and George W. Shepherd, eds. *Global Human*

Rights: Public Policies, Comparative Measures, and NGO Strategies (Boulder, CO: Westview Press, 1981).

Rob Zaagman and Hannie Zaal, "The CSCE High Commissioner on National Minorities: Prehistory and Negotiations," in Arie Bloed, ed., *The Challenges of Change: The Helsinki Summit of the CSCE and the Aftermath* (Dordrecht: Martinus Nijhoff, 1994).

Fareed Zakaria, "Culture is Destiny: A Conversation with Lee Kuan Yew," *Foreign Affairs* (March/April 1994).

Fareed Zakaria, "The Rise of Illiberal Democracy," *Foreign Affairs* 76 (November/December 1997).

U.S. GOVERNMENT DOCUMENTS

(All published in Washington, DC, unless otherwise noted; listed by year of publication.)

1945

Report to the President on the Results of the San Francisco Conference; Department of State Publication No. 2349, Conference Series 71.

1949

Trials of War Criminals Before the Nuremburg Military Tribunals, Vol. IV, "The Einsatzgruppen Case."

1952

Eleanor Roosevelt, "The Universal Validity of Man's Right to Self-Determination," *Department of State Bulletin* 27.

1967

Opening Statement by Senator Thomas J. Dodd, Chairman, Hearings of the Ad-Hoc Sub-Committee on Human Rights, Committee on Foreign Relations, United States Senate (February 23).

1974

Human Rights in the World Community: A Call for World Leadership, Report of the Subcommittee on International Organizations and Movements of the Committee on Foreign Affairs in the House of Representatives.

International Protection of Human Rights: The Work of International Organizations and the Role of US Foreign Policy. Hearings of the Subcommittee on International Organizations and Movements, in the Foreign Affairs Committee, 93rd Congress, 1st Session.

1978

US Department of State, *Country Reports on Human Rights Practices* (plus all subsequent years).

1980

Review of the 36th Session of the United Nations Commission on Human Rights. Hearing before Subcommittee on Human Rights and International Organizations (April 29).

1990

United States Department of State, "Secretary [James] Baker: Power for Good, American Foreign Policy in the New Era," *Current Policy* No. 1162 (1990).

1991

US Department of State, *Dispatch* 2, No. 42.

1996

US Department of State, *Country Reports on Human Rights Practices for 1995.*

United Nations Commission on Human Rights, *Human Rights Near the Turn of the Century by Ambassador Madeleine K. Albright, Permanent Representative of the US to the United Nations* (Geneva: March 20).

1997

Congressional Record—Extension of Remarks, E 996 and E 997, by Representative Frank Wolf (May 21).

Bureau of European and Canadian Affairs, Department of State, *OSCE Implementation Report, 1997* (August 1997).

US Department of State, *United States Policies in Support of Religious Freedom: Focus on Christians.*

Coordinated by Stuart E. Eizenstat, *US and Allied Efforts to Recover and Restore Gold and Other Assets Stolen or Hidden by Germany During World War II: Preliminary Study* (May).

SELECTED DOCUMENTS OF THE COMMISSION ON SECURITY AND COOPERATION IN EUROPE

(All published in Washington, DC, unless otherwise noted; listed by year of publication.)

1982

Human Rights in Czechoslovakia: The Documents of Charter 77, 1977-1982 (July).

1986

Documents of the Helsinki Monitoring Groups in the USSR and Lithuania, 1975-1986, Vols. 1 and 2.

1990

Documents of the Copenhagen Meeting (June).

Documents of the Copenhagen Meeting of the Human Rights Dimension of the CSCE (June).

Statement by Max M. Kampelman, Head of the US Delegation to the Copenhagen CSCE Meeting (June 11).

Charter of Paris for a New Europe (Paris).

Statement by Margaret Thatcher at the Paris CSCE Summit Meeting (November 19).

Statement by Mikhail Gorbachev at the Paris CSCE Meeting (November 19).

1991

The Geneva Experts Meeting on National Minorities, July 1–July 19, 1991 (July).

Hearing on the Conflict in Europe (October 31).

1995

Prosecuting War Crimes in the Former Yugoslavia: An Update. Mimeo (June).

1996

The War Crimes Trials for the Former Yugoslavia: Prospects and Problems (May 28).

SELECTED DOCUMENTS OF THE UNITED NATIONS

Economic and Social Council Official Records (ESCOR): 34 Sess., 1962, Suppl. No. 8 (E/3616/Rev.1).

United Nations Action in the Field of Human Rights, U.N. Doc. ST/HR/2//Rev.2 UN Sales No. E. 83.XIV.2 (1983).

"Report of the [Nuclear] Commission on Human Rights," ESCOR: 2nd Sess., 1946, Annex 4 (E/38).

United Nations, *United Nations Action in the Field of Human Rights* (New York: United Nations, 1983).

United Nations, *The United Nations and the Situation in the Former Yugoslavia* S/ RES.771 (New York: United Nations Department of Public Information, 31 August 1992).

United Nations, *Human Rights International Instruments: Chart of Ratifications as of 31 December 1995* ST/HR/Rev.13 (New York: United Nations, 1995).

United Nations, *Report of the International Tribunal for the Prosecution of Persons Responsible for Serious Violations of International Humanitarian Law Committed in the Territory of the Former Yugoslavia* UN Doc. A/52/375 and S/1997/729 (18 September 1997).

United Nations, *Revised and Updated Report on the Question of the Prevention and Punishment of the Crime of Genocide.*

United Nations World Conference on Human Rights, *The Vienna Declaration and Programme of Action* (New York: United Nations, 1993).

Theo van Boven, *Study Concerning the Right to Restitution, Compensation, and Rehabilitation for Victims of Gross Violations of Human Rights and Fundamental Freedoms* UN Doc. E/CN.4/Sub.2/1993/8, 2 July 1993. Prepared for the Sub-Commission on the Prevention of Discrimination and the Protection of Minorities.

DOCUMENTS OF THE CONFERENCE ON SECURITY AND COOPERATION IN EUROPE

(Later reorganized as the Organization for Security and Cooperation in Europe.)

Report of the CSCE Meeting of Experts on National Minorities (Geneva: CSCE, July 1991).

Program of Events, CSCE Seminar of Experts on Democratic Institutions (Oslo: November 4-5, 1991).

Helsinki Decisions (Helsinki: 1992)

Roma (Gypsies) in the CSCE Region: Report of the High Commissioner on National Minorities Mimeo (September 21-23, 1993).

Budapest Document 1994: Towards a Genuine Partnership in a New Era (Budapest, 1994).

Statement of Max van der Stoel, OSCE High Commissioner on National Minorities at the Seminar on Roma Jointly Convened be the Council of Europe and the OSCE (Warsaw, September 1994).

OSCE Handbook (Vienna: Secretariat of the Organization for Security and Cooperation in Europe, 1996).

Report by Max van der Stoel, OSCE High Commissioner on National Minorities (Vienna: 4 November 1996).

OSCE Decisions 1996: Reference Manual (Prague: 1997).

SELECTED NGO DOCUMENTS AND MATERIALS

(These documents include books, reports, annual reports, and materials for internal circulation made available to the author.)

Americas Watch, *Truth and Political Justice* (Washington, DC: Americas Watch, 1987).

Amnesty International, *Political Killings by Governments* (London: Amnesty International, 1983).

Amnesty International, *Report on Torture* (London: Amnesty International, 1973).

Amnesty International, *Amnesty International 1961-1976: A Chronology* (London: Amnesty International, 1976).

Amnesty International, *Testimony on Secret Detention Camps in Argentina* (London: Amnesty International, 1980).

Amnesty International, *Amnesty International Handbook* (London: Amnesty International, 1977, 1983, 1991).

Amnesty International, *Torture in the Eighties* (London: Amnesty International, 1984).

Amnesty International, *World Conference on Human Rights, Facing Up to the Failures: Proposals for Improving the Protection of Human Rights by the United Nations* (London: Amnesty International, December 1992).

Amnesty International, *Final Report: Review of Amnesty International's Research* (London: Amnesty International, 1993).

Amnesty International, *Establishing a Just, Fair and Effective International Criminal Court* (October, 1994).

Amnesty International, *Peace-keeping and Human Rights* (London: Amnesty International, 1994).

Amnesty International, *Killings in Armed Conflict: Review of Current Policy and Outline of Future Options* (London: Amnesty International, 1995).

Amnesty International, *Liberia: A new peace agreement—an opportunity to introduce human rights protection* (London: Amnesty International, 1995).

Amnesty International, *The quest for justice: Worldwide action for a permanent international criminal court* (London: Amnesty International, 1995).

Amnesty International, *Review of Country Work* (London: Amnesty International, 1995).

Amnesty International, *Rwanda and Burundi: A call for action by the international community* (London: Amnesty International, 1995).

Amnesty International, *Amnesty International's Ljubljana Action Plan* (London: Amnesty International, 1995).

Amnesty International "Memorandum to the Select Committee on Justice: Comments and Recommendations by Amnesty International on the Promotion of National Unity and Reconciliation Bill," unpublished paper (January 13, 1995).

Amnesty International, "The Quest for Justice: Time for a permanent international criminal court," in *Amnesty International Focus* 25, no. 9 (September 1995).

Amnesty International, "Evaluation of Campaign on Women & Human Rights," draft copy of internal report (1996).

Amnesty International, *International Criminal Tribunals: Handbook for Government Cooperation* (London: Amnesty International, August 1996).

Amnesty International, *The International Criminal Court: Making the Right Choices* (London: Amnesty International, January, 1997).

Amnesty International, *Agenda for the New UN High Commissioner for Human Rights* (London: Amnesty International, 1997).

Coordination of Women's Advocacy, *Witness Protection: Third Consultative Working Group on Gender-Specific War Crimes Between the International Criminal Tribunal and the Coordination of Women's Advocacy* (Geneva: Coordination of Women's Advocacy, January 1997).

Asbjorn Eide, *New Approaches to Minority Protection* (London: Minority Rights Group, 1993).

Foundation on Inter-Ethnic Relations, *Defining a Constructive Role for the Kin-State Actors in Minority Situations: An Integrated Program of Research Policy Analysis and Seminars* (The Hague: August 1994).

Foundation on Inter-Ethnic Relations, *Integrated Program in Support of the CSCE High Commissioner on National Minorities* (The Hague: August 1994).

Foundation on Inter-Ethnic Relations, *Project Concerning Minority Education in Albania* (The Hague: August 1994).

Foundation on Inter-Ethnic Relations, *Report of the Seminar on Inter-Ethnic Relations and Regional Cooperation* (Bishkek, Kyrgyzstan: May 17-18, 1995).

Foundation on Inter-Ethnic Relations, *Conclusions and Recommendations: Conclusion of Bilateral Treaties Project,* unpublished typescript (The Hague: November 1995).

Foundation on Inter-Ethnic Relations, *Report from the Seminar on Minority Rights and Mechanisms: Facilitating Government-Minority Dialogue* (Riga, Latvia: May 16, 1996).

Foundation on Inter-Ethnic Relations, *The Hague Recommendations Regarding the Education Rights of National Minorities and Explanatory Note* (The Hague: October 1996).

Foundation on Inter-Ethnic Relations, *Specialized Programmes in Support of the High Commissioner on National Minorities of the OSCE* (The Hague: January 1997).

Foundation on Inter-Ethnic Relations, *Bibliography on the OSCE High Commissioner on National Minorities: Documents, Speeches and Related Publications* (The Hague: 1997).

John Heffernan, *War Criminals Watch* (Washington, DC: Coalition for International Justice, 1996).

Helsinki Watch Committee, *Prologue to Gdansk: A Report on Human Rights by the Polish Helsinki Watch Committee* (New York: US Helsinki Watch Committee, 1980).

Helsinki Watch Committee, *Human Rights in Poland Since December 1981: A Report by the Polish Helsinki Committee to the Human Rights Experts Meeting in Ottawa, May 1985* (New York: US Helsinki Watch Committee, 1985).

Helsinki Watch Committee, *Toward Civil Society: Independent Initiatives in Czechoslovakia* (New York: US Helsinki Watch Committee, August 1989).

Human Rights Watch, *Indivisible Human Rights: The Relationship of Political and Civil Rights to Survival, Subsistence, and Poverty* (New York: September 1992).

Human Rights Watch, *Playing the Communal Card: Communal Violence and Human Rights* (New York: 1995).

Human Rights Watch/Africa & Fédération Internationale des Ligues des Droits de L'Homme, *Democratic Republic of Congo: What Kabila is Hiding* (New York: October 1997).

Human Rights Watch/Arms Project, *Landmines: A Deadly Legacy* (New York: 1993).

Human Rights Watch/Arms Project, *US Cluster Bombs for Turkey?* (New York: 1994).

Human Rights Watch/Asia, *Contemporary Forms of Slavery in Pakistan* (New York: 1995).

Human Rights Watch/Helsinki, *War Crimes in Bosnia-Hercegovina* (New York: 1992), 2 vols.

Human Rights Watch/Helsinki, *Bosnia-Hercegovina: Abuses by Bosnian Croat and Muslim Forces in Central and Southwestern Bosnia-Hercegovina* (New York: September 1993).

Human Rights Watch/Helsinki, *The War Crimes Tribunal: One Year Later* (New York: February 1994).

Human Rights Watch/Helsinki, *War Crimes in Bosnia-Hercegovina: Bosanki Samac, Six War Criminals Named by Victims of Ethnic Cleansing* (New York: April 1994).

Human Rights Watch/Helsinki, *Bosnia-Hercegovina: Sarajevo* (New York: October 1994).

Human Rights Watch/Helsinki, *Bosnia-Hercegovina: "Ethnic Cleansing" Continues in Northern Bosnia* (New York: November 1994).

Human Rights Watch/Helsinki, *Russia's War in Chechnya: Victims Speak Out* (New York: January 1995).

Human Rights Watch/Helsinki, *Russia: War in Chechnya: New Report from the Field* (New York: January 1995).

Human Rights Watch/Helsinki, *Russia: Three Months of War in Chechnya* (New York: May 1995).

Human Rights Watch/Helsinki, *Russia: Partisan War in Chechnya, On the Eve of the WWII Commemoration* (New York: May 1995).

Human Rights Watch/Helsinki, *Former Yugoslavia: War Crimes Trials in the Former Yugoslavia* (New York: June 1995).

Human Rights Watch/Helsinki, *Bosnia-Hercegovina: A Failure in the Making: Human Rights and the Dayton Agreement* (New York: June 1996).

Human Rights Watch/Helsinki, *"Germany for Germans": Xenophobia and Racist Violence in Germany* (New York: 1995).

Lawyers Committee for Human Rights, *Shackling the Defenders: Legal Restrictions on Independent Human Rights Advocacy Worldwide* (New York: Lawyers Committee for Human Rights, 1994).

Lawyers Committee for Human Rights, *In the Name of Development: Human Rights and the World Bank in Indonesia* (New York: Lawyers Committee for Human Rights and the Institute for Policy Research and Advocacy [ELSAM], 1995).

Lawyers Committee for Human Rights, *African Exodus: Refugee Crisis, Human Rights and the 1969 OAU Convention* (New York: Lawyers Committee for Human Rights, June 1995).

Lawyers Committee for Human Rights and the Programma Venezolano de Educacion-Accion en Derechos Humanos, *The World Bank and Judicial Reform in Venezuela: A Case Study* (New York: Lawyers Committee for Human Rights, 1996).

Lawyers Committee for Human Rights, *In the National Interest: 1996 Quadrennial Report on Human Rights and US Foreign Policy* (New York: Lawyers Committee for Human Rights, 1996).

Lawyers Committee for Human Rights, *The Americas: Comments Relating to the Fourth Periodic Report on Colombia before the UN Human Rights Committee* (New York: Lawyers Committee for Human Rights, March 1997).

Minority Rights Group, *World Dictionary of Minorities* (London: St. James Press/Minority Rights Group, 1990).

Minority Rights Group, *Minorities, Justice and Peaceful Development* (London: Minority Rights Group, 1995).

Office of Democratic Institutions and Human Rights, *Situation of Roma and Sinti in the OSCE Region: Background Material for the Review Conference* (Warsaw: ODIHR, October 1, 1996). [The document's reference number is REF. RM/35/96/Add.1 22 October 1996).

Diane Paul, *Beyond Monitoring and Reporting: Strategies for Field-Level Protection of Civilians Under Threat* (New York: Jacob Blaustein Institute for Human Rights and the Center for the Study of Societies in Crisis, 1996).

Physicians for Human Rights, *Investigations in Eastern Congo and Western Rwanda* (Boston: Physicians for Human Rights, July 16, 1997).

Physicians for Human Rights, *Human Rights in the Democratic Republic of Congo and Rwanda: Testimony of Dr. Jennifer Leaning for Physicians for Human Rights* (Boston: Physicians for Human Rights, July 16, 1997).

Patrick Thornberry, *The UN Declaration on the Rights of Minorities* (London: Minority Rights Group, 1993).

Jean-Claude Willame et. al., *Zaire, Predicament and Prospects: A Report of Minority Rights Group* (Washington, DC: US Institute of Peace, 1997).

World Jewish Congress, *The Sinister Face of 'Neutrality': The Role of Swiss Financial Institutions in the Plunder of European Jewry,* Policy Forum No. 13 (Jerusalem: Institute of the World Jewish Congress, 1996).

UNPUBLISHED MATERIAL

Madeleine Albright and Alfred Friendly, *Executive-Legislative Cooperation and East-West Relations: The Birth of the Helsinki Commission* (Washington, DC: December 1984). [Mimeo.] Subsequently published as a chapter in Edmund Muskie, Kenneth Rush, and Kenneth Thompson, eds., *The President, the Congress, and Foreign Policy: A Joint Policy Project of the Association of Former Members of Congress and the Atlantic Council of the United States* (Lanham: University Press of America, 1986).

American Society of International Law, *Proceedings of the 84th Annual Meeting, "Human Rights: The Helsinki Process"* (Washington, DC: 1990).

Amnesty International, *Conference for the Abolition of Torture—Final Report* (10-11 December 1973). [Unpublished.]

Amnesty International, *Report of the Fourth UN World Conference on Women: Beijing, China 4-15 September 1995* (London: Amnesty International, 1995). [Internal document.]

Patrick Ball, *Liberal Hypocrisy and Totalitarian Sincerity: The Social and Ideological Origins of the National Non-Government Human Rights Movement in El Salvador, Pakistan, and Ethiopia* (Ann Arbor: University of Michigan, 1998). Doctoral dissertation.

Joanne Bauer, *Report on UN World Conference on Human Rights* (October 31, 1993). [Mimeo.]

Robert Bernstein, Speech delivered at the University of Virginia (December 14, 1995).

Hillary Rodham Clinton, *Remarks for the United Nations Fourth World Conference on Women* (Beijing: September 5, 1995). [Typescript mimeo.]

Roberta Cohen, *Recommendations for US Policy at the UN in the Human Rights Field*, presented to a meeting of human rights NGOs at the United Nations Association of the US on March 31, 1977.

Helena Cook, *The Role of the High Commissioner for Human Rights: One Step Forward or Two Steps Back?* [Mimeo.]

Coordinating Board of Jewish Organizations (B'nai B'rith), *Memorandum on Discrimination on the Matter of the Right of Everyone to Leave Any Country Including His Own and to Return to His Country* (New York, 1960). [Mimeo.]

Jack Donnelly, *Human Rights and US Foreign Policy: Forty Years of Thinking* (Chapel Hill, NC, fall, 1987). [Mimeo.]

Joseph Eldridge, *Testimony of Joseph Eldridge, Director of the Washington Office of the Lawyers Committee for Human Rights before the Subcommittee on Human Rights and International Organizations of the Committee on Foreign Affairs, US House of Representatives* (February 5, 1992).

Joseph Eldridge, *Testimony of Joseph Eldridge, Director of the Washington Office of the Lawyers Committee for Human Rights before the Subcommittee on Foreign Relations of the Committee on Appropriations for the US Senate* (April 19, 1994).

Joseph T. Eldridge, *Statement of Joseph T. Eldridge, Director of the Washington Office of the Lawyers Committee for Human Rights*, Hearing on Human Rights in

Africa before the US House of Representatives Committee on International Relations, Subcommittee on Africa (May 22, 1996).

Peter Fidler, *The Lawyers Committee for Human Rights and the Shifting Route of Governance at the World Bank*, paper prepared for the author (New York, July 1996).

Felice Gaer, Untitled Draft of Speech on the 50th Anniversary of the United Nations, [1995].

Felice Gaer, *And Never the Twain Shall Meet? The Struggle to Establish Women's Rights as International Human Rights at the United Nations*, draft essay intended for publication and provided to the author by Gaer (October 4, 1997). A shortened version was published by the American Bar Association in *The International Human Rights of Women: Instruments of Change* (1998).

Felice Gaer, *Non-Governmental Organizations and the UN High Commissioner for Human Rights*. Mimeo, prepared for the Carter Center's International Human Rights Council (April 1997).

Jerry Goodman, *Statement by Jerry Goodman, Founding Executive Director, National Conference on Soviet Jewry*, US House of Representatives Committee on International Relations (September 10, 1997).

Stefanie Grant, *Human Rights: Challenge for the XXI Century* (10 December 1996). Speech given before the OAS. [Mimeo.]

Andrew Gray, *Work on Indigenous Peoples from 1983-89*, paper prepared for the Anti-Slavery Society, (n.d.).

Susan Gross and Michael Clark, *Discussion Paper Regarding the Structure, Management and Organizational Development of Human Rights Watch* (Washington, DC: Management Assistance Group, November 5, 1993). [Mimeo.]

Manuel Guzman, *Asia CUSHRID Conference Paper*, Part of a Report on the November 3-5, 1994 CUSHRID Net Inaugural Meeting at the American Association for the Advancement of Science and Human Rights Program.

Peter Hart Research Associates, *Key Findings for a Membership Study* (New York: [1995]).

Ibne Hassan, *Amnesty International as a Human Rights Organization* (Ph.D. dissertation, New York University, 1977).

George Houser, *The International Impact of the South African Struggle for Liberation*, prepared for the UN Centre Against Apartheid, Doc. No. 2/82 (January 1982).

Konrad J. Huber, *Fourth (Final) Quarterly Report* [on the CSCE High Commissioner for National Minorities] (The Hague: March 1, 1994). [Mimeo.]

Human Rights Watch Arms Project, *Funding Renewal Proposal to the Rockefeller Foundation, Fourth Year, 1995-1996* (September 7, 1995). [Mimeo.]

International League for Human Rights, *A NGO Working Paper on Strengthening the Role of the United Nations in the Field of Human Rights* (New York, January 1, 1977). [Mimeo.]

Lawyers Committee for Human Rights, *General Support Proposal*, submitted to Ford Foundation (June 30, 1995).

Lotte Leicht, *IHF and the CSCE, A Discussion Paper* (February, 1994). [Mimeo.]

Raphael Lemkin, *Autobiography* (Typewritten manuscript in the Lemkin Archive, New York Public Library).

Sidney Liskofsky, *NGOs and Human Rights* (July 1974). [Mimeo.]

J. R. P. Montgomery, *Is Slavery Important?*, handwritten report found in the papers of Anti-Slavery International.

William Pace, *Presentation to the "International Conference for the Establishment of an International Criminal Court" in Montevideo, Uruguay* (October 10-11, 1997).

Physicians for Human Rights, *PHR Missions and Investigations 1986-1996* (internal document).

Peter Reddaway, *Soviet Policies on Dissent and Emigration: The Radical Change of Course Since 1979* (Washington, DC: August 28, 1984). [Mimeo.]

E. S. Reddy, *Contribution of Non-Governmental Organizations*, Paper presented at a Symposium entitled "World Peace and the Liberation of South Africa and Namibia," Geneva (June 11-13, 1986).

Lesley Roberts, *Personal Comments*, provided by Roberts to the author.

Baldwin Robertson, *Anti-Slavery International for the Protection of Human Rights* (New York, 1996). [Mimeo.] Prepared for the author's use.

Baldwin Robertson, *The International League for Human Rights* (New York, 1996). [Mimeo.] Prepared for the author's use.

Baldwin Robertson, *Human Rights NGOs in Asia* (New York, 1996) mimeo. Prepared for the author's use. It also includes two addenda on the special case of "China" and "International Human Rights NGOs."

John Shattuck, *Building International Human Rights Institutions*, address given at the twenty-fifth Anniversary dinner of the Jacob Blaustein Institute for the Advancement of Human Rights, mimeo (Washington, DC: May 7, 1997).

Nina Shea, *Testimony of Nina Shea Before the House Committee on International Relations Subcommittee on International Operations and Human Rights* (December 18, 1996).

Timothy D. Sisk, *Democratization in DROC (Democratic Republic of Congo): Options and Recommendations for a Policy of Reciprocal Commitment*, mimeo (Washington, DC: September 10, 1997). Policy paper prepared for an expert's meeting at the State Department on the Congo transition.

H. Gordon Skilling, *Report to the Ford Foundation*, submitted to the Ford Foundation on February 15, 1982.

Leonard Sussman, *NGOs and the Promotion of Human Rights*, paper presented to the 50th Annual DPI/NGO Conference on "Building Partnerships" (New York: September 11, 1997). [DPI is the UN Department of Public Information.]

J.D. Tolbert, *International Non-Governmental Organizations (NGOs) and the Changing Nature of International Law: An Examination of the Emerging Role of NGOs in Human Rights and Environmental Law*, Dissertation (Nottingham: University of Nottingham, 1990).

INTERVIEWS

(All interviews were conducted by the author unless otherwise noted.)

Patricia Armstrong
Alex Arriaga
Frans Baudoin
Robert Bernstein
Arie Bloed
Reed Brody
Cynthia Brown
Thomas Buergenthal
Elizabeth Cabot
Andrew Clapham
Roberta Cohen
Larry Cox
Patricia Derian
Clarence Dias
Richard Dicker
Adama Dieng
Mike Dottridge
Frances D'Souza
Stuart Eizenstat
Joseph Eldridge
Benjamin Ferencz
John Finerty
Felice Gaer
Richard J. Goldstone
Carl-Johan Groth
Jeannine Guthrie
Charles Hall
John Heffernan
Neal Hicks
George Houser
Sidney Jones
Max M. Kampelman
Steve Kass
Helga Klein
John Kornblum
Jeri Laber
Gara LaMarche
José Ayala Lasso
Lotte Leicht
Stephen Marks
Jean-Paul Marthoz
Georg Mauntner-Markhof
Gay McDougall
Tom McCarthy

Michael McClintock
Juan A. Mendes
Aryeh Neier
Ivana Nizich
Susan Osnos
William Pace
Alan Phillips
Thomas Pickering
Vela Pillay (Conducted by Clarity Educational Productions, Inc. of Berkeley, Calif.)
Michael Posner
E. S. Reddy
Bill Richardson
Lesley Roberts
Nigel Rodley
Jemera Rone
Ken Roth
Gavin Ruxton
Pierre Sané
Richard Schifter
William Schulz
John Shattuck
Susanna Sirkin
Malcolm Smart
Elan Steinberg
Leonard Sussman
Frank Sutton
Dorothy Thomas
David Tolbert
Max van der Stoel
Alex Vines
Thomas Warrick
Rachel Weintraub
Joanna Weschler
Lois Whitman

MISCELLANEOUS

Agence France-Presse
American Bar News
American Jewish Committee Press Releases
American Jewish Yearbook (Philadelphia)
Amnesty International, *Amnesty International Report* (London: Amnesty International, annual).
Amnesty International *Newsletter*
Amnesty International Summaries [Press Releases]

Annual Report of the Anti-Slavery Society (London: Anti-Slavery International, [various years]).

Anti-Slavery Reporter (London: Anti-Slavery International, [various years]).

Assembly for Human Rights, *Montreal Statement* (Montreal, 1968).

Beijing Review

Boston Globe

Business Week

CEELI Update (Published by the American Bar Association's Central and East European Law Initiative).

Chicago Tribune

Christian Science Monitor

Congressional Record

Daily Variety

Economist

Far Eastern Economic Review

Financial Times

The First Freedom (published by the Puebla Institute).

Ford Foundation *Archives*

Foundation on Inter-Ethnic Relations Annual Report (The Hague).

Freedom Review

Freedom House News

Freedom Monitor (publications of Freedom House).

Freedom House, *Freedom of the Media Survey* (New York: Freedom House, annual).

General Assembly Official Records (GAOR)

Guardian (London)

Human Rights Commission of Pakistan, *State of Human Rights in Pakistan* (Lahore: Human Rights Commission of Pakistan, annual).

Human Rights Dialogue (newsletter for the Human Rights and Asian Values Project of the Carnegie Council on Ethics and International Affairs).

Human Rights Monitor (Ottawa: Human Rights Internet).

Human Rights Tribune

Human Rights Watch World Report (New York) [Annual; formerly titled (until 1990) *Annual Report*].

Human Rights Watch Quarterly Newsletter

Human Rights Watch Press Releases

International Criminal Court Monitor

International Herald Tribune

International League for Human Rights, *Annual Review* (New York).

International League for Human Rights, *ILHR Human Rights Bulletin*

Jewish Telegraphic Agency dispatches

Jacob Blaustein Institute, *To Reaffirm Faith in Fundamental Human Rights: The UN and Human Rights, 1945-95* (New York: The Jacob Blaustein Institute for the Advancement of Human Rights, 1995).

Lawyers Committee for Human Rights *Annual Report* (New York).

Le Monde

Minority Rights Group *Annual Report* (London).

The National Jewish Post

New Republic

New York Jewish Week

The New York Post

The New York Times

New Yorker

Newsday

Newsweek

NGO Newsletter (Ludwig Boltzmann Institute of Human Rights)

OSCE Newsletter

The Pakistan Times

Petitions, Letters, and Appeals from Soviet Jews (Jerusalem: Hebrew University, 1979).

Physicians for Human Rights Press Releases.

Physicians for Human Rights, *Annual Report* (Boston).

Physicians for Human Rights, *10 Year Report* (Boston).

Physicians for Human Rights, *The Record* (Boston).

Joseph Proskauer, *A New Birth of Freedom, Speech to Carnegie Endowment*, April 28, 1958.

Radio Free Europe dispatches.

Reuters

RFE/RL Research Institute, *Annual Report of the RFE/RL Media and Opinion Research*

San Francisco Chronicle

Terra Viva (Vienna: Newspaper published independently at the World Conference on Human Rights, 1993)

Time Magazine

The Times (London).

The Times Literary Supplement

Union of International Associations, *Yearbook of International Organizations* (Brussels: UIA, Annual).

The United Nations Blue Book Series, Vol. One: The United Nations and Apartheid, 1948-1994 (New York: UN Department of Public Information, 1995).

UN Centre Against Apartheid, *Non-Governmental Organizations, Action Against Apartheid* (New York: UN Centre Against Apartheid, 1978).

UN Monthly Chronicle

UAN (Urgent Action Network) Newsletter (Amnesty International)

US Department of State *Bulletin*

US News & World Report

Village Voice

Wall Street Journal

The Washington Post

World Conference on Religion and Peace Report

INDEX